"I like the Practicing Manager's vocabulary [terms] early so stud...
—Gerald Silver, Professor at Purdue University–Calumet

"I like that the key terms are given at the beginning of the chapter. It helps to know what is important while reading. I also like that the key definitions are put in the margins. It makes it easier for reviewing and studying."
—Joe Hoff, student at University of Wisconsin–LaCrosse

Online Study Center
Prepare for Class

Online Study Center
Improve Your Grade

Online Study Center
ACE the Test

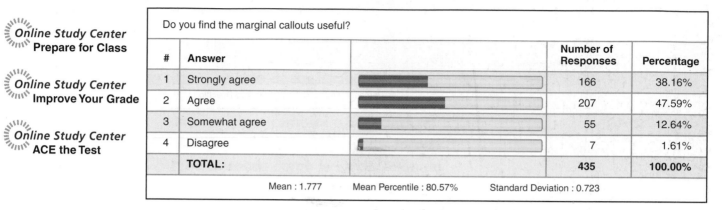

Do you find the marginal callouts useful?

#	Answer		Number of Responses	Percentage
1	Strongly agree		166	38.16%
2	Agree		207	47.59%
3	Somewhat agree		55	12.64%
4	Disagree		7	1.61%
	TOTAL:		**435**	**100.00%**

Mean : 1.777   Mean Percentile : 80.57%   Standard Deviation : 0.723

"It's nice that the book specifically tells you the resources you can use and where you can find them."
—Kristin Chimento, student at Miami University

Do you find the concept checks useful?

#	Answer		Number of Responses	Percentage
1	Strongly agree		117	27.08%
2	Agree		205	47.45%
	Somewhat agree		86	19.91%
	Disagree		24	5.56%
	TOTAL:		**432**	**100.00%**

Mean : 2.039   Mean Percentile : 74.02%   Standard Deviation : 0.831

CONCEPT CHECK 1.2

Recall an interaction you have had with a superior (manager, teacher, group leader, or the like). In that interaction, did the superior use science or art, or both? What could he or she have done to use science? What could he or she have done to use art?

I like the quizzes and that the [text] is short and to the point."
—Fernando Monzon, student at Miami Dade College

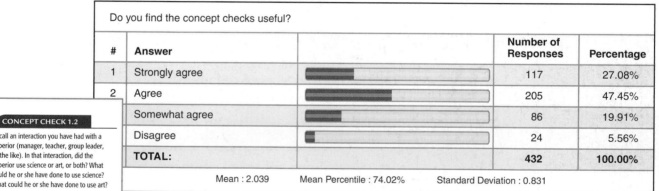

Do you find the test prepper useful?

#	Answer		Number of Responses	Percentage
1	Strongly agree		163	38.08%
2	Agree		194	45.33%
3	Somewhat agree		65	15.19%
4	Disagree		6	1.40%
	TOTAL:		**428**	**100.00%**

Mean : 1.799   Mean Percentile : 80.02%   Standard Deviation : 0.741

Data in barcharts from student survey at San Francisco State University.

INSTRUCTOR'S EDITION

STUDENT ACHIEVEMENT SERIES

Principles of Management

► Ricky W. Griffin

Texas A & M University

Houghton Mifflin Company

Boston   New York

Vice President and Publisher: George Hoffman
Senior Sponsoring Editor: Lise Johnson
Development Editor: Julia Perez
Editorial Associate: Amy Galvin
Senior Project Editor: Carol Merrigan
Editorial Assistant: Anthony D'Aries
Senior Composition Buyer: Chuck Dutton
Art and Design Coordinator: Jill Haber
Senior Photo Editor: Jennifer Meyer Dare
Senior Manufacturing Coordinator: Chuck Dutton
Senior Marketing Manager: Steven Mikels

Cover Photo: © Jim Corwin/Alamy

► FOR W. A. DYER, A TRULY FINE MAN.

Photo Credits

Chapter 1: p. 2: John D. McHugh/AFP/Getty Images; p. 9: © The New Yorker Collection 1996/ Sam Gross from.cartoonbank.com. All rights reserved; p. 15: AT&T Archives; p. 17: AP / Wide World Photos; p. 21: Paul Conklin/PhotoEdit, Inc.; **Chapter 2:** p. 28: AP/Wide World Photos; p. 33: Munshi Ahmed; p. 35: AP/Wide World Photos; p. 38: Chris Kleponis/ZUMA/CORBIS; p. 44: © 2006 Chon Day from cartoonbank.com. All rights reserved; **Chapter 3:** p. 56: Getty Images; p. 65: © Evan Kafka; p. 69: Stan Honda/AFP/Getty Images; p. 75 (top): Reuters/CORBIS SABA; p. 75 (bottom): © King Features Syndicate; **Chapter 4:** p. 84: PHOTOTAKE Inc./Alamy; p. 88: © The New Yorker Collection 2002 Pat Byrnes from.cartoonbank.com. All rights reserved; p. 90: Steve Liss/Getty Images; p. 97: Thaier Al-Sundani / Reuters/CORBIS SABA; **Chapter 5:** p. 108: John Li/Getty Images; p: 116: © The New Yorker Collection 2000/David Sipress from cartoonbank.com. All rights reserved; p. 119: Lon Diehl/PhotoEdit, Inc.; p. 123: AP/Wide World Photos; p: 125: Bob Daemmrich/PhotoEdit Inc.; **Chapter 6:** p. 136: AP/Wide World Photos; p. 140: Eli Reichman; p. 145: DILBERT reprinted by permission of United Features Syndicate, Inc.; p. 150: Michael Geissinger/The Image Works, Inc.; p. 160: Daniel LeClair/Reuters/CORBIS; **Chapter 7:** p. 166: John Gress/Reuters/CORBIS; p. 170: Dennis MacDonald/PhotoEdit, Inc.; p. 173: DILBERT reprinted by permission United Features Syndicate, Inc.; p. 176: Reprinted with permission of Mercedes Benz; p. 183: Kimimasa Mayama/Reuters/CORBIS; **Chapter 8:** p. 190: © Eliane/ZEFA/CORBIS; p. 201: AP/Wide World Photos; p. 206: © 2006 J.P. Rini from cartoonbank.com. All rights reserved; p. 211: Robert Brenner/PhotoEdit, Inc.; p. 212: Business Wire for Getty Images; **Chapter 9:** p. 220: Steve Smith/Getty Images; p. 225: © P.C.Vey; p. 236: Jeff Greenberg/The Image Works, Inc.; p. 225: Tom Carter/PhotoEdit, Inc.; p. 241: AP/Wide World Photos; **Chapter 10:** p. 250: Per-Anders Pettersson/Prestige/Getty; p. 254: Jose Azel/Aurora; p. 265: AP/Wide World Photos; p. 267: Peter McKenzie/Panapress/Getty Images; p. 270: © The New Yorker Collection 1990/James Stevenson from cartoonbank.com. All rights reserved; **Chapter 11:** p. 280: AP/Wide World Photos; p. 284: AP/Wide World Photos; p. 294: © The New Yorker Collection 1988 James Stevenson from cartoonbank.com. All rights reserved; p. 300: Tom Carter/PhotoEdit, Inc.; p. 303: Chip Somodvilla/Getty Images; **Chapter 12:** p. 312: Ken Cedeno/CORBIS; p. 319: © Olivier Laude; p. 329: AP/Wide World Photos; p. 332: © David Deal; p. 334: © 2006 Ted Goff from cartoonbank.com. All rights reserved; **Chapter 13:** p. 340: Eric Feferberg/Getty Images; p. 343: AP/Wide World Photos; p. 346: AP/Wide World Photos; p. 351: © The New Yorker Collection 2003/Leo Cullum from cartoonbank.com. All rights reserved; p. 355: AP/Wide World Photos; **Chapter 14:** p. 366: James Leynse/CORBIS; p. 374: AP/Wide World Photos; p. 379: AP/Wide World Photos; p. 386: Michael Newman/PhotoEdit, Inc.; p. 389: © The New Yorker Collection 2002/Leo Cullum from cartoonbank.com. All rights reserved; **Chapter 15:** p. 396: AP/Wide World Photos; p. 403: AP/Wide World Photos; p. 408: Photri-Microstock; p. 412: AP/Wide World Photos; p.415: © 2006 Roz Chast from cartoonbank.com. All rights reserved.

Printed in the U.S.A.

Library of Congress control number: 2006927992

Instructor's edition:
ISBN 13: 978-0-618-73079-7
ISBN 10: 0-618-73079-6

For orders, use student text ISBNs:
ISBN 13: 978-0-618-73078-0
ISBN 10: 0-618-73078-8

23456789 – CRK – 10 09 08 07

Brief Contents

Contents

CHAPTER 1

UNDERSTANDING THE MANAGER'S JOB   2

CHAPTER 2

THE ENVIRONMENTS OF ORGANIZATIONS AND MANAGERS   28

CHAPTER 3

PLANNING AND STRATEGIC MANAGEMENT   56

CHAPTER 7

ORGANIZATION CHANGE AND INNOVATION   166

CHAPTER 8

MANAGING HUMAN RESOURCES   190

CHAPTER 15

MANAGING OPERATIONS, QUALITY, AND PRODUCTIVITY   396

Instructor's Introduction

Many textbooks are developed to teach the basic fundamentals of management, and these books generally include all of the principles that management professors believe are important for students to learn before entering the "real life" management world. However, it is important to gain other important individual perspectives when developing textbooks so that such learning tools are well rounded and adequately cover the topics that students believe to be important. *Student Achievement Series: Principles of Management* incorporates these various perspectives by including students, as well as professors, in the development process. In particular, Houghton Mifflin, using a variety of data collection methods, compiled information from a diverse national sample of professors and students so that this text could be developed to reflect the interests of both groups. This positions the text as one of the first educational management products that considers the needs and interests of professors, while at the same time utilizing extensive student feedback to enhance the "student friendly" nature of the concepts covered. Students and professors have been included in every basic component of this textbook development process including the structure of the text, the evaluation of key material, the development of concepts, and creation of the title and cover design.

Student involvement in the project has been one of the most important elements of the textbook's development process. The feedback provided by these student participants has facilitated the development of a management text that is quite different from other books that are currently available on the market. In particular, students suggested that, in addition to a reasonable price, a textbook should present the material in a manner that facilitates learning both inside and outside the classroom. With all of their interests and activities both inside and outside of school, students prefer texts that provide a useful overview of the material so that they can learn the information well, perform in an exemplary fashion on examinations, and are prepared for the workplace after the college experience. Taking all of these preferences into consideration, this textbook should represent a good value from an educational standpoint—it should satisfy price-sensitive buyers, as well as enhance the efficiency and effectiveness of student learning.

▶ PEDAGOGY

Satisfying these basic interests and preferences can be a challenge, and many textbooks on the market fall below the mark. In particular, some students learn best by focusing on visual aspects of material, while others learn best by reading the material or participating in practical learning exercises, while still another portion of students learn best by reading aloud or listening to MP3s. To respond to these individual learning styles, we established many different methods of content delivery. We also focused on the student's feedback or "wishlist" of items they wanted to see in their textbook program.

Request #1: We want a straightforward text that contains fewer and shorter chapters/sections and offers brief outlines of content rather than long drawn-out paragraphs (preferably in bulleted format).

Student Achievement Series Response:

▌ Our author has worked laboriously to tighten wording, condense chapter coverage, and critically approach each section. In cases where a concept was introduced, then illustrated by more than one example, close attention was paid to whether or not that additional example (or two) was really vital to student comprehension. In most cases the point was clearly made with one example so why add more words to a page at the risk of being redundant? While it is important to make sure that the concept is adequately explained and illustrated, oftentimes students become bored when given example upon example or re-wordings of the same material. In addition, content, when appropriate, was transformed from running paragraph text to bullets for clear connectivity and to retain student interest.

▌ Boxes were not included, as they are in most all other textbooks, since students commented that they usually skip the boxes and do not deem them integral to concept comprehension. Professors also indicated to us that they often omit the boxed material from their lectures and testing. Opening and Closing Cases were added but closely edited to ensure clarity and succinctness.

Areas of Management

Regardless of their level, managers may work in various areas within an organization.

▪ *Marketing managers* work in areas related to the marketing function. These areas include new-product development, promotion, and distribution.

▪ *Financial managers* deal primarily with an organization's financial resources. They are responsible for such activities as accounting, cash management, and investments. In some businesses, such as banking and insurance, financial managers are found in especially large numbers.

▪ *Operations managers* are concerned with creating and managing the systems that create an organization's products and services. Typical responsibilities of operations managers include production control, inventory control, quality control, plant layout, and site selection.

▪ *Human resource managers* are responsible for hiring and developing employ-

---

Contemporary Management Challenges

Managers today also face an imposing set of challenges as they guide and direct the fortunes of their companies. Coverage of each of these is thoroughly integrated throughout this book. In addition, many of them are also highlighted or given focused coverage in one or more special ways. The following list includes many of the most compelling issues facing managers today:

▪ An erratic economy that constrains managers' abilities to plan for the future

▪ The management of diversity

▪ Employee privacy relative to the organization

▪ The increased capabilities that technology provides for people to work at places other than their office

▪ The appropriate role of the Internet in business strategy

▪ The growth in outsourcing domestic jobs to foreign locations to take advantage of lower labor costs

▪ Globalization

▪ Ethics and social responsibility

▪ Corporate governance

Again, each of these issues is discussed in several places throughout this book.

TEST PREPPER 1.1   ANSWERS CAN BE FOUND ON P. 441

True or False?

____ 1. Arne Sorenson, senior vice president for finance at Marriott, is a middle manager.

____ 2. When a manager forms a team with members from each functional area, she is engaged in organizing.

____ 3. Top managers are using their decision-making skills when they think strategically and monitor a broad area of concern.

Multiple Choice

____ 4. Early in her career Carly Fiorina worked in new-product development, promotion, and distribution. She was a(n) ____ manager.
   a. human resource
   b. specialized
   c. operations
   d. marketing
   e. finance

____ 5. As an operations manager for Cintas, Dave Warns is responsible for motivating subordinates. To accomplish that he must use which skills?
   a. Technical   d. Communication
   b. Interpersonal   e. Time-management
   c. Conceptual

____ 6. Lucia manages a McDonald's. She notices that the morning shift has higher employee turnover, low morale, and low productivity. She must use her ____ skills to develop a solution.
   a. conceptual   d. decision-making
   b. diagnostic   e. time-management
   c. communication

____ 7. Mark prefers to make decisions based on "gut feeling" and experience. He is most likely to describe management as ____.
   a. science   d. theory Y
   b. art   e. theory X
   c. theory Z

New York, market research clearly showed that New Yorkers preferred drip coffee to more exotic espresso-style coffees. After first installing more drip coffee makers and fewer espresso makers than in their other stores, managers had to backtrack when the New Yorkers lined up clamoring for espresso. Starbucks now introduces a standard menu and layout in all its stores, regardless of presumed market differences, and then makes necessary adjustments later. Thus managers must blend an element of intuition and personal insight with hard data and objective facts.[9]

CONCEPT CHECK 1.2

Recall an interaction you have had with a superior (manager, teacher, group leader, or the like). In that interaction, did the superior use science or art, or both? What could he or she have done to use science? What could he or she have done to use art?

Request #2: We want to be ready for our exams. We need assessment tools to prepare us for our tests.

Student Achievement Series Response:

▌ A Test Prepper is included at the end of each major section. Each Test Prepper contains true/false and multiple choice questions that are both recall and application based. The answers can be found at the end of the text.

▌ There are Concept Checks interspersed throughout the margins of the chapter. These questions get the student thinking critically about major concepts. Suggested answers to these Concept Checks can be found in the Instructor's Resource Manual. These can also be used in class as Discussion Starters.

▌ In addition, ACE and ACE+ Practice tests can be found on the Online Study Center.

Request #3: We want a website that's easy to use and worth our time investment.

Student Achievement Series Response:

▌ This text is supported by a comprehensive online support tool. Students also let us know that by far, the most utilized section of a book's supporting website is the Quizzing and Testing portion. The Online Study Center (or student website) contains a plethora of content for students to follow up on what they've read in the chapter. At the conclusion of each chapter, there is a section that outlines all of the valuable assets found on the Online Study Center. To save students time and energy searching an unorganized site, we have categorized assets on the website into 3 categories:

Online Study Center **Prepare for Class**   *Online Study Center* **Improve Your Grade**   *Online Study Center* **ACE the Test**

Many valuable assets are found within these three categories. All assets found on the website are tied to content within the chapter. Icons appear in the text margins to point students to the Online Study Center, the specific bucket, and the asset name. We offer the following assets:

Online Study Center RESOURCES

Prepare for Class, Improve Your Grade, and ACE the Test. These Student Achievement resources include:

ACE Practice Tests	Interactive Skills Assessments	Study Guide to Go
End of Chapter Exercises	Knowledgebank	Video Segments
Glossaries (visual and print)	Reviews (audio and print)	Summaries/Outlines
Flashcards		

To access these learning and study tools, go to: **college.hmco.com/pic/griffinSAS**

▌ We also repeat the website URL on every other page in the text to really drive home the message!

Online Study Center   *college.hmco.com/pic/griffinSAS*

Request #4: We want a text that is visually appealing but uses space economically and with purpose—the longer the book, the heavier it is to carry!

Student Achievement Series Response:

▌ All photographs, cartoons, figures, and tables in this text are included not only to enhance the esthetic appeal of the text but, more importantly, to illustrate the written words. The captions are closely tied to the illustrations as well as the content being discussed in the text. In addition, art was sized substantially smaller than in other texts to avoid waste in the layout.

FIGURE 1.3

The Systems Perspective on Organizations
By viewing organizations as systems, managers can better understand the importance of their environment and the level of interdependence among subsystems within the organization. Managers must also understand how their decisions affect and are affected by other subsystems within the organization.

Inputs from the environment: material inputs, human inputs, financial inputs, and information inputs → Transformation process: technology, operating systems, administrative systems, and control systems → Outputs into the environment: products/services, profits/losses, employee behaviors, and information outputs

Feedback

Online Study Center   *college.hmco.com/pic/griffinSAS*

than management science and can be applied rectly to managerial situations. Indeed, we can **operations management** as a form of applied man-t science. Operations management techniques rally concerned with helping the organization its products or services more efficiently and can ed to a wide range of problems.

example, The Home Depot uses operations ment techniques to manage inventory. (Inven-nagement is concerned with specific inventory s, such as balancing carrying costs and ordering d determining the optimal order quantity.) Lin-ramming (which involves computing simultane-tions to a set of linear equations) helps United plan its flight schedules, helps Consolidated ays develop its shipping routes, and helps man-rs plan what items to produce at various times.

The quantitative management perspective offers many tools and techniques that can help business. For instance, Ford Motor Company is using these crash test dummies to learn more about improving passenger safety. By being able to precisely measure impact points and their effects on these dummies, Ford can better design its products in ways that help reduce injuries.

Request #5: We want cases that cover topics, organizations, or companies that we can relate to.

Student Achievement Series Response:

❚ The author has taken special care to include contemporary companies/organizations and student-friendly topics. For instance, Chapter 13's opening incident focuses on teamwork at the 2006 Winter Olympics, while the Closing Case discusses the burgeoning Video Game Craze.

Teamwork Challenges for the 2006 Winter Olympics U.S. Athletes

The 200-plus members of the 2006 U.S. Winter Olympics team included superstars: Michelle Kwan in figure skating, Bode Miller in downhill skiing, Shaun White in snowboarding, the NHL professionals on the hockey team. In part, the celebrity status of the athletes simply reflects the reality that the public is interested in exceptional athletes. Celebrity status is also hyped by corporate sponsors and network broadcasters to increase viewership, advertising revenues, and sales. Coaches should seek out the best competitors, yet the fame and stardom enjoyed by top performers may have an adverse effect on team cohesion and ultimately, performance.

CLOSING CASE STUDY **363**

CLOSING CASE STUDY

Video Game Teams

Microsoft's new Xbox 360, released in November 2005, was very popular, selling 1.5 million units in the first three months. In addition, Sony and Nintendo both announced new game consoles that would be available in 2006. Sales of hardware and accessories accounted for two-thirds of the industry's $31 billion in worldwide sales in 2005. A focus solely on gaming hardware, however, neglects the real growth engine of the industry, the video games themselves.

Video games can be created by the game console makers or third-party developers under contract to a hardware company or even by independents who self-

"The team dynamic is critical [when developing video games]."

–Laura Fryer, executive producer, Microsoft Game Studios

Moreover, the specialized teams must also work harmoniously with the other subteams. Fryer claims that, when developing video games, "the team dynamic is critical." Managing group conflict is essential, as is team

---

BUILDING EFFECTIVE DECISION-MAKING SKILLS **23**

BUILDING EFFECTIVE DECISION-MAKING SKILLS

Online Study Center
Improve Your Grade
Exercises: Building Effective Skills

Exercise Overview

Decision-making skills enable a manager to recognize and define problems and opportunities correctly and then to select an appropriate course of action to solve the problems and capitalize on the opportunities. This exercise will help you develop your own decision-making skills and also enhance your understanding of the importance of subsystem interdependencies in organizations.

Exercise Background

Assume you are the vice president of a large manufacturing company. Your firm makes home office furniture

lower-skill labor pool and will thus be paid a lower wage. The third option is to replace your existing equipment with newer, more efficient equipment. Although this will require a substantial up-front investment, you are certain that lower production costs can be achieved.

Exercise Task

With this background in mind, respond to the following questions:

---

24 CHAPTER 1 UNDERSTANDING THE MANAGER'S JOB

EXPERIENTIAL EXERCISE

Johari Window

Online Study Center
Improve Your Grade
Exercises: Experiential Exercise

Purpose

This exercise has two purposes: to encourage you to analyze yourself more accurately and to start you working on small-group cohesiveness. This exercise encourages you to share data about yourself and then to assimilate and process feedback. Small groups are typically more trusting and work better together, as you will be able to see after this exercise has been completed. The Johari Window is a particularly good model for under the perceptual process in interpersonal relatio

This skill builder focuses on the human model and will help you develop your mentor

obvious to others. For example, in a working situation, a peer group might observe that your jumping in to get the group moving off dead center is appropriate. At other times, you jump in when the group is not really finished, and you seem to interrupt. A third set of personality characteristics is known to the individual but

Interactive Skills Self-Assessments to accompany
Student Achievement Series: Principles of Management
1st Edition

Ricky W. Griffin
Take these interactive assessments to gauge your management skills:
- Self-Awareness
- Global Awareness
- Are You a Good Planner?
- Decision-Making Styles
- An Entrepreneurial Quiz
- How Is Your Organization Managed?
- Innovative Attitude Scale
- Diagnosing Poor Performance and Enhancing Motivation
- Assessing Your Mental Abilities
- Assessing Your Needs
- Managerial Leader Behavior Questionnaire
- Sex Talk Quiz
- Using Teams
- Understanding Control
- Defining Quality and Productivity

HOUGHTON
new ways to know®

Enter ▶

Request #6: We want material that we can really use in our current or future careers.

Student Achievement Series Response:

❚ Instead of providing a smattering of exercises at the end of each chapter, the author has been precise in selecting only the most appropriate exercises to include in the text and on the Online Study Center. At the conclusion of each chapter, students will find a Building Skills Exercise as well as an Experiential Exercise. On the Online Study Center, students will find the exercises from the text, in addition to two more Building Skills Exercises.

❚ The Interactive Skills Self-Assessments are another great method for students to put this material into practice. The Assessments provide scoring and instant feedback so that students can gauge their managerial "know how."

▌ In addition, at the start of each chapter, the author has listed the important terms found within the chapter. He has distinguished which terms are general Key Terms and which ones are Practicing Manager's Terms. These terms are also found on the Online Study Center as glossaries and flashcards. The terms are color coded (orange for Practicing Manager's Terms and blue for Key Terms.) These important terms also appear in the text margins to further drive home the importance of understanding the language of management.

---

4   CHAPTER 1   UNDERSTANDING THE MANAGER'S JOB

PRACTICING MANAGER'S TERMS

		KEY TERMS
organization *p. 5*	controlling *p. 8*	classical management perspective *p. 12*
management *p. 5*	technical skills *p. 9*	scientific management *p. 13*
efficient *p. 5*	interpersonal skills *p. 9*	soldiering *p. 13*
effective *p. 5*	conceptual skills *p. 9*	administrative management *p. 13*
top managers *p. 6*	diagnostic skills *p. 9*	behavioral management perspective *p. 14*
middle managers *p. 6*	communication skills *p. 10*	human relations movement *p. 15*
first-line managers *p. 7*	decision-making skills *p. 10*	Theory X *p. 16*
planning *p. 8*	time-management skills *p. 10*	Theory Y *p. 16*
decision making *p. 8*	theory *p. 12*	organizational behavior *p. 16*
organizing *p. 8*	system *p. 19*	quantitative management perspective *p. 17*
leading *p. 8*	open system *p. 19*	management science *p. 17*
Online Study Center Improve Your Grade	closed system *p. 19*	operations management *p. 17*
—Flashcards	subsystem *p. 19*	universal perspective *p. 20*
—Glossary	synergy *p. 20*	contingency perspective *p. 20*
	entropy *p. 20*	

You should be able to define and use terms that are part of the practicing manager's vocabulary, as well as those that are integral in the language of management.

stand perception. While working full time at Google, Mayer teaches prog ming to Stanford undergraduates and has won several teaching awards.

Mayer has a strong vision of the website's appearance and function. simplicity of Google's site is deceptive. Every Google search ranks 8 billion

---

Online Study Center Improve Your Grade Knowledgebank 1.1

top managers   The relatively small group of senior executives who manage the overall organization.

middle managers   The relatively large set of managers responsible for implementing the policies and plans developed by top managers and for supervising and coordinating the activities of lower-level managers.

Levels of Management

One way to classify managers is in terms of their level in the organization.

▌ **Top managers** make up the relatively small group of executives who manage the overall organization. Titles found in this group include president, vice president, and chief executive officer (CEO). Top managers create the organization's goals, overall strategy, and operating policies. They also officially represent the organization to the external environment by meeting with government officials, executives of other organizations, and so forth. Marissa Mayer is a top manager.

▌ **Middle managers** are responsible primarily for implementing the policies and plans developed by top managers and for supervising and coordinating the activities of lower-level managers.[3] Common middle-management titles include

---

revitalize itself and keep pace with changes in its environment. A primary objective of management, from a systems perspective, is to re-energize the organization continually to avoid the ill effects of entropy.

The Contingency Perspective

universal perspective   The point of view that there is "one best way" to do something.

contingency perspective   The point of view that appropriate managerial behavior in a given situation depends on, or is contingent on, a wide variety of elements.

Another noteworthy addition to management thinking is the contingency perspective. The classical, behavioral, and quantitative approaches are considered **universal perspectives** because they tried to identify the "one best way" to manage organizations. The contingency perspective, in contrast, suggests that universal theories cannot be applied to organizations because each organization is unique. Instead, the **contingency perspective** suggests that appropriate managerial behavior in a given situation depends on, or is contingent on, unique elements in that situation.[29]

Stated differently, effective managerial behavior in one situation cannot always be generalized to other situations. Recall, for example, that Frederick Taylor

---

We believe that *Student Achievement Series: Principles of Management* fills an important need in the marketplace by listening to students' requests in order to provide a value-based learning tool, not just another textbook.

▶ ORGANIZATION OF THIS TEXT

The text has been arranged into five basic parts to provide students with a knowledge base of management principles and concepts. Part 1 provides students with an overview of management, including an introduction to the job of managing others in organizations, as well as the role of the environment in management. Part 2 covers planning in companies, including the strategic planning process, employee decision making, and entrepreneurial thought and action. Part 3 explores that process of organizing in companies by outlining organizational structure and design, corporate change and innovation, and the supervision of human resources. Part 4 introduces basic leadership concepts such as managing employee conduct, motivating personnel, using leadership to influence others, corporate communication, and group/team management. Finally, Part 5 explores the concept of control in organizations, with a particular focus on operations, quality, and productivity.

In addition to breaking the text into Parts and Chapters, the author has paid a great deal of attention to breaking each chapter into palatable sections. By dividing the chapters into short sections, the content is made more accessible to students. Each section correlates to a learning objective and heading in the chapter outline. The author has taken a systematic approach to structuring the text so that the student will always know where he/she is in the context of the chapter and the text as a whole. The Learning Objectives are reiterated one last time as the last asset in the chapter, the Learning Objective Review. Each individual Learning Objective, major section, and Learning Objective Review section is color coded to divide the text for those who are seeking a more visual connection to the chapter content.

Chapter Outline

▶ AN INTRODUCTION TO MANAGEMENT
 Kinds of managers
 Basic management functions
 Fundamental management skills
 The science and the art of management

▶ THE EVOLUTION OF MANAGEMENT
 The importance of history and theory
 The historical context of management
 The classical management perspective
 The behavioral management perspective
 The quantitative management perspective

▶ CONTEMPORARY MANAGEMENT
 PERSPECTIVES
 The systems perspective
 The contingency perspective
 Contemporary management challenges
  and opportunities

3 ▶ *Identify and discuss key contemporary management perspectives represented by the systems and contingency perspectives and identify the major challenges and opportunities faced by managers today.*

2 ▶ *Justify the importance of history and theory to managers and explain the evolution of management thought through the classical, behavioral, and quantitative perspectives.*

1 ▶ *Define management, describe the kinds of managers found in organizations, identify and explain the four basic management functions, describe the fundamental management skills, and comment on management as science and as art.*

2

AN INTRODUCTION TO MANAGEMENT

1 ▶ *Define management, describe the kinds of managers found in organizations, identify and explain the four basic management functions, describe the fundamental management skills, and comment on management as science and as art.*

THE EVOLUTION OF MANAGEMENT

2 ▶ *Justify the importance of history and theory to managers and explain the evolution of management thought through the classical, behavioral, and quantitative perspectives.*

CONTEMPORARY MANAGEMENT PERSPECTIVES

3 ▶ *Identify and discuss key contemporary management perspectives represented by the systems and contingency perspectives and identify the major challenges and opportunities faced by managers today.*

▶ SUPPLEMENTS FOR INSTRUCTORS

Student Achievement Series: Principles of Management includes an extensive bundle of educational materials and activity-based learning tools that help professors teach a principles of management course:

▌ The ***Online Instructor's Resource Manual*** includes an author introduction, a list of recommended class schedules, and comprehensive outlines for each chapter. The chapter teaching notes contain information that should ideally facilitate the delivery of information to students in the classroom, and contain a chapter summary, various teaching objectives, a comprehensive chapter lecture outline (comprised of opening incident summary, teaching guidelines, suggestions for group activities, discussion topics), extensive teaching notes and outlines, typical/common answers to end-of-chapter case questions, and directions for skills development activities.

- The **_Online Test Bank_** is comprised of over 2,000 multiple choice, true/false, and essay questions, and each individual chapter contains 130 items. Each question is supplemented with a particular learning objective, page reference, an estimation of difficulty level, and category type (knowledge, understanding, or application).

- The **_HMTesting Instructor CD_** is a computerized version of the Test Bank and enables professors to easily select and/or edit questions to be included on a test master for duplication and distribution. There are also Online Testing and Gradebook features that enable professors to give examinations over their local area network or the World Wide Web, organize course content and procedures, tabulate assignment grades, and calculate student grade statistics.

- The **_Online Teaching Center_** is an excellent resource for instructors that offers PowerPoint slides (basic and premium), downloadable Instructor Resource Manual files, the Video Guide, Classroom Response System materials, and other relevant course content.

- A **_video/DVD program_** is included with the text to provide realistic examples of the chapter information and to spark students' interest in material. A discussion-based video guide is also offered, which contains discussion questions and activities.

- **_Eduspace/BlackBoard/WebCT_**—these online course management systems include Instructor Resource Manual files, Test Bank questions, CRS content, video segments, quizzes, discussion threads that facilitate online interaction, various PowerPoint slides, audio chapter summaries and quizzes in MP3 format, _Interactive Skills Self-Assessment,_ homework, and other relevant course content.

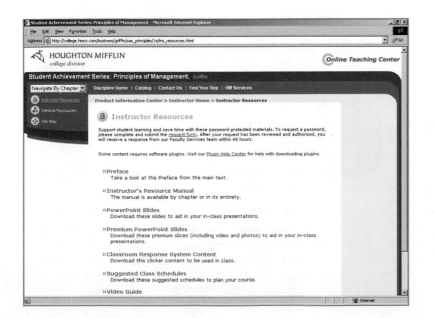

▶ SUPPLEMENTS FOR STUDENTS

▮ The ***Online Study Center*** provides various valuable online assets. As mentioned before, the Online Study Center contains ACE Practice Tests, Knowledgebank material, Video Segments, and much more.

▮ "Your Guide to an 'A'" Media Passkey enables students to access content beyond what is available on the standard Online Study Center. While Chapter 1 is available to all students, the remainder of the chapters contain passkey protected assets. The "Your Guide to an 'A'" Media Passkey is packaged on request with every new textbook. In addition, the "Your Guide to an 'A'" passkey is available for purchase at the bookstore or Houghton Mifflin's eCommerce site for those students using used textbooks. Assets that are housed behind the passkey include:

- ACE+ Practice Tests (10 true/false and 10 multiple choice questions with immediate scoring and feedback)

- Downloadable *Study Guide to Go* (a printable packet containing the chapter outline, learning objective review, a comprehensive list of key terms, and sample quiz questions)

- Online Flash *Interactive Skills Self-Assessments* that provide instant feedback and scoring for students wanting to evaluate their personal management competencies

- Audio Chapter Review and Quiz MP3 files (audio chapter summaries and short quizzes)

- Exercises that enhance student learning (Building Effective Skills Exercises and Experiential Exercises)

- Flashcards (glossary terms in Flash format)

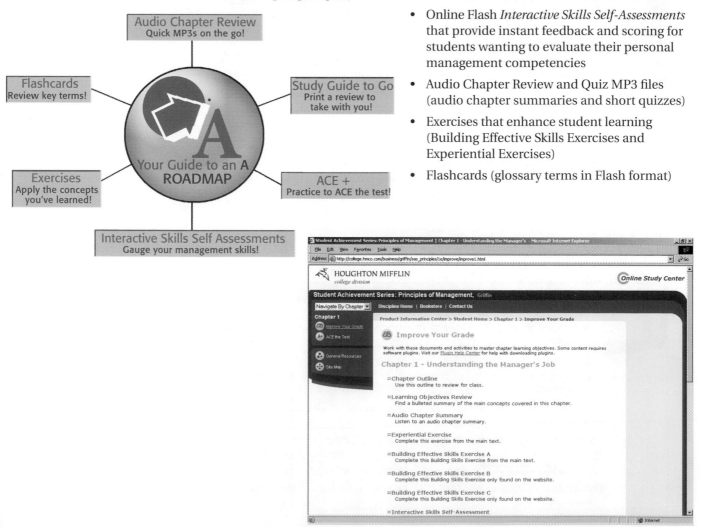

Preface

▶ A Team Approach: Built by Professors and Students, for Professors and Students

Over the past two years Houghton Mifflin has conducted research and focus groups with a diverse cross-section of professors and students from across the country to create the first textbook that truly reflects what professors and students want and need in an educational product. Everything we have learned has been applied to create and build a brand new educational experience and product model, from the ground up, for our two very important customer bases. *Student Achievement Series: Principles of Management* is based on extensive professor and student feedback and is specifically designed to meet the teaching needs of today's instructors as well as the learning, study, and assessment goals of today's students. Professors and students have been involved with every key decision regarding this new product development model and learning system—from content structure, to design, to packaging, to the title of the textbook, and even to marketing and messaging. Professors have also played an integral role as content advisers through their reviews, creative ideas, and contributions to this new textbook.

It has long been a Houghton Mifflin tradition and honor to partner closely with professors to gain valuable insights and recommendations during the development process. Partnering equally as closely with students through the entire product development and product launch process has proved to also be extremely gratifying and productive.

▶ What Students Told Us

Working closely with students has been both rewarding and enlightening. Their honest and candid feedback and their practical and creative ideas have helped us to develop an educational learning model like no other on the market today.

Students have told us many things. While price is important to them, they are just as interested in having a textbook that reflects the way they actually learn and study. As with other consumer purchases and decisions they make, they want a textbook that is of true value to them. *Student Achievement Series: Principles of Management* accomplishes both of their primary goals: it provides them with a price-conscious textbook, and it presents the concepts in a way that pleases them.

Today's students are busy individuals. They go to school, they work, some have families, they have a wide variety of interests, and they are involved in many activities. They take their education very seriously. Their main goal is to master the materials so they can perform well in class, get a good grade, graduate, land a good job, and be successful.

Different students learn in different ways; some learn best by reading, some are more visually oriented, and some learn best by doing through practice and assessment. While students learn in different ways, almost all students told us the same things regarding what they want their textbook to "look like." The ideal textbook for students gets to the point quickly, is easy to understand and read, has fewer and/or shorter chapters, has pedagogical materials designed to reinforce key concepts, has a strong supporting website for quizzing, testing, and assessment of materials, is cost conscious, and provides them with real value for their dollar.

Students want smaller chunks of information rather than the long sections and paragraphs found in traditional textbooks. This format provides them with immediate reinforcement and allows them to assess the concepts they have just studied. They like to read materials in more bulleted formats that are easier to digest than long sections and paragraphs. They almost always pay special attention to key terms and any materials that are boldfaced or highlighted in the text. In general, they spend little time reading or looking at materials that they view as superficial, such as many of the photographs (although they want some photos for visual enhancement) and boxed materials. However, they do want a textbook that is visually interesting, holds their interest, and is designed in an open, friendly, and accessible format. They want integrated study and assessment materials that help them reinforce, master, and test their knowledge of key concepts. They also want integrated Web and technology components that focus on quizzing and provide them with an interactive place to go to for help and assessment. They don't want websites that simply repeat the textual information in the book or that provide superficial information that is not primary to the key concepts in the text.

While students learn and study in a variety of different ways, a number of students told us that they often attend class first to hear their professor lecture and to take notes. Then they go back to read the chapter after (not always before) class. They use their textbook in this fashion to not only get the information they need but to also reinforce what they have learned in class. Students told us that they study primarily by using index or flashcards that highlight key concepts and terms, by reading lecture notes, and by using the supporting book website for quizzing and testing of key concepts. They also told us that they are far more likely to purchase and use a textbook if their professor actively uses the textbook in class and tells them that they need it.

▶ TAKING WHAT PROFESSORS AND STUDENTS TOLD US TO CREATE *Student Achievement Series: Principles of Management*

Student Achievement Series: Principles of Management provides exactly what students want and need pedagogically in an educational product. While other textbooks on the market include some of these features, *Student Achievement Series* is the first textbook to fully incorporate all of these cornerstones, as well as to introduce innovative new learning methods and study processes that completely meet the wishes of today's students. It does this by:

▌ Being concise and to the point.

▌ Presenting more content in bulleted or more succinct formats.

▌ Highlighting and boldfacing key concepts and information.

▌ Organizing content in more bite-size and chunked-up formats.

▌ Providing a system for immediate reinforcement and assessment of materials throughout the chapter.

▌ Creating a design that is open, user friendly, and interesting for today's students.

▌ Developing a supporting and integrated Web component that focuses on quizzing and assessment of key concepts.

▌ Eliminating or reducing traditional chapter components that students view as superficial.

▌ Creating a product that is easier for students to read and study.

▌ Providing students with a price-conscious product.

▌ Providing students with a product they feel is valuable.

When we asked students to compare a chapter from this new learning model to chapters from traditional competing textbooks, students overwhelmingly rated this new product model as far superior. In one focus group, ten students were asked to rank each "blind" chapter on a scale from 1 to 5, with 5 being the highest mark. *Student Achievement Series: Principles of Management* received six 5's, while three competing books collectively received two 5's. Students told us that *Student Achievement Series: Principles of Management* is "a very valuable text," is "easier to read and easier to study from," is "more modern," and is "more of what [they] want in a text."

▶ PROFESSORS AND STUDENTS: WE COULDN'T HAVE DONE IT WITHOUT YOU

We are very grateful to all the students across the country who participated in one form or another in helping us to create and build the first educational product pedagogically designed specifically for them and their learning and educational goals. Working with these students was an honor, as well as a lot of fun, for all of us at Houghton Mifflin. We sincerely appreciate their honesty, candor, creativeness, and interest in helping us to develop a better learning experience. We also appreciate their willingness to meet with us for lengthy periods of time and to allow us to videotape them and use some of their excellent quotes. We wish them much success as they complete their college education, begin their careers, and go about their daily lives.

STUDENT PARTICIPANTS

Adam Delaney-Winn, Tufts University
Adrienne Rayski, Baruch University
Alison Savery, Tufts University
Aliyah Yusuf, Lehman College
Angelique Cooper, DePaul University
Angie Brewster, Boston College
Barry Greenbaum, Cooper Union
Caitlin Offinger, Amherst College
Catie Connolly, Anna Marie College

Cheng Lee, University of Wisconsin–LaCrosse
Christina Fischer, University of Illinois at Chicago
Cyleigh Brez, Miami University
Danielle Gagnon, Boston University
Donna Gonzalex, Florida International University
Durrell Queen, University of New York
Emma Harris, Miami University
Erika Hill, University of Florida
Evan Miller, Parsons School of Design

Fernando Monzon, Miami Dade College
Fritz Kuhnlenz, Boston University
Gabriel Duran, Florida International University
Gerius Brantley, Florida Atlantic University
Giovanni Espinoza, Hunter College
Gregory Toft, Baruch University
Helen Wong, Hunter College
Henry Lopez, Florida International University
Jessie Lynch, Miami University
Joe Barron, Providence College
Joe Hoff, University of Wisconsin–LaCrosse
Jordan Simkovi, Northwestern University
Karissa Teekah, Lehman College
Katie Aiken, Miami University
Kevin Ringel, Northwestern University
Kristin Vayda, Miami University
Kristin Chimento, Miami University
Laura Beal, Miami University
Laura Schaffner, Miami University
Lindsey Lambalot, Northeastern University
Maggie Dolehide, Miami University
Marika Michalos, City College of New York
Matt Janko, University of Massachusetts–Amherst
Matt Nitka, University of Wisconsin–LaCrosse

Matthew Dripps, Miami University
Matthew Konigsberg, Baruch University
Michael Werner, Baruch University
Nichelina Mavros, Fordham University
O'Neil Barrett, Borough of Manhattan Community College
Patrick Thermitus, Bentley College
Paulina Glater, DePaul University
Rachel Hall, Miami University
Rebecca Tolles, Miami University
Rehan Noormohammad, Northeastern Illinois University
Rita Diz, Lehman College
Robert White, DePaul University
Ryan Bis, Boston University
Sam Trzyzewski, Boston University
Sarah Marith, Boston University
Stephanie DiSerio, Miami University
Steven Lippi, Boston College
Tanya Fahrenbach, Benedictine University
Travis Keltner, Boston College
Vanessa Uribe, Florida International University
Veronica Calvo, Keiser College
525 Students in MKTG 431: Principles of Marketing, San Francisco State University

We are equally grateful to all the professors across the country who participated in the development and creation of this new textbook through content reviews, advisory boards, and/or focus group work regarding the new pedagogical learning system. As always, professors provided us with invaluable information, ideas, and suggestions that consistently helped to strengthen our final product. We owe them great thanks and wish them much success in and out of their classrooms.

PROFESSOR PARTICIPANTS and REVIEWERS

Paula E. Brown, Northern Illinois University
Paula Hladik, Waubonsie Community College
Bruce Fisher, Elmhurst College
Mark Fox, Indiana University South Bend
Lisa McConnel, Oklahoma State University
Gerald Silver, Purdue University–Calumet
Nancy Thannert, Robert Morris College
Ron Thomas, Oakton Community College
Kenneth Thompson, DePaul University
Benjamin Weeks, St. Xavier University
Suzanne Peterson, Arizona State University

▶ ORGANIZATION OF THE BOOK

Most management instructors today organize their course around the traditional management functions of planning, organizing, leading, and controlling. Hence, *Principles of Management* uses these functions as its organizing framework. The book consists of five parts, with fifteen chapters.

Part 1 introduces management through two chapters. Chapter 1 provides a basic overview of the management process in organizations, and Chapter 2 introduces students to the environment of management.

Part 2 covers the first basic management function, planning. Chapter 3 introduces the fundamental concepts of planning and discusses strategic management. Managerial decision making is the topic of Chapter 4. Chapter 5 covers entrepreneurship and the management of new ventures.

The second basic management function, organizing, is the subject of Part 3. In Chapter 6 the fundamental concepts of organization structure and design are introduced and discussed. Chapter 7 discusses organization change and innovation. Chapter 8 is devoted to human resource management.

Many instructors and managers believe that the third basic management function, leading, is especially important in contemporary organizations. Thus Part 4 devotes five chapters to this management function. Basic concepts and processes associated with individual behavior are introduced and discussed in Chapter 9. Employee motivation is the subject of Chapter 10. Chapter 11 discusses leadership and influence processes in organizations. Communication in organizations is the topic of Chapter 12, and the management of groups and teams is covered in Chapter 13.

The fourth management function, controlling, is the subject of Part 5. Chapter 14 introduces the fundamental concepts and issues associated with the management of the control process. Finally, operations management is discussed in Chapter 15.

▶ SKILLS-FOCUSED PEDAGOGICAL FEATURES

With this text I have been able to address new dimensions of management education without creating a text that is unwieldy in length. Specifically, each chapter in this book is followed by an exciting set of skills-based exercises. These resources were created to bring an active and behavioral orientation to management education by requiring students to solve problems, make decisions, respond to situations, and work in groups. In short, these materials simulate many of the day-to-day challenges and opportunities faced by real managers.

Among these skills-based exercises are three different *Building Management Skills* organized around the set of basic management skills introduced in Chapter 1 of the text. One of these exercises appears in the text, and two others are found on the student Online Study Center and course management systems. In addition, the *Interactive Skills Self-Assessments,* found on the student Online Study Center and course management systems, help readers learn something about their own approach to management. Students can take these assessments and receive instant scoring and feedback. Finally, the *Experiential Exercises,* found in the text and online, provide additional action-oriented learning opportunities, usually in a group setting.

▶ AN EFFECTIVE TEACHING AND LEARNING PACKAGE

FOR INSTRUCTORS:

▎ ***Online Instructor's Resource Manual*** (Paul Keaton, University of Wisconsin–La Crosse). This resource includes an introduction from the author, suggested class schedules, detailed teaching notes for each chapter, and a video guide. The chapter teaching notes include chapter summaries, learning objectives, detailed chapter lecture outlines (including an opening incident summary, teaching tips, group exercise ideas, and discussion starters), Concept Check teaching notes, suggested responses to end-of-chapter case questions, and information to help facilitate the skills development exercises. This manual is available on the Instructor Website and course management platforms (Eduspace and Black-Board/WebCT CD).

▎ ***Online Test Bank*** (Sean Valentine, University of Wyoming). The Test Bank includes over 2,000 questions, with approximately 130 questions per chapter. Each question is identified by its corresponding learning objective, estimated level of difficulty, page number, and question type (knowledge, understanding, or application). This test bank is available on the Instructor Website and course management platforms (Eduspace and BlackBoard/WebCT CD).

▎ ***Video/DVD***. An expanded video program accompanies the text. Each chapter has its own video designed to illustrate the concepts discussed in the chapter by applying the discussion of the text to real-world case examples. The segments are designed to be shown in the classroom to generate discussion. The video guide for instructors can be found on the Instructor Website and course management platforms (Eduspace and BlackBoard/WebCT CD).

▎ ***HMTesting Instructor CD***. This CD-ROM contains electronic Test Bank items. Through a partnership with the Brownstone Research Group, HM Testing—now powered by *Diploma*®—provides instructors with all the tools they need to create, author/edit, customize, and deliver multiple types of tests. Instructors can import questions directly from the test bank, create their own questions, or edit existing algorithmic questions, all within *Diploma's* powerful electronic platform.

▎ ***Online Teaching Center***. This text-based instructor website offers valuable resources, including basic and premium PowerPoint slides, downloadable Instructor's Resource Manual files, a video guide, classroom response system content, and much more.

▎ ***Eduspace® Course.*** This online course management system, powered by Houghton Mifflin's proprietary, Eduspace, contains Instructor's Resource Manual files, test bank pools, autograded homework, a video guide, classroom response system content, video segments, quizzes, discussion threads, basic and premium PowerPoint slides, audio chapter summaries and quizzes (MP3s), *Interactive Skills Self-Assessments,* homework, and much more.

▎ ***BlackBoard/WebCT.*** This online course management system, powered by BlackBoard, contains Instructor's Resource Manual files, test bank pools, a video guide, classroom response system content, video segments, quizzes, discussion threads, basic and premium PowerPoint slides, audio chapter summaries and quizzes (MP3s), *Interactive Skills Self-Assessments,* homework, and much more.

FOR STUDENTS:

▌ ***Online Study Center***. This text-specific student website offers non-passkey protected content such as ACE practice tests, visual glossary terms, career snapshots, outlines, summaries, glossaries (chapter-based and complete), Knowledgebank content, and much more. Content behind "Your Guide to an 'A'" passkey includes ACE+ quizzes, Flashcards, *Study Guide to Go* content, *Interactive Skills Self-Assessments,* exercises, and audio chapter reviews (MP3 chapter summaries and quizzes).

▶ ACKNOWLEDGMENTS

I would like to acknowledge the many contributions that others have made to this book. My faculty colleagues have contributed enormously both to this book and to my thinking about management education. An outstanding team of professionals, including Lise Johnson, Julia Perez, and Carol Merrigan have made more contributions to this book than I could even begin to list. A special thanks is also due the many reviewers who helped shape the content and form of the materials in this book. While any and all errors are of course my own responsibility, I thank the following people for their help: Robert Ash (Santiago Canyon College), Murray Brunton (Central Ohio Tech), Gary Corona (Florida Community College–Jacksonville), Thomas DeLaughter (University of Florida), Anita Dickson (Northampton Community College), Michael Dutch (University of Houston), Norb Elbert (Eastern Kentucky University), Teri Elkins (University of Houston), Anne Fiedler (Barry University), Eugene Garaventa (College of Staten Island), Phillip Gonsher (Johnson Community College), Patricia Green (Nassau Community College), David Hudson (Spalding University), Judy Nixon (University of Tennessee–Chattanooga), Lisa Reed (University of Portland), Bob Smoot (Hazard Community College), Abe Tawil (Baruch University), Barry Van Hook (Arizona State University), Ruth Weatherly (Simpson College), Mary Williams (Community College of Nevada), Sally Alkazin (Linfield College), Sherryl Berg-Ridenour (DeVry College–Pomona), Alain Broder (Touro College), Sam Chapman (Diablo Valley College), Elizabeth Anne Christo-Baker (Terra Community College), Dr. Anne Cowden (California State University), Joe Dobson (Western Illinois University), Joseph S. Hooker, Jr. (North Greenville College), George W. Jacobs (Middle Tennessee State University), Ranjna Patel (Bethune-Cookman College), Dr. Joan Rivera (Angelo State University), Roberta B. Slater (Pennsylvania College of Technology), and Sheryl A. Stanley (Newman University). I would also like to thank Margaret Hill, who has become an integral part of this project. I sincerely appreciate the high level of professionalism that she brings to her work.

My wife, Glenda, and our children—Dustin, Ashley, and Matt—are, of course, due the greatest thanks. Their love, care, interest, and enthusiasm help sustain me in all that I do.

I would invite your feedback on this book. If you have any questions, suggestions, or issues to discuss, please feel free to contact me. The most efficient way to reach me is through e-mail. My address is ***rgriffin@tamu.edu***.

R.W.G.

Google, the burgeoning search engine company, recently opened a new office complex in London. To celebrate the opening of the new facility, called GooglePlex, the company distributed gifts to employees, investors, and the media in these colorful bags.

1 ▸ *Define management, describe the kinds of managers found in organizations, identify and explain the four basic management functions, describe the fundamental management skills, and comment on management as science and as art.*

2 ▸ *Justify the importance of history and theory to managers and explain the evolution of management thought through the classical, behavioral, and quantitative perspectives.*

3 ▸ *Identify and discuss key contemporary management perspectives represented by the systems and contingency perspectives and identify the major challenges and opportunities faced by managers today.*

> *"I'm the gatekeeper. I have to say no to a lot of people."*
>
> —Marissa Mayer, vice president, Google

Chapter Outline

▶ **An Introduction to Management**
Kinds of managers
Basic management functions
Fundamental management skills
The science and the art of management

▶ **The Evolution of Management**
The importance of history and theory
The historical context of management
The classical management perspective
The behavioral management perspective
The quantitative management perspective

▶ **Contemporary Management Perspectives**
The systems perspective
The contingency perspective
Contemporary management challenges
   and opportunities

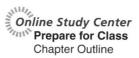
Online Study Center
Prepare for Class
Chapter Outline

Marissa Mayer:
Google's Top Designer

Marissa Mayer interviewed for a position at a start-up called Google in 1998. She wasn't impressed. She says, "[Those Stanford Ph.D. types] eat pizza for breakfast. They don't shower much. And they don't say 'Sorry' when they bump into you." She changed her mind, though, becoming one of the Internet search firm's first hires and its first female engineer.

Today, at thirty, Mayer is one of the top twenty managers at Google and its vice president of "Search Products and User Experience." Mayer rose to the top through a combination of intelligence, ambition, and talent. She was a high school valedictorian, debate leader, and pom-pom squad captain. She earned a Stanford bachelor's and a master's in artificial intelligence, and she patented several of her ideas. Her first task at Google was user interface design, so she read many psychology books to under-

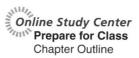
Online Study Center   college.hmco.com/pic/griffinSAS

You should be able to define and use terms that are part of the practicing manager's vocabulary, as well as those that are integral in the language of management.

stand perception. While working full time at Google, Mayer teaches programming to Stanford undergraduates and has won several teaching awards.

Mayer has a strong vision of the website's appearance and function. The simplicity of Google's site is deceptive. Every Google search ranks 8 billion Web pages after solving an equation with over 500 million variables. But Google also offers images, interactive maps, foreign-language translation, and more. It is Mayer's job to make sure that users can quickly and easily find what they want, while at the same time providing enough features. Mayer says, "Google has the functionality of a really complicated Swiss Army knife, but the home page is our way of approaching [the knife] closed. It's simple, it's elegant, you can slip it in your pocket, but it's got the great doodad when you need it."

Mayer is the one who gives the thumbs-up or thumbs-down to any new design idea. Her stringent rule is that any new service must receive millions of page views each day, or it doesn't get added to the home page. She wants the home to remain uncluttered so that Google's site looks different from Yahoo!'s and Microsoft's. The two competitors each have approximately 60 services, 140 links, and numerous advertisements. By comparison, Google's site offers 6 services, 17 links (up from 11 in 2001), and no ads. "[Our site] gives you what you want, when you want it, rather than everything you could ever want, even when you don't," says Mayer. She does not let worry get in the way of innovation, saying, "Customers remember your average over time. That philosophy frees you from fear."

Mayer focuses on the 87 percent of people who rate ease of use as their top priority. To maintain simplicity, lots of good ideas simply don't make the cut. "I'm the gatekeeper," Mayer states. "I have to say no to a lot of people." She is concerned that, once more features are added, they will be impossible to remove. At the same time, she is sensitive to the demands of both engineers and users for more elements. Google now offers a customized website that allows additional complexity. (Try it out by clicking on the "Personalized Home" button on the Google main home page, at www.google.com.)

Although Mayer may be uncompromising in her approach to design, she maintains good relationships with her staff. Two or three times a week, she holds informal "office hours" at Google, a technique she learned from her college professors. "I keep my ears open," she says. "I work at building a reputation for being receptive." Monthly brainstorming sessions for one hundred engineers are another one of Mayer's tools for eliciting creativity.

During her tenure at Google, Mayer has overseen expansion of the site into one hundred languages and helped to add one hundred specialized features. Her colleagues must be doing something right too. The company has grown from a dozen employees in 1998 to 5,000 in 2006. Today, Google controls 60 percent of the search market, up from 45 percent at the end of 2004. (Yahoo! controls 30 percent and MSN just 6 percent.) After a year in which revenues are expected to top $3.5 billion, Google stock is hot. Google went public in August 2004, selling shares for about $100. Eighteen months later, the shares traded for $450. With managers like Mayer leading the firm, Google seems poised to continue this success into the future.[1]

This book is about managers like Marissa Mayer and the work they do. In Chapter 1, we examine the nature of management, its dimensions, and its challenges. We explain the concepts of management and managers, discuss the management process, and summarize the origins of contemporary management thought. We conclude by introducing critical challenges and issues that managers are facing now and will continue to encounter in the future.

AN INTRODUCTION TO MANAGEMENT

1 *Define management, describe the kinds of managers found in organizations, identify and explain the four basic management functions, describe the fundamental management skills, and comment on management as science and as art.*

An **organization** is a group of people working together in a structured and coordinated fashion to achieve a set of goals. Common organizations include businesses (which strive to make profits for their owners) as well as not-for-profit organizations such as those that provide educational, health-care, governmental, and social services. Managers are responsible for using the organization's resources to help achieve its goals. More precisely, **management** is a set of activities (including planning and decision making, organizing, leading, and controlling) directed at using an organization's resources (human, financial, physical, and information) to achieve organizational goals in an efficient and effective manner. By **efficient**, we mean using resources wisely and in a cost-effective way. By **effective**, we mean making the right decisions and successfully implementing them.[2]

Today's managers face a variety of interesting and challenging situations. The average executive works sixty or more hours a week, has enormous demands

organization A group of people working together in a structured and coordinated fashion to achieve a set of goals.

management A set of activities (including planning and decision making, organizing, leading, and controlling) directed at using an organization's resources (human, financial, physical, and information) to achieve organizational goals in an efficient and effective manner.

efficient Using resources wisely and in a cost-effective way.

effective Making and implementing good decisions.

placed on his or her time, and faces increased complexities created by globalization, domestic competition, government regulation, shareholder pressure, and media scrutiny. The task is further complicated by rapid change, unexpected disruptions, and crises both minor and major. The manager's job is unpredictable and fraught with challenges, but it is also filled with excitement and opportunities to make a difference.

Kinds of Managers

Many different kinds of managers work in organizations today. Figure 1.1 shows how various managers can be differentiated by level and by area.

Levels of Management

One way to classify managers is in terms of their level in the organization.

- ▌ **Top managers** make up the relatively small group of executives who manage the overall organization. Titles found in this group include president, vice president, and chief executive officer (CEO). Top managers create the organization's goals, overall strategy, and operating policies. They also officially represent the organization to the external environment by meeting with government officials, executives of other organizations, and so forth. Marissa Mayer is a top manager.

- ▌ **Middle managers** are responsible primarily for implementing the policies and plans developed by top managers and for supervising and coordinating the activities of lower-level managers.[3] Common middle-management titles include

top managers   The relatively small group of senior executives who manage the overall organization.

middle managers   The relatively large set of managers responsible for implementing the policies and plans developed by top managers and for supervising and coordinating the activities of lower-level managers.

FIGURE 1.1

Kinds of Managers by Level and Area
Organizations generally have three levels of management, represented by top managers, middle managers, and first-line managers. Regardless of level, managers are also usually associated with a specific area within the organization, such as marketing, finance, operations, human resources, administration, or some other area.

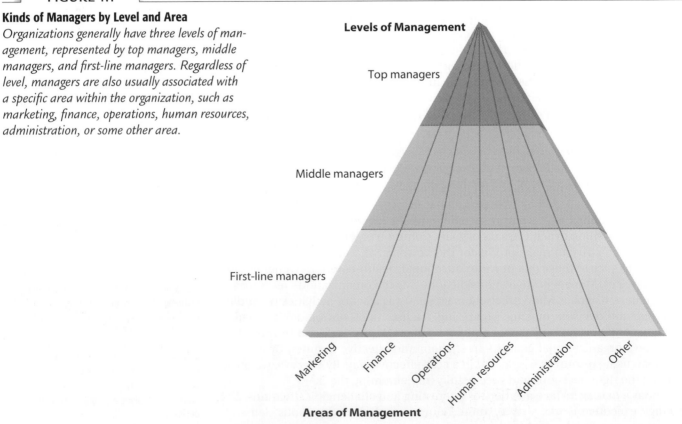

plant manager, operations manager, and division head. Plant managers, for example, handle inventory management, quality control, equipment failures, and minor union problems. They also coordinate the work of supervisors within the plant. James Henderson, general manager for Marriott's flagship hotel, the Marriott Marquis on New York's Times Square, is a middle manager.

▌ **First-line managers** supervise and coordinate the activities of operating employees. Julio Garcia oversees the housekeeping staff at the Marriott Marquis in New York; Roberta Tomlinson is responsible for the hotel's food service operations. Each is a first-line manager. In contrast to top and middle managers, first-line managers typically spend a large proportion of their time supervising the work of subordinates.

first-line managers Managers who supervise and coordinate the activities of operating employees.

Areas of Management

Regardless of their level, managers may work in various areas within an organization.

▌ *Marketing managers* work in areas related to the marketing function. These areas include new-product development, promotion, and distribution.

▌ *Financial managers* deal primarily with an organization's financial resources. They are responsible for such activities as accounting, cash management, and investments. In some businesses, such as banking and insurance, financial managers are found in especially large numbers.

▌ *Operations managers* are concerned with creating and managing the systems that create an organization's products and services. Typical responsibilities of operations managers include production control, inventory control, quality control, plant layout, and site selection.

▌ *Human resource managers* are responsible for hiring and developing employees. They are typically involved in human resource planning, recruiting and selecting employees, training and development, designing compensation and benefit systems, formulating performance appraisal systems, and discharging low-performing and problem employees.

▌ *Administrative*, or *general*, *managers* are not associated with any particular management specialty. Probably the best example of an administrative management position is that of a hospital or clinic administrator. Administrative managers tend to be generalists; they have some basic familiarity with all functional areas of management rather than specialized training in any one area.[4]

Many organizations also have specialized management positions in addition to those already described.

▌ Public relations managers deal with the public and media.

▌ Research and development (R&D) managers coordinate the activities of scientists and engineers working on scientific projects in organizations.

▌ Internal consultants are used in organizations to provide operating managers with specialized expert advice.

▌ International specialists are used to help firms deal with various issues encountered as a firm enters new foreign markets.

Online Study Center
Improve Your Grade
Career Snapshot

Online Study Center
Improve Your Grade
Knowledgebank 1.2

Basic Management Functions

Regardless of level or area, management involves the four basic functions of planning and decision making, organizing, leading, and controlling. This book is organized around these basic functions, as shown in Figure 1.2.

Planning and Decision Making

planning   Setting an organization's goals and deciding how best to achieve them.

decision making   Selecting a course of action from a set of alternatives.

In its simplest form, **planning** means setting an organization's goals and deciding how best to achieve them. **Decision making**, a part of the planning process, involves selecting a course of action from a set of alternatives. Planning and decision making help maintain managerial effectiveness by serving as guides for future activities. Part Two of this text is devoted to planning and decision-making activities and concepts.

Online Study Center
Improve Your Grade
Visual Glossary 1.1

Organizing

organizing   Determining how organizational activities and resources are to be grouped.

Once a manager has set goals and developed a workable plan, the next management function is to organize people and the other resources necessary to carry out the plan. Specifically, **organizing** involves determining how activities and resources are to be grouped. Although some people equate this function with the creation of an organization chart, we will see in Part Three that it is actually much more.

Online Study Center
Improve Your Grade
Visual Glossary 1.2

Leading

leading   The set of processes used to get members of the organization to work together to further the interests of the organization.

The third basic managerial function is leading. Some people consider leading to be both the most important and the most challenging of all managerial activities. **Leading** is the set of processes used to get members of the organization to work together to further the interests of the organization. We cover the leading function in detail in Part Four.

Controlling

controlling   Monitoring organizational progress toward goal attainment.

The final phase of the management process is **controlling**, or monitoring the organization's progress toward its goals. As the organization moves toward its goals,

---

FIGURE 1.2

The Management Process

Management involves four basic activities—planning and decision making, organizing, leading, and controlling. Although there is a basic logic for describing these activities in this sequence (as indicated by the solid arrows), most managers engage in more than one activity at a time and often move back and forth between the activities in unpredictable ways (as shown by the dotted arrows).

"Do you mind? I happen to be on the phone!"

Managers are constantly engaged in many different activities. The types and sequences of activities are often difficult to predict from one day to the next, however, and managers often do their work in impromptu settings or on airplanes, in taxis, over meals, or even when walking down the street. The manager shown here, for example, may be helping a colleague develop goals for the next quarter (planning), discussing a proposed company restructuring (organizing), praising a subordinate for outstanding performance (leading), or checking on last month's sales information (controlling). The pace of this work may be stressful for some people, and exhilarating for others.

managers must monitor progress to ensure that the firm is performing in such a way as to arrive at its "destination" at the appointed time. Part Five explores the control function.

Fundamental Management Skills

To carry out these management functions most effectively, managers rely on a number of specific skills. The most fundamental management skills are technical, interpersonal, conceptual, diagnostic, communication, decision-making, and time-management skills.[5]

▌ **Technical skills** are the skills necessary to accomplish or understand the specific kind of work being done in an organization. Technical skills are especially important for first-line managers. These managers spend much of their time training subordinates and answering questions about work-related problems. They must know how to perform the tasks assigned to those they supervise if they are to be effective managers.

technical skills The skills necessary to accomplish or understand the specific kind of work being done in an organization.

▌ **Interpersonal skills** enable managers to communicate with, understand, and motivate both individuals and groups. As a manager climbs the organizational ladder, she must be able to get along with subordinates, peers, and those at higher levels of the organization. Because of the multitude of roles that managers must play, a manager must also be able to work with suppliers, customers, investors, and others outside of the organization.

interpersonal skills The ability to communicate with, understand, and motivate both individuals and groups.

▌ **Conceptual skills** depend on the manager's ability to think in the abstract. Managers need the mental capacity to understand the overall workings of the organization and its environment, to grasp how all the parts of the organization fit together, and to view the organization in a holistic manner. This allows them to think strategically, to see the "big picture," and to make broad-based decisions that serve the overall organization.

conceptual skills The manager's ability to think in the abstract.

▌ **Diagnostic skills** enable a manager to visualize the most appropriate response to a situation. A physician diagnoses a patient's illness by analyzing symptoms and

diagnostic skills The manager's ability to visualize the most appropriate response to a situation.

determining their probable cause. Similarly, a manager can diagnose and analyze a problem in the organization by studying its symptoms and then developing a solution.

communication skills The manager's ability both to convey ideas and information to others effectively and to receive ideas and information effectively from others.

▌ **Communication skills** refer to the manager's abilities both to convey ideas and information to others effectively and to receive ideas and information effectively from others. These skills enable a manager to transmit ideas to subordinates so that they know what is expected, to coordinate tasks with peers and colleagues so that they work together properly, and to keep higher-level managers informed about what is going on. In addition, they help the manager listen to what others say and understand the real meaning behind letters, reports, and other written communication.

decision-making skills The manager's ability to recognize and correctly define problems and opportunities and then to select an appropriate course of action to solve problems and capitalize on opportunities.

▌ **Decision-making skills** refer to the manager's ability to recognize and correctly define problems and opportunities and then to select an appropriate course of action to solve problems and capitalize on opportunities. No manager makes the right decision all the time. However, effective managers make good decisions most of the time. And when they do make a bad decision, they usually recognize their mistake quickly and then make good decisions to recover with as little cost or damage to their organization as possible.

time-management skills The manager's ability to prioritize work, to work efficiently, and to delegate appropriately.

▌ **Time-management skills** consist of the manager's ability to prioritize work, to work efficiently, and to delegate appropriately. As already noted, managers face many different pressures and challenges. It is all too easy for a manager to get bogged down doing work that could readily be postponed or delegated to others.[6] When this happens, unfortunately, more pressing and higher-priority work may be neglected.[7]

CONCEPT CHECK 1.1

Recall a recent group project or task in which you have participated. Explain how members of the group displayed each of the managerial skills.

The Science and the Art of Management

Given the complexity of the manager's job, it is reasonable to ask whether management is a science or an art. In fact, effective management is a blend of the two. And successful executives recognize the importance of combining both the science and the art of management as they practice their craft.[8]

The Science of Management

Many management problems and issues can be approached in ways that are rational, logical, objective, and systematic. Managers can gather data, facts, and objective information. They can use quantitative models and decision-making techniques to arrive at "correct" decisions. And they need to take such a scientific approach to solving problems whenever possible, especially when they are dealing with relatively routine and straightforward issues. When Marriott considers building a new hotel, its managers look closely at a wide variety of objective details as they formulate their plans. Technical, diagnostic, and decision-making skills are especially important when practicing the science of management.

The Art of Management

Even though managers may try to be scientific as much as possible, they must often make decisions and solve problems on the basis of intuition, experience, instinct, and personal insights. Relying heavily on conceptual, communication, interpersonal, and time-management skills, for example, a manager may have to decide among multiple courses of action that look equally attractive. And even "objective facts" may prove to be misleading. When Starbucks was planning its first store in

New York, market research clearly showed that New Yorkers preferred drip coffee to more exotic espresso-style coffees. After first installing more drip coffee makers and fewer espresso makers than in their other stores, managers had to backtrack when the New Yorkers lined up clamoring for espresso. Starbucks now introduces a standard menu and layout in all its stores, regardless of presumed market differences, and then makes necessary adjustments later. Thus managers must blend an element of intuition and personal insight with hard data and objective facts.[9]

CONCEPT CHECK 1.2

Recall an interaction you have had with a superior (manager, teacher, group leader, or the like). In that interaction, did the superior use science or art, or both? What could he or she have done to use science? What could he or she have done to use art?

TEST PREPPER 1.1

ANSWERS CAN BE FOUND ON P. 441

True or False?

_____ 1. Arne Sorenson, senior vice president for finance at Marriott, is a middle manager.

_____ 2. When a manager forms a team with members from each functional area, she is engaged in organizing.

_____ 3. Top managers are using their decision-making skills when they think strategically and monitor a broad area of concern.

Multiple Choice

_____ 4. Early in her career Carly Fiorina worked in new-product development, promotion, and distribution. She was a(n) _____ manager.
   a. human resource
   b. specialized
   c. operations
   d. marketing
   e. finance

_____ 5. As an operations manager for Cintas, Dave Warns is responsible for motivating subordinates. To accomplish that he must use which skills?
   a. Technical   d. Communication
   b. Interpersonal   e. Time-management
   c. Conceptual

_____ 6. Lucia manages a McDonald's. She notices that the morning shift has higher employee turnover, low morale, and low productivity. She must use her _____ skills to develop a solution.
   a. conceptual   d. decision-making
   b. diagnostic   e. time-management
   c. communication

_____ 7. Mark prefers to make decisions based on "gut feeling" and experience. He is most likely to describe management as _____.
   a. science   d. theory Y
   b. art   e. theory X
   c. theory Z

Online Study Center
ACE the Test
ACE Practice Tests 1.1

THE EVOLUTION OF MANAGEMENT

2 *Justify the importance of history and theory to managers and explain the evolution of management thought through the classical, behavioral, and quantitative perspectives.*

Most managers today recognize the importance of history and theory in their work. For instance, knowing the origins of their organization and the kinds of practices that have led to success—or failure—can be an indispensable tool in managing the contemporary organization. Thus, in our next section, we briefly trace the history of management thought. Then we move forward to the present day by introducing contemporary management issues and challenges.

The Importance of History and Theory

Some people question the value of history and theory. Their arguments are usually based on the assumptions that history has no relevance to contemporary society

Online Study Center
Improve Your Grade
Knowledgebank 1.3

and that theory is abstract and of no practical use. In reality, however, both theory and history are important to all managers today.

A **theory** is simply a conceptual framework for organizing knowledge and providing a blueprint for action.[10] Although some theories may seem abstract and irrelevant, many others are actually very simple and practical. Most management theories that are used to build organizations and guide them toward their goals are grounded in reality.[11] In addition, most managers develop and refine their own beliefs—or theories—about how they should run their organization and manage their employees.

Awareness and understanding of important historical developments are also important to contemporary managers.[12] Understanding the historical context of management provides a sense of heritage and can help managers avoid the mistakes of others. Most courses in U.S. history devote time to business and economic developments in this country, including the Industrial Revolution, the early labor movement, and the Great Depression, and to such captains of U.S. industry as Cornelius Vanderbilt (railroads), John D. Rockefeller (oil), and Andrew Carnegie (steel). The contributions of those and other industrialists left a profound imprint on contemporary culture.[13]

Many managers are also realizing that they can benefit from a greater understanding of history in general. For example, Ian M. Ross of AT&T's Bell Laboratories cites *The Second World War* by Winston Churchill as a major influence on his approach to leadership. Other books that are often mentioned by managers for their relevance to today's business problems include such classics as Plato's *Republic*, Homer's *Iliad*, and Machiavelli's *The Prince*.[14] And, in recent years, new business history books are directed more at women managers and the lessons they can learn from the past.[15]

Managers at Wells Fargo clearly recognize the value of history. For example, the company maintains an extensive archival library of its old banking documents and records and even employs a full-time corporate historian. As part of their orientation and training, new managers at Wells Fargo take courses to become acquainted with the bank's history.[16] And the firm's logo is an old-fashioned stagecoach.

The Historical Context of Management

The serious study of management began in the nineteenth century. Two of its first pioneers were Robert Owen and Charles Babbage. Owen (1771–1858), a British industrialist and reformer, was one of the first managers to recognize the importance of an organization's human resources and to express concern for the personal welfare of his workers. Babbage (1792–1871), an English mathematician, focused his attention on efficiencies of production. He placed great faith in the division of labor and advocated the application of mathematics to such problems as the efficient use of facilities and materials.

The Classical Management Perspective

At the dawn of the twentieth century, the preliminary ideas and writings of these and other managers and theorists converged with the emergence and evolution of large-scale businesses and management practices to create interest in management and to focus attention on how businesses should be operated. The first important ideas to emerge are now called the **classical management perspective**. This perspective actually includes two different branches: scientific management and administrative management.

---

theory A conceptual framework for organizing knowledge and providing a blueprint for action.

classical management perspective An approach to business management that consists of two distinct branches—scientific management and administrative management.

▌ *Scientific Management.*   Productivity emerged as a serious business concern during the early years of the twentieth century. Business was expanding and capital was readily available, but labor was in short supply. Hence managers began to search for ways to use existing labor more efficiently. In response to this need, experts began to focus on ways to improve the performance of individual workers. Their work led to the development of **scientific management**, that branch of the classical management perspective that is concerned with improving the performance of individual workers.

Some of the earliest advocates of scientific management included Frederick W. Taylor (1856–1915), Frank Gilbreth (1868–1924), and Lillian Gilbreth (1878–1972).[17] One of Taylor's first jobs was as a foreman at the Midvale Steel Company in Philadelphia. It was there that he observed what he called **soldiering**—employees' deliberately working at a pace slower than their capabilities would have allowed. Taylor studied and timed each element of the steelworkers' jobs. He determined what each worker should be producing, and then he designed the most efficient way of doing each part of the overall task. Next he implemented a piecework pay system. Rather than paying all employees the same wage, he began increasing the pay of each worker who met and exceeded the target level of output set for his or her job.

After Taylor left Midvale, he worked as a consultant for several companies, including Simonds Rolling Machine Company and Bethlehem Steel. At Simonds he studied and redesigned jobs, introduced rest periods to reduce fatigue, and implemented a piecework pay system. The results were higher quality and quantity of output, and improved morale. At Bethlehem Steel, Taylor studied efficient ways of loading and unloading rail cars and applied his conclusions with equally impressive results.

Frank and Lillian Gilbreth, contemporaries of Taylor, were a husband-and-wife team of industrial engineers. One of Frank Gilbreth's most interesting contributions was to the craft of bricklaying. After studying bricklayers at work, he developed several procedures for doing the job more efficiently. For example, he specified standard materials and techniques, including the positioning of the bricklayer, the bricks, and the mortar at different levels. The results of these changes were a reduction from eighteen separate physical movements to five and an increase in output of about 200 percent. Lillian Gilbreth made equally important contributions to several different areas of work, helped shape the field of industrial psychology, and made substantive contributions to the field of personnel management.

▌ *Administrative Management.*   Whereas scientific management deals with the jobs of individual employees, **administrative management** focuses on managing the total organization. The primary contributors to administrative management were Henri Fayol (1841–1925), Lyndall Urwick (1891–1983), and Max Weber (1864–1920).

Henri Fayol was administrative management's most articulate spokesperson. A French industrialist, Fayol was unknown to U.S. managers and scholars until his most important work, *General and Industrial Management,* was translated into English in 1930.[18] Drawing on his own managerial experience, he attempted to systematize the practice of management to provide guidance and direction to other managers. Fayol also was the first to identify the specific managerial functions of planning, organizing, leading, and controlling. He believed that these functions accurately reflect the core of the management process. Most

scientific management   The branch of the classical management perspective that is concerned with improving the performance of individual workers.

soldiering   Employees' deliberately working at a slow pace.

administrative management   The branch of the classical management perspective that focuses on managing the total organization.

contemporary management books (including this one) still use this framework, and practicing managers agree that these functions are a critical part of their job.

After a career as a British army officer, Lyndall Urwick became a noted management theorist and consultant. He integrated scientific management with the work of Fayol and other administrative management theorists. He also advanced modern thinking about the functions of planning, organizing, and controlling. Like Fayol, he developed a list of guidelines for improving managerial effectiveness. Urwick is noted not so much for his own contributions as for his synthesis and integration of the work of others.

Although Max Weber lived and worked at the same time as Fayol and Taylor, his contributions were not recognized until some years had passed. Weber was a German sociologist, and his most important work was not translated into English until 1947.[19] Weber's work on bureaucracy laid the foundation for contemporary organization theory, discussed in detail in Chapter 6. The concept of bureaucracy, as we discuss later, is based on a rational set of guidelines for structuring organizations in the most efficient manner.

CONCEPT CHECK 1.3

What are the main principles of scientific management and administrative management? What assumptions do these perspectives make about workers?

■ *The Classical Perspective Today.*   The classical management perspective provides many techniques and approaches to management that are still relevant today. For example, thoroughly understanding the nature of the work being performed, selecting the right people for that work, and approaching decisions rationally are all useful ideas—and each was developed during this period. Similarly, some of the core concepts from Weber's bureaucratic model can still be used in the design of modern organizations, as long as their limitations are recognized. Managers should recognize that efficiency and productivity can indeed be measured and controlled in many situations. Recent advances in areas such as business-to-business (B2B) commerce also have efficiency as their primary goal. On the other hand, managers must remember the limitations of the classical perspective and avoid its narrow focus on efficiency to the exclusion of other important perspectives.

The Behavioral Management Perspective

Early advocates of the classical management perspective viewed organizations and jobs from a mechanistic point of view; that is, they sought to conceptualize organizations as machines and workers as cogs within those machines. Even though many early writers recognized the role of individuals, they tended to focus on how managers could control and standardize the behavior of their employees. In contrast, the **behavioral management perspective** placed much more emphasis on individual attitudes and behaviors and on group processes, and it recognized the importance of behavioral processes in the workplace.

behavioral management perspective
An approach to business management that emphasizes individual attitudes and behaviors and group processes.

The behavioral management perspective was stimulated by a number of writers and theoretical movements. One of those movements was industrial psychology, the practice of applying psychological concepts to industrial settings. Hugo Munsterberg (1863–1916), a noted German psychologist, is recognized as the father of industrial psychology. Munsterberg suggested that psychologists could make valuable contributions to managers in the areas of employee selection and motivation. Industrial psychology is still a major course of study at many colleges and universities. Another early advocate of the behavioral approach to management was Mary Parker Follett (1868–1933).[20] Follett worked during the scientific management era but quickly came to recognize the human element in the workplace. Indeed, her work clearly anticipated the behavioral management perspective, and she appreciated the need to understand the role of behavior in organizations.

The Hawthorne Studies

Although Munsterberg and Follett made major contributions to the development of the behavioral approach to management, its primary catalyst was a series of studies conducted near Chicago at Western Electric's Hawthorne plant between 1927 and 1932. The research, originally sponsored by General Electric, was conducted by Elton Mayo and his associates.[21] The first study involved manipulating illumination for one group of workers and comparing their subsequent productivity with the productivity of another group whose illumination was not changed. Surprisingly, when illumination was increased for the experimental group, productivity went up in both groups. And productivity continued to increase in both groups, even when the lighting for the experimental group was decreased. Not until the lighting was reduced to the level of moonlight did productivity begin to decline (and General Electric withdrew its sponsorship).

The Hawthorne studies were a series of early experiments that focused on behavior in the workplace. In one experiment involving this group of workers, for example, researchers monitored how productivity changed as a result of changes in working conditions. The Hawthorne studies and subsequent experiments led scientists to the conclusion that the human element is very important in the workplace.

Another experiment established a piecework incentive pay plan for a group of nine men assembling terminal banks for telephone exchanges. Scientific management would have predicted that each man would try to maximize his pay by producing as many units as possible. Mayo and his associates, however, found that the group itself informally established an acceptable level of output for its members. Workers who overproduced were branded "rate busters," and underproducers were labeled "chiselers." In order to be accepted by the group, workers produced at the acceptable level. And as they approached this acceptable level of output, they slacked off to avoid overproducing.

Other studies, including an interview program involving several thousand workers, led Mayo and his associates to conclude that human behavior was much more important in the workplace than had been previously believed. In the lighting experiment, for example, the results were attributed to the fact that both groups received special attention and sympathetic supervision for perhaps the first time. The incentive pay plans did not work because wage incentives were less important to the individual workers than social acceptance. In short, individual and social processes played a major role in shaping worker attitudes and behavior.

Human Relations

The **human relations movement**, which grew from the Hawthorne studies and which was a popular approach to management for many years, proposed that workers respond primarily to the social context of the workplace, including social conditioning, group norms, and interpersonal dynamics. A basic assumption of the human relations movement was that the manager's concern for workers would lead to increased satisfaction, which would in turn result in improved performance. Two writers who helped advance the human relations movement were Abraham Maslow (1908–1970) and Douglas McGregor (1906–1964).

In 1943 Maslow proposed that people are motivated by a hierarchy of needs, including monetary incentives and social acceptance.[22] Maslow's hierarchy,

human relations movement A school of thought that argued that workers respond primarily to the social context of the workplace.

Theory X   A pessimistic and negative view of workers that is consistent with the views of scientific management.

Theory Y   A positive view of workers that reflects the assumptions that human relations advocates make.

organizational behavior   Contemporary field focusing on behavioral perspectives on management.

perhaps the best-known human relations theory, is described in detail in Chapter 10. Meanwhile, Douglas McGregor's Theory X and Theory Y model best represents the essence of the human relations movement.[23] According to McGregor, Theory X and Theory Y reflect two extreme belief sets that different managers have about their workers. **Theory X** is a relatively pessimistic and negative view of workers and is consistent with the views of scientific management. **Theory Y** is more positive and reflects the assumptions that human relations advocates make. In McGregor's view, Theory Y was a more appropriate philosophy for managers to adhere to. Both Maslow and McGregor notably influenced the thinking of many practicing managers.

Contemporary Behavioral Science in Management

Munsterberg, Mayo, Maslow, McGregor, and others have made many valuable contributions to management. Contemporary theorists, however, have noted that many assertions of the human relationists were simplistic and inadequate descriptions of work behavior. Current behavioral perspectives on management, known as **organizational behavior**, acknowledge that human behavior in organizations is much more complex than the human relationists realized. The field of organizational behavior draws from a broad, interdisciplinary base of psychology, sociology, anthropology, economics, and medicine.[24] Organizational behavior takes a holistic view of behavior and addresses individual, group, and organization processes. These processes are major elements in contemporary management theory. Important topics in this field include job satisfaction, stress, motivation, leadership, group dynamics, organizational politics, interpersonal conflict, and the structure and design of organizations.[25] A contingency orientation also characterizes the field. Our discussions of organizing (Chapters 6–8) and leading (Chapters 9–13) are heavily influenced by organizational behavior. And finally, managers need a solid understanding of human behavior as they address such diversity-related issues as gender, age, ethnicity, and religion in the workplace.

The Behavioral Perspective Today

The primary contributions of this approach are related to ways in which it has changed managerial thinking. Managers are now more likely to recognize the importance of behavioral processes and to view employees as valuable resources instead of mere tools. On the other hand, organizational behavior is still relatively imprecise in its ability to predict behavior, especially the behavior of a specific individual. It is not always accepted or understood by practicing managers. Hence the contributions of the behavioral school have yet to be fully realized.

The Quantitative Management Perspective

The third major school of management thought began to emerge during World War II. During the war, government officials and scientists in England and the United States worked to help the military deploy its resources more efficiently and effectively. These groups took some of the mathematical approaches to management developed as part of the classical perspective and applied them to logistical problems during the war.[26] They learned that problems regarding troop, equipment, and submarine deployment, for example, could all be solved through mathematical analysis. After the war, companies such as DuPont and General Electric began to use the same techniques for deploying employees, choosing plant locations, and planning warehouses. Basically, then, this perspective is concerned with applying quantitative techniques to management. More specifically, the **quantitative management perspective** focuses on decision making, economic effectiveness, mathematical models, and the use of computers. There are two branches of the quantitative approach: management science and operations management.

quantitative management perspective   An approach that applies quantitative techniques to business management.

▌ *Management Science.*   Unfortunately, the term *management science* sounds as though it is related to scientific management. But the two have little in common and should not be confused with each other. **Management science** focuses specifically on the development of mathematical models. A mathematical model is a simplified representation of a system, process, or relationship.

management science   The branch of the quantitative approach to management that focuses specifically on the development of mathematical models.

At its most basic level, management science focuses on models, equations, and similar representations of reality. For example, managers at Detroit Edison use mathematical models to determine how best to route repair crews during blackouts. Banks use models to figure out how many tellers need to be on duty at each location at various times throughout the day. In recent years, paralleling the advent of the personal computer, management science techniques have become increasingly sophisticated. For example, automobile manufacturers use realistic computer simulations to study collision damage to cars. These simulations give them precise information and avoid the costs of crashing so many test cars.

operations management   The branch of the quantitative approach to management that is concerned with helping the organization more efficiently produce its products or services.

▌ *Operations Management.*   Operations management is somewhat less mathematical and statistically sophisticated than management science and can be applied more directly to managerial situations. Indeed, we can think of **operations management** as a form of applied management science. Operations management techniques are generally concerned with helping the organization produce its products or services more efficiently and can be applied to a wide range of problems.

For example, The Home Depot uses operations management techniques to manage inventory. (Inventory management is concerned with specific inventory problems, such as balancing carrying costs and ordering costs, and determining the optimal order quantity.) Linear programming (which involves computing simultaneous solutions to a set of linear equations) helps United Airlines plan its flight schedules, helps Consolidated Freightways develop its shipping routes, and helps manufacturers plan what items to produce at various times.

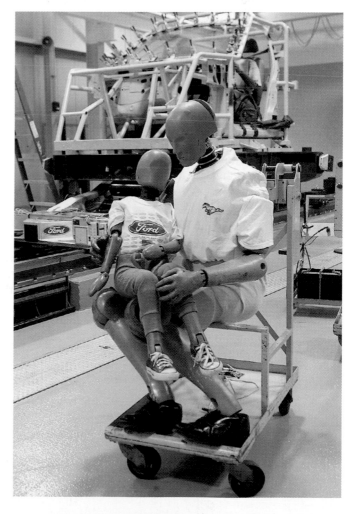

The quantitative management perspective offers many tools and techniques that can help business. For instance, Ford Motor Company is using these crash test dummies to learn more about improving passenger safety. By being able to precisely measure impact points and their effects on these dummies, Ford can better design its products in ways that help reduce injuries.

Other operations management techniques include queuing theory, breakeven analysis, and simulation. All of these techniques and procedures apply directly to operations, but they are also helpful in such areas as finance, marketing, and human resource management.

▌ ***The Quantitative Perspective Today.*** Like the other management perspectives, the quantitative management perspective has made important contributions and has certain limitations. It has provided managers with an abundance of decision-making tools and techniques and has increased understanding of overall organizational processes. It has been particularly useful in the areas of planning and controlling. Relatively new management concepts such as supply chain management and new techniques such as Enterprise Resource Planning, both discussed later in this book, also evolved from the quantitative management perspective. On the other hand, mathematical models cannot fully account for individual behaviors and attitudes. Some believe that the time it takes to develop competence in quantitative techniques retards the development of other managerial skills. Finally, mathematical models typically require a set of assumptions that may not be realistic.

CONCEPT CHECK 1.4

Can a manager use tools and techniques from several different perspectives at the same time? Give an example of a time when a manager used more than one perspective, and explain how this approach enabled him or her to be effective.

TEST PREPPER 1.2

ANSWERS CAN BE FOUND ON P. 441

True or False?

_____ 1. Scientific management focuses on jobs of individual employees.

_____ 2. Administrative management places emphasis on individual attitudes and behaviors. It recognizes the importance of behavior processes in the workplace.

_____ 3. The branches of quantitative management are management science and operations management.

_____ 4. Classical, behavioral, and quantitative approaches make different assumptions and predictions. They are contradictory and mutually exclusive.

Multiple Choice

_____ 5. Which of the following perspectives has a relatively narrow focus on efficiency to the exclusion of other important points of view?
   a. Classical
   b. Behavioral
   c. Quantitative
   d. System
   e. Contingency

_____ 6. When employees deliberately work at a slower pace it is called _____.
   a. bureaucracy
   b. the Hawthorne effect
   c. soldiering
   d. theory Y behavior
   e. synergy

_____ 7. Which of the following is NOT an assumption of Theory X?
   a. People do not like to work
   b. Managers have to control and coerce employees
   c. People avoid responsibility
   d. People want security
   e. Work is a natural part of their lives

_____ 8. Each of the following is a limitation of the quantitative perspective EXCEPT _____.
   a. it cannot explain human behavior
   b. it cannot predict human behavior
   c. models may require unrealistic assumptions
   d. its usefulness in controlling is limited
   e. mathematical sophistication may come at the expense of other important skills

Online Study Center
ACE the Test
ACE Practice Tests 1.2

CONTEMPORARY MANAGEMENT PERSPECTIVES

3 ► *Identify and discuss key contemporary management perspectives represented by the systems and contingency perspectives and identify the major challenges and opportunities faced by managers today.*

It is important to recognize that the classical, behavioral, and quantitative approaches to management are not necessarily contradictory or mutually exclusive. Even though each of the three perspectives makes very different assumptions and predictions, each can also complement the others. Indeed, a complete understanding of management requires an appreciation of all three perspectives. Two additional perspectives, the systems perspective and the contingency perspective, can help us integrate the earlier approaches and enlarge our understanding of all three.

The Systems Perspective

The systems perspective is one important contemporary management perspective. A **system** is an interrelated set of elements functioning as a whole.[27] As shown in Figure 1.3, by viewing an organization as a system, we can identify four basic elements: inputs, transformation processes, outputs, and feedback. First, inputs are the material, human, financial, and information resources the organization gets from its environment. Next, through technological and managerial processes, inputs are transformed into outputs. Outputs include products, services, or both (tangible and intangible); profits, losses, or both (even not-for-profit organizations must operate within their budgets); employee behaviors; and information. Finally, the environment reacts to these outputs and provides feedback to the system.

> **system** An interrelated set of elements functioning as a whole.

Thinking of organizations as systems provides us with a variety of important viewpoints on organizations:

▌ **Open systems** are systems that interact with their environment, whereas **closed systems** do not interact with their environment. Although organizations are open systems, some managers make the mistake of ignoring their environment and behaving as though their environment were not important.

> **open system** A system that interacts with its environment.
> **closed system** A system that does not interact with its environment.

▌ **Subsystems** are systems within a broader system. For example, the marketing, production, and finance functions within Mattel are systems in their own right

> **subsystem** A system within another system.

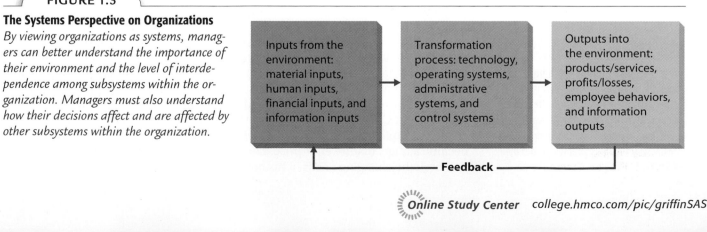

FIGURE 1.3

The Systems Perspective on Organizations
By viewing organizations as systems, managers can better understand the importance of their environment and the level of interdependence among subsystems within the organization. Managers must also understand how their decisions affect and are affected by other subsystems within the organization.

Inputs from the environment: material inputs, human inputs, financial inputs, and information inputs → Transformation process: technology, operating systems, administrative systems, and control systems → Outputs into the environment: products/services, profits/losses, employee behaviors, and information outputs

── **Feedback** ──

Online Study Center college.hmco.com/pic/griffinSAS

but are also subsystems within the overall organization. Because they are interdependent, a change in one subsystem can affect other subsystems as well. If the production department at Mattel lowers the quality of the toys being made (by buying lower-quality materials, for example), the effects are felt in finance (improved cash flow in the short run because of lower costs) and marketing (decreased sales in the long run because of customer dissatisfaction). Managers must therefore remember that although organizational subsystems can be managed with some degree of autonomy, their interdependence should not be overlooked.

synergy Two or more subsystems working together to produce more than the total of what they might produce working alone.

▌ **Synergy** suggests that organizational units (or subsystems) may often be more successful working together than working alone. The Walt Disney Company, for example, benefits greatly from synergy. The company's movies, theme parks, television programs, and merchandise-licensing programs all benefit one another. Children who enjoy a Disney movie such as *Lion King* want to go to Disney World, to see the *Lion King* show there, and to buy stuffed toys of the film's characters. Music from the film generates additional revenues for the firm, as do computer games and other licensing arrangements for lunchboxes, clothing, and so forth. Synergy is an important concept for managers because it emphasizes the importance of working together in a cooperative and coordinated fashion.[28]

entropy A normal process leading to system decline.

▌ **Entropy** is system decline. When an organization does not monitor feedback from its environment and make appropriate adjustments, it may fail. For example, witness the problems of Studebaker (an automobile manufacturer) and Kmart (a major retailer). Each of these organizations went bankrupt because it failed to revitalize itself and keep pace with changes in its environment. A primary objective of management, from a systems perspective, is to re-energize the organization continually to avoid the ill effects of entropy.

The Contingency Perspective

Another noteworthy addition to management thinking is the contingency perspective. The classical, behavioral, and quantitative approaches are considered **universal perspectives** because they tried to identify the "one best way" to manage organizations. The contingency perspective, in contrast, suggests that universal theories cannot be applied to organizations because each organization is unique. Instead, the **contingency perspective** suggests that appropriate managerial behavior in a given situation depends on, or is contingent on, unique elements in that situation.[29]

universal perspective The point of view that there is "one best way" to do something.

contingency perspective The point of view that appropriate managerial behavior in a given situation depends on, or is contingent on, a wide variety of elements.

Stated differently, effective managerial behavior in one situation cannot always be generalized to other situations. Recall, for example, that Frederick Taylor assumed that all workers would generate the highest possible level of output to maximize their own personal economic gain. We can imagine some people being motivated primarily by money—but we can just as easily imagine other people being motivated by the desire for leisure time, status, social acceptance, or any combination of these (as Mayo found at the Hawthorne plant). Leslie Wexner, founder and CEO of The Limited, used one managerial style when his firm was small and rapidly growing, but that style did not match as well when The Limited became a huge, mature enterprise. Thus Wexner had to alter his style at that point to match the changing needs of his business.

CONCEPT CHECK 1.5

Young, innovative, or high-tech firms sometimes adopt the strategy of ignoring historical management approaches and attempting to do something radically new. In what ways will this strategy help them? In what ways will this strategy hinder their efforts?

Contemporary Management Challenges and Opportunities

Interest in management theory and practice has blossomed in recent years as new issues and challenges have emerged. No new paradigm has been formulated that replaces the traditional views, but managers continue to strive to understand how they can better compete and lead their organizations toward improved effectiveness.

Online Study Center
Improve Your Grade
Knowledgebank 1.4

Contemporary Applied Perspectives

In recent years, books written for the popular press have had a major impact on both the theory and the practice of management. This trend first became noticeable in the early 1980s with the success of such modern classics as William Ouchi's *Theory Z* and Thomas Peters's and Robert Waterman's *In Search of Excellence*. Each of these books spent time on the *New York Times* best-seller list and was required reading for any manager who wanted even to appear informed.

Other applied authors have had a major impact on management theory and practice. Among the most popular applied authors today are Peter Senge, Stephen Covey, Tom Peters, Jim Collins, Michael Porter, John Kotter, and Gary Hamel.[30] Their books highlight the management practices of successful firms or outline conceptual or theoretical models or frameworks to guide managers as they formulate strategy or motivate their employees. Scott Adams, creator of the popular comic

Globalization is a major issue facing many managers today. On the one hand, globalization provides business with new opportunities. And many experts agree that the long-term benefits of globalization will be significant. But not everyone agrees with this sentiment. These protesters, for example, believe that globalization hurts the residents of less developed economies and damages our planet's ecosystems. The target of their wrath is often the World Trade Organization (WTO), an international consortium created to promote globalization.

strip Dilbert, is also immensely popular today. Adams is a former communications industry worker who developed his strip to illustrate some of the absurdities that occasionally afflict contemporary organizational life. The daily strip is routinely posted outside office doors, above copy machines, and beside water coolers in hundreds of offices.

Contemporary Management Challenges

Managers today also face an imposing set of challenges as they guide and direct the fortunes of their companies. Coverage of each of these is thoroughly integrated throughout this book. In addition, many of them are also highlighted or given focused coverage in one or more special ways. The following list includes many of the most compelling issues facing managers today:

▎ An erratic economy that constrains managers' abilities to plan for the future

▎ The management of diversity

▎ Employee privacy relative to the organization

▎ The increased capabilities that technology provides for people to work at places other than their office

▎ The appropriate role of the Internet in business strategy

▎ The growth in outsourcing domestic jobs to foreign locations to take advantage of lower labor costs

▎ Globalization

▎ Ethics and social responsibility

▎ Corporate governance

Online Study Center
Improve Your Grade
Knowledgebank 1.5

Again, each of these issues is discussed in several places throughout this book.

TEST PREPPER 1.3

ANSWERS CAN BE FOUND ON P. 441

True or False?

_____ 1. Synergy is important to managers because it emphasizes a cooperative and coordinated effort in working together.

_____ 2. Shannon believes there is one best way to do everything. She has a universal perspective.

_____ 3. Globalization requires managers to more effectively address issues of workforce diversity.

_____ 4. Gloria is a quality control inspector. She focuses on maintaining quality while lowering cost and increasing productivity.

Online Study Center
ACE the Test
ACE Practice Tests 1.3

Multiple Choice

_____ 5. A system that does not interact with its environment is best described as a(n) _____ system.
   a. closed
   b. sub-
   c. operating
   d. open
   e. transformation

_____ 6. Which of the following is NOT a contemporary management challenge faced by managers in the United States?
   a. Stagnant work environment
   b. Erratic economy
   c. Employee privacy
   d. Shift away from manufacturing economy
   e. Ethics and social responsibility

BUILDING EFFECTIVE DECISION-MAKING SKILLS

Online Study Center
Improve Your Grade
Exercises: Building
Effective Skills

Exercise Overview

Decision-making skills enable a manager to recognize and define problems and opportunities correctly and then to select an appropriate course of action to solve the problems and capitalize on the opportunities. This exercise will help you develop your own decision-making skills and also enhance your understanding of the importance of subsystem interdependencies in organizations.

Exercise Background

Assume you are the vice president of a large manufacturing company. Your firm makes home office furniture and cabinets for home theater systems. Because of the growth in each product line, the firm has also grown substantially in recent years. At the same time, this growth has not gone unnoticed, and several competitors have entered the market in the last two years. Your CEO has instructed you to determine how to cut costs by 10 percent so that prices can be cut by the same amount. She feels that this tactic is necessary to retain your market share in the face of new competition.

You have looked closely at the situation and have decided that there are three different ways in which you can accomplish this cost reduction. One option is to begin buying slightly lower-grade materials, such as wood, glue, and stain. Another option is to lay off a portion of your workforce and then pressure the remaining workers to work harder. As part of this same option, employees hired in the future will be selected from a lower-skill labor pool and will thus be paid a lower wage. The third option is to replace your existing equipment with newer, more efficient equipment. Although this will require a substantial up-front investment, you are certain that lower production costs can be achieved.

Exercise Task

With this background in mind, respond to the following questions:

1. Carefully examine each of the three alternatives under consideration. In what ways might each alternative affect other parts of the organization?

2. Which is the most costly option (in terms of impact on other parts of the organization, not absolute dollars)? Which is the least costly?

3. What are the primary obstacles that you might face in pursuing each of the three alternatives?

4. Can you think of other alternatives that might accomplish the cost reduction goal?

EXPERIENTIAL EXERCISE

Johari Window

Online Study Center
Improve Your Grade
Exercises: Experiential Exercise

Purpose

This exercise has two purposes: to encourage you to analyze yourself more accurately and to start you working on small-group cohesiveness. This exercise encourages you to share data about yourself and then to assimilate and process feedback. Small groups are typically more trusting and work better together, as you will be able to see after this exercise has been completed. The Johari Window is a particularly good model for understanding the perceptual process in interpersonal relationships.

This skill builder focuses on the human resources model and will help you develop your mentor role. One of the skills of a mentor is self-awareness.

Introduction

Each individual has four sets of personality characteristics. One set, which includes such characteristics as working hard, is well known to the individual and to others. A second set is unknown to the individual but obvious to others. For example, in a working situation, a peer group might observe that your jumping in to get the group moving off dead center is appropriate. At other times, you jump in when the group is not really finished, and you seem to interrupt. A third set of personality characteristics is known to the individual but not to others. These are situations that you have elected not to share, perhaps because of a lack of trust. Finally, there is a fourth set, which is not known to the individual or to others, such as why you are uncomfortable at office parties.

Instructions

Look at the Johari Window above.

In quadrant 1, list three things that you know about yourself and that you think others know. List three things in quadrant 3 that others do not know about you. Finally, in quadrant 2, list three things that you did not know about yourself last semester that you learned from others.

Sources: Adapted from Joseph Luft, *Group Processes: An Introduction to Group Dynamics* (Palo Alto, CA: Mayfield, 1970), pp. 10–11; William C. Morris and Marshall Sashkin, *Organizational Behavior in Action* (St. Paul, MN: West, 1976), p. 56.

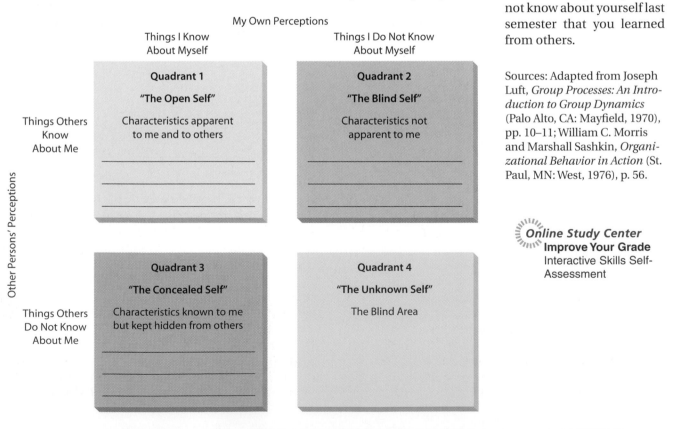

My Own Perceptions

	Things I Know About Myself	Things I Do Not Know About Myself
Things Others Know About Me	**Quadrant 1** "The Open Self" Characteristics apparent to me and to others	**Quadrant 2** "The Blind Self" Characteristics not apparent to me
Things Others Do Not Know About Me	**Quadrant 3** "The Concealed Self" Characteristics known to me but kept hidden from others	**Quadrant 4** "The Unknown Self" The Blind Area

Other Persons' Perceptions

Online Study Center
Improve Your Grade
Interactive Skills Self-Assessment

Taking on All Comers at Southwest

Would you like the opportunity to work for a company that just lost its charismatic founder, replacing him with the company's lawyer and the CEO's one-time secretary? Would you jump at the chance to get a job with a firm that pays one-half to two-thirds as much as its rivals and doubles the workload, then asks employees to clean up their workplace, to avoid hiring a cleaning service? Would you be thrilled to land a position in a business where there is no pension plan, just a stock ownership program, and where the stock has declined 16 percent in the last two years?

As it turns out, yes, you would, if you were one of the 200,000 people who submitted résumés for just 6,000 jobs at Southwest Airlines one year. Positions with the firm are so coveted that Southwest can be more selective than Harvard.

Following the retirement in 2001 of founder and long-time CEO Herb Kelleher, long-time corporate counsel Jim Parker assumed the CEO role and secretary-turned-human-resources-manager Colleen Barrett became president and chief operating officer (COO). These two leaders have done an exemplary job of carrying on the carrier's tradition of success.

From the beginning, Southwest did not adopt the hub-and-spoke system, preferring a short-haul, point-to-point schedule instead. This keeps costs low. The carrier also operates out of smaller, less expensive airports in many major markets; for example, it uses Long Island's Islip rather than New York's LaGuardia or Kennedy. The company flies only one type of jet, the Boeing 737, and so can reduce its expenses in every area from purchasing to maintenance to training. Because of these early, smart decisions, Southwest "has long-term, systematic advantages the other carriers can likely never match," says pilot and industry consultant Vaughn Cordle.

Southwest obtains its most significant advantages in human resources. Although Southwest is highly unionized, it has never experienced a labor strike. The firm's management sits down personally to negotiate every union contract. "The biggest complaint in the industry is that management doesn't listen to employees," says Southwest pilot Brad Bartholomew. "But you can't say that at Southwest. The top guy is in the room." Among the benefits that Southwest employees enjoy

"We aren't in the 'airline business'; we are in the 'Customer Service business,' and we just happen to fly airplanes."

—Colleen Barrett, president and COO, Southwest Airlines

are extensive training, a no-layoffs policy, and generous profit sharing and stock ownership. Even though there are few profits to share just now and the stock price is down, employees are optimistic that this situation will not last. At a time when other airlines are reducing wages, Southwest is giving pay hikes.

Compare Southwest's position to that of other airlines. Over the last three years, United, Northwest, Delta, ATA, U.S. Airways, Aloha Air, and Independence Air all underwent Chapter 11 reorganization for bankruptcy. Further, in the wake of September 11, the major carriers laid off 100,000 employees, most of whom have not been replaced. Layoffs and pay cuts contribute to low morale, which leads to low productivity, further hurting the traditional carriers. Analysts estimate that the major carriers would need to collectively reduce expenses by $18.6 billion, or about 29 percent, to match Southwest's low-cost performance. Consultant Ron Kuhlmann says, "There's no easy way to [cut costs]. The problem is that major carriers are preserving their own model rather than paying attention to what customers are willing to pay for." Consultant Michael Boyd says, "I'm very concerned over whether the airline industry can survive." "JetBlue may be the only [airline] out there that can compete head-to-head with Southwest," says Daryl Jenkins, director of the Aviation Institute.

Every airline has adopted some of Southwest's pioneering concepts, such as eliminating meals. "Stepping up to the new reality is a healthy thing," says Gordon Bethune, CEO of Continental Airlines. "Only those companies that change with it will survive." However, to stay on top, Southwest must learn to compete with firms that are imitating its strategies. And it will have to grow, yet maintain the personalized service and customer loyalty associated with small size. Barrett sums up the carrier's culture, saying, "We aren't in the 'airline business'; we are in the 'Customer Service business,' and we just happen to fly airplanes."

The prevailing, optimistic view is pithily summed up by Michael O'Leary, CEO of Ryanair, a European-based carrier following Southwest's no-frills model. Evaluating the traditional carriers, O'Leary asserts, "They're basket cases. They're incredibly high-cost, very ineffective. . . . These are stupid businesses for the amount of capital tied up in them. They never make any money. . . . I think they'll limp along from crisis to crisis. . . . [Air fares will continue to] decline for another 20, 30, 40 years." When O'Leary is asked, "What about Southwest?" he replies, "If I were Southwest, I wouldn't be worried."

Case Questions

1. Name at least two things that Southwest is doing efficiently. Name at least two things that Southwest is doing effectively. In what ways do efficiency and effectiveness support each other at Southwest? In what ways do they contradict each other?
2. Judging on the basis of information in the case, describe the managerial skills that Colleen Barrett and Jim Parker use in their jobs at Southwest.

3. What roles does history play at Southwest? How does Southwest use tools and techniques derived from the three historical management perspectives? What are some of the contemporary issues facing the airline?

Case References

Andy Serwer, "Southwest Airlines: The Hottest Thing in the Sky," *Fortune*, March 8, 2004, pp. 86–88; Amy Tsao, "Can Airlines Bring Costs Down to Earth?" *BusinessWeek*, October 23, 2002, www.businessweek.com on November 22, 2002; Amy Tsao, "Full-Service Airlines Are 'Basket Cases,'" *BusinessWeek*, September 12, 2002, www.businessweek.com on November 22, 2002; Amy Tsao, "The Wrong Time to Jump on Southwest?" *BusinessWeek*, August 22, 2002, www.businessweek.com on November 22, 2002; "About Southwest Airlines," "The Southwest Difference," Southwest Airlines website, www.iflyswa.com on December 20, 2005 (quote); Peter Coy, "The Airlines: Caught Between a Hub and a Hard Place," *BusinessWeek*, August 5, 2002, www.businessweek.com on November 22, 2002; Sally B. Donnelly, "One Airline's Magic," *Time*, pp. 45–47; Wendy Zellner, "It's Showtime for the Airlines," *BusinessWeek*, September 2, 2002, pp. 36–37.

LEARNING OBJECTIVE REVIEW

Online Study Center
Improve Your Grade
–Learning Objective Review
–Audio Chapter Review
–Study Guide to Go

Online Study Center
ACE the Test
Audio Chapter Quiz

1 ▶ *Define management, describe the kinds of managers found in organizations, identify and explain the four basic management functions, describe the fundamental management skills, and comment on management as science and as art.*

- Management is a set of activities
  planning and decision making
  organizing
  leading
  controlling
- Directed at using an organization's resources
  human resources   physical resources
  financial resources   information resources
- To achieve organizational goals in an efficient and effective manner.
- A manager is someone whose primary responsibility is to carry out the management process within an organization.

- Managers can be classified in terms of level:
  top manager
  middle manager
  first-line manager
- Managers can be classified in terms of area:
  marketing   human resources
  finances   administration
  operations   specialized
- The basic activities of the management process, which are not performed on a systematic and predictable schedule, include:
  planning and decision making: determining courses of action
  organizing: coordinating activities and resources
  leading: motivating and managing people
  controlling: monitoring and evaluating activities

- Effective managers also tend to have the following skills:

  technical   communication
  interpersonal   decision-making
  conceptual   time-management
  diagnostic

- The effective practice of management requires a synthesis of science and art; that is, it calls for a blend of rational objectivity and intuitive insight.

---

2 *Justify the importance of history and theory to managers and explain the evolution of management thought through the classical, behavioral, and quantitative perspectives.*

- Understanding the historical context and precursors of management and organizations provides a sense of heritage and can also help managers avoid repeating the mistakes of others.

- The classical management perspective, which paid little attention to the role of workers, had two major branches:

  scientific management: concerned with improving efficiency and work methods for individual workers

  administrative management: concerned with how organizations themselves should be structured and arranged for efficient operations

- The behavioral management perspective, characterized by a concern for individual and group behavior, emerged primarily as a result of the Hawthorne studies. The human relations movement recognized the importance and potential of behavioral processes in organizations but made many overly simplistic assumptions about those processes. Organizational behavior, a more realistic outgrowth of the behavioral perspective, is of interest to many contemporary managers.

- The quantitative management perspective, which attempts to apply quantitative techniques to decision making and problem solving, has two components:

  management science
  operations management

These areas are also of considerable importance to contemporary managers. Their contributions have been facilitated by the tremendous increase in the use of personal computers and integrated information networks.

---

3 *Identify and discuss key contemporary management perspectives represented by the systems and contingency perspectives and identify the major challenges and opportunities faced by managers today.*

- There are two relatively recent additions to management theory that can serve as frameworks for integrating the other perspectives:

  systems perspective
  contingency perspective

- The important issues and challenges that contemporary managers face include:

  economic instability
  diversity
  privacy
  outsourcing
  ethics and social responsibility
  corporate governance
  globalization

Online Study Center RESOURCES

Prepare for Class, Improve Your Grade, and ACE the Test. These Student Achievement resources include:

ACE Practice Tests	Interactive Skills Assessments	Study Guide to Go
End of Chapter Exercises	Knowledgebank	Video Segments
Glossaries (visual and print)	Reviews (audio and print)	Summaries/Outlines
Flashcards		

To access these learning and study tools, go to: **college.hmco.com/pic/griffinSAS**

STARBUCKS COFFEE ستار بكس كافيه

Starbucks is one of today's most successful businesses. The firm faces significant opportunities and challenges in its business environment. Its recent expansion into numerous foreign markets, such as Saudi Arabia, provides additional opportunities and challenges.

3 > *Discuss the international environment of management, including trends in international business, levels of international business activities, and the context of international business.*

2 > *Describe the ethical and social environment of management, including individual ethics, the concept of social responsibility, and how organizations can manage social responsibility.*

1 > *Discuss the nature of an organization's environments, and identify and describe the components of its general, task, and internal environments.*

Chapter Outline

Online Study Center
Prepare for Class
Chapter Outline

4 ▶ *Describe the importance and
determinants of an organization's
culture, as well as how organization
culture can be managed.*

Brewing Up
Some Competition

A good starting spot for our discussion of the environment is with Starbucks, a firm that has both capitalized on and helped shape its business environment in many different ways.

Starbucks continues to expand everywhere—including Indonesia, Spain, Greece, and Jordan in recent years—and concerns about the company's impact on local business continue to grow also. When Starbucks opened a store near It's A Grind, a Long Beach–based independent coffeehouse, locals feared that the giant retailer would put their neighborhood favorite out of business. Natives of San Diego turned out to protest a Starbucks opening so close to their locally owned coffeehouses. But owners and customers are finding out something surprising about Starbucks stores—sales often increase for all coffeehouses wherever the international chain opens an outlet nearby!

At first glance, customers' qualms appear to be justified. After all, it only makes sense that a huge multinational firm like Starbucks would enjoy advantages in pricing, new-product development, and other areas that would tend to give it an edge. Using size as a competitive weapon has been a common tactic for decades,

You should be able to define and use terms that are part of the practicing manager's vocabulary, as well as those that are integral in the language of management.

used by firms ranging from Standard Oil, Sears, and General Motors to the most contemporary example—Wal-Mart. "A big company like Starbucks can come in and lose money for two years until they wipe everybody else out," editorializes the *Indianapolis Star,* reporting the closing of a local coffeehouse. "It's the old Wal-Mart thing."

Fear of the power of Starbucks has even caused owners to take some extraordinary measures to reduce the possibility of head-to-head competition. One owner, Courtney Bates of Kansas City's City Market Coffee Company, required her landlord to sign a clause preventing rental to any other coffeehouse. Another owner was approached by Starbucks about a possible buyout but was too suspicious of the firm to share any store information with it. "I don't think they really wanted to buy it. They just wanted a peek inside my business," claims Jeff Schmidt, owner of LatteLand in Kansas City. One thousand customers in Kansas City signed a petition asking the city to ban Starbucks. Katerina Carson, owner of Katerina's in Chicago, sums up this view when she says tersely, "Starbucks is a corporate monster."

But the statistics just do not support the assertion that Starbucks is eliminating competition and slashing profits in the coffeehouse industry. In fact, while Starbucks outlets in the United States have grown from 1,000 in 1997 to almost 7,000 today, independents have also increased by 50 percent. And, while the total number of coffeehouses has grown from 8,000 to over 17,000 since 1997, sales have more than doubled, indicating that sales volume per store is also increasing.

Indeed, many coffeehouse owners are now forced to admit that, in spite of their fears, their sales actually increased when a Starbucks located a new store in their vicinity. Jon Cates, co-owner of the Broadway Cafe in Kansas City, says, "Starbucks helped our business, but I don't want to give them any credit for it." Some owners have gone further, embracing the entrance of the chain into local markets. "Competition is good," says Norma Slaman, owner of Newbreak Coffee in San Diego, who saw sales rise 15 percent after Starbucks' arrival. Some chains have even adopted the strategy of following Starbucks into a neighborhood. Doug Zell located his Intelligentsia Coffee Roasters store near not just one, but two, Starbucks locations in Chicago. "It's been double-digit growth every year," says Zell.

Starbucks is increasing competitive pressure on independent coffeehouses, yet the independents are prospering right along with their giant competitor. This might be because the independents are so fearful of Starbucks that they implement improvements even before the chain arrives. It's A Grind fixed up stores, improving customer service and staff training, too, when a Starbucks opened nearby. The independents' sales have been rising 10 percent or more annually since then. Other independents have been prompted to ban smoking or to roast their own beans, two significant aspects of Starbucks' operations. Focusing on local activities and preferences is another way for independents to compete successfully, through poetry readings, live jazz, works by local artists, and regional food choices.

It seems that Starbucks has not merely increased rivalry but also shifted industry dynamics in areas such as customers and new entrants. Although Starbucks and the independent coffeehouses are more profitable than ever, it appears that, for now, the customers are the big winners in this evolving industry.[1]

The business world operates in what can appear to be mysterious ways. Sometimes competition hurts, but sometimes it helps. When Starbucks opens a new store, its closest competitors often benefit. Ford and General Motors compete with each other for consumer dollars but work together to promote the interests of the U.S. auto industry. And CEOs face growing pressure to cut costs and curb their own salaries but grow their businesses. Clearly, the environmental context of business today is changing in unprecedented ways.

THE ORGANIZATION'S ENVIRONMENTS

1 ► *Discuss the nature of an organization's environments, and identify and describe the components of its general, task, and internal environments.*

The **external environment** is everything outside an organization's boundaries that might affect it. There are actually two separate external environments: the *general environment* and the *task environment*. An organization's *internal environment* consists of conditions and forces within the organization.

external environment Everything outside an organization's boundaries that might affect it.

The General Environment

The general environment includes the economy, technology, and the political-legal climate. Each of these embodies conditions and events that have the potential to influence the organization in important ways.

economy The overall health and vitality of the economic system in which the organization operates.

▌ The **economy** commonly refers to the prevailing and projected health and vitality of the economic system in which the organization operates.[2] Particularly important economic factors for business are general economic growth, inflation, interest rates, and unemployment. McDonald's U.S. operation is functioning in an economy currently characterized by moderate growth, low unemployment, and low inflation.[3] These conditions breed paradoxical problems. Low unemployment means that more people can eat out, but McDonald's also has to pay higher wages to attract new employees.[4] Similarly, low inflation means that the prices McDonald's must pay for its supplies remain relatively constant, but it also is somewhat constrained from increasing the prices it charges consumers for a hamburger or milkshake.

technology The methods available for converting resources into products or services.

▌ **Technology** refers to the methods and processes available for converting resources into products or services. Examples of such conversion include molding plastic and other materials into computer keyboards, as well as packaging keyboards made by suppliers with other components to create a personal computer system. Although technology is applied within the organization, the forms and availability of that technology come from the general environment. Although some people associate technology with manufacturing firms, it is also relevant in the service sector. For example, just as an automobile follows a predetermined path along an assembly line as it is built, a hamburger at McDonald's follows a predefined path as the meat is cooked, the burger assembled, and the finished product wrapped and bagged for a customer.

political-legal climate The government regulation of business and the relationship between business and government.

▌ The **political-legal climate** consists of government regulation of business and the relationship between business and government. This dimension is important for three basic reasons.

1. The legal system partially defines what an organization can and cannot do. Although the United States is basically a free market economy, there is still major regulation of business activity. McDonald's, for example, is subject to a variety of political and legal forces, including food preparation standards and local zoning requirements.

2. Pro- or antibusiness sentiment in government influences business activity. During periods of probusiness sentiment, firms find it easier to compete and have fewer concerns about antitrust issues. On the other hand, during a period of antibusiness sentiment, firms may find their competitive strategies more restricted and may have fewer opportunities for mergers and acquisitions because of antitrust concerns.

3. Political stability has ramifications for planning because no business wants to set up shop in another country unless trade relationships with that country are relatively well defined and stable. Hence U.S. firms are more likely to do business with England, Mexico, and Canada than with Haiti and Afghanistan.

The Task Environment

Because the impact of the general environment is often vague, imprecise, and long-term, most organizations tend to focus their attention on their task environment. This environment includes competitors, customers, suppliers, regulators, and strategic partners. Figure 2.1 depicts the task environment of McDonald's.

▌ **Competitors** are other organizations that compete with a particular organization for resources. As we noted earlier, Starbucks competes with independent coffeehouses. McDonald's competes with other fast-food operations, such as Burger King, Wendy's, Subway, and Dairy Queen. But competition also occurs between substitute products; for example, Ford competes with Yamaha (motorcycles) and Schwinn (bicycles) for your transportation dollars, and Walt Disney World theme parks and Carnival Cruise Lines compete for your vacation dollars.

▌ **Customers** are the people who pay money to acquire an organization's products or services. McDonald's customers are individuals who walk into a restaurant to buy food. But customers need not be individuals. Schools, hospitals, government agencies, wholesalers, retailers, and manufacturers are just a few of the many kinds of organizations that may be major customers of other organizations. Some institutional customers, such as schools, prisons, and hospitals, also buy food in bulk from restaurants like McDonald's.

▌ **Suppliers** provide resources for other organizations. McDonald's buys soft-drink products from Coca-Cola; individually packaged servings of ketchup from Heinz; ingredients from wholesale food processors; and napkins, sacks, and wrappers

FIGURE 2.1

McDonald's Task Environment
An organization's task environment includes its competitors, customers, suppliers, strategic partners, and regulators.

Internal environment
Task environment

competitor An organization that competes with other organizations for resources.
customer Whoever pays money to acquire an organization's products or services.
supplier An organization that provides resources for other organizations.

Suppliers are an integral part of an organization's task environment. Hewlett-Packard, for instance, buys keyboards from suppliers in Asia. When it recently ramped up production for a major new product line, it had to call on its suppliers to get their own production going more quickly than had been expected. And because they all responded, HP was able to meet its earlier launch dates for its new product line.

from packaging manufacturers. Besides material resources such as these, businesses also rely on suppliers for information (such as economic statistics), labor (in the form of employment agencies), and capital (from lenders such as banks). Some businesses strive to avoid depending exclusively on particular suppliers. Others, however, find it beneficial to create strong relationships with single suppliers.

regulator A body that has the potential to control, legislate, or otherwise influence the organization's policies and practices.

regulatory agency An agency created by the government to regulate business activities.

interest group A group organized by its members to attempt to influence organizations.

strategic partner (strategically) An organization working together with one or more other organizations in a joint venture or similar arrangement.

■ **Regulators** are elements of the task environment that have the potential to control, legislate, or otherwise influence an organization's policies and practices. There are two important kinds of regulators.

1. **Regulatory agencies** are created by the government to protect the public from certain business practices or to protect organizations from one another. Powerful federal regulatory agencies include the Environmental Protection Agency (EPA), the Securities and Exchange Commission (SEC), the Food and Drug Administration (FDA), which helps ensure that the food we eat is free from contaminants, and the Equal Employment Opportunity Commission (EEOC). Many managers complain that there is too much government regulation. Most large companies must dedicate thousands of labor hours and hundreds of thousands of dollars a year to complying with government regulations.

2. **Interest groups** are organized by their members to attempt to influence organizations. Prominent interest groups include the National Organization for Women (NOW), Mothers Against Drunk Driving (MADD), the National Rifle Association (NRA), the League of Women Voters, the Sierra Club, and industry self-regulation groups such as the Council of Better Business Bureaus. Although interest groups lack the official power of government agencies, they can exert considerable influence by using the media to call attention to their positions. MADD, for example, puts considerable pressure on alcoholic beverage producers (to put warning labels on their products) and on local governments (to stiffen drinking ordinances and penalize bars and restaurants that serve to minors and intoxicated patrons).

■ **Strategic partners** (also called strategic allies) are two or more companies that work together in joint ventures or other partnerships.[5] As shown in Figure 2.1, McDonald's has several strategic partners. For example, it has one arrangement with Wal-Mart whereby small McDonald's restaurants are built in many Wal-Mart stores. The firm also has a long-term deal with Disney: McDonald's will promote Disney movies in its stores, and Disney will build McDonald's restaurants or kiosks in its theme parks. And many of the firm's foreign stores are built in collaboration with local investors. Strategic partnerships help companies get from other companies the expertise they lack. They also help spread risk and open new market opportunities.

The Internal Environment

CONCEPT CHECK 2.1

Identify and discuss each major dimension of the general environment and the task environment. Can you think of dimensions of the task environment that are not discussed in the text? Indicate their linkages to those that are discussed.

internal environment The conditions and forces within an organization.

owner Whoever can claim property rights to an organization.

Organizations also have an **internal environment** that consists of their owners, the board of directors, employees, and the physical work environment. (Another especially important part of the internal environment is the organization's culture, discussed separately later in this chapter.)

■ **Owners** of a business are those who have legal property rights to that business. Owners can be individuals who establish and run small businesses, partners who jointly own a business, individual investors who buy stock in a corporation, or other organizations. McDonald's has 700 million shares of stock, each of which represents one unit of ownership in the firm. McDonald's also owns other businesses. For example, it owns several large regional bakeries that supply its restaurants with buns. McDonald's also has a substantial ownership position in Chipotle Mexican Grill and Pret A Manger.

▌ The **board of directors** is a governing body elected by the stockholders and charged with overseeing the general management of the firm to ensure that it is being run in a way that best serves the stockholders' interests. Recent business scandals have increased this scrutiny, but boards themselves have also been accused of wrongdoings and have sometimes failed to monitor the firm's executives.[6] At issue is the concept of *corporate governance*—who is responsible for governing the actions of a business.

▌ *Employees* are also a major element of the internal environment. Of particular interest to managers today are issues associated with increased diversity in the labor force, the management of knowledge workers (workers who add value through their knowledge), the need to foster flexibility, and the effects of outsourcing. Legal issues associated with accommodating those with disabilities and addressing the complexities of drug and alocohol abuse and worker privacy are also of growing importance.

▌ The *physical environment* of the organization and its employees is important. Some firms have their facilities in downtown skyscrapers, usually spread across several floors. Others locate in suburban or rural settings and may have facilities more closely resembling a college campus. Some facilities have long halls lined with traditional offices. Others have modular cubicles with partial walls and no doors. Increasingly, newer facilities have an even more open arrangement, where people work in large rooms, moving among different tables to interact with different people on different projects. Freestanding computer workstations are available for those who need them, and a few small rooms may be available off to the side for private business.[7]

board of directors Governing body elected by a corporation's stockholders and charged with overseeing the general management of the firm to ensure that it is being run in a way that best serves the stockholders' interests.

Most businesses strive to create a physical work environment that is both efficient and comfortable. Charles Lester (left) and Nicole Peoples (right) are working in their cubicles at the Dell customer contact center in Oklahoma City. While some people might not like cubicles, their use nevertheless allows companies like Dell to provide a modest level of privacy for workers while still making efficient use of space.

TEST PREPPER 2.1

ANSWERS CAN BE FOUND ON P. 44I

True or False?

_____ 1. Some companies use blogs, web logs, to assist human resources with compiling impressions made by an applicant during interviews. This is an example of the technological dimension of the general environment.

_____ 2. Labels on beef such as organic, free-range, and no hormones must be approved by the U.S. Agriculture Department's Food Safety and Inspection Service. This is an example of a strategic partnership.

_____ 3. If you buy stock in a company, you are an owner.

Multiple Choice

_____ 4. The American Association of Retired Persons dispatches volunteers to follow political candidates and ask questions in restaurants, town hall meetings, or anywhere candidates are speaking. They ask questions about issues important to retirees. This is an effort by AARP to influence its _____ dimension.
   a. economic
   b. technological
   c. political-legal
   d. international
   e. cultural

Online Study Center
ACE the Test
ACE Practice Tests 2.1

_____ 5. A state pension fund owns shares of a mutual fund. The pension fund is which part of the task environment?
   a. Competition
   b. Customer
   c. Supplier
   d. Regulatory
   e. Strategic partner

_____ 6. Who is responsible for corporate governance?
   a. Owners
   b. Board of directors
   c. Employees
   d. Shareholders
   e. Regulators

_____ 7. Daniel J. Steininger, chairman of the Catholic Fund, proposed to the SEC that proxy material at seven large U.S. companies allow shareholders to vote on whether to limit chief executive pay to 100 times the average worker. Steininger chose the seven companies based on rapidly growing executive compensation compared to their average workers. The people that support Steininger's proposal _____.
   a. have the threat of substitute products
   b. have the power of buyers
   c. are a regulatory agency
   d. are an interest group
   e. have competitive rivalry

THE ETHICAL AND SOCIAL ENVIRONMENT OF MANAGEMENT

2 ▸ *Describe the ethical and social environment of management, including individual ethics, the concept of social responsibility, and how organizations can manage social responsibility.*

The ethical and social environment has become an especially important area for managers in the last few years. In this section we first explore the concept of individual ethics and then describe social responsibility.

Individual Ethics in Organizations

Online Study Center
Improve Your Grade
Knowledgebank 2.1

ethics An individual's personal beliefs about whether a behavior, action, or decision is right or wrong.

ethical behavior Behavior that conforms to generally accepted social norms.

Ethics are an individual's personal beliefs about whether a behavior, action, or decision is right or wrong.[8] Note that we define ethics in the context of the individual—people have ethics; organizations do not. Likewise, what constitutes ethical behavior varies from one person to another. For example, one person who finds a twenty-dollar bill on the floor of an empty room believes that it is okay to keep it, whereas another feels compelled to turn it in to the lost-and-found department. Further, although **ethical behavior** is in the eye of the beholder, the term usually refers to behavior that conforms to generally accepted social norms. **Unethical behavior**, then, is behavior that does not conform to generally accepted social norms.

unethical behavior Behavior that does not conform to generally accepted social norms.

Managerial Ethics

Managerial ethics consists of the standards of behavior that guide individual managers in their work.[9] One important area of managerial ethics is the treatment of employees by the organization. It includes, for example, hiring and firing, wages and working conditions, and employee privacy and respect. An example of how different managers might approach this area involves minimum wages. While the U.S. government sets a minimum hourly wage, this amount is often not enough to live above the poverty level in high-cost areas such as New York and San Francisco. Some managers might say that paying only the legal minimum is the right business practice, while others might be inclined to pay a wage more attuned to local conditions.

managerial ethics Standards of behavior that guide individual managers in their work.

Numerous ethical issues stem from how employees treat the organization, especially in regard to conflicts of interest, secrecy and confidentiality, and honesty:

▌ *Conflict of interest* occurs when an employee's decision potentially benefits the individual to the possible detriment of the organization.

▌ *Secrecy and confidentiality* issues arise when an employee who works for a business in highly competitive industries—electronics, software, and fashion apparel, for example—might be tempted to sell information about company plans to competitors.

▌ *Honesty* issues include such activities as using a business telephone to make personal long-distance calls, surfing the Internet at work, stealing supplies, and padding expense accounts.

Managerial ethics also comes into play in the relationship between the firm (and its employees) and other economic agents. The primary agents of interest include customers, competitors, stockholders, suppliers, dealers, and unions. The behaviors of the organization and these agents that may be subject to ethical ambiguity include advertising and promotions, financial disclosures, ordering and purchasing, shipping and solicitations, bargaining and negotiation, and other business relationships.

Managing Ethical Behavior

Spurred partially by increased awareness of ethics scandals in business and partially by a sense of enhanced corporate consciousness about the distinction between ethical and unethical behaviors, many organizations have reemphasized ethical behavior on the part of employees. This emphasis takes many forms, but any effort to enhance ethical behavior must begin with top management because top managers establish the organization's culture and define what will and what will not be acceptable behavior. Some companies have also started offering employees training in how to cope with ethical dilemmas. At Boeing, for example, line managers lead training sessions for other employees, covering discussions of ethical dilemmas and how to handle them. The company also has an ethics committee that reports directly to the board of directors.

Organizations are also going to greater lengths to formalize their ethical standards. Whirlpool, Texas Instruments, and Hewlett-Packard have developed formal

code of ethics   A formal, written statement of the values and ethical standards that guide a firm's actions.

CONCEPT CHECK 2.2

Do organizations have ethics? Why or why not? What is the relationship between the law and ethical behavior? Can a behavior be ethical and illegal at the same time?

Online Study Center
Improve Your Grade
Knowledgebank 2.2

Sarbanes-Oxley Act   A 2002 law that requires CEOs and CFOs to vouch personally for the truthfulness and fairness of their firms' financial disclosures and that imposes tough new measures to deter and punish corporate and accounting fraud and corruption.

codes of ethics—written statements of the values and ethical standards that guide the firms' actions. Of course, firms must adhere to such codes if they are to be of value. In one now-infamous case, Enron's board of directors voted to set aside the firm's code of ethics in order to implement a business plan that was in violation of that code.[10]

Of course, no code, guideline, or training program can truly substitute for the quality of an individual's personal judgment about what is right behavior and what is wrong behavior in a particular situation. Such devices may prescribe what people should do, but they often fail to help people understand and live with the consequences of their choices. Making ethical choices may lead to very unpleasant outcomes—firing, rejection by colleagues, and the forfeiture of monetary gain, to name a few. Thus managers must be prepared to confront their own conscience and weigh the options available when making difficult ethical decisions.

Emerging Ethical Issues

Ethical scandals have become almost commonplace in today's world of business, sports, politics, and entertainment. While the moral integrity of our society has been called into question, it is important to remember that one cannot judge everyone by the transgressions of a few.

▪ *Ethical Leadership.*   In recent years the media have been rife with stories about unscrupulous corporate leaders. For every unethical senior manager, of course, there are many highly ethical ones. But the actions of such high-profile deposed executives as Dennis Kozlowski (Tyco), Kenneth Lay (Enron), and Bernard Ebbers (WorldCom) have substantially increased the scrutiny directed at all executives. As a direct result, executives everywhere are being expected to exhibit nothing but the strongest ethical conduct. This leadership, in turn, is expected to help set the tone for the rest of the organization and to establish both norms and a culture that reinforce the importance of ethical behavior.[11] The basic premise behind ethical leadership is that because leaders serve as role models for others, their every action is subject to scrutiny. That is, they must set their company's moral tone by being honest and straightforward and by taking responsibility for any shortcomings that are identified. To support this view, in 2002 Congress passed the **Sarbanes-Oxley Act**, requiring CEOs and CFOs to vouch personally for the truthfulness and fairness of their firms' financial disclosures. The law also imposes tough new measures to deter and punish corporate and accounting fraud and corruption.

▪ *Corporate Governance.*   As discussed earlier, the board of directors of a public corporation is expected to ensure that the business is being properly managed and that the decisions made by its senior management are in the best interests of shareholders and other stakeholders. But many of the recent ethical scandals

The ethical and social environment of management has taken center stage in recent years due to an epidemic of corporate and executive scandals. For example, former WorldCom CEO Bernard Ebbers was sentenced to 25 years for his role in the corporate accounting scandal that bankrupted WorldCom, a multibillion-dollar company. WorldCom re-emerged in 2003 as MCI. Ebbers is shown here during a hearing by the House Committee on Financial Services on the accounting problems of WorldCom.

that we have mentioned have actually started with a breakdown in the corporate governance structure. For instance, WorldCom's board approved a personal loan to the firm's CEO, Bernard Ebbers, for $366 million, when there was little evidence that he could repay it. And Tyco's board approved a $20 million bonus for one of its own members for helping with the acquisition of another firm.

■ ***Ethics and Information Technology.*** Among the specific focal points in this area are individual rights to privacy and the potential abuse of information technology by individuals. Indeed, online privacy has become a hot topic, as companies sort out the related ethical and management issues.

Social Responsibility in Organizations

As we have seen, ethics are associated with individuals and their decisions and behaviors. Organizations themselves do not have ethics, but they relate to their environments in ways that often involve ethical dilemmas and decisions. These situations are generally referred to within the context of the organization's **social responsibility**. Specifically, social responsibility is the set of obligations an organization has to protect and enhance the societal context in which it functions. But not everyone agrees that firms should take on social responsibility. Some of the more salient arguments on both sides of this contemporary debate are summarized in Figure 2.2 and further explained in the following sections.

social responsibility   The set of obligations an organization has to protect and enhance the societal context in which it functions.

Online Study Center
Improve Your Grade
Visual Glossary

FIGURE 2.2

Arguments For and Against Social Responsibility

Although many people want everyone to see social responsibility as a desirable aim, there are in fact several strong arguments that can be advanced both for and against social responsibility. Hence organizations and their managers should carefully assess their own values, beliefs, and priorities when deciding which stance and approach to take regarding social responsibility.

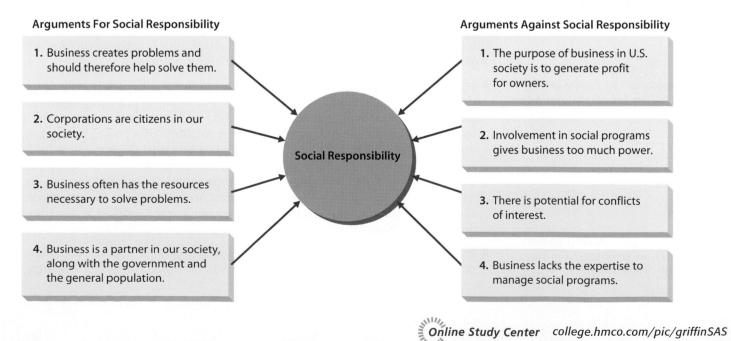

Arguments For Social Responsibility

1. Business creates problems and should therefore help solve them.

2. Corporations are citizens in our society.

3. Business often has the resources necessary to solve problems.

4. Business is a partner in our society, along with the government and the general population.

Social Responsibility

Arguments Against Social Responsibility

1. The purpose of business in U.S. society is to generate profit for owners.

2. Involvement in social programs gives business too much power.

3. There is potential for conflicts of interest.

4. Business lacks the expertise to manage social programs.

Arguments for Social Responsibility

Organizations create many problems, such as air and water pollution and resource depletion; therefore organizations should play a major role in solving them. Since many corporations are legally defined entities with most of the same privileges as private citizens, they are not exempt from their obligations. While governmental organizations have stretched their budgets to the limit, many large businesses often have surplus revenues that could be used to help solve social problems, such as Dell donating surplus computers to schools and many restaurants giving leftover food to homeless shelters.

Arguments Against Social Responsibility

Milton Friedman, famous economist, argues that widening the interpretation of social responsibility will undermine the U.S. economy by detracting from the basic mission of business: to earn profits for owners. A few years ago, shareholders of Ben & Jerry's Homemade Holdings expressed outrage when the firm refused to accept a lucrative exporting deal to Japan simply because the Japanese distributor did not have a strong social agenda.[12] Another objection to deepening the social responsibility of businesses is that corporations already wield enormous power and that involvement in social programs gives them even more power. Still another argument against social responsibility focuses on the potential for conflicts of interest. Finally, critics argue that organizations lack the expertise to understand how to assess and make decisions about worthy social programs. How can a company truly know, they ask, which cause or program is most deserving of its support or how money might best be spent?

Managing Social Responsibility

The demands for social responsibility placed on contemporary organizations by an increasingly sophisticated and educated public are probably stronger than ever. As we have seen, there are pitfalls for managers who fail to adhere to high ethical standards and for companies that try to circumvent their legal obligations. Organizations therefore need to fashion an approach to social responsibility in the same way that they develop any other business strategy. In other words, they should view social responsibility as a major challenge that requires careful planning, decision making, consideration, and evaluation. The formal organizational dimensions through which businesses can manage social responsibility include legal compliance, ethical compliance, and philanthropic giving.

CONCEPT CHECK 2.3

What are the arguments for and against social responsibility on the part of businesses? In your opinion, which set of arguments is more compelling?

▌ **Legal compliance**, generally assigned to the appropriate functional managers, is the extent to which the organization conforms to local, state, federal, and international laws. For example, the organization's top human resource executive is responsible for ensuring compliance with regulations concerning hiring, pay, and workplace safety and health. The organization's legal department is likely to contribute to this effort by providing general oversight and answering queries from managers about the appropriate interpretation of laws and regulations. Unfortunately, though, legal compliance may not be enough—in some cases, for instance, perfectly legal accounting practices have still resulted in deception and other problems.[13]

legal compliance The extent to which an organization complies with local, state, federal, and international laws.

▌ **Ethical compliance** is the extent to which the members of the organization follow basic ethical (and legal) standards of behavior. We noted earlier that organiza-

ethical compliance The extent to which an organization and its members follow basic ethical standards of behavior.

tions have increased their efforts in this area—providing training in ethics and developing guidelines and codes of conduct, for example. Many organizations also establish formal ethics committees, which may be asked to review proposals for new projects, to help evaluate new hiring strategies, to assess a new environmental protection plan, or to serve as a peer review panel to evaluate alleged ethical misconduct by an employee.[14]

▌ **Philanthropic giving** is the awarding of funds or gifts to charities or other worthy causes. Giving across national boundaries is also becoming more common. For example, Alcoa gave $112,000 to a small town in Brazil to build a sewage treatment plant, and Japanese firms such as Sony and Mitsubishi make contributions to a number of social programs in the United States. However, in the current climate of cutbacks, many corporations have had to limit their charitable gifts over the past several years as they continue to trim their own budgets.[15]

philanthropic giving Awarding funds or gifts to charities or other worthy causes.

In addition to these formal dimensions of managing social responsibility, there are also informal ones. Leadership practices, organization culture, and how the organization responds to whistle blowers all help shape and define people's perceptions of the organization's stance on social responsibility.

▌ Leadership practices and organization culture can go a long way toward defining the social responsibility stance an organization and its members will adopt.[16] For example, Johnson & Johnson executives for years provided a consistent message to employees that customers, employees, communities where the company did business, and shareholders were all important—and primarily in that order. Thus, when packages of poisoned Tylenol showed up on store shelves in the 1980s, Johnson & Johnson employees did not need to wait for orders from headquarters to know what to do: They immediately pulled all the packages from shelves before any other customers could buy them.[17]

▌ **Whistle blowing** is the disclosure, by an employee, of illegal or unethical conduct on the part of others within the organization.[18] How an organization responds to this practice often indicates its values as they relate to social responsibility. Whistle blowers may have to proceed through a number of channels to be heard, and they may even get fired for their efforts.[19] Many organizations, however, welcome their contributions. A person who observes questionable behavior typically first reports the incident to his or her boss. If nothing is done, the whistle blower may then inform higher-level managers or an ethics committee, if one exists. Eventually, the person may have to go to a regulatory agency or even the media to be heard. For example, Charles W. Robinson, Jr., worked as a director of a SmithKline lab in San Antonio when one day he noticed a suspicious billing pattern that the firm was using to collect lab fees from Medicare: The bills were considerably higher than the firm's normal charges for those same tests. He pointed out the problem to higher-level managers, but his concerns were ignored. He subsequently took his findings to the U.S. government, which sued SmithKline and eventually reached a settlement of $325 million.[20]

whistle blowing The disclosure, by an employee, of illegal or unethical conduct on the part of others within the organization.

CONCEPT CHECK 2.4

What is your opinion of whistle blowing? If you were aware of criminal activity in your organization but knew that reporting it would probably cost you your job, what would you do?

TEST PREPPER 2.2

ANSWERS CAN BE FOUND ON P. 44I

True or False?

_____ 1. Ethics officers help develop the code of ethics and support whistle blowers.

_____ 2. The most effective board of directors consists of people who do business with the firm and are personally familiar with the CEO.

_____ 3. Milton Friedman supports businesses taking a proactive stance on social responsibility.

Multiple Choice

_____ 4. The Sarbanes-Oxley Act requires who to vouch for the truth and fairness of the firm's financial disclosures?

     a. CEO and CFO   d. Board of directors

     b. CIO   e. SEC

     c. COO

_____ 5. The State of Illinois uses a computer tutorial to train employees on behavior that is not appropriate at work, such as making campaign calls

Online Study Center
ACE the Test
ACE Practice Tests 2.2

for their boss during state time. This tutorial is an attempt to clarify _____.

     a. legal compliance

     b. social responsibility

     c. whistle-blowing

     d. political giving

     e. managerial ethics

_____ 6. Awarding funds to charities or worthy causes is called _____.

     a. legal compliance

     b. ethical compliance

     c. philanthropic giving

     d. social responsibility

     e. corporate privilege

_____ 7. Which of the following is an argument for social responsibility?

     a. Business is a partner in our society

     b. Business has expertise in social programs

     c. Business is powerful

     d. Profits allow businesses to conduct business

     e. All of the above

THE INTERNATIONAL ENVIRONMENT OF MANAGEMENT

3 ▶ *Discuss the international environment of management, including trends in international business, levels of international business activities, and the context of international business.*

Another important competitive issue for managers today is the international environment. After describing recent trends in international business, we examine levels of internationalization and the international context of business.

Trends in International Business

While businesses have engaged in international activities for literally thousands of years, during the last half of the 20th century international business activity began to truly skyrocket. Today, U.S. firms are no longer isolated from global competition or the global market. A few simple numbers help tell the full story of international trade and industry. First of all, the volume of international trade has increased more than 3,100 percent between 1960 and 2005. Further, although 166 of the world's largest corporations are headquartered in the United States, there are also 112 in Japan, 39 in France, 42 in Germany, and 33 in Britain.[21] Within certain industries, the preeminence of non-U.S. firms is even more striking. For example, only two each of the world's ten largest banks and ten largest electronics companies are based in the United States. Only two of the ten largest chemical companies are U.S. firms. On the other hand, U.S. firms account for six of the eight largest aerospace companies, four of the seven largest airlines, five of the ten largest computer companies, four of the five largest diversified financial companies, and six of the ten largest retailers.[22]

U.S. firms are also finding that international operations are an increasingly important element of their sales and profits. For example, in 2004 Exxon Corporation realized 84 percent of its revenues and 65 percent of its profits abroad. For Avon, these percentages were 68 percent and 73 percent, respectively.[23] From any perspective, then, it is clear that we live in a truly global economy. Virtually all businesses today must be concerned with the competitive situations they face in lands far from home and with how companies from distant countries are competing in their homeland.

Online Study Center
Improve Your Grade
Video Segment

Levels of International Business Activity

Firms can choose various levels of international business activity as they seek to gain a competitive advantage in other countries. The general levels are exporting and importing, licensing, strategic alliances, and direct investment. Table 2.1 summarizes the advantages and disadvantages of each approach.

▮ Exporting or importing is usually the first type of international business in which a firm gets involved. **Exporting** is making a product in the firm's domestic marketplace and selling it in another country (examples are automobiles made by Mazda, Ford, and Ferrari and stereo equipment made by Sony, Bang & Olufsen, and Yamaha).

exporting Making a product in the firm's domestic marketplace and selling it in another country.

▮ **Importing** is bringing a good or service into the home country from abroad (as when wine distributors buy products from vineyards in France or California and import them into their own country for resale).

importing Bringing a good, service, or capital into the home country from abroad.

TABLE 2.1

Advantages and Disadvantages of Different Approaches to Internationalization
When organizations decide to increase their level of internationalization, they can adopt several strategies. Each strategy is a matter of degree, as opposed to being a discrete and mutually exclusive category. And each has unique advantages and disadvantages that must be considered.

Approach to Internationalization	Advantages	Disadvantages
Importing or Exporting	1. Small cash outlay 2. Little risk 3. No adaptation necessary	1. Tariffs and taxes 2. High transportation costs 3. Government restrictions
Licensing	1. Increased profitability 2. Extended profitability	1. Inflexibility 2. Competition
Strategic Alliances or Joint Ventures	1. Quick market entry 2. Access to materials and technology	Shared ownership (limits control and profits)
Direct Investment	1. Enhanced control 2. Existing infrastructure	1. Complexity 2. Greater economic and political risk 3. Greater uncertainty

licensing   An arrangement whereby one company allows another company to use its brand name, trademark, technology, patent, copyright, or other assets in exchange for a royalty based on sales.

▌ **Licensing** is an arrangement whereby a firm allows another company to use its brand name, trademark, technology, patent, copyright, or other assets. In return, the licensee pays a royalty, usually based on sales.

Franchising, a special form of licensing, is also widely used in international business. Kirin Brewery, Japan's largest producer of beer, has entered into a number of licensing arrangements with breweries in other markets. These brewers make beer according to strict guidelines provided by the Japanese firm and then package and market it as Kirin Beer. They pay a royalty to Kirin for each case sold.

strategic alliance   A cooperative arrangement between two or more firms for mutual gain.

▌ In a **strategic alliance**, two or more firms jointly cooperate for mutual gain.[24] For example, Kodak and Fuji, along with three other major Japanese camera manufacturers, collaborated on the development of a new film cartridge. This collaboration allowed Kodak and Fuji to share development costs, prevented the advertising war that might have raged if they had developed different cartridges, and made it easier for new cameras to be introduced at the same time as the new film cartridges. A **joint venture** is a special type of strategic alliance in which the partners actually share ownership of a new enterprise. Strategic alliances have enjoyed a tremendous upsurge in the past few years.

joint venture   A special type of strategic alliance in which the partners share in the ownership of an operation on an equity basis.

direct investment   A firm's building or purchasing operating facilities or subsidiaries in a different country from the one where it has its headquarters.

▌ **Direct investment** occurs when a firm headquartered in one country builds or purchases operating facilities or subsidiaries in a foreign country. The foreign operations then become wholly owned subsidiaries of the firm (like Ford's acquisitions of Jaguar, Volvo, and Kia, as well as British Petroleum's acquisition of Amoco). **Maquiladoras** are light assembly plants built in northern Mexico close to the U.S. border. The plants are given special tax breaks by the Mexican government, and the area is populated with workers willing to work for very low wages.

maquiladoras   Light assembly plants that are built in northern Mexico close to the U.S. border and are given special tax breaks by the Mexican government.

CONCEPT CHECK 2.5

Describe the basic levels of international business involvement. Why might a firm use more than one level at the same time?

International business activity continues to expand and affect us in myriad ways. The products we buy, for example, and the standards of living we enjoy are determined in large part by global commerce. Of course, as shown here, the international scope of operations pursued by some companies may also have negative repercussions!

"The repairs will take awhile. We need a part from Mexico, a part from Brazil, and one from Taiwan."

The Context of International Business

Managers involved in international business should also be aware of the cultural environment, controls on international trade, the importance of economic communities, and the role of the GATT and WTO.

The Cultural Environment

A country's culture includes all the values, symbols, beliefs, and language that guide behavior. Cultural values and beliefs are often unspoken; they may even be taken for granted by those who live in a particular country. Cultural factors do not necessarily cause problems for managers when the cultures of two countries are similar. Difficulties can arise, however, when there is little overlap between the home culture of a manager and the culture of the country in which business is to be conducted. For example, most U.S. managers find the culture and traditions of England relatively familiar. The people of both countries speak the same language and share strong historical roots, and there is a history of strong commerce between the two countries. When U.S. managers begin operations in Vietnam or the People's Republic of China, however, many of those commonalities disappear.

Some cultural differences between countries can be very subtle and yet have a major impact on business activities. For example, in the United States most managers clearly agree about the value of time. Most U.S. managers schedule their activities very tightly and then try hard to adhere to their schedules. Other cultures do not put such a premium on time. In the Middle East, managers do not like to set appointments, and they rarely keep appointments set too far into the future. U.S. managers interacting with managers from the Middle East might misinterpret the late arrival of a potential business partner as a negotiation ploy or an insult, when it is merely a simple reflection of different views of time and its value.

Beyond the obvious barriers posed when people speak different languages, subtle differences in meaning can also play a major role. For example, Imperial Oil of Canada markets gasoline under the brand name Esso. When the firm tried to sell its gasoline in Japan, it learned that Esso means "stalled car" in Japanese. Additionally, the color green is used extensively in Muslim countries, but it signifies death in some other lands. The color associated with femininity in the United States is pink, but in many other countries yellow is the most feminine color.

Controls on International Trade

Another element of the international context that managers need to consider is the controls on international trade.

▋ **Tariffs** are taxes collected on goods shipped across national boundaries. Tariffs can be collected by the exporting country, by countries through which goods pass, or by the importing country. Import tariffs, which are the most common, can be levied to protect domestic companies by increasing the cost of foreign goods. Japan charges U.S. tobacco producers a tariff on cigarettes imported into Japan as a way to keep their prices higher than the prices charged by domestic firms. Tariffs can also be levied, usually by less developed countries, to raise money for the government.

> **tariff** A tax collected on goods shipped across national boundaries.

▋ **Quotas**, the most common form of trade restrictions, are limits on the number or value of goods that can be traded. The quota amount is typically designed to ensure that domestic competitors will be able to maintain a certain market share.

> **quota** A limit on the number or value of goods that can be traded.

Honda is allowed to import 425,000 autos each year into the United States. This quota is one reason why Honda opened manufacturing facilities here. The quota applies to cars imported into the United States, but the company can produce as many other cars within our borders as it wants; such cars are not considered imports.

export restraint agreements   Accords reached by governments in which countries voluntarily limit the volume or value of goods they export to or import from one another.

■ **Export restraint agreements** are designed to convince other governments to voluntarily limit the volume or value of goods they export to a particular country. They are, in effect, export quotas. Japanese steel producers voluntarily limit the amount of steel they send to the United States each year.

■ "Buy national" legislation gives preference to domestic producers through content or price restrictions. Several countries have this type of legislation. Brazil requires that Brazilian companies purchase only Brazilian-made computers. The United States requires that the Department of Defense purchase only military uniforms manufactured in the United States, even though the price of foreign uniforms would be only half as much.

Economic Communities

Just as government policies can either increase or decrease the political risk that international managers face, trade relations between countries can either help or hinder international business. Relations dictated by quotas, tariffs, and so forth can hurt international trade. There is currently a movement around the world to reduce many of these barriers. This movement takes its most obvious form in international economic communities.

international economic community   A set of countries that agree to markedly reduce or eliminate trade barriers among member nations (a formalized market system).

An **international economic community** is a set of countries that agree to reduce or eliminate trade barriers among member nations.

European Union (EU)   The first and most important international market system.

■ The **European Union (EU)**: The first (and in many ways still the most important) of these economic communities that has followed a basic plan leading to the systematic elimination of most trade barriers. The EU achieved significantly more potential when eleven member nations eliminated their home currencies (such as French francs and Italian lira) and adopted a new common currency call the *euro*. The current members of the EU are shown in Figure 2.3.

North American Free Trade Agreement (NAFTA)   An agreement between the United States, Canada, and Mexico to promote trade with one another.

■ **North American Free Trade Agreement (NAFTA)**: An economic community encompassing the United States, Canada, and Mexico. These countries have long been major trading partners with one another; more than 70 percent of Mexico's exports go to the United States, and more than 65 percent of what Mexico imports comes from the United States. During the last several years, these countries have negotiated a variety of agreements to make trade even easier. The most important of these eliminates many of the existing trade barriers—quotas and tariffs, for example—that existed previously.[25]

CONCEPT CHECK 2.6

What industries do you think will feel the greatest impact of international business in the future? Are there industries that will remain relatively unaffected by globalization? If so, which ones? If not, explain why not.

The Role of the GATT and WTO

The context of international business is also increasingly being influenced by the General Agreement on Tariffs and Trade (GATT) and the World Trade Organization (WTO).

General Agreement on Tariffs and Trade (GATT)   A trade agreement intended to promote international trade by reducing trade barriers and making it easier for all nations to compete in international markets. Was replaced by the World Trade Organization (WTO) in 1995.

■ The **General Agreement on Tariffs and Trade (GATT)** was first negotiated following World War II in an effort to avoid trade wars that would benefit rich nations and harm poorer ones. It is essentially a trade agreement intended to promote international trade by reducing trade barriers and making it easier for all nations

FIGURE 2.3

European Union Member Nations

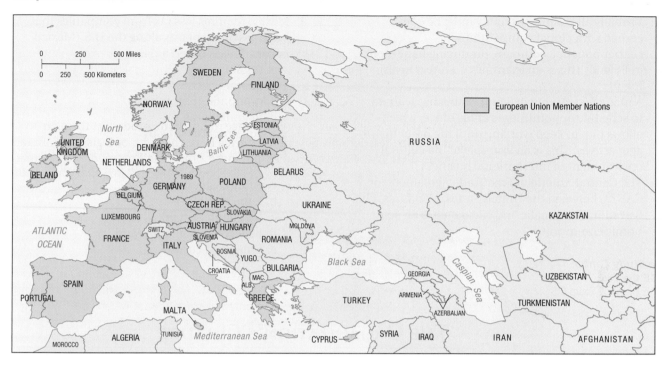

to compete in international markets. The GATT was a major stimulus to international trade after it was first ratified in 1948 by 23 countries; by 1994 a total of 117 countries had signed the agreement. One key component of the GATT was identification of the so-called most favored nation (MFN) principle. This provision stipulates that if a country extends preferential treatment to any other nation that has signed the agreement, then that preferential treatment must be extended to all signatories to the agreement. Members can extend such treatment to nonsignatories as well, but they are not required to do so.

▌ The **World Trade Organization (WTO)** replaced the GATT on January 1, 1995, absorbing its mission. The WTO, headquartered in Geneva, Switzerland, currently includes 140 member nations and 32 observer countries. Members are required to open their markets to international trade and to follow WTO rules. The WTO has three basic goals:

1. To promote trade flows by encouraging nations to adopt nondiscriminatory and predictable trade policies

2. To reduce remaining trade barriers through multilateral negotiations

3. To establish impartial procedures for resolving trade disputes among its members

The World Trade Organization is certain to continue to play a major role in the evolution of the global economy. At the same time, it has also become a lightning rod for protesters and other activists, who argue that the WTO focuses too narrowly on globalization issues to the detriment of human rights and the environment.

World Trade Organization (WTO) An organization, which currently includes 140 member nations and 32 observer countries, that requires members to open their markets to international trade and to follow WTO rules. It replaced the General Agreement on Tariffs and Trade (GATT) in 1995.

True or False?

_____ 1. Virtually all businesses today must be concerned with global competition.

_____ 2. Gerber bought a company producing baby food in Poland. This is an example of a direct investment.

_____ 3. A manager working in Saudi Arabia has learned to schedule appointments at his office, which allows him to keep working until the other manager arrives. This is an example of the cultural environment of international business.

_____ 4. The Central American Free Trade Agreement, or CAFTA, between the United States, Honduras, El Salvador, Guatemala, and Nicaragua is an economic community.

Online Study Center
ACE the Test
ACE Practice Tests 2.3

Multiple Choice

_____ 5. Mexico requires less tax from companies that build assembly plants along the U.S./Mexico border. This is called a _____.
   a. tariff
   b. quota
   c. economic community
   d. maquiladoras
   e. construction subsidy

_____ 6. The advantages of importing and exporting include all EXCEPT which of the following?
   a. Small cash outlay
   b. Little risk
   c. No adaptation necessary
   d. Relatively straightforward
   e. Enhanced control

THE ORGANIZATION'S CULTURE

4 ▸ *Describe the importance and determinants of an organization's culture, as well as how organization culture can be managed.*

organization culture   The set of values, beliefs, behaviors, customs, and attitudes that helps the members of the organization understand what it stands for, how it does things, and what it considers important.

Organization culture is the set of values, beliefs, behaviors, customs, and attitudes that helps the members of the organization understand what it stands for, how it does things, and what it considers important.[26]

The Importance of Organization Culture

Culture determines the "feel" of the organization. A strong and clear culture can play an important role in the competitiveness of a business. At the same time, though, there is no universal culture that will help all organizations. The stereotypic image of Microsoft, for example, is that of a workplace where people dress very casually and work very long hours. In contrast, the image of Bank of America for some observers is that of a formal setting with rigid work rules and people dressed in conservative business attire. And Texas Instruments likes to talk about its "shirtsleeve" culture, in which ties are avoided and few managers ever wear jackets.

Of course, the same culture is not necessarily found throughout an entire organization. For example, the sales and marketing department may have a culture quite different from that of the operations and manufacturing department. Regardless of its nature, however, culture is a powerful force in organizations, one that can shape the firm's overall effectiveness and long-term success. Companies that can develop and maintain a strong culture, such as Starbucks and Procter & Gamble, tend to be more effective than companies that have trouble developing and maintaining a strong culture, such as Kmart.[27]

Determinants of Organization Culture

Where does an organization's culture come from? Typically, it develops and blossoms over a long period of time. Its starting point is often the organization's founder. For example, James Cash Penney believed in treating employees and customers with respect and dignity. Employees at J.C. Penney are still called "associates" rather than "employees" (to reflect partnership), and customer satisfaction is of paramount importance.[28] And many decisions at Walt Disney Company today are still framed by asking, "What would Walt have done?" As an organization grows, its culture is modified, shaped, and refined by symbols, stories, heroes, slogans, and ceremonies.

Corporate success and shared experiences also shape culture. For example, Hallmark Cards has a strong culture derived from its years of success in the greeting card industry. Employees speak of "the Hallmark family" and care deeply about the company; many of them have worked there for years. At Kmart, in contrast, the culture is quite weak, the management team changes rapidly, and few people sense any direction or purpose in the company. The differences in culture at Hallmark and Kmart are in part attributable to past successes and shared experiences.

CONCEPT CHECK 2.7

What is the culture of your college or university? How clear is it? What are its most positive and its most negative characteristics?

Managing Organization Culture

How can managers deal with culture, given its clear importance but intangible nature? Essentially, the manager must understand the current culture and then decide whether it should be maintained or changed. Culture can be maintained by rewarding and promoting people whose behaviors are consistent with the existing culture and by articulating the culture through slogans, ceremonies, and so forth. It can be changed by bringing in newcomers from outside the organization, altering rewards, and using new slogans and symbols.

Managers must walk a fine line between maintaining a culture that still works effectively and changing a culture that has become dysfunctional. For example, some firms take pride in perpetuating their heritage and culture. Shell Oil, for example, has an elaborate display in the lobby of its Houston headquarters that tells the story of the firm's past. But other companies may face situations in which their culture is no longer a strength. For example, some critics feel that the organization culture at General Motors places too much emphasis on product development and internal competition among divisions, and not enough on marketing and competition with other firms.[29]

Culture problems sometimes arise from mergers or from the growth of rival factions within an organization. A few years ago Wells Fargo, which relies heavily on flashy technology and automated banking services, acquired another large bank, First Interstate, which had focused more attention on personal services and customer satisfaction. Blending these two disparate organization cultures was difficult for the firm and took much longer than expected as managers argued over how best to serve customers and operate the new enterprise.[30]

To change culture, managers must have a clear idea of what they want to create. When Continental Airlines "reinvented" itself a few years ago, employees were invited outside the corporate headquarters in Houston to watch the firm's old policies and procedures manuals being set afire. The firm's new strategic direction is known throughout Continental as the "Go Forward" plan, intentionally named to avoid reminding people about the firm's troubled past and to focus on the future instead.

TEST PREPPER 2.4

ANSWERS CAN BE FOUND ON P. 441

True or False?

_____ 1. The set of values, beliefs, customs, and attitudes that helps members of an organization determine how it does things and what it stands for is its code of ethics.

_____ 2. Managers must first understand the existing culture before they determine if it should be changed or maintained.

_____ 3. When Smucker's acquired Jif, managers needed to be concerned with possible culture clashes between the two businesses.

Multiple Choice

_____ 4. Which of the following is NOT an element that goes into organizational culture?
   a. Symbols
   b. Stories
   c. Procedures
   d. Heroes
   e. Ceremonies

Online Study Center
ACE the Test
ACE Practice Tests 2.4

BUILDING EFFECTIVE INTERPERSONAL SKILLS

Online Study Center
Improve Your Grade
Exercises: Building Effective Skills

Exercise Overview

Interpersonal skills reflect the manager's ability to communicate with, understand, and motivate individuals and groups. Managers in international organizations must understand how cultural manners and norms affect communication with people in different areas of the world. This exercise will help you evaluate your current level of cultural awareness and develop insights into areas where you can improve.

Exercise Background

As firms become increasingly globalized, they look for managers with international experience or skills. Yet many American college graduates do not have strong skills in foreign languages, global history, or international cultures.

Exercise Task

Take the International Culture Quiz that follows. Then, on the basis of your score, answer the question at the end. In order to make the quiz more relevant, choose your answers from one or more of the ten largest countries in the world. In order, these are China, India, the United States, Indonesia, Brazil, Pakistan, Bangladesh, Russia, Nigeria, and Japan.

The International Culture Quiz

1. Name the major religion practiced in each of the ten largest countries.

2. When greeting a business associate, in which country or countries is it proper to shake hands? to bow? to hug or kiss?

3. In which country or countries should you avoid wearing the color purple?

4. In which country or countries would smiling be considered suspicious?

5. In which country or countries are laughter and smiling often used as a way of covering up feelings of embarrassment or displeasure?

6. Which part of someone else's body should you never touch in Indonesia? in India? Which part of your own body should you never touch in China?

7. In which country or countries would a server or small-business person require that a tip be paid before the service is rendered?

8. In which country or countries would it be an insult to address someone in Spanish?

9. In which country or countries is whistling considered bad luck?

10. In which country or countries is it important to give printed business cards to all business associates?

11. In which country or countries might you be asked your family size or income upon first meeting with a new business associate?

12. In which country or countries should gum not be chewed at work?

Your instructor will provide the answers. Was your score high or low? What does your score tell you about your cultural awareness?

What do you think you could do to improve your score? Share your ideas with the class.

Reprinted by permission of the author Margaret Hill.

EXPERIENTIAL EXERCISE

Ethics of Employee Appraisal

Online Study Center
Improve Your Grade
Exercises: Experiential Exercise

Purpose

The appraisal of employee performance is one of the management activities that can raise ethical issues. This skill builder focuses on the human resources model. It will help you develop the mentor role of the human resources model. One of the skills of the mentor is the ability to cultivate effective subordinates.

Introduction

Much attention has been given in recent years to ethics in business, yet the ethical issues that arise in the hiring and appraising of employees are often overlooked. Marian Kellogg developed a list of principles to keep in mind when recruiting or appraising.

How to Keep Your Appraisals Ethical: A Manager's Checklist

1. Don't appraise without knowing why the appraisal is required.

2. Appraise on the basis of representative information.

3. Appraise on the basis of sufficient information.

4. Appraise on the basis of relevant information.

5. Be honest in your assessment of all the facts you obtain.

6. Don't write one thing and say another.

7. In offering an appraisal, make it plain that this is only your personal opinion of the facts as you see them.

8. Pass appraisal information along only to those who have good reason to know it.

9. Don't imply the existence of an appraisal that hasn't been made.

10. Don't accept another's appraisal without knowing the basis on which it was made.

Instructions

Read each incident individually and decide which rule or rules it violates, marking the appropriate number beneath the incident. In some cases, more than one rule is violated. In your group, go over each case and come to a consensus on which rules are violated.

Incidents

- Steve Wilson has applied for a transfer to Department O, headed by Marianne Kilbourn. As part of

EXPERIENTIAL EXERCISE (CONTINUED)

her fact finding, Marianne reads through the written evaluation, which is glowing, and then asks Steve's boss, Bill Hammond, for information on Steve's performance. Bill starts complaining about Steve because his last project was not up to par but does not mention that Steve's wife has been seriously ill for two months. Marianne then decides not to accept Steve's transfer.

Rule violation # _____

- Maury Nanner is a sales manager who is having lunch with several executives. One of them, Harvey Gant, asks Maury what he thinks of his subordinate George Williams, and Nanner gives a lengthy evaluation.

Rule violation # _____

- Phillip Randall is working on six-month evaluations of his subordinates. He decides to rate Elisa Donner less than average on initiative because he thinks she spends too much time, energy, and money making herself look attractive. He thinks her attractiveness distracts the male employees.

Rule violation # _____

- Paul Trendant has received an application from an outstanding candidate, Jim Fischer. However, Paul decides not to hire Jim because he has heard from someone that Jim moved to town only because his wife got a good job here. Trendant thinks Jim will quit whenever his wife gets transferred.

Rule violation # _____

- Susan Forman is on the fast track and tries to make herself look good to her boss, Peter Everly. This morning she has a meeting with Pete to discuss which person to promote. Just before the meeting, Pete's golf buddy Harold, a coworker of Susan's, tells Susan that Alice, Jerry, and Joe are favored by Pete. Susan had felt that Darlene was the strongest candidate, but she goes into the meeting with Pete and suggests Alice, Jerry, and Joe as the top candidates.

Rule violation # _____

- Sandy is a new supervisor for seven people. After several months Sandy is certain that Linda is marginally competent and often cannot produce any useful work. Looking over past appraisals, Sandy sees that all of Linda's evaluations were positive, and she is told that Linda "has problems" and not to be "too hard on her." Realizing that this approach is not healthy, Sandy begins documenting Linda's inadequate performance. Several supervisors hint that she should "lighten up because we don't want Linda to feel hurt."

Rule violation # _____

Sources: Marian S. Kellogg, What to Do About Performance Appraisal, AMACOM, a division of the American Management Association, New York, 1975; Marian S. Kellogg, Personnel, American Management Association, New York, July–August 1965; and Dorothy Marcic, *Organizational Behavior: Experiences and Cases*, 3rd ed. (Minneapolis, MN: West, 1992).

Online Study Center
Improve Your Grade
Interactive Skills Self-Assessment

The Final Frontier?

What frontiers are left for an enormous retailer that has become the most profitable corporation on earth? Wal-Mart is gigantic by any measure. Sales totaled $285 billion in 2005, and the discounter employed 1.6 million workers in 6,100 stores. Over 138 million customers per week visit Wal-Mart stores worldwide. In 2005 Wal-Mart topped the Fortune 500 for the fourth year in a row, the first nonmanufacturing firm to ever reach that position.

With domestic sales flattening and the discount market approaching saturation, Wal-Mart is seeking expansion opportunities. It can aggressively attack specialty retailers, such as PETsMART, Albertsons, Toys "R" Us, and Best Buy. It can introduce new categories at its existing stores. "Wal-Mart's aggressive rollout of retail gas stations could be followed closely with the company selling used cars, financial services, home improvement, and food service," says Ira Kalish, a retail consultant. Wal-Mart is negotiating a partnership with Starbucks to put cafes in Wal-Mart stores. The most appealing option, however, is international expansion.

Wal-Mart's international expansion began in 1991, when the firm opened a Sam's Club near Mexico City. Today, the firm's International Division operates 1,100 overseas outlets, with stores located in Argentina, Brazil, Canada, China, Germany, Korea, Mexico, Puerto Rico, and the United Kingdom. In each of these markets, acquisitions have played a more important role than internal growth. For example, in Canada, Wal-Mart purchased 122 Woolco stores to enter that market. In Germany, Wal-Mart began with an acquisition of 21 Wertkauf hypermarkets and then added 74 Interspar stores. The company's U.K.-based acquisitions have been its most ambitious to date, beginning with the 1999 purchase of 230 ASDA stores. The firm integrates the acquired stores into its operations, changes the names, renovates the facilities, brings in store managers from the United States, and changes the product mix.

Wal-Mart is still learning how to deal effectively with differences in culture and business practices across borders. An initial difficulty was the relatively

> "Wal-Mart is formidable, but we aren't afraid of the challenge."
>
> —Ricardo Martin, CEO of Mexican retailer Soriana

small size of most of the acquired stores, with one-third the floor space of a typical Wal-Mart. Wal-Mart's "one-stop" strategy depends, in part, on size, but European customers are turned off by the impersonal feel of very large stores. European customers also dislike greeters. "Germans are skeptical. Customers said that they don't want to be paying the salary of that guy at the door," claims Nikolai Baltruschat, a Deutsche Bank analyst. Also, Europeans typically shop more frequently but buy less at each visit than do Americans, so they do not like pushing around a large cart. Smaller carts could allow the company to cram more products into a small space, but they do not encourage large purchases.

Regulation creates yet another set of hurdles for Wal-Mart. Twenty-four-hour stores are banned in England and Germany. A German court upheld employees' rights to wear earrings and sport facial hair. When the retailer tried to forbid English employees from drinking beer during their lunch break, English labor groups threatened a lawsuit. European laws are much stricter about the sale of "loss leaders," popular products that are sold below cost in order to bring customers into the store. Negotiations with suppliers are also more heavily regulated. In Mexico, Wal-Mart's cost pressure on suppliers is under investigation, after the firm demanded deep discounts on many products.

Wal-Mart's entry into a new market "is a nightmare for a lot of retailers," says Michael P. Godliman, a retail consultant. To fight back, local retailers have imitated Wal-Mart's strategy by cutting costs and increasing variety. In order to attract more customers, firms have also added products and services geared to local tastes. Soriana supermarkets of Mexico are battling Wal-Mart with in-store mariachi concerts. "Wal-Mart is formidable, but we aren't afraid of the challenge," says Soriana CEO Ricardo Martin. Carrefour, a French retailer, is hoping to forestall Wal-Mart's entry into its country, the second-largest retail market in Europe. Carrefour is competing by adding such amenities as travel agents and shoe fitters and by banning fluorescent lighting. Its 2001 merger with France's number-two retailer, Promodes, creates market power for Carrefour. "They're just relentless," says a French retail executive, referring to Carrefour. "The toughest competitor I've ever seen anywhere." Other European retailers, such as Dutch grocer Ahold, are also undergoing preemptive mergers designed to stop Wal-Mart.

In 2004 Wal-Mart's international operations were strong, with 20 percent of its sales from overseas locations. International sales increased by 18 percent over 2003, but its gross margin was just 5.3 percent, compared to 7.4 percent for domestic stores. Flush with the profits from its thousands of domestic stores, Wal-Mart will not be deterred. The international retailing industry will undoubtedly consolidate until just a few very large, cross-border retailers remain. And Wal-Mart, which will open 160 new international stores in 2005, aims to be one of them.

Case Questions

1. What are some of the advantages that Wal-Mart has in terms of its environment? What are some of the environmental challenges it faces?

2. What methods has Wal-Mart used to globalize? Are those the most appropriate methods for the firm? Why or why not?

3. What are some of the key environmental issues related to ethics and social responsibility that Wal-Mart faces?

Case References

Jerry Useem, "Wal-Mart: It's Tough to Be No. 1," *Fortune,* March 8, 2004, pp. 118–122; "2005 Annual Report," "2003 Annual Report," Wal-Mart website, www.walmartstores.com on December 20, 2005; Amy Tsao, "Will Wal-Mart Take Over the World?" *BusinessWeek,* November 27, 2002, www .businessweek.com on December 9, 2002; Geri Smith, "War of the Superstores," *BusinessWeek,* September 23, 2002, p. 60; "The 2003 Global 500," *Fortune,* July 10, 2003, www .fortune.com on April 12, 2004; "California Tries to Slam Lid on Big-Boxed Wal-Mart," *USA Today,* March 2, 2004, pp. B1, B2.

LEARNING OBJECTIVE REVIEW

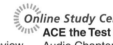

Online Study Center
Improve Your Grade
–Learning Objective Review
–Audio Chapter Review
–Study Guide to Go

Online Study Center
ACE the Test
Audio Chapter Quiz

▶ *Discuss the nature of an organization's environments, and identify and describe the components of its general, task, and internal environments.*

- Managers need to have a thorough understanding of the environment in which they operate and compete.

- The general environment consists of the economy, technology, and the political-legal climate.

- The task environment consists of competitors, customers, suppliers, regulators, and strategic partners. The internal environment consists of the organization's owners, board of directors, employees, physical environment, and culture.

Owners are those who have claims on the property rights of the organization.

The board of directors, elected by stockholders, is responsible for overseeing a firm's top managers.

Individual employees are other important parts of the internal environment.

The physical environment, yet another part of the internal environment, varies greatly across organizations.

2 *Describe the ethical and social environment of management, including individual ethics, the concept of social responsibility, and how organizations can manage social responsibility.*

- Understanding the differences between ethical and unethical behavior, as well as appreciating the special nature of managerial ethics, can help guide effective decision making.

- Understanding the meaning of and arguments for and against social responsibility can help a manager effectively address both the formal and the informal dimensions of social responsibility.

3 *Discuss the international environment of management, including trends in international business, levels of international business activities, and the context of international business.*

- Current trends in the international environment have resulted in the increasing globalization of markets, industries, and businesses.

- Organizations seeking to become more international can rely on importing, exporting, licensing (including franchising), strategic alliances, and direct investment to do so.

- The national culture, controls on international trade, economic communities, and the WTO combine to determine the context of international business.

4 *Describe the importance and determinants of an organization's culture, as well as how organization culture can be managed.*

- Organization culture is the set of values, beliefs, behaviors, customs, and attitudes that helps the members of the organization understand what it stands for, how it does things, and what it considers important. Managers must understand that culture is a key determinant of how well their organization will perform; culture can be assessed and managed in a number of different ways.

Online Study Center **RESOURCES**

Prepare for Class, Improve Your Grade, and ACE the Test. These Student Achievement resources include:

ACE Practice Tests	Interactive Skills Assessments	Study Guide to Go
End of Chapter Exercises	Knowledgebank	Video Segments
Glossaries (visual and print)	Reviews (audio and print)	Summaries/Outlines
Flashcards		

To access these learning and study tools, go to: **college.hmco.com/pic/griffinSAS**

The fastest ball.

Nike continues to explore new global markets across an array of sporting venues. These new Mercurial soccer balls were unveiled at a recent product convention in Germany; at the same show Nike introduced new ski, basketball, and biking equipment.

1 > *Describe the planning process, describe organizational goals, and identify three basic kinds of organizational plans.*

2 > *Discuss the components of strategy, identify the types of strategic alternatives, and describe how to use SWOT analysis in formulating strategy.*

3 > *Identify and describe various alternative approaches to business-level strategy formulation.*

4 > *Identify and describe various alternative approaches to corporate-level strategy formulation.*

> *"We have to be as hungry tomorrow as we were yesterday—as hungry as Phil Knight was back when he was selling shoes out of his car."*
>
> —Bill Perez, CEO, Nike

Chapter Outline

Online Study Center
Prepare for Class
Chapter Outline

6 *Describe the basic types of operational plans used by organizations.*

5 *Discuss how tactical plans are developed and executed.*

Nike Just Does It

From its founding in 1964 through the mid-1990s, Nike was one of the biggest success stories in American business. Since its earliest days, Nike has been an innovator, creating the waffle-sole shoe and the air cushion, as well as pioneering technical shoe design and the acceptance of sportswear as fashionable, casual street wear. The firm's growth peaked in 1997, when sales grew by 50 percent and profits topped $795 million. However, by 1999, profits had fallen to just $451 million, and the firm was clearly struggling.

Founder and legendary former CEO Phil Knight claims, "We got to be a $9 billion company with a $5 billion management." (Knight is retired but remains active at Nike.) The company may have been the victim of its own success. As Nike's premium

Online Study Center college.hmco.com/pic/griffinSAS

Online Study Center
Improve Your Grade
—Flashcards
—Glossary

You should be able to define and use terms that are part of the practicing manager's vocabulary, as well as those that are integral in the language of management.

products became more technologically complex and more expensive to design and manufacture, prices rose. The firm's elite shoes are priced between $150 and $300, far above the budgets of teenagers, who are the biggest consumers of active wear. Another problem was the saturated market for athletic shoes in the United States. There were few new consumers in the footwear industry, which makes up 50 percent of the firm's revenues. And while Nike was seen as a fashion trendsetter, "serious" athletes still preferred to purchase shoes from specialty providers.

To return the firm to its past splendor, Knight began a series of bold moves. In a shocking switch from its promote-from-within, athlete-dominated culture, the firm began to hire top managers from outside the sportswear industry. Donald W. Blair, formerly of PepsiCo, was hired as chief financial officer and charged with bringing fiscal discipline to the free-spending, marketing-driven company. Another outsider, Mindy Grossman, was lured away from Polo Ralph Lauren to head Nike's apparel group. Grossman's focus is on updating Nike's fashion appeal and reducing development time for new products. New CEO Bill Perez is a thirty-four-year veteran of consumer products firm S.C. Johnson, with experience in extension and management of established brands.

The firm has also diversified, moving beyond its traditional strengths in running and basketball. Nike has become a leader in soccer, hockey, and cycling and is actively pursuing the very large and lucrative golf apparel industry. In addition, the company has acquired several related businesses that extend its product lines, such as Converse and Starter. It has moved into the casual shoe and apparel industries, including shoemakers Cole Haan and Hurley, an "up-and-coming surf-culture lifestyle brand." Yet Nike is not making the mistake of neglecting its traditional strengths in running. In the 2004 Olympics, a vast majority of runners wore Nike shoes.

The changes have been pleasing to consumers, as evidenced by increasing sales, especially in the firm's apparel business. The clothing division grew to over 30 percent of Nike sales in 2004. "For the first time, we're an apparel company as well as a shoe company," Knight says. Investors should be happy, too, thanks to higher sales and rising profit margins. And the recent push to increase overseas sales could counteract flattening demand in the United States, which would also benefit shareholders.

Nike seems well on its way to recovering its former glory, but two clouds remain on the horizon. First, the firm has thus far failed to effectively address accusations that it exploits Third World workers. Until the firm sheds its "sweat-shop" image, some consumers will continue to boycott Nike products. Hopefully, Bill Perez's reputation as an ethical leader at S.C. Johnson will soothe social responsibility concerns. Second, in August 2004, Adidas, a German firm, agreed to purchase Reebok, joining the number two and three rivals to form the world's largest athletic shoe company. Nike will face increased competition from the combined firm, but Perez and other leaders are confident.

According to Perez, many companies "make the mistake of narrowly defining the business segments in which they are working so they can talk to themselves about being market leaders." Perez expects Nike to avoid that false sense of complacency and respond to the challenge of renewed competition with even greater efforts. Nike's revenues grew from $10 billion in 2002 to $14 billion in 2005, an annual growth rate of over 20 percent, and plans seek double-digit growth for the foreseeable future. To accomplish this, Perez says, "We have to be as hungry tomorrow as we were yesterday—as hungry as Phil Knight was back when he was selling shoes out of his car."[1]

The actions taken by Nike reflect one of the most critical functions that managers perform for their businesses: strategy and strategic planning. Phil Knight recognized that his firm had both significant strengths and worrisome weaknesses. He also knew that action was required to revitalize the firm. Hence he embarked on a variety of new initiatives and made radical changes in how Nike does business. But each move he made was developed from a strategic perspective.

This chapter is the first of three that explore the planning process in more detail. We begin by examining the nature of planning and organizational goals. We then discuss strategic management, including its components and alternatives, and describe the kinds of analysis needed for firms to formulate their strategies. Finally, we examine how strategies are implemented through tactical and operational planning.

PLANNING AND ORGANIZATIONAL GOALS

1 *Describe the planning process, describe organizational goals, and identify three basic kinds of organizational plans.*

The planning process itself can best be thought of as a generic activity. All organizations engage in planning activities, but no two organizations plan in exactly the same fashion. Figure 3.1 is a general representation of the planning

---

FIGURE 3.1

The Planning Process

The planning process takes place within an environmental context. Managers must develop a complete and thorough understanding of this context to determine the organization's mission and to develop its strategic, tactical, and operational goals and plans.

process that many organizations attempt to follow. But although most firms follow this general framework, each also has its own nuances and variations.[2]

As Figure 3.1 shows, all planning occurs within an environmental context. If managers do not understand this context, they are unable to develop effective plans. Thus understanding the environment is essentially the first step in planning. The previous chapter covers many of the basic environmental issues that affect organizations and how they plan. With this understanding as a foundation, managers must then establish the organization's mission. The mission outlines the organization's purpose, premises, values, and directions. Flowing from the mission are parallel streams of goals and plans. Directly following the mission are strategic goals. These goals and the mission help determine strategic plans. Strategic goals and plans are primary inputs for developing tactical goals. Tactical goals and the original strategic plans help shape tactical plans. Tactical plans, in turn, combine with the tactical goals to shape operational goals. These goals and the appropriate tactical plans determine operational plans. Finally, goals and plans at each level can also be used as input for future activities at all levels.

Organizational Goals

Goals are critical to organizational effectiveness, and they serve a number of purposes. Organizations can also have several different kinds of goals, all of which must be appropriately managed. A number of different kinds of managers must be involved in setting goals.

Purposes of Goals

Goals serve four important purposes.[3]

1. Goals provide guidance and a unified direction for people in the organization. Goals can help everyone understand where the organization is going and why getting there is important.[4] Top managers at General Electric have a goal that every business owned by the firm should be either number one or number

two in its industry. This goal still helps set the tone for most other decisions made by managers at GE.

2. Goal-setting practices strongly affect other aspects of planning. That is, effective goal setting promotes good planning, and good planning facilitates future goal setting. Procter & Gamble recently set a goal of doubling its market share; now its managers must look for opportunities for business growth and work aggressively toward expanding market share and entering new markets.

3. Goals can serve as a source of motivation for employees of the organization. Goals that are specific and moderately difficult can motivate people to work harder, especially if attaining the goal is likely to result in rewards.[5] The Italian furniture manufacturer Industrie Natuzzi SpA uses goals to motivate its workers. Each craftsperson has a goal for how long it should take to perform her or his job, such as sewing leather sheets together to make a sofa cushion or building wooden frames for chair arms. At the completion of assigned tasks, workers enter their ID numbers and job numbers into the firm's computer system. If they get a job done faster than their goal, a bonus is automatically added to their paycheck.[6]

4. Goals provide an effective mechanism for evaluation and control. This means that performance can be assessed in the future in terms of how successfully today's goals are accomplished. For example, suppose that officials of the United Way of America set a goal of collecting $250,000 from a particular small community. If, midway through the campaign, they have raised only $50,000, they know that they need to change or intensify their efforts. If they raise only $100,000 by the end of their drive, they will need to study the situation carefully to determine why they did not reach their goal and what they need to do differently next year. On the other hand, if they succeed in raising $265,000, evaluations of their efforts will take on an entirely different character.

Kinds of Goals

Goals are set for and by different levels within an organization. The four basic levels of goals are mission, strategic, tactical, and operational goals.

1. An organization's **mission** is a statement of its "fundamental, unique purpose that sets [it] apart from other firms of its type and identifies the scope of the business's operations in product and market terms."[7]

2. **Strategic goals** are goals set by and for top management of the organization. They focus on broad, general issues.

3. **Tactical goals** are set by and for middle managers. Their focus is on how to operationalize actions necessary to achieve the strategic goals.

4. **Operational goals** are set by and for lower-level managers. Their concern is with shorter-term issues associated with the tactical goals. While this goal would likely be set by higher-level managers, lower-level managers would be key to actually getting it done. (Some managers use the words *objective* and *goal* interchangeably. When they are differentiated, however, the term *objective* is generally used instead of *operational goal*.)

Kinds of Plans

Organizations establish many different kinds of plans. At a general level, these include strategic, tactical, and operational plans.

CONCEPT CHECK 3.1

What are the four primary purposes of organizational goals?

Online Study Center
Improve Your Grade
Knowledgebank 3.1

mission A statement of an organization's fundamental purpose.

strategic goal A goal set by and for top management of the organization.

tactical goal A goal set by and for middle managers of the organization.

operational goal A goal set by and for lower-level managers of the organization.

strategic plan   A general plan outlining decisions about resource allocation, priorities, and action steps necessary to reach strategic goals.

▌ **Strategic plans** are the plans developed to achieve strategic goals. More precisely, a strategic plan is a general plan outlining decisions about resource allocation, priorities, and action steps necessary to reach strategic goals.[8] These plans are set by the board of directors and top management, generally have an extended time horizon, and address questions of scope, resource deployment, competitive advantage, and synergy. We discuss strategic planning further in the next major section.

tactical plan   A plan aimed at achieving tactical goals and developed to implement parts of a strategic plan.

▌ **Tactical plans** are aimed at achieving tactical goals; they are developed to implement specific parts of a strategic plan. Tactical plans typically involve upper and middle management and, compared with strategic plans, have a somewhat shorter time horizon and a more specific and concrete focus. Thus tactical plans are concerned more with actually getting things done than with deciding what to do. Tactical planning is covered after our discussion of strategic planning.

operational plan   A plan that focuses on carrying out tactical plans to achieve operational goals.

▌ **Operational plans** focus on carrying out tactical plans to achieve operational goals. Developed by middle- and lower-level managers, operational plans have a short-term focus and are relatively narrow in scope. Each one deals with a fairly small set of activities. We cover operational planning in the last section of this chapter.

CONCEPT CHECK 3.2

What are the similarities and differences between tactical and operational planning? Which kind of plan—tactical or operational—should be developed first? Does the order really matter? Why or why not?

Online Study Center
Improve Your Grade
Visual Glossary

TEST PREPPER 3.1

ANSWERS CAN BE FOUND ON P. 441

True or False?

_____ 1. A strategic goal is a statement of an organization's fundamental purpose.

_____ 2. A goal set by and for lower-level managers of the organization is a tactical goal.

_____ 3. A general plan outlining decisions of resource allocation and priorities is a strategic plan.

Multiple Choice

_____ 4. The planning process takes place within an environmental context. Managers must understand the context in order to develop which of the following?
   a. Mission statement
   b. Strategic goals and plans
   c. Tactical goals and plans
   d. Operational goals and plans
   e. All of the above

Online Study Center
ACE the Test
ACE Practice Tests 3.1

_____ 5. Which of the following is NOT a purpose of goals?
   a. Provides guidance and a unified direction for people in the organization
   b. Promotes good planning
   c. Serves as a source of motivation for employees
   d. States an organization's fundamental purpose
   e. Provides an effective mechanism for evaluation and control

_____ 6. American West Airlines introduced tray-table advertising in 2004. This decision was made by top and middle management and involved finding a way to get more revenue for its flights. This is an example of _____ planning.
   a. strategic
   b. tactical
   c. operational
   d. long-range
   e. contingency

THE NATURE OF STRATEGIC MANAGEMENT

> **2** Discuss the components of strategy, identify the types of strategic alternatives, and describe how to use SWOT analysis in formulating strategy.

A **strategy** is a comprehensive plan for accomplishing an organization's goals. **Strategic management**, in turn, is a way of approaching business opportunities and challenges—it is a comprehensive and ongoing management process aimed at formulating and implementing effective strategies. Finally, **effective strategies** are those that promote a superior alignment between the organization and its environment and the achievement of strategic goals.[9]

strategy A comprehensive plan for accomplishing an organization's goals.

strategic management A comprehensive and ongoing management process aimed at formulating and implementing effective strategies; a way of approaching business opportunities and challenges.

effective strategy A strategy that promotes a superior alignment between the organization and its environment and the achievement of strategic goals.

The Components of Strategy

In general, a well-conceived strategy addresses three areas: distinctive competence, scope, and resource deployment.

1. A **distinctive competence** is something the organization does exceptionally well as compared with other firms. A distinctive competence of The Limited is speed in moving inventory. It tracks consumer preferences daily with point-of-sale computers, electronically transmits orders to suppliers in Hong Kong, charters 747s to fly products to the United States, and has products in stores forty-eight hours later. Because other retailers take weeks or sometimes months to accomplish the same things, The Limited relies on this distinctive competence to remain competitive.[10]

   distinctive competence An organizational strength possessed by only a small number of competing firms.

2. The **scope** of a strategy specifies the range of markets in which an organization will compete. Hershey Foods has essentially restricted its scope to the confectionery business, with a few related activities in other food-processing areas. In contrast, its biggest competitor, Mars, has adopted a broader scope by competing in the pet food business and the electronics industry, among others. Some organizations, called conglomerates, compete in dozens or even hundreds of markets.

   scope When applied to strategy, the range of markets in which an organization will compete.

3. A strategy should also include an outline of the organization's projected **resource deployment**—how it will distribute its resources across the areas in which it competes. General Electric, for example, has been using profits from its highly successful U.S. operations to invest heavily in new businesses in Europe and Asia. Alternatively, the firm might have chosen to invest in different industries in its domestic market or to invest more heavily in Latin America. The choices it made about where and how much to invest reflect issues of resource deployment.[11]

   resource deployment How an organization distributes its resources across the areas in which it competes.

Types of Strategic Alternatives

Most businesses today also develop strategies at two distinct levels. These levels provide a rich combination of strategic alternatives for organizations.

▌ **Business-level strategy** is the set of strategic alternatives from which an organization chooses as it conducts business in a particular industry or market. Such alternatives help the organization focus its competitive efforts for each industry or market in a targeted and deliberate manner.

business-level strategy The set of strategic alternatives from which an organization chooses as it conducts business in a particular industry or market.

corporate-level strategy The set of strategic alternatives from which an organization chooses as it manages its operations across several industries and several markets.

strategy formulation The set of processes involved in creating or determining the strategies of the organization; it focuses on the content of strategies.

strategy implementation The methods by which strategies are operationalized, or executed, within the organization; it focuses on the processes through which strategies are achieved.

SWOT An acronym that stands for strengths, weaknesses, opportunities, and threats.

▌ **Corporate-level strategy** is the set of strategic alternatives from which an organization chooses as it manages its operations simultaneously across several industries and several markets.[12] As we will see, most large companies today compete in a variety of industries and markets. Thus, although they develop business-level strategies for each industry or market, they also develop an overall strategy that helps define the mix of industries and markets that are of interest to the firm.

Drawing a distinction between strategy formulation and strategy implementation is also instructive. **Strategy formulation** is the set of processes involved in creating or determining the strategies of the organization, whereas **strategy implementation** consists of the methods by which strategies are implemented within the organization. The primary distinction is along the lines of content versus process: The formulation stage determines what the strategy is, and the implementation stage focuses on how the strategy is achieved.

Using SWOT Analysis to Formulate Strategy

The starting point in formulating strategy is usually SWOT analysis. **SWOT** is an acronym that stands for strengths, weaknesses, opportunities, and threats. As shown in Figure 3.2, SWOT analysis is a careful evaluation of an organization's internal strengths and weaknesses, as well as its environmental opportunities and threats. In SWOT analysis, the best strategies accomplish an organization's mission by (1) exploiting an organization's strengths while (2) avoiding (or correcting) its weaknesses and (3) neutralizing its threats.

FIGURE 3.2

SWOT Analysis

SWOT analysis is one of the most important steps in formulating strategy. Using the organization's mission as a context, managers assess internal strengths (distinctive competencies) and weaknesses as well as external opportunities and threats. The goal is then to develop good strategies that exploit opportunities and strengths, neutralize threats, and avoid weaknesses.

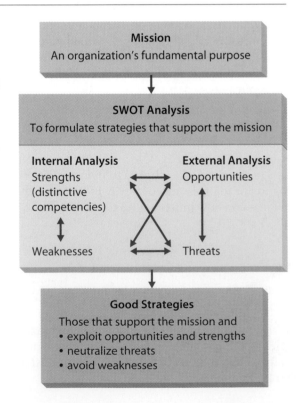

Mission
An organization's fundamental purpose

SWOT Analysis
To formulate strategies that support the mission

Internal Analysis
Strengths (distinctive competencies)

Weaknesses

External Analysis
Opportunities

Threats

Good Strategies
Those that support the mission and
• exploit opportunities and strengths
• neutralize threats
• avoid weaknesses

1. **Organizational strengths** are skills and capabilities that enable an organization to conceive of and implement its strategies. Examples of organizational strengths might include a strong and respected brand name, a highly skilled workforce, proprietary technology, or large cash reserves. A *distinctive competence*, as noted earlier, is a strength possessed by only a small number of competing firms. Organizations that recognize and exploit their distinctive competencies often obtain a *competitive advantage* and achieve above-normal economic performance.[13]

   organizational strength A skill or capability that enables an organization to conceive of and implement its strategies.

2. **Organizational weaknesses** are a deficit in skills or capabilities that prevents an organization from choosing and implementing strategies that support its mission. Potential weaknesses might include an inexperienced top management team, high debt levels, and an aging infrastructure. An organization has essentially two ways of addressing weaknesses. First, it may need to make investments to obtain the strengths required to implement strategies that support its mission. Second, it may need to modify its mission so that it can be accomplished with the skills and capabilities that the organization already possesses.

   organizational weakness A deficit in skills or capabilities that prevents an organization from choosing and implementing strategies that support its mission.

3. Whereas evaluating strengths and weaknesses focuses attention on the internal workings of an organization, evaluating opportunities and threats requires analyzing an organization's environment. **Organizational opportunities** are areas that may generate higher performance. Sears, for example, has a nationwide network of trained service employees who repair Sears appliances. Jane Thompson, a Sears executive, conceived of a plan to consolidate repair and home improvement services nationwide under the well-known Sears brand name and to promote them as a general repair operation for all appliances, not just those purchased from Sears. Thus the firm capitalized on existing capabilities and the strength of its name to launch a new operation.[14] **Organizational threats** are areas that increase the difficulty of an organization's performing at a high level. For instance, Wal-Mart has been experimenting with owning and operating its own bank, with branches located inside its retail stores. Given the retailing giant's track record, this move has to be seen as a threat by other banking enterprises like Bank of America and Wells Fargo.

   organizational opportunity An area in the environment that, if exploited, may generate higher performance.

   organizational threat An area in the environment that increases the difficulty of an organization's achieving high performance.

Effective business strategies generally spell out such things as distinctive competencies, resource deployment, and scope. Consider, for instance, the success currently being enjoyed by Seth Goldman, owner and "Tea-EO" of Honest Tea. The distinctive competence of Honest Tea is its brewing technology: It uses real tea leaves and spring water and adds only a minimum amount of sweetener. It invests heavily in building strong relations with key partners such as socially conscious suppliers and retailers. And it limits operations to packaged tea beverages. Honest Tea has more than doubled its revenues each of the last three years and seems headed toward long-term "prosperi-tea."

TEST PREPPER 3.2

True or False?

_____ 1. GE competes in the appliances, aircraft engines, network television, and medical equipment markets. It has a narrow scope.

_____ 2. An effective strategy promotes superior alignment between the organization, its environment, and strategic goals.

_____ 3. Frequent management changes at Kmart have created an organizational threat due to an unclear vision and inability to support its mission.

Multiple Choice

_____ 4. After the discovery of one cow with mad cow disease in Washington state, Burger King had its advertising agency change its Whopper advertising to include showing the Chicken Whopper option. The specific goal was to demonstrate

confidence in its beef supply and highlight the chicken option if customers were concerned. This is an example of Burger King using which of the following?
  a. Business-level strategy
  b. Corporate-level strategy
  c. Strategy implementation
  d. Distinctive competence
  e. Scope

_____ 5. Newspapers have identified decreasing readership by the 18–34 age group as a long-term _____.
  a. strength
  b. weakness
  c. opportunity
  d. threat
  e. none of the above

Online Study Center
ACE the Test
ACE Practice Tests 3.2

Online Study Center
Improve Your Grade
Knowledgebank 3.2

differentiation strategy   A strategy in which an organization seeks to distinguish itself from competitors through the quality of its products or services.

overall cost leadership strategy   A strategy in which an organization attempts to gain a competitive advantage by reducing its costs below the costs of competing firms.

FORMULATING BUSINESS-LEVEL STRATEGIES

3 ▸ *Identify and describe various alternative approaches to business-level strategy formulation.*

A number of frameworks have been developed for identifying the major strategic alternatives that organizations should consider when choosing their business-level strategies.[15] Two important classification schemes are Porter's generic strategies and strategies based on the product life cycle.

Porter's Generic Strategies

According to Michael Porter, organizations may pursue a differentiation strategy, an overall cost leadership strategy, or a focus strategy at the business level.[16]

▪ A **differentiation strategy** seeks to distinguish the company from competitors through the quality of its products or services. Firms that successfully implement a differentiation strategy are able to charge more than competitors because customers are willing to pay more to obtain the extra value they perceive.[17] Rolex pursues a differentiation strategy with its handmade precious metal watches. They are subjected to strenuous tests of quality and reliability. Therefore, the firm's reputation enables it to charge thousands of dollars for its watches.

▪ An **overall cost leadership strategy** attempts to gain a competitive advantage by reducing the firm's costs below the costs of competing firms. By keeping costs low, the organization is able to sell its products at low prices and still make a profit. Timex uses an overall cost leadership strategy. For decades, this firm has specialized in manufacturing relatively simple, low-cost watches for the mass market. The price of Timex watches, starting around $39.95, is low because of the company's efficient high-volume manufacturing capacity.

▮ A **focus strategy** concentrates on a specific regional market, product line, or group of buyers. This strategy may have either a differentiation focus, whereby the firm differentiates its products in the focus market, or an overall cost leadership focus, whereby the firm manufactures and sells its products at low cost in the focus market. In the watch industry, Tag Heuer follows a focus differentiation strategy by selling only rugged, waterproof watches to active consumers.

Strategies Based on the Product Life Cycle

The **product life cycle** is a model that shows how sales volume changes over the life of products. Understanding the four stages in the product life cycle, as shown in Figure 3.3, helps managers recognize that strategies need to evolve over time.

1. In the *introduction stage,* demand may be very high and sometimes outpace the firm's ability to supply the product. At this stage, managers need to focus their efforts on "getting product out the door" without sacrificing quality. Managing growth by hiring new employees and managing inventories and cash flow are also concerns during this stage.

2. During the *growth stage,* more firms begin producing the product, and sales continue to grow. Important management issues include ensuring quality and delivery and beginning to differentiate an organization's product from competitors' products. Entry into the industry during the growth stage may threaten an organization's competitive advantage; thus strategies to slow the entry of competitors are important.

3. After a period of growth, products enter a third phase. During this *maturity stage,* overall demand growth for a product begins to abate, and the number of new firms producing the product begins to decline. The number of established firms producing the product may also begin to decline. This period of maturity is essential if an organization is going to survive in the long run. Product differentiation concerns are still important during this stage, but keeping costs low and beginning the search for new products or services are also important strategic considerations.

4. In the *decline stage,* demand for the product or technology decreases, the number of organizations producing the product drops, and total sales decline. Demand often sinks because all those who were interested in purchasing a particular product have already done so. Organizations that fail to anticipate the decline stage in earlier stages of the life cycle may go out of business. Those that differentiate their product, keep their costs low, or develop new products or services may do well during this stage.

focus strategy   A strategy in which an organization concentrates on a specific regional market, product line, or group of buyers.

CONCEPT CHECK 3.3

For decades, Procter & Gamble has promoted its Ivory soap as being "99 and 44/100 percent pure." The firm also refuses to use deodorants, perfumes, or colors in Ivory, and it packages the soap in plain paper wrappers with no foil or fancy printing. Is Procter & Gamble using a product differentiation strategy, a cost leadership strategy, or a focus strategy? Or is it using some combination? Explain your answer.

product life cycle   A model that portrays how sales volume for products changes over the life of products.

> **FIGURE 3.3**

The Product Life Cycle

Managers can use the framework of the product life cycle—introduction, growth, maturity, and decline—to plot strategy. For example, management may decide on a differentiation strategy for a product in the introduction stage and a prospector approach for a product in the growth stage. By understanding this cycle and where a particular product falls within it, managers can develop more effective strategies for extending product life.

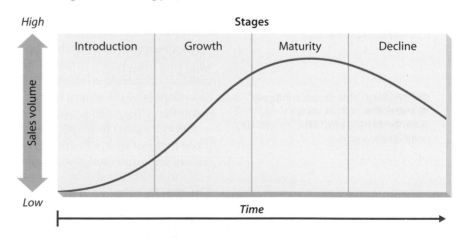

ANSWERS CAN BE FOUND ON P. 441

True or False?

_____ 1. Chelsea Milling Company, maker of Jiffy Mixes, has never spent one cent on advertising. Jiffy mixes sell for one third to one half as much as their competitors. Chelsea Milling Company uses an overall cost leadership strategy.

_____ 2. In the maturity stage of the product life cycle, demand for the product levels off.

Multiple Choice

_____ 3. Radio stations in the United States have begun using Radio Data Systems (RDS). RDS allows stations to transmit a small amount of print information to radios equipped to receive it—

information such as station identification, song title, and traffic information. Stations currently using RDS are using which strategy?
  a. Differentiation
  b. Cost leadership
  c. Focus
  d. Product life cycle
  e. None of the above

_____ 4. In the product life cycle strategy, the period when more firms begin producing the product and sales continue to grow is called the _____ stage.
  a. introduction   d. maturity
  b. expansion   e. decline
  c. growth

Online Study Center
ACE the Test
ACE Practice Tests 3.3

FORMULATING CORPORATE-LEVEL STRATEGIES

> **4** *Identify and describe various alternative approaches to corporate-level strategy formulation.*

Most large organizations are engaged in several businesses, industries, and markets. Each business or set of businesses within such an organization is frequently referred to as a *strategic business unit,* or *SBU.* An organization such as General Electric operates hundreds of different businesses, making and selling products as diverse as jet engines, nuclear power plants, and light bulbs. GE organizes these businesses into approximately twenty SBUs. Even organizations that sell only one product may operate in several distinct markets.

Decisions about which businesses, industries, and markets an organization will enter, and how to manage these different businesses, are based on an organization's corporate strategy. The most important strategic issue at the corporate level concerns the extent and nature of organizational diversification. **Diversification** reflects the number of different businesses that an organization is engaged in and the extent to which these businesses are related to one another. There are three types of diversification strategies: single-product strategy, related diversification, and unrelated diversification.[18]

diversification   The number of different businesses that an organization is engaged in and the extent to which these business are related to one another.

Single-Product Strategy

single-product strategy   A strategy in which an organization manufactures just one product or service and sells it in a single geographic market.

Single-product strategy occurs when an organization pursues and manufactures just one product or service and sells it in a single geographic market. The WD-40 Company, for example, manufactures only a single product, WD-40 spray lubricant, and for years sold it in just one market, North America. WD-40 has started selling its lubricant in Europe and Asia, but it continues to devote all manufacturing, sales, and marketing efforts to one product.

Businesses are always on the alert for new strategies that will enable them to compete more effectively. It's no secret that U.S. automakers like General Motors and Ford have been steadily losing market share, especially to their main Japanese rival Toyota. In an effort to reverse this trend, GM recently introduced a new pricing strategy based on lower sticker prices for most of its cars and trucks. The new lower price for the Chevy HHR LS Sedan was unveiled at the recent North American International Auto Show in Detroit.

The single-product strategy has one major strength and one major weakness. By concentrating its efforts so completely on one product and one market, a firm is likely to be very successful in manufacturing and marketing the product. Because it has staked its survival on a single product, the organization works very hard to make sure that the product is a success. Of course, if the product is not accepted by the market or is replaced by a new one, the firm will suffer.

Related Diversification

In **related diversification**, a company operates in several different, though linked, businesses, industries, or markets.[19] Virtually all larger businesses in the United States use related diversification. Pursuing a strategy of related diversification has three primary advantages.

1. It reduces an organization's dependence on any one of its business activities and thus reduces economic risk. Even if one or two of a firm's businesses lose money, the organization as a whole may still survive because the healthy businesses will generate enough cash to support the others.[20]
2. By managing several businesses at the same time, an organization can reduce the overhead costs associated with managing any one business. In other words, if the normal administrative costs required to operate any business, such as legal services and accounting, can be spread over a large number of businesses, then the overhead costs *per business* will be lower than they would be if each business had to absorb all costs itself.
3. Related diversification enables an organization to exploit its strengths and capabilities in more than one business. When organizations do this successfully, they capitalize on synergies, which are complementary effects that exist among their businesses. *Synergy* exists among a set of businesses when the businesses' economic value together is greater than their economic value separately. McDonald's is using synergy as it diversifies into other restaurant and food businesses. For example, its McCafe premium coffee stands in some McDonald's restaurants and its investments in Donatos Pizza, Chipotle Mexican Grill, and Pret A Manger allow the firm to create new revenue opportunities while utilizing the firm's existing strengths in food product purchasing and distribution.[21]

related diversification A strategy in which an organization operates in several businesses that are somehow linked with one another.

CONCEPT CHECK 3.4

Suppose a firm decides to move from a single-product strategy to a strategy based on related diversification. How might managers use SWOT analysis to select attributes of its current business to serve as bases of relatedness among the potential businesses it may acquire or launch?

Unrelated Diversification

Unrelated diversification is operating multiple businesses that are not logically associated with one another. At one time, for example, Quaker Oats owned clothing chains, toy companies, and a restaurant business. In theory, unrelated diversification has two advantages.

1. A business that uses this strategy should have stable performance over time. During any given period, if some businesses owned by the organization are in a cycle of decline, others may be in a cycle of growth.
2. Unrelated diversification presumably should create resource allocation advantages.

Despite these presumed advantages, research suggests that unrelated diversification usually does not lead to high performance. As a result, unrelated diversification has become an increasingly unpopular corporate-level strategy. There are two basic reasons for this.

1. Corporate-level managers in such a company usually do not know enough about the unrelated businesses to provide helpful strategic guidance or to allocate capital appropriately.
2. Because organizations that implement unrelated diversification are unable to exploit important synergies, they are at a competitive disadvantage compared to organizations that use related diversification. Universal Studios has been at a competitive disadvantage relative to Disney because its theme parks, movie studios, and licensing divisions are less integrated and therefore achieve less synergy.

Managing Diversification

However an organization implements diversification—whether through internal development, vertical integration, or mergers and acquisitions—it must monitor and manage its strategy.[22] **Portfolio management techniques** are methods that diversified organizations use to determine which businesses to engage in and how to manage these businesses to maximize corporate performance. Two important portfolio management techniques are the BCG matrix and the GE Business Screen.

1. The **BCG (for Boston Consulting Group) matrix** provides a framework for evaluating the relative performance of businesses in which a diversified organization operates. It also prescribes the preferred distribution of cash and other resources among these businesses.[23] The BCG matrix uses two factors to evaluate an organization's set of businesses: the growth rate of a particular market and the organization's share of that market. The matrix suggests that fast-growing markets in which an organization has the highest market share are more attractive business opportunities than slow-growing markets in which an organization has small market share. Dividing market growth and market share into two categories (low and high) creates the simple matrix shown in Figure 3.4.

    The matrix describes the types of businesses in which a diversified organization can engage as dogs, cash cows, question marks, and stars.
    * *Dogs* are businesses that have a very small share of a market that is not expected to grow. Because these businesses do not hold much economic promise, the BCG matrix suggests that organizations either should not invest in them or should consider selling them as soon as possible.

- *Cash cows* are businesses that have a large share of a market that is not expected to grow substantially. These businesses characteristically generate high profits that the organization should use to support question marks and stars. (Cash cows are "milked" for cash to support businesses in markets that have more growth potential.)
- *Question marks* are businesses that have only a small share of a quickly growing market. The future performance of these businesses is uncertain. A question mark that is able to capture increasing amounts of this growing market may be very profitable. On the other hand, a question mark unable to keep up with market growth is likely to have low profits. The BCG matrix suggests that organizations should invest carefully in question marks. If their performance does not live up to expectations, question marks should be reclassified as dogs and divested.
- *Stars* are businesses that have the largest share of a rapidly growing market. Cash generated by cash cows should be invested in stars to ensure their pre-eminent position.

2. The **GE Business Screen** responds to the relatively narrow and overly simplistic BCG matrix. It is a more sophisticated approach to managing diversified business units. The Business Screen is a portfolio management technique that can also be represented in the form of a matrix. Rather than focusing solely on market growth and market share, however, the GE Business Screen considers industry attractiveness and competitive position. These two factors are divided into three categories, to make the nine-cell matrix shown in Figure 3.5.[24] These cells, in turn, classify business units as winners, losers, question marks, average businesses, or profit producers.

As Figure 3.5 shows, both market growth and market share appear in a broad list of factors that determine the overall attractiveness of an industry and the overall quality of a firm's competitive position. Other determinants of an industry's attractiveness (in addition to market growth) include market size, capital requirements, and competitive intensity. In general, the greater the market growth, the larger the market, the smaller the capital requirements, and the less the competitive intensity, the more attractive an industry will be. Other determinants of an organization's competitive position in an industry (besides market share) include technological know-how, product quality, service network, price competitiveness, and operating costs. In general, businesses with large market share, technological know-how, high product quality, a quality service network, competitive prices, and low operating costs are in a favorable competitive position.

Think of the GE Business Screen as a way of applying SWOT analysis to the implementation and management of a diversification strategy. The determinants of industry attractiveness are similar to the environmental opportunities and threats in SWOT analysis, and the determinants of competitive position are similar to organizational strengths and weaknesses. By conducting this type of SWOT analysis across several businesses, a diversified organization can decide how to invest its resources to maximize corporate performance.

FIGURE 3.4

The BCG Matrix

The BCG matrix helps managers develop a better understanding of how different strategic business units contribute to the overall organization. By assessing each SBU on the basis of its market growth rate and relative market share, managers can make decisions about whether to commit further financial resources to the SBU or to sell or liquidate it.

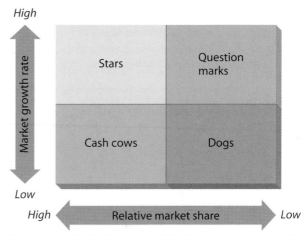

From *Perspectives*, No. 66, "The Product Portfolio." Adapted by permission from The Boston Consulting Group, Inc., 1970.

GE Business Screen   A method of evaluating businesses along two dimensions: (1) industry attractiveness and (2) competitive position; in general, the more attractive the industry and the more competitive the position, the more an organization should invest in a business.

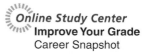

Online Study Center
Improve Your Grade
Career Snapshot

FIGURE 3.5

The GE Business Screen

The GE Business Screen is a more sophisticated approach to portfolio management than the BCG matrix. As shown here, several factors combine to determine a business's competitive position and the attractiveness of its industry. These two dimensions, in turn, can be used to classify businesses as winners, question marks, average businesses, losers, or profit producers. Such a classification enables managers to allocate the organization's resources more effectively across various business opportunities.

From *Strategy Formulation: Analytical Concepts*, 1st edition, by Hofer, © 1978. Reprinted with permission of South-Western, a division of Thomson Learning: www.thomsonrights.com. Fax 800-730-2215.

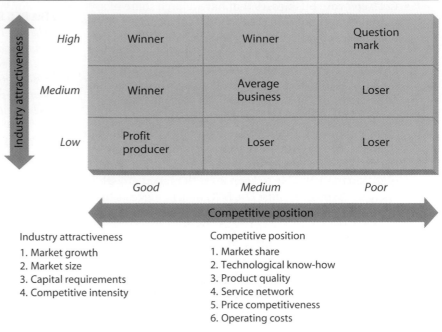

Industry attractiveness	Good	Medium	Poor
High	Winner	Winner	Question mark
Medium	Winner	Average business	Loser
Low	Profit producer	Loser	Loser

Competitive position

Industry attractiveness
1. Market growth
2. Market size
3. Capital requirements
4. Competitive intensity

Competitive position
1. Market share
2. Technological know-how
3. Product quality
4. Service network
5. Price competitiveness
6. Operating costs

In general, organizations should invest in winners and in question marks (where industry attractiveness and competitive position are both favorable); should maintain the market position of average businesses and profit producers (where industry attractiveness and competitive position are average); and should sell losers. For example, Unilever assessed its business portfolio using a similar framework and, as a result, decided to sell off several specialty chemical units that were not contributing to the firm's profitability as much as other businesses. The firm then used the revenues from these divestitures to buy more related businesses such as Ben & Jerry's Homemade and Slim-Fast.[25]

TEST PREPPER 3.4

ANSWERS CAN BE FOUND ON P. 441

True or False?

_____ 1. Nike sells shoes, athletic apparel, and athletic equipment. It uses unrelated diversification.

_____ 2. Synergy is when a combined economic value is greater than economic value separately.

_____ 3. Portfolio management techniques help top executives decide what businesses to engage in.

Multiple Choice

_____ 4. A law firm specializes only in divorce proceedings. It uses which diversification strategy?
  a. Single-product   d. Synergy
  b. Related   e. Portfolio
  c. Unrelated

_____ 5. The Morning News began publishing a free tabloid-sized daily newspaper called *Quick*, designed for readers 18–34. The Morning News is willing to take a short-term loss because it considers the potential advertising revenue to be great. *Quick* is a _____.
  a. star   d. dog
  b. question mark   e. none of the above
  c. cash cow

_____ 6. Which of the following is NOT true about the GE Business Screen?
  a. It is more sophisticated than the BCG matrix
  b. It is a portfolio management technique
  c. It considers industry attractiveness
  d. It considers relative market share
  e. It considers competitive position

Online Study Center
ACE the Test
ACE Practice Tests 3.4

TACTICAL PLANNING

5 ▶ *Discuss how tactical plans are developed and executed.*

As we note earlier, tactical plans are developed to implement specific parts of a strategic plan. You have probably heard the saying about winning the battle but losing the war. Tactical plans are to battles what strategy is to a war: an organized sequence of steps designed to execute strategic plans. Strategy focuses on resources, environment, and mission, whereas tactics focus primarily on people and action.[26]

Developing Tactical Plans

Although effective tactical planning depends on many factors, which vary from one situation to another, we can identify some basic guidelines.

1. First, the manager needs to recognize that tactical planning must address a number of tactical goals derived from a broader strategic goal.[27] An occasional situation may call for a stand-alone tactical plan, but most of the time, tactical plans flow from and must be consistent with a strategic plan.

2. Second, although strategies are often stated in general terms, tactics must specify resources and time frames. A strategy can call for being number one in a particular market or industry, but a tactical plan must specify precisely what activities will be undertaken to achieve that goal.

3. Finally, tactical planning requires the use of human resources. Managers involved in tactical planning spend a great deal of time working with other people. They must be in a position to receive information from others within and outside the organization, to process that information in the most effective way, and then to pass it on to others who might make use of it.

Executing Tactical Plans

Regardless of how well a tactical plan is formulated, its ultimate success depends on the way it is carried out. Successful implementation, in turn, depends on the astute use of resources, effective decision making, and insightful steps to ensure that the right things are done at the right times and in the right ways. A manager can see an absolutely brilliant idea fail because of improper execution.

Proper execution depends on a number of important factors. First, the manager needs to evaluate every possible course of action in light of the goal it is intended to reach. Next, he or she needs to make sure that each decision maker has the information and resources necessary to get the job done. Vertical and horizontal communication and integration of activities must be marshaled to minimize conflict and inconsistent activities. And, finally, the manager must monitor ongoing activities derived from the plan to make sure they are achieving the desired results. This monitoring typically takes place within the context of the organization's ongoing control systems.

TEST PREPPER 3.5

ANSWERS CAN BE FOUND ON P. 441

True or False?

_____ 1. Ultimate success for a tactical plan depends on its execution.

Online Study Center
ACE the Test
ACE Practice Tests 3.5

Multiple Choice

_____ 2. Which of the following is NOT true concerning tactical plans?
- a. They implement specific parts of strategic plans
- b. They are aimed at achieving tactical goals
- c. They focus on resources
- d. They focus on people
- e. They focus on action

OPERATIONAL PLANNING

6 ▸ *Describe the basic types of operational plans used by organizations.*

Another critical element in effective organizational planning is the development and implementation of operational plans. Operational plans are derived from tactical plans and are aimed at achieving operational goals. Thus operational plans tend to be narrowly focused, to have relatively short time horizons, and to involve lower-level managers. The two most basic forms of operational plans (single-use plans and standing plans) and specific types of each are summarized in Table 3.1.

Single-Use Plans

single-use plan   A plan developed to carry out a course of action that is not likely to be repeated in the future.

program   A single-use plan for a large set of activities.

project   A single-use plan of less scope and complexity than a program.

A **single-use plan** is developed to carry out a course of action that is not likely to be repeated in the future. As Disney proceeds with its new theme park in Hong Kong, it developed numerous single-use plans for individual rides, attractions, and hotels. The two most common types of single-use plans are programs and projects.

Programs

A **program** is a single-use plan for a large set of activities. It might consist of identifying procedures for introducing a new product line, opening a new facility, or changing the organization's mission. As part of its own strategic plans for growth, a few years ago Black & Decker bought General Electric's small-appliance business. The deal involved the largest brand-name switch in history: 150 products were converted from the GE to the Black & Decker label. Each product was carefully studied, redesigned, and reintroduced with an extended warranty. A total of 140 steps were used for each product. It took three years to convert all 150 products over to Black & Decker. The total conversion of the product line was a program.

Projects

A **project** is similar to a program but is generally of less scope and complexity. A project may be a part of a broader program, or it may be a self-contained single-use plan. For Black & Decker, the conversion of each of the 150 products

TABLE 3.1

Forms of Operational Plans

Plan	Description
1. SINGLE-USE PLAN	Developed to carry out a course of action not likely to be repeated in the future
Program	Single-use plan for a large set of activities
Project	Single-use plan of less scope and complexity than a program
2. STANDING PLAN	Developed for activities that recur regularly over a period of time
Policy	Standing plan specifying the organization's general response to a designated problem or situation
Standard operating procedure	Standing plan outlining steps to be followed in particular circumstances
Rules and regulations	Standing plans describing exactly how specific activities are to be carried out

Disney developed a single-use plan to design and construct its new theme park in Hong Kong. Disney executives Michael Eisner and Robert Iger are shown here with Hong Kong Chief Executive Tung Chee Hwa and "friends" at the groundbreaking ceremony. Embedded within this over-arching single-use plan are also myriad programs and projects.

was a separate project in its own right. Each product had its own manager, its own schedule, and so forth. Projects are also used to introduce a new product within an existing product line or to add a new benefit option to an existing salary package.

Standing Plans

Whereas single-use plans are developed for nonrecurring situations, a **standing plan** is used for activities that recur regularly over a period of time. Standing plans can greatly enhance efficiency by making decision making routine. Policies, standard operating procedures, and rules and regulations are three kinds of standing plans.

standing plan　A plan developed for activities that recur regularly over a period of time.

Policies

A **policy** specifies the organization's general response to a designated problem or situation. For example, McDonald's has a policy that it will not grant a franchise to an individual who already owns another fast-food restaurant. Similarly, Starbucks has a policy that it will not franchise at all, instead retaining ownership of every Starbucks coffee shop.

policy　A standing plan that specifies the organization's general response to a designated problem or situation.

Standard Operating Procedures

Another type of standing plan is the **standard operating procedure (SOP)**. An SOP is more specific than a policy, in that it outlines the steps to be followed in particular

standard operating procedure (SOP)　A standing plan that outlines the steps to be followed in particular circumstances.

© King Features Syndicate

Standard operating procedures (SOPs), rules, and regulations can all be useful for saving time, improving efficiency, and streamlining decision making and planning but should be reviewed periodically to ensure that they remain useful. For example, an SOP for regularly ordering parts and supplies may become less effective if the demand for those parts and supplies changes or disappears.

circumstances. McDonald's has SOPs explaining exactly how Big Macs are to be cooked, how long they can stay in the warming rack, and so forth, while Starbucks specifies the precise temperature at which coffee must be brewed and kept warm.

Rules and Regulations

rules and regulations Standing plans that describe exactly how specific activities are to be carried out.

The narrowest of the standing plans, **rules and regulations**, describe exactly how specific activities are to be carried out. Rather than guiding decision making, rules and regulations actually take the place of decision making in various situations. Each McDonald's restaurant has a rule prohibiting customers from using its telephones, for example. Rules and regulations and SOPs are similar in many ways. They are both relatively narrow in scope, and each can serve as a substitute for decision making. An SOP typically describes a sequence of activities, however, whereas rules and regulations focus on one activity. In an industrial setting, the SOP for orienting a new employee could involve enrolling the person in various benefit options, introducing him or her to coworkers and supervisors, and providing a tour of the facilities. A pertinent rule for the new employee might involve when to come to work each day.

Contingency Planning and Crisis Management

contingency planning The determination of alternative courses of action to be taken if an intended plan is unexpectedly disrupted or rendered inappropriate.

crisis management The set of procedures the organization will use in the event of a disaster or other unexpected calamity.

Another important type of planning is **contingency planning**, or the determination of alternative courses of action to be taken if an intended plan of action is unexpectedly disrupted or rendered inappropriate.[28] **Crisis management**, a related concept, is the set of procedures the organization will use in the event of a disaster or other unexpected calamity. Some elements of crisis management may be orderly and systematic, whereas others (such as those that unfolded in the aftermath of hurricanes Katrina and Rita in 2005) may be more ad hoc, developing as events unfold.

Because of the aftermath of 9/11, more businesses than ever have developed contingency plans to deal with various potential events. Although airlines have always had contingency plans to deal with a single crash or accident, they now have more complex plans to help deal with a more far-reaching array of events. Similarly, most businesses that rely heavily on electronic communications technology have detailed plans for dealing with viruses, hackers, and other potential problems. Fortunately, most events that prompt the need for contingency plans are less dramatic than these.

The mechanics of contingency planning are shown in Figure 3.6. In relation to an organization's other plans, contingency planning comes into play at four action points. At action point 1, management develops the basic plans of the organization. These may include strategic, tactical, and operational plans. As part of this development process, managers usually consider various contingency events. Some management groups even assign someone the role of devil's advocate to ask, "But what if . . . ?" about each course of action. A variety of contingencies are usually considered.

At action point 2, the plan that management chooses is put into effect. The most important contingency events are also defined. Only the events that are likely to occur and whose effects will have a substantial impact on the organization are used in the contingency-planning process. Next, at action point 3, the company specifies certain indicators or signs that suggest that a contingency event is about to take place. A bank might decide that a 2 percent drop in interest rates should be considered a contingency event. An indicator might be two consecutive months with a drop of 0.5 percent in each. As indicators of contingency events are being

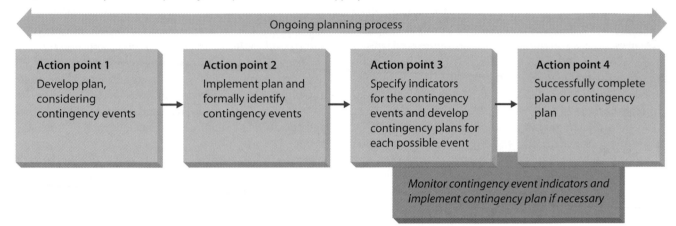

FIGURE 3.6

Contingency Planning

Most organizations develop contingency plans. These plans specify alternative courses of action to be taken if an intended plan is unexpectedly disrupted or rendered inappropriate.

Ongoing planning process

Action point 1
Develop plan, considering contingency events

Action point 2
Implement plan and formally identify contingency events

Action point 3
Specify indicators for the contingency events and develop contingency plans for each possible event

Action point 4
Successfully complete plan or contingency plan

Monitor contingency event indicators and implement contingency plan if necessary

defined, the contingency plans themselves should be developed. Examples of contingency plans for various situations are delaying plant construction, developing a new manufacturing process, and cutting prices.

After this stage, the managers of the organization monitor the indicators identified at action point 3. If the situation dictates, a contingency plan is implemented. Otherwise, the primary plan of action continues in force. Finally, action point 4 marks the successful completion of either the original plan or a contingency plan.

Contingency planning is becoming increasingly important for most organizations, especially those that operate in particularly complex or dynamic environments. Few managers have such an accurate view of the future that they can anticipate and plan for everything. Contingency planning is a useful technique for helping managers cope with uncertainty and change. Crisis management, by its very nature, is more difficult to anticipate. But organizations that have a strong culture, strong leadership, and a capacity to deal with the unexpected stand a better chance than others of successfully weathering a crisis.[29]

CONCEPT CHECK 3.5

In what ways is contingency planning similar to, and how is it different from, crisis management?

TEST PREPPER 3.6

ANSWERS CAN BE FOUND ON P. 441

True or False?

_____ 1. A consequence of September 11, 2001, is the significant increase in contingency planning by virtually all organizations.

Multiple Choice

_____ 2. More than 400 journalists were at the Jet Propulsion Laboratory (JPL) for the landing of the Mars Spirit rover. The JPL media relations staff held weekly meetings for nine months in case

the mission ran into trouble. The staff participated in _____ planning.
   a. contingency   d. operation
   b. strategic   e. long-range
   c. tactical

_____ 3. Opaque websites such as Priceline and Hotwire do not let customers know where they will be staying until they have already paid for their hotel room. This is an example of which of the following?
   a. Program   d. Regulation
   b. Project   e. Planning
   c. Policy

BUILDING EFFECTIVE DIAGNOSTIC SKILLS

Exercise Overview

Diagnostic skills are the skills that enable a manager to visualize the most appropriate response to a situation. As rivalry increases in an industry, competitors develop similar capabilities, making it more difficult to achieve differentiation. In such an industry, price becomes the primary competitive weapon. (The soft-drink, fast-food, airline, and retail industries, for example, are suffering from this problem today.) This in-class demonstration will show you the difficulties of developing an effective competitive response in such a situation.

Exercise Background

Assume that you are the owner of a small business, such as a gas station or fast-food outlet, that is located directly across the street from a rival firm. Your products are not differentiated, and you cannot make them so. Customers prefer the less expensive product, and they switch on the basis of the price difference between the products—the larger the difference, the more customers will switch. Customer switching behavior is shown in Table 3.2.

Further, the following conditions apply to both you and your competitor:

1. You both have a $1.00 cost of production per unit. This number cannot be changed.
2. At the beginning of the game, you are both charging a price of $1.10, for a per-unit profit of $.10.

TABLE 3.2

Customer Switching Behavior

When the price difference is . . .	The market share split is . . .
0 cents	50/50
1 cent	60/40
2 cents	70/30
3 cents	80/20
4 cents	90/10
5 cents	100/0

3. The market consists of exactly 100 customers per period. This number cannot be changed.

Therefore, at the beginning period, you and your rival are charging the same price (0 cents difference) and thus are splitting the market 50/50, or selling 50 units per period. Both you and your rival have per-period profits of $5.00 (50 units × $.10).

For the demonstration, two teams of students, representing your firm and your rival, will separately and independently make a decision about price for the upcoming period. Price is the only variable you can control. Each team will write down its price, and then your professor will disclose the resulting market share and profits for each team. The demonstration will continue for several periods, the exact number of which is not known to the teams. The objective is to be profitable.

Exercise Task

1. Consider volunteering to be part of one of the groups involved in demonstrating this concept in front of the class.
2. Play out the scenario (participants) and observe (class).
3. Did each of the teams choose a strategy that made profit maximization possible? Were the strategies equally profitable? Why or why not?
4. Competing firms are prohibited by law from fixing prices—that is, from jointly deciding on a price. However, price signaling, in which firms do not directly conspire but instead send subtle messages, is legal. Could the two teams in this demonstration use price signaling? What conditions are necessary to make price signaling an effective strategy?
5. What does this demonstration tell you about competitive dynamics in an industry where products are undifferentiated?

Reprinted by permission of the author Margaret Hill.

Online Study Center
Improve Your Grade
Exercises: Experiential
Exercise

EXPERIENTIAL EXERCISE

The SWOT Analysis

Purpose

SWOT analysis provides the manager with a cognitive model of the organization and its environmental forces. By developing the ability to conduct such an analysis, the manager builds both process knowledge and a conceptual skill. This skill builder focuses on the *administrative management model.* It will help you develop the *coordinator role* of the administrative management model. One of the skills of the coordinator is the ability to plan.

Introduction

This exercise helps you understand the complex interrelationships between environmental opportunities and threats and organizational strengths and weaknesses.

Instructions

Step 1: Study the exhibit that follows, "Strategy Formulation at Marriott," and the text materials concerning the matching of organizations with environments.

Step 2: The instructor will divide the class into small groups. Each group will conduct a SWOT (strengths, weaknesses, opportunities, threats) analysis for Marriott and prepare group responses to the discussion questions. Marriott has been successful in its hotel and food services businesses but less than successful in its cruise ship, travel agency, and theme park businesses.

Strategy formulation is facilitated by a SWOT analysis. First, the organization should study its internal operations in order to identify its strengths and weaknesses. Next, the organization should scan the environment to identify existing and future opportunities and threats. Then the organization should identify the relationships that exist among these strengths, weaknesses, opportunities, and threats. Finally, major business strategies usually result from matching an organization's strengths with appropriate opportunities or from matching the threats it faces with weaknesses that have been identified. To facilitate the environmental analysis in search of opportunities and threats, it is helpful to divide the environment into its major components—international, economic, political-legal, sociocultural, and technological.

Step 3: One representative from each group may be asked to report on the group's SWOT analysis and to indicate the group's responses to the discussion questions.

Discussion Questions

1. What was the most difficult part of the SWOT analysis?
2. Why do most firms not develop major strategies for matches between threats and strengths?
3. Under what conditions might a firm develop a major strategy around a match between an opportunity and a weakness? See the list on page 80.

Online Study Center
Improve Your Grade
Interactive Skills Self-
Assessment

Strategy Formulation at Marriott

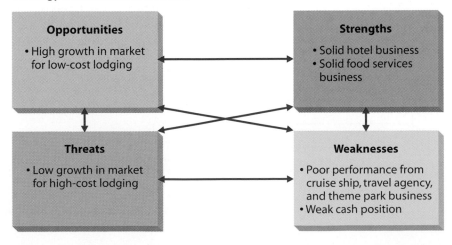

EXPERIENTIAL EXERCISE (CONTINUED)

Marriott SWOT Analysis Sheet

Environmental Analysis

Opportunities
_____
_____
_____
_____
_____
_____
_____
_____
_____
_____

Threats
_____
_____
_____
_____
_____
_____
_____
_____
_____
_____
_____
_____

Organizational Analysis

Strengths
_____
_____
_____
_____
_____
_____
_____
_____
_____
_____

Weaknesses
_____
_____
_____
_____
_____
_____
_____
_____
_____
_____
_____
_____

Relationships Between
Opportunities and Strengths
1. _____
2. _____
3. _____

Relationships Between
Opportunities and Weaknesses
1. _____
2. _____
3. _____

Relationships Between
Threats and Strengths
1. _____
2. _____
3. _____

Relationships Between
Threats and Weaknesses
1. _____
2. _____
3. _____

Major Strategies Matching
Opportunities with Strengths
1. _____
2. _____
3. _____

Major Strategies Matching
Threats with Weaknesses
1. _____
2. _____
3. _____

Source: Gene E. Burton, *Exercises in
Management*, 5th edition. Copyright
© 1996 by Houghton Mifflin Company.
Used with permission.

FEMA's Disastrous Response to Hurricane Katrina

Hurricane Katrina had the following consequences: a $150 billion estimated cost of recovery; 2.5 million persons displaced from their homes; 1,100 deaths, thousands hospitalized, and, as of January 2006, 3,600 individuals still missing; a possible U.S. annual GDP drop of 1 percent, reflecting the $130 billion in annual contributions made by the region; over 100,000 jobs lost in two months in Louisiana alone; a quarter of a million homes destroyed; an estimated 372,000 elementary and secondary students without schools; and eleven universities temporarily closed.

A Category 5 hurricane is one of the most destructive natural events. Hurricane Katrina, which hit the Gulf Coast on August 29, 2005, was the costliest natural disaster in American history and led to vast human suffering. Yet human errors were responsible for much of the economic, physical, and emotional damage, as many individuals, organizations, and governmental bodies failed to respond appropriately. Blame has been placed on everyone, from the citizens to President Bush, but none has received more blame than the Federal Emergency Management Agency, or FEMA.

One factor in the fiasco is FEMA chief Michael Brown's lack of leadership. His e-mails of August 29 discuss rolling up his shirtsleeves to impress television viewers and whining to his deputy director, "Can I quit now? Can I go home?" An employee e-mailed him on August 31, saying New Orleans was "past critical" and mentioning deaths and water shortages. Brown wrote back only: "Thanks for the update. Anything specific I need to do or tweak?" (Amid controversy and shock, Brown resigned on September 12.)

Yet lack of planning was, surprisingly, not one of the causes of FEMA's disastrously inadequate response. The agency was well aware of the possibility of a Katrina-like disaster. In July 2004, FEMA staged "Hurricane Pam," a disaster simulation focused on New Orleans. The exercise hypothesized mass evacuations and levee destruction. In 2005, Brown's superior, Director of Homeland Security Michael Chertoff, introduced a National Preparedness Plan. The plan included scenario-based planning for fifteen disaster scenarios, including a flu pandemic, a major earthquake, a terrorist attack—and a major hurricane.

"We are not as ready as we can be."

—Anderson Cooper, correspondent, CNN

Although the possible extent of the damage was known, as was the responsibility for various actions, there was a lack of clear communication and a failure to coordinate the actions of different organizations and governments. Although Governor Blanco asked FEMA for aid and New Orleans ordered evacuation, FEMA failed to provide the necessary support. The U.S. Army was prepared to drop food and water via helicopter as early as August 30 but was never asked to do so. Yet city and state officials also claim their organizations were overwhelmed and unable to request the help. One *BusinessWeek* editor summed up the situation, saying, "There is no clear strategy for dealing with extraordinary disaster scenarios that can easily overwhelm local officials. And the lack of such unambiguous procedures can lead to chaos." One Louisiana state official commented, "If you do not know what your needs are, you can't request to FEMA what you need."

What can be done to help authorities respond more effectively? One scholar attributes the problems to a failure of imagination. Dr. Lee Clarke, a Rutgers University professor, claims that planners neglected to consider worst-case scenarios. "The usual or recommended way of looking at risk . . . is probabilistic thinking," says Clarke. "Probability says it is highly unlikely that a nuclear power plant will melt down. Possibilism wonders what happens if a nuclear power plant has a particularly bad day. . . . [It] is worst case thinking." Clarke's theory would call for emergency responders to plan for worst-case, as well as most-likely-case, scenarios.

Another approach would focus on grassroots planning efforts. During Katrina, for example, many groups and individuals took heroic actions to help victims. The U.S. Coast Guard, helped by hundreds of privately owned watercraft, rescued 22,000 stranded individuals, more than it rescued in the previous half century. Businesses donated millions, and families opened their homes to victims. In this approach, planning for future Katrinas could be improved by building on local

CLOSING CASE STUDY (CONTINUED)

knowledge and resources. Planning should include those who are not included in the current system, such as the disabled, the elderly, and individuals without transportation.

Anderson Cooper, a CNN correspondent, reflected that the lesson learned in Katrina is that "we are not as ready as we can be." Whatever it takes, we need to improve our planning processes and be ready, because there will surely be a next time. For, as Stanford professor Scott Sagan says, "Things that have never happened before happen all the time."

Case Questions

1. In your opinion, were the problems experienced by agencies coping with Hurricane Katrina occurring at the strategic, tactical, or operational level? Explain.

2. Should FEMA handle planning for hurricanes and other natural disasters with a single-use plan or a standing plan? What would be the advantages of each approach?

3. How would worst-case planning have helped emergency responders react more effectively to Hurricane Katrina?

Case References

"Brown Defends FEMA Response," *Fox News*, September 28, 2005, www.foxnews.com on January 15, 2006; "'Can I Quit Now?' FEMA Chief Wrote as Katrina Raged," *CNN*, November 3, 2005, www.cnn.com on January 15, 2006; Lee Clarke, "Worst Case Katrina," *Understanding Katrina: Perspectives from the Social Sciences*, September 12, 2005, The Social Sciences Research Council website, www.ssrc.org on January 15, 2006; "FEMA Director Brown Resigns," *CNN*, September 12, 2005, www.cnn.com on January 15, 2006; "If Katrina Teaches Us Nothing Else . . ." *BusinessWeek*, October 10, 2005, www.businessweek.com on January 15, 2006; "Labor Market Statistics for Areas Affected by Hurricanes Katrina and Rita," Bureau of Labor Statistics, www.bls.gov on January 15, 2006; Andrew Lakoff, "From Disaster to Catastrophe: The Limits of Preparedness," *Understanding Katrina: Perspectives from the Social Sciences*, September 30, 2005, The Social Sciences Research Council website, www.ssrc.org on January 15, 2006 (quote); "Reported Locations of Katrina/Rita Applicants," January 20, 2006, FEMA website, www.fema.gov on January 22, 2006; Tricia Wachtendorf and James M. Kendra, "Improvising Disaster in the City of Jazz: Organizational Response to Hurricane Katrina," *Understanding Katrina: Perspectives from the Social Sciences*, September 21, 2005, The Social Sciences Research Council website, www.ssrc.org on January 15, 2006.

LEARNING OBJECTIVE REVIEW

Online Study Center
Improve Your Grade
–Learning Objective Review
–Audio Chapter Review
–Study Guide to Go

Online Study Center
ACE the Test
Audio Chapter Quiz

1 *Describe the planning process, describe organizational goals, and identify three basic kinds of organizational plans.*

- The planning process includes understanding the environment, formulating a mission, and creating goals and plans.

- Goals serve four purposes: they provide guidance, facilitate planning, motivate employees, and facilitate evaluation and control.

- By understanding the environmental context, managers develop a number of different types of goals and plans, including
  - strategic plans
  - tactical plans
  - operational plans

2 *Discuss the components of strategy, identify the types of strategic alternatives, and describe how to use SWOT analysis in formulating strategy.*

- A strategy is a comprehensive plan for accomplishing the organization's goals.

- Effective strategies, including business-level and corporate-level strategies, address three organizational issues:
  - distinctive competence
  - scope
  - resource deployment

- SWOT analysis considers an organization's strengths, weaknesses, opportunities, and threats. Using SWOT analysis, an organization chooses strategies that support its mission and
  - exploit its opportunities and strengths
  - neutralize its threats
  - avoid its weaknesses

3 *Identify and describe various alternative approaches to business-level strategy formulation.*

- A business-level strategy is the plan an organization uses to conduct business in a particular industry or market.
- Porter suggests that businesses may formulate a differentiation strategy, an overall cost leadership strategy, or a focus strategy at this level.
- Strategies may also be based on the four stages of the product life cycle: introduction, growth, maturity, and decline.

4 *Identify and describe various alternative approaches to corporate-level strategy formulation.*

- A corporate-level strategy is the plan an organization uses to manage its operations across several businesses.
- A firm that does not diversify is implementing a single-product strategy.
- An organization pursues a strategy of related diversification when it operates a set of businesses that are somehow linked.
- Related diversification
  reduces the financial risk associated with any particular product
  decreases the overhead costs of each business
  enables the organization to create and exploit synergy
- An organization pursues a strategy of unrelated diversification when it operates a set of businesses that are not logically associated with one another.
- Organizations manage diversification through the organization structure that they adopt and through portfolio management techniques.
  The BCG matrix classifies an organization's diversified businesses as dogs, cash cows, question marks, or stars according to their market share and market growth rate.

The GE Business Screen classifies businesses as winners, losers, question marks, average businesses, or profit producers according to their industry attractiveness and competitive position.

5 *Discuss how tactical plans are developed and executed.*

- Tactical plans are formulated at the middle of the organization and have an intermediate time horizon and moderate scope.
- Tactical plans are developed to implement specific parts of a strategic plan and must flow from strategy, specify resource and time issues, and commit human resources.
- Execution of tactical plans depends on evaluation, dissemination of information and resources, and monitoring.

6 *Describe the basic types of operational plans used by organizations.*

- Operational plans, derived from a tactical plan and aimed at achieving one or more operational goals, are carried out at the lower levels of the organization, have a shorter time horizon, and are narrower in scope.
- Two major types of operational plans:
  Single-use plans: Plans designed to carry out a course of action that is not likely to be repeated in the future, including programs and projects.
  Standing plans: Plans designed to carry out a course of action that is likely to be repeated several times, including policies, standard operating procedures, and rules and regulations.
  Contingency planning and crisis management are also emerging as very important forms of operational planning.

Online Study Center **RESOURCES**

Prepare for Class, Improve Your Grade, and ACE the Test. These Student Achievement resources include:

ACE Practice Tests	Interactive Skills Assessments	Study Guide to Go
End of Chapter Exercises	Knowledgebank	Video Segments
Glossaries (visual and print)	Reviews (audio and print)	Summaries/Outlines
Flashcards		

To access these learning and study tools, go to: **college.hmco.com/pic/griffinSAS**

Like most companies in the pharmaceutical industry, Cephalon faces both great opportunities and significant risks. These research and development workers are working on new medications that could generate millions of dollars in revenues or end up with no market potential whatsoever.

1 *Define decision making, discuss types of decisions, and describe decision-making conditions.*

2 *Discuss rational perspectives on decision making, including the steps involved.*

3 *Describe the behavioral aspects of decision making, including the administrative model, political forces, intuition and escalation of commitment, risk, and ethics as they relate to making decisions.*

> *"Cephalon has taken a different path than most biotech companies."*
>
> —Frank Baldino, Jr., CEO, Cephalon

Chapter Outline

▶ **THE NATURE OF DECISION MAKING**
Decision making defined
Types of decisions
Decision-making conditions

▶ **RATIONAL PERSPECTIVES ON DECISION MAKING**
The classical model of decision making
Steps in rational decision making

▶ **BEHAVIORAL ASPECTS OF DECISION MAKING**
The administrative model
Political forces in decision making
Intuition and escalation of commitment
Risk propensity and decision making
Ethics and decision making

▶ **GROUP AND TEAM DECISION MAKING IN ORGANIZATIONS**
Forms of group and team decision making
Advantages of group and team decision making
Disadvantages of group and team decision making
Managing group and team decision-making processes

Online Study Center
Prepare for Class
Chapter Outline

4 ▶ *Discuss group and team decision making, including its advantages and disadvantages and how it can be more effectively managed.*

A Risky Pill

Dr. Frank Baldino, Jr., is a risk taker. After several years working for DuPont, he left the chemical giant at age thirty-three and started his own biotech firm called Cephalon. The company, whose name derives from the Greek word for "brain," focused on neurological diseases. From that start in 1987, Cephalon has grown to employ over 2,500 workers, encompass four facilities, and generate $1.2 billion in annual sales. Baldino still heads the firm and hence is one of the longest-serving CEOs in the volatile biotechnology industry. A large portion of his success comes from his skill in navigating the difficult decisions that are common in the pharmaceutical sector.

One area of considerable risk for biotechnology firms is new-product development, because it entails such long and uncertain lead times. Creation of the complex drug proteins used in such products may take a team of dozens of Ph.D.s ten years or more. During that time, millions of dollars are needed for staffing,

Online Study Center
Improve Your Grade
—Flashcards
—Glossary

You should be able to define and use terms that are part of the practicing manager's vocabulary, as well as those that are integral in the language of management.

equipment, and facilities, but no revenues are generated. The development process creates products that can move on to the next stage—testing—only about half the time. The testing stage is also risky, however, because new drugs must undergo extensive analysis by the U.S. Food and Drug Administration (FDA). The testing is done in three phases that determine safety and effectiveness, and it continues for at least three—and sometimes up to ten—years. The FDA reports that only about 20 percent of drugs that undergo testing are ultimately approved for use.

In addition to the financial risk, drug makers face a great competitive risk. For instance, rivals may quickly create generic versions of popular new medicines. Generics can be sold for much less, because the opportunistic company does not have to recover high development and testing expenses. New medications can be protected by patents, which can last up to twenty years. However, the twenty-year clock starts ticking when the patent is filed, not when the drug hits the market. And companies typically file for a patent before testing, to reduce the risk of having a new drug stolen.

Dr. Baldino made choices that led to a unique strategy for his biotech firm. Cephalon's first product, a potential treatment for Lou Gehrig's disease, failed to gain FDA approval. Rather than engage in an extended regulatory battle, Baldino chose to shelve that product. His next move was unorthodox for a start-up biotech company—he looked for an existing product that could be profitably licensed. He found Provigil, a remedy for narcolepsy. Narcolepsy, which causes sudden attacks of intense sleepiness, is relatively rare; therefore, Provigil had low sales. But Baldino saw that the drug had potential for other uses. After winning FDA approval, extensive testing showed that Provigil was effective against other sleep disorders and even ordinary tiredness. Provigil has become a blockbuster drug, a biotech success story.

Cephalon's other drugs, including treatments for severe pain and epileptic seizures, were also developed elsewhere and licensed by the firm. Sales of each of these drugs are ten or more times their levels before licensing, thanks in part to Cephalon's aggressive marketing and product extension. The company has also acquired smaller companies to further expand its product portfolio.

Baldino clearly uses a rational decision-making process at Cephalon. He did not become emotionally attached to his first, unsuccessful product but quickly abandoned it when it proved unprofitable. He chose a licensing strategy, which is not as glamorous as research but has a higher expected payoff. While many firms stubbornly continue to focus on R&D at the expense of other functions, Baldino balances research with an emphasis on marketing and sales. Baldino performs a thorough analysis of opportunities and the development of specific goals for every product. He then systematically works to expand the usefulness of each drug to its fullest extent.

Thus far, Baldino's decisions have paid off. Cephalon became profitable in 1999, just three years after launching Provigil. Sales revenue is expanding rapidly—42 percent in 2004 alone—allowing the company to finance further research, along with more acquisitions and marketing campaigns. Cephalon is one of only 20 profitable firms among the more than 450 publicly traded biotech companies. Baldino clearly intends to continue with his successful strategy. He says, "Cephalon has taken a different path than most biotech companies. . . . We invested early in developing a sophisticated marketing organization and experienced specialty sales teams. . . . This investment enabled us to build a successful business based upon product sales, and we now let profitability fund our innovative science." And the skillful leadership and decision making will be ongoing at Cephalon. Baldino asserts, "I'll be here until either the shareholders throw me out or the company is acquired."[1]

Frank Baldino, Jr., and other managers at Cephalon make decisions every day. And apparently most of these decisions are good ones. Making effective decisions, as well as recognizing when a bad decision has been made and quickly responding to mistakes, is a key ingredient of organizational effectiveness. Indeed, some experts believe that decision making is the most basic and fundamental of all managerial activities.[2] For this reason we discuss it here in the context of the first management function, planning. However, although decision making is perhaps most closely linked to the planning function, it is also part of organizing, leading, and controlling. We begin our discussion by exploring the nature of decision making. We next describe rational perspectives on decision making, as well as its behavioral aspects. We conclude with a discussion of group and team decision making.

THE NATURE OF DECISION MAKING

1 ▶ *Define decision making, discuss types of decisions, and describe decision-making conditions.*

In the early 2000s, managers at Ford made the decision to buy Land Rover from BMW for nearly $3 billion.[3] At about the same time, the general manager of the Ford dealership in Bryan, Texas, made a decision to sponsor a local youth soccer team for $200. Each of these examples reflects a decision, but the decisions differ in many ways. Thus, as a starting point in understanding decision making, we must first explore the meaning of decision making, as well as the various types of decisions and the conditions under which decisions are made.[4]

Decision Making Defined

decision making The act of choosing one alternative from among a set of alternatives.

Decision making can be either a specific act or a general process.[5] **Decision making** per se is the act of choosing one alternative from among a set of alternatives. The decision-making process, however, is much more than this. One aspect of the process, for example, is that the person making the decision must both recognize that a decision is necessary and identify the set of feasible alternatives before selecting one. Hence the **decision-making process** includes recognizing and defining the nature of a decision situation, identifying alternatives, choosing the "best" alternative, and putting it into practice.[6]

decision-making process Recognizing and defining the nature of a decision situation, identifying alternatives, choosing the "best" alternative, and putting it into practice.

The word *best*, of course, implies effectiveness. Effective decision making requires that the decision maker understand the situation driving the decision. Most people would consider an effective decision to be one that optimizes some set of factors, such as profits, sales, employee welfare, and market share. In some situations, though, an effective decision may be one that minimizes loss, expenses, or employee turnover. It may even mean selecting the best method for going out of business, laying off employees, or terminating a strategic alliance.

We should also note that managers make decisions about both problems and opportunities.[7] For example, making decisions about how to cut costs by 10 percent reflects a problem—an undesirable situation that requires a solution. But decisions are also necessary when opportunities arise. Learning that the firm is earning higher-than-projected profits, for example, requires a subsequent decision. Should the extra funds be used to increase shareholder dividends, to reinvest in current operations, or to expand into new markets? For instance, recall that a few years ago Firestone faced major problems when the most popular line of automobile tires was found to contain serious design defects that could lead to deadly accidents. During this crisis, managers at Goodyear had an opportunity to enlarge the firm's market share significantly by making the right decisions. However, by most accounts, Goodyear executives made poor decisions and lost what observers saw as a golden opportunity.[8]

"Hmm, what would Satan do?"

When confronted with difficult decisions, some managers try to guess what their favorite "role model" might do in the same situation. Walt Disney, James Cash Penny of J.S. Penny, and Herb Kelleher of Southwest Airlines are often invoked as role models for decision making. But when managers use the wrong role model, as this executive is contemplating, things may not turn out so well!

© *The New Yorker* Collection 2002/Pat Byrnes from cartoonbank.com. All Rights Reserved.

Types of Decisions

Managers must make many different types of decisions. In general, however, most decisions fall into one of two categories: programmed and nonprogrammed.[9]

programmed decision A decision that is fairly structured or recurs with some frequency (or both).

1. A **programmed decision** is one that is relatively structured or recurs with some frequency (or both). Starbucks uses programmed decisions to purchase new supplies of coffee beans, cups, and napkins, and Starbucks employees are trained in exact procedures for brewing coffee. Many decisions regarding basic operating systems and procedures and standard organizational transactions are of this variety and can therefore be programmed.[10]

nonprogrammed decision A decision that is relatively unstructured and occurs much less often than a programmed decision.

2. **Nonprogrammed decisions**, on the other hand, are relatively unstructured and occur much less often. Virtually all of the decisions made at Cephalon by Frank Baldino, Jr., are nonprogrammed decisions. Managers faced with such

decisions must treat each one as unique, investing time, energy, and resources in exploring the situation from all perspectives. Intuition and experience are major factors in nonprogrammed decisions. Most of the decisions top managers make that involve strategy (including mergers, acquisitions, and takeovers) and organization design are nonprogrammed. So are decisions about new facilities, new products, labor contracts, and legal issues.

CONCEPT CHECK 4.1

Describe the difference between programmed and nonprogrammed decisions. What are the implications of these differences for decision makers?

Decision-Making Conditions

Just as there are different kinds of decisions, there are also different conditions under which decisions must be made. Managers sometimes have an almost perfect understanding of conditions surrounding a decision, but at other times they have few clues about those conditions. In general, as shown in Figure 4.1, the circumstances that exist for the decision maker are conditions of certainty, risk, or uncertainty.[11]

▌ When the decision maker knows with reasonable certainty what the alternatives are and what conditions are associated with each alternative, a **state of certainty** exists. Suppose, for example, that managers at Singapore Airlines make a decision to buy five new jumbo jets. Their next decision is from whom to buy them. Because there are only two companies in the world that make jumbo jets, Boeing and Airbus, Singapore Airlines knows its options exactly. Each supplier has proven products and will guarantee prices and delivery dates. The airline thus knows the alternative conditions associated with each. There is little ambiguity and relatively little chance of making a bad decision.

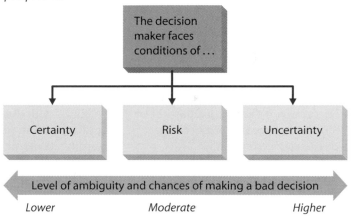

FIGURE 4.1

Decision-Making Conditions

Most major decisions in organizations today are made under conditions of uncertainty. Managers making decisions in these circumstances must be sure to learn as much as possible about the situation and to approach the decision from a logical and rational perspective.

Few organizational decisions, however, are made under conditions of true certainty. The complexity and turbulence of the contemporary business world make such situations rare. Even the airplane purchase decision we just considered has less certainty than it appears. The aircraft companies may not really be able to guarantee delivery dates, so they may write cost-increase or inflation clauses into contracts. Thus the airline may be only partially certain of the conditions surrounding each alternative.

state of certainty A condition in which the decision maker knows with reasonable certainty what the alternatives are and what conditions are associated with each alternative.

▌ A more common decision-making condition is a **state of risk** where the availability of each alternative and its potential payoffs and costs are all associated with probability estimates. Suppose, for example, that a labor contract negotiator for a company receives a "final" offer from the union right before a strike deadline. The negotiator has two alternatives: to accept or to reject the offer. The risk centers on whether the union representatives are bluffing. If the company negotiator accepts the offer, she avoids a strike but commits the firm to a relatively costly labor contract. If she rejects the contract, she may get a more favorable contract if the union is bluffing, but she may provoke a strike if it is not.

On the basis of past experiences, relevant information, the advice of others, and her own judgment, she may conclude that there is about a 75 percent chance that the union representatives are bluffing and about a 25 percent chance

state of risk A condition in which the availability of each alternative and its potential payoffs and costs are all associated with probability estimates.

that they will back up their threats. Thus she can base a calculated decision on the two alternatives (accept or reject the contract demands) and the probable consequences of each. When making decisions under a state of risk, managers must reasonably estimate the probabilities associated with each alternative. For example, if the union negotiators are committed to calling a strike if their demands are not met, and the company negotiator rejects their demands because she guesses they will not strike, her miscalculation will prove costly. As indicated in Figure 4.1, decision making under conditions of risk is accompanied by moderate ambiguity and moderate chances of making a bad decision.[12]

state of uncertainty   A condition in which the decision maker does not know all the alternatives, the risks associated with each, or the consequences each alternative is likely to have.

▌ Most of the major decision making in contemporary organizations is done under a **state of uncertainty**. The decision maker does not know all the alternatives, the risks associated with each, or the probable consequences of each alternative. This uncertainty stems from the complexity and dynamism of contemporary organizations and their environments. The emergence of the Internet as a significant force in today's competitive environment has served to increase both revenue potential and uncertainty for most managers.

To make effective decisions in these circumstances, managers must acquire as much relevant information as possible and approach the situation from a logical and rational perspective. Intuition, judgment, and experience always play major roles in the decision-making process under conditions of uncertainty. Even so, uncertainty is the most ambiguous condition for managers and the one in which errors are most likely to occur.[13] Indeed, many of the problems associated with the downfall of Arthur Andersen resulted from the firm's apparent difficulties in responding to ambiguous and uncertain decision parameters regarding its moral, ethical, and legal responsibilities.[14]

CONCEPT CHECK 4.2

In your opinion, is it easier to make a decision under a condition of risk or under a condition of uncertainty? Why?

Decision making is the act of choosing one alternative from among a set of alternatives. Most decisions take place under conditions of certainty, risk, or uncertainty. Consider, for instance, the decision confronted by Nebraska farmer Bob Roberts during a recent drought. One option was to grow corn, which he could sell for cash. The other was to grow alfalfa to feed his cows. And clearly, each option had a degree of risk.

True or False?

_____ 1. After the discovery of mad cow disease in Washington state, McDonald's launched a public relations campaign designed to assure customers of the safety of its beef supply. This was a programmed decision.

_____ 2. Pranali plans to buy a new car. She has good information on price, reliability, service, and insurance cost. From a financial standpoint she is making her decision in a state of risk.

Multiple Choice

_____ 3. The decision-making process defines the situation, identifies alternatives, chooses the "best" alternative, and _____.
    a. gets feedback
    b. puts it into practice
    c. gets another opinion
    d. presents it to the group
    e. all of the above

_____ 4. Anthony, a platoon leader in the U.S. Army, has to decide which squads to send on each patrol, knowing there is the possibility of a deadly attack. Anthony is making a decision under _____.
    a. certainty
    b. uncertainty
    c. risk
    d. programmed conditions
    e. nonprogrammed conditions

_____ 5. When Kraft Foods monitors its beef-related product sales, it is in which stage of the rational decision-making process?
    a. Identifying alternatives
    b. Evaluating alternatives
    c. Selecting alternatives
    d. Implementing chosen alternatives
    e. Evaluating results

Online Study Center
ACE the Test
ACE Practice Tests 4.1

RATIONAL PERSPECTIVES ON DECISION MAKING

2 ▸ *Discuss rational perspectives on decision making, including the steps involved.*

Most managers like to think of themselves as rational decision makers. And, indeed, many experts argue that managers should try to be as rational as possible in making decisions.[15] This section highlights the fundamental and rational perspectives on decision making.

The Classical Model of Decision Making

The **classical decision model** is a prescriptive approach that tells managers how they should make decisions. It rests on the assumptions that managers are logical and rational and that they make decisions that are in the best interests of the organization.[16] Figure 4.2 indicates how the classical model views the decision-making process. As it shows, the classical model is an idealized construct that makes these assumptions:

classical decision model A prescriptive approach to decision making that tells managers how they should make decisions; assumes that managers are logical and rational and that their decisions will be in the best interests of the organization.

FIGURE 4.2

The Classical Model of Decision Making

The classical model of decision making assumes that managers are rational and logical. It attempts to prescribe how managers should approach decision situations.

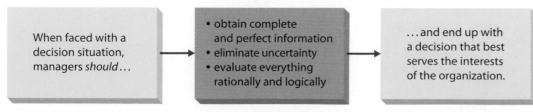

When faced with a decision situation, managers *should*...
→
• obtain complete and perfect information
• eliminate uncertainty
• evaluate everything rationally and logically
→
...and end up with a decision that best serves the interests of the organization.

■ Decision makers have complete information about the decision situation and possible alternatives.

■ They can effectively eliminate uncertainty to achieve a decision condition of certainty.

■ They evaluate all aspects of the decision situation logically and rationally.

As we see later, these conditions rarely, if ever, actually exist.

Steps in Rational Decision Making

steps in rational decision making Recognize and define the decision situation; identify appropriate alternatives; evaluate each alternative in terms of its feasibility, satisfactoriness, and consequences; select the best alternative; implement the chosen alternative; follow up and evaluate the results of the chosen alternative.

A manager who really wants to approach a decision rationally and logically should try to follow the **steps in rational decision making** that are listed in Table 4.1. These steps help keep the decision maker focused on facts and logic and help guard against inappropriate assumptions and pitfalls.

Recognizing and Defining the Decision Situation

To initiate this first step, the individual must recognize that a decision is necessary—that is, there must be some stimulus or spark to initiate the process. Often this

TABLE 4.1

Steps in the Rational Decision-Making Process
Although the conditions assumed in the classical decision model rarely exist, managers can approach decision making with rationality. By following the steps of rational decision making, managers ensure that they are learning as much as possible about the decision situation and the available alternatives.

Step	Detail	Example
1. Recognizing and defining the decision situation	Some stimulus indicates that a decision must be made. The stimulus may be positive or negative.	A plant manager sees that employee turnover has increased by 5 percent.
2. Identifying alternatives	Both obvious and creative alternatives are desired. In general, the more important the decision, the more alternatives should be generated.	The plant manager can increase wages, increase benefits, or change hiring standards.
3. Evaluating alternatives	Each alternative is evaluated to determine its feasibility, its satisfactoriness, and its consequences.	Increasing benefits may not be feasible. Increasing wages and changing hiring standards may satisfy all conditions.
4. Selecting the best alternative	Consider all situational factors and choose the alternative that best fits the manager's situation.	Changing hiring standards will take an extended period of time to cut turnover, so increase wages.
5. Implementing the chosen alternative	The chosen alternative is incorporated into the organizational system.	The plant manager may need permission from corporate headquarters. The human resource department establishes a new wage structure.
6. Following up and evaluating the results	At some time in the future, the manager should ascertain the extent to which the alternative chosen in step 4 and implemented in step 5 has worked.	The plant manager notes that, six months later, turnover has dropped to its previous level.

spark occurs without any prior warning, such as when equipment fails and a manager must decide whether to repair it or replace it. When a major crisis erupts, the manager must quickly decide how to deal with it. As we have noted, the stimulus for a decision may be either positive or negative. A manager who must decide how to invest surplus funds, for example, faces a positive decision situation. A negative financial stimulus could involve having to trim budgets because of cost overruns.

Identifying Alternatives

Once the decision situation has been recognized and defined, the second step is to identify alternative courses of effective action. Developing both obvious, standard alternatives and creative, innovative alternatives is useful. In general, the more important the decision, the more attention is directed to developing alternatives. If the decision involves a multimillion-dollar relocation, a great deal of time and expertise will be devoted to identifying the best locations. J.C. Penney spent two years searching before selecting the Dallas–Fort Worth area for its new corporate headquarters. If the problem is to choose a color for the company softball team uniforms, less time and expertise will be brought to bear.

Although managers should seek creative solutions, they must also recognize that various constraints often limit their alternatives. Common constraints include legal restrictions, moral and ethical norms, authority constraints, and constraints imposed by the power and authority of the manager, available technology, economic considerations, and unofficial social norms.

Evaluating Alternatives

Figure 4.3 presents a decision tree that can be used to evaluate different alternatives. The figure suggests that each alternative be evaluated in terms of its *feasibility*, its *satisfactoriness*, and its *consequences*. The first question to ask is whether an alternative is feasible. Is it within the realm of probability and practicality? For a small, struggling firm, an alternative requiring a huge financial outlay is probably out of the question. Other alternatives may not be feasible because of legal barriers. And limited human, material, and information resources may make other alternatives impractical.

FIGURE 4.3

Evaluating Alternatives in the Decision-Making Process
Managers must thoroughly evaluate all the alternatives in order to increase the chances that the alternative finally chosen will be successful. Failure to evaluate an alternative's feasibility, satisfactoriness, and consequences can lead to a wrong decision.

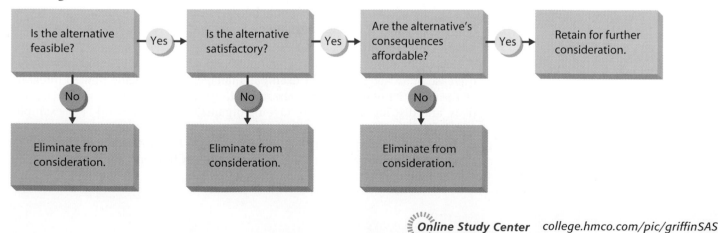

When an alternative has passed the test of feasibility, it must next be examined to see how well it satisfies the conditions of the decision situation. For example, a manager searching for ways to double production capacity might initially consider purchasing an existing plant from another company. If more detailed analysis reveals that the new plant would increase production capacity by only 35 percent, this alternative may not be satisfactory. Finally, when an alternative has proved both feasible and satisfactory, its probable consequences must still be assessed. To what extent will a particular alternative influence other parts of the organization? What financial and nonfinancial costs will be associated with such influences? For example, a plan to boost sales by cutting prices may disrupt cash flows, require a new advertising program, and alter the behavior of sales representatives because it requires a different commission structure. The manager, then, must put "price tags" on the consequences of each alternative. Even an alternative that is both feasible and satisfactory must be eliminated if its consequences are too expensive for the total system.

Selecting an Alternative

Even though many alternatives fail to pass the triple tests of feasibility, satisfactoriness, and affordable consequences, two or more alternatives may remain. Choosing the best of these is the real crux of decision making. One approach is to choose the alternative that offers the optimal combination of feasibility, satisfactoriness, and affordable consequences. Even though most situations do not lend themselves to objective, mathematical analysis, the manager can often develop subjective estimates and weights for choosing an alternative.

Optimization is also a frequent goal. Because a decision is likely to affect several individuals or units, any feasible alternative will probably not maximize all of the relevant goals. Suppose that the manager of the Kansas City Royals needs to select a new outfielder for the upcoming baseball season. Bill hits .350 but has difficulty catching fly balls; Joe hits only .175 but is outstanding in the field; and Sam hits .290 and is a solid but not outstanding fielder. The manager would probably select Sam because of this optimal balance of hitting and fielding. Decision makers should also remember that they might be able to find multiple acceptable alternatives; selecting just one alternative and rejecting all the others might not be necessary. For example, the Royals' manager might decide that Sam will start each game, Bill will be retained as a pinch hitter, and Joe will be retained as a defensive substitute. In many hiring decisions, the candidates remaining after evaluation are ranked. If the top candidate rejects the offer, it may be automatically extended to the number two candidate and, if necessary, to the remaining candidates in order.

Implementing the Chosen Alternative

After an alternative has been selected, the manager must put it into effect. In some decision situations, implementation is fairly easy; in others, it is more difficult. In the case of an acquisition, for example, managers must decide how to integrate all the activities of the new business, including purchasing, human resource practices, and distribution, into an ongoing organizational framework. For example, when Hewlett-Packard announced its acquisition of Compaq, managers also acknowledged that it would take at least a year to integrate the two firms into a single one. Operational plans, which we discuss in Chapter 3, are useful in implementing alternatives.

Managers must also consider people's resistance to change when implementing decisions. The reasons for such resistance include insecurity, inconvenience, and fear of the unknown. Managers should anticipate potential resistance at various stages of the implementation process. (Resistance to change is covered in Chapter 7.) Managers should also recognize that even when all alternatives have been evaluated as precisely as possible and the consequences of each alternative have been weighed, unanticipated consequences are still likely. Any number of factors—unexpected cost increases, a less-than-perfect fit with existing organizational subsystems, or unpredicted effects on cash flow or operating expenses, for example—could develop after implementation has begun.

Following Up and Evaluating the Results

The final step in the decision-making process requires that managers evaluate the effectiveness of their decision—that is, they should make sure that the chosen alternative has served its original purpose. If an implemented alternative appears not to be working, the manager can respond in several ways. Another previously identified alternative (the original second or third choice, for instance) could be adopted. Or the manager might recognize that the situation was not correctly defined to begin with and start the process all over again. Finally, the manager might decide that the original alternative is in fact appropriate but either has not yet had time to work or should be implemented in a different way.

Failure to evaluate decision effectiveness may have serious consequences. The Pentagon once spent $1.8 billion and eight years developing the Sergeant York anti-aircraft gun. From the beginning, tests revealed major problems with the weapon system, but not until it was in its final stages, when it was demonstrated to be completely ineffective, was the project scrapped. The examples in the Opening Incident at the beginning of this chapter illustrate a much more effective approach to evaluating decision effectiveness.

CONCEPT CHECK 4.3

Was your decision about what college or university to attend a rational decision? Did you go through each step in rational decision making? If not, why not?

TEST PREPPER 4.2

Answers can be found on P. 441

True or False?

_____ 1. The classical decision model describes how decisions are actually made.

_____ 2. In the rational decision-making process, selecting the best alternative immediately precedes the follow-up and evaluation of results.

_____ 3. When identifying alternatives, developing obvious standard alternatives and creative innovative alternatives is generally useful.

Multiple Choice

_____ 4. Tonisha is evaluating alternative prices for her financial consulting business. She determines that one alternative has to go because she does not have the human resources and capital necessary to accomplish it. She evaluated the alternatives for _____.
   a. feasibility
   b. satisfactoriness
   c. probable outcomes
   d. consequences
   e. optimization

_____ 5. In selecting an alternative, which of the following is usually the goal?
   a. Feasibility
   b. Satisfactoriness
   c. Probable outcomes
   d. Consequences
   e. Optimization

Online Study Center
ACE the Test
ACE Practice Tests 4.2

BEHAVIORAL ASPECTS OF DECISION MAKING

> **3** ▶ *Describe the behavioral aspects of decision making, including the administrative model, political forces, intuition and escalation of commitment, risk, and ethics as they relate to making decisions.*

If all decision situations were approached as logically as described in the previous section, more decisions would prove successful. Yet decisions are often made with little consideration for logic and rationality. Some experts have estimated that U.S. companies use rational decision-making techniques less than 20 percent of the time.[17] And even when organizations try to be logical, they sometimes fail. For example, when Starbucks opened its first coffee shops in New York, it relied on scientific marketing research, taste tests, and rational deliberation in making a decision to emphasize drip over espresso coffee. However, that decision proved wrong, as it became clear that New Yorkers strongly preferred the same espresso-style coffees that were Starbucks mainstays in the West. Hence, the firm had to reconfigure its stores hastily to meet customer preferences.

On the other hand, sometimes a decision made with little regard for logic can still turn out to be correct.[18] An important ingredient in how these forces work is the behavioral aspect of decision making. The administrative model reflects these subjective considerations. Other behavioral aspects include political forces, intuition and escalation of commitment, risk propensity, and ethics.

The Administrative Model

administrative model   A decision-making model that argues that decision makers (1) have incomplete and imperfect information, (2) are constrained by bounded rationality, and (3) tend to "satisfice" when making decisions.

bounded rationality   The concept that decision makers are limited by their values and unconscious reflexes, skills, and habits.

Herbert A. Simon was one of the first experts to recognize that decisions are not always made with rationality and logic.[19] Simon was subsequently awarded the Nobel Prize in economics. Rather than prescribing how decisions should be made, his view of decision making, now called the **administrative model**, describes how decisions often actually are made. As illustrated in Figure 4.4, the model holds that managers (1) have incomplete and imperfect information, (2) are constrained by bounded rationality, and (3) tend to "satisfice" when making decisions.

Bounded rationality suggests that decision makers are limited by their values and unconscious reflexes, skills, and habits. They are also limited by less-than-complete information and knowledge. Essentially, then, the concept of bounded rationality suggests that although people try to be rational decision makers, their rationality has limits.

FIGURE 4.4

The Administrative Model of Decision Making
The administrative model is based on behavioral processes that affect how managers make decisions. Rather than prescribing how decisions should be made, it focuses more on describing how they actually are made.

| When faced with a decision situation managers *actually*... | → | • use incomplete and imperfect information
• are constrained by bounded rationality
• tend to satisfice | → | ...and end up with a decision that may or may not serve the interests of the organization. |

Another important part of the administrative model is **satisficing**. This concept suggests that, rather than conducting an exhaustive search for the best possible alternative, decision makers tend to search only until they identify an alternative that meets some minimum standard of sufficiency. A manager looking for a site for a new plant, for example, may select the first site she finds that meets basic requirements for transportation, utilities, and price, even though further search might yield a better location. People satisfice for a variety of reasons. Managers may simply be unwilling to ignore their own motives (such as reluctance to spend time making a decision) and therefore may not be able to continue searching after a minimally acceptable alternative is identified. The decision maker may be unable to weigh and evaluate large numbers of alternatives and criteria. Also, subjective and personal considerations often intervene in decision situations.

Because of the inherent imperfection of information, bounded rationality, and satisficing, the decisions made by a manager may or may not actually be in the best interests of the organization. A manager may choose a particular location for the new plant because it offers the lowest price and best availability of utilities and transportation. Or she may choose the location because it is near a community where she wants to live.

In summary, then, the classical and administrative models paint quite different pictures of decision making. Which is more accurate? Actually, each can be used to better understand how managers make decisions. The classical model is prescriptive: It explains how managers can at least attempt to be more rational and logical in their approach to decisions. And managers can use the administrative model to develop a better understanding of their inherent biases and limitations.[20] In the following sections, we describe more fully other behavioral forces that can influence decisions.

satisficing The tendency to search for alternatives only until one is found that meets some minimum standard of sufficiency.

Political Forces in Decision Making

Political forces are another major element that contributes to the behavioral nature of decision making. Organizational politics is covered in Chapter 11, but one major element of politics, coalitions, is especially relevant to decision making. A **coalition** is an informal alliance of individuals or groups formed to achieve a common goal. This common goal is often a preferred decision alternative. For example, coalitions of stockholders frequently band together to force a board of directors to make a certain decision.

The impact of coalitions can be either positive or negative. They can help astute managers get the organization on a path toward effectiveness and profitability, or they can strangle well-conceived strategies

coalition An informal alliance of individuals or groups formed to achieve a common goal.

Coalitions can be a major force in decision making. The Rafadin Women's Coalition, an Iraqi women's rights advocacy group, recently held a news conference to launch the coalition's campaign for the protection of women's rights in the new Iraqi constitution. The coalition asserted that women's rights in Iraq have been overlooked and women have not had the chance to fully participate in the decision-making process.

and decisions. Managers must recognize when to use coalitions, how to assess whether coalitions are acting in the best interests of the organization, and how to constrain their dysfunctional effects.[21]

Intuition and Escalation of Commitment

Two other important decision processes that go beyond logic and rationality are intuition and escalation of commitment to a chosen course of action.

intuition An innate belief about something, without conscious consideration.

Online Study Center
Improve Your Grade
Career Snapshot

1. **Intuition** is an innate belief about something, without conscious consideration. Managers sometimes decide to do something because it "feels right" or they have a "hunch." This feeling is usually not arbitrary, however. Rather, it is based on years of experience and practice in making decisions in similar situations. Such an inner sense may help managers make an occasional decision without going through a full-blown rational sequence of steps.[22] For example, the New York Yankees once contacted three major sneaker manufacturers—Nike, Reebok, and Adidas—and informed them that they were looking to make a sponsorship deal. While Nike and Reebok were carefully and rationally assessing the possibilities, managers at Adidas quickly realized that a partnership with the Yankees made a lot of sense for them. They responded very quickly to the idea and ended up hammering out a contract while the competitors were still analyzing details.[23] Of course, all managers, but most especially inexperienced ones, should be careful not to rely too heavily on intuition. If rationality and logic are continually bypassed for "what feels right," the odds are that disaster will strike one day.

escalation of commitment A decision maker's staying with a decision even when it appears to be wrong.

2. Another important behavioral process that influences decision making is **escalation of commitment** to a chosen course of action. In particular, decision makers sometimes make decisions and then become so committed to the course of action suggested by that decision that they stay with it, even when it appears to have been wrong.[24] For example, when people buy stock in a company, they sometimes refuse to sell it even after repeated drops in price. They choose a course of action—buying the stock in anticipation of making a profit—and then stay with it even in the face of increasing losses. Moreover, after the value drops, they rationalize that they can't sell now because if they do, they will lose money.

For years Pan American World Airways ruled the skies and used its profits to diversify into real estate and other businesses. With the advent of deregulation, however, Pan Am began to struggle and lose market share to other carriers. Experts today point out that when Pan Am managers finally realized how ineffective their airline operations had become, the "rational" decision would have been to sell off the remaining airline operations and concentrate on the firm's more profitable businesses. But because these managers still saw the company as being first and foremost an airline, they instead began slowly selling off the firm's profitable holdings to keep the airline flying. Eventually, the company was left with nothing but an ineffective and inefficient airline and had to sell off its more profitable routes before eventually being taken over by Delta. Had Pan Am managers made the more rational decision years earlier, chances are that the firm could still be a profitable enterprise today, though an enterprise with no involvement in the airline industry.[25]

CONCEPT CHECK 4.4

Under what conditions is escalation of commitment likely to occur? In what ways are escalation of commitment and decision making under conditions of risk closely related to one another?

Risk Propensity and Decision Making

The behavioral element of **risk propensity** is the extent to which a decision maker is willing to gamble when making a decision. Some managers are cautious about every decision they make. They try to adhere to the rational model and are extremely conservative in what they do. Such managers are more likely to avoid mistakes, and they infrequently make decisions that lead to big losses. Other managers are extremely aggressive in making decisions and are willing to take risks.[26] They rely heavily on intuition, reach decisions quickly, and often risk big investments on their decisions. As in gambling, these managers are more likely than their conservative counterparts to achieve big successes with their decisions; they are also more likely to incur greater losses.[27] The organization's culture is a prime ingredient in fostering different levels of risk propensity.

risk propensity The extent to which a decision maker is willing to gamble when making a decision.

Ethics and Decision Making

As we note in Chapter 2, individual ethics are personal beliefs about right and wrong behavior. Ethics are clearly related to decision making in a number of ways. For example, suppose that after careful analysis, a manager realizes that her company could save money by closing her department and subcontracting with a supplier for the same services. But to recommend this course of action would result in the loss of several jobs, including her own. Her personal ethical standards will clearly shape how she proceeds.[28] Indeed, each dimension of managerial ethics (the relationships of the firm to its employees, of employees to the firm, and of the firm to other economic agents) is related to a wide variety of decisions. A manager must remember that, just as behavioral processes such as politics and risk propensity affect the decisions she makes, so, too, do her ethical beliefs.

CONCEPT CHECK 4.5

Recall a decision that you have recently made that had ethical implications. Did these implications make the decision easier or harder?

Ethics often play a major role in how people make decisions. Choosing to engage in illegal or unethical activities is an obvious example. At a more personal level, people sometimes make a decision to become a whistle blower— someone who goes public with apparent misdeeds by her or his employer. Douglas Durand tried to eliminate health-care fraud at his employer, TAP Pharmaceutical Products. When he ran up against too many internal roadblocks, he turned the company in to government officials. The charges were investigated and TAP was eventually fined $875 million.

TEST PREPPER 4.3

True or False?

_____ 1. Satisficing is part of the rational decision-making model.

Multiple Choice

_____ 2. Bounded rationality suggests that _____.
   a. people are limited by values, skills, and habits
   b. people are limited by inadequate information
   c. people are limited by knowledge
   d. rationality has limits
   e. all of the above

_____ 3. At work Tyler, Austin, and Eric eat lunch together and discuss football. At their meeting that afternoon they agree on a course of action. They used _____.
   a. a coalition
   b. escalation of commitment
   c. intuition
   d. satisficing
   e. bounded rationality

_____ 4. Durante is the master of the 70% solution. He prides himself on making quick decisions because he believes most decisions are programmed and of limited significance. He accomplishes more than any of his peers. Additionally, when a decision is important, Durante knows to slow down and thoroughly analyze courses of action. Durante has learned to use _____ to his advantage.
   a. bounded rationality
   b. satisficing
   c. coalitions
   d. intuition
   e. commitment

_____ 5. Decision making is affected by which of the following?
   a. Politics
   b. Risk propensity
   c. Ethical beliefs
   d. Intuition
   e. All of the above

Online Study Center
ACE the Test
ACE Practice Tests 4.3

GROUP AND TEAM DECISION MAKING IN ORGANIZATIONS

4 ▶ *Discuss group and team decision making, including its advantages and disadvantages and how it can be more effectively managed.*

In more and more organizations today, important decisions are made by groups and teams rather than by individuals. Examples include the executive committee of General Motors, product design teams at Texas Instruments, and marketing planning groups at Dell Computer. Managers can typically choose whether to have individuals or groups and teams make a particular decision. Thus it is important that managers be familiar with the various forms of group and team decision making and with their advantages and disadvantages.[29]

Forms of Group and Team Decision Making

The most common methods of group and team decision making are interacting groups, Delphi groups, and nominal groups. Increasingly, these methods of group decision making are being conducted online.[30]

Online Study Center
Improve Your Grade
Knowledgebank 4.1

interacting group or team A decision-making group or team in which members openly discuss, argue about, and agree on the best alternative.

1. **Interacting groups and teams** represent the most common form of decision-making group. The format is simple: Either an existing or a newly designated group or team is asked to make a decision. Existing groups or teams might be functional departments, regular work teams, or standing committees. Newly designated groups or teams can be ad hoc committees, task forces, or newly constituted work teams. The group or team members talk among themselves,

argue, agree, argue some more, form internal coalitions, and so forth. Finally, after some period of deliberation, the group or team makes its decision. An advantage of this method is that the interaction among people often sparks new ideas and promotes understanding. A major disadvantage is that political processes can play too big a role.

2. **Delphi groups** are sometimes used to develop a consensus of expert opinions. Developed by the Rand Corporation, the Delphi procedure solicits input from a panel of experts who contribute individually. Their opinions are combined and, in effect, averaged. Assume, for example, that the problem is to establish an expected date for a major technological breakthrough in converting coal into usable energy. The first step in using the Delphi procedure is to obtain the cooperation of a panel of experts. For this situation, experts might include various research scientists, university researchers, and executives in a relevant energy industry. At first, the experts are asked to predict a time frame for the expected breakthrough anonymously. The persons coordinating the Delphi group collect the responses, average them, and ask the experts for another prediction. In this round, the experts who provided unusual or extreme predictions may be asked to justify them. These explanations may then be relayed to the other experts. When the predictions stabilize, the average prediction is taken to represent the decision of the group of experts. The time, expense, and logistics of the Delphi technique rule out its use for routine, everyday decisions, but it has been successfully used for forecasting technological breakthroughs at Boeing, market potential for new products at General Motors, research and development patterns at Eli Lilly, and future economic conditions by the U.S. government.[31]

3. **Nominal groups** include members that are brought together in a face-to-face setting, unlike with the Delphi method, where members do not see each other. The members represent a group in name only, however; they do not talk to one another freely as the members of interacting groups do. Nominal groups are used most often to generate creative and innovative alternatives or ideas. To begin, the manager assembles a group of knowledgeable experts and outlines the problem for them. The group members are next asked to write down, independently, as many alternatives as they can think of. The members then take turns stating their ideas, which are recorded on a flip chart or board at the front of the room. Discussion is limited to simple clarification. After all alternatives have been listed, more open discussion takes place. Group members then vote, usually by rank-ordering the various alternatives. The highest-ranking alternative represents the decision of the group. Of course, the manager in charge may retain the authority to accept or reject the group decision.

Advantages of Group and Team Decision Making

One advantage of group decision making is that more information is available in a group or team setting—as suggested by the old axiom "Two heads are better than one." A group or team represents a variety of education, experience, and perspective. Partly as a result of this increased information, groups and teams typically can identify and evaluate more alternatives than one person can.[32] The people involved in a group or team decision understand the logic and rationale behind it, are more likely to accept it, and are equipped to communicate the decision to their work group or department.[33] Finally, research evidence suggests that groups may make better decisions than individuals.[34]

Online Study Center
Improve Your Grade
Visual Glossary

Delphi group A form of group decision making in which a group is used to achieve a consensus of expert opinion.

nominal group A structured technique used to generate creative and innovative alternatives or ideas.

CONCEPT CHECK 4.6

What are the major differences between three common methods of group decision making? Which method do you prefer?

Online Study Center
Improve Your Grade
Video Segment

Disadvantages of Group and Team Decision Making

Perhaps the biggest drawback of group and team decision making is the additional time—and hence the greater expense—entailed. The increased time stems from interaction and discussion among group or team members. If a given manager's time is worth $50 an hour, and if the manager spends two hours making a decision, the decision "costs" the organization $100. For the same decision, a group of five managers might require three hours of time. At the same $50-an-hour rate, the decision "costs" the organization $750. If the group or team decision is better, the additional expense may be justified, but the fact remains that group and team decision making is more costly.

Group or team decisions may also represent undesirable compromises.[35] For example, hiring a compromise top manager may be a bad decision in the long run, because he or she may not be able to respond adequately to various subunits in the organization or may not have everyone's complete support. Another problem is that one individual may dominate the group process to the point where others cannot make a full contribution. This dominance may stem from a desire for power or from a naturally forceful personality. The problem is that what appears to emerge as a group decision may actually be the decision of one person.

Finally, a group or team may succumb to a phenomenon known as "groupthink." **Groupthink** occurs when a group or team's desire for consensus and cohesiveness overwhelms its goal of reaching the best possible decision.[36] Under the influence of groupthink, the group may arrive at decisions that are not in the best interests of either the group or the organization but that merely avoid conflict among group members. One of the most clearly documented examples of groupthink involved the space shuttle *Challenger* disaster. As NASA was preparing to launch the shuttle, numerous problems and questions arose. At each step of the way, however, decision makers argued that there was no reason to delay and that everything would be fine. Shortly after its launch, the shuttle exploded, killing all seven crew members.

groupthink A situation that occurs when a group or team's desire for consensus and cohesiveness overwhelms its desire to reach the best possible decision.

Managing Group and Team Decision-Making Processes

Managers can do several things to help promote the effectiveness of group and team decision making. The first step is simply to be aware of the pros and cons of having a group or team make a decision. Time and cost can be managed by setting a deadline by which the decision must be made final. Dominance can be at least partially avoided if a special group is formed just to make the decision. An astute manager, for example, should know who in the organization may try to dominate and can either avoid putting that person in the group or put several strong-willed people together.

To avoid groupthink, each member of the group or team should critically evaluate all alternatives. To ensure that members will present divergent viewpoints, the leader should not make his or her own position known too early. At least one member of the group or team might be assigned the role of devil's advocate. And, after reaching a preliminary decision, the group or team should hold a follow-up meeting wherein divergent viewpoints can be raised again if any group members wish to do so.[37] Gould Paper Corporation used these methods by assigning managers to two different teams. The teams then spent an entire day in a structured debate presenting the pros and cons of each side of an issue to ensure the best possible decision. Sun Microsystems makes most of its major decisions by using this same approach.

CONCEPT CHECK 4.7

Which of the following business decision-making scenarios would be best handled by a group or team? Which would be best handled by an individual?

- A decision about switching pencil suppliers
- A decision about hiring a new CEO
- A decision about firing an employee for stealing
- A decision about calling 911 to report a fire in the warehouse
- A decision about introducing a brand-new product

TEST PREPPER 4.4

True or False?

_____ 1. A Delphi group is best suited for generating creative ideas.

_____ 2. During an episode of *The Apprentice*, two teams were challenged to make the most money selling lemonade. One team chose to sell outside the fish market. It turned out to be a bad choice, but team members were reluctant to challenge the decision until it was too late. This is an example of groupthink.

_____ 3. An astute manager will know who will try to dominate a group and avoid putting other strong-willed people in the group because it will create conflict.

_____ 4. Assigning someone the role of devil's advocate in a group will delay decision making and lead to groupthink.

Multiple Choice

_____ 5. Which of the following is the most common form of decision-making group?
a. Interacting group
b. Delphi group

c. Nominal group
d. Coalition
e. Groupthink

_____ 6. Don, the owner of the Pizza Place, is trying to decide what marketing will be most effective. He gathers various experts he knows to make suggestions. After each has presented his or her idea, Don opens discussion. Finally they vote, and Don has final say on the decision. Don used which form of group decision making?
a. Interacting group   d. Coalition
b. Delphi group   e. Groupthink
c. Nominal group

_____ 7. Which of the following is NOT an advantage of group decision making?
a. More knowledge available
b. Groupthink may occur
c. Increased acceptance of the final decision
d. Better decisions are generally made
e. Enhanced communication

Online Study Center
ACE the Test
ACE Practice Tests 4.4

BUILDING EFFECTIVE TECHNICAL SKILLS

Online Study Center
Improve Your Grade
Exercises: Building Effective Skills

Exercise Overview

Technical skills are the skills necessary to accomplish or understand the specific kind of work being done in an organization. This exercise will enable you to practice technical skills in using the Internet to obtain information for making a decision.

Exercise Background

Assume that you are a business owner seeking a location for a new factory. Your company makes products that are relatively "clean"—that is, they do not pollute the environment, nor will your factory produce any dangerous waste products. Thus most communities would welcome your plant.

You are seeking a place that has a stable and well-educated workforce, a good quality of life, good health care, and a good educational system. You have narrowed your choice to the following towns.
1. Columbia, Missouri
2. Madison, Wisconsin
3. Manhattan, Kansas
4. College Station, Texas
5. Baton Rouge, Louisiana
6. Athens, Georgia

Exercise Task

With this background information as context, do the following:
1. Use the Internet to research each of these cities.
2. Rank-order the cities on the basis of the criteria noted.
3. Select the best city for your new factory.

EXPERIENTIAL EXERCISE

Programmed and Nonprogrammed Decision Making

Purpose

This exercise gives you an opportunity to make decisions and helps you understand the difference between programmed and nonprogrammed decisions. You will also learn how decision making by an individual differs from decision making by a group.

Introduction

You are asked to make decisions both individually and as a member of a group.

Instructions

Following is a list of typical organizational decisions. Your task is to determine whether each is programmed or nonprogrammed. Number your paper, and write P for programmed or N for nonprogrammed beside each number.

Next, your instructor will divide the class into groups of four to seven. All groups should have approximately the same number of members. Your task as a group is to make the decisions that you just made as individuals. In arriving at your decisions, do not use techniques such as voting or negotiating ("OK, I'll give in on this one if you'll give in on that one"). The group should discuss the difference between programmed and nonprogrammed decisions in each decision situation until all members at least partly agree with the decision.

Decision List

1. Hiring a specialist for the research staff in a highly technical field
2. Assigning workers to daily tasks
3. Determining the size of the dividend to be paid to shareholders in the ninth consecutive year of strong earnings growth
4. Deciding whether to excuse an employee's absence for medical reasons
5. Selecting the location for another branch of a 150-branch bank in a large city
6. Approving the appointment of a new law school graduate to the corporate legal staff
7. Making the annual assignment of graduate assistants to the faculty
8. Approving the request of an employee to attend a local seminar in his or her special area of expertise
9. Selecting the appropriate outlets for print advertisements for a new college textbook
10. Determining the location for a new fast-food restaurant in a small but growing town on the major interstate highway between two very large metropolitan areas

Follow-up Questions

1. To what extent did group members disagree about which decisions were programmed and which were nonprogrammed?
2. What primary factors did the group discuss in making each decision?
3. Were there any differences between the members' individual lists and the group lists? If so, discuss the reasons for the differences.

Source: From *Organizational Behavior*, 8th ed., by Ricky Griffin and Gregory Moorhead. Copyright © 2007 by Houghton Mifflin Company. Reprinted by permission.

CLOSING
CASE STUDY

Exploding the Myth of the Superhero CEO

The modern point of view about chief executive officers casts CEOs as celebrities, even heroes. The booming economy that persisted throughout the 1990s was usually attributed to America's business leaders. But the bursting of the dot-com bubble, recent corporate scandals, and the slowing economy have revealed a new truth. CEOs are not heroes. Often, they are not smart or ethical, either. Leave aside examples of blatant fraud, and there are still plenty of bad decisions made by CEOs.

Dick Brown, CEO of Electronic Data Systems (EDS), traveled the country reassuring investors that the technology services company had plenty of new contracts and guaranteed growth. The problem is that this claim was not true. One month later, Brown announced that profits for the year would fall 84 percent. At drug maker Bristol-Myers Squibb, CEO Peter Dolan entered into a $2 billion deal with ImClone to co-develop a new cancer medication. Within months, the Food and Drug Administration rejected ImClone's application. Then ImClone became involved in an insider-trading scandal that implicated CEO Samuel Waksal and shareholder Martha Stewart. To top it off, Bristol came under investigation by the Securities and Exchange Commission (SEC) for misleading financial statements.

Even managers with solid reputations are making poor choices. For example, Citigroup's former CEO Sanford Weill was often cited as an excellent manager and appeared on *BusinessWeek*'s elite "Best Managers" list. However, Weill admitted putting pressure on Jack Grubman, a Citigroup stock analyst, to give favorable evaluations of investment banking clients, in return for donating $1 million to an exclusive preschool to gain admission for Grubman's toddlers. Time Warner's CEO, Gerald Levin, was praised for negotiating the successful sale of his firm to America Online. But after SEC investigations, restatements of earnings, and accumulation of $24 billion in debt, AOL Time Warner stock is worth 75 percent less than it was at the time of the merger.

Why so many bad decisions? Observers say that CEOs today are not much different from those in the past. The difference lies in the increased pressure for

> *"A CEO doesn't make decisions. The job is mostly the art of balancing interests and dealing with shades of gray."*
>
> —Founder of an Internet company

results. Over the last decade, powerful investors have forced CEOs to change strategy or even resign over poor financial performance. David Nadler, consultant and adviser to CEOs, claims, "There was the perception that if you [the CEO] slipped, your stock price could plunge. . . . There are tremendous temptations from the system to cut corners." Former Medtronic chairman William George agrees: "The pressure is always with you. You can't escape it, even for an hour." CEOs must deal with performance demands all by themselves. "Being a CEO is a really lonely job," says James Maxmin, former leader of several businesses. "With your subordinates and peers, you need to have a degree of detachment. There's some detachment from your board too, because they are evaluating you."

In response to pressure, CEOs are careful about what they say and how they say it. "There's a lot you can't share with anyone," says Xerox CEO Anne Mulcahy. Top executives can use "CEO-speak" to reveal or obscure information. After William B. Harrison, Jr., CEO of J.P. Morgan Chase, saw his bank's sales and stock value cut in half in 2001, he said, "No one is happy with our performance this year, but we are positioned well for a rebound in the economy." In plainer words, Harrison could be saying, "When you're at the bottom, there's nowhere to go but up."

From mincing words to bending the rules is just a short step. Stanford professor Jeffrey Pfeffer claims, "There are things that happen when you join a company that cause you to believe that the values in one's outside life aren't relevant any more on the inside." Ethical ambiguity lies everywhere for the CEO. As one Internet company founder says, "A CEO doesn't make decisions. The job is mostly the art of balancing interests and dealing with shades of gray."

At a time when tales of corporate misdeeds are everywhere, leaders may feel justified because "everyone else is doing it." Jim Collins, author of *Good to Great: Why Some Companies Make the Leap . . . and Others Don't*, asserts that most businesspeople are not evil exploiters. Rather, the current crop of CEOs contains many "conscious opportunists"—individuals who deliberately seize an opportunity to get rich quick at the expense of others. Collins believes that more regulatory oversight and enforcement can stop the worst offenders. However, his research has convinced him that greatness springs from a unique decision-making process. "[The greatest company builders] did not craft their strategies principally in reaction to the competitive landscape or in response to external conditions and shocks. . . . The fundamental drive to transform and build their companies was internal and creative. . . . In contrast, the mediocre company leaders displayed a pattern of lurching and thrashing, running about in frantic reaction to threats and opportunities."

Case Questions

1. Describe the decision-making conditions that corporate CEOs face today. What are some probable consequences of their having to make decisions under these conditions?
2. What behavioral aspects of decision making are illustrated in this case? Does the presence of behavioral factors increase or decrease the effectiveness of decision making by CEOs? Why?
3. Over the last decade, investors and boards have played an increasingly important role in making corporate strategic decisions. Now it seems that in the near future, regulators may also play a greater role. In what ways does increasing participation by adding more group members enhance effective decision making? In what ways does it detract from effective decision making?

Case References

Jerry Useem, "From Heroes to Goats . . . and Back Again?" *Fortune*, November 3, 2002, www.fortune.com on January 10, 2003; Keith H. Hammonds and Jim Collins, "The Secret Life of the CEO," *Fast Company*, October 2002, pp. 81–94 (quote p. 105); "The Best (& Worst) Managers of the Year," *Business-Week*, January 13, 2003, pp. 58–92; Jim Collins, "The 10 Greatest CEOs of All Time," *Fortune*, July 21, 2003, pp. 54–68.

LEARNING OBJECTIVE REVIEW

Online Study Center
Improve Your Grade
–Learning Objective Review
–Audio Chapter Review
–Study Guide to Go

Online Study Center
ACE the Test
Audio Chapter Quiz

1 ▶ *Define decision making, discuss types of decisions, and describe decision-making conditions.*

- Decision making, perhaps the most crucial part of the planning process, is the act of choosing one alternative from among a set of alternatives.
- The decision-making process includes
  recognizing and defining the nature of a
  decision situation
  identifying alternatives
  choosing the "best" alternative
  putting the choice into practice

- Two common types of decisions are
  programmed decisions
  nonprogrammed decisions
- Decisions may be made under the states of
  certainty   risk
  uncertainty

2 *Discuss rational perspectives on decision making, including the steps involved.*

- Rational perspectives on decision making rest on the classical model, which assumes that managers have complete information and that they will behave rationally.

- The primary steps in rational decision making are
  recognizing and defining the situation
  identifying alternatives
  evaluating alternatives
  selecting the best alternative
  implementing the chosen alternative
  following up and evaluating the effectiveness of the alternative after it is implemented

3 *Describe the behavioral aspects of decision making, including the administrative model, political forces, intuition and escalation of commitment, risk, and ethics as they relate to making decisions.*

- Behavioral aspects of decision making rely on the administrative model, which recognizes that managers will have incomplete information and that they will not always behave rationally.

- The administrative model also recognizes the concepts of bounded rationality and satisficing.

- Political activities by coalitions, managerial intuition, and the tendency to become increasingly committed to a chosen course of action all play a role.

- Risk propensity is also an important behavioral aspect of decision making.

- Ethics affects how managers make decisions.

4 *Discuss group and team decision making, including its advantages and disadvantages and how it can be more effectively managed.*

- To help enhance decision-making effectiveness, managers often use
  interacting groups and teams
  Delphi groups
  nominal groups

- Group and team decision making in general has several advantages, as well as certain disadvantages, compared to individual decision making. Managers can adopt a number of strategies to help groups and teams make better decisions.

Online Study Center **RESOURCES**

Prepare for Class, Improve Your Grade, and ACE the Test. These Student Achievement resources include:

ACE Practice Tests	Interactive Skills Assessments	Study Guide to Go
End of Chapter Exercises	Knowledgebank	Video Segments
Glossaries (visual and print)	Reviews (audio and print)	Summaries/Outlines
Flashcards		

To access these learning and study tools, go to: **college.hmco.com/pic/griffinSAS**

Pret A Manger, a growing "fast-casual" restaurant chain, has found a lucrative niche for itself.

1. *Discuss the nature of entrepreneurship.*

2. *Describe the role of entrepreneurship in society, including job creation, innovation, and the importance of entrepreneurship to big business.*

3. *Understand the major issues involved in choosing strategies for small firms, such as choosing an industry, emphasizing distinctive competencies, and writing a business plan, as well as the role of international management in entrepreneurship.*

4. *Discuss the structural challenges unique to entrepreneurial firms, most notably issues associated with starting and financing a new business, sources of management advice, and franchising.*

> *"We said, 'We're going to do it our way and see what happens.'"*
> —Andrew Rolfe, CEO, Pret A Manger

Chapter Outline

Online Study Center
Prepare for Class
Chapter Outline

5 ▶ *Understand the determinants of the performance of small firms, including trends in small-business start-ups and common reasons for failure and success.*

Prospecting for Sandwiches

You are hungry. You stop for a fast-food snack. You step into a clean, attractive shop. Along one wall, sandwiches such as Smoked Salmon on Baguette and Indian Spicy Chicken Tikka. Other offerings: yogurt parfaits, freshly squeezed juices, sushi. Homemade cookies and cakes, espresso, Earl Grey tea. You choose, pay, and leave the store, all in just ninety seconds. Yes, this is not your typical "burger-in-a-box" meal. It is Pret A Manger, French for "ready to eat," the name of a British chain that is revolutionizing fast food. Or perhaps spawning a new industry. The term *fast-casual* has been coined to refer to restaurants that fall in the middle ground between traditional fast food and a full-service, sit-down, menu-and-a-waiter dining experience.

At Pret A Manger, the focus is on the food. The company was started in 1986 by two Englishmen, Sinclair Beecham and Julian

Online Study Center
Improve Your Grade
—Flashcards
—Glossary

You should be able to define and use terms that are part of the practicing manager's vocabulary, as well as those that are integral in the language of management.

Metcalfe, who were disenchanted with the unimaginative offerings at London's sandwich shops. To ensure quality, every item is made fresh every morning, at the location where it will be sold. Ingredients are top quality, such as hand-picked fresh basil and homemade mayonnaise. When Chinese crawfish were unavailable, Pret A Manger did not settle for lesser-quality seafood. Instead, it substituted fresh Canadian shrimp. An obsession with quality has led to thirty-three revisions of the firm's brownie recipe. The wall of a Pret A Manger shop in Cambridge states, "A racehorse that runs a mile a few seconds faster is worth twice as much. That little extra proves to be the greatest value." At the end of each day, unsold food is donated to charities that feed the homeless.

Certainly, another important aspect of any retail outlet's success is customer service, and Pret A Manger has adopted a unique approach. In a sharp departure from industry practice, the firm offers no training in customer service, no scripts to follow, no quotas or repetitive tasks. It simply hires enthusiastic people and then lets them do their thing. The company has been named one of the top ten places to work in Europe thanks to a friendly, casual atmosphere—and weekly "pub nights" for all employees probably helped, too. Diversity is high, with less than one-third of its employees of British extraction, and the workforce is also very young: 38 percent of employees are less than twenty-five years old. Every executive spends one day each quarter in stores, making sandwiches and serving coffee. Every worker is given the cell phone number of all Pret A Manger managers, including CEO Andrew Rolfe. Workers can earn Tiffany silver stars for good service and up to $1,500 for suggestions.

Pret A Manger is breaking the fast-food mold in other ways, too. Rolfe says, "We don't believe in focus groups, research, or advertising. We have a very simple principle: If it doesn't take, we stop selling it." As the chain has grown from a single store to 130, consistency has been a key concern. The company has steadfastly refused to consider franchising and has limited growth to no more than 40 new stores annually.

The chain is expanding slowly in the United States, with 10 stores in New York City, but the concept may be "too British." Premade food is essential to the store's business model, because it enables customers to buy quickly, but Americans prefer a custom sandwich. Rolfe remembers seeing workers in New York look at the queue outside a deli, check the time on their watch, and then walk on. He knew then that Pret A Manger could be a success, in spite of its unorthodox approach. "Before we came, everybody we spoke to who is from New York said, 'Americans want to go to their deli and have their sandwich their way,'" Rolfe recollects. "We said, 'We're going to do it our way and see what happens.'"

In an ironic twist, McDonald's purchased 33 percent of Pret A Manger in 2001. The company is quick to distance itself from the burger maker, and so far, McDonald's seems content to let Pret A Manger operate independently. Rolfe admits that maintaining the firm's distinctiveness will be challenging. Yet he feels certain that the firm can hold on to its values and do what is right, saying, "There's no reason I would allow anything to change that."[1]

Just like Sinclair Beecham and Julian Metcalfe, thousands of people all over the world start new businesses each year. Some of these businesses, like Pret A Manger, succeed; unfortunately, many others fail. Some of the people who fail in a new business try again, and sometimes it takes two or more failures before a successful business gets under way. Henry Ford, for example, went bankrupt twice before succeeding with Ford Motor Company.

This process of starting a new business, sometimes failing and sometimes succeeding, is part of what is called "entrepreneurship," the subject of this chapter. We begin by exploring the nature of entrepreneurship. Next we examine the role of entrepreneurship in the business world and discuss strategies for entrepreneurial organizations. We then describe the structure and performance of entrepreneurial organizations.

THE NATURE OF ENTREPRENEURSHIP

▶ **1** ▶ *Discuss the nature of entrepreneurship.*

Entrepreneurship is the process of planning, organizing, operating, and assuming the risk of a business venture. An **entrepreneur** is someone who engages in entrepreneurship. Sinclair Beecham and Julian Metcalfe, as highlighted in our opening incident, fit this description. They put their own resources on the line and had a personal stake in the success or failure of Pret A Manger. Business owners who hire professional managers to run their businesses and then turn their attention to other interests are not true entrepreneurs. Although they are assuming the risk of the venture, they are not actively involved in organizing or operating it. Likewise, professional managers whose job is running someone else's business are not entrepreneurs, for they have a less-than-total personal stake in the success or failure of the business.

Entrpreneurs start new businesses. We define a **small business** as one that is privately owned by one individual or a small group of individuals and has sales and assets that are not large enough to influence its environment. A small, two-person software development company with annual sales of $100,000 would clearly be a small business, whereas Microsoft Corporation is just as clearly a large business. But the boundaries are not always this clear-cut. For example, a regional retailing chain with twenty stores and annual revenues of $30 million may sound large, but it is really very small compared to such giants as Wal-Mart and Sears.

entrepreneurship   The process of planning, organizing, operating, and assuming the risk of a business venture.

entrepreneur   Someone who engages in entrepreneurship.

small business   A business that is privately owned by one individual or a small group of individuals and has sales and assets that are not large enough to influence its environment.

True or False?

_____ 1. Jeffery Immelt, CEO of GE, is an entrepreneur.

Multiple Choice

_____ 2. Which of the following is NOT part of entrepreneurship?
   a. Planning
   b. Operating
   c. Turning management over to a professional
   d. Assuming financial risk
   e. Assuming total personal risk for success or failure

_____ 3. A small business is defined as _____.
   a. sales less than $1,000,000
   b. less than 20 stores
   c. one not large enough to influence its environment
   d. fewer than 100 employees
   e. revenue less than $1,000,000

Online Study Center
ACE the Test
ACE Practice Tests 5.1

THE ROLE OF ENTREPRENEURSHIP IN SOCIETY

2 ▶ *Describe the role of entrepreneurship in society, including job creation, innovation, and the importance of entrepreneurship to big business.*

The history of entrepreneurship and of the development of new businesses is in many ways the history of great wealth and of great failure. Some entrepreneurs have been very successful and have reaped vast fortunes from their entrepreneurial efforts. For example, Bill Gates, founder of Microsoft Corporation, is the richest person in the United States and one of the richest in the world.[2] Many more entrepreneurs, however, have lost a great deal of money. Research suggests that the majority of new businesses fail within the first few years of their founding.[3] Many that last longer do so only because the entrepreneurs themselves work long hours for very little income.

As Figure 5.1 shows, most U.S. businesses employ fewer than 100 people, and most U.S. workers are employed by small firms. For example, Figure 5.1(a) shows that 86.7 percent of all U.S. businesses employ 20 or fewer people; another 11 percent employ between 20 and 99 people. In contrast, only about one-tenth of 1 percent employ 1,000 or more workers. Figure 5.1(b) shows that 25.6 percent of all U.S. workers are employed by firms with fewer than 20 people; another 29.1 percent work in firms that employ between 20 and 99 people. The vast majority of these companies are owner operated.[4] Figure 5.1(b) also shows that 12.7 percent of U.S. workers are employed by firms with a total of 1,000 or more employees.

On the basis of numbers alone, then, small business is a strong presence in the U.S. economy, and this is true in virtually all of the world's mature economies. In Germany, for example, companies with fewer than five hundred employees produce two-thirds of the nation's gross national product, train nine of ten apprentices, and employ four of every five workers. Small businesses also play major roles in the economies of Italy, France, and Brazil. In addition, experts agree that small businesses will be quite important in the emerging economies of countries such as Russia and Vietnam. The contribution of small business can be measured in terms of its effects on key aspects of an economic system. In the United States, these aspects include job creation, innovation, and importance to big business.

FIGURE 5.1

The Importance of Small Business in the United States

Over 86 percent of all U.S. businesses have no more than twenty employees. The total number of people employed by these small businesses is approximately one-fourth of the entire U.S. workforce. Another 29 percent work for companies with fewer than one hundred employees. U.S. Census Bureau, *Statistical Abstract of the United States: 2002* (122nd edition), Washington, DC, 1999.

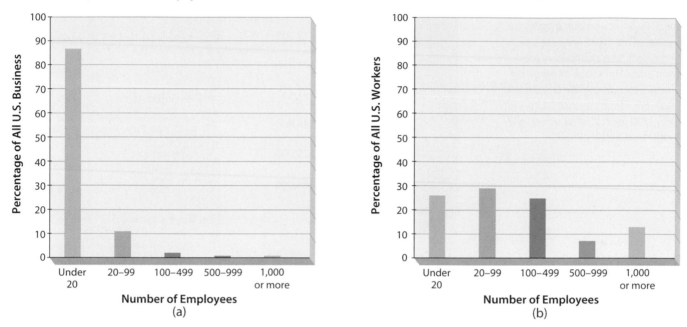

Job Creation

Small business—especially in certain industries—is an important source of new (and often well-paid) jobs in the United States. According to the Small Business Administration (SBA), for example, seven of the ten industries that added the most new jobs are currently in sectors dominated by small businesses. Moreover, small businesses currently account for 38 percent of all jobs in high-technology sectors of the economy.[5] Note that new jobs are also being created by small firms specializing in international business. Indeed, according to the SBA, small businesses account for 96 percent of all U.S. exporters.[6]

Although small businesses certainly create many new jobs each year, the importance of entrepreneurial big businesses in job creation should not be overlooked. Although big businesses cut thousands of jobs in the late 1980s and early 1990s, the booming U.S. economy resulted in large-scale job creation in many larger businesses beginning in the mid-1990s. But this trend was reversed in recent years, as many larger companies began to downsize once again. Figure 5.2 details the changes in the numbers of jobs at sixteen large U.S. companies between 1993 and 2002. As you can see, General Motors eliminated 385,000 jobs, General Mills 91,437, and Kmart 124,000. Wal-Mart alone, however, created 949,000 new jobs during the same period.

The reality, then, is that jobs are created by entrepreneurial companies of all sizes, all of which hire workers and all of which lay them off. Small firms often hire more rapidly than large ones, and they are also likely to eliminate jobs at a far higher rate. Small firms are also the first to hire in times of economic recovery, whereas large firms are the last. Conversely, however, big companies are the last to lay off workers during economic downswings.

CONCEPT CHECK 5.1

Describe the similarities and differences between entrepreneurial firms and large firms in terms of their job creation.

FIGURE 5.2

Representative Jobs Created and Lost by Big Business, 1993–2002

All businesses create and eliminate jobs. Because of their size, the magnitude of job creation and elimination is especially pronounced in bigger businesses. This figure provides several representative examples of job creation and elimination at many big U.S. businesses during the last decade. For example, while General Motors cut 385,000 jobs, Wal-Mart created 949,000 during this period.

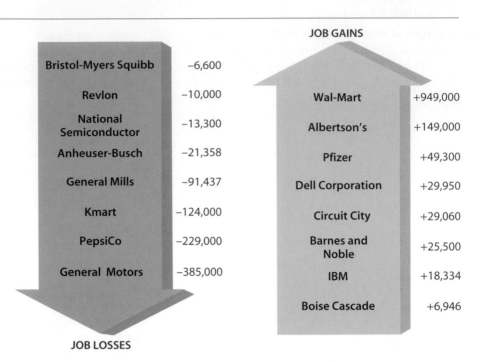

JOB LOSSES	
Bristol-Myers Squibb	–6,600
Revlon	–10,000
National Semiconductor	–13,300
Anheuser-Busch	–21,358
General Mills	–91,437
Kmart	–124,000
PepsiCo	–229,000
General Motors	–385,000

JOB GAINS	
Wal-Mart	+949,000
Albertson's	+149,000
Pfizer	+49,300
Dell Corporation	+29,950
Circuit City	+29,060
Barnes and Noble	+25,500
IBM	+18,334
Boise Cascade	+6,946

Innovation

History has shown that major innovations are as likely to come from small businesses (or individuals) as from big businesses. For example, small firms and individuals invented the personal computer and the stainless steel razor blade, the transistor radio and the photocopying machine, the jet engine and the self-developing photograph. They also gave us the helicopter and power steering, automatic transmissions and air conditioning, cellophane, and the 19-cent ballpoint pen. Today, says the SBA, small businesses supply 55 percent of all "innovations" introduced into the American marketplace.[7]

Not surprisingly, history is repeating itself infinitely more rapidly in the age of computers and high-tech communication. For example, much of today's most innovative software is being written at new start-up companies. Yahoo! and Netscape brought the Internet into the average American living room, and online companies such as Amazon.com and eBay are using it to redefine our shopping habits. Each of these firms started out as a small business.

Importance to Big Business

Most of the products made by big manufacturers are sold to consumers by small businesses. For example, the majority of dealerships selling Fords, Chevrolets, Toyotas, and Volvos are independently owned and operated. Moreover, small businesses provide big businesses with many of the services, supplies, and raw materials they need. Likewise, Microsoft relies heavily on small businesses in the course of its routine business operations. For example, the software giant outsources much of its routine code-writing functions to hundreds of sole proprietorships and other small firms. It also outsources much of its packaging, delivery, and distribution to smaller companies. Dell Computer uses this same strategy, buying most of the parts and components used in its computers from small suppliers around the world.

True or False?

_____ 1. Small businesses are generally the first to hire during economic growth and the first to fire during economic slowdowns.

_____ 2. Dell Computer is essentially a computer assembler. It contracts most of its supplies from numerous vendors. Small business is integral to Dell's success.

Online Study Center
ACE the Test
ACE Practice Tests 5.2

Multiple Choice

_____ 3. The majority of workers in the United States are employed by companies with how many employees?
    a. Less than 20   d. Less than 1,000
    b. Less than 100   e. More than 1,000
    c. Less than 500

_____ 4. Major innovations are likely to come from _____.
    a. small business
    b. large business
    c. global business
    d. small and big business
    e. big and global business

STRATEGY FOR ENTREPRENEURIAL ORGANIZATIONS

3 ▶ *Understand the major issues involved in choosing strategies for small firms, such as choosing an industry, emphasizing distinctive competencies, and writing a business plan, as well as the role of international management in entrepreneurship.*

Would-be entrepreneurs can increase their chances of success by identifying a niche or potential market that no other business is serving. Consider, for instance, the success enjoyed by Boston entrepreneur Chris Murphy. He knew that some dog owners felt that they faced the same day-care problems experienced by parents of small children. In response, he started The Common Dog, a service that picks dogs up on a school bus, takes them to a day-kennel while their owners work, and drops them off at the end of the day. The service costs the dog owners $325 a month. At the kennel, the dogs enjoy their own small swimming pool, several lounging couches, and frequent walks. They do, however, have to bring their own lunches!

One of the most basic challenges facing an entrepreneurial organization is choosing a strategy. The three strategic challenges facing small firms, in turn, are choosing an industry in which to compete, emphasizing distinctive competencies, and writing a business plan.[8]

Choosing an Industry

Not surprisingly, small businesses are more common in some industries than in others. The major industry groups that include successful new ventures and small businesses are services, retailing, construction, financial and insurance, wholesaling, transportation, and manufacturing. In general, the more resources an industry requires, the harder it is to start a business and the less likely that the industry is dominated by small firms. Remember, too, that *small* is a relative term: The criteria (number of employees and total annual sales) differ from industry to industry and are often meaningful only when compared with businesses that are truly large.

▌ *Service businesses* are the fastest-growing segment of small-business enterprises because they require few resources. In addition, no other industry group offers

Entrepreneurs are always on the alert for new business opportunities. In recent years there has been a consistent trend toward online business activity, especially in the retailing sector. Of course, as shown here, if a trend goes too far, new opportunities can be created in the market space vacated by the trend followers.

Online Study Center
Improve Your Grade
Career Snapshot 5.1

a higher return on time invested. Finally, services appeal to the talent for innovation typified by many small enterprises.

Small-business services range from shoeshine parlors to car rental agencies, from marriage counseling to computer software, from accounting and management consulting to professional dog walking. In Dallas, for example, Jani-King has prospered by selling commercial cleaning services to local companies. In Virginia Beach, Virginia, Jackson Hewitt Tax Services has found a profitable niche in providing computerized tax preparation and electronic tax-filing services. Great Clips, Inc., is a fast-growing family-run chain of hair salons headquartered in Minneapolis.

▌ A *retail business* sells directly to consumers products that are manufactured by other firms. There are hundreds of different kinds of retailers, ranging from wig shops and frozen yogurt stands to automobile dealerships and department stores. Usually, however, people who start small businesses favor specialty shops—for example, big-men's clothing or gourmet coffees—which let them focus limited resources on narrow market segments. Retailing accounts for 22.7 percent of all businesses with fewer than twenty employees. John Mackey, for example, launched Whole Foods out of his own frustration at being unable to find a full range of natural foods at other stores. He soon found, however, that he had tapped a lucrative market and started an ambitious expansion program. Today, with over ninety outlets in twenty states and Washington, DC, Whole Foods is the largest natural-foods retailer in the United States, three times larger than its biggest competitor.[9]

▌ *Construction* involves about 10 percent of businesses with fewer than twenty employees. Because many construction jobs are relatively small, local projects, local construction firms are often ideally suited as contractors. Many such firms are begun by skilled craftspeople who start out working for someone else and subsequently decide to work for themselves. Common examples of small construction firms include home builders, wood finishers, roofers, painters, and plumbing, electrical, and roofing contractors. For example, Marek Brothers Construction in College Station, Texas, was started by two brothers, Pat and Joe Marek. They originally worked for other contractors but started their own partnership in 1980. Their only employee is a receptionist. They manage various construction projects, including new-home construction and remodeling, subcontracting out the actual work to other businesses or to individual craftspeople. Marek Brothers has annual gross income of about $5 million.

▌ *Finance and insurance businesses* also account for about 10 percent of all firms with fewer than twenty employees. In most cases, these businesses are either affiliates of larger, national firms or sell products provided by such firms. Although the deregulation of the banking industry has reduced the number of small local banks, other businesses in this sector are still doing quite well. Typically, for example, local State Farm Mutual offices are small businesses. State

Farm itself is a major insurance company, but its local offices are run by 16,500 independent agents. In turn, agents hire their own staff, run their own offices as independent businesses, and so forth. They sell various State Farm insurance products and earn commissions from the premiums paid by their clients. Some local savings and loan operations, mortgage companies, and pawn shops also fall into this category.

■ *Wholesaling* is not generally tackled by small-business owners; however, about 8 percent of businesses with fewer than twenty employees are wholesalers. A whole-sale business buys products from manufacturers or other producers and then sells them to retailers. Wholesalers usually buy goods in bulk and store them in quantity at locations that are convenient for retailers to access. For a given volume of business, therefore, they need fewer employees than manufacturers, retailers, or service pro-viders. Luis Espinoza has found a promising niche for Inca Quality Foods, a midwestern wholesaler that imports and distributes Latino foods for consumers from Mexico, the Caribbean, and Central America. Partnered with the large grocery store chain Kroger, Espinoza's firm continues to grow steadily.[10]

■ *Transportation and transportation-related businesses* account for about 5 percent of all companies with fewer than twenty employees. Such firms include local taxi and limousine companies, charter airplane services, and tour operators. In addition, in many smaller markets, bus com-panies and regional airlines subcontract local equipment maintenance to small businesses. Consider, for example, some of the transportation-related small businesses at a ski resort such as Steamboat Springs, Colorado. Most visi-tors fly to the town of Hayden, about fifteen miles from Steamboat Springs. Although some visitors rent vehi-cles, many others use the services of Alpine Taxi, a small local operation, to transport them to their destinations in Steamboat Springs. While on vacation, they also rely on the local bus service, which is subcontracted by the town to another small business, to get to and from the ski slopes each day. Other small businesses offer van tours of the region, hot-air balloon rides, and helicopter lifts to remote areas for extreme skiers. Still others provide main-tenance support at Hayden for Continental, American, and United aircraft that serve the area during ski season.

■ *Manufacturing*, more than any other industry, lends itself to big business—and for good reason. Because of the investment normally required in equipment, energy, and raw materials, a good deal of money is usually needed to start a manufacturing business. Automobile manufactur-ing, for example, calls for billions of dollars of investment and thousands of workers before the first automobile rolls

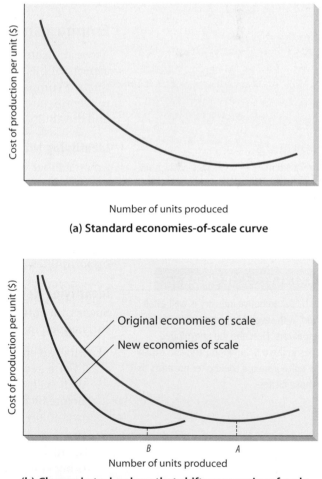

FIGURE 5.3

Economies of Scale in Small-Business Organizations

Small businesses sometimes find it difficult to compete in man-ufacturing-related industries because of the economies of scale associated with plant, equipment, and technology. As shown in (a), firms that produce a large number of units (that is, larger businesses) can do so at a lower per-unit cost. However, new forms of technology occasionally cause the economies-of-scale curve to shift, as illustrated in (b), where smaller firms may be able to compete more effectively because of the drop in per-unit manufacturing cost.

(a) Standard economies-of-scale curve

(b) Change in technology that shifts economies of scale and may make small-business production possible

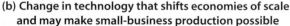

off the assembly line. Obviously, such requirements shut out most individuals. Although Henry Ford began with $28,000, it has been a long time since anyone started a new U.S. car company from scratch.

This is not to say that there are no small-business owners who do well in manufacturing—about 5 percent of businesses with fewer than twenty employees are involved in some aspect of manufacturing. Indeed, it is not uncommon for small manufacturers to outperform big business in such innovation-driven industries as chemistry, electronics, toys, and computer software. Some small manufacturers prosper by locating profitable niches. For example, brothers Dave and Dan Hanlon and Dave's wife Jennie recently started a new motorcycle-manufacturing business called Excelsior-Henderson. (Excelsior and Henderson are actually names of classic motorcycles from the early years of the twentieth century; the Hanlons acquired the rights to these brand names because of the images they evoke among motorcycle enthusiasts.) The Hanlons started by building 4,000 bikes in 1999 and will soon have annual production of 20,000 per year. So far, Excelsior-Henderson motorcycles have been well received (the top-end Excelsior-Henderson Super X sells for about $18,000), and many Harley-Davidson dealers have started to sell these models as a means of diversifying their product lines.[11]

Emphasizing Distinctive Competencies

As we indicate in Chapter 3, an organization's distinctive competencies are the aspects of business that the firm performs better than its competitors. The distinctive competencies of small business usually fall into three areas: the ability to identify new niches in established markets, the ability to identify new markets, and the ability to move quickly to take advantage of new opportunities.

Identifying Niches in Established Markets

An **established market** is one in which several large firms compete on the basis of relatively well-defined criteria. A **niche** is simply a segment of a market that is not currently being exploited. In general, small entrepreneurial businesses are better at discovering these niches than are larger organizations. Large organizations usually have so many resources committed to older, established business practices that they may be unaware of new opportunities. Entrepreneurs can see these opportunities and move quickly to take advantage of them.[12]

Identifying New Markets

Successful entrepreneurs also excel at discovering whole new markets. Discovery can happen in at least two ways.

1. First, an entrepreneur can transfer a product or service that is well established in one geographic market to a second market. This is what Marcel Bich did with ballpoint pens, which occupied a well-established market in Europe before Bich introduced them to the United States. Bich's company, Société Bic, eventually came to dominate the U.S. market.

2. Second, entrepreneurs can sometimes create entire industries. Entrepreneurial innovations such as Yahoo! and Google have spawned the development of other companies and jobs. Again, because entrepreneurs are not encumbered with a history of doing business in a particular way, they are usually better at discovering new markets than are larger, more mature organizations.

CONCEPT CHECK 5.2

What characteristics make an industry attractive to entrepreneurs? Based on these characteristics, which industry would you choose? Why?

---

established market A market in which several large firms compete according to relatively well-defined criteria.

niche A segment of a market not currently being exploited.

CONCEPT CHECK 5.3

The U.S. automotive industry is well established, with several large and many small competitors. Describe the unexploited niches in the U.S. auto industry, and explain how entrepreneurs could offer products that fill those niches.

Exploiting First-Mover Advantages

A **first-mover advantage** is any advantage that comes to a firm because it exploits an opportunity before any other firm does. Sometimes large firms discover niches within existing markets or new markets at just about the same time that small entrepreneurial firms do, but they often are not able to move as quickly as small companies to take advantage of these opportunities. There are two fundamental reasons for this difference.

1. Many large organizations make decisions slowly because each of their many layers of hierarchy has to approve an action before it can be implemented.

2. Large organizations may sometimes put a great deal of their assets at risk when they take advantage of new opportunities. Every time Boeing decides to build a new model of a commercial jet, it is making a decision that could literally bankrupt the company if it does not turn out well.

first-mover advantage Any advantage that comes to a firm because it exploits an opportunity before any other firm does.

Online Study Center
Improve Your Grade
Video Segment

Writing a Business Plan

Once an entrepreneur has chosen an industry to compete in and has determined which distinctive competencies to emphasize, these choices are usually included in a document called a business plan. In a **business plan**, the entrepreneur summarizes the business strategy and how that strategy is to be implemented. The very act of preparing a business plan forces prospective entrepreneurs to crystallize their thinking about what they must do to launch their business successfully and obliges them to develop their business on paper before investing time and money in it. The idea of a business plan is not new. What is new is the growing use of specialized business plans by entrepreneurs, mostly because creditors and investors demand such plans to use as they decide whether to help finance a small business.

business plan A document that summarizes the business strategy and structure.

The plan should describe the match between the entrepreneur's abilities and the requirements for producing and marketing a particular product or service. It should define strategies for production and marketing, legal aspects and organization, and accounting and finance. In particular, it should answer three questions:

Online Study Center
Improve Your Grade
Visual Glossary

1. What are the entrepreneur's goals and objectives?

2. What strategies will the entrepreneur use to achieve these goals and objectives?

3. How will the entrepreneur implement these strategies?

Business plans should also account for the sequential nature of much strategic decision making in small businesses. For example, entrepreneurs cannot forecast sales revenues without first researching markets. The sales forecast itself is one of the most important elements in the business plan. Without such forecasts, it is all but impossible to estimate

Entrepreneurship is becoming an increasingly big part of international business today. But while this trend is picking up steam, some firms have been successfully introducing their products to foreign markets for decades. The Dutch brewer Heineken, for instance, has been selling its flagship brand in the United States for almost one hundred years. And today it exports both its mainstream and niche products to more than 170 nations.

intelligently the size of a plant, store, or office or to determine how much inventory to carry or how many employees to hire.

Another important component of the overall business plan is financial planning, which translates all other activities into dollars. Generally, the financial plan is made up of a cash budget, an income statement, balance sheets, and a breakeven chart. The most important of these statements is the cash budget, because it tells entrepreneurs how much money they will need before they open for business and how much money they will need to keep the business operating.

Entrepreneurship and International Management

Finally, although many people associate international management with big business, many smaller companies are also finding expansion and growth opportunities in foreign countries. For example, Fuci Metals, a small but growing enterprise, buys metal from remote locations in areas such as Siberia and Africa and then sells it to big auto makers such as Ford and Toyota. Similarly, California-based Gold's Gym is expanding into foreign countries and has been especially successful in Russia.[13] And Markel Corporation, a small Philadelphia-based firm that manufactures tubing and insulated wiring, derives 40 percent of its annual revenues (currently around $26 million) from international sales.[14] Although such ventures are accompanied by considerable risks, they also afford entrepreneurs new opportunities and can be a real catalyst for success.

TEST PREPPER 5.3

ANSWERS CAN BE FOUND ON P. 441

True or False?

_____ 1. The service industry appeals to entrepreneurs because it has relatively low start-up cost, it offers a high return on time invested, and it appeals to those with a talent for innovation.

_____ 2. Robert Kiyosaki, known for his best-selling book *Rich Dad, Poor Dad*, created a board game *Cashflow* to complement his books. More than 300,000 copies of the game have sold for $195 each. Mr. Kiyosaki used his success in the publishing market to exploit a niche in the game market.

_____ 3. Amazon.com had a first-mover advantage over Barnes and Noble in online book retailing.

Multiple Choice

_____ 4. Which of the following industries is LEAST likely to have small-business success?
    a. Transportation   d. Construction
    b. Manufacturing   e. Wholesale
    c. Retail

_____ 5. Tim and Nina Zagat started the *Zagat New York City Restaurant Survey* more than 20 years ago. The *Zagat Surveys* now cover more than 45 cities and extend to hotels, resorts, and spas. Prior to the *Zagat Surveys*, there were food critiques available in newspapers and magazines, but the *Zagat Surveys* focused on helping consumers make a decision. Which of the following is NOT true about the *Zagat Surveys*?
    a. It used economy of scale
    b. It found a niche market
    c. It had a first-mover advantage
    d. It showed small-business innovation
    e. It had luck on its side

_____ 6. Economy of scale applies most to which industry?
    a. Transportation   d. Wholesale
    b. Retail   e. Manufacturing
    c. Construction

_____ 7. Healy Brothers is a dealership that sells automobiles. It competes in which industry?
    a. Transportation   d. Wholesale
    b. Retail   e. Manufacturing
    c. Construction

Online Study Center
ACE the Test
ACE Practice Tests 5.3

STRUCTURE OF ENTREPRENEURIAL ORGANIZATIONS

4 ▶ *Discuss the structural challenges unique to entrepreneurial firms, most notably issues associated with starting and financing a new business, sources of management advice, and franchising.*

With a strategy in place and a business plan in hand, the entrepreneur can then proceed to devise a structure that turns the vision of the business plan into a reality. Many of the same concerns in structuring any business, which are described in the next five chapters of this book, are also relevant to small businesses. For example, entrepreneurs need to consider organization design and develop job descriptions, organization charts, and management control systems.

The Internet, of course, is rewriting virtually all of the rules for starting and operating a small business. Getting into business is easier and faster than ever before, there are many more potential opportunities than at any other time in history, and the ability to gather and assimilate information is at an all-time high. Even so, would-be entrepreneurs must still make the right decisions when they start. They must decide, for example, precisely how to get into business. Should they buy an existing business or build from the ground up? In addition, would-be entrepreneurs must find appropriate sources of financing and decide when and how to seek the advice of experts.

Starting the New Business

An old Chinese proverb suggests that a journey of a thousand miles begins with a single step. This is also true of a new business. The first step is the individual's commitment to becoming a business owner. Next comes choosing the goods or services to be offered—a process that means investigating one's chosen industry and market. Making this choice also requires would-be entrepreneurs to assess not only industry trends but also their own skills. Like the managers of existing businesses, new business owners must also be sure that they understand the true nature of the enterprise in which they are engaged.

Buying an Existing Business

After choosing a product and making sure that the choice fits their own skills and interests, entrepreneurs must decide whether to buy an existing business or to start from scratch. Consultants often recommend the first approach. Quite simply, the odds are better: A successful existing business has already proved its ability to draw customers at a profit. It has also established working relationships with lenders, suppliers, and the community. Moreover, the track record of an existing business gives potential buyers a much clearer picture of what to expect than any estimate of a new business's prospects. Around 30 percent of the new businesses started in the past decade were bought from someone else. The McDonald's empire, for example, was started when Ray Kroc bought an existing hamburger business and then turned it into a global fast-food powerhouse. Likewise, Starbucks was a struggling mail-order business when Howard Schultz bought it and turned his attention to retail expansion.

Starting from Scratch

Some people, however, prefer the satisfaction that comes from planting an idea, nurturing it, and making it grow into a strong and sturdy business. There are also practical reasons to start a business from scratch. A new business does not suffer the ill effects of a prior owner's errors. The start-up owner is also free to choose lenders, equipment, inventories, locations, suppliers, and workers, unhindered by a predecessor's commitments and policies. Of the new businesses begun in the past decade, 64 percent were started from scratch.

Not surprisingly, though, the risks of starting a business from scratch are greater than those of buying an existing firm. Founders of new businesses can only make predictions and projections about their prospects. Success or failure thus depends heavily on identifying a genuine business opportunity—a product for which many customers will pay well but which is currently unavailable to them. To find openings, entrepreneurs must study markets and answer the following questions:

▮ Who are my customers?

▮ Where are they?

▮ At what price will they buy my product?

▮ In what quantities will they buy?

▮ Who are my competitors?

▮ How will my product differ from those of my competitors?

Online Study Center
Improve Your Grade
Knowledgebank 5.1

Finding answers to these questions is a difficult task even for large, well-established firms. But where can the new business owner get the necessary information? Other sources of assistance are discussed later in this chapter, but we briefly describe three of the most accessible here. For example, the best way to gain knowledge about a market is to work in it before going into business in it. For example, if you once worked in a bookstore and now plan to open one of your own, you probably already have some idea about the kinds of books people request and buy. Second, a quick scan of the local Yellow Pages or an Internet search will reveal many potential competitors, as will advertisements in trade journals. Personal visits to these establishments and websites can give you insights into their strengths and weaknesses. And third, studying magazines, books, and websites aimed specifically at small businesses can also be helpful, as can hiring professionals to survey the market for you.

Financing the New Business

Although the choice of how to start is obviously important, it is meaningless unless a new business owner can obtain the money to set up shop. Among the more common sources of funding are family and friends, personal savings, banks and similar lending institutions, investors, and government agencies. Lending institutions are more likely to help finance the purchase of an existing business than that of a new business because the risks are better understood. Individuals starting up new businesses, on the other hand, are more likely to have to rely on their personal resources.

▮ *Personal Resources.* According to a study by the National Federation of Independent Business, an owner's personal resources, not loans, are the most important source of money. Including money borrowed from friends and relatives, personal resources account for over two-thirds of all money invested in new small businesses and for one-half of that invested in the purchase of existing businesses.

▌ *Strategic Alliances.*   Strategic alliances are also becoming a popular method for financing business growth. When Steven and Andrew Grundy decided to launch an Internet CD-exchange business called Spun.com, they had very little capital and thus made extensive use of alliances with other firms. They partnered, for example, with wholesaler Alliance Entertainment Corp. as a CD supplier. Orders to Spun.com actually go to Alliance, which ships products to customers and bills Spun.com directly. This setup has allowed Spun.com to promote a vast inventory of labels without actually having to buy inventory. All told, the firm created an alliance network that has provided the equivalent of $40 million in capital.[15]

▌ *Lenders.*   Although banks, independent investors, and government loans all provide much smaller portions of start-up funds than the personal resources of owners, they are important in many cases. Getting money from these sources, however, requires some extra effort. Banks and private investors usually want to see formal business plans—detailed outlines of proposed businesses and markets, owners' backgrounds, and other sources of funding. Government loans have strict eligibility guidelines.

▌ *Venture Capital Companies.*   **Venture capital companies** are groups of small investors seeking to make profits on companies that have the potential for rapid growth. Most of these firms do not lend money: They invest it, supplying capital in return for stock. The venture capital company may also demand a representative on the board of directors. In some cases, managers may even need approval from the venture capital company before making major decisions. Of all venture capital currently committed in the United States, 29 percent comes from true venture capital firms.[16]

▌ *Small-Business Investment Companies.*   Taking a more balanced approach in their choices than venture capital companies, small-business investment companies (SBICs) seek profits by investing in companies with potential for rapid growth. Created by the Small Business Investment Act of 1958, SBICs are federally licensed to borrow money from the SBA and to invest it in or lend it to small businesses. They are themselves investments for their shareholders. Past beneficiaries of SBIC capital include Apple Computer, Intel, and FedEx. In addition, the government has recently begun to sponsor minority enterprise small-business investment companies (MESBICs). As the name suggests, MESBICs specialize in financing businesses that are owned and operated by members of minority groups.

▌ *SBA Financial Programs.*   Since its founding in 1953, the SBA has offered more than twenty financing programs to small businesses that meet certain criteria for size and independence. Eligible firms must also be unable to get private financing on reasonable terms. Because of these and other restrictions, SBA loans have never been a major source of small-business financing. In addition, budget cutbacks at the SBA have reduced the number of firms benefiting from loans. Nevertheless, several SBA programs currently offer funds to qualified applicants.

Financing a new business is a common struggle for many would-be entrepreneurs, but they should leave no stone unturned. Angie Reyes is shown here taking a break from serving breakfast burritos at her restaurant, La India Bonita Burritos, in Kyle, South Dakota. Reyes has been able to expand because of the Lakota Fund, which loans money to start-up and expanding businesses on the Pine Ridge Indian Reservation.

venture capital company   A group of small investors seeking to make profits on companies that have the potential for rapid growth.

CONCEPT CHECK 5.4

Entrepreneurs and small businesses play a variety of important roles in society. Given the importance of these roles, do you think that the government should do more to encourage the development of small business? Why or why not?

Sources of Management Advice

Financing is not the only area in which small businesses need help. Until World War II, for example, the business world involved few regulations, few taxes, few records, few big competitors, and no computers. Since then, simplicity has given way to complexity. Today, few entrepreneurs are equipped with all the business skills they need to survive. Small-business owners can no longer be their own troubleshooters, lawyers, bookkeepers, financiers, and tax experts. For these jobs, they rely on professional help. To survive and grow, however, small businesses also need advice regarding management. This advice is usually available from four sources: advisory boards, management consultants, the SBA, and a process called networking.

Online Study Center
Improve Your Grade
Career Snapshot 5.2

1. *Advisory Boards.* All companies, even those that do not legally need boards of directors, can benefit from the problem-solving abilities of advisory boards. Thus some small businesses create boards to provide advice and assistance. For example, an advisory board might help an entrepreneur determine the best way to finance a plant expansion or to start exporting products to foreign markets.

2. *Management Consultants.* Opinions vary widely about the value of management consultants—experts who charge fees to help managers solve problems. They often specialize in one area, such as international business, small business, or manufacturing. Thus they can bring an objective and trained outlook to problems and provide logical recommendations. They can be quite expensive, however; some consultants charge $1,000 or more for a day of assistance. Like other professionals, consultants should be chosen with care. They can be found through major corporations that have used their services and can provide references and reports on their work. Not surprisingly, they are most effective when the client helps (for instance, by providing schedules and written proposals for work to be done).

3. *The Small Business Administration.* Even more important than its financing role is the SBA's role in helping small-business owners improve their management skills. It is easy for entrepreneurs to spend money; SBA programs are designed to show them how to spend it wisely. The SBA offers small businesses four major management-counseling programs at virtually no cost.

    a. A small-business owner who needs help in starting a new business can get it free through the Service Corps of Retired Executives (SCORE). All SCORE members are retired executives, and all are volunteers. Under this program, the SBA tries to match the expert to the need. For example, if a small-business owner needs help putting together a marketing plan, the SBA will send a SCORE counselor with marketing expertise.

    b. Like SCORE, the Active Corps of Executives (ACE) program is designed to help small businesses that cannot afford consultants. The SBA recruits ACE volunteers from virtually every industry. All ACE volunteers are currently involved in successful activities, mostly as small-business owners themselves. Together, SCORE and ACE have more than 12,000 counselors working out of 350 chapters throughout the United States. They provide assistance to some 140,000 small businesses each year.

    c. The talents and skills of students and instructors at colleges and universities are fundamental to the Small Business Institute (SBI). Under the guidance of seasoned professors of business administration, students seeking advanced degrees work closely with small-business owners to help solve specific problems, such as sagging sales or rising costs. Students earn credit toward their degree, and their grade for that course depends on how well they handle a client's problems. Several hundred colleges and universities counsel thousands of small-business owners through this program every year.

d. Finally, the newest of the SBA's management counseling projects is its Small Business Development Center (SBDC) program. Begun in 1976, SBDCs are designed to consolidate information from various disciplines and institutions, including technical and professional schools. Then they make this knowledge available to new and existing small businesses. In 1995 universities in forty-five states took part in the program.

4. *Networking.*   More and more, small-business owners are discovering the value of networking—meeting regularly with one another to discuss common problems and opportunities and, perhaps most important, to pool resources. Businesspeople have long joined organizations such as the local chamber of commerce and the National Federation of Independent Businesses (NFIB) to make such contacts.

   In particular, women and minorities have found networking to be an effective problem-solving tool. The National Association of Women Business Owners (NAWBO), for example, provides a variety of networking forums. The NAWBO also has chapters in most major cities, where its members can meet regularly. Increasingly, women are relying on other women to help them locate venture capital, establish relationships with customers, and provide such essential services as accounting and legal advice. According to Patty Abramson of the Women's Growth Capital Fund, all of these tasks have traditionally been harder for women because, until now, they have never had friends in the right places. "I wouldn't say this is about discrimination," adds Abramson. "It's about not having the relationships, and business is about relationships."

Networking can prove to be a great source of management advice for entrepreneurs and managers alike. While most networking takes place at more traditional venues, nontraditional locations can also be useful. An Austin nightclub, for example, occasionally hosts a networking event for local businesspeople. These entrepreneurs are exchanging business cards as they discuss how they may be able to help one another.

Franchising

The next time you drive or walk around town, be on the alert for a McDonald's, Taco Bell, Subway, Denny's, or KFC restaurant; a 7-Eleven or Circle K convenience store; a RE/MAX or Coldwell Banker real estate office; a Super 8 or Ramada Inn motel; a Blockbuster Video store; a Sylvan Learning Center educational center; an Express Oil Change or Precision Auto Wash service center; or a Supercuts hair salon. What do these businesses have in common? In most cases, they will be franchised operations, operating under licenses issued by parent companies to local entrepreneurs who actually own and manage them.

CONCEPT CHECK 5.5

Recall the four different sources of advice for entrepreneurs. What type of information would an entrepreneur be likely to get from each source? What are the drawbacks or limitations of each source?

franchising agreement A contract between an entrepreneur (the franchisee) and a parent company (the franchiser); the entrepreneur pays the parent company for the use of its trademarks, products, formulas, and business plans.

As many would-be entrepreneurs have discovered, **franchising agreements** are an accessible doorway to business ownership. A franchise is an arrangement that permits the *franchisee* (buyer) to sell the product of the *franchiser* (seller, or parent company). Franchisees can thus benefit from the selling corporation's experience and expertise. They can also consult the franchiser for managerial and financial help.

For example, the franchiser may supply financing. It may pick the store location, negotiate the lease, design the store, and purchase necessary equipment. It may train the first set of employees and managers and provide standardized policies and procedures. Once the business is open, the franchiser may offer franchisees savings by allowing them to purchase from a central location. Marketing strategy (especially advertising) may also be handled by the franchiser. Finally, franchisees may benefit from continued management counseling. In short, franchisees receive—that is, invest in—not only their own ready-made business but also expert help in running it.

Franchises offer many advantages to both sellers and buyers. For example, franchisers benefit from the ability to grow rapidly by using the investment money provided by franchisees. This strategy has enabled giant franchisers such as McDonald's and Baskin-Robbins to mushroom into billion-dollar concerns. On the other hand, while people might assume that Starbucks coffee shops are franchised operations, in fact the corporation owns all its own stores in order to protect its quality standards.

For the franchisee, the arrangement combines the satisfaction of owning a business with the advantage of access to big-business management skills. Unlike the person who starts from scratch, the franchisee does not have to build a business step by step. Instead, the business is established virtually overnight. Moreover, because each franchise outlet is probably a carbon copy of every other outlet, the chances of failure are reduced. McDonald's, for example, is a model of consistency—Big Macs taste the same everywhere.

Of course, owning a franchise also involves certain disadvantages. Perhaps the most significant is the start-up cost. Franchise prices vary widely. Fantastic Sams hair salon franchise fees are $30,000, but a Gingiss Formalwear franchise can run as high as $125,000. Extremely profitable or hard-to-get franchises are even more expensive. A McDonald's franchise costs at least $650,000 to $750,000, and a professional sports team can cost several hundred million dollars. Franchisees may also have continued obligations to contribute percentages of sales to the parent corporation.

Buying a franchise also entails less tangible costs. For one thing, the small-business owner sacrifices some independence. A McDonald's franchisee cannot change the way its hamburgers or milkshakes are made. Nor can franchisees create an individual identity in their community; for all practical purposes, the McDonald's owner is anonymous. In addition, many franchise agreements are difficult to terminate.

Finally, although franchises minimize risks, they do not guarantee success. Many franchisees have seen their investments—and their dreams—disappear because of poor location, rising costs, or lack of continued franchiser commitment. Moreover, figures on failure rates are artificially low because they do not include failing franchisees bought out by their franchising parent companies. An additional risk is that the chain itself could collapse. In any given year, dozens—sometimes hundreds—of franchisers close shop or stop selling franchises.

ANSWERS CAN BE FOUND ON P. 44I

TEST PREPPER 5.4

True or False?

_____ 1. Eduardo wants to go into business for himself. He is more likely to have success starting from scratch than from buying an existing business.

_____ 2. Most loans to entrepreneurs come from venture capital companies.

_____ 3. As more U.S. consumers are becoming carbavoids, people who are on protein diets, market opportunities have developed. Subway commercials highlight wraps, a low-carbohydrate option. Subway franchisees are restricted by Subway marketing strategies.

Multiple Choice

_____ 4. A business plan should include all EXCEPT which of the following?
   a. Goals and objectives
   b. Strategies and structure
   c. Implementation
   d. Salary expectation
   e. Distinctive competencies

_____ 5. Which of the following is the most important source of financing for entrepreneurs?
   a. Personal resources
   b. Strategic alliances
   c. Lenders
   d. Venture capital companies
   e. SBIC

Online Study Center
ACE the Test
ACE Practice Tests 5.4

THE PERFORMANCE OF ENTREPRENEURIAL ORGANIZATIONS

5 ▷ *Understand the determinants of the performance of small firms, including trends in small-business start-ups and common reasons for failure and success.*

The formulation and implementation of an effective strategy play a major role in determining the overall performance of an entrepreneurial organization. This section examines how entrepreneurial firms evolve over time and the attributes of these firms that enhance their chances of success. For every Henry Ford, Walt Disney, Mary Kay Ash, and Bill Gates—people who transformed small businesses into major corporations—there are many small-business owners and entrepreneurs who fail.

Figure 5.4 illustrates recent trends in new business start-ups and failures. As you can see, between 1991 and 2000, new-business start-ups generally ran between around 150,000 and 180,000 per year, with 155,141 new businesses being launched in 1998. Over this same period, business failures generally ran between 50,000 and 100,000, with a total of 71,857 failing in 1998. In this section, we look first at a few key trends in small-business start-ups. Then we examine some of the main reasons for success and failure in small-business undertakings.

Trends in Small-Business Start-ups

Thousands of new businesses are started in the United States every year. Several factors account for this trend, and in this section we focus on four of them.

1. *Emergence of E-Commerce.* Clearly, one of the most significant recent trends in small-business start-ups is the rapid emergence of electronic commerce. Because the Internet has provided fundamentally new ways of doing business, savvy entrepreneurs have been able to create and expand new businesses more rapidly and more easily than ever before. Such leading-edge firms as America Online and eBay, for example, owe their very existence to the

FIGURE 5.4

Business Start-up Successes and Failures

Over the most recent ten-year period for which data are available, new-business start-ups numbered between 150,000 and 180,000 per year. Business failures during this same period ranged from about 50,000 to nearly 100,000 per year.

U.S. Census Bureau, *Statistical Abstract of the United States: 2002* (122nd edition), Washington, DC, 2002.

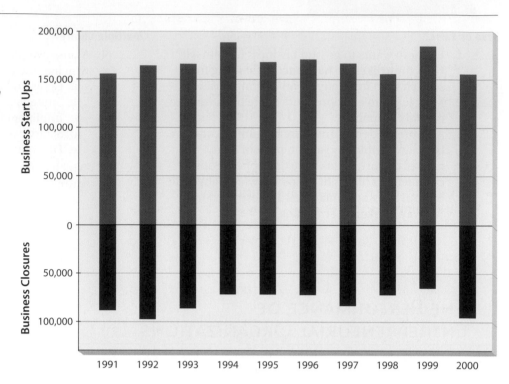

Internet. At the same time, however, many would-be Internet entrepreneurs went under in the last few years, as the so-called dot-com boom quickly faded. Figure 5.5 summarizes trends in online commerce from 1997 through 2001. In addition, one recent study reported that in 1999 the Internet economy grew overall by 62 percent over the previous year and provided jobs for 2.5 million people.[17]

2. *Crossovers from Big Business.* It is interesting to note that more and more businesses are being started by people who have opted to leave big corporations and put their experience and know-how to work for themselves. In some cases, these individuals see great new ideas they want to develop. Often, they get burned out working for a big corporation. Sometimes they have lost their job, only to discover that working for themselves was a better idea anyway.

3. *Opportunities for Minorities and Women.* In addition to big-business expatriates, minorities and women are starting more small businesses. For example, the number of African-American–owned businesses has increased by slightly more than 46 percent during the most recent five-year period for which data are available and now totals about 625,000. Chicago's Gardner family is just one of thousands of examples of this trend. The Gardners are the founders of Soft Sheen Products, a firm specializing in ethnic hair products. Soft Sheen attained sales of $80 million in the year before the Gardners sold it to France's L'Oréal S.A. for more than $160 million. The emergence of such opportunities is hardly surprising, either to African-American entrepreneurs or to the corporate marketers who have taken an interest in their companies. African-American purchasing power topped $575 billion in 2004. Up from just over $300 billion in 1990, that increase of 92 percent far outstrips the 78 percent increase experienced by all Americans.[18]

Latino-owned businesses have grown at an even faster rate of 76 percent and now number over 900,000. Other ethnic groups are also making their presence felt among U.S. business owners. Business ownership among Asians and Pacific Islanders has increased 56 percent, to over 600,000. Although the number of businesses owned by American Indians and Alaska Natives is still somewhat small, at slightly over 100,000, the total nevertheless represents a five-year increase of 93 percent.[19]

Likewise, the number of women-owned businesses is growing rapidly. There are now 9.1 million businesses owned by women—about 40 percent of all businesses in the United States. Combined, they generate nearly $4 trillion in revenue a year—an increase of 132 percent since 1992. The number of people employed nationwide at women-owned businesses since 1992 has grown to around 27.5 million—an increase of 108 percent.[20] Figure 5.6 summarizes the corporate backgrounds of women entrepreneurs and provides some insight into what they like about running their own businesses. Former corporate positions in general management (25 percent), sales (21 percent), and accounting and finance (18 percent) account for almost two-thirds of the women who start their own businesses. Once in charge of their own business, women also report that they like being their own boss, setting their own hours, controlling their own destiny, pleasing customers, having independence, making decisions, and achieving goals.

4. *Better Survival Rates.* Finally, more people are encouraged to test their skills as entrepreneurs because the failure rate among small businesses has been declining in recent years. During the 1960s and 1970s, for example, less than half of all new start-ups survived more than eighteen months; only one in five lasted ten years. Now, however, new businesses have a better chance of surviving. Of new businesses started in the 1980s, for instance, over 77 percent remained in operation for at least three years. Today, the SBA estimates that at least 40 percent of all new businesses can expect to survive for six years. For the reasons discussed in the next section, small businesses suffer a higher mortality rate than larger concerns. Among those that manage to stay in business for six to ten years, however, the survival rate levels off.

Reasons for Failure

Unfortunately, 63 percent of all new businesses will not celebrate a sixth anniversary. Why do some succeed and others fail? Although no set pattern has been established, four general factors contribute to the failure of new businesses.

1. One factor is managerial incompetence or inexperience. Some would-be entrepreneurs assume that they can succeed through common sense, overestimate their own managerial acumen, or think that hard work alone will spell success. But if managers do not know how to make basic business decisions

FIGURE 5.5

The Growth of Online Commerce

Online commerce is becoming an increasingly important part of the U.S. economy. As shown here, for example, online commerce grew from about $2.5 billion in 1997 to an estimated $17.4 billion by 2001. And most indicators suggest that this trend will continue.

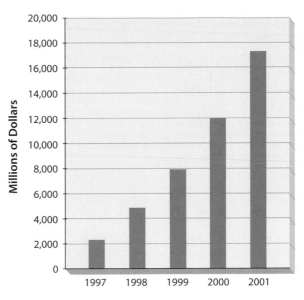

U.S. Census Bureau, *Statistical Abstract of the United States: 1999* (119th edition), Washington, DC, 1999.

FIGURE 5.6

Where Women Entrepreneurs Come from and What They Like About Their Work

Women entrepreneurs come from all sectors of large businesses, although management and sales are especially well represented. Women entrepreneurs indicate that they really like being their own boss, setting their own hours, controlling their own destiny, and being independent.

From *Wall Street Journal*, Eastern Edition (Staff Produced Copy Only) by Wall Street Journal. Copyright © 1999 by Dow Jones & Company, Inc. Reproduced with permission of Dow Jones & Company, Inc. in the format Textbook via Copyright Clearance Center.

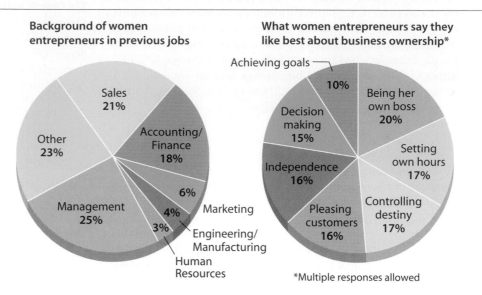

Background of women entrepreneurs in previous jobs

- Sales 21%
- Accounting/Finance 18%
- Other 23%
- Management 25%
- Marketing 6%
- Engineering/Manufacturing 4%
- Human Resources 3%

What women entrepreneurs say they like best about business ownership*

- Achieving goals 10%
- Being her own boss 20%
- Decision making 15%
- Setting own hours 17%
- Independence 16%
- Controlling destiny 17%
- Pleasing customers 16%

*Multiple responses allowed

or do not understand the basic concepts and principles of management, they are unlikely to be successful in the long run.

2. Neglect can also contribute to failure. Some entrepreneurs try either to launch their ventures in their spare time or to devote only a limited amount of time to a new business. But starting a new business requires an overwhelming time commitment. Entrepreneurs who are not willing to put in the time and effort that launching and running a business requires are unlikely to survive.

3. Third, weak control systems can lead to serious problems. Effective control systems are needed to keep a business on track and to help alert entrepreneurs to potential trouble. If control systems are not in place to signal impending problems, managers may be in serious trouble before more visible difficulties alert them.

4. Finally, insufficient capital can contribute to new-business failure. Some entrepreneurs are overly optimistic about how soon they will start earning profits. In most cases, however, it takes months or years before a business starts turning a profit. Amazon.com, for example, has still not earned a profit. Most experts say that a new business should have enough capital to operate for at least six months without earning a profit; some recommend enough to last a year.[21]

Reasons for Success

Similarly, four basic factors are typically cited to explain new-business success.

1. One factor is hard work, drive, and dedication. New-business owners must be committed to succeeding and be willing to put in the time and effort to make it happen. Gladys Edmunds, a single teen-age mother in Pittsburgh, washed laundry, made chicken dinners to sell to cab drivers, and sold fire extinguishers and Bibles door to door to earn money to launch her own business. Today, Edmunds Travel Consultants employs eight people and earns about $6 million in annual revenues.[22]

2. Careful analysis of market conditions can help new-business owners assess the probable reception of their products in the marketplace. This will provide insights about market demand for proposed products and services. Whereas attempts to expand local restaurants specializing in baked potatoes, muffins, and gelato have been largely unsuccessful, hamburger and pizza chains continue to have an easier time expanding into new markets.

3. Managerial competence also contributes to success. Successful new-business owners may acquire competence through training or experience or by drawing on the expertise of others. Few successful entrepreneurs succeed alone or straight out of college. Most spend time working in successful companies or partner with others in order to bring more expertise to a new business.

4. Finally, luck plays a role in the success of some firms. For example, after Alan McKim started Clean Harbors, an environmental cleanup firm based in New England, he struggled to keep his business afloat. Then the U.S. government committed $1.6 billion to toxic waste cleanup—McKim's specialty. He was able to get several large government contracts and put his business on solid financial footing. Had the government fund not been created at just the right time, McKim might well have failed.

CONCEPT CHECK 5.7

Find two entrepreneur-owned businesses in your community. In which industry does each business compete? Judging on the basis of the industry it is in, how do you rate each business's long-term chances for success? Explain your answers.

TEST PREPPER 5.5

ANSWERS CAN BE FOUND ON P. 441

True or False?

_____ 1. Small-business survival rates are better now than in the 1960s and 1970s.

_____ 2. Tight control systems can lead to serious problems in new businesses, because they limit entrepreneurs' responses to potential trouble.

_____ 3. A common path for successful entrepreneurs is to develop a business plan in college and implement it after graduation.

Multiple Choice

_____ 4. Maria joined the National Association of Women Business Owners. She went to a conference and met someone who helped her get venture capital for her business. Maria used which source of management advice?
   a. Management consultants
   b. Advisory board
   c. SBA
   d. Networking
   e. All of the above

_____ 5. Small businesses are increasingly started by whom?
   a. People leaving big business
   b. Minorities
   c. Women
   d. People who were laid off
   e. All of the above

Online Study Center
ACE the Test
ACE Practice Tests 5.5

BUILDING EFFECTIVE CONCEPTUAL SKILLS

Online Study Center
Improve Your Grade
Exercises: Building Effective Skills

Exercise Overview

Conceptual skills reflect the manager's ability to think in the abstract. This exercise will help you relate conceptual skills to entrepreneurship.

Exercise Background

Assume that you have made the decision to open a small business in the local community when you graduate (the community where you are attending college, not your home). Assume that you have funds to start a business without having to worry about finding other investors.

Without regard for market potential, profitability, or similar considerations, list five businesses that you might want to open and operate, solely on the basis of your personal interests. For example, if you enjoy bicycling, you might enjoy opening a shop that caters to cyclists.

Next, without regard for personal attractiveness, list five businesses that you might want to open and operate, solely on the basis of market opportunity. Use the Internet to help you determine which businesses might be profitable in your community, judging on the basis of factors such as population, local economic conditions, local competition, franchising opportunities, and so on.

Evaluate the prospects for success for each of the ten businesses.

Exercise Task

With this background information as context, do the following:

1. Form a small group with three or four classmates and discuss your respective lists. Look for instances where the same type of business appears on multiple lists. Also look for cases where the same business appears with similar or dissimilar prospects for success.

2. How important is personal interest in small-business success?

3. How important is market potential in small-business success?

EXPERIENTIAL EXERCISE

Negotiating a Franchise Agreement

Online Study Center
Improve Your Grade
—Exercises: Experiential Exercise
—Interactive Skills Self-Assessment

Step 1

Assume that you are the owner of a rapidly growing restaurant chain. In order to continue your current level of growth, you are considering the option of selling franchises for new restaurants. Working alone, outline the major points of most concern to you that you would want to have in a franchising agreement. Also note the characteristics you would look for in potential franchisees.

Step 2

Assume that you are an individual investor looking to buy a franchise in a rapidly growing restaurant chain. Again working alone, outline the major factors that might determine which franchise you elect to buy. Also note the characteristics you would look for in a potential franchiser.

Step 3

Now form small groups of four. Randomly select one member of the group to play the role of the franchiser; the other three members will play the roles of potential franchisees. Role-play a negotiation meeting. The franchiser should stick as closely as possible to the major points developed in step 1. Similarly, the potential franchisees should try to adhere to the points they developed in step 2.

Follow-up Questions

1. Did doing both step 1 and step 2 in advance help or hinder your negotiations?

2. Can a franchising agreement be so one-sided as to damage the interests of both parties? How so?

CLOSING CASE STUDY

Laughing All the Way to the Bank

Have you heard the one about the firm that bought laptops so employees could work while traveling—and then bolted the computers to the desks for security? Yes, this is a joke, published in the business-focused *Dilbert* cartoons, drawn by unlikely entrepreneur Scott Adams. But it is also a true story. Adams has found a way to channel the absurdity, frustration, and stress of working life into a productive outlet—the creation of cartoon strips based on his real-life experiences in corporate America.

"I cried because I did not have an office with a door, until I met a man who had no cubicle." Dilbert is the hottest cartoon strip around, carried in 2,000 papers in 65 countries. Scott Adams's comics have spawned 10 million copies of top-selling books, built one of the most-visited websites, and inspired an animated television show. The "hero" of the strip is Dilbert, the prototypical white-collar office worker. Dilbert is a technology geek, and other characters include secretaries, consultants, and bosses.

Scott Adams earned a bachelor's degree in economics and worked for a bank; then he obtained an M.B.A. in hopes of a promotion. "I made the observation that people who didn't have [an M.B.A.] got ahead much more slowly. I thought I was going to become a captain of industry, so I decided it would be good for my career." Adams joined Pacific Bell and began the invention of *Dilbert*. When *Dilbert*'s popularity took off and his corporate career stalled, Adams became a full-time cartoonist. He claims that the variety of jobs he has held led to his achievements, saying, "If I could pick one thing that contributed to my success, it was that I tried many things and I didn't quit."

Most artists sell their work to syndicates, so they have little contact with the comic-reading public. Adams knew this was a faulty model for customer feedback, thanks to his marketing expertise. So he was one of the first to put his e-mail address on every strip, enabling readers to send him hundreds of comments and suggestions daily. He was also one of the first to put *Dilbert* online (at www.dilbert.com).

Another important lesson from M.B.A. school was to identify his target market. Adams claims, "I could get

> *"I cried because I did not have an office with a door, until I met a man who had no cubicle."*
>
> —Dilbert,
> a cartoon character
> created by Scott Adams

people to do my marketing for me through the simple trick of mentioning different occupations in the strip. . . . I'd put an accountant in a strip, and people would cut it out and send a copy to all the accountants they knew. I kept using that technique, including each of the professions, until everyone on earth had been sent a Dilbert cartoon. It was a systematic approach to building the market."

Boss: *"Our policy is to employ only the best technical professionals."* Dilbert: *"Isn't it also our policy to base salaries on the industry average?"* Boss: *"Right. We like them bright but clueless."* Adams used his strip to skewer the incompetence he saw in every profession. "When I originally started drawing Dilbert, I was just writing a funny little comic about a guy who had a job that was a lot like mine. People read into it that workers were brilliant and bosses were stupid. But that's only half true—what I really thought was that everyone was stupid, including me." However, customer feedback altered his original intent. Adams continues, "But it was far more commercial to go with what people wanted. . . . I just did the math: For every boss there are about ten employees. Do you want to sell a product to one boss or to ten employees? I had to go with the ten-to-one advantage."

In Adams's unique philosophy, success is more about luck than about hard work, education, or talent. Adams advises others, "The capitalist system allows nine failures for every winner, so you're either one of the many people who will fail a few times and quit, or you're one of the few people who will keep trying and win. If all the people who quit had kept going, they would have been as successful as I have been with Dilbert."

Adams has a favorite strip, in which Wally, a classic slacker and underperformer, tells the pointy-haired boss, *"Over the past year, most of my co-workers have managed expensive projects that failed. I've done nothing but drink coffee. So on an economic basis that makes me your top performer. Watch and learn."* Advice to aspiring entrepreneurs: Watch Scott Adams and learn.

Case Questions

1. Read some *Dilbert* cartoons in a book or newspaper, or online at www.dilbert.com. What viewpoint is Adams expressing about work and careers? In your opinion, what impact did Adams's viewpoint have on his choice to leave a corporate job and become an entrepreneur?
2. What sources of information and expertise did Adams use in starting and developing his business? Did the start-up of the *Dilbert* cartoon follow the typical pattern of entrepreneurial start-ups? Why or why not?
3. Adams claims that his success is due primarily to luck and persistence. Do you agree or disagree? Do you think his advice is helpful to potential entrepreneurs? Why or why not?

Case References

"Biography of Scott Adams," "Frequently Asked Questions," Dilbert website, www.dilbert.com on December 20, 2005; Scott Adams, *The Dilbert Principle* (New York: HarperCollins, 1996); Scott Adams, *The Joy of Work* (New York: HarperCollins, 1999); "TV Newest Domain for Cultural Icon," *Scripps Howard News*, September/October 1998, www.scripps.com on January 15, 2003 (quote).

Learning Objective Review

Online Study Center
Improve Your Grade
–Learning Objective Review
–Audio Chapter Review
–Study Guide to Go

Online Study Center
ACE the Test
Audio Chapter Quiz

1 *Discuss the nature of entrepreneurship.*

- Entrepreneurship is the process of
  planning
  organizing
  operating
  assuming the risk of a business venture

- An entrepreneur is someone who engages in entrepreneurship and, in general, starts small businesses.

2 *Describe the role of entrepreneurship in society, including job creation, innovation, and the importance of entrepreneurship to big business.*

- Small businesses are an important source of innovation, create numerous jobs, and contribute to the success of large businesses.

3 *Understand the major issues involved in choosing strategies for small firms, such as choosing an industry, emphasizing distinctive competencies, and writing a business plan, as well as the role of international management in entrepreneurship.*

- In choosing strategies, entrepreneurs need to consider the characteristics of the industry in which they are going to conduct business; most small businesses are service or retail businesses.

- A small business must also emphasize its distinctive competencies when choosing its strategy.

- Small businesses are usually skilled at
  identifying niches in established markets
  identifying new markets
  acting quickly to obtain first-mover advantages

- Once an entrepreneur has chosen a strategy, the strategy is normally written down in a business plan to force the entrepreneur to plan thoroughly and to anticipate problems that might occur.

- Many small businesses are expanding internationally.

4 ▶ *Discuss the structural challenges unique to entrepreneurial firms, most notably issues associated with starting and financing a new business, sources of management advice, and franchising.*

- With a strategy and business plan in place, entrepreneurs must choose a structure to implement them; all of the structural issues summarized in the next five chapters of this book are relevant to the entrepreneur.

- The entrepreneur has some unique structural choices to make, including whether to buy an existing business or start a new one.

- In determining financial structure, an entrepreneur has to decide

  how much personal capital to invest in an organization
  whether to enter a strategic alliance
  how much bank and government support to obtain
  whether to encourage venture capital firms to invest

- Small businesses also need management help from advisory boards, management consultants, the SBA, and networking.

- Franchises allow small businesses to benefit from the help of the parent company, but they also have some disadvantages.

5 ▶ *Understand the determinants of the performance of small firms, including trends in small-business start-ups and common reasons for failure and success.*

- Several interesting trends today include the emergence of e-commerce, crossovers from big business, opportunities for minorities and women, and better survival rates.

- New businesses sometimes fail because of managerial incompetence, neglect, weak control systems, and insufficient capital.

- Success often depends on hard work, careful analysis of the market, managerial competence, and luck.

Online Study Center **RESOURCES**

Prepare for Class, Improve Your Grade, and ACE the Test. These Student Achievement resources include:

ACE Practice Tests	Interactive Skills Assessments	Study Guide to Go
End of Chapter Exercises	Knowledgebank	Video Segments
Glossaries (visual and print)	Reviews (audio and print)	Summaries/Outlines
Flashcards		

To access these learning and study tools, go to: **college.hmco.com/pic/griffinSAS**

6 Organization Structure and Design

Viacom recently separated itself into two publicly traded companies: CBS Corp., which will include the CBS network, a group of affiliated TV stations and the Infinity radio broadcaster; and another company, which will keep the Viacom name and include MTV, VH1, several other cable networks, and the Paramount movie studio. These executives are celebrating the event after opening the New York Stock Exchange on the first day the stocks of both companies were available on the market.

1 ▶ *Identify the basic elements of organizations.*

2 ▶ *Describe the bureaucratic perspective on organization design.*

3 ▶ *Identify and explain several situational influences on organization design.*

4 ▶ *Describe the basic forms of organization design that characterize many organizations.*

Chapter Outline

Online Study Center
Prepare for Class
Chapter Outline

5 *Describe emerging issues in organization design.*

Revitalizing Viacom

Viacom is one of the five companies that control 80 percent of the video content viewed in the United States, rivaling Disney, Time Warner, NBC Universal, and News Corporation. Viacom is extremely large and diverse—too much so, in fact. Over the decades, the media giant has grown through mergers and divestitures. By 2005, Viacom owned many successful businesses but had a structure that did not make sense. There were unprofitable units as well as duplicated services and too little knowledge sharing.

So on January 1, 2006, majority owner Sumner Redstone split Viacom into two parts. One piece, still called Viacom, owns most of the cable networks and its Paramount movie studios. The other part, now called CBS, owns most of the broadcasting operations and also publishing and theme parks. Though the businesses have been reshuffled, the separation echoes the company's makeup

Online Study Center
Improve Your Grade
—Flashcards
—Glossary

You should be able to define and use terms that are part of the practicing manager's vocabulary, as well as those that are integral in the language of management.

before the 1999 merger of CBS and Viacom. That merger, the largest ever up to that time, was hailed as a groundbreaking effort to expand and diversify into "new" online media.

By splitting Viacom, Redstone hopes to increase the coordination between different lines of business, more effectively control operations, and better realize synergies between units. However, the new structure suffers from the same weaknesses. For example, Viacom now owns businesses as different as Comedy Central, MTV, BET, Nickelodeon, CMT, and Spike, along with Paramount studios. CBS owns the CBS cable station, local broadcasters, Showtime, UPN, Paramount television, Simon & Schuster publishers, and Paramount Parks. The split has only slightly increased the focus of each of the two companies, which are still very diversified.

Paul R. La Monica, writing in *BusinessWeek*, says, "It used to be that bigger is better, but now Wall Street may think that leaner is meaner." Redstone hopes that investors will appreciate the growth opportunities of the new Viacom in addition to the cash-generating CBS. "Shakespeare said that a rose by any other name smells as sweet, and now I've got two roses," Redstone quips. Yet today the stock of Viacom and CBS, combined, is worth about as much as the stock of the old firm before the split. Apparently, investors are not convinced that the breakup increases the firm's value.

On the other hand, the split has increased creativity, as shown in the new ventures the companies are undertaking. CBS, for example, is entering into a joint venture between UPN and Warner Brothers to create a new cable network called The CW. "This new network will . . . clearly be greater than the sum of its parts," says CBS CEO Leslie Moonves, showing his belief in synergy.

In the company's most innovative move thus far, CBS is at the forefront of a movement to deliver television shows in new ways. CBS will break from television's all-powerful schedule to deliver hit shows through ComCast on Demand. The shows will be available the day following broadcast for a 99-cent fee. Media experts believe that the switch to on-demand broadcasting will soon be followed by advertising support, much as traditional shows are now financed. This would do away with user fees and help Viacom to better compete against satellite providers. Analysts from Forrester Research claim that "the TV schedule will become obsolete." CBS is even partnering with Apple to offer Comedy Central shows on iTunes, enabling viewers to watch episodes on iPods or even cell phones.

Other creative moves include Paramount's acquisition of movie studio DreamWorks SKG and MTV's acquisition of the NeoPets website. Viacom and CBS are both adding new media units to deliver broadband video and specialized programming tied to specific television shows and channels. Viacom executives hope people will view online clips, say from *The Colbert Report,* at Comedy Central online and then e-mail them to friends, providing free promotion. Another new media unit, ifilm, was just purchased by Viacom's MTV. Ifilm provides user-created as well as professionally produced videos and content about movies. CBS's theme parks are up for sale.

Viacom is working to find the most effective organizational structure. And it's not the only one. For example, competitor Time Warner merged with AOL in 2000 and today is considering divestiture. Most of the entertainment companies are creating new online businesses. Media technology and users' desires are changing rapidly at this time, requiring companies to adapt. Leo Hindery, Jr., formerly a media CEO, says, "Audiences are diverse, complex, and changing—and the best media companies are similarly so."[1]

One of the major ingredients in managing any business is the creation of an organization structure and design to link the various elements that make up the organization. Managers in any given organization may select its design from a wide array of alternatives. Managers at Viacom continue to work to create the right organization for the firm. Each addition and subtraction of a business unit from the company requires that the firm reconfigure how it functions. This chapter, the first of three devoted to organizing, discusses many of the critical elements of organization structure and design that managers can control. We first identify and describe the various elements of organization. We then summarize the first common approach to organization, bureaucracy. Next we introduce situational influences on organization design and then discuss the basic forms of design used today. We conclude with a look at emerging issues in organization design.

THE BASIC ELEMENTS OF ORGANIZING

1 ▶ *Identify the basic elements of organizations.*

The phrase **organization structure and design** refers to the overall set of elements that can be used to configure an organization. This section introduces and describes these elements: job specialization, departmentalization, reporting relationships, distribution of authority, and coordination.[2]

organization structure and design   The set of elements that can be used to configure an organization.

Job Specialization

The first element of organization structure is job specialization. **Job specialization** is the degree to which the overall task of the organization is broken down into smaller component parts. Job specialization is a normal extension of organizational growth. For example, when Walt Disney started his company, he did everything himself—wrote cartoons, drew them, and then marketed them to theaters. As the business grew, he eventually hired others to perform many of these same functions. As growth continued, so did specialization. For example, as animation artists work on Disney movies today, they may specialize in drawing only a single character or doing only background scenery. And today, the Walt Disney Company has thousands of different specialized jobs. Clearly, no one person could perform them all.

job specialization   The degree to which the overall task of the organization is broken down into smaller component parts.

Online Study Center
Improve Your Grade
Visual Glossary 6.1

Benefits and Limitations of Specialization

Job specialization provides four benefits to organizations.[3]

1. Workers performing small, simple tasks will become very proficient at each task.
2. Transfer time between tasks decreases. If employees perform several different tasks, some time is lost as they stop doing one task and start doing the next.
3. The more narrowly defined a job is, the easier it is to develop specialized equipment to assist with that job.
4. When an employee who performs a highly specialized job is absent or resigns, the manager is able to train someone new at relatively low cost.

Designing jobs is a fundamental cornerstone of organizing. Most organizations today rely on a blend of job specialization and such alternatives to specialization as job enrichment and work teams. Take this Cessna factory in Independence, Kansas. All of its assembly employees are expected to have a base specialization. But each is also expected to learn new skills continuously while working as part of a team that has a lot to say about how its work gets done.

On the other hand, job specialization can have negative consequences.

1. Workers who perform highly specialized jobs may become bored and dissatisfied. The job may be so specialized that it offers no challenge or stimulation. Boredom and monotony set in, absenteeism rises, and the quality of the work may suffer.

2. The anticipated benefits of specialization do not always occur. For example, a study conducted at Maytag found that the time spent moving work in process from one worker to another was greater than the time needed for the same individual to change from job to job.[4]

Thus, although some degree of specialization is necessary, it should not be carried to extremes because of the possible negative consequences. Managers must be sensitive to situations in which extreme specialization should be avoided. And indeed, several alternative approaches to designing jobs have been developed in recent years.

Alternatives to Specialization

To counter the problems associated with specialization, managers have sought other approaches to job design that achieve a better balance between organizational demands for efficiency and productivity and individual needs for creativity and autonomy. Five alternative approaches are job rotation, job enlargement, job enrichment, the job characteristics approach, and work teams.[5]

1. **Job rotation** involves systematically moving employees from one job to another. A worker in a warehouse might unload trucks on Monday, carry incoming inventory to storage on Tuesday, verify invoices on Wednesday, pull outgoing inventory from storage on Thursday, and load trucks on Friday. Thus the jobs do not change, but workers move from job to job. Unfortunately, for this very reason, job rotation has not been particularly successful in enhancing employee motivation or satisfaction. Jobs that are amenable to rotation tend to be relatively standard and routine. Workers who are rotated to a "new" job may be more satisfied at first, but their satisfaction soon wanes. Although many companies have tried job rotation, it is most often used today as a training device to improve worker skills and flexibility.

2. **Job enlargement** was developed to increase the total number of tasks that workers perform. As a result, all workers perform a wide variety of tasks, which presumably reduces the level of job dissatisfaction. At Maytag, for example, the assembly line for producing washing machine water pumps was systematically changed so that work that had originally been performed by six workers, who passed the work sequentially from one person to another, was performed by four workers, each of whom assembled a complete pump.[6] Unfortunately, although job enlargement does have some positive consequences, they are often offset by some disadvantages:
   - Training costs usually rise.
   - Unions have argued that pay should increase because the worker is doing more tasks.
   - In many cases the work remains boring and routine even after job enlargement.

job enrichment   An alternative to job specialization that involves increasing both the number of tasks the worker does and the control the worker has over the job.

3. A more comprehensive approach, **job enrichment**, assumes that increasing the range and variety of tasks is not by itself sufficient to improve employee motivation.[7] Thus job enrichment attempts to increase both the number of tasks a worker does and the control the worker has over the job. To implement job enrichment, managers remove some controls from the job, delegate more authority to employees, and structure the work in complete, natural units. These changes increase subordinates' sense of responsibility. Another part of job enrichment is to assign new and challenging tasks continually, thereby increasing employees' opportunities for growth and advancement. Texas Instruments, IBM, and General Foods have all used job enrichment.

job characteristics approach   An alternative to job specialization that suggests that jobs should be diagnosed and improved along five core dimensions, taking into account both the work system and employee preferences.

4. The **job characteristics approach** is an alternative to job specialization that more systematically accounts for the work system and employee preferences.[8] As illustrated in Figure 6.1, the job characteristics approach suggests that jobs should be diagnosed and improved along five core dimensions:
   - *Skill variety*, the number of things a person does in a job
   - *Task identity*, the extent to which the worker does a complete or identifiable portion of the total job
   - *Task significance*, the perceived importance of the task
   - *Autonomy*, the degree of control the worker has over how the work is performed
   - *Feedback*, the extent to which the worker knows how well the job is being performed

FIGURE 6.1

The Job Characteristics Approach
The job characteristics approach to job design provides a viable alternative to job specialization. Five core job dimensions may lead to critical psychological states that, in turn, may enhance motivation, performance, and satisfaction while also reducing absenteeism and turnover.

Reprinted from *Organizational Behavior and Human Decision Processes,* formerly known as *Organizational Behavior and Human Performance,* Vol. 16, 1976, pp. 150–179, Hackman et al., "Motivation Through the Design of Work: Test of a Theory in Organizational Behavior and Human Performance." Copyright © 1976 with permission from Elsevier.

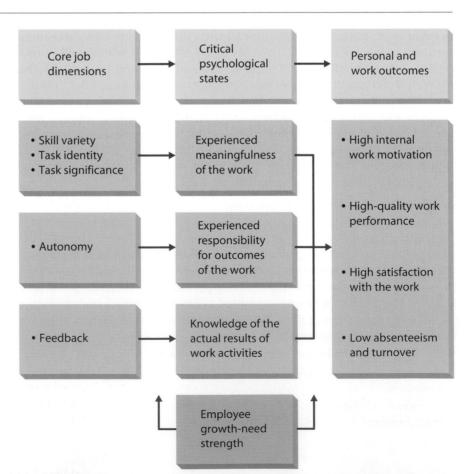

Increasing the presence of these dimensions in a job presumably leads to higher motivation, high-quality work performance, high satisfaction, and low absenteeism and turnover. Numerous studies have been conducted to test the usefulness of the job characteristics approach. The Southwestern Division of Prudential Insurance, for example, used this approach in its claims division. Results included moderate declines in turnover and a small but measurable improvement in work quality. Other research findings have not supported this approach as strongly. Thus, although the job characteristics approach is one of the most promising alternatives to job specialization, it is probably not the final answer.

5. Another alternative to job specialization is **work teams**. Under this arrangement, a group is given responsibility for designing the work system to be used in performing an interrelated set of tasks. In the typical assembly-line system, the work flows from one worker to the next, and each worker has a specified job to perform. In a work team, however, the group itself decides how jobs will be allocated. For example, the work team assigns specific tasks to members, monitors and controls its own performance, and has autonomy over work scheduling.[9]

work team An alternative to job specialization that allows an entire group to design the work system it will use to perform an interrelated set of tasks.

Online Study Center
Improve Your Grade
Visual Glossary 6.2

Grouping Jobs: Departmentalization

The second basic element of organization structure is the grouping of jobs according to some logical arrangement. This process is called **departmentalization**. When organizations are small, the owner-manager can personally oversee the work of everyone employed there. As an organization grows, however, personally supervising all the employees becomes more and more difficult for the owner-manager. Consequently, new managerial positions are created to supervise the work of others. Employees are not assigned to particular managers randomly. Rather, jobs are grouped according to some plan. The logic embodied in such a plan is the basis for all departmentalization.[10]

departmentalization The process of grouping jobs according to some logical arrangement.

1. **Functional departmentalization**, the most common basis for departmentalization, groups together jobs that involve the same or similar activities. (The word *function* is used here to mean organizational functions such as finance and production, rather than the basic managerial functions, such as planning and controlling.) This approach, which is most common in smaller organizations, has three primary advantages.
   - Each department can be staffed by experts in that functional area. Marketing experts can be hired to run the marketing function, for example.
   - Supervision is facilitated, because an individual manager needs to be familiar with only a relatively narrow set of skills.
   - Coordinating activities inside each department is easier.

functional departmentalization Grouping jobs that involve the same or similar activities.

Online Study Center
Improve Your Grade
Visual Glossary 6.3

On the other hand, as an organization begins to grow in size, several disadvantages of this approach may emerge.
   - Decision making tends to become slower and more bureaucratic.
   - Employees may begin to concentrate too narrowly on their own unit and lose sight of the total organizational system.
   - Accountability and performance become increasingly difficult to monitor. For example, it may not be possible to determine whether a new product fails because of production deficiencies or a poor marketing campaign.

product departmentalization Grouping activities around products or product groups.

2. **Product departmentalization** involves grouping and arranging activities around products or product groups. Product departmentalization has three major advantages.
   - All activities associated with one product or product group can be easily integrated and coordinated.
   - The speed and effectiveness of decision making are enhanced.
   - The performance of individual products or product groups can be assessed more easily and objectively, thereby improving the accountability of departments for the results of their activities.

   Product departmentalization also has two major disadvantages.
   - Managers in each department may focus on their own product or product group to the exclusion of the rest of the organization. (For example, a marketing manager may see her or his primary duty as helping the group rather than helping the overall organization.)
   - Administrative costs rise, because each department must have its own functional specialists for areas such as market research and financial analysis.

customer departmentalization Grouping activities to respond to and interact with specific customers or customer groups.

3. **Customer departmentalization** involves structuring activities to respond to and interact with specific customers or customer groups. The lending activities in most banks, for example, are usually tailored to meet the needs of different kinds of customers (business, consumer, mortgage, and agricultural loans). The basic advantage of this approach is that the organization is able to use skilled specialists to deal with unique customers or customer groups. It takes one set of skills to evaluate a balance sheet and lend a business $500,000 for operating capital, and a different set of skills to evaluate an individual's creditworthiness and lend $20,000 for a new car. However, a fairly large administrative staff is required to integrate the activities of the various departments. In banks, for example, coordination is necessary to make sure that the organization does not overcommit itself in any one area and to handle collections on delinquent accounts from a diverse set of customers.

location departmentalization Grouping jobs on the basis of defined geographic sites or areas.

4. **Location departmentalization** groups jobs on the basis of defined geographic sites or areas. The defined sites or areas may range in size from an entire hemisphere to only a few blocks of a large city. Transportation companies, police departments (precincts represent geographic areas of a city), and the Federal Reserve Bank often use location departmentalization. The primary advantage of location departmentalization is that it enables the organization to respond easily to unique customer and environmental characteristics in the various regions. On the negative side, a larger administrative staff may be required if the organization must keep track of units in scattered locations.

CONCEPT CHECK 6.2

Learn how your school or workplace is organized. Analyze the advantages and disadvantages of this form of departmentalization, and then comment on how well or how poorly other forms of departmentalization might work.

Establishing Reporting Relationships

The third basic element of organizing is the establishment of reporting relationships among positions. The purpose of this activity is to clarify the chain of command and the span of management.

chain of command A clear and distinct line of authority among the positions in an organization.

1. **Chain of command** is a traditional concept that suggests that clear and distinct lines of authority need to be established among all positions in an organization. The popular saying "The buck stops here" is derived from this

DILBERT reprinted by permission of United Feature Syndicate, Inc.

Distributing authority is a key building block in creating an effective organization. Unfortunately, some managers prefer to avoid accountability for decisions and work to ensure that someone else can always be held responsible for mistakes and errors. This Dilbert cartoon offers a whimsical view of a manager teaching others how to avoid accountability and pass the buck.

idea—someone in the organization must ultimately be responsible for every decision.

2. **Span of management** (sometimes called the *span of control*) describes how relationships are determined and how many people will report to each manager. Even though the span of management is a crucial factor in structuring organizations, there are no universal, cut-and-dried prescriptions for an ideal or optimal span. Instead, managers must carefully assess their situation and context when making decisions about the span best suited for their needs.[11]

span of management   The number of people who report to a particular manager.

3. *Tall versus flat organizations* refers to the layers in the organizational hierarchy. Having more layers results in a taller organization, whereas having fewer layers leads to a flatter organization. What difference does it make whether the organization is tall or flat? One early study at Sears, Roebuck and Company found that a flat structure led to higher levels of employee morale and productivity.[12] Researchers have also argued that a tall structure is more expensive (because of the larger number of managers involved) and that it fosters more communication problems (because of the increased number of people through whom information must pass). On the other hand, a wide span of management in a flat organization may result in a manager's having more administrative responsibility (because there are fewer managers) and more supervisory responsibility (because there are more subordinates reporting to each manager). If these additional responsibilities become excessive, the flat organization may suffer.[13]

Online Study Center
Improve Your Grade
Career Snapshot 6.1

Many experts agree that businesses can function effectively with fewer layers of organization than they currently have. The Franklin Mint, for example, reduced its number of management layers from six to four. At the same time, the CEO increased his span of management from six to twelve. One additional reason for this trend is that electronic communication enables managers to stay in touch with a larger number of subordinates than was possible even just a few years ago.[14]

Distributing Authority

Another important element in structuring organizations is the determination of how authority is to be distributed among positions. **Authority** is power that has been legitimized by the organization.[15] Two specific issues that managers must address when distributing authority are delegation and decentralization.[16]

authority   Power that has been legitimized by the organization.

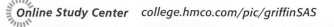

delegation   The process by which a manager assigns a portion of his or her total workload to others.

Online Study Center
Improve Your Grade
Visual Glossary 6.4

decentralization   The process of systematically delegating power and authority throughout the organization to middle and lower-level managers.

centralization   The process of systematically retaining power and authority in the hands of higher-level managers.

Online Study Center
Improve Your Grade
Visual Glossary 6.5

The Delegation Process

Delegation is the establishment of a pattern of authority between a superior and one or more subordinates. Specifically, **delegation** is the process by which managers assign a portion of their total workload to others.[17] In theory, the delegation process involves three steps.

1. The manager assigns responsibility or gives the subordinate a job to do. The assignment of responsibility might range from telling a subordinate to prepare a report to placing the person in charge of a task force.
2. Along with the assignment, the individual is also given the authority to do the job. The manager may give the subordinate the power to requisition needed information from confidential files or to direct a group of other workers.
3. The manager establishes the subordinate's accountability—that is, the subordinate accepts an obligation to carry out the task assigned by the manager.

Decentralization and Centralization

Just as authority can be delegated from one individual to another, organizations also develop patterns of authority across a wide variety of positions and departments. **Decentralization** is the process of systematically delegating power and authority throughout the organization to middle and lower-level managers. It is important to remember that decentralization is actually one end of a continuum anchored at the other end by **centralization**, the process of systematically retaining power and authority in the hands of higher-level managers. Hence a decentralized organization is one in which decision-making power and authority are delegated as far down the chain of command as possible. Conversely, in a centralized organization, decision-making power and authority are retained at the higher levels of management.

What factors determine an organization's position on the decentralization-centralization continuum?

▎ The organization's external environment: Usually, the greater the complexity and uncertainty of the environment, the greater the tendency to decentralize.

▎ The history of the organization: Firms have a tendency to do what they have done in the past, so there is likely to be some relationship between what an organization did in its early history and what it chooses to do today in terms of centralization or decentralization.

▎ The nature of the decisions being made: The costlier and riskier the decisions, the more pressure there is to centralize.

In short, a manager has no clear-cut guidelines for determining whether to centralize or decentralize. Many successful organizations, such as Sears and General Electric, are quite decentralized. Equally successful firms, however, such as McDonald's and Wal-Mart, have remained centralized.

Coordinating Activities

A fifth major element of organizing is coordination. As we noted earlier, job specialization and departmentalization involve breaking jobs down into small units and then combining those jobs into departments. Once this has been accomplished, the activities of the departments must be linked—that is, systems must be put into place to keep the activities of each department focused on the attainment of organizational goals. This is accomplished by **coordination**—the process of linking the activities of the various departments of the organization.[18]

The Need for Coordination

The primary reason for coordination is that departments and work groups are interdependent—they depend on one another for information and resources to perform their respective activities. The greater the interdependence between departments, the more coordination the organization requires if departments are to be able to perform effectively. There are three major forms of interdependence: pooled, sequential, and reciprocal.[19]

1. **Pooled interdependence** represents the lowest level of interdependence. Units that exhibit pooled interdependence operate with little interaction—the output of the units is pooled at the organizational level. Gap clothing stores operate with pooled interdependence. Each store is considered a "department" by the parent corporation. Each has its own operating budget, staff, and so forth. The profits or losses from each store are "added together" at the organizational level. The stores are interdependent to the extent that the final success or failure of one store affects the others, but they do not generally interact on a day-to-day basis.

2. In **sequential interdependence**, the output of one unit becomes the input for another in sequential fashion. This creates a moderate level of interdependence. At Nissan, for example, one plant assembles engines and then ships them to a final assembly site at another plant, where the cars are completed. The plants are interdependent in that the final assembly plant must have the engines from engine assembly before it can perform its primary function of producing finished automobiles. But the interdependence is largely one-way—the engine plant is not necessarily dependent on the final assembly plant.

3. **Reciprocal interdependence** exists when activities flow both ways between units. This form is clearly the most complex. Within a Marriott hotel, for example, the reservations department, front-desk check-in, and housekeeping are all reciprocally interdependent. Reservations has to provide front-desk employees with information about how many guests to expect each day, and housekeeping needs to know which rooms require priority cleaning. If any of the three units does not do its job properly, all the others will be affected.

Structural Coordination Techniques

Because of the obvious coordination requirements that characterize most organizations, many techniques for achieving coordination have been developed. Some of the most useful devices for maintaining coordination among interdependent units are the managerial hierarchy, rules and procedures, liaison roles, task forces, and integrating departments.[20]

▮ The *managerial hierarchy* is used to achieve coordination: that is, one manager is put in charge of interdependent departments or units. In Wal-Mart distribution centers, major activities include receiving and unloading bulk shipments from railroad cars and loading other shipments onto trucks for distribution to

---

Sidebar definitions:

coordination The process of linking the activities of the various departments of the organization.

pooled interdependence A form of interdependence in which units operate with little interaction, and their output is simply pooled.

sequential interdependence A form of interdependence in which the output of one unit becomes the input for another in sequential fashion.

Online Study Center
Improve Your Grade
Video Segment

reciprocal interdependence A form of interdependence in which activities flow both ways between units.

Online Study Center
Improve Your Grade
Career Snapshot 6.2

retail outlets. The two groups (receiving and shipping) are interdependent in that they share the loading docks and some equipment. To ensure coordination and minimize conflict, one manager is in charge of the whole operation.

▮ *Rules and standard procedures* aid in the coordination of activities. In the Wal-Mart distribution center, an outgoing truck shipment has priority over an incoming rail shipment. Thus, when trucks are to be loaded, the shipping unit is given access to all of the center's auxiliary forklifts. This priority is specifically stated in a rule. As useful as rules and procedures often are in routine situations, however, relying on them is not particularly effective when coordination problems are complex or unusual.

▮ A manager in a *liaison role* coordinates interdependent units by acting as a common point of contact. This individual may not have any formal authority over the groups but instead simply facilitates the flow of information between units. Two engineering groups working on component systems for a large project might interact through a liaison. The liaison maintains familiarity with each group as well as with the overall project. She can answer questions and otherwise serve to integrate the activities of all the groups.

▮ A *task force* may be created when the need for coordination is acute. When interdependence is complex and several units are involved, a single liaison person may not be sufficient. Instead, a task force might be assembled by drawing one representative from each group. The coordination function is thus spread across several individuals, each of whom has special information about one of the groups involved. When the project is completed, task force members return to their original positions. For example, a college in the process of overhauling its degree requirements might establish a task force made up of representatives from each department affected by the change. Each person retains her or his regular departmental affiliation and duties but also serves on the special task force. After the new requirements are agreed on, the task force is dissolved.

▮ *Integrating departments* are occasionally used for coordination. These are somewhat similar to task forces but are of longer duration. An integrating department generally has some permanent members as well as members who are assigned temporarily from units that are particularly in need of coordination. One study found that successful firms in the plastics industry, which is characterized by complex and dynamic environments, used integrating departments to maintain internal integration and coordination.[21] An integrating department usually has more authority than a task force and may even be given some budgetary control by the organization.

True or False?

_____ 1. Yu Soon works in the public relations office of a university. Her boss initially gave her assignments working with alumni and then added arranging some interviews. Eventually she was given power to accept or reject interview requests. Her boss uses job rotation.

_____ 2. The pastry chef at an upscale restaurant sees each dessert before it leaves the kitchen. He has high task identity.

_____ 3. In a small organization the most common departmentalization is by customer.

Multiple Choice

_____ 4. At Harley-Davidson a production-line worker has the authority to shut down assembly when she sees a minor defect in a part. According to the job characteristics approach she has _____.
  a. skill variety   d. feedback
  b. task identity   e. task significance
  c. autonomy

_____ 5. An alternative to job specialization that allows an entire group to design the work system it will use to perform an interrelated set of tasks is called _____.
  a. functional departmentalization
  b. product departmentalization
  c. customer departmentalization
  d. location departmentalization
  e. a work team

_____ 6. The principle that each employee should have only one boss to report to is called _____.
  a. chain of command
  b. unity of command
  c. scalar principle
  d. narrow span of control
  e. tall organization

_____ 7. Which of the following is the most complex form of interdependence?
  a. Pooled   d. Organizational
  b. Sequential   e. Centralized
  c. Reciprocal

Online Study Center
ACE the Test
ACE Practice Tests 6.1

THE BUREAUCRATIC MODEL OF ORGANIZATION DESIGN

2 ▶ *Describe the bureaucratic perspective on organization design.*

Max Weber, an influential German sociologist, was a pioneer of classical organization theory. At the core of Weber's writings was the bureaucratic model of organizations.[22] The Weberian perspective suggests that a **bureaucracy** is a model of organization design based on a legitimate and formal system of authority. Many people associate bureaucracy with "red tape," rigidity, and passing the buck. For example, how many times have you heard people refer disparagingly to "the federal bureaucracy"? And many U.S. managers believe that bureaucracy in the Japanese government is a major impediment to U.S. firms' ability to do business there.

Weber viewed the bureaucratic form of organization as logical, rational, and efficient. He offered the model as a framework to which all organizations should aspire—the "one best way" of doing things. According to Weber, the ideal bureaucracy exhibits five basic characteristics:

1. The organization should adopt a distinct division of labor, and each position should be filled by an expert.

2. The organization should develop a consistent set of rules to ensure that task performance is uniform.

3. The organization should establish a hierarchy of positions or offices that creates a chain of command from the top of the organization to the bottom.

bureaucracy   A model of organization design based on a legitimate and formal system of authority.

4. Managers should conduct business in an impersonal way and maintain an appropriate social distance between themselves and their subordinates.

5. Employment and advancement in the organization should be based on technical expertise, and employees should be protected from arbitrary dismissal.

Perhaps the best examples of bureaucracies today are government agencies and universities. Consider, for example, the steps you must go through and the forms you must fill out to apply for admission to college, request housing, register each semester, change majors, submit a degree plan, substitute a course, and file for graduation. Even when paper is replaced with electronic media, the steps are often the same. The reason why these procedures are necessary is that universities deal with large numbers of people who must be treated equally and fairly. Hence rules, regulations, and standard operating procedures are needed. Large labor unions are also generally organized as bureaucracies.[23]

A primary strength of the bureaucratic model is that several of its elements (such as reliance on rules, and employment based on expertise) do, in fact, often improve efficiency. Bureaucracies also help prevent favoritism (because everyone must follow the rules) and make procedures and practices very clear to everyone. Unfortunately, however, this approach also has several disadvantages. One major disadvantage is that the bureaucratic model spawns inflexibility and rigidity. Once rules are created and put in place, making exceptions or changing them is often difficult. In addition, the bureaucracy often results in the neglect of human and social processes within the organization.

Many government offices still rely on the bureaucratic model of organization design. This is the main search room at the U.S. Patent and Trademark Office, in Arlington, Virginia. Anyone wanting to apply for a patent must follow a detailed set of procedures. The office itself also relies on precise rules and regulations, extensive paper documentation, and elaborate review and approval procedures as mainstays for getting its work done.

TEST PREPPER 6.2

ANSWERS CAN BE FOUND ON P. 441

True or False?

_____ 1. Bureaucracies create favoritism in an organization.

Online Study Center
ACE the Test
ACE Practice Tests 6.2

Multiple Choice

_____ 2. Max Weber, the sociologist, viewed the bureaucratic model as _____.
   a. the "one best way" of doing things
   b. intuitive
   c. motivational
   d. situational
   e. flexible

SITUATIONAL INFLUENCES ON ORGANIZATION DESIGN

3 *Identify and explain several situational influences on organization design.*

The **situational view of organization design** is based on the assumption that the optimal design for any given organization depends on a set of relevant situational factors. In other words, situational factors play a role in determining the best organization design for any particular circumstance. Four basic situational factors—technology, environment, size, and organizational life cycle—are discussed here.

situational view of organization design A view of organization design that is based on the assumption that the optimal design for any given organization depends on a set of relevant situational factors.

Core Technology

Technology consists of the conversion processes used to transform inputs (such as materials or information) into outputs (such as products or services). Most organizations use multiple technologies, but an organization's most important one is called its *core technology*. Although most people visualize assembly lines and machinery when they think of technology, the term can also be applied to service organizations. For example, an investment firm such as Vanguard uses technology to transform investment dollars into income in much the same way that Union Carbide uses natural resources to manufacture chemical products.

technology Conversion processes used to transform inputs into outputs.

The link between technology and organization design was first recognized by Joan Woodward.[24] Woodward studied one hundred manufacturing firms in southern England. She collected information about such aspects as the history of each organization, its manufacturing processes, its forms and procedures, and its financial performance. Woodward expected to find a relationship between the size of an organization and its design, but no such relationship emerged. As a result, she began to seek other explanations for differences. Close scrutiny of the firms in her sample led her to recognize a potential relationship between technology and organization design. This follow-up analysis led Woodward first to classify the organizations according to their technology. She identified three basic forms of technology:

1. *Unit or small-batch technology.* The product is custom-made to customer specifications or produced in small quantities. Organizations using this form of technology include a tailor shop such as Brooks Brothers (custom suits), a printing shop such as Kinko's (business cards, company stationery), and a photography studio.

Online Study Center
Improve Your Grade
Knowledgebank 6.2

2. *Large-batch or mass-production technology.* The product is manufactured in assembly-line fashion by combining component parts into another part or finished product. Examples include automobile manufacturers such as Subaru, appliance makers such as Whirlpool Corporation, and electronics firms such as Philips.

3. *Continuous-process technology.* Raw materials are transformed into a finished product by a series of machine or process transformations. The composition of the materials themselves is changed. Examples include petroleum refineries such as ExxonMobil and Shell and chemical refineries such as Dow Chemical and Hoescht AG.

These forms of technology are listed in order of their assumed levels of complexity. In other words, unit or small-batch technology is presumed to be the least complex

and continuous-process technology the most complex. Woodward found that different configurations of organization design were associated with each technology.

Specifically, Woodward found that the two extremes (unit or small-batch and continuous-process) tended to have little bureaucracy, whereas the middle-range organizations (large-batch or mass-production) tended to have much more bureaucracy. The large-batch and mass-production organizations also had a higher level of specialization.[25] Finally, she found that organizational success was related to the extent to which organizations followed the typical pattern. For example, more successful continuous-process organizations tended to have less bureaucracy, whereas less successful firms with the same technology tended to have more bureaucracy.

Environment

Environmental elements and organization design are specifically linked in a number of ways. The first widely recognized analysis of environment–organization design linkages was provided by Tom Burns and G. M. Stalker.[26] Like Woodward, Burns and Stalker worked in England. Their first step was identifying two extreme forms of organizational environment: stable (tending to remain relatively constant over time) and unstable (subject to uncertainty and rapid change). Next they studied the designs of organizations in each type of environment. Not surprisingly, they found that organizations in stable environments tended to have a different kind of design than organizations in unstable environments. The two kinds of design that emerged were called mechanistic organization and organic organization.

mechanistic organization An organization design that is similar to the bureaucratic model but is most frequently found in stable environments.

1. A **mechanistic organization**, quite similar to the bureaucratic model, was most frequently found in stable environments. Free from uncertainty, organizations structured their activities in rather predictable ways by means of rules, specialized jobs, and centralized authority. Mechanistic organizations are also quite similar to bureaucracies. Although no environment is completely stable, Kmart and Wendy's use mechanistic designs. Each Kmart store, for example, has prescribed methods for store design and merchandise-ordering processes. No deviations are allowed from these methods.

organic organization A very flexible and informal model of organization design, most often found in unstable and unpredictable environments.

2. An **organic organization**, on the other hand, was most often found in unstable and unpredictable environments, in which constant change and uncertainty usually necessitate a much higher level of fluidity and flexibility. Motorola (facing rapid technological change) and The Limited (facing constant change in consumer tastes) both use organic designs. A manager at Motorola, for example, has considerable discretion over how work is performed and how problems can be solved.

These ideas were extended in the United States by Paul R. Lawrence and Jay W. Lorsch.[27] They agreed that environmental factors influence organization design but believed that this influence varies among different units of the same organization. In fact, they predicted that each organizational unit has its own unique environment and responds by developing unique attributes. Lawrence and Lorsch suggested that organizations could be characterized along two primary dimensions.

differentiation The extent to which an organization is broken down into subunits.

1. **Differentiation** is the extent to which an organization is broken down into subunits. A firm with many subunits is highly differentiated; one with few subunits has a low level of differentiation.

2. **Integration** is the degree to which the various subunits must work together in a coordinated fashion. For example, if each unit competes in a different market and has its own production facilities, they may need little integration. Lawrence and Lorsch reasoned that the degree of differentiation and integration needed by an organization depends on the stability of the environments that its subunits face.

integration The degree to which the various subunits in an organization must work together in a coordinated fashion.

Organizational Size and Life Cycle

The size and life cycle of an organization may also affect organization design.[28] Although several definitions of size exist, we define **organizational size** as the total number of full-time or full-time-equivalent employees. A team of researchers at the University of Aston in Birmingham, England, believed that Woodward had failed to find a relationship between size and structure (which was her original expectation) because nearly all of the organizations she studied were relatively small (three-fourths had fewer than 500 employees).[29] Thus they decided to undertake a study of a wider array of organizations to determine how size and technology both individually and jointly affect an organization's design.

organizational size The total number of full-time or full-time-equivalent employees.

Their primary finding was that technology did in fact influence structural variables in small firms, probably because all of their activities tend to be centered on their core technology. In large firms, however, the strong link between technology and design broke down, most likely because technology is not as central to ongoing activities in large organizations. The Aston studies yielded a number of basic generalizations: When compared to small organizations, large organizations tend to be characterized by higher levels of job specialization, more standard operating procedures, more rules, more regulations, and a greater degree of decentralization. Wal-Mart is a good case in point. The firm expects to continue its dramatic growth for the foreseeable future, adding as many as 800,000 new jobs in the next few years. But the firm acknowledges that as it grows, it will have to become more decentralized for its first-line managers to stay in tune with their customers.[30]

Although no clear pattern explains changes in size, many organizations progress through a four-stage **organizational life cycle**.[31]

organizational life cycle Progression through which organizations evolve as they grow and mature.

1. The first stage is the *birth* of the organization.
2. The second stage, *youth,* is characterized by growth and by the expansion of organizational resources.
3. *Midlife* is a period of gradual growth evolving eventually into stability.
4. *Maturity* is a period of stability, perhaps eventually evolving into decline.

Managers must confront a number of organization design issues as the organization progresses through these stages. In general, as an organization passes from one stage to the next, it becomes bigger, more mechanistic, and more decentralized. It also becomes more specialized, devotes more attention to planning, and takes on an increasingly large staff component. Finally, coordination demands increase, formalization increases, organizational units become geographically more dispersed, and control systems become more extensive. Thus an organization's size and design are clearly linked, and this link is dynamic because of the organizational life cycle.[32]

True or False?

_____ 1. The process H & R Block uses to transform tax information into tax returns is an example of technology in the situational view of organization design.

_____ 2. Integration is the extent to which an organization is broken down into subunits.

_____ 3. Kmart is an example of a youthful organization characterized by gradual growth evolving into stability.

Multiple Choice

_____ 4. The situational view of organization design is based on four factors. Which of the following is NOT one of them?

a. Leadership   d. Organization life cycle
b. Environment   e. Technology
c. Size

_____ 5. Siemens AG, a large German conglomerate, manufactures many products. One product is telecommunication equipment, which is produced in high volume. What production technology would you expect Siemens to use for that product?

a. Unit   d. Large-batch
b. Small-batch   e. Continuous-process
c. Medium-batch

_____ 6. Microsoft operates in an environment that is uncertain and requires flexibility. You would expect them to use which organization design?

a. Mechanistic   d. Bureaucratic
b. Organic   e. Hybrid
c. Virtual

Online Study Center
ACE the Test
ACE Practice Tests 6.3

BASIC FORMS OF ORGANIZATION DESIGN

4 *Describe the basic forms of organization design that characterize many organizations.*

Because technology, environment, size, life cycle, and strategy can all influence organization design, it should come as no surprise that organizations adopt many different kinds of designs. Most designs, however, fall into one of four basic categories. Others are hybrids based on two or more of the basic forms.

Functional (U-Form) Design

functional (U-form) design An organization design based on the functional approach to departmentalization.

The **functional design** is an arrangement based on the functional approach to departmentalization. This design is also called the **U form** (for "unitary").[33] Under the U-form arrangement, the members and units in the organization are grouped into functional departments such as marketing and production. For the organization to operate efficiently in this design, there must be considerable coordination across departments. This integration and coordination are most commonly the responsibility of the CEO and members of senior management. Figure 6.2 shows the U-form design applied to the corporate level of a small manufacturing company. In a U-form organization, none of the functional areas can survive without the others. Marketing, for example, needs products from operations to sell and funds from finance to pay for advertising. The WD-40 Company, which makes a popular lubricating oil, and the McIlhenny Company, which makes Tabasco sauce, both use the U-form design.

In general, this approach shares the basic advantages and disadvantages of functional departmentalization. It allows the organization to staff all important positions with functional experts and facilitates coordination and integration. On the other hand, it also promotes a functional, rather than an organizational, focus and may promote centralization. Functionally based designs are most commonly

FIGURE 6.2

Functional (U-Form) Design for a Small Manufacturing Company

The U-form design is based on functional departmentalization. This small manufacturing firm uses managers at the vice presidential level to coordinate activities within each functional area of the organization. Note that each functional area is dependent on the others.

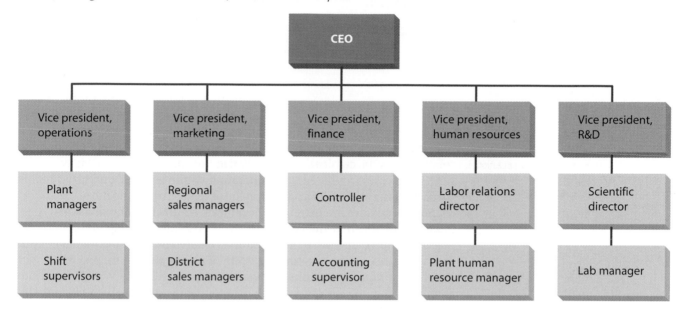

used in small organizations. In a small company, an individual CEO can relatively easily oversee and coordinate the entire organization. But as an organization grows, the CEO will find staying on top of all functional areas increasingly difficult.

Conglomerate (H-Form) Design

Another common form of organization design is the **conglomerate (H-form) design**.[34] This design is used by an organization made up of a set of unrelated businesses. Thus the H-form design is essentially a holding company that results from unrelated diversification. (The *H* in this term stands for "holding.") This approach is based loosely on the product form of departmentalization. Each business or set of businesses is operated by a general manager who is responsible for its profits or losses, and each general manager functions independently of the others. Samsung Electronics Co., a South Korean firm, uses the H-form design. As illustrated in Figure 6.3, Samsung is structured around four business groups that, on the surface at least, have little relationship to one another.

In an H-form organization, a corporate staff usually evaluates the performance of each business, allocates corporate resources across companies, and shapes decisions about buying and selling businesses. The basic shortcoming of the H-form design is the complexity associated with holding diverse and unrelated businesses. Managers usually find comparing and integrating activities across a large number of diverse operations difficult. Research suggests that many organizations following this approach achieve only average to weak financial performance.[35] Thus, although some U.S. firms are still using the H-form design, many have also abandoned it for other approaches.

conglomerate (H-form) design   An organization design used by an organization made up of a set of unrelated businesses.

FIGURE 6.3

Conglomerate (H-Form) Design at Samsung

Samsung Electronics Co., a South Korean firm, uses the conglomerate form of organization design. This design, which results from a strategy of unrelated diversification, is a complex one to manage. Managers find that it is difficult to compare and integrate activities among the dissimilar operations. Companies may abandon this design for another approach, such as the M-form design.

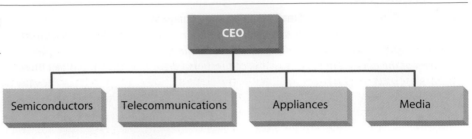

divisional (M-form) design An organization design based on multiple businesses in related areas operating within a larger organizational framework.

Divisional (M-Form) Design

In the divisional design, which is becoming increasingly popular, a product form of organization is also used; in contrast to the H-form, however, the divisions are related. Thus the **divisional (M-form) design** (for "multidivisional") is based on multiple businesses in related areas operating within a larger organizational framework. This design results from a strategy of related diversification.

Some activities are extremely decentralized down to the divisional level; others are centralized at the corporate level.[36] As shown in Figure 6.4, The Limited uses this approach. Each of its divisions is headed by a general manager and operates with reasonable autonomy, but the divisions also coordinate their activities as is appropriate. Other firms that use this approach are the Walt Disney Company (theme parks, movies, and merchandising units, all interrelated) and Hewlett-Packard (computers, printers, scanners, electronic medical equipment, and other electronic instrumentation).

The opportunities for coordination and shared resources represent one of the biggest advantages of the M-form design. The Limited's market research and purchasing departments are centralized. Thus a buyer can inspect a manufacturer's entire product line and buy some designs for The Limited chain, others for Express, and still others for Lerner New York. The M-form design's basic objective is to optimize internal competition and cooperation. Healthy competition for resources among divisions can enhance effectiveness, but cooperation should also be promoted. Research suggests that the M-form organization that can achieve and maintain this balance will outperform large U-form and all H-form organizations.[37]

FIGURE 6.4

Multidivisional (M-Form) Design at The Limited

The Limited uses the multidivisional approach to organization design. Although each unit operates with relative autonomy, all units function in the same general market. This design resulted from a strategy of related diversification. Other firms that use M-form designs include PepsiCo and Woolworth Corporation.

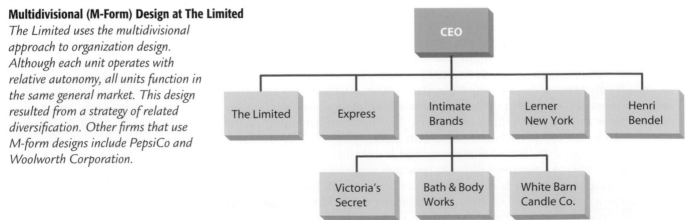

Matrix Design

The **matrix design**, another common approach to organization design, is based on two overlapping bases of departmentalization.[38] The foundation of a matrix is a set of functional departments. A set of product groups, or temporary departments, is then superimposed across the functional departments. Employees in a matrix are simultaneously members of a functional department (such as engineering) and of a project team.

Figure 6.5 shows a basic matrix design. At the top of the organization are functional units headed by vice presidents of engineering, production, finance, and marketing. Each of these managers has several subordinates. Along the side of the organization are a number of positions called *project manager*. Each project manager heads a project group composed of representatives or workers from the functional departments. Note from the figure that a matrix reflects a *multiple-command structure:* Any given individual reports to both a functional superior and one or more project managers.

The project groups, or teams, are assigned to designated projects or programs. For example, the company might be developing a new product. Representatives are chosen from each functional area to work as a team on the new product. They

matrix design An organization design based on two overlapping bases of departmentalization.

FIGURE 6.5

A Matrix Organization

A matrix organization design is created by superimposing a product form of departmentalization on an existing functional organization. Project managers coordinate teams of employees drawn from different functional departments. Thus a matrix relies on a multiple-command structure.

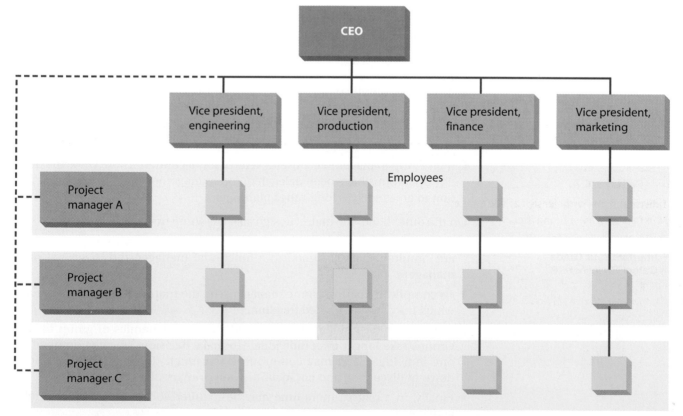

also retain membership in the original functional group. At any given time, a person may be a member of several teams as well as a member of a functional group. Ford used this approach in creating its popular Focus automobile. It formed a group called "Team Focus" made up of designers, engineers, production specialists, marketing specialists, and other experts from different areas of the company. This group facilitated getting a very successful product to the market at least a year earlier than would have been possible using Ford's previous approaches.

The matrix form of organization design is most often used in one of three situations.[39]

1. First, a matrix may work when there is strong pressure from the environment. For example, intense external competition may dictate the sort of strong marketing thrust that is best spearheaded by a functional department, but the diversity of a company's products may argue for product departments.

2. Second, a matrix may be appropriate when large amounts of information need to be processed. For example, creating lateral relationships by means of a matrix is one effective way to increase the organization's capacity for processing information.

3. Third, the matrix design may work when there is pressure for shared resources. For example, a company with ten product departments may have resources for only three marketing specialists. A matrix design would allow all the departments to share the company's scarce marketing resources.

The matrix design has several advantages.

▌ It enhances flexibility because teams can be created, redefined, and dissolved as needed.

▌ When team members assume a major role in decision making, they are likely to be highly motivated and committed to the organization.

▌ Employees in a matrix organization have considerable opportunity to learn new skills.

▌ It provides an efficient way for the organization to take full advantage of its human resources.

▌ Team members retain membership in their functional unit so that they can serve as a bridge between the functional unit and the team, enhancing cooperation.

▌ It gives top management a useful vehicle for decentralization. Once the day-to-day operations have been delegated, top management can devote more attention to areas such as long-range planning.

On the other hand, the matrix design also has some major disadvantages.

▌ Employees may be uncertain about reporting relationships, especially if they are simultaneously assigned to a functional manager and to several project managers.

▌ To complicate matters, some managers see the matrix as a form of anarchy in which they have unlimited freedom.

▌ Another set of problems is associated with the dynamics of group behavior. Groups take longer than individuals to make decisions, may be dominated by one individual, and may compromise too much. They may also get bogged down in discussion and not focus on their primary objectives.

▌ Finally, in a matrix, more time may be required for coordinating task-related activities.[40]

Online Study Center
Improve Your Grade
Career Snapshot 6.3

Hybrid Designs

Some organizations use a design that represents a hybrid of two or more of the common forms of organization design.[41] For example, an organization may have five related divisions and one unrelated division, making its design a cross between an M-form and an H-form design. Indeed, few companies use a design in its pure form; most firms have one basic organization design as a foundation for managing the business but maintain enough flexibility to make temporary or permanent modifications for strategic purposes. Ford, for example, used the matrix approach to design the Taurus and the Mustang, but the company is basically a U-form organization showing signs of moving to an M-form design. As we note earlier, any combination of factors may dictate the appropriate organization design for any particular company.

> **CONCEPT CHECK 6.3**
>
> Describe the characteristics that a firm using the U-form design should have. Do the same for the H-form, the M-form, and the matrix design. For each item, explain the relationship between that set of characteristics and the choice of organization design.

TEST PREPPER 6.4

ANSWERS CAN BE FOUND ON P. 441

True or False?

_____ 1. A doctor's office using a single service strategy is likely to use functional design.

_____ 2. The matrix design structure breaks the unity of command principle.

Multiple Choice

_____ 3. Kristen Runyon owns her own photography studio. She is the only photographer. You would expect her to use _____ organization design.
   a. U-form   d. matrix
   b. H-form   e. hybrid
   c. M-form

_____ 4. Don and Jane Stiriz own a bed-and-breakfast, restaurant, pizza shop, and antique store. You would expect them to use which organization design?
   a. Functional
   b. Conglomerate
   c. Divisional
   d. Matrix
   e. Hybrid

Online Study Center
ACE the Test
ACE Practice Tests 6.4

EMERGING ISSUES IN ORGANIZATION DESIGN

5 ▸ *Describe emerging issues in organization design.*

Finally, in today's complex and ever-changing environment, it should come as no surprise that managers continue to explore and experiment with new forms of organization design. Many organizations today are creating designs for themselves that maximize their ability to adapt to shifting circumstances and to a fluid environment. They try to accomplish this by not becoming too compartmentalized or too rigid. As we noted earlier, bureaucratic organizations are hard to change, slow, and inflexible. To avoid these problems, organizations can try to be as different from bureaucracies as possible by imposing relatively few rules, writing general job descriptions, and so forth. This final section highlights some of the more important emerging issues in organization design.[42]

1. The **team organization** relies almost exclusively on project-type teams, with little or no underlying functional hierarchy. In such an organization, people float from project to project as consistent with their skills and as necessitated by the demands of those projects.[43]

team organization An organization that relies almost exclusively on project-type teams, with little or no underlying functional hierarchy.

virtual organization An organization that has little or no formal structure.

learning organization An organization that works to facilitate the lifelong learning and personal development of all of its employees, while continuously transforming itself to respond to changing demands and needs.

2. The **virtual organization** is one that has little or no formal structure. Such an organization typically has only a handful of permanent employees and a very small staff and administrative headquarters facility. As the needs of the organization change, its managers bring in temporary workers, lease facilities, and outsource basic support services to meet the demands of each unique situation. As the situation changes, the temporary workforce changes accordingly, with some people leaving the organization and others entering. Facilities and the services subcontracted to others change as well. Thus the organization exists only in response to its needs. And increasingly, virtual organizations are conducting most—if not all—of their business online.[44]

3. The **learning organization** is one that works to facilitate the lifelong learning and personal development of all of its employees, while continuously transforming itself to respond to changing demands and needs.[45]

   Although managers might approach the concept of a learning organization from a variety of perspectives, their goals often include improved quality, continuous improvement, and performance measurement. The idea is that the most consistent and logical strategy for achieving continuous improvement is constantly to upgrade employee talent, skill, and knowledge. For example, if each employee in an organization learns one new thing each day and can translate that knowledge into work-related practice, continuous improvement will logically follow. Indeed, organizations that wholeheartedly embrace this approach believe that continuous improvement can occur only through constant learning by employees.

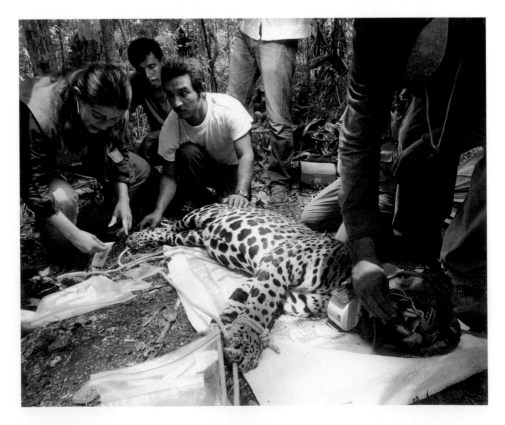

Teams are being increasingly used in organizations today. Guatemalan veterinarian Janette Udiales and her assistants are shown taking samples from a sleeping jaguar in Laguna del Tigre, Guatemala. A binational team of biologists, veterinarians, and hunters are working in the Peten jungle region on a high-tech project using satellite tracking to try to save from extinction the jaguar and the habitat in which it lives.

TEST PREPPER 6.5

True or False?

_____ 1. A management consulting company where consultants come together for projects and then disband is designed as a virtual organization.

Multiple Choice

_____ 2. An organization with little or no formal structure is which type of organization?
  a. Team organziation
  b. Virtual organization
  c. Learning organization
  d. International organization
  e. Hybrid organization

_____ 3. American Fidelity Assurance offers free professional growth courses on company time. It could be described as a(n) _____ organization.
  a. team
  b. virtual
  c. learning
  d. international
  e. hybrid

Online Study Center
ACE the Test
ACE Practice Tests 6.5

BUILDING EFFECTIVE TECHNICAL SKILLS

Exercise Overview

Technical skills are the skills necessary to accomplish or understand the specific work being done in an organization. This exercise asks you to develop technical skills related to understanding the impact of an organization's strategy on its structure.

Exercise Background

Assume that you are a manager of a firm that has developed a new, innovative system of personal transportation, such as the Segway HT. (If you are not familiar with the Segway, visit the website at www.segway.com and learn about the product.)

Exercise Task

Using the information about strategy given in each question below and your knowledge of the Segway product, choose the appropriate form of organization structure.

1. What would be the most appropriate organization structure if Segway's corporate-level strategy were to continue to produce a limited line of very similar products for sale in the United States?

Online Study Center
Improve Your Grade
Exercises: Building Effective Skills

2. What would be the most appropriate organization structure if Segway's corporate-level strategy were to continue to produce only its original product but to sell it in Asia and Europe as well as in North America?

3. What would be the most appropriate organization structure if Segway's corporate-level strategy were to move into related areas, using the innovations developed for the Segway to help design several other innovative products?

4. What would be the most appropriate organization structure if Segway's corporate-level strategy were to use its expertise in personal ground transportation to move into other areas, such as personal air or personal water transport?

5. What would be the most appropriate organization structure if Segway's corporate-level strategy were to use the funds generated by Segway sales to finance moves into several unrelated industries?

6. For each of the five strategies listed above, tell how that strategy influenced your choice of organization design.

EXPERIENTIAL EXERCISE

Purpose

The purpose of this exercise is to help you better understand how new forms of technology can affect organization structure and design.

Introduction

Amazon.com, Inc., is generally cited as one of the first—and best—examples of a new business created solely to capitalize on the potential of the Internet. Amazon.com started up in 1991 as a supplier of hard-to-find books. It rapidly grew and soon began selling all kinds of books, often at significant discounts. Amazon.com went public in May 1997.

Amazon.com essentially serves as a book distributor. The firm receives orders from customers and fills those orders from one of several different wholesalers with whom it works. As a result, Amazon.com has little warehouse space, low distribution costs, and modest sales costs. In recent times, the firm has started to branch out. It now sells CDs, videos, DVDs, and electronic equipment as well.

Instructions

Step 1: Working alone, draw an organization chart of how you think Amazon.com is likely to be structured.

Online Study Center
Improve Your Grade
–Exercises: Experiential Exercise
–Interactive Skills Self-Assessment

Step 2: Still working alone, draw an organization chart of how a firm like Amazon.com might look if the Internet did not exist.

Step 3: Now form small groups with three or four classmates, and discuss similarities and differences between the two organization charts each of you developed.

Follow-up Questions

1. Even though Amazon.com has yet to make a profit, it is a darling among investors. How do you explain this?
2. How might the Internet affect the organization structure and design of an existing business?
3. Research Amazon.com and see whether you can find out what its organization chart actually looks like.

CLOSING CASE STUDY

Customers Say "Yum!"

Mom likes roast chicken, Dad prefers nachos, and Junior will eat only pepperoni pizza. Now, thanks to a restructuring of Yum! Brands restaurants, everybody can eat together. Yum! developed the concept of putting more than one brand together at a single location. Co-location of multiple restaurants, called "multibranding," has proved to be immensely popular, increasing store revenues by 25 percent or more. But the tactic is just the latest in a long line of structural changes in the ever-evolving fast-food business.

Typical fast-food restaurants offer just one type of food, such as burgers or sub sandwiches. To attract customers in a slow-growing industry, fast-food chains have tried to offer new products, such as the McPizza. Yet, according to David C. Novak, CEO and president of Yum!, "every time we've tried to venture into a new category, we've failed because we've lacked credibility. Nobody is waiting with bated breath for a Taco Bell burger." Another growth tactic calls for fast-food chains to add new brands. For example, McDonald's bought Boston Market, Donato's, and Chipotle Mexican Grill. Wendy's acquired Baja Fresh Mexican Grill. Every chain is also trying a third strategy—upgrading existing restaurants, with fresher ingredients, more cooked-to-order items, and upscale ambience. The new type of restaurant is called "fast-casual." "[Baby] boomers want more and will pay for it," claims Charles Rawley, Yum!'s chief development officer.

Multibranding offers a fourth option for growth. Yum! owns Pizza Hut, Taco Bell, Kentucky Fried Chicken (KFC), A&W Restaurants, and Long John Silver's. The mix of businesses increases market share, but Yum! has found a way to wring even more value from the diverse chains. The chain has nearly two thousand stores that combine two or more brands, such as KFC and Taco Bell. At a time when the fast-food industry on the whole is averaging just 2 percent annual growth in sales, Yum!'s multibranded stores can see a 25 percent increase.

Multibranding is not the first structural innovation made by fast-food firms, which have a long history

> *"[I]t's harder to run a restaurant with two brands. With more variety comes more complexity."*
>
> —David C. Novak, CEO and president, Yum! Brands, Inc.

of changes in structure and ownership. For example, each of Yum!'s five brands began as an independently owned, entrepreneurial start-up. Pizza Hut was begun by two brothers, college students at Wichita State University. From humble beginnings, Pizza Hut grew to become the number-one pizza restaurant in the world by selling franchises and expanding internationally. After becoming a publicly traded company in the 1960s, Pizza Hut was acquired by PepsiCo in 1977. World War II veteran Glen Bell opened the first Taco Bell in 1962. Taco Bell also developed many domestic and international franchisees. When Bell was ready to retire in 1978, he sold Taco Bell to PepsiCo. Harland Sanders, founder of KFC, began offering franchises in 1952, built up the firm's international operations, and sold out in 1964. The company was owned by distiller Heublein, tobacco conglomerate R.J. Reynolds, and others before its sale to PepsiCo in 1986.

PepsiCo's purchase of Pizza Hut, Taco Bell, and KFC was designed to give the firm an edge over competitor Coca-Cola. The firm was looking to diversify beyond the stagnant soft-drink market and believed that the food industry would make a good complement for the beverage industry. Soon, however, PepsiCo realized that its competencies in marketing did not compensate for its weaknesses in customer service and food products. After years of disappointing sales and synergy that never materialized, PepsiCo spun off the three businesses into a separate firm, called Tricon Global Restaurants, in 1997.

In 2002 Tricon changed its name to Yum! Brands and purchased A&W. A&W grew from a single California root beer stand in 1919 to a nationwide chain of restaurants by the 1950s. After several changes of ownership, in 1999 the chain bought Long John Silver's (founded in 1969). Yum! is continuing with the franchising and international growth strategies. In 2004 Yum! realized gross profit margins of around 14 percent. Domestic store sales grew by 3 percent, while international sales grew 9 percent.

Imitation is the sincerest form of flattery, and others are copying Yum!'s multibranding structure. Allied Domecq Quick Service Restaurants has taken the multibranding concept one step further, combining Dunkin' Donuts, Togo's sandwich shops, and Baskin-Robbins. This allows a store to maintain consistent sales throughout the day, from early-morning pastries to late-night desserts.

Yum! has probably reached the logical limit of adding new brands, with the possible exception of a sandwich chain, a segment in which Yum! is not currently competing. Changes implemented over the last several years have begun to show results, yet CEO Novak concedes, "[I]t's harder to run a restaurant with two brands. With more variety comes more complexity, so we've been dedicated to improving the capability of our people to deliver our customers a great experience." However, Yum!'s structure—including upgrades, multibranding, global growth, and development of fast-casual restaurants—is working, for now.

Case Questions

1. Examine the development of the fast-food industry, including the impact that core technology, environment, organizational size, and organizational life cycle have had on organization structure.

2. What seems to be Yum!'s current corporate structure?

3. Look at your answer to question 2. How has Yum!'s corporate-level strategy influenced that structure?

Case References

"2004 Annual Report," "About Yum! Brands," Yum! Brands, Inc., website, www.yum.com on January 20, 2006; "About A&W," A&W Restaurants website, www.awrestaurants.com on January 24, 2003; "About KFC," Kentucky Fried Chicken website, www.kfc.com on April 18, 2004; Gerry Khermouch, "Tricon's Fast-Food Smorgasbord," *BusinessWeek*, February 11, 2002, www.businessweek.com on January 16, 2003; "History," Taco Bell website, www.tacobell.com on April 18, 2004; "Long John Silver's," Long John Silver's website, www.ljsilvers.com on January 24, 2003; Melanie Wells, "Happier Meals," *Forbes*, January 8, 2003, story.news.yahoo .com on January 16, 2003 (quote); "The Pizza Hut Story," Pizza Hut website, www.pizzahut.com on April 18, 2004.

Online Study Center
Improve Your Grade
–Learning Objective Review
–Audio Chapter Review
–Study Guide to Go

Online Study Center
ACE the Test
Audio Chapter Quiz

LEARNING OBJECTIVE REVIEW

1 *Identify the basic elements of organizations.*

- Organizations are made up of five basic elements:
  job specialization
  departmentalization
  reporting relationships
  distribution of authority
  coordination

2 *Describe the bureaucratic perspective on organization design.*

- One early universal model of organization design is the bureaucratic model, which attempts to prescribe how all organizations should be designed.

- It is based on the presumed need for legitimate, logical, and formal rules, regulations, and procedures.

3 ▶ *Identify and explain several situational influences on organization design.*

- The situational view of organization design is based on the assumption that the optimal organization design is a function of situational factors.

- Four important situational factors are
  technology
  environment
  size
  organizational life cycle

4 ▶ *Describe the basic forms of organization design that characterize many organizations.*

- Many organizations today adopt one of four basic organization designs:
  functional (U-form)
  conglomerate (H-form)
  divisional (M-form)
  matrix design

- Other organizations use a hybrid design derived from two or more of these.

5 ▶ *Describe emerging issues in organization design.*

- Three emerging forms of organization design are
  the team organization
  the virtual organization
  the learning organization

Online Study Center **RESOURCES**

Prepare for Class, Improve Your Grade, and ACE the Test. These Student Achievement resources include:

ACE Practice Tests	Interactive Skills Assessments	Study Guide to Go
End of Chapter Exercises	Knowledgebank	Video Segments
Glossaries (visual and print)	Reviews (audio and print)	Summaries/Outlines
Flashcards		

To access these learning and study tools, go to: **college.hmco.com/pic/griffinSAS**

7 Organization Change and Innovation

Sears has undergone numerous changes in recent years. This Sears store in Illinois has a prominent display of Lands' End merchandise. After Sears bought Lands' End, Sears itself was subsequently bought by Kmart. Each of these moves resulted in numerous major changes.

1 *Describe the nature of organization change, including forces for change and planned versus reactive change.*

2 *Discuss the steps in organization change and how to manage resistance to change.*

3 *Identify and describe major areas of organization change, and discuss the assumptions, techniques, and effectiveness of organization development.*

*"Organizationally, the table is being set.
Culturally, we are coming together."*

—Edward S. Lampert, chairman, Sears Holdings

Chapter Outline

▶ THE NATURE OF ORGANIZATION CHANGE
Forces for change
Planned versus reactive change

▶ MANAGING CHANGE IN ORGANIZATIONS
Steps in the change process
Understanding resistance to change
Overcoming resistance to change

▶ AREAS OF ORGANIZATION CHANGE
Changing organization structure and design
Changing technology and operations
Changing people, attitudes, and behaviors
Changing business processes
Organization development

▶ ORGANIZATIONAL INNOVATION
The innovation process
Forms of innovation
The failure to innovate
Promoting innovation in organizations

Online Study Center
Prepare for Class
Chapter Outline

4 ▶ *Describe the innovation process,
forms of innovation, the failure to
innovate, and how organizations can
promote innovation.*

Teaching an
Old Dog New Tricks

*"C*onservative, wealthy, respectable but outdated suitor seeks
younger, energetic, modern partner."* A personals ad? No—this is
a description of the recent "marriage" between venerable retailer
Sears, Roebuck and Co. and online and catalog e-tailer Lands' End.
Sears, which has struggled with stagnant sales in recent years,
acquired Lands' End recently, hoping to revitalize its leadership of
the fiercely competitive retailing industry.

Sears, founded in 1886, was for decades an important store
for rural customers. Over the years, Sears added retail stores for
city shoppers and also was at the forefront of private-label brand-
ing, creating the DieHard, Kenmore, and Craftsman labels. Today,
Sears has no catalog operations. It is also one of the last of the traditional department stores, providing everything from lawn mow-
ers to wedding gowns to auto repair. Sears enjoys an outstanding
reputation for its appliances, tools, and other "hard" goods, but

You should be able to define and use terms that are part of the practicing manager's vocabulary, as well as those that are integral in the language of management.

its "soft" goods are often seen as lacking in style and of poor quality. Many shoppers seeking lower-priced clothing prefer Target, Kohl's, or Wal-Mart. Sears's recent major ad campaign, "Come see the softer side of Sears," and store upgrades did not increase sales of soft goods. In fact, apparel sales fell throughout 2004 and 2005.

Lands' End had some things in common with Sears. The firm began in 1963 as a mail-order-only retailer, mimicking Sears's early strategy. Tom Filline, a retired Sears executive, helped Lands' End develop its efficient mail-order operations. The firm also quickly established a reputation for selling clothing and housewares that are sturdy and reliable, echoing Sears's reputation in hard goods. Finally, Lands' End had strict quality standards and tests products at its in-house facility, a practice initiated by Sears over a hundred years ago.

In three significant ways, however, Lands' End and Sears were quite different. First, Lands' End was a pioneer in online technology, creating an early online catalog. "We were one of the first companies to recognize that selling online was not an end in itself, but another channel in a multichannel sales environment," says Lands' End spokesperson Emily C. Leuthner. Second, whereas Sears failed to master the apparel industry, Lands' End clearly hit on a winning formula. It offers timeless designs and high-quality materials and workmanship. It appeals to women in the thirty-five- to fifty-four-year-old category, the top spenders on apparel. Third, although Lands' End had grown, it remained a direct merchant, not opening any retail outlets. The firm ran all of its operations out of its rural Dodgeville, Wisconsin, headquarters. The enforced closeness led to the development of a unique, cohesive, and high-achieving culture, unlike Sears's bureaucratic and impersonal atmosphere. As a result, Lands' End was named to *Fortune*'s new "Best Companies to Work For" list.

The acquisition is called "bricks and clicks," because it combines a traditional bricks-and-mortar retailer with an online e-tailer. Sears carries Lands' End upscale apparel and home products in its stores. Lands' End contributes its skill in selling higher-quality soft goods and its online expertise. "The transaction could bring a breath of fresh air to Sears' apparel operations," declares analyst Filippe Goossens. Sears brings to the table capabilities in managing stores, which can introduce Lands' End goods to a wider market.

It sounds like a marriage made in heaven, but there have been some difficulties. Although Sears intended to blend the two firms' strengths without diluting them, some changes have been required. One springs from the two firms' different target customers. Lands' End's typical customers, with annual income over $100,000, have not been shopping at Sears, where typical customers earn less than $50,000. Sears's price-conscious customers have not been willing to pay more, causing Sears to lower prices. Analyst Kevin Murphy said, "Sears must maintain the distinctiveness of the Lands' End brand and the quality of service that Lands' End customers are used to." While customer service remains high, many dedicated Lands' End shoppers have become dissatisfied with quality, as Sears has begun to use less costly materials. In another cost-cutting move, Sears has combined apparel design staff into one group.

In March 2005, Sears merged with Kmart, which was emerging from bankruptcy. Sears Holding Company has begun to integrate the two stores, putting Kenmore and Craftsman products in Kmarts, for example.

In 2006, the firm will completely merge all of the stores' functions. The chairman of Sears Holdings, Edward S. Lampert, claims, "Organizationally, the table is being set. Culturally, we are coming together. We are shedding our separate . . . identities and becoming Sears Holdings." Change will come slowly, but if the merged firms can share their abilities, Sears can regain some of its former glory as an icon of American retailing.[1]

Managers at Sears and Lands' End have had to grapple with something all managers must eventually confront: the need for change. Sears, especially, was in dire need of an infusion of energy and opportunity, and Lands' End seems like the perfect tonic. And, for Lands' End, becoming a part of Sears introduces it to a whole new customer base and gives it the financial strength to continue to grow, expand into new markets, and develop new distribution and marketing options. In short, both firms are changing in dramatic ways.

Understanding when and how to implement change is a vital part of management. This chapter describes how organizations manage change. We first examine the nature of organization change and identify the basic issues of managing change. We then identify and describe major areas of change, including business process change, a major type of change that has been undertaken by many firms recently. We then examine organization development and conclude by discussing a related area, organizational innovation.

THE NATURE OF ORGANIZATION CHANGE

1 ▶ *Describe the nature of organization change, including forces for change and planned versus reactive change.*

Organization change is any substantive modification to some part of the organization.[2] Thus change can involve virtually any aspect of an organization: work schedules, bases for departmentalization, span of management, machinery, organization design, people themselves, and so on. It is important to remember that any change in an organization may have effects extending beyond the actual area where the change is implemented. For example, when Northrop Grumman recently installed a new automated production system at one of its plants, employees were trained to operate new equipment, the compensation system was adjusted

organization change   Any substantive modification to some part of the organization.

There are a variety of forces that can create a need for change, some external and some internal. This shopper is checking out her own purchases at a Kroger supermarket. Several factors—new technology (that facilitates cashless transactions), customer preferences for convenience (that cause them to want to get in and out of the store quickly), and the firm's interests in lowering costs (by hiring fewer checkout operators)—have together led to this increasingly popular change.

to reflect new skill levels, the span of management for supervisors was altered, and several related jobs were redesigned. Selection criteria for new employees were also changed, and a new quality control system was installed.[3] In addition, it is quite common for activities involving several different kinds of organization change to be going on simultaneously.[4]

Forces for Change

Why do organizations find change necessary? The basic reason is that something relevant to the organization either has changed or is likely to change in the foreseeable future. The organization therefore may have little choice but to change as well. Indeed, a primary reason for the problems that organizations often face is failure to anticipate or respond properly to changing circumstances. The forces that compel change may be external or internal to the organization.[5]

External Forces

External forces for change derive from the organization's general and task environments. For example, two energy crises, an aggressive Japanese automobile industry, floating currency exchange rates, and floating international interest rates—all manifestations of the international dimension of the general environment—profoundly influenced U.S. automobile companies. New rules of production and competition forced them to alter the way they do business. In the political area, new laws, court decisions, and regulations affect organizations. The technological dimension may yield new production techniques that the organization needs to explore. The economic dimension is affected by inflation, the cost of living, and money supplies. The sociocultural dimension, reflecting societal values, determines what kinds of products or services will be accepted in the market.

Because of its immediacy to the organization, the task environment is an even more powerful force for change. Competitors influence an organization through their price structures and product lines. When Dell lowers the prices it charges for computers, Gateway may have little choice but to follow suit. Because customers determine what products can be sold at what prices, organizations must be concerned with consumer tastes and preferences. Suppliers affect organizations by raising or lowering prices or changing product lines. Regulators can have dramatic effects on an organization. For example, if the Occupational Safety & Health Administration (OSHA) rules that a particular production process is dangerous to workers, it can force a firm to close a plant until that facility meets higher safety standards. Unions can force change when they negotiate for higher wages or go on strike.[6]

Internal Forces

A variety of forces inside the organization may cause change. If top management revises the organization's strategy, organization change is likely to result. A decision by an electronics company to enter the home computer market or a decision to increase a ten-year product sales goal by 3 percent would occasion many organization changes. Other internal forces for change may be reflections of external forces. As sociocultural values shift, for example, workers' attitudes toward their job may also shift—and they may demand a change in working hours or working conditions. In such a case, even though the force is rooted in the external environment, the organization must respond directly to the internal pressure it generates.[7]

Planned Versus Reactive Change

Some change is planned well in advance; other change comes about as a reaction to unexpected events.

▋ **Planned change** is change that is designed and implemented in an orderly and timely fashion in anticipation of future events. Planned change is nearly always preferable to reactive change.[8] Georgia-Pacific, a large forest products business, is an excellent example of a firm that went through a planned and well-managed change process. When A. D. Correll became CEO, he quickly grew alarmed at the firm's high accident rate—nine serious injuries per hundred employees each year, and twenty-six deaths during the most recent five-year period. Although the forest products business is inherently dangerous, Correll believed that the accident rate was far too high and launched a major effort to improve things. He and other top managers developed a multistage program intended to educate workers about safety, improve safety equipment in the plant, and eliminate a long-standing part of the firm's culture that made injuries almost a badge of courage. Today, Georgia-Pacific has the best safety record in the industry, with relatively few injuries.[9]

planned change Change that is designed and implemented in an orderly and timely fashion in anticipation of future events.

▋ **Reactive change** is a piecemeal response to circumstances as they develop. Because reactive change may be hurried, the potential for poorly conceived and executed change is increased. Caterpillar was caught flat-footed by a worldwide recession in the construction industry, suffered enormous losses, and took several years to recover. Had managers at Caterpillar anticipated the need for change, they might have been able to respond more quickly. The importance of approaching change from a planned perspective is reinforced by the frequency of organization change. Most companies and most divisions of large companies implement some form of moderate change at least every year and effect one or more major changes every four to five years.[10] Managers who sit back, responding only when they have to, are likely to spend a lot of time hastily changing and re-changing things. A more effective approach is to anticipate forces that will necessitate change and plan ahead to deal with them.[11]

reactive change A piecemeal response to circumstances as they develop.

TEST PREPPER 7.1

ANSWERS CAN BE FOUND ON P. 441

True or False?

_____ 1. Organizations change because something relevant to the organization has already changed or is about to change.

_____ 2. Planned change is a piecemeal response to circumstances as they develop.

_____ 3. Reactive change is generally executed better than planned change.

Multiple Choice

_____ 4. Passage of the Sarbanes-Oxley Act, which required CEOs and CFOs to personally vouch for the accuracy of their business's financial statement, is an example of a _____.
   a. reactive change
   b. planned change
   c. general force of change
   d. internal force of change
   e. external force of change

_____ 5. Which of the following is an example of an internal force that affects the performance of an organization?
   a. A change in the organization's strategy
   b. Customers
   c. Competition
   d. Regulators
   e. A sociocultural values shift

Online Study Center
ACE the Test
ACE Practice Tests 7.1

MANAGING CHANGE IN ORGANIZATIONS

> **2** *Discuss the steps in organization change and how to manage resistance to change.*

Organization change is a complex phenomenon. A manager cannot simply wave a wand and implement a planned change like magic. Instead, any change must be systematic and logical to have a realistic opportunity to succeed.[12] To carry this off, the manager needs to understand the steps of effective change and how to counter employee resistance to change.[13]

Steps in the Change Process

Experts have over the years developed a number of models or frameworks outlining steps for change.[14] A comprehensive approach is generally most useful in today's complex business environment.

A Comprehensive Approach to Change

The comprehensive approach to change takes a systems view and delineates a series of specific steps that often leads to successful change. This expanded model is illustrated in Figure 7.1.

1. Recognizing the need for change: Reactive change might be triggered by employee complaints, declines in productivity, a court injunction, sales slumps, or labor strikes. A planned change might be the result of a forecast indicating new market potential, the accumulation of a cash surplus for possible investment, or an opportunity to achieve and capitalize on a major technological

FIGURE 7.1

Steps in the Change Process

Managers must understand how and why to implement change. A manager who, when implementing change, follows a logical and orderly sequence such as the one shown here is more likely to succeed than a manager who launches a change process that is haphazard and poorly conceived.

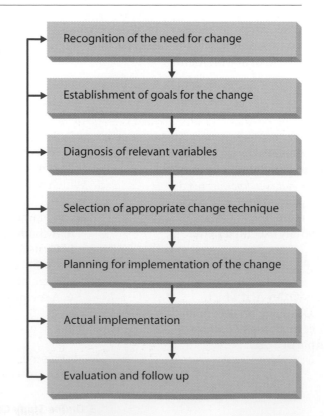

Recognition of the need for change

Establishment of goals for the change

Diagnosis of relevant variables

Selection of appropriate change technique

Planning for implementation of the change

Actual implementation

Evaluation and follow up

breakthrough. Managers might also initiate change today because indicators suggest that it will be necessary in the near future.[15]

2. Setting goals for the change: These could include increasing market share, entering new markets, restoring employee morale, settling a strike, and identifying investment opportunities.

3. Diagnosing the situation to determine what brought on the need for change: Turnover, for example, might be caused by low pay, poor working conditions, poor supervisors, or employee dissatisfaction. Although turnover may be the immediate stimulus for change, managers must understand its causes in order to make the right changes.

4. Selecting a change technique that will accomplish the intended goals: If turnover is caused by low pay, a new reward system may be needed. If the cause is poor supervision, training in interpersonal skills may be called for. (Various change techniques are summarized later in this chapter.)

5. Planning for the implementation: Issues to consider include the costs of the change, its effects on other areas of the organization, and the degree of employee participation appropriate to the situation.

6. Implementing the change.

7. Evaluating the results: If the change was intended to reduce turnover, managers must check turnover after the change has been in effect for a while. If turnover is still too high, other changes may be necessary.[16]

Understanding Resistance to Change

Another element in the effective management of change is understanding the resistance that often accompanies change.[17] Managers need to know why people resist change and what can be done about their resistance.

▌ *Uncertainty.*   In the face of impending change, employees may become anxious and nervous. They may worry about their ability to meet new job demands, they may think that their job security is threatened, or they may simply dislike ambiguity.

Change is a common event in most organizations today. And although much of this change is necessary and beneficial, managers sometimes engage in change activities that are either unnecessary or poorly conceived. When this happens, it increases the chances that employees will resist the change—they will experience uncertainty, are likely to perceive a threat to their self-interests, may see things differently than those who decided upon the change, and may experience feelings of loss. Indeed, as shown in this cartoon, change can be so poorly managed that employees sense it before it even occurs and develop resistance without even knowing the details.

CONCEPT CHECK 7.1

What are the symptoms that a manager should look for in determining whether an organization needs to change? What are the symptoms that indicate that an organization has been through too much change?

DILBERT reprinted by permission of United Features Syndicate Inc.

▌ ***Threats to self-interests.*** Many impending changes threaten the self-interests of some managers within the organization. A change might diminish their power or influence within the company, so they fight it. Before deciding to merge with Lands' End, managers at Sears developed a plan calling for a new type of store. The new stores would be somewhat smaller than typical Sears stores and would be located in smaller strip centers rather than in large shopping malls. They would carry clothes and other "soft goods," but not hardware, appliances, furniture, or automotive products. When executives in charge of the excluded product lines heard about the plan, they raised such strong objections that the plan was canceled.

▌ ***Different perceptions.*** A manager may make a decision and recommend a plan for change on the basis of her own assessment of a situation. Others in the organization may resist the change because they do not agree with the manager's assessment or because they perceive the situation differently.[18]

▌ ***Feelings of loss.*** Many changes involve altering work arrangements in ways that disrupt existing social networks. Because social relationships are important, most people resist any change that might adversely affect those relationships. Other intangibles threatened by change include power, status, security, familiarity with existing procedures, and self-confidence.

Overcoming Resistance to Change

Of course, a manager should not give up in the face of resistance to change. Although there are no sure-fire cures, there are several techniques that at least have the potential to overcome resistance.[19]

▌ Participation is often the most effective technique for overcoming resistance to change. Employees who participate in planning and implementing a change are better able to understand the reasons for the change. Uncertainty is reduced, and self-interests and social relationships are less threatened. Having had an opportunity to express their ideas and assume the perspectives of others, employees are more likely to accept the change gracefully.

▌ Educating employees about the need for and the expected results of an impending change should reduce their resistance. If open communication is established and maintained during the change process, uncertainty can be minimized.

▌ Facilitation procedures are also advisable. For instance, making only necessary changes, announcing those changes well in advance, and allowing time

---

FIGURE 7.2

Force-Field Analysis for Plant Closing at General Motors

A force-field analysis can help a manager facilitate change. A manager who is able to identify both forces acting for and forces acting against a change can see where to focus efforts to remove barriers to change (such as offering training and relocation to displaced workers). Removing the forces against the change can at least partially overcome resistance.

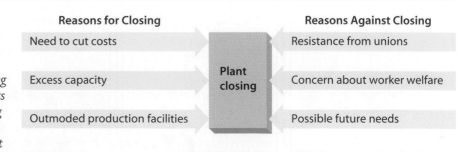

for people to adjust to new ways of doing things can help reduce resistance to change.[20]

▮ "Force-field analysis" may sound like something out of a *Star Trek* movie, but it can help overcome resistance to change. In almost any change situation, some forces are acting for and others against the change. To facilitate the change, managers start by listing each set of forces and then trying to tip the balance so that the forces facilitating the change outweigh those hindering it. It is especially important to try to remove, or at least to minimize, some of the forces acting against the change. Suppose, for example, that General Motors is considering a plant closing as part of a change. As shown in Figure 7.2, three factors are reinforcing the change: GM needs to cut costs, it has excess capacity, and the plant includes outmoded production facilities. At the same time, there is resistance from the International Union, United Automobile, Aerospace and Agricultural Implement Workers of America (UAW), concern for workers being put out of their jobs, and a feeling that the plant might be needed again in the future. GM might start by convincing the UAW that the closing is necessary by presenting profit-and-loss figures. It could then offer relocation and retraining to displaced workers. And GM might shut down the plant and put it in "mothballs" so that it can be renovated later. The three major factors hindering the change are thus eliminated or reduced in importance.

CONCEPT CHECK 7.2

Think back to a time when a professor or employer announced a change that you did not want to adopt. What were the reasons for your resistance to this change? Was the professor able to overcome your resistance? If so, tell what he or she did. If not, tell what he or she could have done that might have been successful.

TEST PREPPER 7.2

ANSWERS CAN BE FOUND ON P. 441

True or False?

_____ 1. Making change announcements well in advance of implementation is called facilitation.

_____ 2. Isabelle has been relatively secure in knowing her job performance was good to excellent. However, with a pending merger, she feels less secure. She hopes the merger will fail. Her resistance to change is caused by different perceptions.

Multiple Choice

_____ 3. The marketing department is getting better furniture for the office. Remarkably, many workers are complaining about the change. They are experiencing _____.
   a. uncertainty
   b. threatened self-interest
   c. different perceptions
   d. feelings of loss
   e. the grapevine

_____ 4. Which of the following techniques has NOT been identified as often being effective in battling resistance to change?
   a. Participation   d. Cost analysis
   b. Education   e. Communication
   c. Force-field analysis

Online Study Center
ACE the Test
ACE Practice Tests 7.2

AREAS OF ORGANIZATION CHANGE

3 ▶ *Identify and describe major areas of organization change, and discuss the assumptions, techniques, and effectiveness of organization development.*

We note earlier that change can involve virtually any part of an organization. In general, however, most change interventions involve organization structure and design, technology and operations, or people. In addition, many organizations have gone through massive and comprehensive programs of business process change.

Changing Organization Structure and Design

Organization change might be focused on any of the basic components of organization structure or on the organization's overall design. Thus the organization might change the way it designs its jobs or its bases of departmentalization. Likewise, it might change reporting relationships or the distribution of authority. For example, we noted in Chapter 6 the trend toward flatter organizations. Coordination mechanisms are also subject to change. On a larger scale, the organization might change its overall design. For example, a growing business could decide to drop its functional design and adopt a divisional design. Or it might transform itself into a matrix. Changes in culture usually involve the structure and design of the organization as well. Finally, the organization might change any part of its human resource management system, such as its selection criteria, its performance appraisal methods, or its compensation package.[21] Toyota has been undergoing a significant series of changes in its organization structure and design—changes intended to make it a flatter and more decentralized enterprise and thus more responsive to its external environment.[22]

New technologies represent a major form of organization change. Due in part to rising consumer demand and in part to government pressure, many automobile companies today are developing and marketing so-called hybrid cars. These cars use fuel cells and/or electric power to augment their internal combustion engines, resulting in much greater fuel efficiency. But designing, manufacturing, and marketing these new automobiles requires different methods than in the past, hence prompting a variety of organization changes.

Changing Technology and Operations

Technology is the conversion process that an organization uses to transform inputs into outputs. Because of the rapid rate of all technological innovation, technological changes are becoming increasingly important to many organizations. One important area of change today revolves around information technology. The adoption and institutionalization of information technology innovations is almost constant in most firms today. Sun Microsystems, for example, has adopted a very short-range planning cycle in order to be prepared for frequent environmental changes.[23] Another important form of technological change involves equipment. To keep pace with competitors, firms periodically find that they must replace existing machinery and equipment with newer models. And changes in work processes or work activities may be necessary when new equipment is introduced or new products are manufactured. Organizational control systems may also be the targets of change.

Many large businesses have been working to implement change in technology and operations by installing and using complex and integrated software systems. Such a system—called *enterprise resource planning*—links virtually all facets of the business, making it easier for managers to keep abreast of related developments. **Enterprise resource planning, or ERP**, is a large-scale information system for integrating and synchronizing the many activities in the extended enterprise. In most cases these systems are purchased from external vendors, who then tailor their products to the client's unique needs and requirements. Companywide processes—such as materials management, production planning, order management, and financial reporting—can all be managed via ERP. In effect, these are the processes that cut across product lines, departments, and geographic locations.

enterprise resource planning (ERP)   A large-scale information system for integrating and synchronizing the many activities in the extended enterprise.

Changing People, Attitudes, and Behaviors

A third area of organization change has to do with human resources. For example, an organization might decide to change the skill level of its workforce. This change might be prompted by changes in technology or by a general desire to upgrade the quality of the workforce. Thus training programs and new selection criteria might be needed. The organization might also decide to improve its workers' performance level. In this instance, a new incentive system or performance-based training might be in order. Reader's Digest has been attempting to implement significant changes in its workforce. For example, the firm has eliminated 17 percent of its employees, reduced retirement benefits, and taken away many of the "perks" (perquisites, or job benefits) that they once enjoyed. Part of the reason for the changes was to instill in the remaining employees a sense of urgency and the need to adopt a new perspective on how they do their job.[24] Employee perceptions and expectations are also a frequent focus of organization change.

Changing Business Processes

Many organizations today have gone through massive and comprehensive change programs involving all aspects of organization design, technology, and people. Although various descriptions are used, the terms currently in vogue for these changes are *business process change* and *reengineering*. Specifically, **business process change, or reengineering**, is the radical redesign of all aspects of a business to achieve major improvements in cost, service, or time.[25] ERP, as described above, is a common platform for changing business processes. However, business process change is a more comprehensive set of changes that transcends software and information systems.

business process change (reengineering) The radical redesign of all aspects of a business to achieve major improvements in cost, service, or time.

The Need for Business Process Change

Why are so many organizations finding it necessary to undergo business process change? We noted in Chapter 1 that all systems, including organizations, are subject to entropy—a normal process leading to system decline. An organization is behaving most typically when it maintains the status quo, does not change in synch with its environment, and starts consuming its own resources to survive. In a sense, that is what happened to Kmart. In the early and mid-1970s, Kmart was in such a high-flying growth mode that it passed first J.C. Penney and then Sears to become the world's largest retailer. But then the firm's managers grew complacent and assumed that the discount retailer's prosperity would continue and that they didn't need to worry about environmental shifts, the growth of Wal-Mart, and so forth—and entropy set in. The key is to recognize the beginning of the decline and immediately move toward changing relevant business processes. Major problems occur when managers either do not recognize the onset of entropy until it is well advanced or fail to take steps immediately to counter it.

Approaches to Business Process Change

Figure 7.3 shows general steps in changing business processes, or reengineering.

1. The first step is setting goals and developing a strategy for the changes. The organization must know in advance what new business processes are supposed to accomplish and how those accomplishments will be achieved.

2. Next, top managers must begin to direct the reengineering effort. If a CEO simply announces that business process change is to occur and does nothing else, the program is unlikely to be successful. But if the CEO is constantly involved in the process, underscoring its importance and taking the lead, business process change stands a much better chance of success.

FIGURE 7.3

The Reengineering Process

Reengineering is a major redesign of all areas of an organization. To be successful, reengineering requires a systematic and comprehensive assessment of the entire organization. Goals, the support of top management, and a sense of urgency help the organization re-create itself and blend both top-level and bottom-up perspectives.

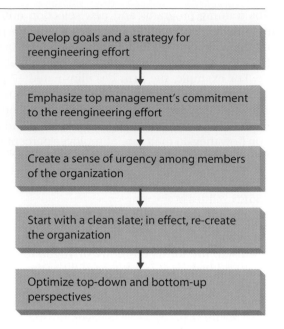

Develop goals and a strategy for reengineering effort

Emphasize top management's commitment to the reengineering effort

Create a sense of urgency among members of the organization

Start with a clean slate; in effect, re-create the organization

Optimize top-down and bottom-up perspectives

3. Most experts also agree that successful business process change is usually accompanied by a sense of urgency. People in the organization must see the clear and present need for the changes being implemented and must appreciate their importance.

4. In addition, most successful reengineering efforts start with a new, clean slate. In other words, rather than assuming that the existing organization is a starting point and then trying to modify it, business process change usually starts by asking questions, such as inquiring how customers are best served and competitors best neutralized. New approaches and systems are then created and imposed in place of existing ones.

5. Finally, business process change requires a careful blend of top-down and bottom-up involvement. On the one hand, strong leadership is necessary, but too much involvement by top management can make the changes seem autocratic. Similarly, employee participation is vital, but too little involvement by leaders can undermine the program's importance and create a sense that top managers do not care. Thus care must be taken to balance these two countervailing forces.

CONCEPT CHECK 7.3

Do you think it is possible for a change made in one area of an organization—in technology, for instance—not to lead to change in other areas? If you think that change in one area must lead to change in other areas, describe an example of an organization change to illustrate your point. If you think that change can occur in just one area without causing change in other areas, describe an example of an organization change that illustrates your point.

Organization Development

We have noted in several places the importance of people and change, and indeed, people have figured prominently in all the aspects of organization change that we have discussed. However, a special area of interest that focuses almost exclusively on people is organization development (OD).

OD Assumptions

Organization development is concerned with changing people's:

attitudes	behaviors
perceptions	expectations

More precisely, **organization development (OD)** is a planned effort that is organization-wide and managed from the top, intended to increase organizational effectiveness and health through planned interventions in the organization's process, using behavioral science knowledge.[26] The theory and practice of OD are based on several very important assumptions:

▌ Employees have a desire to grow and develop.

▌ Employees have a strong need to be accepted by others within the organization.

▌ The total organization and the way it is designed influence the way individuals and groups within the organization behave. Thus some form of collaboration between managers and their employees is necessary to:
1. take advantage of the skills and abilities of the employees
2. eliminate aspects of the organization that retard employee growth, development, and group acceptance

Because of the intense personal nature of many OD activities, many large organizations rely on one or more OD consultants (either full-time employees assigned to this function or outside experts hired specifically for OD purposes) to implement and manage their OD program.[27]

organization development (OD) An effort that is planned, organization-wide, and managed from the top, intended to increase organizational effectiveness and health through planned interventions in the organization's process, using behavioral science knowledge.

OD Techniques

Several kinds of interventions or activities are generally considered part of organization development.[28] Some OD programs may use only one or a few of these; other programs use several of them at once.

▌ *Diagnostic activities:* Just as a physician examines patients to diagnose their current condition, an OD diagnosis analyzes the current condition of an organization. To carry out this diagnosis, managers use:

questionnaires	archival data
opinion or attitude surveys	meetings
interviews	

The results of this diagnosis may generate profiles of the organization's activities, which can then be used to identify problem areas in need of correction.

▌ *Team-building activities* are intended to enhance the effectiveness and satisfaction of individuals who work in groups or teams and to promote overall group effectiveness. Given the widespread use of teams today, these activities have taken on increased importance. An OD consultant might interview team members to determine how they feel about the group; then an off-site meeting could be held to discuss the issues that surfaced and to iron out any problem areas or member concerns. Caterpillar used team building as one method for changing the working relationships between workers and supervisors from confrontational to cooperative. An interesting new approach to team building involves having executive teams participate in group cooking classes to teach them the importance of interdependence and coordination.[29]

▌ In *survey feedback*, each employee responds to a questionnaire intended to measure perceptions and attitudes (for example, satisfaction and supervisory style). Everyone involved, including the supervisor, receives the results of the survey. The aim of this approach is usually to change the behavior of supervisors by showing them how their subordinates view them. After the feedback has been provided, workshops may be conducted to evaluate results and suggest constructive changes.

▍ *Third-party peacemaking* is most often used when substantial conflict exists within the organization. Third-party peacemaking can be appropriate on the individual, group, or organizational level. The third party, usually an OD consultant, uses a variety of mediation or negotiation techniques to resolve any problems or conflicts among individuals or groups.

▍ In *process consultation*, an OD consultant observes groups in the organization to develop an understanding of their communication patterns, decision-making and leadership processes, and methods of cooperation and conflict resolution. The consultant then provides feedback to the involved parties about the processes he or she has observed. The goal of this form of intervention is to improve the observed processes. A leader who is presented with feedback outlining deficiencies in his or her leadership style, for example, might be expected to change to overcome them.

▍ *Coaching and counseling* provides nonevaluative feedback to individuals. The purpose is to help people develop a better sense of how others see them and learn behaviors that will assist others in achieving their work-related goals. The focus is not on how the individual is performing today; instead, it is on how the person can perform better in the future.

▍ *Planning and goal setting* is designed to help managers improve their planning and goal setting. Emphasis still falls on the individual, however, because the intent is to help individuals and groups integrate themselves into the overall planning process. The OD consultant might use the same approach as in process consultation, but the focus is more technically oriented, on the mechanics of planning and goal setting.

TEST PREPPER 7.3

ANSWERS CAN BE FOUND ON P. 441

True or False?

_____ 1. Organization development is planned change that bubbles up from line managers intending to increase effectiveness using behavioral science knowledge.

_____ 2. Xavier is looking for a mentor who will help guide him to work-related goals and give him a better idea of how people see him in the organization. This is the organization development technique of coaching.

_____ 3. Organization development processes and techniques are generally effective and easy to evaluate.

Multiple Choice

_____ 4. When an organization creates a radical redesign of all aspects of its business in order to achieve major cost savings, this is an example of _____.
  a. refreezing
  b. sponsorship
  c. a product champion
  d. intrapreneurship
  e. reengineering

_____ 5. When a conflict arose at Procter & Gamble between two groups, one of the internal organization development consultants was asked to intervene and help reach a resolution. The organization development technique used was _____.
  a. coaching and counseling
  b. planning and goal setting
  c. survey feedback
  d. team building
  e. third-party peacemaking

_____ 6. Which of the following is NOT one of the diagnostic techniques in organization development?
  a. Team building
  b. Survey feedback
  c. Technostructural activities
  d. Conjecture
  e. Coaching

Online Study Center
ACE the Test
ACE Practice Tests 7.3

ORGANIZATIONAL INNOVATION

4 ▶ *Describe the innovation process, forms of innovation, the failure to innovate, and how organizations can promote innovation.*

A final element of organization change that we address is innovation. **Innovation** is the managed effort of an organization to develop new products or services or new uses for existing products or services. Innovation is clearly important, because without new products or services, any organization will fall behind its competition.[30]

innovation The managed effort of an organization to develop new products or services or new uses for existing products or services.

The Innovation Process

The organizational innovation process consists of developing, applying, launching, growing, and managing the maturity and decline of creative ideas.[31] This process is depicted in Figure 7.4.

1. *Innovation development* involves the evaluation, modification, and improvement of creative ideas. Innovation development can transform a product or service with only modest potential into a product or service with significant potential. Parker Brothers, for example, decided during innovation development not to market an indoor volleyball game but instead to sell separately the appealing little foam ball designed for the game. The firm will never know how well the volleyball game would have sold, but the Nerf ball and numerous related products generated millions of dollars in revenues for Parker Brothers.

2. *Innovation application* is the stage in which an organization takes a developed idea and uses it in the design, manufacturing, or delivery of new products, services, or processes. At this point the innovation emerges from the laboratory and is transformed into tangible goods or services. One example of innovation application is the use of radar-based focusing systems in Polaroid's instant cameras. The idea of using radio waves to discover the location, speed, and

---

FIGURE 7.4

The Innovation Process

Organizations actively seek to manage the innovation process. These steps illustrate the general life cycle that characterizes most innovations. Of course, just like creativity, the innovation process will suffer if it is approached too mechanically and rigidly.

Development
Organization evaluates, modifies, and improves on a creative idea.

Application
Organization uses developed idea in design, manufacturing, or delivery of new products, services, or processes.

Launch
Organization introduces new products or services to the marketplace.

Decline
Demand for an innovation decreases, and substitute innovations are developed and applied.

Maturity
Most competing organizations have access to the idea.

Growth
Demand for new products or services grows.

direction of moving objects was first applied extensively by Allied forces during World War II. As radar technology developed during the following years, the electrical components needed became smaller and more streamlined. Researchers at Polaroid applied this well-developed technology in a new way.[32]

3. *Application launch* is the stage at which an organization introduces new products or services to the marketplace. The important question is not "Does the innovation work?" but "Will customers want to purchase the innovative product and service?" Unfortunately, despite development and application, new products and services can still fail at the launch phase.

4. *Application growth* is the stage that occurs once an innovation has been successfully launched. This is a period of high economic performance for an organization, because demand for the product or service is often greater than supply. Organizations that do not anticipate this stage may unintentionally limit their growth. At the same time, overestimating demand for a new product can be just as detrimental to performance. Unsold products can sit in warehouses for years.

5. *Innovation maturity* is the stage at which most organizations in an industry have access to an innovation and are applying it in approximately the same way. The technological application of an innovation during this stage of the innovation process can be very sophisticated. Because most firms have access to the innovation, however, as a result of their either developing it on their own or copying it from others, the innovation does not give any one of them a competitive advantage. The time that elapses between innovation development and innovation maturity varies notably, depending on the particular product or service. Whenever an innovation involves the use of complex skills (such as a complicated manufacturing process or highly sophisticated teamwork), moving from the growth phase to the maturity phase takes longer. In addition, if the skills needed to implement these innovations are rare and difficult to imitate, then strategic imitation may be delayed, and the organization may enjoy a period of sustained competitive advantage.

6. *Innovation decline* is the stage during which demand for an innovation decreases and substitute innovations are developed and applied. Because an organization does not gain a competitive advantage from an innovation at maturity, it must encourage its creative scientists, engineers, and managers to begin looking for new innovations. This continued search for competitive advantage usually leads new products and services to move from the creative process through innovation maturity, and finally to innovation decline.

Forms of Innovation

Each creative idea that an organization develops poses a different challenge for the innovation process. Innovations can be radical or incremental, they can be technical or managerial, and they can involve products or processes.

radical innovation   A new product, service, or technology that completely replaces an existing one.

incremental innovation   A new product, service, or technology that modifies an existing one.

▍ *Radical versus incremental innovations.*   **Radical innovations** are new products, services, or technologies developed by an organization that completely replace the existing products, services, or technologies in an industry.[33] **Incremental innovations** are new products, services, or technologies that modify existing ones. Firms that implement radical innovations fundamentally shift the nature of competition and the interaction of firms within their environments. Firms that

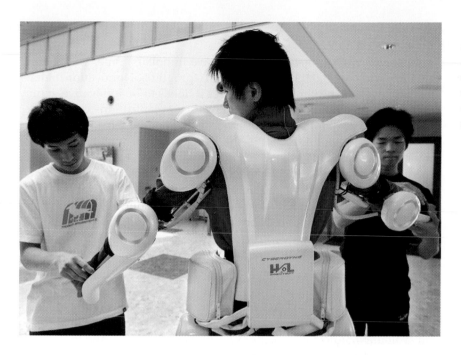

Innovation plays a critical role in our modern world. These graduate students in Japan demonstrate a new robot suit developed by their professor to help the elderly in their everyday lives. The suit is capable of doubling the normal strength of its wearer.

implement incremental innovations alter, but do not fundamentally change, competitive interaction in an industry.

▍ *Technical versus managerial innovations.* **Technical innovations** are changes in the physical appearance or performance of a product or service, or in the physical processes through which a product or service is manufactured. Many of the most important innovations over the last fifty years have been technical. For example, the serial replacement of the vacuum tube with the transistor, of the transistor with the integrated circuit, and of the integrated circuit with the microchip has greatly enhanced the power, ease of use, and speed of operation of a wide variety of electronic products. Not all innovations developed by organizations are technical, however. **Managerial innovations** are changes in the management process by which products and services are conceived, built, and delivered to customers. Managerial innovations do not necessarily affect the physical appearance or performance of products or services directly. In effect, business process change, or reengineering, which we discussed earlier, represents a managerial innovation.

▍ *Product versus process innovations.*   Perhaps the two most important types of technical innovations are product innovations and process innovations. **Product innovations** are changes in the physical characteristics or performance of existing products or services or the creation of brand-new products or services. **Process innovations** are changes in the way products or services are manufactured, created, or distributed. Whereas managerial innovations generally affect the broader context of development, process innovations directly affect manufacturing.

The Failure to Innovate

To remain competitive in today's economy, organizations must be innovative. And yet many organizations that should be innovative either are not successful at bringing out new products or services or do so only after innovations created

technical innovation   A change in the appearance or performance of products or services, or in the physical processes through which a product or service passes.

Online Study Center
Improve Your Grade
Knowledgebank 7.1

managerial innovation   A change in the management process in an organization.

product innovation   A change in the physical characteristics or performance of an existing product or service or the creation of new products or services.

process innovation   A change in the way a product or service is manufactured, created, or distributed.

CONCEPT CHECK 7.4

Categorize each of the following products along all three dimensions of innovation, if possible (radical versus incremental, technical versus managerial, and product versus process). Explain your answers.

- Teaching college courses by videotaping the instructor and sending the image over the Internet
- The rise in popularity of virtual organizations (discussed in Chapter 6)
- Checking the security of packages on airlines with the type of MRI scanning devices that are common in health care
- A device combining features of a cell phone and a handheld computer with Internet capability
- Robotic arms that can perform surgery that is too precise for a human surgeon's hands
- Hybrid automobiles, which run on both batteries and gasoline
- Using video games to teach soldiers how to plan and execute battles

Online Study Center
Improve Your Grade
Knowledgebank 7.2

by others are very mature. Organizations may fail to innovate for at least three reasons.

1. *Lack of resources.*   Innovation is expensive in dollars, time, and energy. If a firm does not have enough money to fund a program of innovation or does not currently employ the kinds of employees it needs to be innovative, it may lag behind in innovation. Even highly innovative organizations cannot become involved in every new product or service its employees think up. For example, numerous other commitments in the electronic instruments and computer industry discouraged Hewlett-Packard from investing in Steve Jobs and Steve Wozniak's original idea for a personal computer. With infinite resources of money, time, and technical and managerial expertise, HP might have entered this market early. Because the firm did not have this flexibility, however, it had to make some difficult choices about which innovations to invest in.

2. *Failure to recognize opportunities.*   Because firms cannot pursue all innovations, they need to develop the capability to evaluate innovations carefully and to select the ones that have the greatest potential. To obtain a competitive advantage, an organization usually must make investment decisions before the innovation process reaches the mature stage. The earlier the investment, however, the greater the risk. If organizations are not skilled at recognizing and evaluating opportunities, they may be overly cautious and fail to invest in innovations that later turn out to be successful for other firms.

3. *Resistance to change.*   As we discussed earlier, many organizations tend to resist change. Innovation means giving up old products and old ways of doing things in favor of new products and new ways of doing things. These kinds of changes can be personally difficult for managers and other members of an organization. Thus resistance to change can slow the innovation process.

Promoting Innovation in Organizations

A great many ideas for promoting innovation in organizations have been developed over the years. Three specific ways to promote innovation are through the reward system, through the organization's culture, and through a process called *intrapreneurship.*[34]

1. The *reward system* is the means by which the company encourages and discourages certain behaviors by employees. Major components of the reward system include salaries, bonuses, and perquisites. Using the reward system to promote innovation is a fairly mechanical but nevertheless effective management technique. The idea is to provide financial and nonfinancial rewards to people and groups who develop innovative ideas. Once the members of an organization understand that they will be rewarded for such activities, they are more likely to work creatively. With this end in mind, Monsanto gives a $50,000 award each year to the scientist or group of scientists that develops the biggest commercial breakthrough.

   It is important for organizations to reward creative behavior, but it is vital to avoid punishing creativity when it does not result in highly successful innovations. It is the nature of the creative and innovative processes that many new product ideas simply do not work out in the marketplace. Each process is fraught with too many uncertainties to generate positive results every time. An individual may have prepared herself to be creative, but an insight may not be forthcoming. Or managers may attempt to apply a developed innovation, only to recognize that it does not work. Indeed, some organizations operate according to the assumption that if all their innovative efforts succeed, then they are probably not taking enough risks in research and development. At 3M, nearly 60 percent of the creative ideas suggested each year do not succeed in the marketplace.

Managers need to be very careful in responding to innovative failure. If innovative failure is due to incompetence, systematic errors, or managerial sloppiness, then the firm should respond appropriately—for example, by withholding raises or reducing promotion opportunities. People who act in good faith to develop an innovation that simply does not work out, however, should not be punished for failure. If they are, they will probably not be creative in the future. A punitive reward system will discourage people from taking risks and therefore reduce the organization's ability to obtain competitive advantages.

2. *Organization culture* is the set of values, beliefs, and symbols that help guide behavior within it. A strong, appropriately focused organization culture can be used to support innovative activity. A well-managed culture can communicate a sense that innovation is valued and will be rewarded and that occasional failure in the pursuit of new ideas is not only acceptable but even expected. In addition to reward systems and intrapreneurial activities (see below), firms such as 3M, Corning, Monsanto, Procter & Gamble, Texas Instruments, Johnson & Johnson, and Merck are all known to have strong, innovation-oriented cultures that value individual creativity, risk taking, and inventiveness.[35]

Online Study Center
Improve Your Grade
Career Snapshot

3. In recent years, many large businesses have realized that the *entrepreneurial spirit* that propelled their growth becomes stagnant after they transform themselves from a small but growing concern into a larger one. To help revitalize this spirit, some firms today encourage what they call "intrapreneurship." **Intrapreneurs** are similar to entrepreneurs except that they develop a new business in the context of a large organization. There are three intrapreneurial roles in large organizations.[36] To use intrapreneurship successfully to encourage creativity and innovation, the organization must find one or more individuals to play these roles.

intrapreneurs   Similar to entrepreneurs except that they develop new businesses in the context of a large organization.

- The *inventor* is the person who actually conceives of and develops the new idea, product, or service by means of the creative process. Because the inventor may lack the expertise or motivation to oversee the transformation of the product or service from an idea into a marketable entity, however, a second role comes into play.

- A *product champion* is usually a middle manager who learns about the project and becomes committed to it. He or she helps overcome organizational resistance and convinces others to take the innovation seriously. The product champion may have only limited understanding of the technological aspects of the innovation. Nevertheless, product champions are skilled at knowing how the organization works, whose support is needed to push the project forward, and where to go to secure the resources necessary for successful development.

- A *sponsor* is a top-level manager who approves of and supports a project. This person may fight for the budget needed to develop an idea, overcome arguments against a project, and use organizational politics to ensure the project's survival. With a sponsor in place, the inventor's idea has a much better chance of being successfully developed.

True or False?

_____ 1. The stage where innovation decreases and sub-stitute innovations are developed and applied is called innovation maturity.

_____ 2. You are given the task of purchasing $500 worth of a product and reselling it at a flea market for a profit. You decide to buy white T-shirts and embellish them with beading and silk screen-ing. You have utilized process innovation.

_____ 3. The reward system is a fairly mechanical yet effective management technique for promoting innovation.

Online Study Center
ACE the Test
ACE Practice Tests 7.4

Multiple Choice

_____ 4. The replacement of standard radios with Radio Data Systems, RDS that display print information is an example of which type of innovation?
 a. Technical   c. Incremental   e. Product
 b. Radical   d. Process

_____ 5. The creation of one-handed foods that can be consumed while driving a car is an example of what kind of innovation?
 a. Technical   c. Incremental   e. Product
 b. Radical   d. Process

_____ 6. An employee at IBM invented a smart credit card that makes credit card purchases more secure. A top manager at IBM, called the _____, will be responsible for bringing the invention to market.
 a. inventor   d. entrepreneur
 b. intrapreneur   e. sponsor
 c. champion

BUILDING EFFECTIVE DIAGNOSTIC SKILLS

Online Study Center
Improve Your Grade
Exercises: Building Effective Skills

Exercise Overview

Diagnostic skills help a manager visualize the most appropriate response to a situation and are especially important during a period of organization change.

Exercise Background

Assume that you are the general manager of a hotel that is situated along a beautiful stretch of beach and is one of six large resorts on a tropical island. The hotel is owned by a group of foreign investors and is one of the oldest on the island. For several years, the hotel has been operated as a franchise unit of a large international hotel chain, as are all of the others on the island.

Recently, the owners have been taking most of the profits for themselves and putting relatively little back into the hotel. They have also let you know that their business is not in good financial health; the money earned from your hotel is being used to offset losses they are incurring elsewhere. In contrast, most of the other hotels on the island have been refurbished, and plans for two new ones have just been announced.

Executives from franchise headquarters have just visited your hotel and expressed disappointment that the hotel has not kept pace with the other island resorts. If the property is not brought up to their standards, the franchise agreement, which comes up for review in a year, will be revoked. You see this move as potentially disastrous because you would lose their "brand name," access to their reservation system, and so forth. Sitting alone in your office, you have identified several alterna-tives that seem viable:

1. Try to convince the owners to remodel the hotel. You estimate that it will take $5 million to meet the franchiser's minimum standards and another $5 million to match the top resort on the island.

2. Try to convince the franchiser to give you more time and more options for upgrading the facility.

3. Allow the franchise agreement to terminate and try to succeed as an independent hotel.

4. Assume that the hotel will fail, and start looking for another job. You have a good reputation, although you might have to start at a lower level (perhaps as an assistant manager) with another firm.

Exercise Task

With the background information presented above, do the following:

1. Rank-order the four alternatives in terms of their potential success. Make assumptions as appropriate.

2. Identify other alternatives not noted above.

3. Can any alternatives be pursued simultaneously?

4. Develop an overall strategy for trying to save the hotel while also protecting your own interests.

Innovation in Action: Egg Drop

Purpose

Managers are continuously improving work flow, products, and the packaging of products. This is what total quality management is all about. To do this means thinking creatively and acting innovatively. This skill builder focuses on the *open systems model*. It helps you develop the *innovator role*. One of the skills of the innovator is thinking creatively and acting innovatively.

Introduction

This activity is a practical and entertaining demonstration of creativity and innovation in action. The "Egg Drop" exercise provides practice in identifying, defining, or refining a problem or opportunity; developing options and alternatives; choosing the best option or alternative; actually launching the alternative into reality; and verifying the results within a specified time period. Your instructor will provide you with further instructions.

Source: Reproduced with permission from "Metaphorically Speaking," from *50 Activities on Creativity and Problem Solving* by Geof Cox, Chuck DuFault, and Walt Hopkins, Gower, Aldershot, 1992.

Innovative Whole Foods

Austin, Texas, in 1979 was a counterculture haven. A twenty-five-year-old student named John Mackey began a natural foods store called SaferWay. He and his friends sold groceries from a storefront, lived above the store, and showered in the commercial dishwasher. A quarter of a century later, Mackey looks back at that time and says, "When you're young, you don't know what you can't do." Today, it seems there is nothing Mackey can't do. He is the CEO of Whole Foods Markets, the nation's largest natural and organic food store, with 181 locations, 39,000 employees, and $4.7 billion of sales in 2005. From its unusual beginning, Whole Foods developed into the supermarket industry leader, at the forefront of new ideas and change in its industry.

Traditional grocers are mimicking Wal-Mart, driving down prices and optimizing the supply chain, but at Whole Foods, it's all about innovative food. "Selling the highest quality natural and organic products available" is the first of the firm's core values. Its website claims, "We feature foods that are free of artificial preservatives, colors, flavors, sweeteners, and hydrogenated oils." Instead of standard grocery items, offerings are more numerous and varied, with a focus on handmade, local products. In the Austin store, shoppers can choose from 600 cheeses, 400 beers, and a wide variety of ready-to-eat food.

Whole Foods is moving beyond the traditional grocery chain in other ways, too. In 2006, the company expects to open its first store in the U.K., making it the first multinational organic foods operation. In Los Angeles, Whole Foods is experimenting with a Lifestyle store to sell home and personal items such as bamboo furniture, hemp purses, and organic cotton baby clothes. Whole Foods subsidiaries process natural seafood, inspect organic produce, and purchase fair-trade coffee.

Workers at Whole Foods enjoy an organization culture, benefits plan, and human resource policies that surpass that of any other foods company. For example, the CEO makes a salary just fourteen times that of the average pay of hourly workers. Employees vote on their choices of benefits, resulting in no-cost health insurance. A new employee must be "voted in" by two-thirds of his or her work team to become a permanent employee. Walter Robb, former Whole Foods president, says, "Happy team members make happy customers. Our job as management is simply to make that a reality."

"It's better to ask forgiveness than permission."

—John Mackey, CEO,
Whole Foods Markets

To foster innovation, store managers may spend up to $100,000 each year without asking for permission. According to Mackey, his policy is that "it's better to ask forgiveness than permission." These funds are used for experimentation, and successes are adopted throughout the organization. "Most businesses have . . . a mass market football model of executing the game plan—don't fumble the ball," says Mackey. "Whole Foods is more like a fast-breaking basketball team. We're driving down the court, but we don't exactly know how the play is going to evolve." He adds, "We're creating an organization based on love instead of fear."

Most grocery chains now offer more organic and natural foods, thanks in part to the success of Whole Foods. When Whole Foods asked Dole to provide organic pineapples, Dole complied but was surprised to find that half of their demand comes from traditional grocers. Even Wal-Mart announced in October 2005 that it would increase its healthy offerings. Whole Foods, called "Whole Paycheck" by some critics, seems vulnerable to Wal-Mart-style price competition. So far, though, no competitors have matched the leader, where annual same-store sales growth is 13 percent, higher than the industry average of 1 percent and Wal-Mart's 8 percent. "I keep waiting for the competition I've been hearing about, but nobody else is doing quite what we're doing," claims Mackey.

Yet Whole Foods is not content with revolutionizing the grocery industry; it wants to change the world. From improving health to saving the planet, managers at the firm have always had big agendas, as shown in this excerpt from the mission statement: "Our mission is to promote the vitality and well-being of all individuals by supplying the highest quality, most wholesome foods available. . . . [We are] devoted to the promotion of organically grown foods, food safety concern, and sustainability of our entire eco-system." The biggest goal, however, may be changing the way that corporate managers view their companies. CEO Mackey feels that profitability will follow when companies have a strong vision and purpose. "To be sustainable, business has to be profitable," says Mackey. "[Yet] neither does business exist primarily to make a profit. It exists to fulfill its purpose, whatever that might be." He goes on to add, "[Business] can make money and do good."

Case Questions

1. What internal and external forces for change have supported the innovations made at Whole Foods?
2. Traditional grocers try unsuccessfully to compete with Wal-Mart on price, when instead they could be developing a new model of competition, as Whole Foods has. What types of resistance to change contribute to this situation? What could managers do to overcome this resistance?
3. What specific actions does Whole Foods take to encourage and promote continuous innovation throughout the company? In your opinion, will these actions continue to be successful in promoting further innovation in the future?

Case References

"2005 Annual Report," Whole Foods website, www .wholefoodsmarket.com on January 22, 2006; Parija Bhatnagar, "Eat Tofu, Drink Aloe, Wear Soy?" *CNN Money*, November 1, 2004, www.cnnmoney.com on January 22, 2006; Parija Bhatnagar, "What's for Dinner in 2006," *CNN Money*, January 11, 2006, www.cnnmoney.com on January 22, 2006; Diane Brady, "Eating Too Fast at Whole Foods," *Business-Week*, October 24, 2005, www.businessweek.com on January 22, 2006; Michael V. Copeland, "The Whole Lifestyle," *Business 2.0*, November 1, 2005, www.cnnmoney.com on January 22, 2006; Charles Fishman, "The Anarchist's Cookbook," *Fast Company*, July 2004, www.fastcompany.com on January 22, 2006; Evan Smith, "John Mackey," *Texas Monthly*, March 2005, pp. 122–132; Ryan Underwood, "Employee Innovator Runner-Up," *Fast Company*, October 2005, www.fastcompany .com on January 22, 2006.

LEARNING OBJECTIVE REVIEW

1 ▸ *Describe the nature of organization change, including forces for change and planned versus reactive change.*

- Organization change is any substantive modification to some part of the organization that may be prompted by forces internal or external to the organization.
- In general, planned change is preferable to reactive change.

2 ▸ *Discuss the steps in organization change and how to manage resistance to change.*

- A comprehensive model is usually most effective for managing change.
- People tend to resist change because of
  uncertainty
  threats to their self-interests
  perceptions different from those of others
  feelings of loss
- Methods for overcoming resistance include
  participation
  education
  facilitation procedures
  force-field analysis

3 ▸ *Identify and describe major areas of organization change, and discuss the assumptions, techniques, and effectiveness of organization development.*

- The most common interventions involve changing
  organization structure and design
  technology
  people
  business processes

- Organization development (OD) is concerned with changing attitudes, perceptions, behaviors, and expectations, and its effective use relies on an important set of assumptions and techniques.

4 ▸ *Describe the innovation process, forms of innovation, the failure to innovate, and how organizations can promote innovation.*

- The innovation process has six steps:
  development   growth
  application   maturity
  launch   decline
- Innovation may be
  radical or incremental
  technical or managerial
  involved with products or processes
- Despite the importance of innovation, many organizations fail to innovate for a number of reasons:
  They either lack creative individuals or are committed to too many other creative activities.
  They fail to recognize opportunities.
  They resist the change that innovation requires.
- Organizations can use a variety of tools to overcome these problems:
  the reward system
  the organization's culture
  intrapreneurship

Online Study Center RESOURCES

Prepare for Class, Improve Your Grade, and ACE the Test. These Student Achievement resources include:

ACE Practice Tests	Interactive Skills Assessments	Study Guide to Go
End of Chapter Exercises	Knowledgebank	Video Segments
Glossaries (visual and print)	Reviews (audio and print)	Summaries/Outlines
Flashcards		

To access these learning and study tools, go to: **college.hmco.com/pic/griffinSAS**

8 Managing Human Resources

REI has become quite successful by catering to those interested in outdoor activities. The firm hires employees who also pursue active lifestyles and provides them with incentives that motivate them to help REI continue to prosper.

4 *Discuss how organizations maintain human resources, including the determination of compensation and benefits.*

3 *Describe how organizations develop human resources, including training and development, performance appraisal, and performance feedback.*

2 *Discuss how organizations attract human resources, including human resource planning, recruiting, and selecting.*

1 *Describe the environmental context of human resource management, including its strategic importance and its relationship to legal and social factors.*

190

> *"REI is a big team, with a little of the small 'family' shop feel."*
>
> —Chris, REI employee

Chapter Outline

▶ **THE ENVIRONMENTAL CONTEXT OF HUMAN RESOURCE MANAGEMENT**
The strategic importance of HRM
The legal environment of HRM

▶ **ATTRACTING HUMAN RESOURCES**
Human resource planning
Recruiting human resources
Selecting human resources

▶ **DEVELOPING HUMAN RESOURCES**
Training and development
Performance appraisal
Performance feedback

▶ **MAINTAINING HUMAN RESOURCES**
Determining compensation
Determining benefits

▶ **MANAGING WORKFORCE DIVERSITY**
The meaning of diversity
The impact of diversity
Managing diversity in organizations

▶ **MANAGING LABOR RELATIONS**
How employees form unions
Collective bargaining

▶ **MANAGING KNOWLEDGE WORKERS AND CONTINGENT AND TEMPORARY WORKERS**
The nature of the knowledge worker
Knowledge worker management and labor markets
Contingent and temporary workers

Online Study Center
Prepare for Class
Chapter Outline

5 *Discuss the nature of diversity, including its meaning, associated trends, impact, and management.*

6 *Discuss labor relations, including how employees form unions and the mechanics of collective bargaining.*

7 *Describe the issues associated with managing knowledge workers and contingent and temporary workers.*

REI:
A Place for Serious Fun

Imagine you're looking for the perfect kayak for your local lake and the sales clerk is a kayaker who shares her expertise and experiences with you. Imagine shopping for hiking boots and being able to try them out on the store's test "mountain." Imagine a store that sells you exactly the right tent and then helps you practice setting it up. Welcome to REI, an outdoor gear retailer, known for high-quality products as well as excellent customer service. REI's new CEO, Sally Jewell, is beating competitors by providing buyers with experiences, advice, and quality interactions with knowledgeable store staff. "We used to be product-driven . . .

Online Study Center college.hmco.com/pic/griffinSAS

PRACTICING MANAGER'S TERMS

human resource management
   (HRM)   *p. 194*
human capital   *p. 194*
Title VII of the Civil Rights Act of
   1964   *p. 195*
adverse impact   *p. 195*
Equal Employment Opportunity
   Commission   *p. 195*
Age Discrimination in Employment
   Act   *p. 195*
affirmative action   *p. 195*
Americans with Disabilities Act   *p. 195*
Fair Labor Standards Act   *p. 195*
Equal Pay Act of 1963   *p. 196*
Family and Medical Leave Act of
   1993   *p. 196*
National Labor Relations Act   *p. 196*

Online Study Center
Improve Your Grade
   –Flashcards
   –Glossary

National Labor Relations Board
   (NLRB)   *p. 196*
Labor-Management Relations
   Act   *p. 196*
Occupational Safety and Health
   Act of 1970 (OSHA)   *p. 196*
recruiting   *p. 199*
realistic job preview (RJP)   *p. 199*
training   *p. 202*
development   *p. 202*
performance appraisal   *p. 203*
Behaviorally Anchored Rating Scale
   (BARS)   *p. 205*
360-degree feedback   *p. 205*
compensation   *p. 207*
benefits   *p. 208*
diversity   *p. 209*
labor relations   *p. 211*
collective bargaining   *p. 212*
grievance procedure   *p. 212*
knowledge workers   *p. 213*

KEY TERMS

job analysis   *p. 197*
internal recruiting   *p. 199*
external recruiting   *p. 199*
validation   *p. 200*
job evaluation   *p. 207*

*You should be able to define and use
terms that are part of the practicing
manager's vocabulary, as well as those
that are integral in the language of
management.*

relying on customers to trust us to pick the right products," says Jewell. "[Now we are] market-driven, paying attention to who those customers are and how we can adapt to the way they want to recreate."

REI's new strategy is called "experience marketing," and it is powering phenomenal growth for the retailer. The key to the new approach is store personnel. REI needs expert, enthusiastic workers, all the way from top managers to the sales floor. Typically, retail operations have difficulty recruiting enough hourly workers, and the annual personnel turnover rate is 30 percent or more. In contrast, REI's turnover is just 12 percent. The firm is ranked 9th on *Fortune*'s 2006 list of "100 Best Companies to Work For." It is also in *Fortune*'s "Hall of Fame" as one of just 22 firms that have appeared on the list every year since it began in 1998. How does REI attract and keep the kind of employees it needs to provide that exceptional experience for its customers?

To attract the right employees, REI seeks outdoor enthusiasts. The REI website says, "People work for REI because of their passion for outdoor sports." Betty Fujikado, an advertiser for REI, agrees. "Employees are expected to live the brand," she says. REI does a careful job of screening applicants, so it makes sense that they also seek to fill most job vacancies through promotion-from-within. Former CEO Dennis Madsen worked for REI for thirty-nine years.

Several factors contribute to REI's ability to retain good personnel. The company's culture reflects and supports employees' values. REI is organized as a member cooperative, owned by its approximately 2.5 million customers. This may contribute to its workplace environment, which is characterized by open communication, friendship, and a respect for employees' lives outside of work. Community involvement and social responsibility are also important at REI. Employees are encouraged to volunteer with community organizations that support outdoor recreation. The company makes conservation grants to protect the natural environment and has environmentally friendly policies, such as energy-efficient buildings and recycling programs. Although REI donates millions of dollars in cash and equipment, grant requests are not accepted from outsiders. Instead, REI gives to causes that employees select. REI uses responsible sourcing, ensuring that its products have been made in a way that protects workers and the environment. All of these values have a clear connection to the store's products and mission.

REI's culture has three additional core values that help in employee retention. The first is teamwork. One employee says, "REI is a big team, with a little of the small 'family' shop feel." The company does not pay commissions to sales personnel, who insist that commissions would introduce destructive competition and reduce teamwork. Personal growth is second. Every employee is encouraged to try more activities, acquire training, and learn. Third, REI calls itself "the place for serious fun." The company promotes active lifestyles, adventure, and play through such activities as company-sponsored cycling teams, weekend camping, and lunchtime Frisbee and yoga. "We . . . balance hard work with time off to play," the company's website states.

REI also improves retention through a progressive employee benefit program. Everyone qualifies for life and health insurance, even part-timers and seasonal employees. "This move sends a clear message to its employees that each is highly valued regardless of how many hours they clock," says human resources consultant Thomas Pursley. Additional benefits include generous retirement and profit-sharing plans; vacation time, sick pay, and paid holidays for both full- and part-time workers; and subsidy pay for those who commute via public transportation. In addition, employees get discounts that range from 30 to 50 percent and free use of any of REI's rental equipment. Thus, salespeople become familiar with REI's products, improving their ability to offer good service.

"REI is a way of life," says one employee. And it seems like a healthy, happy life for both workers and customers.[1]

REI has gone from a modestly successful retailer to a phenomenally successful one. While other firms may offer the same products, REI has put its performance into overdrive by developing a new relationship with its employees. This chapter is about how organizations manage the people who constitute them. This set of processes is called "human resource management," or HRM. We start by describing the environmental context of HRM. We then discuss how organizations attract human resources. Next we describe how organizations seek to develop the capacities of their human resources further. We also examine how high-quality human resources are maintained by organizations. Diversity in organizations is discussed next. We conclude by describing labor relations.

THE ENVIRONMENTAL CONTEXT OF HUMAN RESOURCE MANAGEMENT

1 ▶ *Describe the environmental context of human resource management, including its strategic importance and its relationship to legal and social factors.*

human resource management (HRM) The set of organizational activities directed at attracting, developing, and maintaining an effective workforce.

Human resource management (HRM) is the set of organizational activities directed at attracting, developing, and maintaining an effective workforce.[2] Human resource management takes place within a complex and ever-changing environmental context. Three particularly vital components of this context are HRM's strategic importance and the legal and social environments of HRM.

The Strategic Importance of HRM

Human resources are critical for effective organizational functioning. HRM (or "personnel," as it is sometimes called) was once relegated to second-class status in many organizations, but its importance has grown dramatically in the last two decades. Its new importance stems from increased legal complexities, the recognition that human resources are a valuable means for improving productivity, and the awareness today of the costs associated with poor human resource management.[3]

Indeed, managers now realize that the effectiveness of their HR function has a substantial impact on the bottom-line performance of the firm. Poor human resource planning can result in spurts of hiring followed by layoffs—costly in terms of unemployment compensation payments, training expenses, and morale. Haphazard compensation systems do not attract, keep, and motivate good employees, and outmoded recruitment practices can expose the firm to expensive and embarrassing discrimination lawsuits. Consequently, the chief human resource executive of most large businesses is a vice president directly accountable to the CEO, and many firms are developing strategic HR plans and integrating those plans with other strategic planning activities.[4]

Online Study Center
Improve Your Grade
Career Snapshot 8.1

Even organizations with as few as two hundred employees usually have a human resource manager and a human resource department charged with overseeing these activities. Responsibility for HR activities, however, is shared between the HR department and line managers. The HR department may recruit and initially screen candidates, but the final selection is usually made by managers in the department where the new employee will work. Similarly, although the HR department may establish performance appraisal policies and procedures, the actual evaluation and coaching of employees is done by their immediate superiors.

The growing awareness of the strategic significance of human resource management has even led to new terminology to reflect a firm's commitment to people. **Human capital** reflects the organization's investment in attracting, retaining, and motivating an effective workforce. Hence, just as the phrase *financial capital* is an indicator of a firm's financial resources and reserves, the phrase *human capital* serves as a tangible indicator of the value of the people who make up an organization.[5]

human capital A term that reflects the organization's investment in attracting, retaining, and motivating an effective workforce.

The Legal Environment of HRM

A number of laws regulate various aspects of employee-employer relations, especially in the areas of equal employment opportunity, compensation and benefits, labor relations, and occupational safety and health.

Equal Employment Opportunity

There are numerous laws and related regulations that affect equal employment opportunity.

1. **Title VII of the Civil Rights Act of 1964** forbids discrimination in all areas of the employment relationship. The intent of Title VII is to ensure that employment decisions are made on the basis of an individual's qualifications rather than on the basis of personal biases. The law has reduced the incidence of direct forms of discrimination (refusing to promote African-Americans into management, failing to hire men as flight attendants, refusing to hire women as construction workers) as well as indirect forms of discrimination (using employment tests that whites pass at a higher rate than African-Americans). Employment requirements such as test scores and other qualifications are legally defined as having an **adverse impact** on minorities and women when such individuals meet or pass the requirement at a rate less than 80 percent of the rate of majority group members. Criteria that have an adverse impact on protected groups can be used only when there is solid evidence that they effectively identify individuals who are better able than others to do the job. The **Equal Employment Opportunity Commission** is charged with enforcing Title VII and several other employment-related laws.

2. The **Age Discrimination in Employment Act**, passed in 1967, amended in 1978, and amended again in 1986, is an attempt to prevent organizations from discriminating against older workers. In its current form, it outlaws discrimination against people older than forty years. Both the age discrimination act and Title VII mandate no more than passive nondiscrimination, or equal employment opportunity. That is, employers are not required to seek out and hire minorities, but they must treat fairly all who apply.

3. Several executive orders, however, require that employers holding government contracts engage in **affirmative action**—intentionally seeking and hiring employees from groups that are underrepresented in the organization. These organizations must have a written affirmative action plan that spells out employment goals for underutilized groups and how those goals will be met.

4. These same employers are required to act affirmatively in hiring Vietnam-era veterans (as a result of the *Vietnam Era Veterans Readjustment Assistance Act*) and qualified handicapped individuals.

5. The *Pregnancy Discrimination Act* forbids discrimination against women who are pregnant.

6. In 1990 Congress passed the **Americans with Disabilities Act**, which forbids discrimination on the basis of disabilities and requires employers to provide reasonable accommodations for disabled employees.

7. The *Civil Rights Act of 1991* amended the original Civil Rights Act as well as other related laws by both making it easier to bring discrimination lawsuits and limiting the amount of punitive damages that can be awarded in those lawsuits.

Compensation and Benefits

Laws also regulate compensation and benefits.

1. The **Fair Labor Standards Act**, passed in 1938 and amended frequently since then, sets a minimum wage and requires the payment of overtime rates for work in excess of forty hours per week. Salaried professional, executive, and

---

Title VII of the Civil Rights Act of 1964 Forbids discrimination on the basis of sex, race, color, religion, or national origin in all areas of the employment relationship.

Online Study Center
Improve Your Grade
Knowledgebank 8.1

adverse impact A selection standard for employment is said to have an adverse impact when minority group members or women pass that standard at a rate less than 80 percent of the pass rate of majority group members.

Equal Employment Opportunity Commission The body charged with enforcing Title VII of the Civil Rights Act of 1964.

Age Discrimination in Employment Act A law that prohibits discrimination against people older than forty years; passed in 1967, amended in 1978 and 1986.

affirmative action Intentionally seeking and hiring employees from groups that are underrepresented in the organization.

Americans with Disabilities Act A law that prohibits discrimination against people with disabilities.

Online Study Center
Improve Your Grade
Knowledgebank 8.2

Fair Labor Standards Act A law that sets a minimum wage and requires overtime pay for work in excess of forty hours per week; passed in 1938 and amended frequently since then.

Equal Pay Act of 1963   A law that requires that men and women be paid the same amount for doing the same job.

Family and Medical Leave Act of 1993   A law that requires employers to provide up to twelve weeks of unpaid leave for family and medical emergencies.

CONCEPT CHECK 8.1

The Family and Medical Leave Act of 1993 is seen as providing much-needed flexibility and security for families and workers. Others think that it places an unnecessary burden on business. Yet another opinion is that the act hurts women, who are more likely to ask for leave, and shuffles them off onto a low-paid "mommy track" career path. In your opinion, what are the probable consequences, if any, of this act?

National Labor Relations Act   A law passed in 1935 to set up procedures for employees to vote on whether to have a union; also known as the Wagner Act.

National Labor Relations Board (NLRB)   A body established by the Wagner Act to enforce its provisions.

Labor-Management Relations Act   A law passed in 1947 to limit union power; also known as the Taft-Hartley Act.

Online Study Center
Improve Your Grade
Knowledgebank 8.3

Occupational Safety and Health Act of 1970 (OSHA)   A law that directly mandates the provision of safe working conditions.

Online Study Center
Improve Your Grade
Knowledgebank 8.4

administrative employees are exempt from the minimum hourly wage and overtime provisions.

2. The **Equal Pay Act of 1963** requires that men and women be paid the same amount for doing the same job. Attempts to circumvent the law by having different job titles and pay rates for men and women who perform the same work are also illegal. Basing an employee's pay on seniority or performance is legal, however, even if it means that a man and a woman are paid different amounts for doing the same job.

3. Certain benefits are mandatory—for example, worker's compensation insurance for employees who are injured on the job.

4. Employers who provide a pension plan for their employees are regulated by the *Employee Retirement Income Security Act of 1974 (ERISA)*. The purpose of this act is to help ensure the financial security of pension funds by regulating how they can be invested.

5. The **Family and Medical Leave Act of 1993** requires employers to provide up to twelve weeks of unpaid leave for family and medical emergencies.

Labor Relations

Union activities and management's behavior toward unions constitute another heavily regulated area.

1. The **National Labor Relations Act** (also known as the Wagner Act), passed in 1935, sets up a procedure for employees to vote on whether to have a union. If they vote for a union, management is required to bargain collectively with the union.

2. The **National Labor Relations Board (NLRB)** was established by the Wagner Act to enforce its provisions.

3. Following a series of severe strikes in 1946, the **Labor-Management Relations Act** (also known as the Taft-Hartley Act) was passed in 1947 to limit union power. The law increases management's rights during an organizing campaign. The Taft-Hartley Act also contains the National Emergency Strike provision, which allows the president of the United States to prevent or end a strike that endangers national security. Taken together, these laws balance union and management power. Employees can be represented by a legally created and managed union, but the business can make non-employee-related business decisions without interference.

Health and Safety

1. The **Occupational Safety and Health Act of 1970 (OSHA)** directly mandates the provision of safe working conditions. It requires that employers (1) provide a place of employment that is free from hazards that may cause death or serious physical harm and (2) obey the safety and health standards established by the Department of Labor. Safety standards are intended to prevent accidents, whereas occupational health standards are concerned with preventing occupational disease. For example, standards limit the concentration of cotton dust in the air, because this contaminant has been associated with lung disease in textile workers. The standards are enforced by OSHA inspections, which are conducted when an employee files a complaint of unsafe conditions or when a serious accident occurs. Spot inspections of plants in especially hazardous industries such as mining and chemicals are also made. Employers who fail to meet OSHA standards may be fined.

TEST PREPPER 8.1

True or False?

_____ 1. The Fair Labor Standards Act requires that men and women be paid the same amount for doing the same jobs.

_____ 2. Affirmative action requires all organizations to actively seek and hire employees from under-represented groups.

_____ 3. The Age Discrimination in Employment Act sets standards for pension plan management and provides federal insurance if pension funds go bankrupt.

Multiple Choice

_____ 4. The set of organizational activities directed at attracting, developing, and maintaining an effective workforce is called _____.
   a. human resource management
   b. affirmative action
   c. equal employment opportunity
   d. fair labor
   e. equal pay

_____ 5. The National Labor Relations Act _____.
   a. spells out procedures by which employees can establish labor unions
   b. requires organizations to bargain collectively with legally formed unions
   c. is also known as the Wagner Act
   d. established the National Labor Relations Board
   e. all of the above

_____ 6. Which of the following directly mandates the provision of safe working conditions?
   a. Family and Medical Leave Act of 1993
   b. National Labor Relations Act
   c. Labor-Management Relations Act
   d. Americans with Disabilities Act
   e. Occupational Safety and Health Act of 1970

Online Study Center
ACE the Test
ACE Practice Tests 8.1

ATTRACTING HUMAN RESOURCES

2 *Discuss how organizations attract human resources, including human resource planning, recruiting, and selecting.*

With an understanding of the environmental context of human resource management as a foundation, we are now ready to address its first substantive concern—attracting qualified people who are interested in employment with the organization.

Human Resource Planning

The starting point in attracting qualified human resources is planning. HR planning, in turn, involves job analysis and forecasting the demand and supply of labor.

Job Analysis

Job analysis is a systematic analysis of jobs within an organization. A job analysis is made up of two parts.

1. The *job description* lists the duties of a job, the job's working conditions, and the tools, materials, and equipment used to perform it.

2. The *job specification* lists the skills, abilities, and other credentials needed to do the job. Job analysis information is used in many human resource activities. For instance, knowing about job content and job requirements is essential to developing appropriate selection methods and job-relevant performance appraisal systems and to setting equitable compensation rates.

job analysis A systematized procedure for collecting and recording information about jobs within an organization.

Online Study Center
Improve Your Grade
Career Snapshot 8.2

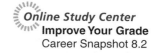

Forecasting Human Resource Demand and Supply

After managers fully understand the jobs to be performed within the organization, they can start planning for the organization's future human resource needs. Figure 8.1 summarizes the steps most often followed.

1. The manager starts by *assessing trends* in past human resources usage, future organizational plans, and general economic trends. A good sales forecast is often the foundation, especially for smaller organizations. Historical ratios can then be used to predict demand for such employees as operating employees and sales representatives. Of course, large organizations use much more complicated models to predict their future human resource needs. Wal-Mart recently completed an exhaustive planning process that projects that the firm will need to hire 1 million people over the next five years. Of this total, 800,000 will fill new positions created as the firm grows, and the other 200,000 will replace current workers who leave for various reasons.[6]

2. *Forecasting the supply of labor* is really two tasks: forecasting the internal supply (the number and type of employees who will be in the firm at some future date) and forecasting the external supply (the number and type of people who will be available for hiring in the labor market at large). The simplest approach merely adjusts present staffing levels for anticipated turnover and promotions. Again, though, large organizations use extremely sophisticated models to make forecasts. Forecasting the external supply of labor is a different problem altogether. How does a manager, for example, predict how many electrical engineers will be seeking work in Georgia three years from now? To get an idea

---

FIGURE 8.1

Human Resource Planning

Attracting human resources cannot be left to chance if an organization expects to function at peak efficiency. Human resource planning involves assessing trends, forecasting supply of and demand for labor, and then developing appropriate strategies for addressing any differences between project supply and demand.

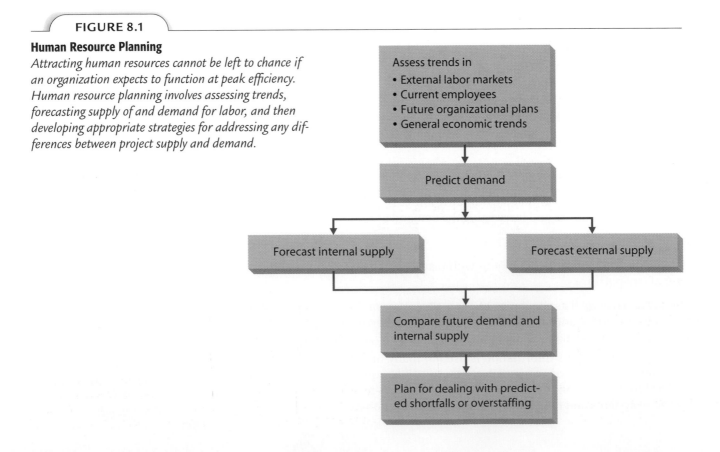

of the future availability of labor, planners must rely on information from such outside sources as state employment commissions, government reports, and figures supplied by colleges on the numbers of students in major fields.

Matching Human Resource Supply and Demand

After comparing future demand and internal supply, managers can make plans to manage predicted shortfalls or overstaffing. If a shortfall is predicted, new employees can be hired, present employees can be retrained and transferred into the understaffed area, individuals approaching retirement can be convinced to stay on, or labor-saving or productivity-enhancing systems can be installed. If the organization needs to hire, the external labor supply forecast helps managers plan how to recruit, with some idea whether the type of person needed will be readily available or scarce in the labor market. The trend in temporary workers also helps managers in staffing by affording them extra flexibility. If overstaffing is expected to be a problem, the main options are transferring the extra employees, not replacing individuals who quit, encouraging early retirement, and laying people off.

Recruiting Human Resources

Once an organization has an idea of its future human resource needs, the next phase is usually recruiting new employees. **Recruiting** is the process of attracting qualified persons to apply for jobs that are open.

> **recruiting** The process of attracting individuals to apply for jobs that are open.

1. **Internal recruiting** means considering present employees as candidates for openings. Promotion from within can help build morale and keep high-quality employees from leaving the firm. In unionized firms, the procedures for notifying employees of internal job change opportunities are usually spelled out in the union contract. For higher-level positions, a skills inventory system may be used to identify internal candidates, or managers may be asked to recommend individuals who should be considered. Most businesses today routinely post job openings on their internal communication network, or intranet. One disadvantage of internal recruiting is its ripple effect. When an employee moves to a different job, someone else must be found to take his or her old job. In one organization, 454 job movements were necessary as a result of filling 195 initial openings!

> **internal recruiting** Considering current employees as applicants for higher-level jobs in the organization.

2. **External recruiting** involves attracting persons outside the organization to apply for jobs. External recruiting tools include advertising, campus interviews, employment agencies or executive search firms, union hiring halls, referrals by present employees, and hiring "walk-ins" or "gate-hires" (people who show up without being solicited). Increasingly, firms are using the Internet to post job openings and to solicit applicants. Of course, a manager must select the most appropriate methods, using the state employment service to find maintenance workers but not a nuclear physicist, for example. Private employment agencies can be a good source of clerical and technical employees, and executive search firms specialize in locating top-management talent. Newspaper ads are often used because they reach a wide audience and thus allow members of minority groups equal opportunity to find out about and apply for job openings.

> **external recruiting** Attempting to attract job applicants from outside the organization.

3. One generally successful method for facilitating effective recruiting is the so-called **realistic job preview (RJP)**. As the term suggests, the RJP involves providing the applicant with a realistic picture of what it will be like to perform the

> **realistic job preview (RJP)** The practice of providing the applicant with a realistic picture of what it will be like to perform the job that the organization is trying to fill.

CONCEPT CHECK 8.2

Consider a job that you have held or with which you are familiar. Describe how you think an organization could best provide a realistic job preview for that position. What types of information and experiences should be conveyed to applicants? What techniques should be used to convey the information and experiences?

validation Determining the extent to which a selection device is really predictive of future job performance.

Online Study Center
Improve Your Grade
Career Snapshot 8.3

job that the organization is trying to fill.[7] For example, it would not make sense for a firm to tell an applicant that the job is exciting and challenging when in fact it is routine and straightforward, yet some managers do this in an effort to hire the best people. The likely outcome is a dissatisfied employee who will quickly be looking for a better job. If the company is more realistic about the job, on the other hand, the person hired will be more likely to remain in the job for a longer period of time.

Selecting Human Resources

Once the recruiting process has attracted a pool of applicants, the next step is to decide whom to hire. The intent of the selection process is to gather from applicants information that will predict their job success and then to hire the candidates likely to be most successful. Of course, the organization can gather information only about factors that are predictive of future performance. The process of determining the predictive value of information is called **validation**.

Applications

The first step in selection is usually asking the candidate to fill out an application blank. Application blanks are an efficient method of gathering information about the applicant's previous work history, educational background, and other job-related demographic data. They should not contain questions about areas not related to the job, such as gender, religion, or national origin. Application blank data are generally used informally to decide whether a candidate merits further evaluation, and interviewers use application blanks to familiarize themselves with candidates before interviewing them. Unfortunately, in recent years there has been a trend toward job applicants' either falsifying or inflating their credentials in order to stand a better chance of getting a job. Indeed, one recent survey of 2.6 million job applications found that an astounding 44 percent of them contained some false information.[8]

Tests

Tests of ability, skill, aptitude, or knowledge that is relevant to the particular job are usually the best predictors of job success, although tests of general intelligence or personality are occasionally useful as well. In addition to being validated, tests should be administered and scored consistently. All candidates should be given the same directions, should be allowed the same amount of time, and should experience the same testing environment (the same temperature, lighting, level of distractions, and the like).[9]

Interviews

Although they are a popular selection device, interviews are sometimes poor predictors of job success. For example, biases inherent in the way people perceive and judge others at a first meeting affect subsequent evaluations by the interviewer. Interview validity can be improved by training interviewers to be aware of potential biases and by increasing the structure of the interview. In a structured interview, questions are written in advance, and all interviewers follow the same question list with each candidate they interview. This procedure introduces consistency into the interview procedure and allows the organization to validate the content of the questions to be asked.[10]

Assessment Centers

Assessment centers are a popular method used to select managers and are particularly good for selecting current employees for promotion. The assessment center is a simulation of major parts of the managerial job. A typical center lasts two to three days, with groups of six to twelve persons participating in a variety of managerial exercises. Centers may also include interviews, public speaking, and standardized ability tests. Candidates are assessed by several trained observers, usually managers several levels above the job for which the candidates are being considered. Assessment centers are quite valid if properly designed and are fair to members of minority groups and women.[11] For some firms, the assessment center is a permanent facility created for these activities. For other firms, assessment activities are performed in a multipurpose location such as a conference room.

Job fairs are a common method used by many organizations to recruit prospective new employees. For instance, the City University of New York sponsors the Big Apple Job Fair in April each year. Christian Ruiz, who just earned his master's degree in economic, reviews his documents before he starts to make the rounds at the job fair to meet recruiters.

Other Techniques

Organizations also use other selection techniques depending on the circumstances. Polygraph tests, once popular, are declining in popularity. On the other hand, more and more organizations are requiring that applicants in whom they are interested take physical exams. Organizations are also increasingly using drug tests, especially in situations in which drug-related performance problems could create serious safety hazards. For example, applicants for jobs in a nuclear power plant are likely to be tested for drug use. And some organizations today even run credit checks on prospective employees.

CONCEPT CHECK 8.3

How is it possible to tell whether a selection device is valid? What are the possible consequences of using invalid selection methods? How can an organization ensure that its selection methods are valid?

TEST PREPPER 8.2

ANSWERS CAN BE FOUND ON P. 441

True or False?

_____ 1. Campus interviews, executive search firms, referrals by present employees, and "gate-hires" are examples of internal recruiting.

Multiple Choice

_____ 2. A systematized procedure for collecting and recording information about jobs is called a _____.

     a. job analysis
     b. job description
     c. job specification
     d. replacement chart
     e. skills inventory

_____ 3. A disadvantage of internal recruiting is _____.

     a. the ripple effect
     b. recruiting expense
     c. too much information on a recruit
     d. irrelevance of a replacement chart
     e. all of the above

_____ 4. Providing the applicant with a real picture of job requirements is called _____.

     a. realistic job previews
     b. reliability
     c. measurement
     d. validation
     e. external recruiting

Online Study Center
ACE the Test
ACE Practice Tests 8.2

DEVELOPING HUMAN RESOURCES

> **3** ▶ *Describe how organizations develop human resources, including training and development, performance appraisal, and performance feedback.*

Regardless of how effective a selection system is, most employees need additional training if they are to grow and develop in their jobs. Evaluating their performance and providing feedback are also necessary.

Training and Development

training Teaching operational or technical employees how to do the job for which they were hired.

development Teaching managers and professionals the skills needed for both present and future jobs.

Online Study Center
Improve Your Grade
Visual Glossary 8.1

In HRM, **training** consists of teaching operational or technical employees how to do the job for which they were hired. **Development** consists of teaching managers and professionals the skills needed for both present and future jobs. Most organizations provide regular training and development programs for managers and employees.

Assessing Training Needs

The first step in developing a training plan is to determine what needs exist. For example, if employees do not know how to operate the machinery they must use to do their job, a training program on how to operate the machinery is clearly needed. On the other hand, when a group of office workers is performing poorly, training may not be the answer. The problem could be motivation, aging equipment, poor supervision, inefficient work design, or a deficiency of skills and knowledge. Only the last could be remedied by training. As training programs are being developed, the manager should set specific and measurable goals specifying what participants are to learn. Managers should also plan to evaluate the training program after employees complete it.

Common Training Methods

Online Study Center
Improve Your Grade
Video Segment

Many different training and development methods are available. What method is chosen depends on many considerations, but perhaps the most important is the nature of the training content.

1. If the training content is factual material (such as company rules or explanations of how to fill out forms), then assigned reading, programmed learning, and lecture methods work well.
2. If the content is interpersonal relations or group decision making, however, then firms must use a method that allows interpersonal contact, such as role-playing or case discussion groups.
3. If employees must learn a physical skill, then methods allowing practice and the actual use of tools and materials are needed, as in on-the-job training or vestibule training. (Vestibule training enables participants to focus on safety, learning, and feedback rather than on productivity.)
4. Web-based and other electronic media–based training are also becoming popular. Such methods accommodate a mix of training content, are relatively easy to update and revise, let participants use a variable schedule, and lower travel costs. On the other hand, they are limited in their capacity to simulate real activities and facilitate face-to-face interaction. Xerox, Massachusetts Mutual Life Insurance, and Ford have all reported tremendous success with these methods.

5. Finally, some larger businesses have started creating their own self-contained training facility, often called a *corporate university*. McDonald's was among the first to start this practice with its so-called Hamburger University in Illinois. All management trainees for the firm attend training programs there to learn exactly how long to grill a burger, how to maintain good customer service, and so on. Other firms that are using this approach include Shell Oil and General Electric.

Evaluation of Training

Typical evaluation approaches include:

▌ choosing one or more relevant criteria (such as attitudes or skills)

▌ measuring the trainees' performance on those criteria before and after the training

▌ determining whether their performance changed significantly

Evaluation measures collected at the end of training are easy to get, but actual performance measures collected when the trainee is on the job are more important. Trainees may say that they enjoyed the training and learned a lot, but the true test is whether their job performance improves after their training.

Performance Appraisal

Once employees are trained and settled into their jobs, one of management's next concerns is performance appraisal. **Performance appraisal** is a formal assessment of how well an employee is doing his or her job. Employees' performance should be evaluated regularly for many reasons, including:

▌ performance appraisal may be necessary for validating selection devices or assessing the impact of training programs.

▌ performance appraisal assists in making decisions about pay raises, promotions, and training.

▌ performance appraisal provides feedback to employees to help them improve their present performance and plan their future careers.

Because performance evaluations often help determine wages and promotions, they must be fair, valid, and nondiscriminatory.

performance appraisal A formal assessment of how well an employee is doing his or her job.

Common Appraisal Methods

1. *Objective measures of performance* include actual output (that is, number of units produced), scrap rate, dollar volume of sales, and number of claims processed. Objective performance measures may be contaminated by "opportunity bias" if some persons have a better chance to perform well than others. For example, a sales representative selling snow blowers in Michigan has a greater opportunity than a colleague selling the same product in Arkansas. Fortunately, it is often possible to adjust raw performance figures for the effect of opportunity bias and thereby to arrive at figures that accurately represent each individual's performance.

   Another type of objective measure, the special performance test, is a method in which each employee is assessed under standardized conditions. For example, Verizon has a series of prerecorded calls that operators in a test booth answer. The operators are graded on speed, accuracy, and courtesy in

Online Study Center
Improve Your Grade
Knowledgebank 8.5

handling the calls. Performance tests measure ability but do not measure the extent to which one is motivated to use that ability on a daily basis. (A high-ability person may be a lazy performer except when being tested.) Special performance tests must therefore be supplemented by other appraisal methods to provide a complete picture of performance.

2. *Judgmental methods,* including ranking and rating techniques, are the most common way to measure performance. Ranking compares employees directly with one another and orders them from best to worst. Ranking has a number of drawbacks:
   - Ranking is difficult for large groups, because the persons in the middle of the distribution may be hard to distinguish from one another accurately.
   - Comparisons of people in different work groups are also difficult. For example, an employee ranked third in a strong group may be more valuable than an employee ranked first in a weak group.
   - The manager must rank people on the basis of overall performance, even though each person probably has both strengths and weaknesses.
   - Rankings do not provide useful information for feedback. To be told that one is ranked third is not nearly as helpful as to be told that the quality of one's work is outstanding, its quantity is satisfactory, one's punctuality could use improvement, or one's paperwork is seriously deficient.

   Rating differs from ranking in that it compares each employee with a fixed standard rather than with other employees. A rating scale provides the standard. Figure 8.2 gives examples of three graphic rating scales for a bank teller.

FIGURE 8.2

Graphic Rating Scales for a Bank Teller

Graphic rating scales are very common methods for evaluating employee performance. The manager who is doing the rating circles the point on each scale that best reflects her or his assessment of the employee on that scale. Graphic rating scales are widely used for many different kinds of jobs.

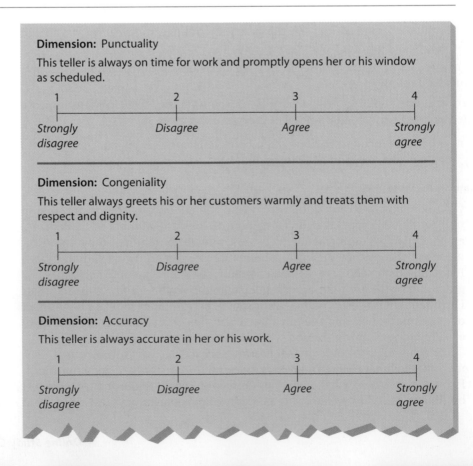

Dimension: Punctuality

This teller is always on time for work and promptly opens her or his window as scheduled.

1	2	3	4
Strongly disagree	Disagree	Agree	Strongly agree

Dimension: Congeniality

This teller always greets his or her customers warmly and treats them with respect and dignity.

1	2	3	4
Strongly disagree	Disagree	Agree	Strongly agree

Dimension: Accuracy

This teller is always accurate in her or his work.

1	2	3	4
Strongly disagree	Disagree	Agree	Strongly agree

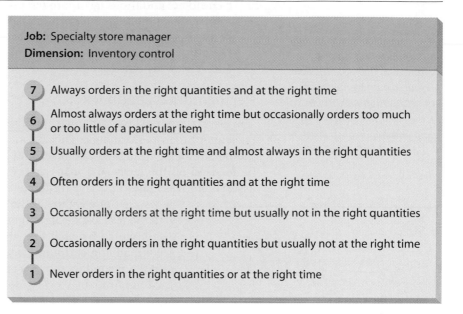

FIGURE 8.3

Behaviorally Anchored Rating Scale
Behaviorally anchored rating scales help overcome some of the limitations of standard rating scales. Each point on the scale is accompanied by a behavioral anchor—a summary of an employee behavior that fits that spot on the scale.

Job: Specialty store manager
Dimension: Inventory control

7 Always orders in the right quantities and at the right time

6 Almost always orders at the right time but occasionally orders too much or too little of a particular item

5 Usually orders at the right time and almost always in the right quantities

4 Often orders in the right quantities and at the right time

3 Occasionally orders at the right time but usually not in the right quantities

2 Occasionally orders in the right quantities but usually not at the right time

1 Never orders in the right quantities or at the right time

Each consists of a performance dimension to be rated (punctuality, congeniality, and accuracy) followed by a scale on which to make the rating. In constructing graphic rating scales, one must select performance dimensions that are relevant to job performance. In particular, they should reflect job behaviors and results rather than personality traits or attitudes.

The **Behaviorally Anchored Rating Scale (BARS)** is a sophisticated and useful rating method. Supervisors construct rating scales with associated behavioral anchors. They first identify relevant performance dimensions and then generate anchors—specific, observable behaviors typical of each performance level. Figure 8.3 shows an example of a behaviorally anchored rating scale for the dimension "Inventory control" for the job of specialty store manager.

Behaviorally Anchored Rating Scale (BARS) A performance rating method that is tied to behavioral anchors.

Errors in Performance Appraisal

1. One common problem is *recency error*—the tendency to base judgments on the subordinate's most recent performance because it is most easily recalled. Often a rating or ranking is intended to evaluate performance over an entire time period, such as six months or a year, so overemphasis on recent performance does introduce error into the judgment. Other errors include overuse of one part of the scale—being too lenient, being too severe, or giving everyone a rating of "average."

2. *Halo error* is allowing the assessment of an employee on one dimension to "spread" to ratings of that employee on other dimensions. For instance, if an employee is outstanding on quality of output, a rater might tend to give her or him higher marks than deserved on other dimensions. Errors can also occur because of race, sex, or age discrimination, intentionally or unintentionally. The best way to offset these errors is to ensure that a valid rating system is developed at the outset and then to train managers carefully in its use.

A recent innovation in performance appraisal that is used in many organizations today is called **360-degree feedback**, in which managers are evaluated by everyone around them—their boss, their peers, and their subordinates. Such

360-degree feedback An appraisal method in which managers are evaluated by everyone around them.

Evaluating employee performance and providing appropriate feedback are an important component of effective human resource management. Of course, the evaluation needs to be valid and objective, and the feedback should be developmental and constructive in nature—unlike what is shown here!

"We've done a computer simulation of your projected performance in five years. You're fired."

a complete and thorough approach provides people with a far richer array of information about their performance than a conventional appraisal given just by the boss. It also helps minimize the common sources of error noted here. Of course, such a system also takes considerable time and must be handled in such a way as not to breed fear and mistrust in the workplace.[12]

Performance Feedback

The last step in most performance appraisal systems is giving subordinates feedback about their performance. This is usually done in a private meeting between the person being evaluated and his or her boss. The discussion should generally be focused on the facts—the assessed level of performance, how and why that assessment was made, and how it can be improved in the future. Feedback interviews are not easy to conduct. Many managers are uncomfortable with the task, especially if feedback is negative and subordinates are disappointed by what they hear. These points are amplified in the accompanying cartoon. Properly training managers, however, can help them conduct more effective feedback interviews.[13]

Some firms use a very aggressive approach to terminating people who do not meet expectations. General Electric actually implemented a system whereby each year the bottom 10 percent of its workforce is terminated and replaced with new employees. Company executives claim that this approach, although stressful for all employees, helps it to upgrade its workforce continuously. Other firms have started using this same approach. However, both Ford and Goodyear recently agreed to abandon similar approaches in response to age discrimination lawsuits.[14]

TEST PREPPER 8.3

ANSWERS CAN BE FOUND ON P. 441

True or False?

_____ 1. A 360-degree feedback appraisal evaluates a manager by her boss, peers, and subordinates.

_____ 2. Development is teaching managers and professionals the skills needed for both present and future jobs.

_____ 3. Vestibular training focuses on productivity and cost savings.

_____ 4. NetSolve uses ranking and rating techniques to measure performance. NetSolve uses objective methods.

Multiple Choice

_____ 5. When determining the training method, the most important consideration is the _____.
    a. trainee   d. duration
    b. evaluation   e. cost
    c. content

_____ 6. Verizon Southwest has a series of prerecorded calls that operators in a booth answer. The operators are graded on speed, accuracy, and courtesy in handling the calls. This is an example of which method of performance appraisal method.
    a. Interview
    b. Performance appraisal
    c. 360-degree appraisal
    d. Performance test
    e. Behaviorally anchored rating scale

_____ 7. A sophisticated rating method in which supervisors construct a rating scale associated with behavioral anchors is called a(n) _____.
    a. interview
    b. performance appraisal
    c. 360-degree appraisal
    d. performance test
    e. behaviorally anchored rating scale

Online Study Center
ACE the Test
ACE Practice Tests 8.3

MAINTAINING HUMAN RESOURCES

4 ▶ *Discuss how organizations maintain human resources, including the determination of compensation and benefits.*

After organizations have attracted and developed an effective workforce, they must also make every effort to maintain that workforce. To do so requires effective compensation and benefits.

Determining Compensation

Compensation is the financial remuneration given by the organization to its employees in exchange for their work. There are three basic forms of compensation.

▌ *Wages* are the hourly compensation paid to operating employees. The minimum hourly wage paid in the United States today is $5.15.

▌ *Salary* is compensation paid for total contributions, as opposed to pay based on hours worked. For example, managers earn an annual salary, which is usually paid monthly. They receive the salary regardless of the number of hours they work. Most managers and other professionals are paid on this basis.

▌ *Incentives* are special compensation opportunities that are usually tied to performance. Sales commissions and bonuses are among the most common incentives.

A good compensation system can help attract qualified applicants, retain present employees, and stimulate high performance at a cost reasonable for one's industry and geographic area. To set up a successful system, management must make decisions about wage levels, the wage structure, and the individual wage determination system.

1. A *wage-level decision* is a management policy decision about whether the firm wants to pay above, at, or below the going rate for labor in the industry or the geographic area. Most firms choose to pay near the average, although those that cannot afford more pay below average. Large, successful firms may like to cultivate the image of being "wage leaders" by intentionally paying more than average and thus attracting and keeping high-quality employees. IBM, for example, pays top dollar to get the new employees it wants. McDonald's, on the other hand, often pays close to the minimum wage. The level of unemployment in the labor force also affects wage levels. Pay declines when labor is plentiful and increases when labor is scarce.

2. *Wage-structure decisions* are usually set up through a procedure called **job evaluation**—an attempt to assess the worth of each job relative to other jobs. The simplest method for creating a wage structure is to rank jobs from those that should be paid the most (for example, the president) to those that should be paid the least (for example, a mail clerk or a janitor). In a small firm with few jobs this method is quick and practical, but larger firms with many job titles require more sophisticated methods. The next step is setting actual wage rates on the basis of a combination of survey data and the wage structure that results from job evaluation. Jobs of equal value are often grouped into wage grades for ease of administration.

3. *Individual wage decisions* concern how much to pay each employee in a particular job. Although the easiest decision is to pay a single rate for each job,

Online Study Center
Improve Your Grade
Visual Glossary 8.2

compensation The financial remuneration given by the organization to its employees in exchange for their work.

job evaluation An attempt to assess the worth of each job relative to other jobs.

more typically a range of pay rates is associated with each job. For example, the pay range for an individual job might be $5.85 to $6.39 per hour, with different employees earning different rates within the range. A system is then needed for setting individual rates. This may be done on the basis of seniority (enter the job at $6.85, for example, and increase 10 cents per hour every six months on the job), initial qualifications (inexperienced people start at $6.85; more experienced people start at a higher rate), or merit (raises above the entering rate are given for good performance). Combinations of these bases may also be used.

Determining Benefits

benefits   Things of value other than compensation that the organization provides to its employees.

Benefits are things of value other than compensation that the organization provides to its workers. The average company spends an amount equal to more than one-third of its cash payroll on employee benefits. Thus an average employee who is paid $18,000 per year averages about $6,588 more per year in benefits. Benefits come in several forms. Pay for time not worked includes sick leave, vacation, holidays, and unemployment compensation. Insurance benefits often include life and health insurance for employees and their dependents. Workers' compensation is a legally required insurance benefit that provides medical care and disability income for employees injured on the job. Social security is a government pension plan to which both employers and employees contribute. Many employers also provide a private pension plan to which they and their employees contribute. Employee service benefits include such extras as tuition reimbursement and recreational opportunities.

Some organizations have instituted "cafeteria benefit plans," whereby basic coverage is provided for all employees but employees are then allowed to choose which additional benefits they want (up to a cost limit based on salary). An employee with five children might choose medical and dental coverage for dependents, a single employee might prefer more vacation time, and an older employee might elect increased pension benefits. Flexible systems are expected to encourage people to stay in the organization and even to help the company attract new employees.[15]

TEST PREPPER 8.4

ANSWERS CAN BE FOUND ON P. 441

True or False?

_____ 1. Compensation has three basic forms: wages, salary, and incentives.

_____ 2. Some organizations have instituted "cafeteria benefit plans," whereby basic coverage is provided for all employees, but employees are then allowed to choose which additional benefits they want (up to a cost limit based on salary).

Online Study Center
ACE the Test
ACE Practice Tests 8.4

Multiple Choice

_____ 3. A worker who is paid $20.00 per hour is being paid on what type of compensation basis?
   a. Straight commission   d. Wages
   b. Straight salary   e. Benefits
   c. Incentives

_____ 4. An attempt to assess the worth of each job relative to other jobs is called _____.
   a. benefits evaluation
   b. salary evaluation
   c. wage evaluation
   d. job evaluation
   e. compensation evaluation

MANAGING WORKFORCE DIVERSITY

5 ▶ *Discuss the nature of diversity, including its meaning, associated trends, impact, and management.*

Workforce diversity has become a very important issue in many organizations. The management of diversity is often seen as a key human resource function.

The Meaning of Diversity

Diversity exists in a community of people when its members differ from one another along one or more important dimensions. In the business world, the term *diversity* is generally used to refer to demographic differences among people—differences in gender, age, ethnicity, and so forth. For instance, the average age of the U.S. workforce is gradually increasing; and so is the number of women in the labor force. Likewise, the labor force reflects growing numbers of African-Americans, Latinos, and Asians, as well as more dual-career couples, same-gender couples, single parents, and physically challenged employees.

diversity A characteristic of a group or organization whose members differ from one another along one or more important dimensions, such as age, gender, or ethnicity.

The Impact of Diversity

There is no question that organizations are becoming ever more diverse. But how does this affect organizations? Diversity provides both opportunities and challenges for organizations.

Diversity as a Competitive Advantage

Many organizations are finding that diversity can be a source of competitive advantage in the marketplace (in addition to the fact that hiring and promoting in such a way as to enhance diversity is simply the right thing to do). For instance, organizations that manage diversity effectively often have higher levels of productivity and lower levels of turnover and absenteeism. Likewise, organizations that manage diversity effectively become known among women and minorities as good places to work. These organizations are thus better able to attract qualified employees from among these groups. Organizations with a diverse workforce are also better able to understand different market segments than are less diverse organizations. For example, a cosmetics firm such as Avon, which wants to sell its products to women and African-Americans, can better understand how to create such products and effectively market them if women and African-American managers are available to provide and solicit inputs into product development, design, packaging, advertising, and so forth.[16] Finally, organizations with diverse workforces are generally more creative and innovative than other organizations.

Online Study Center
Improve Your Grade
Knowledgebank 8.6

Diversity as a Source of Conflict

Unfortunately, diversity in an organization can also create conflict. This conflict can arise when:[17]

▪ An individual thinks that someone else has been hired, promoted, or fired because of her or his diversity status.

▪ Diversity is misunderstood or misinterpreted or consists of inappropriate interactions among people of different groups.[18]

■ There is an environment of fear, distrust, or individual prejudice. Members of the dominant group in an organization may worry that newcomers from other groups pose a personal threat to their own position in the organization. For example, when U.S. firms have been taken over by Japanese firms, U.S. managers have sometimes been resentful about or hostile toward Japanese managers assigned to work with them.

■ People are unwilling to accept people different from themselves. Personal bias and prejudices are still very real among some people today and can lead to potentially harmful conflict.

Online Study Center
Improve Your Grade
Career Snapshot 8.4

CONCEPT CHECK 8.4

In your opinion, what are the potential benefits of diversity? How can individuals and organizations more effectively manage diversity?

Managing Diversity in Organizations

Because of the tremendous potential that diversity holds for competitive advantage, as well as the importance of trying to avoid the negative consequences of associated conflict, much attention has been focused in recent years on how individuals and organizations can function more effectively in diverse contexts.

■ *Individual strategies* include the following:
　　Trying to understand differences between people
　　Tolerating and accepting people who are different
　　Communicating with people who are different

■ *Organizational strategies* include the following:
　　Policies regarding the treatment of people who are different
　　Practices and procedures that reflect and support those policies
　　Diversity training to help educate people about differences
　　Creating and maintaining an organizational culture that values diversity

TEST PREPPER 8.5

ANSWERS CAN BE FOUND ON P. 441

True or False?

_____ 1. Problems often get minimized over diversity issues because people are afraid or otherwise unwilling to openly discuss issues that relate to diversity.

Multiple Choice

_____ 2. _____ exists in a group or organization when its members differ from one another along one or more important dimensions.
　　　a. Diversity　　d. Homogeneity
　　　b. Community　　e. Affirmative action
　　　c. Culture

_____ 3. Which of the following is NOT true about an organization that manages diversity effectively?
　　a. High levels of productivity
　　b. Lower levels of turnover
　　c. It becomes known as a good place to work and attracts well-qualified people
　　d. It understands different market segments better
　　e. The use of quotas simplifies hiring and promotion decisions

Online Study Center
ACE the Test
ACE Practice Tests 8.5

MANAGING LABOR RELATIONS

6 ▶ *Discuss labor relations, including how employees form unions and the mechanics of collective bargaining.*

Labor relations is the process of dealing with employees who are represented by a union.[19] Managing labor relations is an important part of HRM. However, most large firms have separate labor relations specialists apart from other human resource functions to handle these activities.

labor relations   The process of dealing with employees who are represented by a union.

How Employees Form Unions

For employees to form a new local union, several things must happen.

1. First, employees must become interested in having a union. Nonemployees who are professional organizers employed by a national union (such as the Teamsters or the United Auto Workers) may generate interest by making speeches and distributing literature outside the workplace. Inside, employees who want a union try to convince other workers of the benefits of union representation.

2. The second step is to collect employees' signatures on authorization cards. These cards state that the signer wishes to vote to determine whether the union will represent him or her. To show the National Labor Relations Board (NLRB) that interest is sufficient to justify holding an election, 30 percent of the employees in the potential bargaining unit must sign these cards. The bargaining unit consists of all employees who will be eligible to vote in the election and to join and be represented by the union if one is formed.

3. The election is supervised by an NLRB representative (or, if both parties agree, by the American Arbitration Association—a professional association of arbitrators) and is conducted by secret ballot.

4. If a simple majority of those voting (not of all those eligible to vote) votes for the union, then the union becomes certified as the official representative of the bargaining unit.[20] If not, the process ends at this point, and no unionization occurs.

5. If the union is certified, it organizes itself by officially signing up members and electing officers; it will soon be ready to negotiate the first contract.

6. If workers later become disgruntled with their union or if management presents strong evidence that the union is not representing workers appropriately, the NLRB can arrange a decertification election. The results of such an election determine whether the union remains certified.

Online Study Center
Improve Your Grade
Knowledgebank 8.7

Labor unions sometimes feel that they must resort to strikes in order to protect the interests of their members. These workers, for instance, are striking over wage issues. They believe that their employer should increase their wages to a higher level than the firm has offered. Sometimes strikes are effective, but in other cases they end up not generating many, if any, new concessions from employers.

How would managing nonunionized workers differ from managing workers who have elected to be in a union? Which would be easier? Why?

Organizations usually prefer that employees not be unionized because unions limit management's freedom in many areas. Management may thus wage its own campaign to convince employees to vote against the union. "Unfair labor practices" are often committed at this point. For instance, it is an unfair labor practice for management to promise to give employees a raise (or any other benefit) if the union is defeated. Experts agree that the best way to avoid unionization is to practice good employee relations all the time—not just when threatened by a union election. Providing absolutely fair treatment with clear standards in the areas of pay, promotion, layoffs, and discipline; having a complaint or appeal system for persons who feel unfairly treated; and avoiding any kind of favoritism will help convince employees that a union is unnecessary. Wal-Mart strives to avoid unionization through these practices.[21]

Collective Bargaining

collective bargaining   The process of agreeing on a satisfactory labor contract between management and a union.

grievance procedure   The means by which a labor contract is enforced.

The intent of **collective bargaining** is to agree on a labor contract between management and the union that is satisfactory to both parties. The contract contains agreements about such issues as wages, hours, conditions of employment, promotion, layoffs, discipline, benefits, methods of allocating overtime, vacations, rest periods, and the grievance procedure. The process of bargaining may go on for weeks, months, or longer, with representatives of management and the union meeting to make proposals and counterproposals. The resulting agreement must be ratified by the union membership. If the agreement is not approved, the union may strike to put pressure on management, or it may choose not to strike and simply continue negotiating until a more acceptable agreement is reached.

Working Mother magazine recently named Allstate Insurance Company a "Best Company for Women of Color" for the second consecutive year. Only seven other companies were named to this exclusive list. Anise Wiley-Little is Allstate's Director of Diversity & Work/Life. Allstate views diversity as a competitive advantage and devotes significant resources to its diversity strategies. African-American, Asian-American, Latina, and Native American women make up 20 percent of Allstate's workforce.

The **grievance procedure** is the means by which the contract is enforced. Most of what is in a contract concerns how management will treat employees. When employees feel that they have not been treated fairly under the contract, they file a grievance to correct the problem. The first step in a grievance procedure is for the aggrieved employee to discuss the alleged contract violation with her immediate superior. Often the grievance is resolved at this stage. If the employee still believes that she is being mistreated, however, the grievance can be appealed to the next level. A union official can help an aggrieved employee present her case. If the manager's decision is also unsatisfactory to the employee, additional appeals to successively higher levels are made until, finally, all in-company steps are exhausted. The final step is to submit the grievance to binding arbitration. An arbitrator is a labor law expert who is paid jointly by the union and management. The arbitrator studies the contract, hears both sides of the case, and renders a decision that both parties must obey. The grievance system for resolving disputes about contract enforcement prevents any need to strike during the term of the contract.

As we have seen throughout this chapter, human resource managers face several ongoing challenges in their efforts to keep their organization staffed with an effective workforce. To complicate matters, new challenges arise as the economic and social environments of business change. We conclude this chapter with a look at two of the most important human resource management issues facing business today.

True or False?

_____ 1. The process of dealing with employees when they are represented by a union is called collective bargaining.

_____ 2. When Ford negotiates a new contract with the United Auto Workers they are engaged in grievance procedures.

_____ 3. If less than 30 percent of bargaining unit members sign authorization cards, the process ends.

Multiple Choice

_____ 4. What percent of voters in a bargaining unit must support a union for it to be certified?

    a. 30   d. 66

    b. 40   e. 33

    c. 50

Online Study Center
ACE the Test
ACE Practice Tests 8.6

MANAGING KNOWLEDGE WORKERS AND CONTINGENT AND TEMPORARY WORKERS

7 ▸ *Describe the issues associated with managing knowledge workers and contingent and temporary workers.*

Employees traditionally added value to organizations because of what they did or because of their experience. In the "information age," however, many employees add value because of what they know.[22]

The Nature of the Knowledge Worker

Knowledge workers, including, for example, computer scientists, engineers, and physical scientists, pose special challenges for managers. They tend to work in high-technology firms and are usually experts in some abstract knowledge base. They often like to work independently and tend to identify more strongly with their profession than with any organization—even to the extent of defining performance largely in terms recognized by other members of their profession.

As the importance of information-driven jobs grows, the need for knowledge workers continues to grow as well. But these employees require extensive and highly specialized training, and not every organization is willing to make the human capital investments necessary to make the most of their contribution to the firm. In fact, even after knowledge workers are on the job, retraining and training updates are critical to prevent their skills from becoming obsolete. It has been suggested, for example, that the "half-life" of a technical education in engineering is about three years. The failure to update such skills will not only result in the loss of competitive advantage but also increase the likelihood that the knowledge worker will go to another firm that is more committed to providing such workers with opportunities to update their skills.

Knowledge Worker Management and Labor Markets

Even though overall demand for labor has slowed in recent years in the wake of the economic downturn, the demand for knowledge workers remains strong. As a result, organizations that need these workers must introduce regular salary increases in order to pay them enough to keep them. This is especially critical in areas in which demand is growing, because even entry-level salaries for these employees are high. Once an employee accepts a job with a firm, the employer

knowledge workers Workers whose contributions to an organization are based on what they know.

faces yet another dilemma. Once hired, workers are more subject to the company's internal labor market, which is not likely to be growing as quickly as the external market for knowledge workers as a whole. Consequently, the longer an employee remains with a firm, the further behind the market his or her pay falls—unless, of course, it is regularly adjusted (upward).

Not surprisingly, the growing demand for these workers has inspired some fairly extreme measures for attracting them in the first place.[23] High starting salaries and sign-on bonuses are common. BP Exploration was recently paying starting petroleum engineers with undersea platform-drilling knowledge—not experience, just knowledge—salaries in the six figures, plus sign-on bonuses of over $50,000 and immediate profit sharing. Even with these incentives, managers complain that in the Gulf Coast region, they cannot retain specialists because young engineers soon leave to accept sign-on bonuses with competitors. Laments one executive, "We wind up six months after we hire an engineer having to fight off offers for that same engineer for more money."[24]

Contingent and Temporary Workers

A final contemporary issue of note involves the use of contingent or temporary workers. Indeed, recent years have seen an explosion in the use of such workers by organizations. The FBI, for example, routinely employs a cadre of retired agents in various temporary jobs.[25]

Trends in Contingent and Temporary Employment

In recent years, the number of contingent workers in the workforce has increased dramatically. A *contingent worker* is a person who works for an organization on something other than a permanent or full-time basis. Categories of contingent workers include independent contractors, on-call workers, temporary employees (usually hired through outside agencies), and contract and leased employees. Another category is part-time workers. The financial services giant Citigroup, for example, makes extensive use of part-time sales agents to pursue new clients. About 10 percent of the U.S. workforce is currently involved in one of these alternative forms of employment relationships. Experts suggest, however, that this percentage is increasing at a consistent pace.

Managing Contingent and Temporary Workers

Given the widespread use of contingent and temporary workers, managers must understand how to use such employees most effectively. In other words, they need to understand how to manage contingent and temporary workers.

▌ Careful planning.   Even though one of the presumed benefits of using contingent workers is flexibility, it is still important to integrate such workers in a coordinated fashion. Rather than having to call in workers sporadically and with no prior notice, organizations try to bring in specified numbers of workers for well-defined periods of time.

▌ Understanding contingent workers and acknowledging both the advantages and the disadvantages of using them.   In other words, the organization must recognize what it can and what it cannot achieve via the use of contingent and temporary workers. Expecting too much from such workers, for example, is a mistake that managers should avoid.

▌ Careful assessment of the real cost of using contingent workers.   We noted above that many firms adopt this course of action to save labor costs. The organization should be able to document those savings precisely. How much would it be paying people in wages and benefits if they were on permanent staff? How does this cost compare with the amount spent on contingent workers?

▌ Full understanding of how to integrate contingent workers into the organizational structure.   On a very simplistic level, for example, an organization with a large contingent workforce must make some decisions about the treatment of contingent workers relative to the treatment of permanent, full-time workers. Should contingent workers be invited to the company holiday party? Should they have access to such employee benefits as counseling services and childcare? There are no right or wrong answers to these questions. Managers must understand that they must develop a sound and logical strategy for integrating contingent workers into the organization and then must follow that strategy consistently over time.[26]

CONCEPT CHECK 8.6

In what respects would managing temporary employees be easier than managing traditional permanent employees? In what ways would it be more difficult? How might you personally choose to behave if you were in a contingent or temporary job, compared to the way you would behave in a traditional, permanent job?

TEST PREPPER 8.7

ANSWERS CAN BE FOUND ON P. 441

True or False?

_____ 1. The demand for knowledge workers has dwindled in the past ten years.

Online Study Center
ACE the Test
ACE Practice Tests 8.7

Multiple Choice

_____ 2. Categories of contingent workers include _____ .
   a. independent contractors
   b. on-call workers
   c. temporary employees
   d. contract and leased employees
   e. all of the above

BUILDING EFFECTIVE COMMUNICATION SKILLS

Exercise Overview

Communication skills reflect the manager's ability both to convey ideas and information effectively to others and to receive ideas and information effectively from others. This exercise gives you practice in presenting yourself in the best possible light to others.

Exercise Background

One of the first tasks that you will be called upon to do in your job search is to introduce yourself to company recruiters at a job fair, career day, informational meeting, or interview. This exercise gives you a two-minute self-introduction tool for making a quick but memorable impression on anyone who might help you in your career advancement. It can be used to make a professional impression on anyone, not just potential employers.

The hour or so that you take to write this introduction and practice using it can be the difference between getting and not getting the job or interview you want.

Online Study Center
Improve Your Grade
Exercises: Building Effective Skills

The most common request is "Tell me about yourself." If you can respond to this briefly, by saying something distinctive and memorable, you rise above the crowd.

The two-minute self-introduction should

- Be brief, so the listener will not get bored.
- Highlight what makes you unique.
- Reveal information not necessarily found in your résumé.
- Explain your interest in the firm.
- Show how your goals and background can benefit the firm.
- Encourage the listener to want to know more.
- Highlight aspects that the listener is interested in.
- Sell you—your skills, knowledge, and ability.
- Be truthful but positive.
- Be adapted to the particular listener and to his or her firm.
- Tell an interesting story in a conversational way.

- Not mention dates or years, because they are too hard to remember.
- Not include anything that is potentially biasing.

Exercise Task

1. Write a two-minute self-introduction following the format below. Make minor adjustments, if necessary, to accommodate your unique history.
   - *Early Life—15 seconds.* Who are you? Where do you come from? What are your roots? "How" did you grow up? Include any unique or memorable fact or early experience or interest that connects to the desired job, even by inference.
   - *Education—15 seconds.* Degrees, honors, awards? Major? Significant leadership, interests, or community activity while in school?
   - *Work Life—45 seconds.* What are your work habits? Accomplishments (not duties)? How did your interests lead you in this direction? Projects you were enthusiastic about or your proudest moment? What have you learned that is relevant to the listener? If you do not have enough work experience, spend more time talking about your education.
   - *Sales Pitch—45 seconds.* What do you have to offer? Key skills you have gained, from school, work, leadership, or relationships? How do you want to use your key skills? How do your key skills fit the job or firm? End with "I want to work for [or I am considering] your company because . . . ." Do not forget to thank them for the opportunity to talk with them!

2. Practice speaking your introduction aloud, with a firm handshake and a smile, until you can say everything in two minutes. One approach is to start alone or in front of a mirror and then work up to saying it to friends.

3. Practice your two-minute self-introduction in class, using classmates as stand-ins for interviewers. Or take turns presenting it in front of the class, with the professor or another student as a partner. Share constructive comments with one another.

Reprinted by permission of the author Margaret Hill.

Experiential Exercise

Choosing a Compensation Strategy

Online Study Center
Improve Your Grade
—Exercises: Experiential Exercise
—Interactive Skills Self-Assessment

Purpose

This exercise helps you better understand how internal and external market forces affect compensation strategies.

Introduction

Assume that you are the head of a large academic department in a major research university. Your salaries are a bit below external market salaries. For example, your assistant professors make between $45,000 and $55,000 a year; your associate professors make between $57,000 and $65,000 a year; and your full professors make between $67,000 and $75,000 a year.

Faculty who have been in your department for a long time enjoy the work environment and appreciate the low cost of living in the area. They know that they are somewhat underpaid but have tended to regard the advantages of being in your department as offsetting this disadvantage. Recently, however, external market forces have caused salaries for people in your field to escalate rapidly. Unfortunately, although your university acknowledges this problem, you have been told that no additional resources can be made available to your department.

You currently have four vacant positions that need to be filled. One of these is at the rank of associate professor, and the other three are at the rank of assistant professor. You have surveyed other departments in similar universities, and you realize that to hire the best new assistant professors, you will need to offer at least $58,000 a year and that to get a qualified associate professor, you will need to pay at least $70,000. You have been given the budget to hire new employees at more competitive salaries but cannot do anything to raise the salaries of faculty currently in your department. You have identified the following options:

1. You can hire new faculty from lower-quality schools that pay salaries below market rate.
2. You can hire the best people available, pay market salaries, and deal with internal inequities later.
3. You can hire fewer new faculty, use the extra money to boost the salaries of your current faculty, and cut class offerings in the future.

EXPERIENTIAL EXERCISE (CONTINUED)

Instructions

Step 1: Working alone, decide how you will proceed.

Step 2: Form small groups with your classmates and compare solutions.

Step 3: Identify the strengths and weaknesses of each option.

Follow-up Questions

1. Are there other options that might be pursued?
2. Assume that you chose option 2. How would you go about dealing with the internal inequity problems?
3. Discuss with your instructor the extent to which this problem exists at your school.

CLOSING CASE STUDY

The Retirement That Isn't

After they both completed thirty-year careers at United Airlines, Terry and Judith Parsley anticipated retiring on $90,000 annually. However, when United declared bankruptcy, the Pension Benefit Guaranty Corporation (PBGC), a federal agency, assumed responsibility for United's $7 billion pension obligation. The PBGC may be forced to pay at a reduced rate, and the Parsleys may have a very different retirement than the one they anticipated.

Today, many retirees, such as the Parsleys, are returning to work. More than 30 percent of Americans over fifty-five are employed, and that number is expected to grow to 50 percent by 2012. That's good news for employers, but the bad news is that many are working because their retirement benefits do not cover their living expenses. PBS reports that more than half of full-time workers in the United States have no employee-sponsored pension plan. Pressure from global competition, low profits, and bankruptcies have caused many companies to reduce or even eliminate postretirement benefits. Of those who have a plan, fewer than 10 percent have a defined benefits plan, which provides a specified level of retirement pay. Even among those fortunate 10 percent, many are discovering, to their surprise, that "promised" benefits cannot be legally enforced if the fine print of the contract gives the firm the right to modify the program. The federal government guarantees pensions for some employers, but well under half of Americans are covered by this insurance, so millions are at risk. "These people were promised a secure retirement, and now they're not getting it," says retiree advocate James Leas.

Even worse off are the millions of retirees who depend entirely on their own investments, such as savings or 401(k) accounts, where stock market fluctuations have made returns unstable in recent years. Ironically, the higher an individual's salary during his or her career, the more likely it is that the person will depend heavily on investments. "It's the higher-income retirees who are out seeking jobs," reports economics professor William Rodgers.

Many retirees have opted to return to work, but "they're apprehensive about having to compete for positions with younger workers who may be more technologically advanced," says counselor Dr. Michael Nuccitelli. Retirees often take technology classes or begin exercise regimens to increase their knowledge and stamina. Others find it too humiliating to accept an entry-level job and the modest paycheck that goes along with it.

Some firms are happy to employ seniors, finding them more reliable, more experienced, and even more honest than younger employees. Shel Hart, a staffing expert, thinks older workers have an advantage in the stagnant economy. "Companies are tied at the purse strings, and they can't afford to take risks," says Hart. "They need a quick return on investment. They need people with expertise." Bill Coleman, a compensation consultant, agrees. "Position yourself as a bargain," Coleman tells retirees. "Tout the fact that you have 40 years' experience. . . . Don't say, 'I'm old.' By doing that, you're admitting to a defect that's probably not even there."

Yet recruiter Jeff Kaye claims, "In many fields, retirees are considered washed up." This is particularly true in fields that require technical knowledge. Author Barbara M. Morris concurs, saying, "Those who return after retiring have lost a lot of their skills. Their thinking slows, their response time is slower, and they just can't

Online Study Center college.hmco.com/pic/griffinSAS

"These people were promised a secure retirement, and now they're not getting it."

—James Leas, former IBM engineer and retiree advocate

grasp the technological changes." Kaye goes on to say, "The people who used to work in the [telecommunications and technology] fields aren't even getting in to see recruiters. They're getting jobs ripping tickets at movie theaters or punching the clock at Wal-Mart."

Age discrimination may be part of the problem, but employers are also wary of investing in someone whose sole reason for working is financial. "Nobody wants to hire somebody . . . they think is just temporary," says Professor Dennis A. Ahlburg. His advice to older job seekers: "Don't say you're out of money. Say that you were bored in retirement and you want to be an active part of the labor force."

Some retirees are filing lawsuits against their former employers, who are cutting retirement benefits while realizing high profits. Nynex retiree C. William Jones asserts, "[Companies] view retirees as a cost center, and they're cutting their losses." Others are willing to return to work, but the barriers, especially the psychological ones, can be formidable. Norman Doroson, a pharmacist who returned to work after four years of retirement, sighs and says, "Most days at work, I just sit here thinking, 'I would rather be at home.' That's a little bit depressing."

Case Questions

1. What are the benefits that firms can obtain by hiring older workers? What are the potential problems that might be experienced by the organization and by the older workers themselves?
2. How would the hiring of retirees affect a company's human resource management? Consider the impact on recruiting and selecting, training, and compensation.
3. One expert recommends that retirees be treated as contingent or temporary workers. What would be the advantages and disadvantages of this approach for the organization, compared to offering full-time, permanent employment? What would be the advantages and disadvantages of this approach from the older worker's point of view?

Case References

Tom Abate, "Bankruptcies Strain Agency That Backs Retirement Plans," *San Francisco Chronicle*, December 22, 2004, www.sfgate.com on January 18, 2006; "Can Retiree Health Benefits Provided by Your Employer Be Cut?" U.S. Department of Labor website, www.dol.gov on January 30, 2003; Kathy Gurchiek, "Older Employees Prompt New Work, Retirement Trends," Society for Human Resource Management website, December 15, 2005, www.shrm.org on January 18, 2006; David Henry and Michael Arndt, "Where's My Pension?" *BusinessWeek*, December 2, 2002, pp. 96–97; Melinda Ligos, "As Portfolios Shrink, Retirees Warily Seek Work," *New York Times*, September 8, 2002, p. BU10; Michelle Conlin, "Grandpa? He's Busy at the Office," *BusinessWeek*, January 3, 2003, www.businessweek.com on January 30, 2003; Michelle Conlin, "Revenge of the Retirees," *BusinessWeek*, November 18, 2002, p. 125 (quote).

LEARNING OBJECTIVE REVIEW

Online Study Center
Improve Your Grade
–Learning Objective Review
–Audio Chapter Review
–Study Guide to Go

Online Study Center
ACE the Test
Audio Chapter Quiz

1 *Describe the environmental context of human resource management, including its strategic importance and its relationship to legal and social factors.*

- Human resource management is concerned with attracting, developing, and maintaining the human resources an organization needs.
- Numerous laws and other regulations impact human resource management, including those related to
  equal employment opportunity   labor relations
  compensation and benefits   health and safety

- Its environmental context consists of its strategic importance and the legal and social environments that affect it.

2 *Discuss how organizations attract human resources, including human resource planning, recruiting, and selecting.*

- Attracting human resources is an important part of the HRM function that starts with job analysis and then focuses on the following:
  forecasting the organization's future need for employees

forecasting the availability of employees both within and outside the organization

planning programs to ensure that the proper number and type of employees will be available when needed

- Recruitment can be internal or external, and it can sometimes involve a realistic job interview.

- Methods of selection (which should all be properly validated) include

application blanks	interviews
tests	assessment centers

---

3 ▶ *Describe how organizations develop human resources, including training and development, performance appraisal, and performance feedback.*

- Training and development enable employees to perform their present job effectively and to prepare for future jobs.

- Performance appraisals are important for
  validating selection devices
  assessing the impact of training programs
  deciding on pay raises and promotions
  determining training needs

- Both objective and judgmental methods of appraisal can be applied, and a good system usually includes several methods.

- The validity of appraisal information is always a concern, because it is difficult to evaluate accurately the many aspects of a person's job performance.

---

4 ▶ *Discuss how organizations maintain human resources, including the determination of compensation and benefits.*

- Compensation rates must be fair compared with rates for other jobs within the organization and with rates for the same or similar jobs in other organizations in the labor market.

- Properly designed incentive or merit pay systems can encourage high performance, and a good benefits program can help attract and retain employees.

---

5 ▶ *Discuss the nature of diversity, including its meaning, associated trends, impact, and management.*

- Diversity exists in an organization when its members differ from one another along one or more important dimensions, including
  - gender,
  - age, or
  - ethnicity

- Individual strategies for managing diversity include being understanding, tolerant, and communicative with those who are different.

- Organizational strategies include having fair policies, practices, and procedures; providing diversity training; and maintaining a tolerant culture.

---

6 ▶ *Discuss labor relations, including how employees form unions and the mechanics of collective bargaining.*

- If a majority of a company's nonmanagement employees so desire, they have the right to be represented by a union.

- Management must engage in collective bargaining with the union in an effort to agree on a contract.

- While the contract is in effect, the grievance system is used to settle disputes with management.

---

7 ▶ *Describe the issues associated with managing knowledge workers and contingent and temporary workers.*

- Knowledge workers are those with specialized knowledge. They need to have their skills updated frequently and to be paid well.

- The increased use of temporary and contingent workers requires several management techniques and assessments, such as whether they actually are cost-effective.

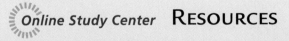 *Online Study Center* **RESOURCES**

Prepare for Class, Improve Your Grade, and ACE the Test. These Student Achievement resources include:

ACE Practice Tests	Interactive Skills Assessments	Study Guide to Go
End of Chapter Exercises	Knowledgebank	Video Segments
Glossaries (visual and print)	Reviews (audio and print)	Summaries/Outlines
Flashcards		

To access these learning and study tools, go to: **college.hmco.com/pic/griffinSAS**

9 Managing Individual Behavior

Many workers today are so busy and so connected with their jobs that they work through lunch. For instance, this team of workers is carrying on with their discussion as they take a few minutes to eat.

1 *Explain the nature of the relationship between the individual and the organization.*

2 *Define personality and describe personality attributes that affect behavior in organizations.*

3 *Discuss how attitudes affect the behavior of individuals in organizations.*

4 *Describe basic perceptual processes and the role of attributions in organizations.*

> *"...formerly, personal success was evinced by the ability to not work. ... Today, we measure our success by how much we work."*
>
> —Ilene Philipson, psychotherapist
> and author of *Married to the Job*

Chapter Outline

▶ **Understanding Individuals in Organizations**
The psychological contract
The person-job fit

▶ **Personality and Individual Behavior**
The "Big Five" personality traits
The Myers-Briggs framework
Other personality traits at work
Emotion intelligence

▶ **Attitudes and Individual Behavior**
Work-related attitudes
Affect and mood in organizations

▶ **Perception and Individual Behavior**
Basic perceptual processes
Perception and attribution

▶ **Stress and Individual Behavior**
Causes and consequences of stress
Managing stress

▶ **Creativity in Organizations**
The creative individual
The creative process
Enhancing creativity in organizations

▶ **Types of Workplace Behavior**
Performance behaviors
Withdrawal behaviors
Organizational citizenship
Dysfunctional behavior

Online Study Center
Prepare for Class
Chapter Outline

5 ▶ *Discuss the causes and consequences of stress and describe how it can be managed.*

6 ▶ *Describe creativity and its role in organizations.*

7 ▶ *Explain how workplace behaviors can directly or indirectly influence organizational effectiveness.*

Loving Your Job. . .
Too Much?

Y ou can love your job, but will it love you back? Psychologists and other experts who study job-related mental health report a disturbing trend—more and more workers say that they prefer long hours. Many employees routinely put in twelve-hour days or work from home every weekend. Bill George, former CEO of a Fortune 500 company who routinely worked sixty hours per week, says, "It didn't use to be this intense [until] we went to this eighty-hour week." It is an ironic twist in a society where "formerly, personal success was evinced by the ability to not work, to be a part of a leisure class, to be idle," says psychotherapist and author Ilene Philipson. "Today, we measure our success by how *much* we work," she adds.

Online Study Center   college.hmco.com/pic/griffinSAS

PRACTICING MANAGER'S TERMS

psychological contract   *p. 224*
individual differences   *p. 226*
personality   *p. 226*
emotional intelligence (EQ)   *p. 230*
attitudes   *p. 231*
job satisfaction or dissatisfaction   *p. 232*
organizational commitment   *p. 232*
stereotyping   *p. 233*
stress   *p. 235*
Type A   *p. 236*
Type B   *p. 236*
burnout   *p. 238*
creativity   *p. 239*
absenteeism   *p. 243*
turnover   *p. 243*

Online Study Center
Improve Your Grade
—Flashcards
—Glossary

KEY TERMS

contributions   *p. 224*
inducements   *p. 224*
person-job fit   *p. 225*
"Big Five" personality
   traits   *p. 226*
agreeableness   *p. 226*
conscientiousness   *p. 227*
negative emotionality   *p. 227*
extraversion   *p. 227*
openness   *p. 227*
locus of control   *p. 228*
self-efficacy   *p. 229*
authoritarianism   *p. 229*
Machiavellianism   *p. 229*

self-esteem   *p. 229*
risk propensity   *p. 229*
cognitive dissonance   *p. 231*
positive affectivity   *p. 232*
negative affectivity   *p. 232*
perception   *p. 233*
selective perception   *p. 233*
attribution   *p. 234*
General Adaptation Syndrome
   (GAS)   *p. 235*
workplace behavior   *p. 243*
performance behaviors   *p. 243*
organizational citizenship   *p. 244*
dysfunctional behaviors   *p. 244*

You should be able to define and use terms that are part of the practicing manager's vocabulary, as well as those that are integral in the language of management.

Philipson's book *Married to the Job: Why We Live to Work and What We Can Do About It* contains numerous examples. One high-performing manager fell out of favor after asking for a raise. The lack of praise caused deep depression and anxiety attacks. Philipson says that this client is typical of the career-obsessed worker: "What they have done is to transfer all of their unmet emotional needs to the workplace." For many, work is their top priority, to which Philipson responds, "Your boss is not your friend. Your colleagues are not your family. Workplaces are intensely political environments. If you bring your heart and soul there, you're likely setting yourself up for feeling betrayed."

Benjamin Hunnicutt, a professor, claims, "Work has become how we define ourselves. It is now answering the traditional religious questions: 'Who am I? How do I find meaning and purpose?' Work is no longer just about economics; it's about identity." Most of Philipson's patients have few social relationships outside of work. Many use work to help them through tough times. Yet the praise they receive at work is powerfully addictive, and that can also be dangerous. Yolanda Perry-Pastor, a patient of Philipson's, kept assuming more job duties until she suffered a nervous breakdown. She says, "I've been through a lot in my life," referring to domestic abuse and single parenthood. "But that was nothing compared with this."

Another contributing factor is companies that "ensnare" workers by offering a homelike environment, providing personal services, or just encouraging workers to consider their coworkers as family. For example, hot technology company Google offers free chef-prepared meals and snacks, as well as an on-site doctor, oil changes, car wash, dry cleaning, massage therapy, gym, hair stylist, fitness classes, sauna, roller hockey, outdoor volleyball court, and bike repair. Psychologist Maynard Brusman explains: "The workplace has become [workers'] community. They come to me anxious, and they don't know why. They've become caught up in the culture. The question is 'Is that healthy?' From what I've seen, it isn't."

Workers who are obsessed with their career find that work consumes all their passion and time, leaving nothing for other relationships. Perry-Pastor says of her two children during the time she was overworking, "They were never allowed to be sick. . . . I would pay for baby sitters, lessons, tutors, whatever they needed. I thought they were taken care of." Work relationships become more rewarding than relationships at home. Sociologist Arlie Hochschild theorizes that dual-income couples work long hours to escape their hectic home lives. "At home, you don't always get a pat on the back," says Karin Hanson, formerly of Microsoft. "In your office, you can hear, 'Hey, good work.'" Some managers may believe that an all-consuming interest in work is acceptable and even desirable, but the quality and quantity of work drop, and the incidence of absence, turnover, accidents, and workplace violence increases with stress. Many workers drop out of the workforce entirely—a loss for families and for society.

Philipson claims that career-obsessed individuals are not weak or insecure. "These people are in the same boat with all of the rest of us who work longer hours, take fewer vacations, and wake up and go to sleep thinking about work," she asserts. So how can one avoid becoming overinvolved in work? The psychotherapists recommend that you start by defining yourself and your worth in nonwork terms. Look to religion, family, or community for praise and comfort. Develop compelling interests and strong friendships outside of work. Take "real" nights, weekends, vacations—no work allowed. Focus less on praise, which can put you under someone else's control, and more on developing your own sense of self-worth. And, oh yes, miss work every now and then. Play hooky. Take an occasional day off and just relax.[1]

People and the organizations where they work are continually defining and redefining their relationship—in much the same way as the relationship between people evolves and changes over time. As evidenced in the opening vignette, some people even risk developing an unhealthy attachment to or dependence on their work. Of course, many other people develop and maintain a healthy and productive relationship with their employer. A variety of characteristics unique to each employee affect this relationship and reflect the basic elements of individual behavior in organizations.

This chapter describes several of these basic elements and is the first of several chapters that examine the leading function of management. In the next section we investigate the psychological nature of individuals in organizations. The following section introduces the concept of personality and discusses several important personality attributes that can influence behavior in organizations. We next examine attitudes and their role in the behavior of individuals in organizations. The role of stress in the workplace is then addressed, followed by a discussion of individual creativity. Finally, we describe a number of basic individual behaviors that are important to organizations.

UNDERSTANDING INDIVIDUALS IN ORGANIZATIONS

1 ▶ *Explain the nature of the relationship between the individual and the organization.*

As a starting point in understanding human behavior in the workplace, we must consider the nature of the relationship between individuals and organizations. We must also gain an appreciation of the nature of individual differences.

The Psychological Contract

Most people have a basic understanding of a contract. A psychological contract is similar in some ways to a standard legal contract but is less formal and less well defined. In particular, a **psychological contract** is the overall set of expectations held by an individual with respect to what he or she will contribute to the organization and what the organization will provide in return.[2] Thus a psychological contract is not written on paper, nor are all of its terms explicitly negotiated.

The essential elements of a psychological contract are contributions and inducements.

▌ The individual makes a variety of **contributions** to the organization—effort, skills, ability, time, loyalty, and so forth. These contributions presumably satisfy various needs and requirements of the organization. In other words, because the organization may have hired the person because of her skills, it is reasonable for the organization to expect that she will subsequently display those skills in the performance of her job.

▌ In return for these contributions, the organization provides **inducements** to the individual. Some inducements, such as pay and career opportunities, are tangible rewards. Others, such as job security and status, are more intangible. Just as the contributions provided by the individual must satisfy needs of the organization, the inducements offered by the organization must serve the needs of the individual. Thus, if a person accepts employment with an organization because he thinks he will earn an attractive salary and have an opportunity to advance, he will subsequently expect that those rewards will actually be forthcoming.

If both the individual and the organization perceive that the psychological contract is fair and equitable, they will be satisfied with the relationship and will most likely continue it. On the other hand, if either party sees an imbalance or inequity in the contract, that party may initiate a change. For example, the individual may request a pay raise or promotion, decrease her contributed effort, or look for a better job elsewhere. The organization can initiate change by requesting that the individual improve his skills through training, transferring the person to another job, or terminating the person's employment.

A basic challenge faced by the organization, then, is to manage psychological contracts. The organization must ensure that it is getting value from its employees. At the same time, it must be certain that it is providing employees with appropriate inducements. If the organization is underpaying its employees for their contributions, for example, they may perform poorly or leave for better jobs elsewhere.

---

psychological contract   The overall set of expectations held by an individual with respect to what he or she will contribute to the organization and what the organization will provide in return.

contributions   In the "psychological contract" that governs employment, what the individual provides to the organization.

inducements   In the "psychological contract" that governs employment, what the organization provides to the individual.

CONCEPT CHECK 9.1

List some things that might be included in the psychological contract as employed individuals' contributions. List some things that might be included in organizational inducements. Which do you find to be the most appealing or the least appealing?

On the other hand, if they are being overpaid relative to their contributions, the organization is incurring unnecessary costs.[3]

The Person-Job Fit

One specific aspect of managing psychological contracts is managing the person-job fit. **Person-job fit** is the extent to which the contributions made by the individual match the inducements offered by the organization. In theory, each employee has a specific set of needs that he wants fulfilled and a set of job-related behaviors and abilities to contribute. Thus, if the organization can take perfect advantage of those behaviors and abilities and can exactly fulfill his needs, it will have achieved a perfect person-job fit.

Of course, such a precise level of person-job fit is seldom achieved. There are three reasons for this:

1. Organizational selection procedures are imperfect. Organizations can make approximations of employee skill levels when making hiring decisions and can improve them through training. But even simple performance dimensions are hard to measure objectively and validly. The accompanying cartoon provides a humorous example of poor "person"-job fit.
2. Both people and organizations change. An individual who finds a new job stimulating and exciting may find the same job boring and monotonous after performing it for a few years. And when the organization adopts new technology, it has changed the skills it needs from its employees.
3. Each individual is unique. Measuring skills and performance is difficult enough. Assessing needs, attitudes, and personality is far more complex. Each of these individual differences serves to make matching individuals with jobs a difficult and complex process.

person-job fit The extent to which the contributions made by the individual match the inducements offered by the organization.

Online Study Center
Improve Your Grade
Career Snapshot

Effective person-job fit is an important element in dealing with individual behavior in organizations. For instance, these hazardous materials handlers were hired because of both their technical understanding of hazardous materials and their confidence and abilities in handling those materials. On the other hand, as illustrated in the cartoon, a poor person-job fit can lead to a number of undesirable outcomes, including dissatisfaction and low performance (or, in this case, glass breakage!)

"I'M PUTTING YOU ON THE CHINA SHOP ACCOUNT. DO YOU THINK YOU CAN HANDLE IT?"

©P. C. Vey

individual differences   Personal attributes that vary from one person to another.

Individual differences are personal attributes that vary from one person to another. Individual differences may be physical, psychological, or emotional. Taken together, all of the individual differences that characterize any specific person serve to make that individual unique. Much of the remainder of this chapter is devoted to individual differences. We start with personality, which represents some of the most fundamental sets of individual differences.

TEST PREPPER 9.1

ANSWERS CAN BE FOUND ON P. 441

True or False?

_____ 1. The extent to which individual contributions match organizational inducements is called attitude.

Multiple Choice

_____ 2. When an individual exhibits effort, skill, ability, and loyalty to satisfy needs and requirements of the organization, it is known as _____.
    a. the person-job fit
    b. a psychological contract

    c. inducements
    d. contributions
    e. individual differences

_____ 3. What the organization provides to the individual is known as _____.
    a. the person-job fit
    b. a psychological contract
    c. inducements
    d. contributions
    e. individual differences

Online Study Center
ACE the Test
ACE Practice Tests 9.1

PERSONALITY AND INDIVIDUAL BEHAVIOR

2   *Define personality and describe personality attributes that affect behavior in organizations.*

personality   The relatively permanent set of psychological and behavioral attributes that distinguish one person from another.

Personality is the relatively stable set of psychological attributes that distinguish one person from another.[4] Managers should strive to understand basic personality attributes and the ways they can affect people's behavior in organizational situations, not to mention their perceptions of and attitudes toward the organization.

The "Big Five" Personality Traits

Psychologists have identified literally thousands of personality traits and dimensions that differentiate one person from another. But in recent years, researchers have identified five fundamental personality traits that are especially relevant to organizations. Because these five traits are so important, they are now commonly referred to as the **"Big Five" personality traits**.[5] Figure 9.1 illustrates the Big Five traits.

"Big Five" personality traits   A popular personality framework based on five key traits.

agreeableness   In the "Big Five" model of personality, an individual's ability to get along with others.

1. **Agreeableness** is a person's ability to get along with others. Some people are usually gentle, cooperative, forgiving, understanding, and good-natured in their dealings with others. Other people are often irritable, short-tempered, uncooperative, and generally antagonistic toward other people. These people differ on the dimension of agreeableness. Although research has not yet fully investigated the effects of agreeableness, it would seem likely that highly agreeable people will be better able to develop good working relationships with coworkers, subordinates, and higher-level managers, whereas less agreeable people will not have particularly good working relationships. This same

pattern might also extend to relationships with customers, suppliers, and other key organizational constituents.

2. **Conscientiousness** is related to the number of goals on which a person focuses. People who focus on relatively few goals at one time are likely to be organized, systematic, careful, thorough, responsible, and self-disciplined as they work to pursue those goals. By contrast, people who take on a wider array of goals tend to be more disorganized, careless, and irresponsible, as well as less thorough and self-disciplined. Research has found that more conscientious people tend to be higher performers than less conscientious people across a variety of different jobs. This pattern seems logical, of course, because more conscientious people will take their job seriously and will approach the performance of their job in a highly responsible fashion.

FIGURE 9.1

The "Big Five" Model of Personality

The "Big Five" personality model is a widely accepted framework for understanding personality traits in organizational settings. In general, experts tend to agree that personality traits toward the left end of each dimension, as illustrated in this figure, are more positive in organizational settings, whereas traits closer to the right are less positive.

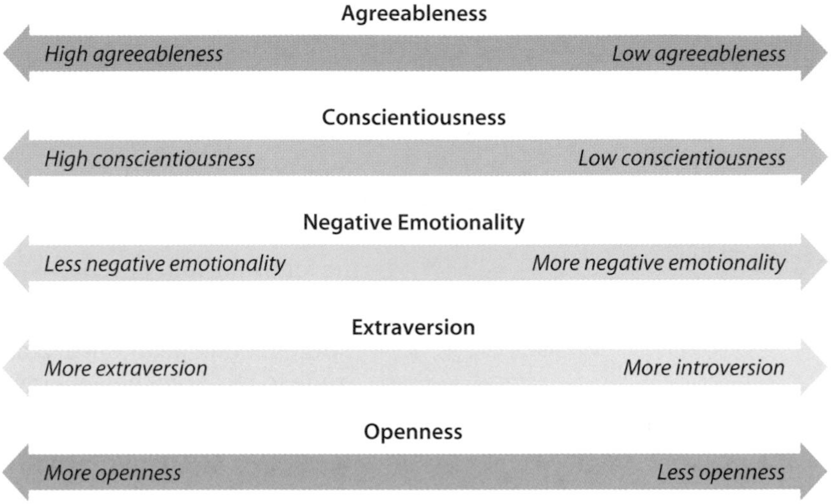

Agreeableness

High agreeableness ← → Low agreeableness

Conscientiousness

High conscientiousness ← → Low conscientiousness

Negative Emotionality

Less negative emotionality ← → More negative emotionality

Extraversion

More extraversion ← → More introversion

Openness

More openness ← → Less openness

---

3. **Negative emotionality** is the third trait. People with less negative emotionality are relatively poised, calm, resilient, and secure. But people with more negative emotionality are more excitable, insecure, reactive, and subject to extreme mood swings. People with less negative emotionality might be expected to handle job stress, pressure, and tension better. Their stability might also lead them to be seen as more reliable than their less stable counterparts.

4. **Extraversion** reflects a person's comfort level with relationships. Extraverts are sociable, talkative, assertive, and open to establishing new relationships, whereas introverts are much less sociable, more withdrawn, less garrulous, less inclined to assert themselves, and less open to establishing new relationships. Research suggests that extraverts tend to be higher overall job performers than introverts and that they are also more likely to be attracted to jobs based on personal relationships, such as sales and marketing positions.

5. **Openness** reflects a person's rigidity of beliefs and range of interests. People with high levels of openness are willing to listen to new ideas and to change their own ideas, beliefs, and attitudes as a result of new information. They also tend to have broad interests and to be curious, imaginative, and creative. On the other hand, people with low levels of openness tend to be less receptive to new ideas and less willing to change their minds. Further, they tend to have fewer and narrower interests and to be less curious and creative. People with more openness might be expected to be better performers in the organization, owing to their flexibility and the likelihood that they will be better accepted by others. Openness may also encompass an individual's willingness to accept change. For example, people with high levels of openness may be more receptive to change, whereas people with low levels of openness may be more likely to resist change.

conscientiousness   In the "Big Five" model of personality, the number of goals on which an individual focuses.

negative emotionality   In the "Big Five" model of personality, a measure of the extent to which an individual is poised, calm, resilient, and secure.

extraversion   In the "Big Five" model of personality, an individual's comfort level with relationships.

openness   In the "Big Five" model of personality, a measure of an individual's rigidity of beliefs and range of interests.

The Big Five framework continues to attract the attention of both researchers and managers. The potential value of this framework is that it offers an integrated set of traits that appear to be valid predictors of certain behaviors in certain situations. Thus managers who can develop both an understanding of the framework and the ability to assess these traits in their employees will be in a good position to understand how and why employees behave as they do.[6] On the other hand, managers must also be careful not to overestimate their ability to assess the Big Five traits in others. Even assessment via the most rigorous and valid measures is likely to be somewhat imprecise.

The Myers-Briggs Framework

Another interesting approach to understanding personalities in organizations is the Myers-Briggs framework. This framework, based on the classic work of Carl Jung, differentiates people in terms of four general dimensions. These are defined by the following four criteria:

1. *Extroversion (E) versus Introversion (I).*   Extroverts get their energy from being around other people, whereas introverts are worn out by others and need solitude to recharge their energy.

2. *Sensing (S) versus Intuition (N).*   The sensing type prefers concrete things, whereas intuitives prefer abstract concepts.

3. *Thinking (T) versus Feeling (F).*   Thinking individuals base their decisions more on logic and reason, whereas feeling individuals base their decisions more on feelings and emotions.

4. *Judging (J) versus Perceiving (P).*   People who are the judging type enjoy completion or being finished, whereas perceiving types enjoy the process and open-ended situations.

To use this framework, people complete a questionnaire designed to measure their personality on each dimension. Higher or lower scores in each of the dimensions are used to classify people into one of sixteen different personality categories.

The Myers-Briggs Type Indicator (MBTI) is one popular questionnaire that some organizations use to assess personality types. Indeed, it is among the most popular selection instruments used today; as many as 2 million people take it each year. Research suggests that the MBTI is a useful method for determining communication styles and interaction preferences. In terms of personality attributes, however, questions exist about both the validity and the reliability of the MBTI.

Other Personality Traits at Work

Besides the Big Five and the Myers-Briggs framework, there are several other personality traits that influence behavior in organizations.

locus of control   The degree to which an individual believes that his or her behavior has a direct impact on the consequences of that behavior.

▌ **Locus of control** is the extent to which people believe that their behavior has a real effect on what happens to them.[7] Some people, for example, believe that if they work hard, they will succeed. They also may believe that people who fail do so because they lack ability or motivation. People who believe that individuals are in control of their lives are said to have an *internal locus of control*. Other people think that fate, chance, luck, or other people's behavior determines what happens to them. For example, an employee who fails to get a promotion may attribute that failure to a politically motivated boss or just bad luck, rather than to her or his own lack of skills or poor performance record. People who think that forces outside their control dictate what happens to them are said to have an *external locus of control.*

▪ **Self-efficacy** is a related but subtly different personality characteristic. Self-efficacy is a person's beliefs about his or her capabilities to perform a task.[8] People with high self-efficacy believe that they can perform well on a specific task, whereas people with low self-efficacy tend to doubt their ability to perform a specific task. Although self-assessments of ability contribute to self-efficacy, so, too, does the individual's personality. Some people simply have more self-confidence than others. This belief in their ability to perform a task effectively results in their being more self-assured and more able to focus their attention on performance.

self-efficacy   An individual's beliefs about her or his capabilities to perform a task.

▪ **Authoritarianism** is the extent to which an individual believes that power and status differences are appropriate within hierarchical social systems such as organizations.[9] For example, a person who is highly authoritarian may accept directives or orders from someone with more authority purely because the other person is "the boss." On the other hand, although a person who is not highly authoritarian may still carry out appropriate and reasonable directives from the boss, he or she is also more likely to question things, express disagreement with the boss, and even refuse to carry out orders if they are for some reason objectionable.

authoritarianism   The extent to which an individual believes that power and status differences are appropriate within hierarchical social systems such as organizations.

▪ **Machiavellianism** is another important personality trait. This concept is named after Niccolò Machiavelli, a sixteenth-century Italian political philosopher. In his book *The Prince,* Machiavelli explained how the nobility could more easily gain and use power. The term *Machiavellianism* is now used to describe behavior directed at gaining power and controlling the behavior of others. Research suggests that Machiavellianism is a personality trait that varies from person to person. More Machiavellian individuals tend to be rational and nonemotional, may be willing to lie to attain their personal goals, may place little value on loyalty and friendship, and may enjoy manipulating others' behavior. Less Machiavellian individuals are more emotional, are less willing to lie to succeed, value loyalty and friendship highly, and get little personal pleasure from manipulating others.

Machiavellianism   Behavior directed at gaining power and controlling the behavior of others.

▪ **Self-esteem** is the extent to which a person believes that she is a worthwhile and deserving individual.[10] A person with high self-esteem is more likely to seek high-status jobs, to be confident in her ability to achieve higher levels of performance, and to derive greater intrinsic satisfaction from her accomplishments. In contrast, a person with less self-esteem may be more content to remain in a lower-level job, be less confident of his ability, and focus more on extrinsic rewards.

self-esteem   The extent to which a person believes that he or she is a worthwhile and deserving individual.

▪ **Risk propensity** is the degree to which an individual is willing to take chances and make risky decisions. A manager with a high risk propensity, for example, might be expected to experiment with new ideas and gamble on new products. She might also lead the organization in new and different directions. This manager might be a catalyst for innovation. On the other hand, the same individual might also jeopardize the continued well-being of the organization if the risky decisions prove to be bad ones. Hiring a manager with low risk propensity might lead to a stagnant and overly conservative organization or help the organization successfully weather turbulent and unpredictable times by maintaining stability and calm. Thus the potential consequences of risk propensity to an organization are heavily dependent on that organization's environment.

risk propensity   The degree to which an individual is willing to take chances and make risky decisions.

CONCEPT CHECK 9.2

Assume that you are going to hire three new employees for the department store you manage. One will sell shoes, one will manage the toy department, and one will work in the stockroom. Identify the basic characteristics you want in each of these people in order to achieve a good person-job fit.

Emotional Intelligence

emotional intelligence (EQ)   The extent to which people are self-aware, can manage their emotions, can motivate themselves, express empathy for others, and possess social skills.

Emotional intelligence, or EQ, only identified in recent years, refers to the extent to which people are self-aware, can manage their emotions, can motivate themselves, express empathy for others, and possess social skills.[11] These various dimensions can be described as follows:

▮ *Self-Awareness.*   This is the basis for the other components. It refers to a person's capacity for being aware of how he or she is feeling. In general, more self-awareness allows people to guide their own life and behaviors more effectively.

▮ *Managing Emotions.*   This refers to a person's capacity to balance anxiety, fear, and anger so that these emotions do not overly interfere with getting things accomplished.

▮ *Motivating Oneself.*   This dimension reflects a person's ability to remain optimistic and to continue striving in the face of setbacks, barriers, and failure.

▮ *Empathy.*   Empathy is a person's ability to understand how others are feeling, even without being explicitly told.

▮ *Social Skill.*   This refers to a person's ability to get along with others and to establish positive relationships.

Preliminary research suggests that people with high EQs may perform better than others, especially in jobs that require a high degree of interpersonal interaction and that involve influencing or directing the work of others. Moreover, EQ appears to be something that is not biologically based but can be developed.[12]

TEST PREPPER 9.2

ANSWERS CAN BE FOUND ON P. 442

True or False?

_____ 1. Personal attributes that vary from one person to another are called personality.

_____ 2. Conscientiousness refers to the number of goals on which a person focuses.

_____ 3. Someone who enjoys manipulating others would be classified as highly Machiavellian.

Multiple Choice

_____ 4. Which of the following is represented in the "Big Five" personality traits model?
   a. Sensing
   b. Extraversion
   c. Intuition
   d. Feeling
   e. Judging

_____ 5. The relatively permanent set of psychological and behavioral attributes that distinguish one person from another is called _____.
   a. the "Big Five" personality traits
   b. agreeableness
   c. openness
   d. negative emotionality
   e. personality

_____ 6. Managers who believe that they are NOT in control of their own destiny and success in the organization are said to have a(n) _____.
   a. external locus of control
   b. internal locus of control
   c. negative emotionality
   d. psychological contract
   e. positive emotionality

Online Study Center
ACE the Test
ACE Practice Tests 9.2

ATTITUDES AND INDIVIDUAL BEHAVIOR

3 ▶ *Discuss how attitudes affect the behavior of individuals in organizations.*

Attitudes are complexes of beliefs and feelings that people have about specific ideas, situations, or other people. Attitudes are important because they are the mechanism through which most people express their feelings. An employee's statement that he feels underpaid by the organization reflects his feelings about his pay. Similarly, when a manager says that she likes the new advertising campaign, she is expressing her feelings about the organization's marketing efforts.

Attitudes have three components.

1. The *affective component* of an attitude reflects feelings and emotions that an individual has toward a situation.

2. The *cognitive component* of an attitude is derived from knowledge that an individual has about a situation. It is important to note that cognition is subject to individual perceptions (something we discuss more fully later). Thus one person might "know" that a certain political candidate is better than another, whereas someone else might "know" just the opposite.

3. The *intentional component* of an attitude reflects how an individual expects to behave toward or in the situation.

To illustrate these three components, consider the case of a manager who places an order for some supplies for his organization from a new office supply firm. Suppose many of the items he orders are out of stock, others are overpriced, and still others arrive damaged. When he calls someone at the supply firm for assistance, he is treated rudely and gets disconnected before his claim is resolved. When asked how he feels about the new office supply firm, he might respond, "I don't like that company [affective component]. They are the worst office supply firm I've ever dealt with [cognitive component]. I'll never do business with them again [intentional component]."

People try to maintain consistency among the three components of their attitudes as well as among all their attitudes. However, circumstances sometimes lead to conflicts. The conflict that individuals may experience among their own attitudes is called **cognitive dissonance**.[13] Say, for example, that an individual who has vowed never to work for a big, impersonal corporation intends instead to open her own business and be her own boss. Unfortunately, because of a series of financial setbacks, she later has no choice but to take a job with a large company and work for someone else. Thus cognitive dissonance occurs: The affective and cognitive components of the individual's attitude conflict with her intended behavior. In order to reduce cognitive dissonance, which is usually an uncomfortable experience for most people, this individual might tell herself that the situation is only temporary and that she can go back out on her own in the near future. Or she might revise her cognitions and decide that working for a large company is more pleasant than she had expected.

Work-Related Attitudes

People in organizations form attitudes about many different things. For example, employees are likely to have attitudes about their salary, promotion possibilities, their boss, employee benefits, the food in the company cafeteria, and the color of

attitudes   Complexes of beliefs and feelings that people have about specific ideas, situations, or other people.

cognitive dissonance   An uncomfortable feeling that results when an individual has conflicting attitudes.

Online Study Center
Improve Your Grade
Knowledgebank 9.1

job satisfaction or dissatisfaction   An attitude that reflects the extent to which an individual is gratified by or fulfilled in his or her work.

organizational commitment   An attitude that reflects an individual's identification with and attachment to the organization itself.

CONCEPT CHECK 9.3

As a manager, how can you tell whether an employee is experiencing job satisfaction? If a worker is not satisfied, what can a manager do to improve satisfaction? How can you tell whether employees are highly committed to the organization? What can a manager do to improve organizational commitment?

---

positive affectivity   A tendency to be relatively upbeat and optimistic, to have an overall sense of well-being, to see things in a positive light, and to seem to be in a good mood.

negative affectivity   A tendency to be generally downbeat and pessimistic, to see things in a negative way, and to seem to be in a bad mood.

the company softball team uniforms. Of course, some of these attitudes are more important than others. There are two especially important attitudes:[14]

1. **Job satisfaction or dissatisfaction** is an attitude that reflects the extent to which an individual is gratified by or fulfilled in his or her work. Extensive research conducted on job satisfaction has indicated that personal factors, such as an individual's needs and aspirations, determine this attitude, along with group factors, such as relationships with coworkers and supervisors, and organizational factors, such as working conditions, work policies, and compensation.[15]

   A satisfied employee tends to be absent less often, to make positive contributions, and to stay with the organization.[16] In contrast, a dissatisfied employee may be absent more often, may experience stress that disrupts coworkers, and may be continually looking for another job. Contrary to what many managers believe, however, high levels of job satisfaction do not necessarily lead to higher levels of performance.

2. **Organizational commitment** is an attitude that reflects an individual's identification with and attachment to the organization itself. A person with a high level of commitment is likely to see herself as a true member of the organization (for example, referring to the organization in personal terms: "We make high-quality products"), to overlook minor sources of dissatisfaction with the organization, and to see herself remaining a member of the organization. In contrast, a person with less organizational commitment is more likely to see himself as an outsider (for example, referring to the organization in less personal terms: "They don't pay their employees very well"), to express more dissatisfaction, and not to see himself as a long-term member of the organization.

Affect and Mood in Organizations

Researchers have recently taken renewed interest in the affective component of attitudes. Recall from our discussion above that the affective component of an attitude reflects our feelings and emotions. Although managers once believed that emotion and feelings varied among people from day to day, research now suggests that, although some short-term fluctuation does indeed occur, there are also underlying stable predispositions toward fairly constant and predictable moods and emotional states.[17]

▍ Some people, for example, tend to have a higher degree of **positive affectivity**. This means that they are relatively upbeat and optimistic, have an overall sense of well-being, and usually see things in a positive light. Thus they always seem to be in a good mood.

▍ Other people, those with more **negative affectivity**, are just the opposite. They are generally downbeat and pessimistic, and they usually see things in a negative way. Thus they seem to be in a bad mood most of the time.

Of course, there can be short-term variations among even the most extreme types. People with a lot of positive affectivity, for example, may still be in a bad mood if they have just received some bad news—being passed over for a promotion, getting extremely negative performance feedback, or being laid off or fired, for instance. Similarly, those with negative affectivity may still be in a good mood—at least for a short time—if they have just been promoted, received very positive performance feedback, or had other good things befall them. After the initial impact of these events wears off, however, those with positive affectivity will generally return to their normal positive mood, whereas those with negative affectivity will gravitate back to their normal bad mood.

True or False?

_____ 1. A tendency to believe in yourself and that you are worthwhile shows organizational commitment.

Multiple Choice

_____ 2. A manager who says, "I'll never work with that person again," is focusing on which component of an attitude?
  a. Cognitive
  b. Affective
  c. Intentional
  d. Risk propensity
  e. None of the above

_____ 3. Tosha prides herself on always telling the truth. When confronted by her marginally performing boss about his 360-degree review, she felt _____.
  a. self-efficacy   d. locus of control
  b. introversion   e. cognitive dissonance
  c. extraversion

_____ 4. _____ is an attitude that reflects the extent to which an individual is gratified by or fulfilled in his or her work.
  a. Organizational commitment
  b. Cognitive dissonance
  c. Perception
  d. Attitudes
  e. Job satisfaction

Online Study Center
ACE the Test
ACE Practice Tests 9.3

PERCEPTION AND INDIVIDUAL BEHAVIOR

4 ▸ *Describe basic perceptual processes and the role of attributions in organizations.*

As noted earlier, an important element of an attitude is the individual's perception of the object about which the attitude is formed. Because perception plays a role in a variety of other workplace behaviors, managers need to have a general understanding of basic perceptual processes.[18] The role of attributions is also important.

Basic Perceptual Processes

Perception is the set of processes by which an individual becomes aware of and interprets information about the environment. As shown in Figure 9.2, two basic perceptual processes that are particularly relevant to organizations are selective perception and stereotyping.

1. **Selective perception** is the process of screening out information that we are uncomfortable with or that contradicts our beliefs. For example, suppose a manager is exceptionally fond of a particular worker. The manager has a very positive attitude about the worker and thinks he is a top performer. One day the manager notices that the worker seems to be goofing off. Selective perception may cause the manager to quickly forget what he observed. Similarly, suppose a manager has formed a very negative image of a particular worker. She thinks this worker is a poor performer and never does a good job. When she happens to observe an example of high performance from the worker, she, too, may not remember it very long. In one sense, selective perception is beneficial because it allows us to disregard minor bits of information. Of course, this holds true only if our basic perception is accurate. If selective perception causes us to ignore important information, it can be quite detrimental.

2. **Stereotyping** is the process of categorizing or labeling people on the basis of a single attribute. Attributes on the basis of which people often stereotype

perception The set of processes by which an individual becomes aware of and interprets information about the environment.

selective perception The process of screening out information that we are uncomfortable with or that contradicts our beliefs.

CONCEPT CHECK 9.4

How does selective perception help a manager? How does it create difficulties for a manager? How can a manager increase the "good" selective perception and decrease the "bad"?

stereotyping The process of categorizing or labeling people on the basis of a single attribute.

FIGURE 9.2

Perceptual Processes

Two of the most basic perceptual processes are selective perception and stereotyping. As shown here, selective perception occurs when we screen out information (represented by the — symbols) that causes us discomfort or that contradicts our beliefs. Stereotyping occurs when we categorize or label people on the basis of a single attribute, illustrated here by color.

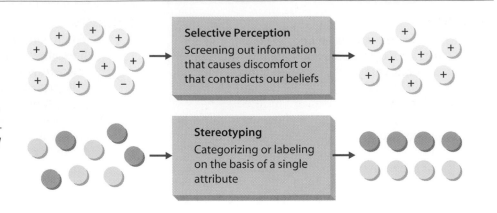

Selective Perception
Screening out information that causes discomfort or that contradicts our beliefs

Stereotyping
Categorizing or labeling on the basis of a single attribute

include race and sex. Of course, stereotypes along these lines are inaccurate and can be harmful. For example, suppose a manager forms the stereotype that women can perform only certain tasks and that men are best suited for other tasks. To the extent that this affects the manager's hiring practices, the manager is

- costing the organization valuable talent for both sets of jobs
- violating federal law
- behaving unethically

On the other hand, certain forms of stereotyping can be useful and efficient. Suppose, for example, that a manager believes that communication skills are important for a particular job and that speech communication majors tend to have exceptionally good communication skills. As a result, whenever he interviews candidates for jobs, he pays especially close attention to speech communication majors. To the extent that communication skills truly predict job performance and that majoring in speech communication does indeed enhance those skills, this form of stereotyping can be beneficial.

Perception and Attribution

attribution The process of observing behavior and attributing it to a cause.

Perception is closely linked with another process, **attribution**, which is a mechanism through which we observe behavior and then attribute it to a cause.[19] The behavior that is observed may be our own or that of others. For example, suppose someone realizes one day that she is working fewer hours than before, that she talks less about her work, and that she calls in sick more frequently. She might conclude from this that she must have become disenchanted with her job and might subsequently decide to quit. Thus she observed her own behavior, attributed it to a cause, and developed what she thought was a consistent response.

More common is attributing the behavior of others to some cause. For example, if the manager of the individual described above has observed the same behavior, he might form exactly the same attribution. On the other hand, he might instead decide that she has a serious illness, that he is driving her too hard, that she is experiencing too much stress, that she has a drug problem, or that trouble has arisen in her family.

TEST PREPPER 9.4   ANSWERS CAN BE FOUND ON P. 442

True or False?

_____ 1. William believes that an MBA is essential to performing well as a manager. In interviewing candidates he always stresses educational background and education opportunity with the company. William engages in stereotyping.

Multiple Choice

_____ 2. The process of screening out information we are uncomfortable with is known as _____.
   a. positive emotionality
   b. negative affectivity
   c. authoritarianism
   d. selective perception
   e. stereotyping

Online Study Center
ACE the Test
ACE Practice Tests 9.4

STRESS AND INDIVIDUAL BEHAVIOR

5 ▷ *Discuss the causes and consequences of stress and describe how it can be managed.*

Another important element of behavior in organizations is stress. **Stress** is an individual's response to a strong stimulus.[20] This stimulus is called a *stressor*. Stress generally follows a cycle referred to as the **General Adaptation Syndrome, or GAS,**[21] which is illustrated in Figure 9.3. According to this view, when an individual first encounters a stressor, the GAS is initiated, and the first stage, alarm, is activated. He may sense impending panic, wonder how to cope, and feel helpless. For example, suppose a manager is told to prepare a detailed evaluation of a plan his firm has made to buy one of its competitors. His first reaction may be "How will I ever get this done by tomorrow?"

If the stressor is too intense, the individual may feel unable to cope and may never really try to respond to its demands. In most cases, however, after a short period of alarm, the individual gathers some strength and starts to resist the negative effects of the stressor. For example, the manager with the evaluation to write may calm down, call home to say he is working late, roll up his sleeves, order out for coffee, and get to work. Thus, at stage 2 of the GAS, the person is resisting the effects of the stressor.

In many cases, the resistance phase may end the GAS. If the manager is able to complete the evaluation earlier than expected, he may drop it in his briefcase,

stress An individual's response to a strong stimulus, which is called a stressor.

General Adaptation Syndrome (GAS) General cycle of the stress process.

Online Study Center
Improve Your Grade
Knowledgebank 9.2

FIGURE 9.3

The General Adaptation Syndrome

The General Adaptation Syndrome represents the normal process by which we react to stressful events. At stage 1—alarm—we feel panic and alarm, and our level of resistance to stress drops. Stage 2—resistance—represents our efforts to confront and control the stressful circumstance. If we fail, we may eventually reach stage 3—exhaustion—and just give up or quit.

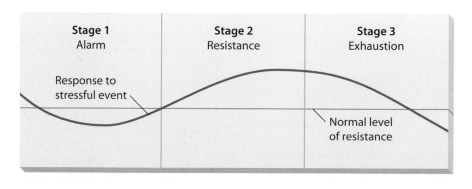

A variety of techniques and methods have been proposed as ways in which people can better manage the stress in their lives. Both meditation and yoga, as practiced by these individuals, are increasingly popular methods that many people find helpful.

Type A   Individuals who are extremely competitive, are very devoted to work, and have a strong sense of time urgency.

Type B   Individuals who are not particularly competitive, are only moderately devoted to work, and do not have a strong sense of time urgency.

smile to himself, and head home tired but satisfied. On the other hand, prolonged exposure to a stressor without resolution may bring on stage 3 of the GAS—exhaustion. At this stage, the individual literally gives up and can no longer resist the stressor. The manager, for example, might fall asleep at his desk at 3:00 A.M. and never finish the evaluation.

We should note that stress is not all bad. In the absence of stress, we may experience lethargy and stagnation. An optimal level of stress can result in motivation and excitement. Too much stress, however, can have negative consequences. It is also important to understand that stress can be caused by "good" as well as "bad" things. Excessive pressure, unreasonable demands on our time, and bad news can all cause stress. But even receiving a bonus and then having to decide what to do with the money can be stressful. So, too, can receiving a promotion, gaining recognition, and similar good things.

One important line of thinking about stress focuses on **Type A** and **Type B** personalities.[22]

1. Type A individuals are extremely competitive, are very devoted to work, and have a strong sense of time urgency. They are likely to be aggressive, impatient, and very preoccupied with work. They have a lot of drive and want to accomplish as much as possible as quickly as possible.

2. Type B individuals are less competitive, are less devoted to work, and have a weaker sense of time urgency. Such individuals are less likely to experience conflict with other people and more likely to have a balanced, relaxed approach to life. They are able to work at a constant pace without time urgency. Type B people are not necessarily more or less successful than Type A people. But they are less likely to experience stress.

Causes and Consequences of Stress

Stress is obviously not a simple phenomenon. As Figure 9.4 suggests, several different things can cause stress. Note that this list includes only work-related conditions. We should keep in mind that stress can also be the result of personal circumstances.[23]

Causes of Stress

Work-related stressors fall into one of four categories.

1. *Task demands* are associated with the task itself. Some occupations are inherently more stressful than others. Having to make fast decisions, decisions with less than complete information, or decisions that have relatively serious consequences can make some jobs stressful. The jobs of surgeon, airline pilot, and stockbroker are relatively more stressful than the jobs of general practitioner, baggage handler, and office receptionist. Although a general practitioner makes important decisions, he is also likely to have time to make a considered diagnosis and fully explore a number of different treatments. But during surgery, the surgeon must make decisions quickly and is constantly aware that the wrong one may endanger her patient's life.

FIGURE 9.4

Causes of Work Stress

There are several causes of work stress in organizations. Four general sets of organizational stressors are task demands, physical demands, role demands, and interpersonal demands.

2. *Physical demands* are stressors associated with the job setting. Working outdoors in extremely hot or cold temperatures, or even in an improperly heated or cooled office, can lead to stress. A poorly designed office—say, one that makes it difficult for people to have privacy or promotes too little social interaction—can result in stress, as can poor lighting and inadequate work surfaces. Even more severe are actual threats to health. Examples include jobs such as coal mining, poultry processing, and toxic waste handling.

3. *Role demands* can also cause stress. A role is a set of expected behaviors associated with a position in a group or organization. Stress can result from either role conflict or role ambiguity. For example, an employee who is feeling pressure from her boss to work longer hours or to travel more, while also being asked by her family for more time at home, will almost certainly experience stress as a result of role conflict.[24] Similarly, a new employee who is experiencing role ambiguity because the orientation and training that the organization has provided have been poor will also suffer from stress.

4. *Interpersonal demands* are stressors associated with relationships that confront people in organizations. For example, group pressures regarding restriction of output and norm conformity can lead to stress. Leadership styles may also cause stress. An employee who feels a strong need to participate in decision making may feel stress if his boss refuses to allow participation. And individuals with conflicting personalities may experience stress if they are required to work too closely together. For example, a person with an internal locus of control might be frustrated when working with someone who prefers to wait and just let things happen.

Consequences of Stress

As noted earlier, the results of stress may be positive or negative. The negative consequences may be one of three things: behavioral, psychological, or medical.

1. Behavioral: Stress may lead to detrimental or harmful behavior, such as smoking, alcoholism, overeating, and drug abuse. Other stress-induced behaviors include accident proneness, violence toward self or others, and appetite disorders.

2. Psychological: Consequences of stress interfere with an individual's mental health and well-being. These outcomes include sleep disturbances, depression, family problems, and sexual dysfunction. Managers are especially prone to sleep disturbances when they experience stress at work.[25]

3. Medical: Consequences of stress affect an individual's physiological well-being. Heart disease and stroke have been linked to stress, as have headaches, backaches, ulcers and related disorders, and skin conditions such as acne and hives.

Individual stress has direct consequences for businesses as well.

▌ For an operating employee, stress may translate into poor-quality work and lower productivity.

▌ For a manager, it may mean faulty decision making and disruptions in working relationships.

▌ Withdrawal behaviors can also result from stress. People who are having difficulties with stress in their job are more likely to call in sick or to leave the organization. More subtle forms of withdrawal may also occur. A manager may start missing deadlines, for example, or taking longer lunch breaks. Employees may withdraw by developing feelings of indifference.

▌ The irritation displayed by people under great stress can make them difficult to get along with.

▌ Job satisfaction, morale, and commitment can all suffer as a result of excessive levels of stress. Another consequence of stress is **burnout**—a feeling of exhaustion that may develop when someone experiences too much stress for an extended period of time. Burnout results in constant fatigue, frustration, and helplessness. Increased rigidity follows, as do a loss of self-confidence and psychological withdrawal. The individual dreads going to work, often puts in longer hours but get less accomplished than before, and exhibits mental and physical exhaustion. Because of the damaging effects of burnout, some firms are taking steps to help avoid it. For example, British Airways provides all of its employees with training designed to help them recognize the symptoms of burnout and develop strategies for avoiding it.

Managing Stress

Given the potential consequences of stress, it follows that both people and organizations should be concerned about how to limit its more damaging effects. Numerous ideas and approaches have been developed to help manage stress for the individual.

▌ *Exercise.*   People who exercise regularly experience less tension and stress, are more self-confident, and feel more optimistic.

▌ *Relaxation.*   Relaxation allows individuals to adapt to, and therefore better deal with, their stress.

▌ *Time management.*   The idea behind time management is that many daily pressures can be reduced or eliminated if individuals do a better job of managing time.

▌ *Support groups.*   A support group can be as simple as a group of family members or friends to enjoy leisure time with. Going out after work with a couple of

Online Study Center
Improve Your Grade
Knowledgebank 9.4

burnout   A feeling of exhaustion that may develop when someone experiences too much stress for an extended period of time.

Online Study Center
Improve Your Grade
Knowledgebank 9.5

coworkers to a basketball game or a movie, for example, can help relieve stress built up during the day.

Organizations themselves are beginning to realize that they should be involved in helping employees cope with stress. Hence, there are also organizational strategies for enabling people to better handle stress.

▌ Wellness programs include stress management programs, health promotion programs, and other kinds of programs for this purpose. Wellness programs are ongoing activities that commonly include exercise-related activities as well as classroom instruction programs dealing with smoking cessation, weight reduction, and general stress management.

▌ Some companies are developing their own programs or using existing programs of this type. Johns Manville, for example, has a gym at its corporate headquarters. Other firms negotiate discounted health club membership rates with local establishments. For the instructional part of the program, the organization can either sponsor its own training or jointly sponsor seminars with a local YMCA, civic organization, or church. Organization-based fitness programs facilitate employee exercise, a very positive consideration, but such programs are also quite costly. Even so, more and more companies are developing fitness programs for employees.

TEST PREPPER 9.5

ANSWERS CAN BE FOUND ON P. 442

True or False?

____ 1. The stress process is also known as pressure adaptation syndrome (PAS).

____ 2. People with a weaker sense of time urgency are Type B.

____ 3. Type A people are more likely to experience stress than Type B people.

Multiple Choice

____ 4. An employee who feels a strong need to participate in decision making may feel stress if his boss refuses to allow participation. This is an example of ____.
   a. task demands
   b. physical demands
   c. role demands
   d. interpersonal demands
   e. organizational stressors

____ 5. Which of the following is a productive way for managers to manage stress?
   a. Avoid medical attention
   b. "Happy hour"
   c. Physical exercise
   d. Sleep
   e. Work longer hours

Online Study Center
ACE the Test
ACE Practice Tests 9.5

CREATIVITY IN ORGANIZATIONS

6 ▸ *Describe creativity and its role in organizations.*

Creativity is yet another important component of individual behavior in organizations. **Creativity** is the ability of an individual to generate new ideas or to conceive of new perspectives on existing ideas. What makes a person creative? How do people become creative? How does the creative process work? Although psychologists have not yet discovered complete answers to these questions, examining a few general patterns can help us understand the sources of individual creativity within organizations.[26]

creativity   The ability of an individual to generate new ideas or to conceive of new perspectives on existing ideas.

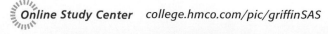

The Creative Individual

Numerous researchers have attempted to describe the attributes that characterize creative individuals. These attributes generally fall into three categories: background experiences, personal traits, and cognitive abilities.

Background Experiences and Creativity

Researchers have observed that many creative individuals were raised in an environment in which creativity was nurtured. Mozart was raised in a family of musicians and began composing and performing music at age six. Pierre and Marie Curie, great scientists in their own right, also raised a daughter, Irène, who won the Nobel Prize in chemistry. Thomas Edison's creativity was nurtured by his mother. However, people with background experiences very different from these have also been creative. Frederick Douglass was born into slavery in Tuckahoe, Maryland, and had very limited opportunities for education. Nonetheless, his powerful oratory and creative thinking helped lead to the Emancipation Proclamation, which outlawed slavery in the United States.

Personal Traits and Creativity

Certain personal traits have also been linked to creativity in individuals. The traits shared by most creative people are openness, an attraction to complexity, high levels of energy, independence and autonomy, self-confidence, and a strong belief that one is, in fact, creative. Individuals who possess these traits are more likely to be creative than are those who do not have them.

Cognitive Abilities and Creativity

Cognitive abilities are an individual's power to think intelligently and to analyze situations and data effectively. Intelligence may be a precondition for individual creativity, but even though most creative people are highly intelligent, not all intelligent people are creative. Creativity is also linked with the ability to think divergently and convergently.

1. *Divergent thinking* enables people to see differences among situations, phenomena, or events.

2. *Convergent thinking* enables people to see similarities among situations, phenomena, or events.

Creative people are generally very skilled at both divergent and convergent thinking.

The Creative Process

Although creative people often report that ideas seem to come to them "in a flash," individual creative activity actually tends to progress through a series of stages. Not all creative activity has to follow these four stages, but much of it does.

1. *Preparation:* To make a creative contribution to business management or business services, individuals must usually receive formal training and education in business. Formal education and training are generally the most efficient ways of becoming familiar with this vast amount of research and knowledge. This is one reason for the strong demand for undergraduate and master's-level business education. Formal business education can be an effective way for an individual to get "up to speed" and begin making creative contributions

quickly. Experiences that managers have on the job after their formal training is over can also contribute to the creative process. In an important sense, the education and training of creative people never really ends. It continues as long as they remain interested in the world and curious about the way things work. Bruce Roth, for example, earned a Ph.D. in chemistry and then spent years working in the pharmaceutical industry learning more and more about chemical compounds and how they work in human beings.

2. *Incubation:*   Incubation is a period of less intense concentration during which the knowledge and ideas acquired during preparation mature and develop. A curious aspect of incubation is that it is often helped along by pauses in concentrated rational thought. Some creative people rely on physical activity such as jogging or swimming to provide a break from thinking. Others may read or listen to music. Sometimes sleep may even supply the needed pause. Bruce Roth eventually joined Warner-Lambert, an up-and-coming drug company, to help develop medication to lower cholesterol. In his spare time, Roth read mystery novels and hiked in the mountains. He later acknowledged that this was when he did his best thinking.

People will do some interesting things to promote creative thinking. Haverford College physics professor Walter Smith is shown here playing a baritone ukulele and singing a song about physics to his class. Smith said the admittedly "kooky" tunes, co-written with his wife, help students think more creatively about science. Of course, coming up with this idea took some creative thinking by Smith himself!

3. *Insight:*   Insight occurs as a spontaneous breakthrough in which the creative person achieves a new understanding of some problem or situation. Insight represents a coming together of all the scattered thoughts and ideas that were maturing during incubation. It may occur suddenly or develop slowly over time. Insight can be triggered by some external event, such as a new experience or an encounter with new data, which forces the individual to think about old issues and problems in new ways, or it can be a completely internal event in which patterns of thought finally coalesce in ways that generate new understanding. One day Bruce Roth was reviewing data from some earlier studies that had found the new drug under development to be no more effective than other drugs already available. But this time he noticed some statistical relationships that had not been identified previously. He knew then that he had a major breakthrough on his hands.

4. *Verification:*   The validity or truthfulness of the insight is essential. For many creative ideas, verification includes scientific experiments to determine whether the insight actually leads to the results expected. Verification may also include the development of a product or service prototype. A prototype is one product or a very small number of products built just to see whether the ideas behind this new product actually work. Product prototypes are rarely sold to the public but are very valuable in verifying the insights developed in the creative process. Once the new product or service is developed, verification in the marketplace is the ultimate test of the creative idea behind it. Bruce Roth and his colleagues set to work testing the new drug compound and eventually

won FDA approval. The drug, named Lipitor, is already the largest-selling pharmaceutical in history. And Pfizer, the firm that bought Warner-Lambert in a hostile takeover, is expected soon to earn more than $10 billion a year on the drug.[27]

Enhancing Creativity in Organizations

Managers who wish to enhance and promote creativity in their organization can do so in a variety of ways.[28]

1. One important method for enhancing creativity is to make it a part of the organization's culture, often through explicit goals. Firms that truly want to stress creativity, such as 3M and Rubbermaid, state goals that some percentage of future revenues is to be gained from new products. This clearly communicates that creativity and innovation are valued.

2. Another important part of enhancing creativity is to reward creative successes, while being careful not to punish creative failures. Many ideas that seem worthwhile on paper fail to pan out. If the first person to come up with an idea that fails is fired or otherwise punished, others in the organization will become more cautious in their own work. And as a result, fewer creative ideas will emerge.

CONCEPT CHECK 9.5

What can an organization do to increase employees' creativity?

TEST PREPPER 9.6

ANSWERS CAN BE FOUND ON P. 442

True or False?

_____ 1. A feeling of exhaustion that may develop when someone experiences too much stress for an extended period of time is called burnout.

_____ 2. Creative individuals believe they are creative. They demonstrate openness, energy, and autonomy.

_____ 3. German managers have recently questioned their own creative ability. Their emphasis on group harmony has perhaps stifled individual initiative and hampered the development of individual creativity.

Multiple Choice

_____ 4. Sung is good at assimilating information from diverse sources and recognizing similarities between situations. This is known as _____.
   a. contradictory thinking
   b. divergent thinking
   c. convergent thinking
   d. creative thinking
   e. creative preparation

_____ 5. For many creative ideas, _____ includes scientific experiments to determine whether or not the insight actually leads to the results expected.
   a. convergent thinking
   b. preparation
   c. incubation
   d. insight
   e. verification

Online Study Center
ACE the Test
ACE Practice Tests 9.6

TYPES OF WORKPLACE BEHAVIOR

 7 Explain how workplace behaviors can directly or indirectly influence organizational effectiveness.

Now that we have looked closely at how individual differences can influence behavior in organizations, let's turn our attention to what we mean by workplace behavior. **Workplace behavior** is a pattern of action by the members of an organization that directly or indirectly influences organizational effectiveness. Important workplace behaviors include performance and productivity, absenteeism and turnover, and organizational citizenship. Unfortunately, a variety of dysfunctional behaviors can also occur in organizational settings.

workplace behavior A pattern of action by the members of an organization that directly or indirectly influences organizational effectiveness.

Performance Behaviors

Performance behaviors are the total set of work-related behaviors that the organization expects the individual to display. Thus they derive from the psychological contract. For some jobs, performance behaviors can be narrowly defined and easily measured. For example, an assembly-line worker who sits by a moving conveyor and attaches parts to a product as it passes by has relatively few performance behaviors. He or she is expected to remain at the workstation and correctly attach the parts. Performance can often be assessed quantitatively by counting the percentage of parts correctly attached.

performance behaviors The total set of work-related behaviors that the organization expects the individual to display.

For many other jobs, however, performance behaviors are more diverse and much more difficult to assess. For example, consider the case of a research and development scientist at Merck. The scientist works in a lab trying to find new scientific breakthroughs that have commercial potential. The scientist must apply knowledge learned in graduate school, along with experience gained from previous research. Intuition and creativity are also important elements. And the desired breakthrough may take months or even years to accomplish. As we discuss in Chapter 8, organizations rely on a number of different methods for evaluating performance. The key, of course, is to match the evaluation mechanism with the job being performed.

Withdrawal Behaviors

Withdrawal behaviors include absenteeism and turnover.

1. **Absenteeism** occurs when an individual does not show up for work. The cause may be legitimate (illness, jury duty, death in the family, and so forth) or feigned (reported as legitimate but actually just an excuse to stay home). When an employee is absent, her or his work does not get done at all, or a substitute must be hired to do it. In either case, the quantity or quality of actual output is likely to suffer. Obviously, some absenteeism is expected. The key concern of organizations is to minimize feigned absenteeism and to reduce legitimate absences as much as possible. High absenteeism may be a symptom of other problems as well, such as job dissatisfaction and low morale.

absenteeism An individual's not showing up for work.

2. **Turnover** occurs when people quit their job. An organization usually incurs costs in replacing individuals who have quit, but if turnover involves especially productive people, it is even more costly. Turnover seems to result from a number of factors, including aspects of the job, of the organization, and of

turnover The loss of employees that occurs when people quit their job.

the individual; the labor market; and family influences. In general, a poor person-job fit is also a likely cause of turnover. The labor shortage among some knowledge-related jobs has resulted in higher turnover in some companies as a result of the abundance of more attractive alternative jobs that are available to highly qualified individuals.[29]

Efforts to manage turnover directly are frequently fraught with difficulty, even in organizations that concentrate on rewarding good performers. Of course, some turnover is inevitable, and in some cases it may even be desirable. For example, if the organization is trying to cut costs by reducing its staff, having people leave voluntarily is preferable to terminating them. And if the people who choose to leave are low performers or express high levels of job dissatisfaction, the organization itself may benefit from turnover.

Organizational Citizenship

organizational citizenship Behavior of individuals that makes a positive overall contribution to the organization.

Organizational citizenship is the behavior of individuals that makes a positive overall contribution to the organization.[30] Consider, for example, an employee who does work that is acceptable in both quantity and quality. However, she refuses to work overtime, will not help newcomers learn the ropes, and is generally unwilling to make any contribution to the organization beyond the strict performance of her job. Although this person may be seen as a good performer, she is not likely to be seen as a good organizational citizen. Another employee may exhibit a comparable level of performance. In addition, however, he will always work late when the boss asks him to, often helps newcomers learn their way around, and is perceived as being helpful and committed to the organization's success. Although his level of performance is equal to that of the first worker, he is likely to be seen as a better organizational citizen.

The determinant of organizational citizenship behaviors is likely to be a complex mosaic of individual, social, and organizational variables. For example, for organizational citizenship to flower, the personality, attitudes, and needs of the individual must be consistent with citizenship behaviors. Similarly, the social context in which the individual works, or her or his work group, will have to facilitate and promote such behaviors (we discuss group dynamics in Chapter 13). And the organization itself, especially its culture, must be capable of promoting, recognizing, and rewarding these types of behaviors if they are to be maintained. Although the study of organizational citizenship is still in its infancy, preliminary research suggests that it may play a powerful role in organizational effectiveness.[31]

Dysfunctional Behaviors

dysfunctional behaviors Behaviors that detract from, rather than contribute to, organizational performance.

Dysfunctional behaviors are behaviors that detract from, rather than contribute to, organizational performance. Two of the more common ones, absenteeism and turnover, are discussed above. But other forms of dysfunctional behavior may be even more costly for an organization. Theft and sabotage, for example, result in direct financial costs. Sexual and racial harassment also cost an organization, both indirectly (by lowering morale, producing fear, and driving off valuable employees) and directly (through financial liability if the organization responds inappropriately). So, too, can politicized behavior, intentionally misleading others in the organization, spreading malicious rumors, and similar activities. Workplace violence is also a growing concern in many organizations. Violence by disgruntled workers or former workers results in dozens of deaths and injuries each year.[32]

True or False?

_____ 1. Performance behaviors are separate and distinct from the psychological contract.

_____ 2. Turnover occurs when an organization downsizes.

Multiple Choice

_____ 3. Which of the following is a performance workplace behavior that organizations expect individuals to display?
- a. Absenteeism
- d. Harassment
- b. Turnover
- e. Low morale
- c. Intuition

Online Study Center
ACE the Test
ACE Practice Tests 9.7

BUILDING EFFECTIVE INTERPERSONAL SKILLS

Online Study Center
Improve Your Grade
Exercises: Building Effective Skills

Exercise Overview

Interpersonal skills reflect the ability to communicate with, understand, and motivate individuals and groups. This exercise introduces a widely used tool for personality assessment. It shows how an understanding of personality can aid in developing effective interpersonal relationships within organizations.

Exercise Background

There are many different ways of viewing personality, and one that is widely used is called the Myers-Briggs Type Indicator. According to Isabel Myers, each individual's personality type varies in four dimensions:

1. *Extraversion (E) versus Introversion (I).* Extraverts get their energy from being around other people, whereas introverts are worn out by others and need solitude to recharge their energy.

2. *Sensing (S) versus Intuition (N).* The sensing type prefers concrete things, whereas the intuitivist prefers abstract concepts.

3. *Thinking (T) versus Feeling (F).* Thinking individuals base their decisions more on logic and reason, whereas feeling individuals base their decisions more on feelings and emotions.

4. *Judging (J) versus Perceiving (P).* People who are the judging type enjoy completion or being finished, whereas perceiving types enjoy the process and open-ended situations.

On the basis of their answers to a survey, individuals are classified into sixteen personality types—all the possible combinations of the four dimensions above. The resulting personality type is then expressed as a four-character code, such as ESTP or INFJ. These four-character codes can then be used to describe an individual's preferred way of interacting with others.

Exercise Task

1. Use an online Myers-Briggs assessment form to determine your own personality type. One place to find the form online is www.keirsey.com/scripts/ newkts.cgi. This website also contains additional information about personality type. (*Note:* You do *not* need to pay fees or agree to receive e-mails in order to take the Temperament Sorter.)

2. When you have determined the four-letter code for your personality type, obtain a handout from your professor. The handout will show how your personality type affects your preferred style of working and your leadership style.

3. Conclude by addressing the following questions:
   - How easy is it to measure personality?
   - Do you feel that the online test accurately assessed your personality?
   - Why or why not? Share your assessment results and your answers with the class.

Reprinted by permission of the author Margaret Hill.

EXPERIENTIAL EXERCISE

Online Study Center
Improve Your Grade
–Exercises: Experiential Exercise
–Interactive Skills Self-Assessment

Assumptions That Color Perceptions

Purpose

Perceptions rule the world. In fact, everything we know or think we know is filtered through our perceptions. Our perceptions are rooted in past experiences and in socialization by significant others in our lives. This exercise is designed to help you become aware of how much our assumptions influence our perceptions and evaluations of others. It also illustrates how we compare our perceptions with those of others to find similarities and differences.

Instructions

1. Read the personal descriptions of four individuals that follow.
2. Then, for each of the occupations listed, decide which of these people would best fill that position, and place the name of that person in the blank beside the job.

Personal Descriptions

R. B. Red is a trim, attractive woman in her early thirties. She holds an undergraduate degree from an eastern women's college and is active in several professional organizations. She is an officer (on the national level) of Toastmistress International. Her hobbies include classical music, opera, and jazz. She is an avid traveler who is planning a sojourn to China next year.

W.C. White is a quiet, meticulous person. W.C. is tall and thin with blond hair and wire-framed glasses. Family, friends, and church are very important, and W.C. devotes any free time to community activities. W.C. is a wizard with figures but can rarely be persuaded to demonstrate this ability to do mental calculations.

G. A. Green grew up on a small farm in rural Indiana. He is an avid hunter and fisherman. In fact, he and his wife joke about their "deer-hunting honeymoon" in Colorado. One of his primary goals is to "get back to the land," and he hopes to be able to buy a small farm before he is fifty. He drives a pickup truck and owns several dogs.

B. E. Brown is the child of wealthy professionals who live on Long Island. B.E.'s father is a "self-made" financial analyst who never missed an opportunity to stress the importance of financial security as B.E. grew up. B.E. values the ability to structure one's use of time and can often be found on the golf course on Wednesday afternoons. B.E. dresses in a conservative upper-class manner and professes to be "allergic to polyester."

Occupations

Indicate which of these people you think would best "fit" each of the following jobs.

Banker
Labor negotiator
Production manager
Travel agent
Accountant
Teacher
Clerk
Army general
Salesperson
Truck driver
Physician
Financial analyst
Computer operations manager

Source: Adapted from Jerri L. Frantzve, *Behaving in Organizations* (Boston: Allyn & Bacon, 1983), pp. 63–65.

CLOSING CASE STUDY

Too Much Character Building?

There is good stress and there is bad stress. Dr. Allen Elkin, stress expert, says, "Stress is like a violin string. If there's no tension, there's no music. But if the string is too tight, it will break." Good stress helps us to do our best work, motivates us to complete projects on time, and inspires creativity as we attempt to resolve the conflicting tensions we feel. Bad stress, on the other hand, makes our personality characteristics more pronounced. If you are naturally shy, you become reclusive. If you are naturally irritable, you become explosively angry. Bad stress leads to negative physical outcomes, from headaches to heart attacks; to negative psychological outcomes such as depression, indecision, and forgetfulness; and to negative social outcomes—anger, impatience, rudeness. "Don't let anyone tell you [stress] is just in your head," says professor Jim Quick. "It is in your body too."

The bad news, according to stress experts, is that Americans are experiencing the highest levels of stress ever. Author and stress expert Dr. Stephen Schoonover says, "People are absolutely nuts, stressed off the map. I've never seen it this bad." Stress experts, including physicians, psychiatrists, professors, and career counselors, back up their opinion with some scary statistics. Half of American workers report that stress is their major problem—double the rate ten years ago. The number of people missing work due to stress has tripled in the last four years. And 42 percent of employees think that their coworkers are suffering from dangerously high stress and need professional help to manage it.

What is causing this national epidemic of stress? Sally Helgesen, author of *Thriving in 24/7*, blames technology. The rise of the knowledge-based economy means that work is more competitive and unstable, so workers experience more chaos, rivalry, and conflict. Helgesen also sees technology (such as pagers) as "intrusive," because it allows workers to work all the time. Workers cannot, and cannot afford to, "turn their job off." A McKinsey consulting firm study of top managers around the world reported that half of them spend at least one full day per week on communications that are not valuable and that 25 percent say their communications are "completely unmanageable."

> *"Stress is like a violin string. If there's no tension, there's no music. But if the string is too tight, it will break."*
>
> —Dr. Allen Elkin of the Stress Management and Counseling Center

Everyone experiences stress. The traditional view holds that middle managers have the most, because they are squeezed between their superiors and their subordinates. However, experts see a rise in stress among top executives, perhaps because of the increased financial and ethical pressure on business leaders today. CEOs complain that they do not have as much autonomy; others whine that no one takes them seriously because scandals have destroyed their credibility. The stress of success also hits CEOs hard, because high achievers may be expected to keep up that level of performance forever.

Stress is tougher on top-level executives, because overcoming adversity is a hallmark trait of a successful leader. The myth of executive stress says that managers who cannot manage their own stress cannot possibly handle the pressure of managing a corporation. Therefore, many managers hide their stress, which results in . . . more stress! CEO Alexandra Lebenthal admits, "Fortunately or unfortunately, stress is part of our character building. But there is a moment when you think, I don't need any more character building. What I need is a vacation." Executives would rather admit to depression or alcoholism than own up to an inability to manage stress.

On the positive side, the experts also have plenty of ideas for coping with stress. Clearly, for stress that may result in harm to the employee or to others, a professional counselor is required. There are even inpatient stress-management programs. However, for moderate stress, a stress-management workshop, such as those offered by the American Management Association, would be helpful. Other suggestions include the mundanely practical, such as turning off your pager during dinner. More complex solutions include setting up a napping area at your workplace or visiting an Indian ashram to learn yoga and deep-breathing techniques.

However, the suggestions that are the most difficult to implement—those that involve radical life changes—are also the most likely to lead to success. Experts recommend that managers rethink and revolutionize their life strategies. Suggestions include volunteering in order to feel a connection with others, developing exciting and active hobbies outside of work, and budgeting large blocks of time for important relationships with family and friends. In other words, do what Helgesen calls "making a living *and* making a life." These answers may sound obvious and simplistic, but to those with stress-impaired reason and emotion, following these proposals could literally save a life.

Case Questions

1. Consider the causes of stress experienced by CEOs in terms of the four types of demands listed in your text. What demands are made on CEOs? How do these demands affect them and their performance?

2. The case suggests a number of actions that managers can take to cope with stress. What can or-

ganizations do to help their employees cope with stress? In your opinion, should companies take these steps? Why or why not?

3. Some firms are subjecting prospective employees to "stress tests" to assess the job candidate's ability to cope with stress. Judging on the basis of what you have read in the case, what positive and negative consequences will firms experience that try to hire people who can cope with a lot of stress?

Case References

Mark Albion, "The Beauty of Burnout," *Fast Company*, May 2001, www.fastcompany.com on February 3, 2003; Diane Brady, "Rethinking the Rat Race," *BusinessWeek*, August 26, 2002, www.businessweek.com on February 3, 2003; Michael Lewis, "The Last Taboo," *Fortune*, October 28, 2002, pp. 137–144 (quote p. 144); Michael Mandel, "The Real Reason You're Working So Hard . . ." *BusinessWeek*, October 3, 2005, www.businessweek.com on January 19, 2006; Jody Miller and Matt Miller, "Get A Life!" *Fortune*, November 16, 2005, www .fortune.com on December 19, 2005; Anni Layne Rodgers, "Surviving la Vida Loca," *Fast Company*, September 2001, www.fastcompany.com on February 3, 2003.

LEARNING OBJECTIVE REVIEW

Online Study Center
Improve Your Grade
–Learning Objective Review
–Audio Chapter Review
–Study Guide to Go

Online Study Center
ACE the Test
Audio Chapter Quiz

1 ▶ *Explain the nature of the relationship between the individual and the organization.*

- A basic framework that managers can use to facilitate understanding individuals is the psychological contract—the set of expectations held by people with respect to what they will contribute to the organization and what they will get in return.

- Organizations strive to achieve an optimal person-job fit, but this process is complicated by the existence of individual differences.

2 ▶ *Define personality and describe personality attributes that affect behavior in organizations.*

- Personality is the relatively stable set of psychological and behavioral attributes that distinguish one person from another.

- The "Big Five" personality traits are
  agreeableness
  conscientiousness
  negative emotionality
  extraversion
  openness

- The Myers-Briggs framework can also be a useful mechanism for understanding personality.

- Other important traits include the following:
  locus of control   Machiavellianism
  self-efficacy   self-esteem
  authoritarianism   risk propensity

- Emotional intelligence, a fairly new concept, may provide additional insights into personality.

3 ► *Discuss how attitudes affect the behavior of individuals in organizations.*

- Attitudes are based on
  emotion
  knowledge
  intended behavior

- Job satisfaction or dissatisfaction and organizational commitment are important work-related attitudes.

- People tend to be either generally positive or negative in their mood.

4 ► *Describe basic perceptual processes and the role of attributions in organizations.*

- Perception is the set of processes by which an individual becomes aware of and interprets information about the environment. Two forms of perception are
  selective perception
  stereotyping

- Perception and attribution—identifying a cause for a behavior—are also closely related.

5 ► *Discuss the causes and consequences of stress and describe how it can be managed.*

- Stress is an individual's response to a strong stimulus.

- The General Adaptation Syndrome outlines the basic stress process.

- Stress can be caused by the following demands:
  task   role
  physical   interpersonal

- Consequences of stress include
  harmful behaviors
  psychological problems
  medical problems

- Stress can also influence work performance, sometimes leading to burnout.

- Stress can be managed through such things as exercise, and some organizations have stress-reduction programs.

6 ► *Describe creativity and its role in organizations.*

- Creativity is the capacity to generate new ideas.

- Creative people tend to have certain profiles of background experiences, personal traits, and cognitive abilities.

- The creative process itself includes
  preparation
  incubation
  insight
  verification

- Firms can encourage a creative culture.

7 ► *Explain how workplace behaviors can directly or indirectly influence organizational effectiveness.*

- Workplace behavior is a pattern of action by the members of an organization that directly or indirectly influences organizational effectiveness.

- Performance behaviors are the set of work-related behaviors that the organization expects the individual to display in order to fulfill the psychological contract.

- Withdrawal behaviors include absenteeism and turnover.

- Organizational citizenship consists of behavior that makes a positive overall contribution to the organization.

- Dysfunctional behaviors can be very harmful to an organization.

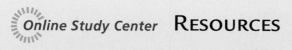 **Online Study Center** **RESOURCES**

Prepare for Class, Improve Your Grade, and ACE the Test. These Student Achievement resources include:

ACE Practice Tests	Interactive Skills Assessments	Study Guide to Go
End of Chapter Exercises	Knowledgebank	Video Segments
Glossaries (visual and print)	Reviews (audio and print)	Summaries/Outlines
Flashcards		

To access these learning and study tools, go to: **college.hmco.com/pic/griffinSAS**

Doctors Without Borders capitalizes on the motivation of many people to help those less fortunate than themselves. A worker, Anja, from German Médecins Sans Frontières (Doctors Without Borders) is shown here helping one of the youngest victims of the recent flooding in Chokwe, Mozambique.

4 ▸ *Describe reinforcement perspectives on motivation.*

3 ▸ *Identify and describe the major process perspectives on motivation.*

2 ▸ *Identify and describe the major content perspectives on motivation.*

1 ▸ *Characterize the nature of motivation, including its importance and basic historical perspectives.*

Chapter Outline

Online Study Center
Prepare for Class
Chapter Outline

5 ▶ Identify and describe
popular motivational
strategies.

6 ▶ Describe the role of
organizational reward systems
in motivation.

Motivation
Without Borders

It's not just your imagination. The world is becoming a more disastrous place. There were 2.6 times more natural disasters from 1993 to 2002 than there were in the 1960s. When an Indian Ocean tsunami struck, volunteers from Doctors Without Borders were the first responders. When civil wars broke out in Sudan and Congo, Doctors Without Borders went. They also went to an earthquake in Pakistan, election violence in Haiti, and flooding in Guatemala, wherever a population was in danger. The nonprofit, nongovernmental organization (NGO) treats medical crises, provides aid to

PRACTICING MANAGER'S TERMS

motivation   *p. 254*
need for achievement   *p. 258*
positive reinforcement   *p. 264*
punishment   *p. 265*
empowerment   *p. 267*
participation   *p. 267*
compressed work schedule   *p. 268*
job sharing   *p. 268*
telecommuting   *p. 268*
reward system   *p. 269*
merit pay   *p. 269*
merit pay plan   *p. 269*
gainsharing programs   *p. 271*
stock option plan   *p. 273*

Online Study Center
Improve Your Grade
–Flashcards
–Glossary

KEY TERMS

content perspectives   *p. 255*
Maslow's hierarchy of
     needs   *p. 256*
two-factor theory of
     motivation   *p. 257*
need for affiliation   *p. 258*
need for power   *p. 258*
process perspectives   *p. 259*
expectancy theory   *p. 259*
effort-to-performance
     expectancy   *p. 259*
performance-to-outcome
     expectancy   *p. 260*
outcomes   *p. 260*

valence   *p. 260*
equity theory   *p. 261*
reinforcement theory   *p. 264*
avoidance   *p. 265*
extinction   *p. 265*
fixed-interval schedule   *p. 265*
variable-interval
     schedule   *p. 266*
fixed-ratio schedule   *p. 266*
variable-ratio schedule   *p. 266*
piece-rate incentive plan
     p. 270
Scanlon plan   *p. 272*

You should be able to define and use terms that are part of the practicing manager's vocabulary, as well as those that are integral in the language of management.

victims of war and famine, builds health-care facilities, fights epidemics, and gives care to excluded groups and refugees.

Doctors Without Borders, another name for Médecins Sans Frontières (MSF), began in France in 1971. MSF now include sections in nineteen countries and served seventy countries in 2005. African nations received the most aid, $260 million in all, while millions more were spent in Afghanistan, Chechnya, Iraq, and Cambodia.

Aid ranges from vaccinations and food to mental health counseling and antiviral medicines. In addition, MSF offers public health education and training for local caregivers. The nonprofit's list of the "Top 10 Most Underreported Humanitarian Stories" raises public awareness about the lack of attention given to worldwide medical crises. In 2005, of the 14,529 minutes of major evening newscasts in the United States, just 8 minutes reported humanitarian stories. MSF also participates in a research consortium for drug research and development.

Volunteers are physicians and other health professionals, in addition to experts in communications, information technology, water and sanitation engineering, and distribution. MSF recruits volunteers through word of mouth and public relations. Applicants must have specialized and professional qualifications as well as personal characteristics such as adaptability, teamwork, commitment, and ability to function under stress. Volunteers are expected to work continuously, in primitive and stressful conditions, with risky, infectious diseases. MSF volunteers often work in hostile areas and under armed guards, and employees are sometimes the target of violence, as were the five workers killed in a 2004 ambush in Afghanistan. Experienced MSF member and nurse Pierre LePlante tells of working seven days a week, for ten to sixteen hours daily, and being threatened with automatic weapons in Rwanda and Somalia.

Why are highly qualified people, who could be earning top salaries in more conventional and comfortable jobs, volunteering to work under brutal conditions for so little compensation? And why do 70 percent of the members return after their first year's experience? Although experienced volunteers qualify for a small salary and benefits, the pay is low, even compared to that of other nonprofits and NGOs.

Nayana Somaiah, an Indian-trained physician who practiced in Canada, explains her initial motivation: "I was drawn to going back to the developing world. . . . I was going to . . . join an organization that could put my skills and sense of adventure to use." After beginning work in Nigeria, her feelings changed. "Slowly the poverty that surrounded me took away my naïve sense of adventure . . . it hit me really hard." Somaiah's realization of the true nature of her work is echoed in the words of Lisabeth List, a nurse and MSF volunteer. "MSF is not a working holiday," List says, "nor a way to see the world."

What most MSF volunteers cherish most is the chance to make a difference in someone's life. "There is nothing like seeing a child deathly skinny and watching that child become healthy," states List. "It's amazing. I think working with starving people is the best thing I've done." Other members mention the career opportunities and valuable experience they gained as MSF volunteers, including everything from patient care to training to advising local governments.

Surgeon Wei Cheng and his wife Karin Moorhouse recently wrote *No One Can Stop the Rain*, a book about their MSF volunteer experience in Angola. By writing, they fulfill MSF's commitment to *témoignage*, or bearing witness. They discuss their motives: "The flickering light of humanity we witness almost daily in this world of conflict and tragedy is not about to be extinguished, but rather can be given new energy through the efforts of ordinary people. . . . [T]he rewards are tremendous. The [Angolans'] ability to endure in terrible circumstances touched us to the core. Our experience was both inspiring and humbling."[1]

Those who work for Doctors Without Borders are strongly motivated by the desire to do good, despite the absence of safe working conditions and decent pay. Indeed, they chose this work knowing all too well the implicit sacrifices they were making. In most settings, people can choose how hard they work and how much effort they expend. Thus managers need to understand how and why employees make different choices regarding their own performance. The key ingredient behind this choice is motivation, the subject of this chapter. We first examine the nature of employee motivation and then explore the major perspectives on motivation. Newly emerging approaches are then discussed. We conclude with a description of rewards and their role in motivation.

THE NATURE OF MOTIVATION

1 ▸ *Characterize the nature of motivation, including its importance and basic historical perspectives.*

Motivation is the set of forces that cause people to behave in certain ways.[2] On any given day, an employee may choose to work as hard as possible at a job, to work just hard enough to avoid a reprimand, or to do as little as possible. The goal for the manager is to maximize the likelihood of the first behavior and minimize the likelihood of the last. This goal becomes all the more critical when we understand how important motivation is in the workplace. Individual performance is generally determined by three things:

1. Motivation (the desire to do the job)
2. Ability (the capability to do the job)
3. The work environment (the resources needed to do the job)

If an employee lacks ability, the manager can provide training or replace the worker. If there is a resource problem, the manager can correct it. But if motivation is the problem, the manager's task is more challenging.[3] Individual behavior is a complex phenomenon, and it may be difficult for the manager to figure out the precise nature of the problem and how to solve it. Thus motivation is important because of its significance as a determinant of performance and because of its intangible character.[4]

The motivation framework shown in Figure 10.1 is a good starting point for understanding how motivated behavior occurs. The motivation process begins with a need or deficiency. For example, when a worker feels that she is underpaid, she experiences a need for more income. In response, the worker searches for ways to satisfy the need, such as working harder to try to earn a raise or seeking a new job. Next she chooses an option to pursue. After carrying out the chosen option—working harder and putting in more hours for a reasonable period of time, for example—she then evaluates her success. If her hard work resulted in a pay raise, she probably feels good about things and will continue to work hard. But if no raise has been provided, she is likely to try another option.

motivation   The set of forces that cause people to behave in certain ways.

Online Study Center
Improve Your Grade
Knowledgebank 10.1

Motivation is both an incredibly important and an extremely complex phenomenon. Take Hank Schmelzer, for example. After several years as a successful CEO, Schmelzer decided that he wanted to do something different—and more meaningful. He eventually took the job as president of the Maine Community Foundation. Although he gave up both prestige and a huge salary to take this job, he says he feels content and at peace for the first time in years.

FIGURE 10.1

The Motivation Framework

The motivation process progresses through a series of discrete steps. Content, process, and reinforcement perspectives on motivation address different parts of this process.

Need or deficiency → Search for ways to satisfy need → Choice of behavior to satisfy need → Evaluation of need satisfaction → Determination of future needs and search/choice for satisfaction ⤏ (back to Need or deficiency)

TEST PREPPER 10.1

ANSWERS CAN BE FOUND ON P. 442

True or False?

_____ 1. The motivation framework supports the statement "necessity is the mother of invention."

Multiple Choice

_____ 2. Which of the following determines performance?
   a. Motivation
   b. Ability
   c. Work environment
   d. The capability to do the job
   e. All of the above

_____ 3. Individual behavior is a complex phenomenon, and the manager may be hard pressed to figure out the precise nature of the problem and how to solve it. Thus _____ is important because of its significance as a determinant of performance and because of its intangible character.
   a. security
   b. motivation
   c. esteem
   d. leadership
   e. self-actualization

Online Study Center
ACE the Test
ACE Practice Tests 10.1

CONTENT PERSPECTIVES ON MOTIVATION

2 | *Identify and describe the major content perspectives on motivation.*

Content perspectives on motivation deal with the first part of the motivation process—needs and deficiencies. More specifically, **content perspectives** address the issue of what factors in the workplace motivate people. Labor leaders often argue that workers can be motivated by more pay, shorter working hours, and improved working conditions. Meanwhile, some experts suggest that motivation can be more effectively enhanced by providing employees with more autonomy and greater responsibility.[5] Both of these views represent content perspectives on motivation. The former asserts that motivation is a function of pay, working hours, and working conditions; the latter suggests that autonomy and responsibility contribute significantly to motivation. Two widely known content perspectives on motivation are the needs hierarchy and the two-factor theory.

content perspectives Approaches to motivation that try to determine what factor or factors motivate people.

The Needs Hierarchy Approach

Needs hierarchies assume that people have different needs that can be arranged in a hierarchy of importance. The best-known needs hierarchy was advanced by

FIGURE 10.2

Maslow's Hierarchy of Needs

Maslow's hierarchy suggests that human needs can be classified into five categories and that these categories can be arranged in a hierarchy of importance. A manager should understand that an employee may not be satisfied with only a salary and benefits; he or she may also need challenging job opportunities to experience self-growth and satisfaction.

Adapted from Abraham H. Maslow, "A Theory of Human Motivation," *Psychology Review*, vol. 50, 1943, pp. 370–396.

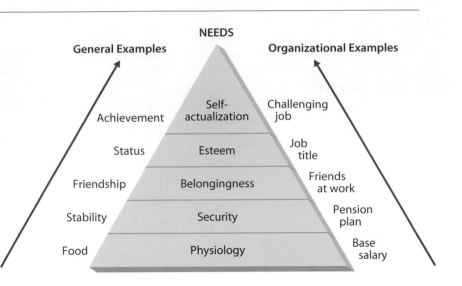

Maslow's hierarchy of needs   A content perspective on motivation that suggests that people must satisfy the following five levels of needs in the following order—physiological, security, belongingness, esteem, and self-actualization needs.

Online Study Center
Improve Your Grade
Knowledgebank 10.2

Abraham Maslow, a human relationist, who argued that people are motivated to satisfy five levels of needs.[6] **Maslow's hierarchy of needs** is shown in Figure 10.2.

1. *Physiological needs*—basic needs of survival and biological function, such as food, sex, and air. In organizations, these needs are generally satisfied by adequate wages and the work environment itself, which provides restrooms, adequate lighting, comfortable temperatures, and ventilation.

2. *Security needs*—a secure physical and emotional environment. Examples include the desire for housing and clothing and the need to be free from worry about money and job security. These needs can be satisfied in the workplace by job continuity (no layoffs), a grievance system (to protect against arbitrary supervisory actions), and an adequate insurance and retirement benefit package (for the security of knowing that medical care will be available in the event of illness and the security of knowing that one will have an income in later life). Even today, however, depressed industries and economic decline can put people out of work and threaten the satisfaction of security needs.

3. *Belongingness needs*—needs related to social processes. They include the need for love and affection and the need to be accepted by one's peers. These needs are satisfied for most people by family and community relationships outside of work and by friendships on the job. A manager can help satisfy these needs by allowing social interaction and by making employees feel like part of a team or work group.

4. *Esteem needs*—the need for a positive self-image and self-respect and the need for recognition and respect from others. A manager can help address these needs by providing a variety of extrinsic symbols of accomplishment, such as job titles, nice offices, and similar rewards as appropriate. At a more intrinsic level, the manager can provide challenging job assignments and opportunities for the employee to experience a sense of accomplishment.

5. *Self-actualization needs*—realizing one's potential for continued growth and individual development. The self-actualization needs are perhaps the most difficult for a manager to address. In fact, it can be argued that these needs must be met entirely from within the individual. But a manager can help by promoting a culture wherein self-actualization is possible. For instance, a

manager could give employees a chance to participate in making decisions about their work and the opportunity to learn new things.

Maslow suggests that the five categories of needs constitute a hierarchy. An individual is motivated first and foremost to satisfy physiological needs. As long as these remain unsatisfied, the individual is motivated to fulfill only them. When satisfaction of physiological needs is achieved, they cease to act as primary motivational factors, and the individual moves "up" the hierarchy and becomes concerned with security needs. This process continues until the individual reaches the self-actualization level. Maslow's concept of the hierarchy of needs has a certain intuitive logic and has been accepted by many managers. But research has revealed the following shortcomings or defects:

▌ Some research has found that five levels of needs are not always present and that the order of the levels is not always the same.[7]

▌ In addition, people from different cultures are likely to exhibit different categories and hierarchies of needs.

The Two-Factor Theory

Another popular content perspective is the **two-factor theory of motivation**.[8] Frederick Herzberg developed his theory by interviewing two hundred accountants and engineers. He asked them to recall occasions when they had been satisfied and motivated and occasions when they had been dissatisfied and unmotivated. Surprisingly, he found that different sets of factors were associated with satisfaction and with dissatisfaction—that is, a person might identify "low pay" as causing dissatisfaction but would not necessarily mention "high pay" as a cause of satisfaction. Instead, different factors—such as recognition or accomplishment—were cited as causing satisfaction and motivation.

This finding led Herzberg to conclude that the traditional view of job satisfaction was incomplete. That view assumed that satisfaction and dissatisfaction are at opposite ends of a single continuum. People might be satisfied, dissatisfied, or somewhere in between. But Herzberg's interviews had identified two different dimensions altogether: one ranging from satisfaction to no satisfaction and the other ranging from dissatisfaction to no dissatisfaction. This perspective, along with several examples of factors that affect each continuum, is illustrated in Figure 10.3. Note that the factors influencing the satisfaction continuum—called *motivation factors*—are related specifically to the work content. The factors presumed to cause dissatisfaction—called *hygiene factors*—are related to the work environment.

On the basis of these findings, Herzberg argued that there are two stages in the process of motivating employees.

1. First, managers must ensure that the hygiene factors are not deficient. Pay and security must be appropriate, working conditions must be safe, technical supervision must be acceptable, and so on. By providing hygiene factors at an appropriate level, managers do not stimulate motivation

two-factor theory of motivation   A content perspective on motivation that suggests that people's satisfaction and dissatisfaction are influenced by two independent sets of factors—motivation factors and hygiene factors.

FIGURE 10.3

The Two-Factor Theory of Motivation
The two-factor theory suggests that job satisfaction has two dimensions. A manager who tries to motivate an employee using only hygiene factors, such as pay and good working conditions, is not likely to succeed. To motivate employees and produce a high level of satisfaction, managers must also offer factors such as responsibility and the opportunity for advancement (motivation factors).

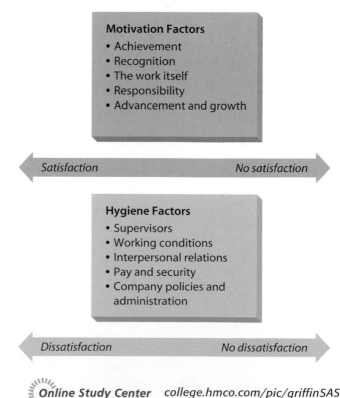

Motivation Factors
• Achievement
• Recognition
• The work itself
• Responsibility
• Advancement and growth

Satisfaction ——————— *No satisfaction*

Hygiene Factors
• Supervisors
• Working conditions
• Interpersonal relations
• Pay and security
• Company policies and administration

Dissatisfaction ——————— *No dissatisfaction*

but merely ensure that employees are "not dissatisfied." Employees whom managers attempt to "satisfy" through hygiene factors alone will usually do just enough to get by.

2. Thus managers should proceed to the second stage—giving employees the opportunity to experience motivation factors such as achievement and recognition. The result is predicted to be a high level of satisfaction and motivation. Herzberg also went a step further than most other theorists and described exactly how to use the two-factor theory in the workplace. Specifically, he recommended job enrichment, as discussed in Chapter 6. He argued that jobs should be redesigned to provide higher levels of the motivation factors.

Although widely accepted by many managers, Herzberg's two-factor theory is not without its critics. One criticism is that the findings in Herzberg's initial interviews are subject to different explanations. Another charge is that his sample was not representative of the general population and that subsequent research often failed to uphold the theory.[9]

At the present time, Herzberg's theory is not held in high esteem by researchers in the field. The theory has had a major impact on managers, however, and has played a key role in increasing their awareness of motivation and its importance in the workplace.

Individual Human Needs

In addition to these theories, research has focused on specific individual human needs that are important in organizations. The three most important individual needs are achievement, affiliation, and power.[10]

1. The **need for achievement**, the best known of the three, is the desire to excel and accomplish important goals.
2. The **need for affiliation** is the desire for human companionship and acceptance.
3. The **need for power** is the desire to be influential in a group and to have control over one's environment.

CONCEPT CHECK 10.1

Summarize Maslow's needs hierarchy and the two-factor theory. In what ways are they similar and in what ways are they different?

need for achievement The desire to accomplish a goal or task more effectively than in the past.

need for affiliation The desire for human companionship and acceptance.

need for power The desire to be influential in a group and to control one's environment.

ANSWERS CAN BE FOUND ON P. 442

TEST PREPPER 10.2

True or False?

_____ 1. Approaches to motivation that try to answer the question "What factor or factors motivate people?" are called needs perspectives.

_____ 2. Herzberg's two-factor theory of motivation suggests that people's satisfaction and dissatisfaction are influenced by two independent sets of factors: need for achievement and need for affiliation.

_____ 3. The need for achievement is higher in the United States than in Japan.

Multiple Choice

_____ 4. An organization contributes to the bottom of Maslow's need hierarchy through _____.
   a. job challenges   d. pension plan
   b. socialization   e. job sharing
   c. adequate wages

_____ 5. Which of the following is the desire for human companionship and acceptance?
   a. Need for motivation
   b. Need for affiliation
   c. Need for accomplishment
   d. Need for power
   e. Need for encouragement

_____ 6. Herzberg recommended _____ to provide higher levels of motivation.
   a. job specialization   d. departmentalization
   b. job rotation   e. job sharing
   c. job enrichment

Online Study Center
ACE the Test
ACE Practice Tests 10.2

PROCESS PERSPECTIVES ON MOTIVATION

3 ▷ *Identify and describe the major process perspectives on motivation.*

Process perspectives are concerned with how motivation occurs. Rather than attempting to identify motivational stimuli, **process perspectives** focus on why people choose certain behavioral options to satisfy their needs and how they evaluate their satisfaction after they have attained these goals. Three useful process perspectives on motivation are expectancy theory, equity theory, and goal-setting theory.

Expectancy Theory

Expectancy theory suggests that motivation depends on two things:
1. How much we want something and
2. How likely we think we are to get it.[11]

Assume that you are approaching graduation and looking for a job. You see an ad on monster.com from General Motors seeking a new vice president with a starting salary of $500,000 per year. Even though you might want the job, you will not apply because you realize that you have little chance of getting it. The next ad you see is for someone to scrape bubble gum from underneath theater seats for a starting salary of $6 an hour. Even though you could probably get this job, you do not apply because you do not want it. Then you see an ad for a management trainee at a big company, with a starting salary of $40,000. You will probably apply for this job because you want it and because you think you have a reasonable chance of getting it.

Expectancy theory rests on four basic assumptions.
1. It assumes that behavior is determined by a combination of forces in the individual and in the environment.
2. It assumes that people make decisions about their own behavior in organizations.
3. It assumes that different people have different types of needs, desires, and goals.
4. It assumes that people make choices from among alternative plans of behavior on the basis of their perceptions of the extent to which a given behavior will lead to desired outcomes.

Figure 10.4 summarizes the basic expectancy model. The model suggests that motivation leads to effort and that effort, combined with employee ability and environmental factors, results in performance. Performance, in turn, leads to various outcomes, each of which has an associated value, called its *valence*. The most important parts of the expectancy model cannot be shown in the figure, however. These are the individual's expectation that effort will lead to high performance, that performance will lead to outcomes, and that each outcome will have some kind of value.

Effort-to-Performance Expectancy

The **effort-to-performance expectancy** is the individual's perception of the probability that effort will lead to high performance. When the individual believes that effort will lead directly to high performance, expectancy will be quite strong (close to 1.00). When the individual believes that effort and performance are unrelated, the effort-to-performance expectancy is very weak (close to 0). The belief that effort

process perspectives Approaches to motivation that focus on why people choose certain behavioral options to fulfill their needs and how they evaluate their satisfaction after they have attained these goals.

expectancy theory A process perspective on motivation that suggests that motivation depends on two things—how much we want something and how likely we think we are to get it.

effort-to-performance expectancy The individual's perception of the probability that effort will lead to high performance.

FIGURE 10.4

The Expectancy Model of Motivation

The expectancy model of motivation is a complex but relatively accurate portrayal of how motivation occurs. According to this model, a manager must understand what employees want (such as pay, promotions, or status) to begin to motivate them.

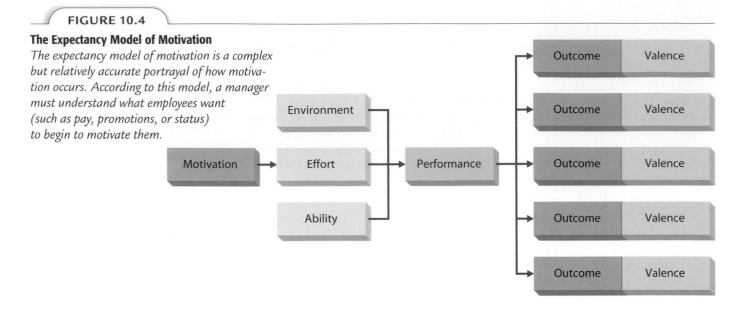

is somewhat but not strongly related to performance carries with it a moderate expectancy (somewhere between 0 and 1.00).

Performance-to-Outcome Expectancy

performance-to-outcome expectancy The individual's perception that performance will lead to a specific outcome.

The **performance-to-outcome expectancy** is the individual's perception that performance will lead to a specific outcome. For example, if the individual believes that high performance will result in a pay raise, the performance-to-outcome expectancy is high (approaching 1.00). The individual who believes that high performance may lead to a pay raise has a moderate expectancy (between 1.00 and 0). The individual who believes that performance has no relationship to rewards has a low performance-to-outcome expectancy (close to 0).

Outcomes and Valences

outcomes Consequences of behaviors in an organizational setting, usually rewards.

valence An index of how much an individual desires a particular outcome; the attractiveness of the outcome to the individual.

Expectancy theory recognizes that an individual's behavior results in a variety of **outcomes**, or consequences, in an organizational setting. A high performer, for example, may get bigger pay raises, faster promotions, and more praise from the boss. On the other hand, she may also be subject to more stress and incur resentment from coworkers. Each of these outcomes also has an associated value, or **valence**—an index of how much an individual values a particular outcome. If the individual wants the outcome, its valence is positive; if the individual does not want the outcome, its valence is negative; and if the individual is indifferent to the outcome, its valence is zero.

It is this part of expectancy theory that goes beyond the content perspectives on motivation. Different people have different needs, and they will try to satisfy these needs in different ways. For an employee who has a high need for achievement and a low need for affiliation, the pay raise and promotions cited above as outcomes of high performance might have positive valences, the praise and resentment zero valences, and the stress a negative valence. For a different employee, who has a low need for achievement and a high need for affiliation, the pay raise, promotions, and praise might all have positive valences, whereas both resentment and stress could have negative valences.

For motivated behavior to occur, three conditions must be met.

1. The effort-to-performance expectancy must be greater than 0 (the individual must believe that if effort is expended, high performance will result).

2. The performance-to-outcome expectancy must also be greater than 0 (the individual must believe that if high performance is achieved, certain outcomes will follow).

3. The sum of the valences for the outcomes must be greater than 0. (One or more outcomes may have negative valences if these are more than offset by the positive valences of other outcomes. For example, the attractiveness of a pay raise, a promotion, and praise from the boss may outweigh the unattractiveness of experiencing more stress and incurring resentment from coworkers.)

Expectancy theory suggests that when these conditions are met, the individual is motivated to expend effort.

Starbucks credits its unique stock ownership program with maintaining a dedicated and motivated workforce. In a plan that reflects the fundamental concepts of expectancy theory, Starbucks employees earn stock as a function of their seniority and performance. Thus their hard work helps them earn shares of ownership in the company.[12]

Equity Theory

After needs have stimulated the motivation process and the individual has chosen an action that is expected to satisfy those needs, the individual assesses the fairness, or equity, of the outcome. **Equity theory** contends that people are motivated to seek social equity in the rewards they receive for performance.[13] In this context, a sense of equity is an individual's belief that the treatment he or she is receiving is fair relative to the treatment received by others. According to equity theory, outcomes from a job include the following:

- Pay
- Recognition
- Promotions
- Social relationships
- Intrinsic rewards

equity theory   A process perspective on motivation that suggests that people are motivated to seek social equity in the rewards they receive for performance.

To get these rewards, the individual makes inputs to the job, such as the following:

- Time
- Experience
- Effort
- Education
- Loyalty

The theory suggests that people view their outcomes and inputs as a ratio and then compare it to someone else's ratio. This other "person" may be someone in the work group or some sort of group average or composite. The process of comparison looks like this:

$$\frac{\text{Outcomes (self)}}{\text{Inputs (self)}} = \frac{\text{Outcomes (other)}}{\text{Inputs (other)}}$$

Both the formulation of the ratios and the comparisons between them are very subjective, being based on individual perceptions. As a result of such comparisons, one of three conditions may result: The individual may feel equitably rewarded, underrewarded, or overrewarded.

▮ A person who feels equitably rewarded has two ratios that are equal. This may occur even though the other person's outcomes are greater than the individual's own outcomes—provided that the other's inputs are also proportionately greater. Suppose that Mark has a high school education and earns $30,000. He may still feel equitably treated relative to Susan, who earns $35,000, because she has a college degree.

■ People who feel underrewarded try to reduce the inequity. Such an individual might decrease her inputs by exerting less effort, increase her outcomes by asking for a raise, distort the original ratios by rationalizing, try to get the other person to change her or his outcomes or inputs, leave the situation, or change the object of comparison.

■ An individual may also feel overrewarded relative to another person. This is not likely to be terribly disturbing to most people, but research suggests that some people who experience inequity under these conditions are somewhat motivated to reduce it. Under such a circumstance, the person might increase his inputs by exerting more effort, reduce his outcomes by producing fewer units (if paid on a per-unit basis), distort the original ratios by rationalizing, or try to reduce the inputs or increase the outcomes of the other person.

CONCEPT CHECK 10.2

Using equity theory as a framework, explain how a person can experience inequity because he or she is paid too much. What are the potential outcomes of this situation?

Goal-Setting Theory

The goal-setting theory of motivation assumes that behavior is a result of conscious goals and intentions.[14] Therefore, by setting goals for people in the organization, a manager should be able to influence their behavior. Given this premise, the challenge is to develop a thorough understanding of the processes by which people set goals and then work to reach them. In the original version of goal-setting theory, two specific goal characteristics—goal difficulty and goal specificity—were expected to shape performance.

1. *Goal difficulty* is the extent to which a goal is challenging and requires effort. If people work to achieve goals, it is reasonable to assume that they will work harder to achieve more difficult goals. But a goal must not be so difficult that it is unattainable. If a new manager asks her sales force to increase sales by 300 percent, the group may become discouraged. A more realistic but still difficult goal—perhaps a 30 percent increase—would be a better incentive. A substantial body of research supports the importance of goal difficulty. In one study, for example, managers at Weyerhauser set difficult goals for truck drivers hauling loads of timber from cutting sites to wood yards. Over a nine-month period, the drivers increased the quantity of wood they delivered by an amount that would have required $250,000 worth of new trucks at the previous per-truck average load.[15]

2. *Goal specificity* is the clarity and precision of the goal. A goal of "increasing productivity" is not very specific; a goal of "increasing productivity by 3 percent in the next six months" is quite specific. Some goals, such as those involving costs, output, profitability, and growth, are readily amenable to specificity. Other goals, such as improving employee job satisfaction, morale, company image and reputation, ethics, and socially responsible behavior, may be much harder to state in specific terms. Like difficulty, specificity has been shown to be consistently related to performance. The study of timber truck drivers mentioned above, for example, also examined goal specificity. The initial loads that the truck drivers were carrying were found to be 60 percent of the maximum weight each truck could haul. The managers set a new goal for drivers of 94 percent, which the drivers were soon able to reach. Thus the goal was both specific and difficult.

FIGURE 10.5

The Expanded Goal-Setting Theory of Motivation

One of the most important emerging theories of motivation is goal-setting theory. This theory suggests that goal difficulty, specificity, acceptance, and commitment combine to determine an individual's goal-directed effort. This effort, when complemented by appropriate organizational support and individual abilities and traits, results in performance. Finally, performance is seen as leading to intrinsic and extrinsic rewards that, in turn, result in employee satisfaction.

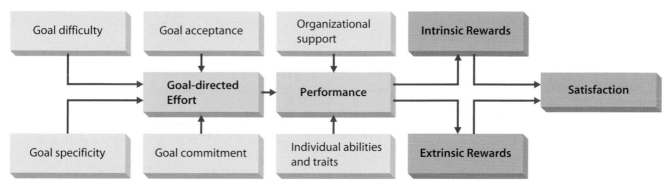

Reprinted from *Organizational Dynamics,* Autumn 1979, Gary P. Latham and Edwin A. Locke, "A Motivational Technique That Works," p. 79. Copyright © 1979 with permission from Elsevier Science.

Because the theory attracted so much widespread interest and support from researchers and managers alike, an expanded model of the goal-setting process was eventually proposed. The expanded model, shown in Figure 10.5, attempts to capture more fully the complexities of goal setting in organizations.

The expanded theory argues that goal-directed effort is a function of four goal attributes: difficulty and specificity, as already discussed, and acceptance and commitment.

▌ *Goal acceptance* is the extent to which a person accepts a goal as his or her own.

▌ *Goal commitment* is the extent to which she or he is personally interested in reaching the goal. The manager who vows to take whatever steps are necessary to cut costs by 10 percent has made a commitment to achieve the goal.

Factors that can foster goal acceptance and commitment include the following:

▌ Participating in the goal-setting process

▌ Making goals challenging but realistic

▌ Believing that goal achievement will lead to valued rewards

The interaction of goal-directed effort, organizational support, and individual abilities and traits determines actual performance.

▌ Organizational support is whatever the organization does to help or hinder performance. Positive support might mean making available adequate personnel and a sufficient supply of raw materials; negative support might mean failing to fix damaged equipment.

▌ Individual abilities and traits are the skills and other personal characteristics necessary for doing a job. As a result of performance, a person receives various intrinsic and extrinsic rewards, which in turn influence satisfaction.

CONCEPT CHECK 10.3

Choose one theory from the content perspectives and one from the process perspectives. Describe actions that a manager might take to increase worker motivation under each of the theories. What differences do you see between the theories in terms of their implications for managers?

TEST PREPPER 10.3

ANSWERS CAN BE FOUND ON P. 442

True or False?

_____ 1. Process perspectives are approaches to motivation that focus on why people choose certain behavioral options to fulfill their needs and how they evaluate their satisfaction after they have attained these goals.

_____ 2. People who feel underrewarded try to reduce the inequity. Such an individual might decrease her inputs, distort the original ratios of rationalizing, or leave the situation.

_____ 3. Your supervisor tells you to increase productivity by 10 percent. This manager has created goal commitment.

Online Study Center
ACE the Test
ACE Practice Tests 10.3

Multiple Choice

_____ 4. According to the expectancy theory, an index of how much an individual values an outcome is called _____.
   a. effort-to-performance
   b. performance-to-outcome
   c. valence
   d. outcomes
   e. none of the above

_____ 5. Natasha was happy making what she calculated to be about $25 per hour as a line manager. Then she learned a housekeeper earned $75 for cleaning a house her size. You would expect her motivation to decrease according to which theory?
   a. Maslow's hierarchy   c. Reinforcement
      of needs   d. Equity
   b. Goal setting   e. Expectancy

_____ 6. The extent to which a goal is challenging and requires effort is called _____.
   a. punishment   d. goal commitment
   b. goal difficulty   e. goal specificity
   c. goal acceptance

REINFORCEMENT PERSPECTIVES ON MOTIVATION

4 ▶ *Describe reinforcement perspectives on motivation.*

reinforcement theory An approach to motivation that argues that behavior that results in rewarding consequences is likely to be repeated, whereas behavior that results in punishing consequences is less likely to be repeated.

A third approach to the motivational process addresses why some behaviors are maintained over time and why other behaviors change. As we have seen, content perspectives deal with needs, and process perspectives explain why people choose various behaviors to satisfy needs and how they evaluate the equity of the rewards they get for those behaviors. Reinforcement perspectives explain the role of those rewards as they cause behavior to change or to remain the same over time. Specifically, **reinforcement theory** argues that behavior that results in rewarding consequences is likely to be repeated, whereas behavior that results in punishing consequences is less likely to be repeated.[16]

Kinds of Reinforcement in Organizations

There are four basic kinds of reinforcement that can result from behavior—positive reinforcement, avoidance, punishment, and extinction.[17] Two kinds of reinforcement strengthen or maintain behavior, whereas the other two weaken or decrease behavior.

positive reinforcement A method of strengthening behavior by administering rewards or positive outcomes after a desired behavior is performed.

1. **Positive reinforcement**, a method of strengthening behavior, is a reward or a positive outcome after a desired behavior is performed. When a manager observes an employee doing an especially good job and offers praise, that praise serves

Reinforcement plays a big role in encouraging desirable behaviors. Brooke County High School, in Charleston, West Virginia, adopted a positive reinforcement strategy for encouraging students to be prepared, strive to do their best, and show and give respect to fellow students and teachers. The rewards are certificates good for free or discounted meals at popular local restaurants. The program has been so successful that it was expanded to all eleven schools in the Northern Panhandle county, including Grandview Elementary. Grandview principal Sherrie Davis is shown here handing out a restaurant certificate to fourth-grader Jarrell Carter as recognition for his good behavior.

to reinforce the behavior of good work. Other positive reinforcers in organizations include pay raises, promotions, and awards. Employees who work at General Electric's customer service center receive clothing, sporting goods, and even trips to Disney World as rewards for outstanding performance.

2. **Avoidance** allows individuals to avoid, or escape, an unpleasant consequence by engaging in desired behaviors. An employee may come to work on time to avoid a reprimand. In this instance, the employee is motivated to perform the behavior of punctuality to avoid an unpleasant consequence that is likely to follow tardiness.

3. **Punishment** is used by some managers to weaken undesired behaviors. When an employee is loafing, coming to work late, doing poor work, or interfering with the work of others, the manager might resort to reprimands, discipline, or fines. The assumption is that the unpleasant consequence will reduce the likelihood that the employee will choose that particular behavior again. Given the counterproductive side effects of punishment (such as resentment and hostility), it is often advisable to use the other kinds of reinforcement instead, whenever possible.

4. **Extinction** can also be used to weaken behavior, especially behavior that has previously been rewarded. When an employee tells an off-color joke and the boss laughs, that laughter reinforces the behavior, and the employee may continue to tell off-color jokes. By simply ignoring this behavior and not reinforcing it, the boss can cause the behavior to subside and eventually become "extinct."

Providing Reinforcement in Organizations

Not only is the kind of reinforcement important, but so is when or how often it occurs. Various strategies are possible for providing reinforcement.

1. The **fixed-interval schedule** provides reinforcement at fixed intervals of time, regardless of behavior. A good example of this schedule is the weekly or

Online Study Center
Improve Your Grade
Career Snapshot

avoidance A method of strengthening behavior by making it clear that there will be unpleasant consequences if the behavior is not performed.

punishment A method of weakening undesired behaviors by administering negative outcomes or unpleasant consequences when the behavior is performed.

extinction A method of weakening undesired behaviors by simply ignoring or not reinforcing them.

CONCEPT CHECK 10.4

How do rewards increase motivation? What would happen if an organization gave too few rewards? What would happen if it gave too many?

fixed-interval schedule Provides reinforcement at fixed intervals of time, such as regular weekly paychecks.

monthly paycheck. This method provides the least incentive for good work, because employees know they will be paid regularly regardless of how much (or little) effort they exert.

variable-interval schedule Provides reinforcement at varying intervals of time, such as occasional visits by the supervisor.

2. A **variable-interval schedule** also uses time as the basis for reinforcement, but the time interval varies from one reinforcement to the next. This schedule is appropriate for praise or other rewards based on visits or inspections. When employees do not know when the boss is going to drop by, they tend to maintain a reasonably high level of effort all the time.

fixed-ratio schedule Provides reinforcement after a fixed number of behaviors.

3. A **fixed-ratio schedule** gives reinforcement after a fixed number of behaviors, regardless of the time that elapses between behaviors. This results in an even higher level of effort. For example, when Sears is recruiting new credit card customers, salespersons get a small bonus for every fifth application returned from their department. Under this arrangement, motivation is high because each application gets the person closer to the next bonus.

variable-ratio schedule Provides reinforcement after varying numbers of behaviors are performed, such as the use of compliments by a supervisor on an irregular basis.

4. The **variable-ratio schedule**, the most powerful in terms of maintaining desired behaviors, varies the number of behaviors needed for each reinforcement. A supervisor who praises an employee for the second order she generates, the seventh order after that, the ninth after that, then the fifth, and then the third is using a variable-ratio schedule. The employee is motivated to increase the frequency of the desired behavior because each performance increases the probability of receiving a reward. Of course, a variable-ratio schedule is difficult (if not impossible) to use for formal rewards such as pay, because it would be too complicated to keep track of who was rewarded when.

TEST PREPPER 10.4

ANSWERS CAN BE FOUND ON P. 442

True or False?

_____ 1. You are paid the last day of the month. This is a fixed-ratio schedule.

Multiple Choice

_____ 2. At Build-a-Bear customers receive a card for $10 off their next purchase after every $100 they spend. This is an example of _____.
   a. variable-ratio schedule
   b. variable-interval schedule
   c. fixed-ratio schedule
   d. fixed-interval schedule
   e. extinction

_____ 3. Scheduling and starting a meeting at 9:48 and ignoring anyone who comes in late is an example of _____.
   a. punishment   d. avoidance
   b. extinction   e. aloofness
   c. positive reinforcement

_____ 4. Which of the following strengthens behavior after a desired behavior is performed?
   a. Punishment   d. Avoidance
   b. Extinction   e. Aloofness
   c. Positive reinforcement

Online Study Center
ACE the Test
ACE Practice Tests 10.4

POPULAR MOTIVATIONAL STRATEGIES

5 ▷ *Identify and describe popular motivational strategies.*

Although the various theories that we have discussed so far provide a solid explanation for motivation, managers must use various techniques and strategies to apply them. Among the most popular motivational strategies today are empowerment and participation, and alternative forms of work arrangements.

Empowerment and Participation

Empowerment and participation represent important methods that managers can use to enhance employee motivation. **Empowerment** is the process of enabling workers to set their own work goals, make decisions, and solve problems within their sphere of responsibility and authority. **Participation** is the process of giving employees a voice in making decisions about their own work. Thus empowerment is a somewhat broader concept that promotes participation in a wide variety of areas, including (but not limited to) work itself, work context, and work environment.[18]

The role of participation and empowerment in motivation can be expressed in terms of both content perspectives and expectancy theory. Employees who participate in decision making may be more committed to executing decisions properly. Furthermore, the rewarding experience of making a decision, executing it, and then seeing the positive consequences can help satisfy one's need for achievement, provide recognition and responsibility, and enhance self-esteem. Simply being asked to participate in organizational decision making may enhance an employee's self-esteem. In addition, participation should help clarify expectancies; that is, by participating in decision making, employees may better understand the link between their performance and the rewards they want most.

empowerment　The process of enabling workers to set their own work goals, make decisions, and solve problems within their sphere of responsibility and authority.

participation　The process of giving employees a voice in making decisions about their own work.

Empowerment can help motivate people in organizations. Winemaker Patrick Kroukamp makes Thandi wine at the Paul Kluver wine cellars in South Africa. The Thandi wine project, a black empowerment venture, is a partnership between the farm workers from the villages of Lebanon and De Rust and the well-known Paul Kluver Wine brand. Before becoming a winemaker, Kroukamp was a truck driver. His new position affords him a better lifestyle and the opportunity to develop a new skill set.

Alternative Forms of Work Arrangements

Alternative forms of work arrangements are generally intended to enhance employee motivation and performance by providing employees with greater flexibility in how and when they work. Among the more popular alternative work arrangements are variable work schedules, flexible work schedules, job sharing, and telecommuting.[19]

Online Study Center
Improve Your Grade
Knowledgebank 10.3

▍ ***Variable Work Schedules.***　Although there are many exceptions, the traditional work schedule starts at 8:00 or 9:00 in the morning and ends at 5:00 in the evening, five days a week (and, of course, many managers work many additional

hours outside of these times). Unfortunately, this schedule makes it difficult to attend to routine personal business—going to the bank, seeing a doctor or dentist for a routine checkup, having a parent-teacher conference, getting an automobile serviced, and so forth. At a practical level, then, employees locked into this sort of arrangement may find it necessary to take a sick day or a vacation day to handle these activities. At a more unconscious level, some people may also feel so constrained by their job schedule as to harbor increased resentment and frustration.

compressed work schedule   A schedule whereby employees work a full forty-hour week in fewer than the traditional five days.

To help counter these problems, some businesses have adopted a **compressed work schedule**, in which employees work a full forty-hour week in fewer than the traditional five days.[20] One approach involves working ten hours a day for four days, leaving an entire extra day off. Another alternative is for employees to work slightly less than ten hours a day but to complete the forty hours by lunchtime on Friday. Organizations that have used these forms of compressed workweeks include John Hancock, BP Amoco, and Philip Morris. One problem with this schedule is that when employees put in too much time in a single day, they tend to get tired and perform at a lower level later in the day.

Online Study Center
Improve Your Grade
Visual Glossary 10.1

A schedule that some organizations today are beginning to use is what they call a "nine-eighty" schedule. Under this arrangement, an employee works a traditional schedule one week and a compressed schedule the next, getting every other Friday off. In other words, employees work eighty hours (the equivalent of two weeks of full-time work) in nine days. By alternating the regular and compressed schedules across half of its workforce, the organization can be staffed at all times, while still giving employees two full days off each month. Shell Oil and BP Amoco Chemicals are two of the firms that currently use this schedule.

Online Study Center
Improve Your Grade
–Visual Glossary 10.2
–Video Segment

▌ *Flexible Work Schedules.*   These schedules are sometimes called flextime. Flextime gives employees more personal control over the times they work. The workday is broken down into two categories: flexible time and core time. All employees must be at their workstations during core time, but they can choose their own schedules during flexible time. Thus one employee may choose to start work early in the morning and leave in midafternoon, another to start in late morning and work until late afternoon, and still another to start early in the morning, take a long lunch break, and work until late afternoon. Organizations that use flexible work schedules include Hewlett-Packard, Microsoft, and Texas Instruments.

job sharing   A work arrangement in which two part-time employees share one full-time job.

▌ *Job Sharing.*   **Job sharing** occurs when two part-time employees share one full-time job. One person may perform the job from 8:00 A.M. to noon and the other from 1:00 P.M. to 5:00 P.M. Job sharing may be desirable for people who want to work only part time or when job markets are tight. For its part, the organization can accommodate the preferences of a broader range of employees and may benefit from the talents of more people.

Online Study Center
Improve Your Grade
Visual Glossary 10.3

telecommuting   A work arrangement that allows employees to spend part of their time working offsite, usually at home.

▌ *Telecommuting.*   **Telecommuting**, a relatively new approach to alternative work arrangements, allows employees to spend part of their time working offsite, usually at home. By using e-mail, the Internet, and other forms of information technology, many employees can maintain close contact with their organization and still get just as much work done at home as if they were in their office. The increased power and sophistication of modern communication technology are making telecommuting easier and easier.

Online Study Center
Improve Your Grade
Visual Glossary 10.4

TEST PREPPER 10.5

True or False?

_____ 1. Participation is the process of enabling workers to set their own work goals, make decisions, and solve problems within their sphere of responsibility and authority.

_____ 2. Karen goes to work from 6:00 A.M. to 2:00 P.M. Core time is from 9:00 A.M. to 2:00 P.M. Karen uses flextime.

Multiple Choice

_____ 3. Bob works from 6:00 A.M. to 4:00 P.M. four days a week. He uses which alternative work arrangement?
   a. Job sharing
   b. Telecommuting
   c. A compressed workweek
   d. A part-time schedule
   e. All of the above

Online Study Center
ACE the Test
ACE Practice Tests 10.5

USING REWARD SYSTEMS TO MOTIVATE PERFORMANCE

6 ▶ *Describe the role of organizational reward systems in motivation.*

Online Study Center
Improve Your Grade
Knowledgebank 10.4

Aside from these types of motivational strategies, an organization's reward system is its most basic tool for managing employee motivation. An organizational **reward system** is the formal and informal mechanisms by which employee performance is defined, evaluated, and rewarded. Rewards that are tied specifically to performance, of course, have the greatest impact on enhancing both motivation and actual performance.

Performance-based rewards play a number of roles and address a variety of purposes in organizations. The major purposes involve the relationship of rewards to motivation and to performance. Specifically, organizations want employees to perform at relatively high levels and need to make it worth their effort to do so. When rewards are associated with higher levels of performance, employees will presumably be motivated to work harder in order to obtain those rewards. At that point, their own self-interests coincide with the organization's interests. Performance-based rewards are also relevant regarding other employee behaviors, such as punctuality, attendance, and so forth.

reward system The formal and informal mechanisms by which employee performance is defined, evaluated, and rewarded.

Merit Reward Systems

Merit reward systems are one of the most fundamental forms of performance-based rewards. **Merit pay** is generally pay awarded to employees on the basis of the relative value of their contributions to the organization. Employees who make greater contributions are given higher pay than those who make lesser contributions. **Merit pay plans**, then, are compensation plans that formally base at least some meaningful portion of compensation on merit.

The most general form of merit pay plan is to provide annual salary increases to individuals in the organization on the basis of their relative merit. Merit, in turn, is usually determined or defined in terms of the individual's performance and overall contributions to the organization. For example, an organization using such a traditional merit pay plan might instruct its supervisors to give all their employees an average pay raise of, say, 4 percent. But the individual supervisor is further instructed to differentiate among high, average, and low performers.

merit pay Pay awarded to employees on the basis of the relative value of their contributions to the organization.

merit pay plan Compensation plan that formally bases at least some meaningful portion of compensation on merit.

Incentives are a very popular approach to providing rewards to employees. By making rewards contingent on performance, experts agree that an organization is likely to increase employee motivation to work toward achieving those rewards. Of course, left to their own devices (as shown here), some employees might expect an ever-expanding array of rewards.

"My client wants a fifty-per-cent salary boost, a bonus guarantee, and a snappy choreographed victory dance he can do after he makes a touchdown."

Under a simple system, for example, a manager might give the top 25 percent of her employees a 6 percent pay raise, the middle 50 percent a 4 percent or average pay raise, and the bottom 25 percent a 2 percent pay raise.

Incentive Reward Systems

Incentive reward systems are among the oldest forms of performance-based rewards. For example, some companies were using individual piece-rate incentive plans over a hundred years ago.[21] Under a **piece-rate incentive plan**, the organization pays an employee a certain amount of money for every unit she or he produces. For example, an employee might be paid one dollar for every dozen units of products that are successfully completed. But such simplistic systems fail to account for such facts as minimum wage levels and rely very heavily on the assumptions that performance is totally under an individual's control and that the individual employee does a single task continuously throughout his or her work time. Thus most organizations today that try to use incentive compensation systems apply more sophisticated methodologies.

Individual incentive plans reward individual performance on a real-time basis. In other words, rather than receiving an increase in base salary at the end of the year, an individual instead receives some level of salary increase or financial reward in conjunction with demonstrated outstanding performance and close to the time when that performance occurred. Individual incentive systems are most likely to be used in cases in which performance can be objectively assessed in terms of number of units of output or similar measures, rather than on the basis of a subjective assessment of performance by a superior.

Perhaps the most common form of individual incentive is *sales commissions* that are paid to people engaged in sales work. For example, sales representatives for consumer products firms and retail sales agents may be compensated under

piece-rate incentive plan A reward system wherein the organization pays an employee a certain amount of money for every unit she or he produces.

Online Study Center
Improve Your Grade
Visual Glossary 10.5

this type of commission system. In general, the person might receive a percentage of the total volume of attained sales as her or his commission for a period of time. Some sales jobs are based entirely on commission, whereas others use a combination plan, paying a minimum salary as a base and additional commission as an incentive. Note that these plans put a considerable amount of the salespersons' earnings "at risk." In other words, although organizations often have drawing accounts to allow the salesperson to live during lean periods (the person then "owes" this money back to the organization), if he or she does not perform well, he or she will not be paid much. The portion of salary based on commission is simply not guaranteed and is paid only if sales reach some target level.

Other Forms of Incentives

Occasionally organizations also use other forms of incentives to motivate people. A nonmonetary incentive, such as additional time off or a special perk, might be a useful incentive. For example, a company might establish a sales contest in which the sales group that attains the highest level of sales increase over a specified period of time will receive an extra week of paid vacation, perhaps even at an arranged place, such as a tropical resort or a ski lodge.[22]

A major advantage of incentives over merit systems is that incentives are typically one-shot rewards and do not accumulate by becoming part of the individual's base salary. In other words, an individual whose outstanding performance entitles him or her to a financial incentive gets the incentive only once, at the time that level of performance occurs. If the individual's performance begins to erode in the future, then the individual may receive a lesser incentive or perhaps no incentive at all. As a consequence, his or her base salary remains the same or is perhaps increased at a relatively moderate pace; he or she receives one-time incentive rewards as recognition for exemplary performance. Furthermore, because these plans, by their very nature, focus on one-time events, it is much easier for the organization to change the focus of the incentive plan. At a simple level, for example, an organization can set up an incentive plan for selling one product during one quarter but can then shift the incentive to a different product the next quarter, as the situation requires. Automobile companies such as Ford and GM routinely do this by reducing sales incentives for models that are selling very well and increasing sales incentives for models that are selling below expectations or are about to be discontinued.

Team and Group Incentive Reward Systems

The merit compensation and incentive compensation systems described in the preceding sections deal primarily with performance-based reward arrangements for individuals. A different set of performance-based reward programs are targeted for teams and groups. These programs are particularly important for managers to understand today, given the widespread trends toward team- and group-based methods of work and organizations.[23]

Common Team and Group Reward Systems

There are two commonly used types of team and group reward systems.

1. **Gainsharing programs** are designed to share the cost savings from productivity improvements with employees. The underlying assumption of gainsharing is that employees and the employer have the same goals and thus should appropriately share in incremental economic gains.[24]

> ### CONCEPT CHECK 10.5
>
> Think about the worst job you have held. What approach to motivation was used in that organization? Now think about the best job you have held. What approach to motivation was used there? Can you base any conclusions on this limited information? If so, what are they?

gainsharing programs Programs designed to share the cost savings from productivity improvements with employees.

In general, organizations that use gainsharing start by measuring team- or group-level productivity. It is important that this measure be valid and reliable and that it truly reflect current levels of performance by the team or group. The team or work group itself is then given the charge of attempting to lower costs and otherwise improve productivity through any measures that its members develop and its manager approves. Resulting cost savings or productivity gains that the team or group is able to achieve are quantified and translated into dollar values. A predetermined formula is next used to divide these dollar savings between the employer and the employees themselves. A typical formula for distributing gainsharing savings is to allocate 25 percent to the employees and 75 percent to the company.

Scanlon plan A program similar to gainsharing, but the distribution of gains is tilted much more heavily toward employees.

2. The **Scanlon plan**, developed by Joseph Scanlon in 1927, has the same basic strategy as gainsharing plans, in that teams or groups of employees are encouraged to suggest strategies for reducing costs. However, the distribution of these gains is usually tilted much more heavily toward employees, with employees usually receiving between two-thirds and three-fourths of the total cost savings that the plan achieves. Furthermore, the cost savings resulting from the plan are distributed not just among the team or group that suggested and developed the ideas, but across the entire organization.

Other Types of Team and Group Rewards

Gainsharing and Scanlon-type plans are among the most popular group incentive reward systems, but other systems are also used. Some companies, for example, have begun to use true incentives at the team or group level. Just as with individual incentives, team or group incentives tie rewards directly to performance increases. And, like individual incentives, team or group incentives are paid as they are earned rather than being added to employees' base salary. The incentives are distributed at the team or group level, however, rather than at the individual level. In some cases, the distribution may be based on the existing salary of each employee, with incentive bonuses being given on a proportionate basis. In other settings, each member of the team or group receives the same incentive pay.

Some companies also use nonmonetary rewards at the team or group level— most commonly in the form of prizes and awards. For example, a company might announce which team in a plant or subunit of the company achieved the highest level of productivity increase, the highest level of reported customer satisfaction, or a similar index of performance. The reward itself might take the form of additional time off, as described earlier in this chapter, or it might be a tangible award, such as a trophy or plaque. In any event, the idea is that the reward is at the team level and serves as recognition of exemplary performance by the entire team.

There are also other kinds of team- or group-level incentives that go beyond the contributions of a specific work group. These are generally organization-wide kinds of incentives. One time-honored example is *profit sharing*. In a profit-sharing approach, at the end of the year some portion of the company's profits is paid into a profit-sharing pool that is then distributed to all employees. Either this amount is distributed at that time, or it is put into an escrow account and payment is deferred until the employee retires.

Executive Compensation

The top-level executives of most companies have separate compensation programs and plans. These are intended to reward such executives for their performance and for the performance of the organization.

Standard Forms of Executive Compensation

Most senior executives receive their compensation in two forms:

1. *Base salary.* As with the base salary of any staff member or professional member of an organization, the base salary of an executive is a guaranteed amount of money that the individual will be paid.

2. *Bonuses.* Most executives also receive this traditional method of incentive pay above their base salary. Bonuses are usually determined by the performance of the organization. At the end of the year, some portion of a corporation's profits may be diverted into a bonus pool. Senior executives then receive a bonus expressed as a percentage of this bonus pool. The chief executive officer and president are likely to get a larger percentage bonus than a vice president. The exact distribution of the bonus pool is usually specified in advance in the individual's employment contract. Some organizations intentionally leave the distribution unspecified so that the board of directors will have the flexibility to give larger rewards to those individuals deemed most deserving.

Stock Option Plans

Beyond base salary and bonuses, many executives receive stock option plans and other kinds of compensation. A **stock option plan** is established to give senior managers the option to buy company stock in the future at a predetermined fixed price. The basic idea underlying stock option plans is that if the executives contribute to higher levels of organizational performance, then the company stock should increase in value. Then the executive will be able to purchase the stock at the predetermined price, which theoretically should be lower than its future market price. The difference then becomes profit for the individual.

stock option plan An aspect of compensation established to give senior managers the option to buy company stock in the future at a predetermined fixed price.

Stock options continue to grow in popularity as a means of compensating top managers. Options are seen as a means of aligning the interests of the manager with those of the stockholders, and given that they do not cost the organization much (other than some possible dilution of stock values), they will probably be even more popular in the future. In fact, a recent study by KPMG Peat Marwick indicates that for senior management whose salary exceeds $250,000, stock options represent the largest share of the salary mix (relative to salary and other incentives). Furthermore, when we consider all of top management (annual salary over $750,000), stock options account for a full 60 percent of their total compensation. And the Peat Marwick report indicates that even among exempt employees at the $35,000-a-year level, stock options represent 13 percent of total compensation.

However, events in recent years have raised serious questions about the use of stock options as incentives for executives. For example, it has been alleged that several executives at Enron withheld critical financial information from the markets, cashed in their stock options (while Enron stock was trading at $80 a share), and then watched as the financial information was made public and the stock fell to less than $1 a share. Of course, these actions (if they occurred) are illegal, but they raise questions in the public's mind about the role of stock options and about the way organizations treat stock options from an accounting perspective. Most organizations have *not* treated stock options as liabilities, even though, when exercised, they are exactly that. There is concern that by not carrying stock options as liabilities, the managers are overstating the value of the company, which, of course, can help raise the stock price. Finally, when stock markets generally fell during the middle of 2002, many executives found that their options were worthless, as the price of the stock fell below the option price. When stock options go "under water" in this way, they have no value to anyone.

Other kinds of executive compensation are also used by some companies. Among the more popular are the following:

- Memberships in private clubs
- Access to company recreational facilities
- Low- or no-interest loans (these are often given to new executives whom the company is hiring from other companies and serve as an incentive for the individual to leave his or her current job and join the new organization)

Criticisms of Executive Compensation

In recent years, executive compensation has come under fire for a variety of reasons:

- Levels of executive compensation.   These figures seem simply too large for the average shareholder to understand. It is not uncommon, for instance, for a senior executive of a major corporation to earn, in a given year, total income from his or her job well in excess of $1 million. Sometimes the income of chief executive officers can be substantially more than this. Thus, just as the typical person has difficulty comprehending the astronomical salaries paid to some movie stars and sports stars, so, too, would the average person be aghast at the astronomical salaries paid to some senior executives.

- Disconnect between the performance of the organization and the compensation paid to its senior executives.[25]   Certainly, if an organization is performing at an especially high level and its stock price is increasing consistently, then most observers would agree that the senior executives responsible for this growth are entitled to attractive rewards.[26] It is more difficult to understand a case in which executives are paid huge salaries and other forms of rewards when their company is performing at only a marginal level, yet this is fairly common today. For example, in 2002 Oracle's CEO, Lawrence Ellison, pocketed over $700 million from the sale of previously granted stock options, while the value of Oracle stock was dropping by 57 percent.

- The enormous gap between the earnings of the CEO and the earnings of a typical employee.   First of all, the size of the gap has been increasing in the United States. In 1980 the typical CEO earned forty-two times the earnings of an ordinary worker, but by 1990 this ratio had increased to eighty-five times the earnings of an ordinary worker. In Japan, on the other hand, the relationship in 1990 was that a typical CEO made less than twenty times the earnings of an ordinary worker.[27]

New Approaches to Performance-Based Rewards

Some organizations have started to recognize that they can leverage the value of the incentives that they offer to their employees and to groups in their organization by allowing those individuals and groups to have a say in how rewards are distributed. For example, at the extreme, a company could go so far as to grant salary-increase budgets to work groups and then allow the members of those groups themselves to determine how the rewards are going to be allocated among the various members of the group. This strategy would appear to hold considerable promise if everyone understands the performance arrangements that exist in the work group and everyone is committed to being fair. Unfortunately, it can also create problems if people in a group feel that rewards are not being distributed fairly.[28]

Organizations are also getting increasingly innovative in their incentive programs. For example, some now offer stock options to all their employees, rather than just to top executives. In addition, some firms are looking into ways to individualize reward systems entirely. For instance, a firm might offer one employee a paid three-month sabbatical every two years in exchange for a 20 percent reduction in salary. Another employee in the same firm might be offered a 10 percent salary increase in exchange for a 5 percent reduction in company contributions to the person's retirement account. Corning, General Electric, and Microsoft are among the firms that are closely studying this option.[29]

Regardless of the method used, however, it is also important that managers in an organization effectively communicate what rewards are being distributed and the basis for that distribution. If pay increases and other incentives are being distributed on the basis of perceived individual contributions to the organization, then members of the organization should be informed of that fact.

TEST PREPPER 10.6

ANSWERS CAN BE FOUND ON P. 442

True or False?

_____ 1. Incentive pay plans usually increase base pay.

_____ 2. Performance-based rewards play a number of roles and address a variety of purposes in organizations.

_____ 3. Executive compensation plans have come under fire because there seems to be little relationship between pay and performance.

Multiple Choice

_____ 4. When a factory work team receives 25 percent of the cost savings for a suggestion made, this is an example of _____.
   a. gainsharing   d. compensation plan
   b. Scanlon plan   e. benefits plan
   c. stock option plan

Online Study Center
ACE the Test
ACE Practice Tests 10.6

BUILDING EFFECTIVE INTERPERSONAL AND COMMUNICATION SKILLS

Online Study Center
Improve Your Grade
Exercises: Building Effective Skills

Exercise Overview

Interpersonal skills reflect the manager's ability to understand and motivate individuals and groups, and communication skills reflect the ability to send and receive information effectively. This exercise shows, in a very explicit way, how essential understanding and communicating are for motivating workers.

Exercise Background

One implication of reinforcement theory is that both positive reinforcement (reward) and punishment can be effective in altering employee behavior. However, the use of punishment may also cause resentment on the worker's part, which can reduce the effectiveness of punishment over the long term. Therefore, over time, positive reinforcement is more effective.

Exercise Task

Your professor will ask for volunteers to perform a demonstration in front of the class. Consider volunteering or observe the demonstration. Then answer the following questions:

1. Judging on the basis of what you saw, which is more effective, positive reinforcement or punishment?

2. How did positive reinforcement and punishment affect the "employee" in the demonstration? How did it affect the "boss"?

3. What do you think are the probable long-term consequences of positive reinforcement and of punishment?

Reprinted by permission of the author Margaret Hill.

EXPERIENTIAL EXERCISE

An Exercise in Thematic Apperception

Online Study Center
Improve Your Grade
–Exercises: Experiential Exercise
–Interactive Skills Self-Assessment

Purpose

All people have needs, and those needs make people pursue different goals. This exercise introduces one of the tools by which managers can identify both their own needs and those of their employees.

Introduction

Over the last thirty years, behaviorists have researched the relationship between a person's fantasies and his or her motivation. One popular instrument used to establish this relationship is the Thematic Apperception Test (TAT).

Instructions

Step 1:

1. Examine each of six pictures (provided by your instructor) for about one minute. Then cover the picture.
2. Using the picture as a guide, write a story that could be used in a TV soap opera. Make your story continuous, dramatic, and interesting. Do not just answer the questions. Try to complete the story in less than ten minutes.
3. Do not be concerned about obtaining negative results from this instrument. There are no right or wrong stories.
4. After finishing one story, repeat the same procedure until all six stories are completed.

Step 2: Conduct a story interpretation in groups of three persons each. Taking turns reading one story at a time, each person will read a story out loud to the other two people in the group. Then all three will examine the story for statements that fall into one of the following three categories:

- Category AC—Statements that refer to:
    High standards of excellence
    A desire to win, do well, or succeed
    Unique accomplishments
    Long-term goals
    Careers
- Category PO—Statements that refer to:
    Influencing others
    Controlling others

The desire to instruct others
The desire to dominate others
Concern over weakness, failure, or humiliation
Superior-subordinate relationships or status relationship

- Category AF—Statements that refer to:
    Concern over establishing positive emotional relationships
    Warm friendships or their loss
    A desire to be liked
    One person's liking another
    Parties, reunions, or visits
    Relaxed small talk
    Concern for others when not required by social custom

To assist in the interpretation of the test results, assign ten points to each story. Divide the ten points among the three categories on the basis of the frequency of statements that refer to AC, PO, and AF behaviors in the story. Once the allocation of the ten points is determined, record the results in the following scoring table.

Divide ten points among the following categories:

Story Scored	AC		PO		AF		TOTAL
Story 1		+		+		=	10
Story 2		+		+		=	10
Story 3		+		+		=	10
Story 4		+		+		=	10
Story 5		+		+		=	10
Story 6		+		+		=	10
TOTAL		+		+		=	60

Divide totals by ten times number of stories scored ____ + ____ + ____

Category percentages ____% ____% ____ % = ____ 100%

CLOSING CASE STUDY

You've Got to Love this Job

For most of us, dreams jobs are just that, a dream. Yet some individuals are lucky enough to land the perfect job, one that combines their unique talents and interests in a way that is rewarding and also offers unique benefits to employers. Dana Gioia, a Stanford MBA who ultimately became a marketing vice president at General Foods, is one example. For fun, he wrote poetry and was skilled enough to see many of his poems published. After leaving corporate America and spending a decade as a serious writer, President Bush offered him the job of chairman of the National Endowment for the Arts. Gioia says, "This is the only job I've ever had in which I use pretty much everything I know."

Others are wise enough to let their dream job evolve over time. Tim Brosnan turned his childhood interest in baseball into a business position with the New York Yankees and today heads corporate sponsorships for Major League Baseball. Rick Steves, a piano teacher, enjoyed travel to Europe to listen to concerts. Ultimately, he began to make presentations about his travel experiences, then to write travel guidebooks. "I'm real thankful that I found something I love doing that works from a business point of view," says Steves. "The joy and reward in my work have always been about teaching." Today he produces a PBS television travel series and owns a travel company.

Firms find that creating positions based on an employee's interests can be a reward for high performance. Steve Gluckman is a bicycle designer for REI, a supplier of outdoor gear. Gluckman worked his way up from service manager to designer over thirteen years. An avid cyclist, he says, "Some people sing. Some people paint. I ride my bike. Like a ballet dancer, like a gymnast, like a skateboarder, I express myself in my job." Starbucks' coffee education manager, Aileen Carrell, travels around the world educating employees about coffee. "I was hired as temporary Christmas help . . . and I fell madly in love with the fact that coffees came from the most amazing places, like Sulawesi." After working as a store manager for several years, Carrell moved into her exciting and challenging position.

Sometimes individuals are so motivated by an activity that they look around for an employer who will allow

> *"I enjoy what I do. I'm living a dream. It was a round peg in a round hole."*
>
> —Pat Connors,
> recreational site manager, Agilent

them to do what they love. Holly Brewster Jones was an independent artist for years but wanted more job security. She says, "I applied for a graphic design job at SAS Institute, which I really wasn't qualified for. They called me about a week later for the artist-in-residence job." She paints about sixty works a year for display in the company's campuslike headquarters. "I'll paint until I retire, probably," asserts Jones. "And even then I'll still be an artist."

When high-performing workers define their dream jobs, they can come up with offbeat ideas that take the company in new and interesting directions. At financial services firm Citigroup, Sandra Feagan Stern has carved out a unique niche: ranching. Stern is a private banker, serving clients who invest $3 million or more. The combination of her extensive knowledge of ranching and her financial savvy makes Stern the perfect person to recommend and manage investments in thoroughbreds and second homes.

Pat Connors found his dream job—managing Agilent's corporate retreat in the Pennsylvania Poconos. He previously worked on the firm's manufacturing line but wanted a change. "I'm a naturalist at heart," says Connors. "I enjoy what I do. I'm living a dream." Connors finds the work itself rewarding, because it utilizes his talents and skills. "It was a round peg in a round hole," he claims.

As these examples show, if companies want to motivate workers, maybe they should focus less on offering incentives to individuals who are doing tasks they find unexciting and uninspiring. Instead, firms could ask employees to tell them how to make their jobs more motivating. Employees are the experts in what motivates them. Perhaps they are also the most effective job designers.

CLOSING CASE STUDY (CONTINUED)

Case Questions

1. For each of the employees mentioned in the case, determine which needs they are working to fulfill, using Maslow's hierarchy. Explain how you arrived at your answers.

2. Tell whether the workers described in the case are high or low on satisfaction and dissatisfaction, according to Herzberg's theory. Do the examples tend to support Herzberg's claim that satisfaction and dissatisfaction are based on two independent sets of factors?

3. Allowing employees control over their job design is empowering. What are some benefits that firms might expect from empowering their employees? What are some problems that firms might

encounter as they empower their employees? In the case, are there any examples of the benefits or problems associated with empowerment? If so, describe them.

Case References

Lee Clifford, "Citigroup Bets (on) the Ranch," *Fortune*, January 8, 2002, www.fortune.com on February 6, 2003; Michael A. Prospero, "Dream Jobs," *Fast Company*, July 2005, www.fastcompany.com on January 20, 2006; Curtis Sittenfeld, "Poet-In-Chief," *Fast Company*, November 7, 2005, www.fastcompany.com on January 20, 2006; Eric Wahlgren, "Online Extra: Goodbye, 'Guru of Fun,'" *BusinessWeek*, August 27, 2001, www.businessweek.com on February 6, 2003; "You Get Paid to Do What?" *Fortune*, January 20, 2003, www.fortune.com on January 13, 2003 (quote).

Online Study Center
Improve Your Grade
—Learning Objective Review
—Audio Chapter Review
—Study Guide to Go

Online Study Center
ACE the Test
Audio Chapter Quiz

LEARNING OBJECTIVE REVIEW

1 *Characterize the nature of motivation, including its importance and basic historical perspectives.*

- Motivation is the set of forces that cause people to behave in certain ways.

- It is an important consideration for managers because it, along with ability and environmental factors, determines individual performance.

2 *Identify and describe the major content perspectives on motivation.*

- Content perspectives on motivation are concerned with what factor or factors enhance motivation.

- Popular content theories include
  Maslow's needs hierarchy
  Herzberg's two-factor theory

- Other important needs are the needs for achievement, affiliation, and power.

3 *Identify and describe the major process perspectives on motivation.*

- Process perspectives on motivation deal with how motivation occurs.

- Expectancy theory suggests that people are motivated to perform if they believe that their effort will result in high performance, that this performance will lead to rewards, and that the positive aspects of the outcomes outweigh the negative aspects.

- Equity theory is based on the premise that people are motivated to achieve and to maintain social equity.

- Goal-setting theory assumes that people are motivated by goals and intentions.

4 *Describe reinforcement perspectives on motivation.*

- The reinforcement perspective focuses on how motivation is maintained.
  Its basic assumption is that behavior that results in rewarding consequences is likely to be repeated, whereas behavior that results in negative consequences is less likely to be repeated.

- Reinforcement contingencies can be arranged in the form of
  positive reinforcement
  avoidance
  punishment
  extinction

- Reinforcement contingencies can be provided on the following schedules:
  fixed-interval
  variable-interval
  fixed-ratio
  variable-ratio

5 *Identify and describe popular motivational strategies.*

- Managers use a variety of motivational strategies derived from the various theories of motivation.

- Common strategies include
  empowerment and participation
  alternative forms of work arrangements (such as variable work schedules, flexible work schedules, job sharing, and telecommuting)

6 *Describe the role of organizational reward systems in motivation.*

- Reward systems play a key role in motivating employee performance; they include
  merit reward systems
  incentive reward systems
  team and group incentive reward systems

- Executive compensation, which is intended to serve as motivation for senior managers, has recently come under close scrutiny and criticism.

Online Study Center RESOURCES

Prepare for Class, Improve Your Grade, and ACE the Test. These Student Achievement resources include:

ACE Practice Tests	Interactive Skills Assessments	Study Guide to Go
End of Chapter Exercises	Knowledgebank	Video Segments
Glossaries (visual and print)	Reviews (audio and print)	Summaries/Outlines
Flashcards		

To access these learning and study tools, go to: **college.hmco.com/pic/griffinSAS**

Influence Processes

While society has always expected business to be ethical, recent scandals at firms like Enron, WorldCom, and Tyco have shaken this belief. Former Enron CEO Jeff Skilling, one of the more visible figures to emerge from these scandals, is shown here arriving at the federal courthouse in Houston during his trial for fraud and conspiracy charges.

1 Describe the nature of leadership and relate leadership to management.

2 Discuss and evaluate the two generic approaches to leadership.

3 Identify and describe the major situational approaches to leadership.

4 Identify and describe three related approaches to leadership.

Chapter Outline

▶ **THE NATURE OF LEADERSHIP**
The meaning of leadership
Leadership and management
Leadership and power

▶ **GENERIC APPROACHES TO LEADERSHIP**
Leadership traits
Leadership behaviors

▶ **SITUATIONAL APPROACHES TO LEADERSHIP**
LPC theory
Path-goal theory
Vroom's decision tree approach
The leader-member exchange approach

▶ **RELATED APPROACHES TO LEADERSHIP**
Substitutes for leadership
Charismatic leadership
Transformational leadership

▶ **EMERGING APPROACHES TO LEADERSHIP**
Strategic leadership
Cross-cultural leadership
Ethical leadership

▶ **POLITICAL BEHAVIOR IN ORGANIZATIONS**
Common political behaviors
Impression management
Managing political behavior

Online Study Center
Prepare for Class
Chapter Outline

6 *Discuss political behavior in organizations and how it can be managed.*

5 *Describe three emerging approaches to leadership.*

CEOs Behaving Badly

Starting in 2001, the U.S. economy has been hit with one scandal after another. Ethical leadership seems to be at an all-time low. Enron is a classic case. Top managers, including CEOs Ken Lay and Jeffrey Skilling, used nonstandard accounting, lied to government regulators and shareholders, deceived Wall Street analysts, and ordered employees to perform illegal actions. As the company faltered, Lay encouraged stockholders to buy, while quietly selling 300 million shares.

For their misconduct, Lay and Skilling, accounting head Richard Causey, CFO Andrew Fastow, and others were charged in federal court with fraud and conspiracy. Sixteen managers pled guilty and made deals with the prosecution. Causey, for example, will be imprisoned for five years, and Fastow will serve ten. Lay's trial began in January 2006. He claimed he was unaware of any wrong-

Online Study Center college.hmco.com/pic/griffinSAS

You should be able to define and use terms that are part of the practicing manager's vocabulary, as well as those that are integral in the language of management.

doing, which he blames on subordinates. Yet is it possible that Lay, a Ph.D. economist, former federal energy regulator, and CEO with decades of leadership experience, did not know about or did not understand what was happening at the company he founded?

It's not clear whether Lay was truly ignorant of events or is merely using an "ostrich" legal defense tactic. The ostrich defense may work for Lay, as it has for others. HealthSouth's former CEO, Richard Scrushy, was recently cleared of fraud charges when he successfully argued that underlings were responsible for the mistakes. Jeffrey Sonnenfeld, a Yale professor who studies leadership, sees the failure as a moral one. He says, "When [Lay] sensed dangerous truths, he saw his job as one of containment, rather than showing courage or character."

Enron is not the only one. In 2002, the telecommunications industry was rocked by a scandal that began when WorldCom lied about expenses. As competitors desperately tried to keep up with what seemed to be a very profitable firm, they too began to lie. Today, Qwest, Global Crossing, and Adelphia, in addition to WorldCom, have all been through bankruptcy and their former CEOs are in prison or under indictment. Accounting firm Arthur Andersen, which audited the books of Enron, WorldCom, and Qwest, has suffered the same fate and no longer exists.

In 2005, Dennis Kozlowski, former CEO of giant conglomerate Tyco, was convicted of fraud and of misappropriating $400 million for his personal use. He is currently serving 8-to-25 in a federal penitentiary. January of 2006 brought news of indictments against several managers at General Re and AIG, insurance companies that conspired in issuing $500 million in false contracts.

These blatant failures of leadership are costly for all of us. Although the companies pay fines, the trials cost the taxpayers plenty and most of the money is gone, spent. Bankrupt firms cost the economy thousands of jobs—31,000 at Enron alone. Retirements are endangered when 401(k) plans fail. Shareholders lose billions of dollars in value when their stock declines. Suppliers are adversely affected, as are accounting, banking, and real estate firms. Local economies are hard hit when businesses fail and tax revenues cease.

The federal government has responded with new, tougher accounting rules, including the Sarbanes-Oxley Act, and made boards of directors legally liable when they fail to provide adequate oversight. Penalties are tougher too. AIG, for example, is expected to pay a record $1.5 billion in fines, and WorldCom directors are forced to pay penalties from their personal funds. Some of the companies are ruined, yet several emerged from bankruptcy with only a moderate penalty and immediately resumed business.

Insurance companies that insure executives, investment fund managers, and regulators are working to predict the next Enron or Tyco before it happens. They look for danger signs such as suspiciously high executive compensation, obscure accounting practices, or a CEO who exerts a lot of control over the company's directors. Looking ahead, these experts are issuing warnings about some of today's top companies, including Home Depot, Lucent, Wells Fargo, and Viacom, among others.

Companies, shareholders, and regulators are increasingly dedicated to holding leaders accountable for criminal behavior. Experienced board member Robert S. Miller, Jr., says that, with enhanced regulation, "It is going to be much more difficult today for anyone to pull off the gross accounting scandals." Yet most of the CEOs' actions listed above, while unethical, are not clearly illegal. Until there's a way to legislate against greed, there will be unethical CEOs.[1]

Kenneth Lay illustrates what some people would call the best and the worst things about leadership. On the one hand, he took bold risks early in his career, founded a small firm that grew to become an industry giant, and created tremendous wealth for shareholders and the charities he supported. On the other hand, he also exhibited questionable behaviors, made controversial decisions, and alienated key people. But love him or hate him, just about everyone agrees that Ken Lay exemplifies strong leadership.

This chapter examines leadership and its role in management. We characterize the nature of leadership and examine the three major approaches to studying leadership—traits, behaviors, and situations. After examining related and emerging perspectives on leadership, we conclude by describing another approach to influencing others—political behavior in organizations.

THE NATURE OF LEADERSHIP

1 ▶ *Describe the nature of leadership and relate leadership to management.*

In Chapter 10, we described various models and perspectives on employee motivation. From the manager's standpoint, trying to motivate people is an attempt to influence their behavior. In many ways, leadership, too, is an attempt to influence the behavior of others. In this section, we first define leadership, then differentiate it from management, and conclude by relating it to power.

Power is usually a foundation for leadership. Australian actress Nicole Kidman, left, has agreed to help advance women's rights around the globe in her new role as a goodwill ambassador for the U.N. (working with the United Nations Development Fund for Women). Noeleen Heyzer, the organization's executive director, is shown here presenting Kidman with a T-shirt during a news conference at the United Nations in January 2006. Kidman's referent power will give her visibility in this work, and the legitimate power conveyed by this position will further enhance her ability to influence others.

The Meaning of Leadership

leadership   As a process, the use of noncoercive influence to shape the group's or organization's goals, motivate behavior toward the achievement of those goals, and help define group or organization culture; as a property, the set of characteristics attributed to individuals who are perceived to be leaders.

leaders   People who can influence the behaviors of others without having to rely on force; those accepted by others as leaders.

Leadership is both a process and a property.[2] As a process—focusing on what leaders actually do—leadership is the use of noncoercive influence to shape the group or organization's goals, motivate behavior toward the achievement of those goals, and help define group or organization culture.[3] As a property, leadership is the set of characteristics attributed to individuals who are perceived to be leaders. Thus **leaders** are people who can influence the behaviors of others without having to rely on force, and sometimes they are simply people whom others accept as leaders.

Leadership and Management

From these definitions, it should be clear that leadership and management are related, but they are not the same. A person can be a manager, a leader, both, or neither.[4] Table 11.1 summarizes four elements that differentiate leadership from management. The two columns at the right show how each element differs when considered from a management point of view and from a leadership point of view. For example, when executing plans, managers focus on monitoring results, comparing them with goals, and correcting deviations. In contrast, the leader focuses on energizing people to overcome bureaucratic hurdles to reach goals.

Organizations need both management and leadership if they are to be effective. Leadership is necessary to create change, and management is necessary to achieve orderly results. Management in conjunction with leadership can produce orderly change, and leadership in conjunction with management can keep the organization properly aligned with its environment. Indeed, perhaps part of the reason why executive compensation has soared in recent years is the belief that management and leadership skills reflect a critical but rare combination that can lead to organizational success.

Online Study Center
Improve Your Grade
Visual Glossary 11.1

Leadership and Power

power   The ability to affect the behavior of others.

To understand leadership, it is necessary to understand power. **Power** is the ability to affect the behavior of others. One can have power without actually using it. For example, a football coach has the power to bench a player who is not performing up to par. The coach seldom has to use this power, because players recognize that the power exists and work hard to keep their starting positions. In organizational settings, there are usually five kinds of power: legitimate, reward, coercive, referent, and expert power.[5]

TABLE 11.1

Distinctions Between Management and Leadership

Management and leadership are related, but distinct, constructs. Managers and leaders differ in how they create an agenda, develop a rationale for achieving the agenda, and execute plans, and in the types of outcomes they achieve.

Activity	Management	Leadership
Creating an agenda	*Planning and Budgeting.* Establishing detailed steps and time-tables for achieving needed results; allocating the resources necessary to make those needed results happen	*Establishing Direction.* Developing a vision of the future, often the distant future, and strategies for producing the changes needed to achieve that vision
Developing a human network for achieving the agenda	*Organizing and Staffing.* Establishing some structure for accomplishing plan requirements, staffing that structure with individuals, delegating responsibility and authority for carrying out the plan, providing policies and procedures to help guide people, and creating methods or systems to monitor implementation	*Aligning People.* Communicating the established direction by words and deeds to everyone whose cooperation may be needed to influence the creation of teams and coalitions that understand the visions and strategies and accept their validity
Executing plans	*Controlling and Problem Solving.* Monitoring results versus planning in some detail, identifying deviations, and then planning and organizing to solve these problems	*Motivating and Inspiring.* Energizing people to overcome major political, bureaucratic, and resource barriers by satisfying very basic, but often unfulfilled, human needs
Outcomes	*Producing* a degree of predictability and order and having the potential to produce, consistently, major results expected by various stakeholders (for example, for customers, always being on time; for stockholders, being on budget)	*Producing change,* often dramatically, and having the potential to produce useful change (for example, new products that customers want, new approaches to labor relations that make a firm more competitive)

Reprinted with the permission of The Free Press, a division of Simon & Schuster Adult Publishing Group, from *A Force for Change: How Leadership Differs from Management* by John P. Kotter. Copyright © 1990 by John P. Kotter, Inc. All rights reserved.

1. **Legitimate power** is power granted through the organizational hierarchy; it is the power defined by the organization to be accorded to people occupying a position. A manager can assign tasks to a subordinate. A subordinate who refuses to do them can be reprimanded or fired. Such outcomes stem from the manager's legitimate power as vested in her or him by the organization. Legitimate power, then, is authority. The mere possession of legitimate power, however, does not by itself make someone a leader. Some subordinates follow only orders that are strictly within the letter of organizational rules and policies. If asked to do something not in their job description, they refuse or do a poor job. A manager of such employees is exercising authority but not leadership.

legitimate power Power granted through the organizational hierarchy; the power defined by the organization to be accorded to people occupying particular positions.

2. **Reward power** is the power to give or withhold rewards. Rewards that a manager may control include the following:

- Salary increases
- Praise
- Promotion recommendations
- Bonuses
- Recognition
- Interesting job assignments

In general, the greater the number of rewards a manager controls and the more important the rewards are to subordinates, the greater is the manager's reward power. If the subordinate sees as valuable only the formal organizational rewards provided by the manager, then that manager is not a leader. However, if the subordinate also wants and appreciates the manager's informal rewards, such as praise, gratitude, and recognition, then the manager is also exercising leadership.

reward power The power to give or withhold rewards, such as salary increases, bonuses, promotions, praise, recognition, and interesting job assignments.

3. **Coercive power** is the power to force compliance by means of psychological, emotional, or physical threat. In the past, physical coercion in organizations was relatively common. In most organizations, coercion is limited to:

- Verbal reprimands
- Fines, demotion
- Disciplinary layoffs
- Written reprimands
- Termination

coercive power The power to force compliance by means of psychological, emotional, or physical threat.

CONCEPT CHECK 11.1

Consider the following list of leadership situations. For each situation, describe in detail the kinds of power the leader has. If the leader were the same but the situation changed—for example, if you thought of the president as the head of his family rather than of the military—would your answers change? Why?

- The president of the United States is commander-in-chief of the U.S. military.
- An airline pilot is in charge of a particular flight.
- Fans look up to a movie star.
- Your professor is the head of your class.

referent power   The personal power that accrues to someone on the basis of identification, imitation, loyalty, or charisma.

expert power   The personal power that accrues to someone as a consequence of the information or expertise that she or he possesses.

Some managers occasionally go so far as to use verbal abuse, humiliation, and psychological coercion in an attempt to manipulate subordinates. (Most people would agree that these are not appropriate managerial behaviors.) The more punitive the elements under a manager's control and the more important they are to subordinates, the more coercive power the manager possesses. On the other hand, the more a manager uses coercive power, the more likely he is to provoke resentment and hostility and the less likely he is to be seen as a leader.[6]

4. **Referent power** is more abstract than legitimate, reward, and coercive power, which are relatively concrete and grounded in objective facets of organizational life. Referent power is based on identification, imitation, loyalty, or charisma. Followers may react favorably because they identify in some way with a leader who may be like them in personality, background, or attitudes. In other situations, followers might choose to imitate a leader with referent power by wearing the same kinds of clothes, working the same hours, or espousing the same management philosophy. Referent power may also take the form of charisma, an intangible attribute of the leader that inspires loyalty and enthusiasm. Thus a manager might have referent power, but it is more likely to be associated with leadership.

5. **Expert power** is derived from information or expertise. A manager who knows how to interact with an eccentric but important customer, a scientist who is capable of achieving an important technical breakthrough that no other company has dreamed of, and a secretary who knows how to unravel bureaucratic red tape all have expert power over anyone who needs that information. The more important the information and the fewer the people who have access to it, the greater is the degree of expert power possessed by any one individual. In general, both leaders and managers tend to have a lot of expert power.

TEST PREPPER 11.1

ANSWERS CAN BE FOUND ON P. 442

True or False?

_____ 1. Management, as a process, is the use of noncoercive influences to shape the organization's goals, motivate behavior toward the achievement of those goals, and help define organization culture.

_____ 2. Legitimate power is power granted through the organizational hierarchy; it is the power defined by the organization that is to be accorded to people occupying particular positions.

_____ 3. Leadership is both something you do and something you have.

_____ 4. A sports figure viewed by some as a role model can use referent power through personal identification and imitation.

Online Study Center
ACE the Test
ACE Practice Tests 11.1

Multiple Choice

_____ 5. Leaders and managers differ in the types of outcomes they are expected to produce. Which of the following is an expected leader outcome?
   a. Produce a degree of predictability
   b. Produce a degree of order
   c. Consistently produce major results
   d. Produce results on time and on budget
   e. Produce dramatic change

_____ 6. The power to give salary increases, bonuses, promotions, praise, recognition, and interesting job assignments is called _____ power.
   a. reward   c. referent   e. legitimate
   b. expert   d. coercive

_____ 7. The administrative assistant for a state college has held that particular job for thirty-five years. When the staff need to accomplish a task, they often get her advice. She has which kind of power?
   a. Reward   c. Referent   e. Legitimate
   b. Expert   d. Coercive

GENERIC APPROACHES TO LEADERSHIP

2 ▶ *Discuss and evaluate the two generic approaches to leadership.*

Early approaches to the study of leadership adopted what might be called a "universal" or "generic" perspective. Specifically, they assumed that there was one set of answers to the leadership puzzle. One generic approach focused on leadership traits, and the other looked at leadership behavior.

Leadership Traits

The first organized approach to studying leadership analyzed the personal, psychological, and physical traits of strong leaders. The trait approach assumed that some basic trait or set of traits differentiated leaders from nonleaders. If those traits could be defined, potential leaders could be identified. Researchers thought that leadership traits might include intelligence, assertiveness, above-average height, good vocabulary, attractiveness, self-confidence, and similar attributes.[7]

During the first half of the twentieth century, hundreds of studies were conducted in an attempt to identify important leadership traits. For the most part, the results of the studies were disappointing. For every set of leaders who possessed a common trait, a long list of exceptions was also found, and the list of suggested traits soon grew so long that it had little practical value. Alternative explanations usually existed even for relationships between traits and leadership that initially appeared valid. For example, it was observed that many leaders have good communication skills and are assertive. Rather than those traits being the cause of leadership, however, successful leaders may begin to display those traits after they have achieved a leadership position.

Although most researchers gave up trying to identify traits as predictors of leadership ability, many people still explicitly or implicitly adopt a trait orientation.[8] For example, politicians are all too often elected on the basis of personal appearance, speaking ability, or an aura of self-confidence. In addition, traits such as honesty and integrity may very well be fundamental leadership traits that serve an important purpose.

Online Study Center
Improve Your Grade
Video Segment

CONCEPT CHECK 11.2

Even though the trait approach to leadership has no empirical support, it is still widely used. In your opinion, why is this so? In what ways is the use of the trait approach helpful to those who use it? In what ways is it harmful to those who use it?

Leadership Behaviors

Spurred on by their lack of success in identifying useful leadership traits, researchers soon began to investigate other variables, especially the behaviors or actions of leaders. The new hypothesis was that effective leaders somehow behaved differently than less effective leaders. Thus the goal was to develop a fuller understanding of leadership behaviors.

Michigan Studies

Researchers at the University of Michigan, led by Rensis Likert, began studying leadership in the late 1940s.[9] On the basis of extensive interviews with both leaders (managers) and followers (subordinates), this research identified two basic forms of leader behavior: job-centered and employee-centered.

1. Managers who exhibit **job-centered leader behavior** pay close attention to subordinates' work, explain work procedures, and are keenly interested in performance.

job-centered leader behavior   The behavior of leaders who pay close attention to the job and to work procedures involved with that job.

employee-centered leader behavior   The behavior of leaders who develop cohesive work groups and ensure employee satisfaction.

2. Managers who exhibit **employee-centered leader behavior** are interested in developing a cohesive work group and in ensuring that employees are satisfied with their jobs. Their primary concern is the welfare of subordinates.

The two styles of leader behavior were presumed to be at the ends of a single continuum. Although this suggests that leaders may be extremely job-centered, extremely employee-centered, or somewhere in between, Likert studied only the two "end styles" for contrast. He argued that employee-centered leader behavior generally tends to be more effective.

Ohio State Studies

At about the same time that Likert was beginning his leadership studies at the University of Michigan, a group of researchers at Ohio State University also began studying leadership.[10] The extensive questionnaire surveys conducted during the Ohio State studies also suggested that there are two basic leader behaviors or styles: initiating-structure behavior and consideration behavior.

initiating-structure behavior   The behavior of leaders who define the leader-subordinate role in such a way that everyone knows what is expected, establish formal lines of communication, and determine how tasks will be performed.

consideration behavior   The behavior of leaders who show concern for subordinates and attempt to establish a warm, friendly, and supportive climate.

1. When using **initiating-structure behavior**, the leader clearly defines the leader-subordinate role so that everyone knows what is expected, establishes formal lines of communication, and determines how tasks will be performed.
2. Leaders using **consideration behavior** show concern for subordinates and attempt to establish a warm, friendly, and supportive climate. The behaviors identified at Ohio State are similar to those described at Michigan, but there are important differences. One major difference is that the Ohio State researchers did not interpret leader behavior as being one-dimensional; each behavior was assumed to be independent of the other. Presumably, then, a leader could exhibit varying levels of initiating structure and, at the same time, varying levels of consideration.

At first, the Ohio State researchers thought that leaders who exhibit high levels of both behaviors would tend to be more effective than other leaders. A study at International Harvester (now Navistar International), however, suggested a more complicated pattern.[11] The researchers found that employees of supervisors who ranked high on initiating structure were high performers but expressed low levels of satisfaction and had a higher absence rate. Conversely, employees of supervisors who ranked high on consideration had low performance ratings but high levels of satisfaction and few absences from work. Later research isolated other variables that make consistent prediction difficult and determined that situational influences also played a part. (This body of research is discussed in the section on situational approaches to leadership.)

Leadership Grid

concern for production   The part of the Leadership Grid that deals with the job and task aspects of leader behavior.

concern for people   The part of the Leadership Grid that deals with the human aspects of leader behavior.

Yet another behavioral approach to leadership is the Leadership Grid.[12] The Leadership Grid provides a means for evaluating leadership styles and then training managers to move toward an ideal style of behavior. The Leadership Grid is shown in Figure 11.1. The horizontal axis represents **concern for production** (similar to job-centered behavior and initiating-structure behavior), and the vertical axis represents **concern for people** (similar to employee-centered behavior and consideration behavior). Note the five extremes of leadership behavior:

1. The 1,1 manager (impoverished management), who exhibits minimum concern for both production and people;

FIGURE 11.1

The Leadership Grid

The Leadership Grid® is a method of evaluating leadership styles. The overall objective of an organization using the Grid® is to train its managers using organization development techniques so that they are simultaneously more concerned for both people and production (9,9 style on the Grid®).

The Leadership Grid Figure for *Leadership Dilemmas— Grid Solutions*, p. 29, by Robert R. Blake, Ph.D., and Anne Adams McCanse. Copyright © 1991 by Robert R. Blake and the Estate of Jane S. Morton. Reprinted with permission of GRID International.

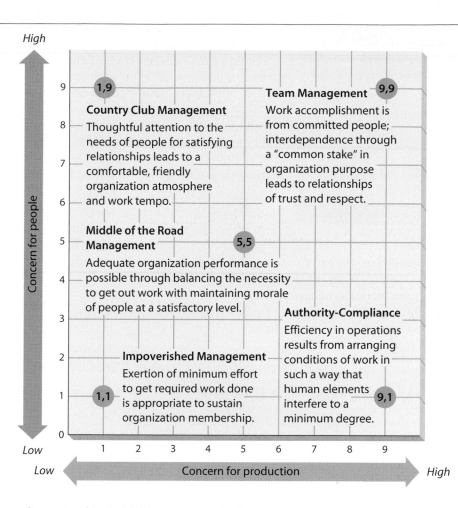

2. The 9,1 manager (authority-compliance), who is highly concerned about production but exhibits little concern for people;

3. The 1,9 manager (country club management), who has exactly opposite concerns from the 9,1 manager;

4. The 5,5 manager (middle-of-the-road management), who maintains adequate concern for both people and production;

5. The 9,9 manager (team management), who exhibits maximum concern for both people and production.

According to this approach, the ideal style of leadership behavior is 9,9. There is a six-phase program to assist managers in achieving this style of behavior. A.G. Edwards, Westinghouse, the FAA, Equicor, and other companies have used the Leadership Grid with reasonable success. However, there is little published scientific evidence regarding its true effectiveness.

The leader-behavior theories have played an important role in the development of contemporary thinking about leadership. In particular, they urge us not to be preoccupied with what leaders are (the trait approach) but to concentrate on what leaders do (their behaviors). Unfortunately, these theories also make universal generic prescriptions about what constitutes effective leadership. When we are dealing with complex social systems composed of complex individuals, however,

CONCEPT CHECK 11.3

What can managers today learn from the two generic approaches to leadership?

few if any relationships are consistently predictable, and certainly no formulas for success are infallible. Yet the behavior theorists tried to identify consistent relationships between leader behaviors and employee responses in the hope of finding a dependable prescription for effective leadership. As we might expect, they often failed. Other approaches to understanding leadership were therefore needed. The catalyst for these new approaches was the realization that although interpersonal and task-oriented dimensions might be useful for describing the behavior of leaders, they were not useful for predicting or prescribing it. The next step in the evolution of leadership theory was the creation of situational models.

TEST PREPPER 11.2

ANSWERS CAN BE FOUND ON P. 442

True or False?

_____ 1. According to the Ohio State studies, leaders could exhibit only initiating-structure behavior or consideration behavior.

_____ 2. When using the Leadership Grid, managers should aspire to be 1,1 leaders.

Multiple Choice

_____ 3. Fred is primarily concerned with the efficiency and performance of his subordinates. Accord-

ing to the Michigan studies, he exhibits which leader behavior?
   a. Job-centered
   b. Employee-centered
   c. Initiating-structure
   d. Consideration
   e. Initiating-structure and consideration

_____ 4. In the Leadership Grid, which type of leader has a high concern for production and a high concern for people?
   a. 5,5   b. 1,1   c. 9,9   d. 1,9   e. 9,1

Online Study Center
ACE the Test
ACE Practice Tests 11.2

SITUATIONAL APPROACHES TO LEADERSHIP

3 ▶ *Identify and describe the major situational approaches to leadership.*

Situational models assume that appropriate leader behavior varies from one situation to another. The goal of a situational theory, then, is to identify key situational factors and to specify how they interact to determine appropriate leader behavior. In the following sections, we describe four of the most important and widely accepted situational theories of leadership: the LPC theory, the path-goal theory, Vroom's decision tree approach, and the leader-member exchange approach.

LPC Theory

LPC theory A theory of leadership that suggests that the appropriate style of leadership varies with situational favorableness.

The **LPC theory**, developed by Fred Fiedler, was the first truly situational theory of leadership.[13] As we will discuss later, LPC stands for least-preferred coworker. Beginning with a combined trait and behavioral approach, Fiedler identified two styles of leadership: task-oriented leadership (analogous to job-centered and initiating-structure behavior) and relationship-oriented leadership (similar to employee-centered and consideration behavior). He went beyond the earlier behavioral approaches by arguing that the style of behavior is a reflection of the leader's personality and that most personalities fall by nature into one or the other of his two categories. Fiedler measures leadership style by means of a controversial questionnaire called the **least-preferred coworker (LPC) measure**. To use the measure, a manager or leader is asked to describe the specific person with whom he or she is able to work least well—the LPC—by filling in a set of sixteen scales anchored at each end by a positive or negative adjective. For example, three of the sixteen scales are as follows:

least-preferred coworker (LPC) measure A measuring scale that asks leaders to describe the person with whom they are able to work least well.

The leader's LPC score is then calculated by adding up the numbers below the lines that the respondent has checked on these scales. Note in these three examples that the higher numbers are associated with positive qualities (helpful, relaxed, and interesting), whereas the negative qualities (frustrating, tense, and boring) have low point values. A high total score is assumed to reflect a relationship orientation and a low score a task orientation on the part of the leader. The LPC measure is controversial because researchers disagree about its validity. Some question exactly what an LPC measure reflects and whether the score is an index of behavior, personality, or some other factor.[14]

Favorableness of the Situation

The underlying assumption of situational models of leadership is that appropriate leader behavior varies from one situation to another. According to Fiedler, the key situational factor is the favorableness of the situation from the leader's point of view. This factor is determined by leader-member relations, task structure, and position power.

▮ *Leader-member relations* reflect the nature of the relationship between the leader and the work group. If the leader and the group have a high degree of mutual trust, respect, and confidence, and if they like one another, relations are assumed to be good. If there is little trust, respect, or confidence, and if they do not like one another, relations are poor. Naturally, good relations are more favorable.

▮ *Task structure* is the degree to which the group's task is well defined. The task is structured when it is routine, easily understood, and unambiguous and when the group has standard procedures and precedents to rely on. An unstructured task is nonroutine, ambiguous, and complex, with no standard procedures or precedents. You can see that high structure is more favorable for the leader, whereas low structure is less favorable. For example, if the task is unstructured, the group will not know what to do, and the leader will have to play a major role in guiding and directing its activities. If the task is structured, the leader will not have to get so involved and can devote time to nonsupervisory activities.

▮ *Position power* is the power vested in the leader's position. If the leader has the power to assign work and to reward and punish employees, position power is assumed to be strong. But if the leader must get job assignments approved by someone else and does not administer rewards and punishment, position power is weak, and it is more difficult to accomplish goals. From the leader's point of view, strong position power is clearly preferable to weak position power. However, position power is not as important as task structure and leader-member relations.

Favorableness and Leader Style

Fiedler and his associates conducted numerous studies linking the favorableness of various situations to leader style and the effectiveness of the group.[15] The results of these studies—and the overall framework of the theory—are shown in Figure 11.2. To interpret the model, look first at the situational factors at the top of the figure. Good or bad leader-member relations, high or low task structure, and strong or weak leader position power can be combined to yield six unique situations. For example, good leader-member relations, high task structure, and strong leader position power (at the far left) are presumed to define the most favorable situation; bad leader-member relations, low task structure, and weak leader power (at the far right) are the least favorable. The other combinations reflect intermediate levels of favorableness.

Below each set of situations are shown the degree of favorableness and the form of leader behavior found to be most strongly associated with effective group performance for those situations. When the situation is either most or least favorable, Fiedler found that a task-oriented leader is most effective. When the situation is only moderately favorable, however, a relationship-oriented leader is predicted to be most effective.

Flexibility of Leader Style

Fiedler argued that for any given individual, leader style is essentially fixed and cannot be changed; leaders cannot change their behavior to fit a particular

---

FIGURE 11.2

The Least-Preferred Coworker Theory of Leadership

Fiedler's LPC theory of leadership suggests that appropriate leader behavior varies as a function of the favorableness of the situation. Favorableness, in turn, is defined by task structure, leader-member relations, and the leader's position power. According to the LPC theory, the most and least favorable situations call for task-oriented leadership, whereas moderately favorable situations suggest the need for relationship-oriented leadership.

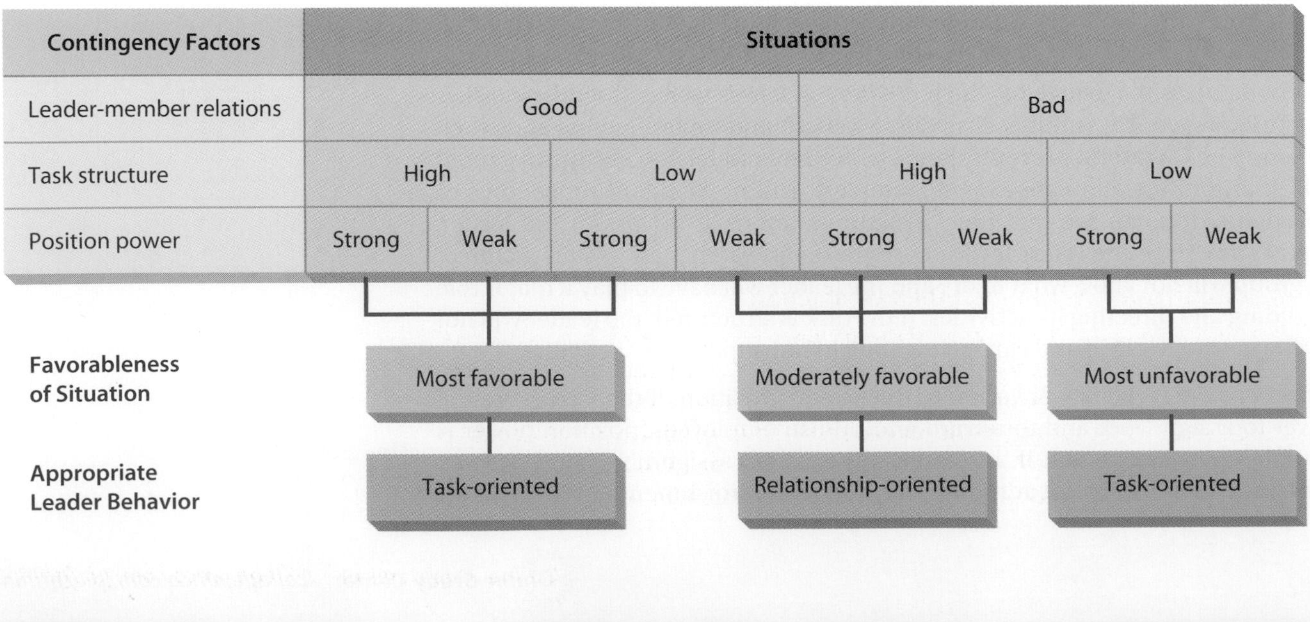

Contingency Factors	Situations							
Leader-member relations	Good				Bad			
Task structure	High		Low		High		Low	
Position power	Strong	Weak	Strong	Weak	Strong	Weak	Strong	Weak

Favorableness of Situation	Most favorable	Moderately favorable	Most unfavorable
Appropriate Leader Behavior	Task-oriented	Relationship-oriented	Task-oriented

situation, because their behavior is linked to their particular personality traits. Thus Fiedler argued that when a leader's style and the situation do not match, the situation should be changed to fit the leader's style. When leader-member relations are good, task structure low, and position power weak, the relationship-oriented leader style is most likely to be effective. If the leader is task-oriented, a mismatch exists. According to Fiedler, the leader can make the elements of the situation more congruent by structuring the task (by developing guidelines and procedures, for instance) and increasing power (by requesting additional authority or by other means).

Fiedler's contingency theory has been attacked on the grounds that it is not always supported by research, that his findings are subject to other interpretations, that the LPC measure lacks validity, and that his assumptions about the inflexibility of leader behavior are unrealistic.[16] However, Fiedler's theory was one of the first to adopt a situational perspective on leadership. It has helped many managers recognize the important situational factors they must contend with, and it has fostered additional thinking about the situational nature of leadership. Moreover, in recent years Fiedler has attempted to address some of the concerns about his theory by revising it and adding such additional elements as cognitive resources.

Path-Goal Theory

The **path-goal theory** of leadership—associated most closely with Martin Evans and Robert House—is a direct extension of the expectancy theory of motivation discussed in Chapter 10.[17] Recall that the primary components of expectancy theory included the likelihood of attaining various outcomes and the value associated with those outcomes. The path-goal theory of leadership suggests that the primary functions of a leader are to make valued or desired rewards available in the workplace and to clarify for the subordinate the kinds of behavior that will lead to goal accomplishment and valued rewards—that is, the leader should clarify the paths to goal attainment.

path-goal theory A theory of leadership that suggests that the primary functions of a leader are to make valued or desired rewards available in the workplace and to clarify for the subordinate the kinds of behavior that will lead to those rewards.

Leader Behavior

The most fully developed version of path-goal theory identifies four kinds of leader behavior.

1. *Directive leader behavior* consists of letting subordinates know what is expected of them, gives guidance and direction, and schedules work.

2. *Supportive leader behavior* is being friendly and approachable, showing concern for subordinate welfare, and treating members as equals.

3. *Participative leader behavior* includes consulting with subordinates, soliciting suggestions, and allowing participation in decision making.

4. *Achievement-oriented leader behavior* entails setting challenging goals, expecting subordinates to perform at high levels, encouraging subordinates, and showing confidence in subordinates' abilities.

In contrast to Fiedler's theory, path-goal theory assumes that leaders can change their style or behavior to meet the demands of a particular situation. For example, when encountering a new group of subordinates and a new project, the leader may be directive in establishing work procedures and in outlining what needs to be done. Next, the leader may adopt supportive behavior to foster group cohesiveness and a positive climate. As the group becomes familiar with the task and as new problems are encountered, the leader may exhibit participative behavior to enhance group members' motivation. Finally, achievement-oriented behavior may be used to encourage continued high performance.

Situational Factors

Like other situational theories of leadership, path-goal theory suggests that appropriate leader style depends on situational factors. Path-goal theory focuses on the situational factors of the personal characteristics of subordinates and the environmental characteristics of the workplace.

Important personal characteristics include the subordinates' perception of their own ability and their locus of control. If people perceive that they are lacking in ability, they may prefer directive leadership to help them understand path-goal relationships better. If they perceive themselves to have a lot of ability, however, employees may resent directive leadership. Locus of control is a personality trait that is explained in Table 11.2.

Managers can do little or nothing to influence the personal characteristics of subordinates, but they can shape the environment to take advantage of these personal characteristics by, for example, providing rewards and structuring tasks. Environmental characteristics include factors outside the subordinates' control, such as the following:

▌ ***Task structure.***   When structure is high, directive leadership is less effective than when structure is low. Subordinates do not usually need their boss to tell them repeatedly how to do an extremely routine job.

TABLE 11.2

Internal vs. External Locus of Control

Internal Locus of Control	External Locus of Control
Belief that what happens to them is a function of their own efforts and behavior	Belief that fate, luck, or "the system" determines what happens to them
Prefer participative leadership	Prefer directive leadership

Most effective leaders demonstrate sincere interest in their employees, their jobs, and their families. When the interest is real, employees will feel more valued and appreciated by their leader, and develop stronger job satisfaction and commitment. But when the interest is clearly false, as in this case, employees are likely to both resent and lose respect for the leader.

"Keep up the good work, whatever it is, whoever you are."

FIGURE 11.3

The Path-Goal Framework

The path-goal theory of leadership suggests that managers can use four types of leader behavior to clarify subordinates' paths to goal attainment. Both the personal characteristics of the subordinate and environmental characteristics within the organization must be taken into account when determining which style of leadership will work best for a particular situation.

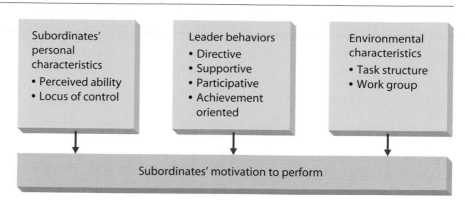

- **Formal authority system.** Again, the higher the degree of formality, the less directive is the leader behavior that will be accepted by subordinates.

- **Nature of the work group.** When the work group provides the employee with social support and satisfaction, supportive leader behavior is less critical. When social support and satisfaction cannot be derived from the group, the worker may look to the leader for this support.

The basic path-goal framework as illustrated in Figure 11.3 shows that different leader behaviors affect subordinates' motivation to perform. Personal and environmental characteristics are seen as defining which behaviors lead to which outcomes. The path-goal theory of leadership is a dynamic and incomplete model. The original intent was to state the theory in general terms so that future research could explore a variety of interrelationships and modify the theory. Research that has been done suggests that the path-goal theory offers a reasonably good description of the leadership process and that future investigations along these lines should enable us to discover more about the link between leadership and motivation.[18]

Vroom's Decision Tree Approach

The third major contemporary approach to leadership is **Vroom's decision tree approach**. Like the path-goal theory, this approach attempts to prescribe a leadership style appropriate to a given situation. It also assumes that the same leader may display different leadership styles. But Vroom's approach concerns itself with only a single aspect of leader behavior: subordinate participation in decision making.

Vroom's decision tree approach An approach to leadership that predicts what kinds of situations call for different degrees of group participation.

Basic Premises

Vroom's decision tree approach assumes that the degree to which subordinates should be encouraged to participate in decision making depends on the characteristics of the situation. In other words, no one decision-making process is best for all situations. After evaluating a variety of problem attributes (characteristics of the problem or decision), the leader determines an appropriate decision style that specifies the amount of subordinate participation.

Vroom's current formulation suggests that managers should use one of two different decision trees.[19] To decide which to use, the manager first assesses the situation in terms of several factors. This assessment involves determining whether the given factor is high or low for the decision that is to be made. For instance, the first factor is decision significance. If the decision is extremely important and may have a major impact on the organization (such as choosing a location for a new plant), its significance is high. But if the decision is routine and its consequences are not terribly important (such as selecting a color for the firm's softball team uniforms), its significance is low. This assessment guides the manager through the paths of the decision tree to a recommended course of action. One decision tree is to be used when the manager is interested primarily in making the decision as quickly as possible; the other is to be used when time is less critical and the manager is interested in helping subordinates to improve and develop their own decision-making skills.

The two decision trees are shown in Figures 11.4 and 11.5. The problem attributes (situational factors) are arranged along the top of the decision tree. To use the model, the decision maker starts at the left side of the diagram and assesses the first problem attribute (decision significance). The answer determines the path to the second node on the decision tree, where the next attribute (importance of commitment) is assessed. This process continues until a terminal node is reached. In this way, the manager identifies an effective decision-making style for the situation.

FIGURE 11.4

Vroom's Time-Driven Decision Tree

This matrix is recommended for situations where time is of the greatest importance in making a decision. The matrix operates like a funnel. The leader starts at the left with a specific decision problem in mind. The column headings denote situational factors that may or may not be present in that problem. The leader next selects high or low (H or L) for each relevant situational factor. Then she or he proceeds down the funnel, judging only those situational factors where a judgment is called for, until the recommended process is reached.

Adapted and reprinted from *Leadership and Decision-Making,* by Victor H. Vroom and Philip W. Yetton, by permission of the University of Pittsburgh Press. Copyright © 1973 by University of Pittsburgh Press.

PROBLEM STATEMENT	Decision Significance	Importance of Commitment	Leader Expertise	Likelihood of Commitment	Group Support	Group Expertise	Team Competence	
	H	H	H	H	—	—	—	Decide
	H	H	H	L	H	H	H	Delegate
	H	H	H	L	H	H	L	Consult (group)
	H	H	H	L	H	L	—	Consult (group)
	H	H	H	L	L	—	—	Consult (group)
	H	H	L	H	H	H	H	Facilitate
	H	H	L	H	H	H	L	Consult (individually)
	H	H	L	H	H	L	—	Consult (individually)
	H	H	L	H	L	—	—	Consult (individually)
	H	H	L	L	H	H	H	Facilitate
	H	H	L	L	H	H	L	Consult (group)
	H	H	L	L	H	L	—	Consult (group)
	H	H	L	L	L	—	—	Consult (group)
	H	L	H	—	—	—	—	Decide
	H	L	L	—	H	H	H	Facilitate
	H	L	L	—	H	H	L	Consult (individually)
	H	L	L	—	H	L	—	Consult (individually)
	H	L	L	—	L	—	—	Consult (individually)
	L	H	—	H	—	—	—	Decide
	L	H	—	L	—	—	H	Delegate
	L	H	—	L	—	—	L	Facilitate
	L	L	—	—	—	—	—	Decide

FIGURE 11.5

Vroom's Development-Driven Decision Tree

This matrix is to be used when the leader is more interested in developing employees than in making the decision as quickly as possible. Just as with the time-driven tree shown in Figure 11.4, the leader assesses up to seven situational factors. These factors, in turn, funnel the leader to a recommended process for making the decision.

Adapted and reprinted from *Leadership and Decision-Making*, by Victor H. Vroom and Philip W. Yetton, by permission of the University of Pittsburgh Press. Copyright © 1973 by University of Pittsburgh Press.

Decision Significance	Importance of Commitment	Leader Expertise	Likelihood of Commitment	Group Support	Group Expertise	Team Competence	
H	H	—	H	H	H	H	Decide
						L	Facilitate
					L	—	Consult (group)
				L	—	—	Consult (group)
			L	H	H	H	Delegate
						L	Facilitate
					L	—	Facilitate
				L	—	—	Consult (group)
	L	—	—	H	H	H	Delegate
						L	Facilitate
					L	—	Consult (group)
				L	—	—	Consult (group)
L	H	—	H	—	—	—	Decide
			L	—	—	—	Delegate
	L	—	—	—	—	—	Decide

PROBLEM STATEMENT

Decision-Making Styles

The various decision styles reflected at the ends of the tree branches represent different levels of subordinate participation that the manager should attempt to adopt in a given situation. The five styles are defined as follows:

1. *Decide.* The manager makes the decision alone and then announces or "sells" it to the group.

2. *Consult (individually).* The manager presents the program to group members individually, obtains their suggestions, and then makes the decision.

3. *Consult (group).* The manager presents the problem to group members at a meeting, gets their suggestions, and then makes the decision.

4. *Facilitate.* The manager presents the problem to the group at a meeting, defines the problem and its boundaries, and then facilitates discussion among group members as they make the decision.

5. *Delegate.* The manager allows the group to define for itself the exact nature and parameters of the problem and then to develop a solution.

Vroom's decision tree approach represents a very focused but quite complex perspective on leadership. To compensate for this difficulty, Vroom has developed elaborate expert system software to help managers assess a situation accurately and quickly and then to make an appropriate decision regarding employee participation.[20] Many firms, including Halliburton Company, Litton Industries, and Borland International, have provided their managers with training in how to use the various versions of this model.

The Leader-Member Exchange Approach

Because leadership is such an important area, managers and researchers continue to study it. As a result, new ideas, theories, and perspectives are continuously being developed. The **leader-member exchange (LMX) model** of leadership, conceived by George Graen and Fred Dansereau, stresses that supervisors have different relationships with different subordinates.[21] Each superior-subordinate pair is referred to as a "vertical dyad." The model differs from earlier approaches in that it focuses on leaders' establishing different relationships with different subordinates. Figure 11.6 shows the basic concepts of the leader-member exchange theory.

The model suggests that supervisors establish a special relationship with a small number of trusted subordinates, referred to as the in-group. The in-group usually receives special duties requiring responsibility and autonomy; they may also receive special privileges. Subordinates who are not a part of this group are called the out-group, and they receive less of the supervisor's time and attention. Note in the figure that the leader has a dyadic, or one-to-one, relationship with each of the five subordinates.

Early in his or her interaction with a given subordinate, the supervisor initiates either an in-group or an out-group relationship. It is not clear how a leader selects members of the in-group, but the decision may be based on personal compatibility and subordinates' competence. Research has confirmed the existence of in-groups and out-groups. In addition, studies generally have found that in-group members have a higher level of performance and satisfaction than out-group members.[22]

---

leader-member exchange (LMX) model   A model of leadeship that stresses that leaders have different kinds of relationships with different subordinates.

CONCEPT CHECK 11.4

Describe a time when you or someone you know was part of an in-group or an out-group. What was the relationship between each of the groups and the leader? What was the relationship between the members of the two different groups? What was the outcome of the situation for the leader? for the members of the two groups? for the organization?

FIGURE 11.6

The Leader-Member Exchange (LMX) Model

The LMX model suggests that leaders form a unique, independent relationship with each of their subordinates. As illustrated here, a key factor in the nature of this relationship is whether the individual subordinate is in the leader's out-group or in-group.

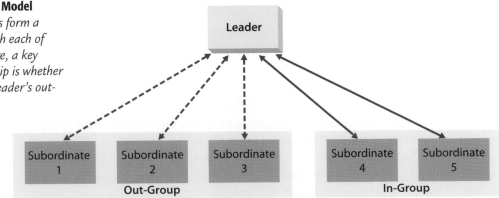

True or False?

_____ 1. The least-preferred coworker (LPC) model was one of the first to adopt a situational perspective on leadership.

_____ 2. When a manager "sells" her decision to the group, she uses the consulting style of decision making.

Multiple Choice

_____ 3. Fiedler's least-preferred coworker theory has been attacked on the grounds that _____.
   a. it is not always supported by research
   b. his findings are subject to other interpretations
   c. the LPC measure lacks validity
   d. his assumptions about the inflexibility of leader behavior are unrealistic
   e. all of the above

_____ 4. Which leadership theory is a direct extension of the expectancy theory of motivation?
   a. Vroom's decision tree
   b. LPC
   c. Path-goal
   d. Leader-member exchange
   e. Michigan studies

_____ 5. Which of the following is NOT a Vroom decision-making style?
   a. Decide   d. Exchange
   b. Facilitate   e. Consult
   c. Delegate

_____ 6. A manager presents a problem to the team and helps them make the decision. He is exhibiting which decision-making style?
   a. Decide   d. Exchange
   b. Facilitate   e. Consult
   c. Delegate

Online Study Center
ACE the Test
ACE Practice Tests 11.3

RELATED APPROACHES TO LEADERSHIP

4   *Identify and describe three related approaches to leadership.*

Because of its importance to organizational effectiveness, leadership continues to be the focus of a great deal of research and theory building. New approaches that have attracted much attention are the concepts of substitutes for leadership, charismatic leadership, and transformational leadership.

Substitutes for Leadership

The concept of **substitutes for leadership** was developed because existing leadership models and theories do not account for situations in which leadership is not needed.[23] They simply try to specify what kind of leader behavior is appropriate. The substitutes concept, however, identifies situations in which leader behaviors are neutralized or replaced by characteristics of the subordinate, the task, and the organization. For example, when a patient is delivered to a hospital emergency room, the professionals on duty do not wait to be told what to do by a leader. Nurses, doctors, and attendants all go into action without waiting for directive or supportive leader behavior from the emergency room supervisor.

Characteristics of the subordinate that may serve to neutralize leader behavior include the following:

- Ability
- Experience
- Need for independence
- Professional orientation
- Indifference to organizational rewards

For example, employees with a high level of ability and experience may not need to be told what to do. Similarly, a subordinate's strong need for independence may

substitutes for leadership A concept that identifies situations in which leader behaviors are neutralized or replaced by characteristics of subordinates, the task, and the organization.

While leadership is clearly important, the fact remains that in at least some settings people function very effectively without a leader. Take this team of paramedics, for example. Each is highly trained and very motivated to help patients who have been hurt or injured. They do not need an on-site supervisor to tell them what to do or how to handle each emergency situation. They know how to work together, with or without supervision, to carry out their responsibilities.

render leader behavior ineffective. Task characteristics that may substitute for leadership include the following:

- Routineness
- The availability of feedback
- Intrinsic satisfaction

When the job is routine and simple, the subordinate may not need direction. When the task is challenging and intrinsically satisfying, the subordinate may not need or want social support from a leader.

Organizational characteristics that may substitute for leadership include the following:

- Formalization
- Group cohesion
- Inflexibility
- A rigid reward structure

Leadership may not be necessary when policies and practices are formal and inflexible, for example. Similarly, a rigid reward system may rob the leader of reward power and thereby decrease the importance of the role. Preliminary research has provided support for the concept of substitutes for leadership.[24]

Charismatic Leadership

charismatic leadership The concept that charisma is an individual characteristic of the leader.

charisma A form of interpersonal attraction that inspires support and acceptance.

The concept of **charismatic leadership**, like trait theories, assumes that charisma is an individual characteristic of the leader. **Charisma** is a form of interpersonal attraction that inspires support and acceptance. All else being equal, then, a highly charismatic supervisor will be more successful in influencing subordinate behavior than a supervisor who lacks charisma. Thus influence is again a fundamental element of this perspective.

Robert House first proposed a theory of charismatic leadership on the basis of research findings from a variety of social science disciplines.[25] His theory suggests that charismatic leaders are likely to have a lot of self-confidence, a firm conviction in their beliefs and ideals, and a strong need to influence people. They also tend to communicate high expectations about follower performance and to express confidence in followers. Donald Trump is an excellent example of a charismatic leader.

Even though he has made his share of mistakes and generally is perceived as only an "average" manager, many people view him as larger than life.[26]

There are three elements of charismatic leadership in organizations that most experts acknowledge today.[27]

1. The leader needs to be able to envision the future, set high expectations, and model behaviors consistent with meeting those expectations.
2. The leader must be able to energize others through a demonstration of personal excitement, personal confidence, and patterns of success.
3. The leader enables others by supporting them, empathizing with them, and expressing confidence in them.

The concept of charismatic leadership is quite popular among managers today, and it has recently been the subject of numerous books and articles. Unfortunately, few studies have attempted rigorously to test the meaning and impact of charismatic leadership. There are also lingering ethical issues about charismatic leadership that trouble some people. For instance, President Bill Clinton was a charismatic leader. But some of his critics argue that this very charisma caused his supporters to overlook his flaws and to minimize some of his indiscretions.

Transformational Leadership

A variety of names have been used to describe another new perspective on leadership, including inspirational leadership, symbolic leadership, and transformational leadership. We use the term **transformational leadership** and define it as leadership that goes beyond ordinary expectations by transmitting a sense of mission, stimulating learning experiences, and inspiring new ways of thinking.[28] Because of rapid change and turbulent environments, transformational leaders are increasingly being seen as vital to the success of business.

A recent article in the popular press identified seven keys to successful leadership: trusting one's subordinates, developing a vision, keeping cool, encouraging risk, being an expert, inviting dissent, and simplifying things.[29] Although this list grew out of a simplistic survey of the leadership literature, it is nevertheless consistent with the premises underlying transformational leadership. So, too, are recent examples cited as illustrating effective leadership. Take the case of 3M. The firm's CEO has been working to make the firm more efficient and profitable, while retaining its leadership role in new-product innovation. He also changed the reward system, overhauled procedures, and restructured the entire firm. And so far, at least, analysts have applauded these changes.[30]

transformational leadership Leadership that goes beyond ordinary expectations by transmitting a sense of mission, stimulating learning experiences, and inspiring new ways of thinking.

Online Study Center
Improve Your Grade
Career Snapshot 11.2

TEST PREPPER 11.4

Answers can be found on p. 442

True or False?

_____ 1. Charisma seldom inspires support and acceptance.

_____ 2. Leadership that goes beyond ordinary expectations by transmitting a sense of mission, stimulating learning experiences, and inspiring new ways of thinking is called charismatic leadership.

Multiple Choice

_____ 3. Which of the following is a substitute for leadership?
   a. Subordinates' strong need for independence
   b. Experienced subordinates
   c. Rigid reward structure
   d. Routine tasks
   e. All of the above

Online Study Center
ACE the Test
ACE Practice Tests 11.4

Online Study Center   college.hmco.com/pic/griffinSAS

EMERGING APPROACHES TO LEADERSHIP

5 ▷ *Describe three emerging approaches to leadership.*

Recently, three potentially very important new approaches to leadership have emerged. One is called strategic leadership; the others deal with cross-cultural leadership and ethical leadership.

Strategic Leadership

strategic leadership The capability to understand the complexities of both the organization and its environment and to lead change in the organization in order to achieve and maintain a superior alignment between the organization and its environment.

Strategic leadership is a new concept that explicitly relates leadership to the role of top management. We will define **strategic leadership** as the capability to understand the complexities of both the organization and its environment and to lead change in the organization in order to achieve and maintain a superior alignment between the organization and its environment. This definition reflects an integration of the leadership concepts covered in this chapter with our discussion of strategic management in Chapter 3.

To be effective in this role, a manager needs to have a thorough and complete understanding of the organization—its history, its culture, its strengths, and its weaknesses. In addition, the leader needs a firm grasp of the organization's environment. This understanding must encompass current conditions and circumstances as well as significant trends and issues on the horizon. The strategic leader also needs to recognize how the firm is currently aligned with its environment— where it relates effectively and where it relates less effectively with that environment. Finally, looking at environmental trends and issues, the strategic leader works to improve both the current alignment and the future alignment.

Andrea Jung (CEO of Avon Products), Fujio Cho (CEO of Toyota), Michael Dell (founder and CEO of Dell Computer), and A. G. Lafley (CEO of Procter & Gamble) have all been recognized as strong strategic leaders. Reflecting on his dramatic turnaround at Procter & Gamble, for instance, Lafley commented, "I have made a lot of symbolic, very physical changes so people understand we are in the business of leading change." On the other hand, Sandy Weill (CEO of Citigroup), Dick Brown (CEO of Electronic Data Systems), and Peter Dolan (CEO of Bristol-Myers Squibb) have been cited as less effective strategic leaders. For instance, following Dolan's appointment as CEO of Bristol-Myers Squibb the firm's stock price dropped steadily for over two years. While a number of factors contributed to the decline, ineffective strategic leadership clearly played a role.[31]

Cross-Cultural Leadership

Another new approach to leadership is based on cross-cultural issues. In this context, culture is used as a broad concept to encompass both international differences and diversity-based differences within one culture. For instance, when a Japanese firm sends an executive to head the firm's operations in the United States, that person will need to become acclimated to the cultural differences that exist between the two countries and to change his or her leadership style accordingly. For example, Japan is generally characterized by collectivism, whereas the United States is based more on individualism. The Japanese executive, then, will find it necessary to recognize the importance of individual contributions and rewards, as well as the differences in individual and group roles that exist between Japanese and U.S. businesses.

BUILDING EFFECTIVE DECISION-MAKING SKILLS

Online Study Center
Improve Your Grade
Exercises: Building Effective Skills

Exercise Overview

Vroom's decision tree approach to leadership is an effective method for determining how much participation a manager might allow his or her subordinates in making a decision. This exercise will enable you to refine your decision-making skills by applying Vroom's approach to a hypothetical situation.

Exercise Background

Assume that you are the branch manager of the West Coast region of the United States for an international manufacturing and sales company. The company is making a major effort to control costs and boost efficiency. As part of this effort, the firm recently installed a networked computer system linking sales representatives, customer service employees, and other sales support staff. The goal of this network was to increase sales while simultaneously cutting sales expenses.

Unfortunately, just the opposite has resulted—sales are down slightly, but expenses are increasing. You have looked into this problem and believe that the computer hardware that people are using is fine. You also believe, however, that the software that is used to run the system is flawed: It is too hard to use and provides less than complete information.

Your employees disagree with your assessment, however. They believe that the entire system is fine. They attribute the problems to poor training in using the system and to a lack of incentive for using it to solve many problems that they already know how to handle using other methods. Some of them also think that their colleagues are merely resistant to change.

Your boss has just called and instructed you to "solve the problem." She indicated that she has complete faith in your ability to do so, that decisions about how to proceed will be left to you, and that she wants a report suggesting a course of action in five days.

Exercise Task

Using the information presented above, do the following:

1. Using your own personal preferences and intuition, describe how you think you would proceed.

2. Now use Vroom's approach to determine a course of action.

3. Compare and contrast your initial approach with the actions suggested by Vroom's approach.

The Leadership/Management Interview Experiment

Purpose

Leadership and management are in some ways the same, but more often they are different. This exercise offers you an opportunity to develop a conceptual framework for leadership and management.

Introduction

Because most management behaviors and leadership behaviors are a product of individual work experience, each leader/manager tends to have a unique leadership/management style. Analyzing leadership/management styles, comparing such styles, and relating them to different organizational contexts are often rewarding experiences in learning.

Instructions

Fact-finding and Execution of the Experiment

1. Develop a list of questions related to issues you have studied in this chapter that you want to ask a practicing manager and leader during a face-to-face interview. Prior to the actual interview, submit your list of questions to your instructor for approval.

2. Arrange to interview a practicing manager and a practicing leader. For purposes of this assignment, a manager or leader is a person whose job involves supervising the work of other people. The leader/manager may work in a business or in a public or private agency.

3. Interview at least one manager and at least one leader, using the questions you developed. Take good notes on their comments and on your own observations. Do not take more than one hour of each leader's/manager's time.

Online Study Center
Improve Your Grade
    –Exercises: Experiential Exercise
    –Interactive Skills Self-Assessment

Oral Report

Prepare an oral report using the questions here and your interview information. Complete the following report after the interview. (Attach a copy of your interview questions.)

The Leadership/Management Interview Experiment Report

1. How did you locate the leader(s)/manager(s) you interviewed? Describe your initial contacts.
2. Describe the level and responsibilities of your leader(s)/manager(s). Do not supply names—their responses should be anonymous.
3. Describe the interview settings. How long did the interview last?
4. In what ways were the leaders/managers similar or in agreement about issues?
5. What were some of the major differences between the leaders/managers and between the ways in which they approached their jobs?
6. In what ways would the managers agree or disagree with ideas presented in this course?
7. Describe and evaluate your own interviewing style and skills.
8. How did your managers feel about having been interviewed? How do you know that?

CLOSING CASE STUDY

The "New and Improved" Procter & Gamble

Low-key, bespectacled Alan G. Lafley is the unlikely-looking yet successful CEO of Procter & Gamble (P&G), the largest household products company and the maker of megabrands such as Tide, Crest, Charmin, Downy, Pampers, Folgers, Bounty, and Pringles. "If there were 15 people sitting around the conference table, it wouldn't be obvious that he was the CEO," says analyst Ann Gillin-Lefever. Johnathan Rodgers, a P&G board member, says, "He doesn't have that superstar CEO personality." *Fortune* writer Katrina Booker calls Lafley "the un-CEO." But quiet and unassuming Lafley has succeeded in turning around the once-ailing manufacturer when other, more flamboyant leaders have failed. His victory demonstrates the power of a back-to-basics strategy and straightforward leadership.

Procter & Gamble was troubled before Lafley took the reins in 2000. After phenomenal growth through the 1980s, P&G was struggling to expand when sales already topped $40 billion. In the 1990s, for the first time, P&G did not meet its target of doubling sales growth each decade.

The firm had three different CEOs during the 1990s, and the most recent, Durk Jager, served just seventeen months. Jager's aggressive reorganization plan called for focusing attention on new products rather than on best-sellers, but the innovations, such as Olay cosmetics, bombed. Jager moved 110,000 workers into new jobs. P&G began putting American brand names on its global products, but shoppers in Germany and Hong Kong did not recognize "Pantene" and "Dawn." Jager sought to acquire drug makers Warner-Lambert and American Home Products but dropped the idea in response to pressure from investors. Under Jager's strategies, P&G missed earnings targets and lost $70 billion in market value. An aggressive personality did not endear Jager to P&G employees either. "I was lost," says Chris Start, a P&G vice president. "It was like no one knew how to get anything done anymore." After Jager, there was little confidence in Lafley, and P&G stock fell $4 when Lafley's promotion was announced.

Lafley had worked at P&G for twenty-five years before becoming CEO. He knew that the firm could do a better job of selling its winners. Lafley gave the managers of P&G's top ten brands more resources. Lafley

> *"I have made a lot of symbolic, very physical changes so people understand we are in the business of change."*
>
> —A. G. Lafley, CEO, Procter & Gamble

claims, "The trick was to find the few things that were really going to sell, and sell as many of them as you could." He adds, "The essence of our strategy is incredibly simple, but I believe the simplicity is its power. . . . It's Sesame Street—simple, but it works." For example, hair-care managers reinvented top-selling Pantene. Rather than group products by hair type—oily, fine, normal—new groups focused on the look the customer wanted—curls, volumizing. Sales of those top ten products grew by 7 percent annually in 2005.

Rather than insisting that new products be developed internally, Lafley acquired small, idea-driven firms. Lafley states that 50 percent of innovation should come through acquisitions. He says, "That means we would double the productivity of our current investment in R&D." Lafley is demanding better marketability of new products, telling researchers, "Innovation is in the consumer's eyes. . . . It isn't a great innovation until she loves it and purchases it."

Lafley is shaking up the firm's staid culture in other ways, too. "I have made a lot of symbolic, very physical changes so people understand we are in the business of change," he says. At the company's historic Cleveland headquarters, product managers are leaving their executive suites to move closer to their employees. Wood paneling and oil paintings are coming down so that top managers can work as a team in one open, modern space. The rest of the penthouse floor is now a learning center, where top executives deliver some of the training. Lafley asked for these changes because, as he says, "I really believe knowledge is power, and translating knowledge into action in the marketplace is one of the things that distinguishes leadership." Communication among managers, workers, board members, and even competitors has opened up. "You can tell him bad news or things you'd be afraid to tell other bosses," says vice president Start. Lafley rewards managers for financial results and is harsh on poor performers—half of the top team is new.

With a series of small changes, Lafley had a powerful impact on P&G's performance. Earnings beat expectations for four years in a row, and stock prices rose from their 2000 level of $100 per share to over $200 in 2005. P&G grew internationally too, as ten countries each generated more than $1 billion in sales. Lafley continues to emphasize the basics. "Nearly two billion times a day, P&G products are put to the test when consumers use [them]," Lafley reminds his employees. "When we get this right . . . then we begin to earn the trust on which great brands are built." Under Lafley's leadership, P&G is again earning consumers' trust—and their dollars.

Case Questions

1. In what ways is Procter & Gamble's CEO A. G. Lafley acting as a leader? In what ways is he acting as a manager?

2. Does Lafley show job-centered leader behavior, employee-centered leader behavior, or some combination of the two? Explain your answer.

3. Using one or more of the leadership theories presented in the chapter, explain why Lafley is a more effective leader than his predecessor, Durk Jager.

Case References

2002 Annual Report, 2005 Annual Report, www.pg.com on January 28, 2006; Daniel Eisenberg, "A Healthy Gamble," *Time*, September 16, 2002, pp. 46–48; Katrina Booker, "The Un-CEO," *Fortune*, September 16, 2002, pp. 88–96; Robert Berner, "Procter & Gamble's Renovator-in-Chief," *Business-Week*, December 11, 2002, www.businessweek.com on February 9, 2003; Robert Berner, "Why P&G's Smile Is So Bright," *BusinessWeek Small Biz*, www.businessweek.com on February 10, 2003; "The Best and Worst Managers: A. G. Lafley, Procter & Gamble," *BusinessWeek*, January 13, 2003, p. 67 (quote).

Online Study Center
Improve Your Grade
–Learning Objective Review
–Audio Chapter Review
–Study Guide to Go

Online Study Center
ACE the Test
Audio Chapter Quiz

LEARNING OBJECTIVE REVIEW

1 *Describe the nature of leadership and relate leadership to management.*

- As a process, leadership is the use of noncoercive influence to
    shape the group's or organization's goals
    motivate behavior toward the achievement of
      those goals
    help define group or organization culture

- As a property, leadership is the set of characteristics attributed to those who are perceived to be leaders.

- Leadership and management are often related but are also different.

- Managers and leaders use the following types of power:
    legitimate
    reward
    coercive
    referent
    expert

2 *Discuss and evaluate the two generic approaches to leadership.*

- The trait approach to leadership assumed that some basic trait or set of traits differentiated leaders from nonleaders.

- The leadership behavior approach to leadership assumed that the behavior of effective leaders was somehow different from the behavior of nonleaders.

- Research at the University of Michigan and Ohio State University identified two basic forms of leadership behavior:
    that which concentrates on work and performance
    that which concentrates on employee welfare and
      support

- The Leadership Grid attempts to train managers to exhibit high levels of both forms of behavior.

3 *Identify and describe the major situational approaches to leadership.*

- Situational approaches to leadership recognize that no single form of leadership behavior is universally applicable and attempt to specify situations in which various behaviors are appropriate.

- The LPC theory suggests that a leader's behaviors should be either task-oriented or relationship-oriented, depending on the favorableness of the situation.

- The path-goal theory suggests that the following leader behaviors may be appropriate, depending on the personal characteristics of subordinates and on the characteristics of the environment:
    directive
    supportive
    participative
    achievement-oriented

- Vroom's decision tree approach maintains that leaders should vary the extent to which they allow subordinates to participate in making decisions as a function of problem attributes.

- The leader-member exchange model focuses on individual relationships between leaders and followers and on in-group versus out-group considerations.

4 *Identify and describe three related approaches to leadership.*

- Other, related leadership perspectives include
    the concept of substitutes for leadership
    charismatic leadership
    the role of transformational leadership in organizations

5 *Describe three emerging approaches to leadership.*

- Emerging approaches include
    strategic leadership
    cross-cultural leadership
    ethical leadership

6 *Discuss political behavior in organizations and how it can be managed.*

- Political behavior is another influence process frequently used in organizations.

- Impression management, one especially important form of political behavior, is a direct and intentional effort by someone to enhance his or her image in the eyes of others.

- Managers can take steps to limit the effects of political behavior.

Online Study Center **RESOURCES**

Prepare for Class, Improve Your Grade, and ACE the Test. These Student Achievement resources include:

ACE Practice Tests	Interactive Skills Assessments	Study Guide to Go
End of Chapter Exercises	Knowledgebank	Video Segments
Glossaries (visual and print)	Reviews (audio and print)	Summaries/Outlines
Flashcards		

To access these learning and study tools, go to: **college.hmco.com/pic/griffinSAS**

Instant messaging is becoming an increasingly popular method for communication. Wendy Moniz is shown here instant messaging various people at work. A growing number of people say they now use instant messaging at work to get answers, make business decisions, and even interact with clients or customers.

4 ▸ *Discuss informal communication, including its various forms and types.*

3 ▸ *Describe the role of electronic communication in organizations.*

2 ▸ *Identify the basic forms of communication in organizations.*

1 ▸ *Describe the role and importance of communication in the manager's job.*

> *"E-mail is as private as sending a message in a postcard."*
>
> — Common saying among computer experts

Chapter Outline

▶ COMMUNICATION AND THE MANAGER'S JOB
A definition of communication
Characteristics of useful information
The communication process

▶ FORMS OF COMMUNICATION IN ORGANIZATIONS
Interpersonal communication
Communication in networks and work teams
Organizational communication

▶ ELECTRONIC COMMUNICATION
Information systems
Personal electronic technology

▶ INFORMAL COMMUNICATION IN ORGANIZATIONS
The grapevine
Management by wandering around
Nonverbal communication

▶ MANAGING ORGANIZATIONAL COMMUNICATION
Barriers to communication
Improving communication effectiveness

Online Study Center
Prepare for Class
Chapter Outline

---

5 ▶ *Describe how the communication process can be managed to recognize and overcome barriers.*

Information Tidal Wave

The last twenty-five years have seen an explosion of new communication technology. Cell phones, videoconferencing, chat rooms, e-bulletin boards, and instant messaging have revolutionized the way we communicate at home and at work. Out of all these innovations, e-mail has had perhaps the most powerful impact on interpersonal communication. Although that impact has been largely positive, it has also created a host of unique dangers for organizations.

E-mail seems like a dream come true for managers, allowing rapid, inexpensive communication to almost anywhere. E-mail can substitute for written communications, which are slow over distances; for phone calls, which are not possible in some areas; and for face-to-face meetings, which are expensive for far-flung attendees. E-mail offers some of the immediacy of a conversation,

Online Study Center college.hmco.com/pic/griffinSAS

You should be able to define and use terms that are part of the practicing manager's vocabulary, as well as those that are integral in the language of management.

while also enabling the participants to keep a written record of what was "said." Through features such as mailing lists and auto reply, e-mail can broadcast to a large group simultaneously or tell senders that the receiver is unavailable.

Yet e-mail also poses some problems as well. For one thing, it encourages poor communication skills. Conversations provide context—such as tone of voice and body language—along with the message content. But e-mail provides no context. Traditional written communication also provides no context, but because it takes time to prepare, it encourages the sender to reflect carefully before transmission. E-mail, on the other hand, is quick and easy. Thus it sometimes combines the worst of both verbal and written communications by allowing the sender to convey a thoughtless message that does not contain context clues. When intentional, these messages are called "flames," but offensive and confusing messages are often sent by accident, too.

The Direct Marketing Association has released a list of guidelines for eliminating unsolicited junk e-mail, or spam, but few companies have adopted the guidelines. Spam can cost an organization thousands of dollars each year in lost productivity and increased resource demand, simply through the time it takes employees to delete the messages. One expert estimates that legitimate e-mails will make up only 8 percent of the messages in the typical corporate manager's in-box this year, down from 12 percent in 2005.

Critics also worry that e-mail is making workplace relationships more impersonal. Fewer direct interactions between employees can lessen organizational commitment, reduce teamwork, and block creativity.

E-mail, unlike mail or phone conversations, is not protected by any privacy laws. Corporate monitoring of employee e-mail is very common. A Pillsbury employee, for example, lost a privacy suit against his employer. The judges wrote, "We do not find a reasonable expectation of privacy in e-mail communications . . . notwithstanding any assurances that such communications would not be intercepted by management . . . [and] the company's interest in preventing inappropriate and unprofessional comments or even illegal activity over its e-mail system outweighs any privacy interest the employee may have." In other words, it is perfectly legal for employers to monitor employees' e-mail, even if they promise not to.

Liability and legal issues related to e-mail have become problematic also. E-mails provided a "smoking gun" in a number of recent corporate scandals, including those at Enron, Citigroup, and AIG. E-mail messages sent over the Internet or through a firm's internal network allow individuals to intercept or view messages not intended for them. One expert says, "E-mail is as private as sending a message in a postcard." Confidential information is easy to steal from an e-mail. At the *New York Times,* hacker Adrian Lamo obtained illegal access to reporters' online address books. Lamo discovered private home phone numbers and addresses for *Times* contributors, including commentator Rush Limbaugh, Robert Redford, and former president Jimmy Carter.

Of course, e-mail is no longer the "latest and greatest" communication tool. Companies are now turning to text messaging, blogs, wikis (sites that allow groups of workers to share and edit documents), and RSS, which stands for Really Simple Syndication. RSS allows users to ask for information through "subscriptions," rather than accepting whatever information is delivered. Early adopters of wikis and other technologies can cut e-mail volume by 75 percent and overall project time by 50 percent. Of course, these technologies don't eliminate concerns about human error or poor judgment. They only make the process faster![1]

E-mail has become a ubiquitous part of the manager's job. And new technology that provides quick and easy wireless access to the Internet from virtually anywhere promises to continue to revolutionize electronic communication. But communication has always been a vital part of managerial work. Indeed, managers around the world agree that communication is one of their most important tasks. It is important for them to communicate with others in order to convey their vision and goals for the organization. And it is important for others to communicate with them so that they will better understand what is going on in their environment and how they and their organization can become more effective.

This chapter discusses communication, one of the most basic forms of interaction among people. We begin by examining communication in the context of the manager's job. We then identify and discuss forms of interpersonal, group, and organizational communication. After discussing informal means of communication, we describe how organizational communication can be effectively managed.

COMMUNICATION AND THE MANAGER'S JOB

1 ▶ *Describe the role and importance of communication in the manager's job.*

A typical day for a manager includes attending meetings (both scheduled and unscheduled), placing and receiving telephone calls, reading and answering correspondence (both print and electronic), reviewing websites, and walking around the workplace.[2] Most of these activities involve communication. In fact, managers usually spend well over half their time on some form of communication. Communication always involves two or more people, so other behavioral processes, such as motivation, leadership, and group and team interactions, all come into play. Top executives must handle communication effectively if they are to be true leaders.

A Definition of Communication

Imagine three managers working in an office building. The first is all alone but is nevertheless yelling for a subordinate to come help. No one appears, but he continues to yell. The second is talking on the telephone to a subordinate, but static on the line causes the subordinate to misunderstand some important numbers being provided by the manager. As a result, the subordinate sends 1,500 crates of eggs to 150 Fifth Street, when he should have sent 150 crates of eggs to 1500 Fifteenth Street. The third manager is talking in her office with a subordinate who clearly hears and understands what is being said. Each of these managers is attempting to communicate, but with different results.

communication   The process of transmitting information from one person to another.

Communication is the process of transmitting information from one person to another. Did any of our three managers communicate? The last did, and the first did not. How about the second? In fact, she did communicate. She transmitted information, and information was received. The problem was that the message transmitted and the message received were not the same. The words spoken by the manager were distorted by static and noise. **Effective communication**, then, is the process of sending a message in such a way that the message received is as close in meaning as possible to the message intended. Although the second manager engaged in communication, it was not effective.

effective communication   The process of sending a message in such a way that the message received is as close in meaning as possible to the message intended.

A key element in effective communication is differentiating between data and information. **Data** are raw figures and facts reflecting a single aspect of reality. The facts that a plant has 35 machines, that each machine is capable of producing 1,000 units of output per day, that current and projected future demand for the units is 30,000 per day, and that workers sufficiently skilled to run the machines make $20 an hour are data. **Information**, meanwhile, is data presented in a way or form that has meaning.[3] Thus combining and summarizing the four pieces of data given above provides information: The plant has excess capacity and is therefore incurring unnecessary costs. Information has meaning to a manager and provides a basis for action. The plant manager might use the information and decide to sell four machines (perhaps keeping one as a backup) and transfer five operators to other jobs.

data   Raw figures and facts reflecting a single aspect of reality.

information   Data presented in a way or form that has meaning.

Online Study Center
Improve Your Grade
Career Snapshot 12.1

Characteristics of Useful Information

What characteristics make the difference between information that is useful and information that is not useful? In general, information is useful if it is accurate, timely, complete, and relevant.

accurate information   Information that provides a valid and reliable reflection of reality.

1. *Accurate.*   For information to be of real value to a manager, it must be **accurate information**. *Accuracy* means that the information provides a valid and reliable reflection of reality. A Japanese construction company once bought information from a consulting firm about a possible building site in London. The Japanese were told that the land, which would be sold in a sealed-bid auction, would attract bids of close to $250 million. They were also told that the land currently held an old building that could readily be demolished. Thus the

Japanese bid $255 million—which ended up being $90 million more than the next-highest bid. And to make matters worse, a few days later the British government declared the building historic, preventing any possibility of demolition. Clearly, the Japanese acted on information that was less than accurate. More recently, President Bush's decision to invade Iraq was apparently based, at least in part, on faulty information regarding that country's possession of weapons of mass destruction.

2. *Timely.* Timeliness does not necessarily mean speediness; it means only that information needs to be available in time for appropriate managerial action. What constitutes **timely information** is a function of the situation facing the manager. When Marriott was gathering information for a new hotel project a few years ago, managers allowed themselves a six-month period for data collection. They felt this would give them an opportunity to do a good job of getting the information they needed while not delaying things too much. In contrast, Marriott's computerized reservation and accounting system can provide a manager today with last night's occupancy level at any Marriott facility.[4]

   timely information Information that is available in time for appropriate managerial action.

3. *Complete.* If information is less than **complete information**, the manager is likely to get an inaccurate or distorted picture of reality. For example, managers at Kroger used to think that house-brand products were more profitable than national brands because they yielded higher unit profits. On the basis of this information, they gave house brands a great deal of shelf space and organized promotional activities around them. As Kroger's managers became more sophisticated in understanding their information, however, they realized that national brands were actually more profitable over time, because they sold many more units than house brands during any given period of time. Hence, although a store might sell 10 cans of Kroger coffee in a day, with a profit of 50 cents per can (total profit of $5), it would also sell 15 cans of Maxwell House, with a profit of 40 cents per can (total profit of $6), and 10 vacuum bags of Starbucks coffee, with a profit of $1 per bag (total profit of $10). With this more complete picture, managers could do a better job of selecting the right mix of Kroger, Maxwell House, and Starbucks coffee to display and promote.

   complete information Information that provides the manager with all the information he or she needs.

4. *Relevant.* **Relevant information**, like timely information, is defined according to the needs and circumstances of a particular manager. Operations managers need information on costs and productivity; human resource managers need information on hiring needs and turnover rates; and marketing managers need information on sales projections and advertising rates. As Wal-Mart contemplates various countries as possible expansion opportunities, it gathers information about local regulations, customs, and so forth. But the information about any given country is not really relevant until the decision is made to enter that market.

   relevant information Information that is useful to managers in their particular circumstances for their particular needs.

The Communication Process

Figure 12.1 illustrates how communication generally takes place between people. The process of communication begins when one person (the sender) wants to transmit a fact, idea, opinion, or other information to someone else (the receiver). This fact, idea, or opinion has meaning to the sender, whether it be simple and concrete or complex and abstract. The next step is to encode the meaning into a form appropriate to the situation. The encoding might take the form of words, facial expressions, gestures, or even artistic expressions and physical actions.

FIGURE 12.1

The Communication Process

"Noise" can disrupt the communication process at any step. Managers must therefore understand that a conversation in the next office, a fax machine out of paper, and the receiver's worries may all thwart the manager's best attempts to communicate. The numbers in the diagram indicate the sequence in which steps take place.

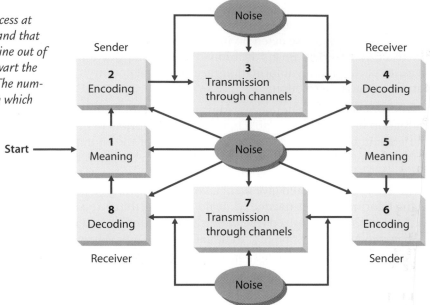

After the message has been encoded, it is transmitted through the appropriate channel or medium. The channel by which this encoded message is being transmitted to you is the printed page. Common channels in organizations include meetings, e-mail, memos, letters, reports, and telephone calls. After the message is received, it is decoded back into a form that has meaning for the receiver. As noted earlier, the consistency of this meaning can vary dramatically. In many cases, the meaning prompts a response, and the cycle is continued when a new message is sent, by the same steps, back to the original sender.

"Noise" may disrupt communication anywhere along the way. Noise can be the sound of someone coughing, a truck driving by, or two people talking close at hand. It can also include disruptions such as a letter lost in the mail, a dead telephone line, an interrupted cell phone call, an e-mail misrouted or infected with a virus, or one of the participants in a conversation being called away before the communication process is completed.

Online Study Center
Improve Your Grade
Knowledgebank 12.1

TEST PREPPER 12.1
ANSWERS CAN BE FOUND ON P. 442

True or False?

_____ 1. Effective communication occurs when the message received is as close as possible to the message sent.

_____ 2. Information is raw facts and figures reflecting a single aspect of reality.

_____ 3. "Statistics lie" is a cliché reflecting the challenge of using data in a way that is accurate.

Online Study Center
ACE the Test
ACE Practice Tests 12.1

Multiple Choice

_____ 4. Managers spend most of their time_____.
   a. working with other people
   b. communicating with other people
   c. interacting with other people
   d. e-mailing other people
   e. doing all of the above

_____ 5. Ben and Jerry's relies heavily on inventory information to ensure customer satisfaction. Data that Cherry Garcia sales have gone flat would be categorized as_____.
   a. timely   d. accurate
   b. complete   e. all of the above
   c. relevant

FORMS OF COMMUNICATION IN ORGANIZATIONS

2 ► *Identify the basic forms of communication in organizations.*

Managers need to understand several kinds of communication that are common in organizations today. These include interpersonal communication, communication in networks and teams, organizational communication, and electronic communication. The first three are discussed in this section; electronic communication is the subject of the next section.

Interpersonal Communication

Interpersonal communication generally takes one of two forms: oral and written. As we will see, each has clear strengths and weaknesses.

Oral Communication

Oral communication takes place in conversations, group discussions, telephone calls, and other situations in which the spoken word is used to express meaning. One study (conducted before the advent of e-mail) demonstrated the importance of oral communication when it revealed that most managers spent between 50 and 90 percent of their time talking to people.[5] Oral communication is very popular for several reasons.

People communicate with one another in a variety of ways and in many different settings. Consider this team of Netscape employees. They are using oral communication as they talk while they eat lunch. They are also using written communication from the papers stacked on the table and electronic communication in the form of e-mail. Moreover, they are using nonverbal communication with their body language and facial expressions.

▌ It promotes prompt feedback and interchange in the form of verbal questions or agreement, facial expressions, and gestures.

▌ It is easy (all the sender needs to do is talk), and it can be done with little preparation (though careful preparation is advisable in certain situations).

▌ The sender does not need pencil and paper, computer, or other equipment.

▌ In one survey, 55 percent of the executives sampled felt that their own written communication skills were fair or poor, so they chose oral communication to avoid embarrassment.[6]

However, oral communication also has drawbacks.

▌ It may suffer from problems of inaccuracy if the speaker chooses the wrong words to convey meaning or leaves out pertinent details, if noise disrupts the process, or if the receiver forgets part of the message.[7]

▌ In a two-way discussion, there is seldom time for a thoughtful, considered response or for introducing many new facts, and there is no permanent record of what has been said.

▌ Although most managers are comfortable talking to people individually or in small groups, fewer enjoy speaking to larger audiences.[8]

oral communication Face-to-face conversation, group discussions, telephone calls, and other circumstances in which the spoken word is used to transmit meaning.

Written Communication

written communication Memos, letters, reports, notes, and other circumstances in which the written word is used to transmit meaning.

"Putting it in writing" in a letter, report, memorandum, handwritten note, or e-mail can solve many of the problems inherent in oral communication. Nevertheless, and perhaps surprisingly, **written communication** is not as common as one might imagine, nor is it a mode of communication much respected by managers. One sample of managers indicated that only 13 percent of the printed mail they received was of immediate use to them.[9] Over 80 percent of the managers who responded to another survey indicated that the written communication they received was of fair or poor quality.[10]

Oral communication has its drawbacks.

▋ It inhibits feedback and interchange. When one manager sends another manager a letter, it must be written or dictated, typed, mailed, received, routed, opened, and read. If there is a misunderstanding, it may take several days for it even to be recognized, let alone rectified.

▋ The use of e-mail is much faster, but both sender and receiver must still have access to a computer, and the receiver must open and read the message in order for it actually to be received. A phone call could settle the whole matter in just a few minutes. Thus written communication is usually more difficult and time-consuming than oral communication.

However, written communication has its advantages.

▋ It is often quite accurate and provides a permanent record of the exchange.

▋ The sender can take the time to collect and assimilate the information and can draft and revise it before it is transmitted.

▋ The receiver can take the time to read it carefully and can refer to it repeatedly, as needed.

For these reasons, written communication is generally preferable when important details are involved. At times it is important to one or both parties to have a written record available as evidence of exactly what took place. Julie Regan, founder of Toucan-Do, an importing company based in Honolulu, relies heavily on formal business letters in establishing contacts and buying merchandise from vendors in Southeast Asia. She believes that such letters give her an opportunity to think through carefully what she wants to say, tailor her message to each individual, and avoid later misunderstandings.

Choosing the Right Form

The best form of interpersonal communication will be determined by the situation. Oral communication or e-mail is often preferred when the message is personal, nonroutine, and brief. More formal written communication is usually best when the message is more impersonal, routine, and longer. And, given the prominent role that e-mails have played in several recent court cases, managers should always use discretion when sending messages electronically.[11] For example, private e-mails made public during legal proceedings have played major roles in litigation involving Enron, Tyco, and WorldCom.[12]

The manager can also combine media to capitalize on the advantages of each. For example, a quick telephone call to set up a meeting is easy and gets an immediate response. Following up the call with a reminder e-mail or handwritten note helps ensure that the recipient will remember the meeting, and it provides a record of the meeting's having been called. Electronic communication, discussed more fully later, blurs the differences between oral and written communication and can help each be more effective.

Communication in Networks and Work Teams

Although communication among team members in an organization is clearly interpersonal in nature, substantial research also focuses specifically on how people in networks and work teams communicate with one another. A **communication network** is the pattern through which the members of a group or team communicate. Researchers studying group dynamics have discovered several typical networks in groups and teams consisting of three, four, and five members.[13]

- *The wheel pattern.* All communication flows through one central person, who is probably the group's leader. The wheel is the most centralized network, because one person receives and disseminates all information.

- *The Y pattern.* This is slightly less centralized—two people are close to the center.

- *The chain pattern.* This offers a more even flow of information among members, although two people (the people at either end) interact with only one other person. This path is closed in the circle pattern.

- *The all-channel network.* This is the most decentralized, allowing a free flow of information among all group members. Everyone participates equally, and the group's leader, if there is one, is not likely to have excessive power.

Research conducted on networks suggests some interesting connections between the type of network and group performance:

- When the group's task is *relatively simple and routine*, centralized networks tend to perform with greatest efficiency and accuracy. The dominant leader facilitates performance by coordinating the flow of information.

- When the task is *complex and nonroutine*, such as when making a major decision about organizational strategy, decentralized networks tend to be most effective, because open channels of communication permit more interaction and a more efficient sharing of relevant information.

Managers should recognize the effects of communication networks on group and organization performance and should try to structure networks appropriately.

Organizational Communication

Still other forms of communication in organizations are those that flow among and between organizational units or groups. Each of these involves oral or written communication, but each also extends to broad patterns of communication across the organization.[14] As shown in Figure 12.2, two of these forms of communication follow vertical and horizontal linkages in the organization.

Vertical Communication

Vertical communication flows up and down the organization, usually along formal reporting lines—that is, it is the communication that takes place between managers and their superiors and subordinates. Vertical communication may involve only two people, or it may flow through several different organizational levels.

communication network The pattern through which the members of a group communicate.

Online Study Center
Improve Your Grade
Career Snapshot 12.2

vertical communication Communication that flows up and down the organization, usually along formal reporting lines; takes place between managers and their subordinates and may involve several different levels of the organization.

FIGURE 12.2

Formal Communication in Organizations

Formal communication in organizations follows official reporting relationships or prescribed channels. For example, vertical communication, shown here with solid lines, flows between levels in the organization and involves subordinates and their managers. Horizontal communication, shown with dashed lines, flows between people at the same level and is generally used to facilitate coordination.

← ———— Vertical communication

← – – – – Horizontal communication

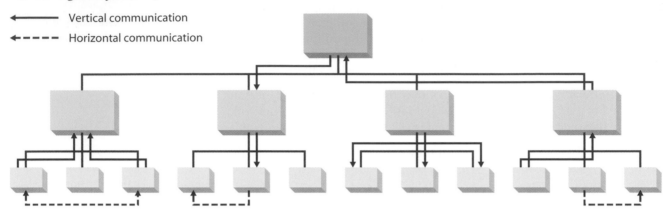

■ *Upward communication* consists of messages from subordinates to superiors, usually from subordinates to their direct superior, then to that person's direct superior, and so on up the hierarchy. Occasionally, a message might bypass a particular superior. The typical content of upward communication is requests, information that the lower-level manager thinks is of importance to the higher-level manager, responses to requests from the higher-level manager, suggestions, complaints, and financial information. Research has shown that upward communication is more subject to distortion than downward communication. Subordinates are likely to withhold or distort information that makes them look bad. The greater the degree of difference in status between superior and subordinate and the greater the degree of distrust, the more likely the subordinate is to suppress or distort information.[15] For example, subordinates might choose to withhold information about problems from their boss if they think the news will make the boss angry and if they think they can solve the problem themselves without her or his ever knowing about it.

■ *Downward communication* occurs when information flows down the hierarchy from superiors to subordinates. The typical content of these messages is directives on how something is to be done, the assignment of new responsibilities, performance feedback, and general information that the higher-level manager thinks will be of value to the lower-level manager. Vertical communication can and usually should be two-way in nature. In other words, give-and-take communication with active feedback is generally likely to be more effective than one-way communication.[16]

Horizontal Communication

horizontal communication Communication that flows laterally within the organization; involves colleagues and peers at the same level of the organization and may involve individuals from several different organizational units.

Horizontal communication involves colleagues and peers at the same level of the organization. For example, an operations manager might communicate to a marketing manager that inventory levels are running low and that projected delivery dates should be extended by two weeks. Horizontal communication probably occurs more among managers than among nonmanagers. This type of communication serves a number of purposes.[17]

▌ It facilitates coordination among interdependent units. For example, a manager at Motorola was once researching the strategies of Japanese semiconductor firms in Europe. He found a great deal of information that was relevant to his assignment. He also uncovered some additional information that was potentially important to another department; so he passed it along to a colleague in that department, who used it to improve his own operations.

▌ It can be used for joint problem solving, as when two plant managers at Northrop Grumman got together to work out a new method to improve productivity.

▌ It plays a major role in work teams made up of members drawn from several departments.

TEST PREPPER 12.2

ANSWERS CAN BE FOUND ON P. 442

True or False?

_____ 1. A standard operating procedure is best communicated orally.

_____ 2. Studies show that managers generally prefer written communication to oral communication.

_____ 3. The marketing director tells the operations director that a new campaign will start next week. This is horizontal communication.

Multiple Choice

_____ 4. Which of the following is an example of noise in communication?
   a. A lost memo
   b. Telephone static
   c. An e-mail infected with a virus
   d. A helicopter flying overhead
   e. All of the above

_____ 5. Which of the following is NOT an advantage of oral communication?
   a. Prompt feedback   d. Ease
   b. Accuracy   e. Voice inflection
   c. Little preparation

_____ 6. Which form of communication is most appropriate for a performance appraisal?
   a. Oral   d. E-mail
   b. Written   e. All of the above
   c. Oral and written

_____ 7. Which type of network exists when all communication flows through one person?
   a. Chain   d. Wheel
   b. Circle   e. Y
   c. All-channel

_____ 8. The team approach to problem solving would most likely use which type of communication network?
   a. Chain   d. Wheel
   b. Circle   e. Y
   c. All-channel

_____ 9. Communication that usually flows along formal reporting lines and takes place between managers and their subordinates and may involve several different levels of the organization is called _____ communication.
   a. vertical   d. virtual
   b. horizontal   e. circular
   c. diagonal

Online Study Center
ACE the Test
ACE Practice Tests 12.2

ELECTRONIC COMMUNICATION

3 ▷ *Describe the role of electronic communication in organizations.*

An increasingly important form of organizational communication relies on electronic communication technology. **Information technology**, or **IT**, consists of the resources used by an organization to manage information that it needs in order to carry out its mission. IT may consist of computers, computer networks, telephones, fax machines, and other pieces of hardware. In addition, IT involves software that facilitates the system's ability to manage information in a way that is useful for managers. Both formal information systems and personal information technology have reshaped how managers communicate with one another.[18]

Information Systems

Advances in information technology have made it increasingly easy for managers to use many different kinds of information systems. In this section we discuss ten of the most common kinds of information systems used by businesses today.

1. **Transaction-processing systems (TPS)** are applications of information processing for basic day-to-day business transactions. Customer order taking by online retailers, approval of claims at insurance companies, receipt and confirmation of reservations by airlines, payroll processing and bill payment at almost every company—all are routine business processes. Typically, the TPS for first-level (operational) activities is well defined, with predetermined data requirements, and follows the same steps to complete all transactions in the system.

2. *Systems for knowledge workers and office applications* support the activities of both knowledge workers and employees in clerical positions. They provide assistance for data processing and other office activities, including the creation of communications documents. Like other departments, the information systems (IS) department includes both knowledge workers and data workers.

3. *Systems for operations and data workers* make sure that the right programs are run in the correct sequence, and they monitor equipment to ensure that it is operating properly. Many organizations also have employees who enter data into the system for processing.

4. *Knowledge-level and office systems.* Needless to say, the explosion of new support systems—word processing, document imaging, desktop publishing, computer-aided design, simulation modeling—has increased the productivity of both knowledge and office workers. Desktop publishing combines graphics and word-processing text to publish professional-quality print and Web documents. Document-imaging systems can scan paper documents and images, convert them into digital form for storage on disks, retrieve them, and transmit them electronically to workstations throughout the network.

5. **Management information systems (MIS)** support an organization's managers by providing daily reports, schedules, plans, and budgets. Each manager's information activities vary according to his or her functional area (say, accounting or marketing) and management level. Whereas midlevel managers focus mostly on internal activities and information, higher-level managers are also

---

information technology (IT) Consists of the resources used by an organization to manage information that it needs in order to carry out its mission.

transaction-processing system (TPS) An application of information processing for basic day-to-day business transactions.

Online Study Center
Improve Your Grade
Knowledgebank 12.2

management information system (MIS) An information system that supports an organization's managers by providing daily reports, schedules, plans, and budgets.

engaged in external activities. Middle managers, the largest MIS user group, need networked information to plan such upcoming activities as personnel training, materials movements, and cash flows. They also need to know the current status of the jobs and projects being carried out in their department: What stage is it at now? When will it be finished? Is there an opening so we can start the next job? Many of a firm's management information systems—cash flow, sales, production scheduling, shipping—are indispensable in helping managers find answers to such questions.

6. **Decision support systems (DSS)** are interactive systems that locate and present information needed to support the decision-making process. Whereas some DSSs are devoted to specific problems, others serve more general purposes, allowing managers to analyze different types of problems. Thus a firm that often faces decisions on plant capacity, for example, may have a capacity DSS: The manager inputs data on anticipated levels of sales, working capital, and customer delivery requirements. Then the DSS's built-in transaction processors manipulate the data and make recommendations on the best levels of plant capacity for each future time period. In contrast, a general-purpose system, such as a marketing DSS, might respond to a variety of marketing-related problems. It may be programmed to handle "what if" questions, such as "When is the best time to introduce a new product if my main competitor introduces one in three months, our new product has an eighteen-month expected life, demand is seasonal with a peak in autumn, and my goal is to gain the largest possible market share?" The DSS can help managers make decisions for which predetermined solutions are unknown by using sophisticated modeling tools and data analysis.

> **decision support system (DSS)**   An interactive system that locates and presents information needed to support the decision-making process.

7. An **executive support system (ESS)** is a quick-reference, easy-access application of information systems specially designed for instant access by upper-level managers. ESSs are designed to assist with executive-level decisions and problems, ranging from "What lines of business should we be in five years from now?" to "Based on forecasted developments in electronic technologies, to what extent should our firm be globalized in five years? in ten years?" The ESS also uses a wide range of both internal information and external sources, such as industry reports, global economic forecasts, and reports on competitors' capabilities. Because senior-level managers do not usually possess advanced computer skills, they prefer systems that are easily accessible and adaptable. Accordingly, ESSs are not designed to address only specific, predetermined problems. Instead, they allow the user some flexibility in attacking a variety of problem situations. They are easily accessible by means of simple keyboard strokes or even voice commands.

> **executive support system (ESS)**   A quick-reference, easy-access application of information systems specially designed for instant access by upper-level managers.

8. **Artificial intelligence (AI)** can be defined as the construction of computer systems, both hardware and software, to imitate human behavior—in other words, systems that perform physical tasks, use thought processes, and learn. In developing AI systems, knowledge workers (business specialists, modelers, and information technology experts) try to design computer-based systems capable of reasoning, so that computers, instead of people, can perform certain business activities. Examples include the following:
   - A credit evaluation system that decides which loan applicants are creditworthy and which ones are risky and then composes acceptance and rejection letters accordingly.

> **artificial intelligence (AI)**   The construction of computer systems, both hardware and software, to imitate human behavior—that is, to perform physical tasks, use thought processes, and learn.

- An *expert system* that is designed to imitate the thought processes of human experts in a particular field. Expert systems incorporate the rules that an expert applies to specific types of problems, such as the judgments a physician makes in diagnosing illnesses. In effect, expert systems supply everyday users with "instant expertise." A system called MOCA (for Maintenance Operations Center Advisor), by imitating the thought processes of a maintenance manager, schedules routine maintenance for American Airlines' entire fleet.

intranet A communications network similar to the Internet but operating within the boundaries of a single organization.

9. **Intranets**, or private Internet networks, are accessible only to employees via entry through electronic firewalls. Firewalls are used to limit access to an intranet. Ford's intranet connects 120,000 workstations in Asia, Europe, and the United States to thousands of Ford websites containing private information on Ford activities in production, engineering, distribution, and marketing. Sharing such information has helped reduce the lead time for getting models into production from thirty-six to twenty-four months. Ford's latest project in improving customer service through internal information sharing is called manufacturing on demand. Now, for example, the Mustang that required fifty days' delivery time in 1996 is available in less than two weeks. The savings to Ford, of course, will be billions of dollars in inventory and fixed costs.[19]

extranet A communications network that allows selected outsiders limited access to an organization's internal information system, or intranet.

10. **Extranets** allow outsiders limited access to a firm's intranet. The most common application allows buyers to enter the seller's system to see which products are available for sale and delivery, thus providing product availability information quickly to outside buyers. Industrial suppliers, too, are often linked into their customers' intranets so that they can see planned production schedules and make supplies ready as needed for customers' upcoming operations.

Personal Electronic Technology

In recent years, the nature of organizational communication has changed dramatically, mainly because of breakthroughs in personal electronic communication technology, and the future promises even more change. Electronic typewriters and photocopying machines were early breakthroughs. The photocopier, for example, makes it possible for a manager to have a typed report distributed to large numbers of other people in an extremely short time. Personal computers have accelerated the process even more. E-mail networks, the Internet, and corporate intranets are carrying communication technology ever further.

It is also becoming common to have teleconferences in which managers stay at their own location (such as offices in different cities) but are seen on television or computer monitors as they "meet." A manager in New York can keyboard a letter or memorandum at her personal computer, point and click with a mouse, and have it delivered to hundreds or even thousands of colleagues around the world in a matter of seconds. Highly detailed information can be retrieved with ease from large electronic databanks. This has given rise to a new version of an old work arrangement—the cottage industry. In a cottage industry, people work at home (in their "cottage") and periodically bring the products of their labors in to the company. "Telecommuting" is the label given to a new electronic cottage industry. In telecommuting, people work at home on their computer and transmit their work to the company via telephone line or cable modem.

Cellular telephones and facsimile machines have made it even easier for managers to communicate with one another. Many now use cell phones to make calls while commuting to and from work, and some carry them in their briefcases so that they can receive calls while at lunch. Facsimile machines make it easy for people to use written communication media and get rapid feedback. And new personal computing devices, such as Palm Pilots, are revolutionizing how people communicate with one another. Wi-Fi technology is further extending the impact of these devices.

Psychologists, however, are beginning to associate some problems with these communication advances. For one thing, managers who are seldom in their "real" office are likely to fall behind in their field and to be victimized by organizational politics because they are not present to keep in touch with what is going on and to protect themselves. They drop out of the organizational grapevine and miss out on much of the informal communication that takes place. Moreover, the use of electronic communication at the expense of face-to-face meetings and conversations makes it hard to build a strong culture, develop solid working relationships, and create a mutually supportive atmosphere of trust and cooperativeness.[20] Finally, electronic communication is opening up new avenues for dysfunctional employee behavior, such as the passing of lewd or offensive materials to others. For example, the *New York Times* recently fired almost 10 percent of its workers at one of its branch offices for sending inappropriate e-mails at work.[21]

CONCEPT CHECK 12.1

How are electronic communication devices likely to affect the communication process in the future? Describe both the advantages and the disadvantages of these devices over traditional communication methods, such as face-to-face conversations, written notes, and phone calls.

TEST PREPPER 12.3

ANSWERS CAN BE FOUND ON P. 442

True or False?

_____ 1. Transaction-processing systems are used primarily for first-level activities.

_____ 2. Artificial intelligence systems "see, hear, and feel."

_____ 3. A decision support system supports an organization's manager by providing daily reports, schedules, plans, and budgets.

_____ 4. Wal-Mart shares inventory information with Procter & Gamble. The two firms are part of an intranet.

_____ 5. Jill writes for a publishing company. Information systems enable her to work whenever she chooses from a computer at home. Telecommuting created by information systems allows her to have flextime.

_____ 6. An information system designed to imitate the thought processes of human experts in a particular field is called an intranet.

Multiple Choice

_____ 7. _____ refers to the resources used by an organization to manage information that it needs to carry out its mission.
    a. Information technology   d. DSS
    b. TSS   e. ESS
    c. MIS

_____ 8. When you make a reservation on Travelocity, you have just used a(n) _____.
    a. TPS   d. ESS
    b. MIS   e. intranet
    c. DSS

_____ 9. The computer ranking system used in college football to imitate the thought processes of humans to determine the national champion is (debatably) classified as a(n) _____.
    a. MIS   d. ESS
    b. expert system   e. intranet
    c. DSS

Online Study Center
ACE the Test
ACE Practice Tests 12.3

INFORMAL COMMUNICATION IN ORGANIZATIONS

▶ 4 *Discuss informal communication, including its various forms and types.*

The forms of organizational communication that we have discussed up to this point generally represent planned and relatively formal communication mechanisms. However, in many cases some of the communication that takes place in an organization transcends these formal channels and instead follows any of several informal paths. Figure 12.3 illustrates numerous examples of informal communication. Common forms of informal communication in organizations include the grapevine, management by wandering around, and nonverbal communication.

The Grapevine

grapevine An informal communication network among people in an organization.

The **grapevine** is an informal communication network that can permeate an entire organization. Grapevines are found in all organizations except the very smallest, but they do not always follow the same patterns as, nor do they necessarily coincide with, formal channels of authority and communication. Research has identified several kinds of grapevines.[22] The two most common are illustrated in Figure 12.4.

There is some disagreement about how accurate the information carried by the grapevine is, but research is increasingly finding it to be fairly accurate, especially when the information is based on fact rather than speculation. One study found that the grapevine may be between 75 percent and 95 percent accurate.[23] That same study also found that informal communication is increasing in many organizations for two basic reasons. One contributing factor is the recent increase in merger, acquisition, and takeover activity. Because such activity can greatly affect the people within an organization, it is natural for them to spend more time talking about it.[24] The second contributing factor is that as more and more corporations move facilities from inner cities to suburbs, employees tend to talk less and less to others outside the organization and more and more to one another.

FIGURE 12.3

Informal Communication in Organizations

Informal communication in organizations may or may not follow official reporting relationships or prescribed channels. It may cross different levels and different departments or work units, and it may or may not have anything to do with official organizational business.

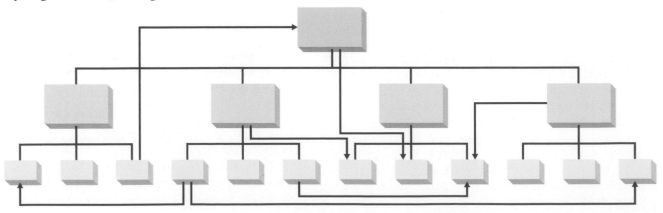

FIGURE 12.4

Common Grapevine Chains Found in Organizations

The two most common grapevine chains in organizations are the gossip chain (in which one person communicates messages to many others) and the cluster chain (in which many people pass messages to a few others).

From Keith Davis and John W. Newstrom, *Human Behavior at Work: Organizational Behavior,* Eighth Edition, 1989. Copyright © 1989 The McGraw-Hill Companies, Inc. Reprinted with permission.

Gossip Chain
One person tells many

Cluster Chain
Many people tell a few

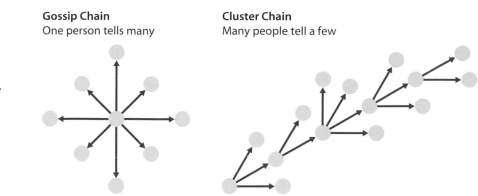

Attempts to eliminate the grapevine are fruitless, but fortunately the manager does have some control over it. By maintaining open channels of communication and responding vigorously to inaccurate information, the manager can minimize the damage the grapevine can do. In fact, the grapevine can actually be an asset. By learning who the key people in the grapevine are, for example, the manager can partially control the information they receive and use the grapevine to sound out employee reactions to new ideas, such as a possible change in human resource policies or benefit packages. The manager can also get valuable information from the grapevine and use it to improve decision making.[25]

Management by Wandering Around

The basic idea of **management by wandering around**[26] is that some managers keep in touch with what is going on by wandering around and talking with people—immediate subordinates, subordinates far down the organizational hierarchy, delivery people, customers, or anyone else who is involved with the company in some way. Bill Marriott, for example, frequently visits the kitchens, loading docks, and custodial work areas whenever he tours a Marriott hotel. He claims that by talking with employees throughout the hotel, he gets new ideas and gains a better feel for the entire company. A related form of organizational communication, for which there is really no specific term, is the informal interchange that takes place outside the normal work setting. Employees attending the company picnic, playing on the company softball team, or taking fishing trips together nearly always spend part of their time talking about work. For example, Texas Instruments engineers at TI's Lewisville, Texas, facility often frequent a local bar in town after work. On any given evening, they talk about the Dallas Cowboys, the newest government contract received by the company, the weather, their boss, the company's stock price, local politics, and problems at work. There is no set agenda, and the key topics of discussion vary from group to group and from day to day. Still, the social gatherings play an important role. They promote a strong culture and enhance understanding of how the organization works.

management by wandering around   An approach to communication that involves the manager's literally wandering around and having spontaneous conversations with others.

Management by wandering around can be an effective method for communicating with others. Jim Whitehurst, Delta Airlines chief operating officer (wearing tie), talks with Delta Technical Operations Center employees at the facility in Atlanta. A former industry consultant, Whitehurst has rapidly moved up the ladder in his four years at Delta. The 38-year-old executive says he's focused on winning over employees who have been concerned about job and pay cuts at the bankrupt airline. Informal and spontaneous discussions like this one may help turn the company around.

Nonverbal Communication

nonverbal communication Any communication exchange that does not use words or that amplifies the meanings of words to convey more than the strict definition of the words themselves.

Nonverbal communication, a powerful but little-understood form of communication, is an exchange that does not use words or that amplifies the meanings of words to convey more than the strict definition of the words themselves. It often relies on facial expressions, body movements, physical contact, and gestures. One study found that as much as 55 percent of the content of a message is transmitted by facial expressions and body posture and that another 38 percent derives from inflection and tone. Words themselves account for only 7 percent of the content of the message.[27] Research has identified three kinds of nonverbal communication practiced by managers—images, settings, and body language.[28]

1. *Images* are the kinds of words people elect to use. "Damn the torpedoes, full speed ahead" and "Even though there are some potential hazards, we should proceed with this course of action" may convey the same meaning. Yet the person who uses the first expression may be perceived as a maverick, a courageous hero, an individualist, or a reckless and foolhardy adventurer. The person who uses the second might be described as aggressive, forceful, diligent, or narrow-minded and resistant to change. In short, our choice of words conveys much more than the strict meaning of the words themselves.

2. The *setting* for communication also plays a major role in nonverbal communication. Boundaries, familiarity, the home turf, and other elements of the setting are all important. Much has been written about the symbols of power in organizations. The size and location of an office, the kinds of furniture in the office, and the accessibility of the person in the office all communicate useful information. For example, H. Ross Perot positions his desk so that it is always between him and a visitor. This keeps him in charge. When he wants a less formal dialogue, he moves around to the front of the desk and sits beside his visitor.

3. A third form of nonverbal communication is *body language*.[29] The distance we stand from someone as we speak has meaning. In the United States, standing very close to someone you are talking to generally signals either familiarity or aggression. The English and Germans stand farther apart than Americans when talking, whereas the Arabs, Japanese, and Mexicans stand closer together.[30] Eye contact is another effective means of nonverbal communication. For example, prolonged eye contact might suggest either hostility or romantic interest. Other kinds of body language include body and hand movement, pauses in speech, and mode of dress.

The manager should be aware of the importance of nonverbal communication and recognize its potential impact. Giving an employee good news about a reward with the wrong nonverbal cues can destroy the reinforcement value of the reward. Likewise, reprimanding an employee but providing inconsistent nonverbal cues can limit the effectiveness of the sanctions. The tone of the message, where and how the message is delivered, facial expressions, and gestures can all amplify or weaken the message or change the message altogether.

CONCEPT CHECK 12.2

What forms of communication have you experienced today? What form of communication is involved in the following situations:
1. A face-to-face conversation with a friend?
2. A telephone call from a customer?
3. A traffic light or crossing signal?
4. A picture of a cigarette in a circle with a slash across it?

True or False?

_____ 1. Craig makes a point of leaving the office and talking to assembly-line workers. He practices management by wandering around.

Multiple Choice

_____ 2. The _____ is an informal communication network among people in an organization.
  a. channel   d. intranet
  b. e-mail   e. grapevine
  c. network

_____ 3. Which of the following statements is true of the grapevine?
  a. The information is 75 to 95 percent accurate.
  b. Employees rely on it more during mergers and acquisitions.

  c. It is impossible to eliminate.
  d. It is used more often as employees talk less to others outside the organization.
  e. All of the above

_____ 4. Nonverbal communication does which of the following?
  a. Accounts for more than 90 percent of communication
  b. Includes images
  c. Includes size of an office
  d. Includes body language
  e. All of the above

Online Study Center
ACE the Test
ACE Practice Tests 12.4

MANAGING ORGANIZATIONAL COMMUNICATION

5 ▶ *Describe how the communication process can be managed to recognize and overcome barriers.*

In view of the importance and pervasiveness of communication in organizations, it is vital for managers to understand how to manage the communication process.[31] Managers should understand how to maximize the potential benefits of communication and minimize the potential problems. We begin our discussion of communication management by considering the factors that might disrupt effective communication and then discuss how to deal with them.

Barriers to Communication

Individual Barriers

Several individual barriers may disrupt effective communication.

▌ *Conflicting or inconsistent signals* are sent when a manager says on Monday that things should be done one way but then prescribes an entirely different procedure on Wednesday. Inconsistent signals are being sent by a manager who says that he has an "open-door" policy and wants his subordinates to drop by but keeps his door closed and becomes irritated whenever someone stops in.

▌ *Credibility* problems arise when the sender is not considered a reliable source of information. He may not be trusted or may not be perceived as knowledgeable about the subject at hand. When a politician is caught withholding information or when a manager makes a series of bad decisions, the extent to which she will be listened to and believed thereafter diminishes. In extreme cases, people may talk about something they obviously know little or nothing about.

BUILDING EFFECTIVE TECHNICAL SKILLS

Exercise Overview

Technical skills are the skills necessary to perform the work of the organization. This exercise will help you develop and apply technical skills involving the Internet and its potential for gathering information relevant to important decisions.

Exercise Background

Assume that you are a manager for a large national retailer. You have been assigned the responsibility for identifying potential locations for the construction of a warehouse and distribution center. The idea behind such a center is that the firm can use its enormous purchasing power to buy many products in bulk quantities at relatively low prices. Individual stores can then order the specific quantities they need from the warehouse.

The location must include a great deal of land. The warehouse itself, for example, will occupy more than four square acres. In addition, it must be close to railroads and major highways, because shipments will be arriving by both rail and truck, although outbound shipments will be exclusively by truck. Other important

Online Study Center
Improve Your Grade
Exercises: Building Effective Skills

considerations are that land prices and the cost of living should be relatively low and weather conditions should be mild (to minimize disruptions to shipments).

The firm's general experience is that small to mid-size communities work best. Moreover, warehouses are already in place in the western and eastern parts of the United States, so this new one will most likely be in the central or south-central area. Your boss has asked you to identify three or four possible sites.

Exercise Task

With the information above as a framework, do the following:

1. Use the Internet to identify as many as ten possible locations.
2. Using additional information from the Internet, narrow the set of possible locations to three or four.
3. Again using the Internet, find out as much as possible about the potential locations.

EXPERIENTIAL EXERCISE

Developing Communication Skills

Online Study Center
Improve Your Grade
–Exercises: Experiential Exercise
–Interactive Skills Self-Assessment

Purpose

Some ways of giving instructions to people are quicker or more accurate than others. Some generate more satisfaction in the recipient or spur greater compliance. It is important for you to recognize the "costs and benefits" of different communication models. This exercise identifies the types of behaviors that enhance or interfere with the effective transmission of instructions. It also illustrates forms of communication and investigates the differing outcomes of these means of communication, as well as the processes resulting from them. The exercise allows you to explore possible techniques for dealing with dysfunctional communication behaviors.

Instructions

Your instructor will provide further instructions.

Source: From *Organization and People*, 3rd edition, by Ritchie, © 1984. Reprinted with permission of South-Western, a division of Thomson Learning: www.thomsonrights.com. Fax: 1-800-730-2215.

Communicating the Truth About Smoking

A young man stands near a pile of body bags outside the high-rise headquarters of Philip Morris. He shouts up: "We're gonna leave these here, so you can see what 1,200 people actually look like!" The body bags represent the 1,200 daily deaths in the United States attributable to tobacco products. The American Legacy Foundation developed this ad as part of an innovative television campaign to inform and warn teens about the dangers of smoking. So far, the commercials have been remarkably effective.

In 1998 Big Tobacco agreed to pay $206 billion as part of a legal settlement against various individual tobacco makers. Of that money, $300 million was earmarked each year for smoking education and prevention, especially among youth. The not-for-profit American Legacy Foundation (ALF) was established to administer those programs.

ALF developed their unique "truth" ads to raise awareness of the dangers of smoking. The commercials feature diverse teens taking direct action against tobacco companies. The style is edgy and confrontational. Market researcher Peter Zollo calls the ads "the 'un-marketing' of high-risk youth behaviors." He explains why the commercials have been so effective with teenagers: "The truth campaign creates a brand with which [teens] want to affiliate. Truth understands teenagers' emotional needs to rebel, defy authority, and assert their independence. So instead of rebelling by smoking, truth encourages teens to rebel by confronting and rejecting the tobacco industry."

The messages appeal to young people's distrust of big business and their desire for nonconformity. Zollo claims, "We've found that humor also goes a long way in gaining teens' acceptance and establishing credibility." High schooler Katie Hardison agrees. "They're not saying we're smarter than you; we know what you should do," says Hardison. "They never say don't smoke." In fact, the ads show a teen saying, "If I want to smoke that's my own decision," and another ad claims, "We totally respect people's freedom of choice—different strokes for different folks." Philip Morris's own ad campaign features the tag line "Think. Don't Smoke." ALF contends that the ads present smoking as a behavior that is reserved for adults, which makes smoking

> *"'Please don't smoke; it's not good for your health' doesn't work for kids."*
>
> —Colleen Stevens, spokeswoman, California Department of Health

appear forbidden and therefore more desirable. Surveys show that teens who view the Philip Morris ads are more likely to smoke.

A young woman pushes a baby carriage on a busy city sidewalk. She abruptly runs away, abandoning the carriage near the curb. Bewildered pedestrians approach. Inside, they see a baby doll, and a sign proclaims, "Every year, smoking leaves about 13,000 kids motherless." An ALF ad that aired during Superbowl XXXVIII won an Emmy for the best community service advertisement. ALF not only produces commercials but also creates print ads for publications geared to teens and maintains a website, www.thetruth.com. A truth tour visits beaches and concerts with vans full of DJs, video monitors, and game consoles. The nonprofit provides money to fund grassroots, youth-led antismoking activities. ALF's research division conducts surveys to evaluate the organization's effectiveness.

Thus far, performance has been high. ALF CEO Cheryl G. Healton claims that after one year of the truth campaign, "75 percent of all 12 to 17 year olds . . . could accurately describe at least one of the truth ads." Even more encouraging, truth ads were judged most effective by those at the highest risk—young people who are already smoking or are considering smoking. Best of all, in 2005, the *American Journal of Public Health* published research showing that, as a result of the truth campaign, youth smoking declined 22 percent during the first two years, resulting in 300,000 fewer young smokers.

Unfortunately, despite the unprecedented success of the truth campaign, ALF is facing a funding crisis. The payments from tobacco companies ended in 2003, and the company is struggling to find the financing to keep its message in the public view. Focusing on the thousands of expected fatalities if the youth smoking rate climbs to previous levels, the ALF website claims, "If truth dies, it won't die alone." *A teen holds an electronic display, showing the digit 8. The view is grainy, off-center, unsteady. The text reads, "Every 8 seconds, big tobacco loses another customer." Pause. "They die."*

Case Questions

1. Describe the steps in the communication process that occur as ALF attempts to educate teens about smoking. Use specific examples from the case.
2. Show how ALF is using oral, written, electronic, and nonverbal communication.
3. In your opinion, why is ALF successful when other organizations sending the same basic message are not? Is there anything ALF could do to increase its effectiveness?

Case References

"American Legacy Foundation," "Applied Research and Evaluation," "Fact Sheet on College Students and Smoking," "First Look Report 9," "Remarks as Prepared for Delivery by Peter Zollo," "Truth Advertising Campaign Takes Home Emmy," American Legacy Foundation website, www.americanlegacy.org on February 1, 2006; Cara B. DiPasquale, "Anti-Tobacco Group Blasts Philip Morris Ads," *Ad Age*, May 29, 2002, www.adage.com on February 16, 2003; Wendy McElroy, "Paying for the Rope That Hangs Them," September 25, 2000, Wendy McElroy's website, www.zetetics.com on February 16, 2003; Alina Tugend, "Cigarette Makers Take Anti-Smoking Ads Personally," *New York Times*, October 27, 2002, p. BU4 (quote).

LEARNING OBJECTIVE REVIEW

Online Study Center
Improve Your Grade
 –Learning Objective Review
 –Audio Chapter Review
 –Study Guide to Go

Online Study Center
ACE the Test
 Audio Chapter Quiz

1 *Describe the role and importance of communication in the manager's job.*

- Communication is the process of transmitting information from one person to another.
- Effective communication is the process of sending a message in such a way that the message received is as close in meaning as possible to the message intended.
- For information to be useful, it must be accurate, timely, complete, and relevant.
- The communication process consists of a sender's encoding meaning and transmitting it to one or more receivers, who receive the message and decode it into meaning.
- In two-way communication, the process continues with the roles reversed.
- Noise can disrupt any part of the overall process.

2 *Identify the basic forms of communication in organizations.*

- Interpersonal communication focuses on communication among a small number of people.
    Two important forms of interpersonal communication, oral and written, both offer unique advantages and disadvantages.
    The manager should weigh the pros and cons of each when choosing a medium for communication.
- Communication networks are recurring patterns of communication among members of a group or work team.
- Vertical communication between superiors and subordinates may flow upward or downward.
- Horizontal communication involves peers and colleagues at the same level in the organization.

3 ▶ *Describe the role of electronic communication in organizations.*

- There are several basic levels of information systems:
  - transaction-processing systems
  - systems for various types of workers
  - basic management information systems
  - decision support systems and executive support systems
  - artificial intelligence, including expert systems

- Intranets and extranets are also growing in popularity.

- Electronic communication is having a profound effect on managerial and organizational communication.

4 ▶ *Discuss informal communication, including its various forms and types.*

- The grapevine is the informal communication network among people in an organization.

- Management by wandering around is also a popular informal method of communication.

- Nonverbal communication is expressed through
  - images
  - settings
  - body language

5 ▶ *Describe how the communication process can be managed to recognize and overcome barriers.*

- Managing the communication process entails recognizing the barriers to effective communication and understanding how to overcome them.

- Barriers can be identified at both the individual and the organizational level.

- Likewise, both individual and organizational skills can be used to overcome these barriers.

Online Study Center RESOURCES

Prepare for Class, Improve Your Grade, and ACE the Test. These Student Achievement resources include:

ACE Practice Tests	Interactive Skills Assessments	Study Guide to Go
End of Chapter Exercises	Knowledgebank	Video Segments
Glossaries (visual and print)	Reviews (audio and print)	Summaries/Outlines
Flashcards		

To access these learning and study tools, go to: **college.hmco.com/pic/griffinSAS**

While work teams in organizations are growing in popularity, sports teams have been around for a long time. For instance, these athletes comprise the U.S. Olympic team that competed in the 2006 games in Italy.

3 *Discuss interpersonal and intergroup conflict in organizations.*

2 *Identify and discuss four essential characteristics of groups and teams.*

1 *Define and identify types of groups and teams in organizations, discuss reasons why people join groups and teams, and list the stages of group and team development.*

Chapter Outline

Online Study Center
Prepare for Class
Chapter Outline

4 ▶ *Describe how organizations manage conflict.*

Teamwork Challenges for the 2006 Winter Olympics U.S. Athletes

The 200-plus members of the 2006 U.S. Winter Olympics team included superstars: Michelle Kwan in figure skating, Bode Miller in downhill skiing, Shaun White in snowboarding, the NHL professionals on the hockey team. In part, the celebrity status of the athletes simply reflects the reality that the public is interested in exceptional athletes. Celebrity status is also hyped by corporate sponsors and network broadcasters to increase viewership, advertising revenues, and sales. Coaches should seek out the best competitors, yet the fame and stardom enjoyed by top performers may have an adverse effect on team cohesion and ultimately, performance.

Superstars may have little loyalty to their country or to their sport. Bode Miller is one who puts his own interests above all else.

Online Study Center college.hmco.com/pic/griffinSAS

PRACTICING MANAGER'S TERMS

group   *p. 343*
team   *p. 345*
norms   *p. 351*
socialization   *p. 352*
cohesiveness   *p. 352*
informal leader   *p. 354*
conflict   *p. 355*

Online Study Center
Improve Your Grade
—Flashcards
—Glossary

KEY TERMS

functional group   *p. 344*
informal or interest group   *p. 345*
task group   *p. 345*
roles   *p. 349*
role structure   *p. 349*
role ambiguity   *p. 349*
role conflict   *p. 350*
role overload   *p. 350*

You should be able to define and use terms that are part of the practicing manager's vocabulary, as well as those that are integral in the language of management.

"I kind of take pride in the fact that I do things my own way," Miller states. "I don't really care what anybody else says." The champion refuses to offer a professional appearance at press conferences, bragging on air about skiing drunk and the resulting hangovers. He doesn't associate with other athletes. Year-round, he trains alone, shunning team workouts. In Turin in 2006, he declined to stay in the Olympic Village and slept in his own mobile home, as did teammate Daron Rahlves. Miller claims, "The athletes' village is competitive . . . not a healthy living environment."

Miller isn't the only one with teamwork issues. In speed skating, Americans Shani Davis and Chad Hedrick both took gold medals. They were signed up for a three-man event, but Davis opted to sit out, conserving strength for another event. Afterwards, Hedrick said, "I felt betrayed. He didn't participate in the race, and he didn't discuss it with me, as the leader of the team." "I'm one of a kind," replies Davis, the first black to win an individual medal at a Winter Olympics, shrugging off the criticism. "A lot of people don't understand me." Davis got his gold but Hedrick would not congratulate him. The resulting feud spilled over into a "frigid and nasty" press conference complete with shouts and traded insults.

A few American competitors received top honors, including Shaun White in halfpipe snowboarding and Joey Cheek in speed skating. Overall, however, the U.S. team was disappointing. Some wonder if the setbacks are a consequence of poor teamwork. Miller, a favorite going in, failed to complete the course more than once. He didn't win any medals, although initial estimates predicted as many as four golds. Davis and Hedrick both lost to Italian skater Enrico Fabris in the 1500-meter speed skate, placing second and third. The two stood on the same podium to receive their medals but didn't shake hands or speak.

While the skiing and skating teams are clearly troubled, some Americans have gone to extraordinary lengths. Emily Hughes quickly flew to Turin to replace Michelle Kwan, who was hurt and withdrew. Lindsey Kildow got back in the race just 48 hours after a fall hard enough to cause her to black out. Cheek donated his $40,000 in U.S. Olympic Committee bonus money to a charity for Sudanese children.

The American athletes are talented and have great resources. With better teamwork, who knows what they could accomplish?[1]

Teamwork can be a powerful force in any competitive setting. When people work together and put the greater good ahead of personal gain, the sky is often the limit. But when people on a team refuse to work together, the likely result will be disappointing performance. Who knows what might have happened if Bode Miller had taken his role more seriously, or if Shani Davis and Chad Hedrick had been more supportive of one another? Indeed, one of the most glorious moments in U.S. Olympic history was when a bunch of collegiate hockey players put team first to win the gold medal in 1980. This stands in stark contrast to the current hockey team populated by professionals who often put their own interests first.

This chapter is about processes that lead to and follow from people working together, primarily those processes involving groups and teams of people. It discusses the roles and importance of groups and teams in organizations. We first introduce basic concepts of group and team dynamics. Subsequent sections explain the characteristics of groups and teams in organizations. We then describe interpersonal and intergroup conflict. And we conclude with a discussion of how conflict can be managed.

GROUPS AND TEAMS IN ORGANIZATIONS

1 ▶ *Define and identify types of groups and teams in organizations, discuss reasons why people join groups and teams, and list the stages of group and team development.*

Groups are a ubiquitous part of organizational life. They are the basis for much of the work that gets done, and they evolve both inside and outside the normal structural boundaries of the organization. We will define a **group** as two or more people who interact regularly to accomplish a common purpose or goal.[2] The purpose of a group or team may range from preparing a new advertising campaign, to sharing information informally, to making important decisions, to fulfilling social needs.

group Two or more people who interact regularly to accomplish a common purpose or goal.

A task group is one that is created by the organization to accomplish a relatively narrow range of purposes within a stated or implied time horizon. In the aftermath of the crash of the space shuttle Columbia, numerous task groups were assembled to collect debris, analyze information, and attempt to determine what went wrong. This team, for instance, is working on debris from the wreckage in a hangar at Cape Canaveral. By attempting to reconstruct sections of the shuttle, the team hopes to develop new methods for avoiding future disasters.

Types of Groups and Teams

In general, three basic kinds of groups are found in organizations—functional groups, informal or interest groups, and task groups and teams.[3] These are illustrated in Figure 13.1.

functional group A permanent group created by the organization to accomplish a number of organizational purposes with an unspecified time horizon.

1. A **functional group** is a permanent group created by the organization to accomplish a number of organizational purposes with an unspecified time horizon. The advertising department at Target, the management department at the University of North Texas, and the nursing staff at the Mayo Clinic are functional groups. The advertising department at Target, for example, seeks to plan effective advertising campaigns, increase sales, run in-store promotions, and develop a unique identity for the company. It is assumed that the functional group will remain in existence after it attains its current objectives—those objectives will be replaced by new ones.

FIGURE 13.1

Types of Groups in Organizations
Every organization has many different types of groups. In this hypothetical organization, a functional group is shown within the blue area, a cross-functional team within the yellow area, and an informal group within the green area.

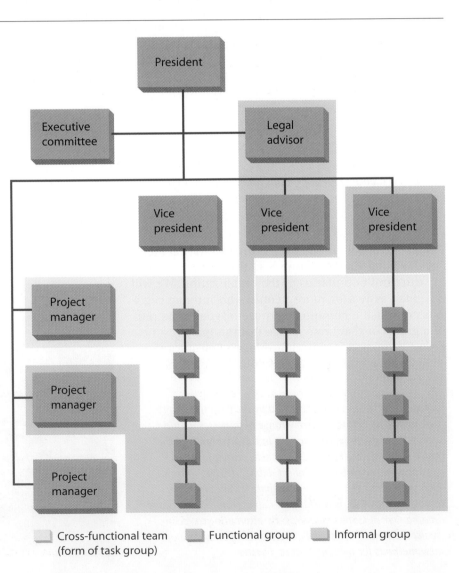

◻ Cross-functional team (form of task group) ◻ Functional group ◻ Informal group

2. An **informal or interest group** is created by its own members for purposes that may or may not be relevant to organizational goals. It also has an unspecified time horizon. A group of employees who lunch together every day may be discussing how to improve productivity, how to embezzle money, or local politics and sports. As long as the group members enjoy eating together, they will probably continue to do so. When lunches cease to be pleasant, they will seek other company or a different activity.

> **informal or interest group** A group created by its members for purposes that may or may not be relevant to those of the organization.

Informal groups can be a powerful force that managers cannot ignore.[4] One writer described how a group of employees at a furniture factory subverted their boss's efforts to increase production. They tacitly agreed to produce a reasonable amount of work but not to work too hard. One man kept a stockpile of completed work hidden as a backup in case he got too far behind. In another example, auto workers described how they left out gaskets and seals and put soft-drink bottles inside doors.[5] Of course, informal groups can also be a positive force, as was demonstrated when Continental Airlines employees worked together to buy a new motorcycle for Gordon Bethune, the company's former CEO, to show their support and gratitude for his excellent leadership.

In recent years the Internet has served as a platform for the emergence of more and different kinds of informal or interest groups. As one example, Yahoo! includes a wide array of interest groups that bring together people with common interests. And increasingly, workers who lose their jobs as a result of layoffs are banding together electronically to boost each other's morale and facilitate networking as they all look for new jobs.[6]

Online Study Center
Improve Your Grade
Knowledgebank 13.1

3. A **task group** is a group created by the organization to accomplish a relatively narrow range of purposes within a stated or implied time horizon. Most committees and task forces are task groups. The organization specifies group membership and assigns a relatively narrow set of goals, such as developing a new product or evaluating a proposed grievance procedure. The time horizon for accomplishing these purposes is either specified (a committee may be asked to make a recommendation within sixty days) or implied (the project team will disband when the new product is developed).

> **task group** A group created by the organization to accomplish a relatively narrow range of purposes within a stated or implied time horizon.

> **team** A group of workers that functions as a unit, often with little or no supervision, to carry out work-related tasks, functions, and activities.

Teams are a special form of task group that have become increasingly popular.[7] In the sense used here, a **team** is a group of workers that functions as a unit, often with little or no supervision, to carry out work-related tasks, functions, and activities. Table 13.1 lists and defines some of the various types of teams that are being used today. Earlier forms of teams included autonomous work groups and quality circles. Today, teams are also sometimes called self-managed teams, cross-functional teams, or high-performance teams. Many firms today are routinely using teams to carry out most of their daily operations.[8]

Organizations create teams for a variety of reasons:

1. Teams give more responsibility for task performance to the workers who are actually performing the tasks.

TABLE 13.1

Types of Teams

Problem-Solving Team Most popular type of team; comprises knowledge workers who gather to solve a specific problem and then disband.

Management Team Consists mainly of managers from various functions like sales and production; coordinates work among other teams.

Work Team An increasingly popular type of team; work teams are responsible for the daily work of the organization; when empowered, they are self-managed teams.

Virtual Team A new type of work team that interacts by computer; members enter and leave the network as needed and may take turns serving as leader.

Quality Circle Declining in popularity, quality circles, comprising workers and supervisors, meet intermittently to discuss workplace problems.

Reprinted by permission from Brian Dumaine, "The Trouble with Teams," *Fortune*, Sept. 5, 1994, p. 87, © 1994 Time Inc. All rights reserved.

2. Teams empower workers by giving them greater authority and decision-making freedom.

3. Teams allow the organization to capitalize on the knowledge and motivation of their workers.

4. Teams enable the organization to shed its bureaucracy and to promote flexibility and responsiveness.

When an organization decides to use teams, it is essentially implementing a major form of organization change, as discussed in Chapter 7. Thus it is important to follow a logical and systematic approach to planning and implementing teams in an existing organization design. It is also important to recognize that resistance may be encountered. This resistance is most likely to come from first-line managers who will be giving up much of their authority to the team. Many organizations find that they must change the whole management philosophy of such managers from thinking of themselves as supervisors to acting as coaches or facilitators.[9]

After teams are in place, managers should continue to assess their contributions and monitor how effectively they are functioning. In the best circumstances, teams will become very cohesive groups with high performance norms. To achieve this state, the manager can use any or all of the techniques described later in this chapter for enhancing cohesiveness. If implemented properly, and with the support of the workers themselves, performance norms are likely to be relatively high. In other words, if the change is properly implemented, the team participants will understand the value and potential of teams and the rewards they may expect to get as a result of their contributions. On the other hand, poorly designed and implemented teams will do a less effective job and may detract from organizational effectiveness.[10]

Why People Join Groups and Teams

People join groups and teams for a variety of reasons. They join functional groups simply by virtue of joining organizations. People accept employment to earn money or to practice their chosen profession. Once inside the organization, they are assigned to jobs and roles and thus become members of functional groups. People in existing functional groups are told, are asked, or volunteer to serve on committees, task forces, and teams. People join informal or interest groups for a variety of reasons, most of them quite complex.[11] Indeed, the need for employees to be team players has grown so strong today that many organizations actively resist hiring someone who does not want to work with others.[12]

1. *Interpersonal Attraction.* Many different factors contribute to interpersonal attraction. When people see a lot of each other, pure proximity increases the likelihood that interpersonal attraction will develop. Attraction is increased when people are similar in attitudes, personality, or economic standing.

2. *Group Activities.* Jogging, playing bridge, bowling, discussing poetry, playing war games, and flying model airplanes are all activities that some people enjoy. Many of them are more enjoyable to participate in as a member of a group, and most require more than one person. Many large firms, such as Shell Oil and Apple Computer, have a football, softball, or bowling league. A person may join a bowling team, not because of any particular attraction to other group members, but simply because being a member of the group enables that person to participate in a pleasant activity.

People join groups for a variety of reasons. These volunteers, Jose Luis Rodriguez, Houston's Mexican Consul General Carlos Gonzalez, Consul Jose Borson, and Enrique Lara are all interested in increasing voter awareness and participation in their home country. They are shown here displaying some of the completed application forms for Mexico's absentee voting in Houston. Their common goal led them to form a group to further their interests.

3. *Group Goals.* The Sierra Club, which is dedicated to environmental conservation, is a good example of this kind of interest group. Various fund-raising groups are another illustration. Members may or may not be personally attracted to the other fundraisers, and they probably do not enjoy the activity of knocking on doors asking for money, but they join the group because they subscribe to its goal. Workers join unions such as the United Auto Workers because they support its goals.

4. *Need Satisfaction.* New residents in a community may join the Newcomers Club partly as a way to meet new people and partly just to be around other people. Likewise, newly divorced people often join support groups as a way to find companionship.

5. *Instrumental Benefits.* It is fairly common for college students entering their senior year to join several professional clubs or associations, because they believe that listing such memberships on a résumé will enhance their chances of getting a good job. Similarly, a manager might join a certain racquet club not because she is attracted to its members (although she might be) and not because of the opportunity to play tennis (although she may enjoy it). The club's goals are not relevant, and her affiliation needs may be satisfied in other ways. However, she may feel that being a member of this club will lead to important and useful business contacts. The racquet club membership is instrumental in establishing those contacts. Membership in civic groups such as the Junior League and Rotary may be solicited for similar reasons.

Stages of Group and Team Development

Imagine the differences between a collection of five people who have just been brought together to form a group or team and a group or team that has functioned like a well-oiled machine for years. Members of a new group or team are not sure how they will function together and are tentative in their interactions. In a group or team with considerable experience, members are familiar with one another's strengths and weaknesses and are more secure in their role in the group. The former group or team is generally considered to be immature, the latter to be mature. To progress from the immature phase to the mature phase, a group or team must go through certain stages of development, as shown in Figure 13.2.[13]

1. *Forming.* Members of a group or team get acquainted and begin to test which interpersonal behaviors are acceptable and which are unacceptable to the other members. The members are very dependent on others at this point to provide cues about what is acceptable. The basic ground rules for the group or team are established, and a tentative group structure may emerge. At Reebok, for example, a merchandising team was created to handle its sportswear business. The team leader and his members were barely acquainted and had to spend a few weeks getting to know one another.

2. *Storming.* This stage may be characterized by uneven patterns of interaction and a general lack of unity. At the same time, some members of the group or team may begin to exert themselves to become recognized as the group leader or at least to play a major role in shaping the group's agenda. In Reebok's team, some members advocated a rapid expansion into the marketplace; others argued for a slower entry. The first faction won, with disastrous results. Because of the rush, product quality was poor and deliveries were late. As a result, the team leader was fired and a new manager was placed in charge.

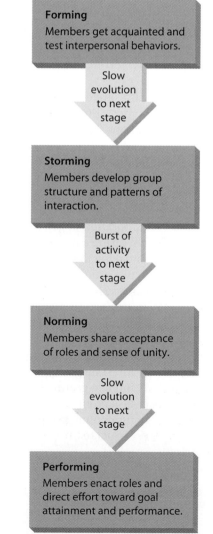

FIGURE 13.2

Stages of Group Development
Groups evolve through four stages of development. Managers must understand that group members need time to become acquainted, accept one another, develop a group structure, and become comfortable with their role in the group before they can begin to work directly to accomplish goals.

Forming
Members get acquainted and test interpersonal behaviors.

Slow evolution to next stage

Storming
Members develop group structure and patterns of interaction.

Burst of activity to next stage

Norming
Members share acceptance of roles and sense of unity.

Slow evolution to next stage

Performing
Members enact roles and direct effort toward goal attainment and performance.

CONCEPT CHECK 13.1

CONCEPT CHECK 13.1

What is likely to be the result when members join a group for different reasons? What can a group leader do to reduce the negative impact of a conflict in reasons for joining the group?

3. *Norming.* During this stage, which usually begins with a burst of activity, each person begins to recognize and accept her or his role and to understand the roles of others. Members also begin to accept one another and to develop a sense of unity. Temporary regressions to the previous stage may occur. For example, the group or team might begin to accept one particular member as the leader. If this person later violates important norms or otherwise jeopardizes his or her claim to leadership, conflict might reemerge as the group rejects this leader and searches for another. Reebok's new leader transferred several people away from the team and set up a new system and structure for managing things. The remaining employees accepted his new approach and settled into doing their job.

4. *Performing.* The team really begins to focus on the problem at hand. The members enact the roles they have accepted, interaction occurs, and the efforts of the group are directed toward goal attainment. The basic structure of the group or team is no longer an issue but, rather, has become a mechanism for accomplishing the purpose of the group. Reebok's sportswear business is now growing consistently and has successfully avoided the problems that plagued it at first.

TEST PREPPER 13.1

ANSWERS CAN BE FOUND ON P. 442

True or False?

_____ 1. Quality circles exist when workers and supervisors meet intermittently to discuss workplace problems. They are increasing in popularity.

_____ 2. A team is a group of workers that functions as a unit, often with little or no supervision, to carry out work-related tasks, functions, and activities.

Multiple Choice

_____ 3. A corporation began a unique interview process when hiring a new sales executive. They began by breaking the sixteen-person candidate pool into two groups. The groups competed in daily business challenges while being observed by members of top management, in addition to evaluating each other's performance. At the end of the interview process, only one applicant was left standing. Each group was a(n) _____.
   a. informal group
   b. interest group
   c. task group
   d. functional group
   e. virtual team

_____ 4. _____ teams are the most popular type of team. They are knowledge workers who answer a challenge and then disband.
   a. Problem-solving
   b. Quality circle
   c. Management
   d. Work
   e. Virtual

_____ 5. Tonisha joined a country club because she thinks it will help her make contacts that will support her career. Which reason best describes why she joined the club?
   a. To satisfy a need for affiliation
   b. Because the group's activities appeal to her
   c. Because of the goals of the group
   d. Because of instrumental benefits
   e. All of the above

_____ 6. Which of the following is the last stage of group development?
   a. Norming
   b. Storming
   c. Forming
   d. Performing
   e. None of the above

Online Study Center
ACE the Test
ACE Practice Tests 13.1

CHARACTERISTICS OF GROUPS AND TEAMS

> **2** ▶ *Identify and discuss four essential characteristics of groups and teams.*

As groups and teams mature and pass through the four basic stages of development, they begin to take on four important characteristics—a role structure, behavioral norms, cohesiveness, and informal leadership.[14]

Role Structure

Each individual in a team has a part, or **role**, to play in helping the group reach its goals. Some people are leaders, some do the work, some interface with other teams, and so on. Indeed, a person may take on a *task specialist role* (concentrating on getting the group's task accomplished) or a *socioemotional role* (providing social and emotional support to others on the team). A few people, usually the leaders, perform both roles; a few others may do neither. The group's **role structure** is the set of defined roles and interrelationships among those roles that the group or team members define and accept. Each of us belongs to many groups and therefore plays multiple roles—in work groups, classes, families, and social organizations.[15]

Role structures emerge as a result of role episodes, as shown in Figure 13.3. The process begins with the expected role—what other members of the team expect the individual to do. The expected role gets translated into the sent role—the messages and cues that team members use to communicate the expected role to the individual. The perceived role is what the individual perceives the sent role to mean. Finally, the enacted role is what the individual actually does in the role. The enacted role, in turn, influences future expectations of the team. Of course, role episodes seldom unfold this easily. When major disruptions occur, individuals may experience role ambiguity, conflict, or overload.[16]

1. **Role ambiguity** arises when the sent role is unclear. If your instructor tells you to write a term paper but refuses to provide more information, you will probably experience role ambiguity. You do not know what the topic is, how long the paper should be, what format to use, or when the paper is due. In work settings, role ambiguity can stem from poor job descriptions, vague instructions from a supervisor, or unclear cues from coworkers. The result is likely to be a subordinate who does not know what to do. Role ambiguity can be a significant problem for both the individual who must contend with it and the organization that expects the employee to perform.

roles   The parts that individual members of a group play in helping the group reach its goals.

role structure   The set of defined roles and interrelationships among those roles that the group members define and accept.

Online Study Center
Improve Your Grade
Career Snapshot 13.1

role ambiguity   Ambiguity that arises in the role structure within a group when the sent role is unclear and the individual does not know what is expected of him or her.

FIGURE 13.3

The Development of a Role

Roles and role structures within a group generally evolve through a series of role episodes. The first two stages of role development are group processes, as the group members let individuals know what is expected of them. The other two parts are individual processes, as the new group members perceive and enact their roles.

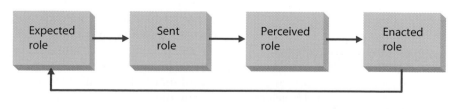

Expected role → Sent role → Perceived role → Enacted role

role conflict Conflict that arises within the role structure of a group when the messages and cues that make up the sent role are clear but contradictory or mutually exclusive.

2. **Role conflict** occurs when the messages and cues composing the sent role are clear but contradictory or mutually exclusive.[17] There are several kinds of role conflict.

  • *Interrole conflict* is conflict between roles. For example, if a person's boss says that one must work overtime and on weekends to get ahead, and the same person's spouse says that more time is needed at home with the family, conflict may result. In a matrix organization, interrole conflict often arises between the roles one plays in different teams as well as between team roles and one's permanent role in a functional group.

  • *Intrarole conflict* may occur when the person is subject to conflicting demands from different sources within the context of the same role. A manager's boss may tell her that she needs to put more pressure on subordinates to follow new work rules. At the same time, her subordinates may indicate that they expect her to get the rules changed. Thus the cues are in conflict, and the manager may be unsure about which course to follow.

  • *Intrasender conflict* occurs when a single source sends clear but contradictory messages. This might arise if the boss says one morning that there can be no more overtime for the next month but then, after lunch, tells someone to work late that same evening.

  • *Person-role conflict* results from a discrepancy between the role requirements and the individual's personal values, attitudes, and needs. If a person is told to do something unethical or illegal, or if the work is distasteful (for example, firing a close friend), person-role conflict is likely.

Role conflict of all varieties is of particular concern to managers. Research has shown that conflict may occur in a variety of situations and lead to a variety of adverse consequences, including stress, poor performance, and rapid turnover.

role overload A consequence of a weak role structure within a group, which occurs when expectations for the role assigned to an individual exceed his or her capabilities to perform.

3. A final consequence of a weak role structure is **role overload**, which occurs when expectations for the role exceed the individual's capabilities. When a manager gives an employee several major assignments at once and at the same time increases the person's regular workload, the employee will probably experience role overload. Role overload may also result when an individual takes on too many roles at one time. For example, a person trying to work extra hard at the office, run for election to the school board, serve on a committee in church, coach Little League baseball, maintain an active exercise program, and be a contributing member to her or his family will probably encounter role overload.

In a functional group or team, the manager can take steps to avoid role ambiguity, conflict, and overload. Having clear and reasonable expectations and sending clear and straightforward cues go a long way toward eliminating role ambiguity. Consistent expectations that take into account the employee's other roles and personal value system may minimize role conflict. Role overload can be avoided simply by recognizing the individual's capabilities and limits. In friendship and interest groups, role structures are likely to be less formal, so role ambiguity, conflict, and overload may not be so likely to arise. However, if one or more of these problems do occur, they may be difficult to handle. Because roles in friendship and interest groups are less likely to be partially defined by a formal authority structure or written job descriptions, the individual cannot turn to those sources to clarify a role.

CONCEPT CHECK 13.2

Do you think teams are a valuable new management technique that will endure, or are they just a fad that will be replaced with something else in the near future?

Behavioral Norms

Norms are standards of behavior that the group or team accepts for its members and to which it expects them to adhere. Most committees, for example, develop norms governing their discussions. A person who talks too much is perceived as doing so to make a good impression or to get his or her own way. Other members may not talk much to this person, may not sit nearby, may glare at the person, and may otherwise "punish" the individual for violating the norm. Norms, then, define the boundaries between acceptable and unacceptable behavior.[18] Some groups develop norms that limit the upper bounds of behavior to "make life easier" for the group. In general, these norms are counterproductive—examples include not making more than two comments in a committee discussion and not producing any more than you have to. Other groups may develop norms that limit the lower bounds of behavior. These norms tend to reflect motivation, commitment, and high performance—examples include not coming to meetings unless you have read the reports to be discussed and producing as much as you can. Managers can sometimes use norms for the betterment of the organization. For example, Kodak has successfully used group norms to reduce injuries in some of its plants.[19] Three key elements of norms are generalization, variation, and conformity.

1. Norms will not always generalize from group to group. In some academic departments, for example, it may be the norm that faculty members dress up on teaching days. People who fail to observe this norm are "punished" by sarcastic remarks or even formal reprimands. In other departments, the norm may be casual clothes, and the person unfortunate enough to wear dress clothes may be punished just as vehemently. Even within the same work area, similar groups or teams can develop different norms. One team may strive always to produce above its assigned quota; another may maintain productivity just below its quota. The norm of one team may be to be friendly and cordial to its supervisor; that of another team may be to remain aloof and distant. Some differences are due primarily to the composition of the teams.

2. In some cases, norms may vary within a group or team. A common norm is that the least senior member of a group is expected to perform unpleasant or trivial tasks for the rest of the group. These tasks might be to wait on customers who are known to be small tippers (in a restaurant), to deal with complaining customers (in a department store), or to handle the low-commission line of merchandise (in a sales department). Another example occurs when certain individuals, especially informal leaders, are able to violate some norms. If the team is going to meet at 8:00 A.M., anyone arriving late will be chastised for holding things up. Occasionally, however, the informal leader may arrive a few minutes late. As long as this does not happen too often, the group will probably not do anything about it.

3. Four sets of factors contribute to *norm conformity*.
   - Factors associated with the group are important. For example, some groups or teams may exert more pressure for conformity than others.
   - The initial stimulus that prompts behavior can affect conformity. The more ambiguous the stimulus (for

I don't <u>have</u> to be a team player, Crawford. I'm the team owner.

CONCEPT CHECK 13.3

Consider the case of a developed group, where all members have been socialized. What are the benefits to the individuals of norm conformity? What are the benefits of not conforming to the group's norms? What are the benefits to an organization of conformity? What are the benefits to an organization of nonconformity?

example, news that the team is going to be transferred to a new unit), the more pressure there is to conform.

- Individual traits determine the individual's propensity to conform. For example, more intelligent people are often less subject to pressure to conform.
- Situational factors, such as team size and unanimity, influence conformity. As an individual learns the group's norms, she or he can do several different things. The most obvious is to adopt the norms. For example, the new male professor who notices that all the other men in the department dress up to teach can also start wearing a suit. A variation is to try to obey the "spirit" of the norm while retaining individuality. The professor may recognize that the norm is actually to wear a tie; thus he might succeed in conforming adequately by wearing a tie with his sport shirt, jeans, and sneakers.

The individual may also ignore the norm. When a person does not conform, several things can happen. At first the group may increase its communication with the deviant individual to try to bring him or her back in line. If this does not work, communication may decline. Over time, the group may begin to exclude the individual from its activities and, in effect, ostracize the person.

socialization Generalized norm conformity that occurs as a person makes the transition from being an outsider to being an insider in the organization.

4. **Socialization** is generalized norm conformity that occurs as a person makes the transition from being an outsider to being an insider. A newcomer to an organization, for example, gradually begins to learn the norms about dress, working hours, and interpersonal relations. As the newcomer adopts these norms, she or he is being socialized into the organization culture. Some organizations, such as Texas Instruments, work actively to manage the socialization process; others leave it to happenstance.

Cohesiveness

cohesiveness The extent to which members are loyal and committed to the group; the degree of mutual attractiveness within the group.

Cohesiveness is the extent to which members are loyal and committed to the group. In a highly cohesive team, the members work well together, support and trust one another, and are generally effective at achieving their chosen goal.[20] In contrast, a team that lacks cohesiveness is not very coordinated, its members do not necessarily support one another fully, and it may have a difficult time reaching goals. Of particular interest are the factors that increase and those that reduce cohesiveness, and the consequences of team cohesiveness.

Factors That Increase Cohesiveness

▌ One of the strongest is intergroup competition. When two or more groups are in direct competition (for example, three sales groups competing for top sales honors or two football teams competing for a conference championship), each group is likely to become more cohesive.

▌ Just as personal attraction sometimes plays a role in the formation of a group, so, too, does attraction seem to enhance cohesiveness.

▌ Favorable evaluation of the entire group by outsiders can increase cohesiveness. Thus a group's winning a sales contest or a conference title, or receiving recognition and praise from a superior, will tend to increase cohesiveness.

▌ If all the members of the group or team agree on their goals, cohesiveness is likely to increase.[21]

▌ The more frequently members of the group interact with one another, the more likely the group is to become cohesive.

A manager who wants to foster a high level of cohesiveness in a team might do well to establish some form of intergroup competition, assign members to the group who are likely to be attracted to one another, provide opportunities for success, establish goals that all members are likely to accept, and allow ample opportunities for interaction.

Factors That Reduce Cohesiveness

▌ Cohesiveness tends to decline as a group increases in size.

▌ When members of a team disagree on what the goals of the group should be, cohesiveness may decrease. For example, when some members believe the group should maximize output and others think output should be restricted, cohesiveness suffers.

▌ Intragroup competition reduces cohesiveness. When members are competing among themselves, they focus more on their own actions and behaviors than on those of the group.

▌ Domination by one or more persons in the group or team may cause overall cohesiveness to decline. Other members may feel that they are not being given an opportunity to interact and contribute, and they may become less attracted to the group as a consequence.

▌ Unpleasant experiences that result from group membership may reduce cohesiveness. A sales group that comes in last in a sales contest, an athletic team that sustains a long losing streak, and a work group reprimanded for poor-quality work may all become less cohesive as a result of their unpleasant experience.

CONCEPT CHECK 13.4

Describe the several different types of groups and indicate the similarities and differences between them. What is the difference between a group and a team?

Consequences of Cohesiveness

In general, as teams become more cohesive, their members tend to interact more frequently, conform more to norms, and become more satisfied with the team. Cohesiveness may influence team performance as well. However, performance is also influenced by the team's performance norms. Figure 13.4 shows how cohesiveness and performance norms interact to help shape team performance.

▌ When both cohesiveness and performance norms are high, high performance should result, because the team wants to perform at a high level (norms) and its members are working together toward that end (cohesiveness).

▌ When norms are high and cohesiveness is low, performance will be moderate. Although the team wants to perform at a high level, its members are not necessarily working well together.

▌ When norms are low, performance will be low, regardless of whether group cohesiveness is high or low.

▌ The least desirable situation occurs when low performance norms are combined with high cohesiveness. In this case, all team members embrace the standard of restricting performance (owing to the low performance norm), and the group is united in its efforts to maintain that standard (owing to the high cohesiveness).

FIGURE 13.4

The Interaction Between Cohesiveness and Performance Norms

Group cohesiveness and performance norms interact to determine group performance. From the manager's perspective, high cohesiveness combined with high performance norms is the best situation, and high cohesiveness combined with low performance norms is the worst situation. Managers who can influence the level of cohesiveness and performance norms can greatly improve the effectiveness of a work group.

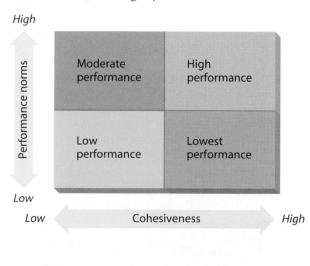

Formal and Informal Leadership

Most functional groups and teams have a formal leader—that is, one appointed by the organization or chosen or elected by the members of the group. Because friendship and interest groups are formed by the members themselves, however, any formal leader must be elected or designated by the members. Although some groups do designate such a leader (a softball team may elect a captain, for example), many do not. Moreover, even when a formal leader is designated, the group or team may also look to others for leadership. An **informal leader** is a person who engages in leadership activities but whose right to do so has not been formally recognized. The formal leader and the informal leader in any group or team may be the same person, or they may be different people. We noted earlier the distinction between the task specialist and socioemotional roles within groups. An informal leader is likely to be a person capable of playing both roles effectively. If the formal leader can perform one role but not the other, an informal leader often emerges to supplement the formal leader's functions. If the formal leader can fill neither role, one or more informal leaders may emerge to carry out both sets of functions.

Is informal leadership desirable? In many cases, informal leaders are quite powerful because they draw from referent or expert power. When they are working in the best interests of the organization, they can be a tremendous asset. Notable athletes such as Tom Brady and Derek Jeter are classic examples of informal leaders. However, when informal leaders work counter to the goals of the organization, they can cause significant difficulties. Such leaders may lower performance norms, instigate walkouts or wildcat strikes, or otherwise disrupt the organization.

informal leader   A person who engages in leadership activities but whose right to do so has not been formally recognized by the organization or group.

Online Study Center
Improve Your Grade
Career Snapshot 13.2

CONCEPT CHECK 13.5

Identify two examples of informal leaders. Can a person be a formal and an informal leader at the same time?

TEST PREPPER 13.2

ANSWERS CAN BE FOUND ON P. 442

True or False?

_____ 1. A norm is the part that an individual plays in a group in order to help the group reach its goals. The person may take on a task specialist norm or a socioemotional norm.

_____ 2. Jim, the informal leader of the work team, seems to get away with behavior that others cannot. This is due to norm variation.

_____ 3. Socialization is generalized norm conformity that occurs as a person makes the transition from being an outsider to being an insider in the organization.

_____ 4. A great deal of cohesiveness in a group is always a good thing.

Multiple Choice

_____ 5. Role _____ is the relationship among roles that a group accepts.
     a. conflict
     b. structure
     c. ambiguity
     d. overload
     e. implications

_____ 6. The last stage of role development is which of the following?
     a. Sent role
     b. Expected role
     c. Task-specialist role
     d. Perceived role
     e. Enacted role

_____ 7. Raj knows Mikela's performance has been slipping. She is supporting her mother through frequent medical treatments, and this is taking its toll on her. Raj was just informed that he has to fire Mikela. He is experiencing which conflict?
     a. Expected role conflict
     b. Person-role conflict
     c. Intrasender conflict
     d. Intrarole conflict
     e. Interrole conflict

_____ 8. Which of the following is a factor that increases cohesiveness in a group or team?
     a. Group size
     b. Intergroup competition
     c. Domination
     d. Unpleasant experiences
     e. Personal attraction

Online Study Center
ACE the Test
ACE Practice Tests 13.2

INTERPERSONAL AND INTERGROUP CONFLICT

3 ▶ *Discuss interpersonal and intergroup conflict in organizations.*

Of course, when people work together in an organization, things do not always go smoothly. Indeed, conflict is an inevitable element of interpersonal relationships in organizations. In this section, we will look at how conflict affects overall performance. We also explore the causes of conflict between individuals, between groups, and between an organization and its environment.

The Nature of Conflict

Conflict is a disagreement among two or more individuals, groups, or organizations. This disagreement may be relatively superficial or very strong. It may be short-lived or exist for months or even years, and it may be work-related or personal. Conflict may manifest itself in a variety of ways. People may compete with one another, glare at one another, shout, or withdraw. Groups may band together to protect popular members or oust unpopular members. Organizations may seek legal remedies.

Most people assume that conflict is something to be avoided because it connotes antagonism, hostility, unpleasantness, and dissension. Indeed, managers and management theorists have traditionally viewed conflict as a problem to be avoided.[22] In recent years, however, we have come to recognize that although conflict can be a major problem, certain kinds of conflict may also be beneficial.[23] For example, when two members of a site selection committee disagree over the best location for a new plant, each may be forced to more thoroughly study and defend his or her preferred alternative. As a result of more systematic analysis and discussion, the committee may make a better decision and be better prepared to justify it to others than if everyone had agreed from the outset and accepted an alternative that was perhaps less well analyzed.

conflict   A disagreement among two or more individuals or groups.

Conflict can be caused by any number of things. Philippine President Gloria Macapagal Arroyo has angered many people with her antipoverty policies, increased taxes, electoral fraud, and widespread corruption. These protesters, led by government leaders Loretta Ann Rosales (second from left) and Risa Hontiveros (third from left seated) make an "X" gesture while shouting slogans during the launching of the "Ayaw Ko Na!" (I've Had Enough) campaign against the president in 2006 in Manila. The protesters are urging their fellow citizens to put an "X" mark on their homes, cars, and other places in symbolic protest.

FIGURE 13.5

The Nature of Organizational Conflict

Either too much or too little conflict can be dysfunctional for an organization. In either case, performance may be low. However, an optimal level of conflict that sparks motivation, creativity, innovation, and initiative can result in higher levels of performance. T. J. Rodgers, CEO of Cypress Semiconductor, maintains a moderate level of conflict in his organization as a way of keeping people energized and motivated.

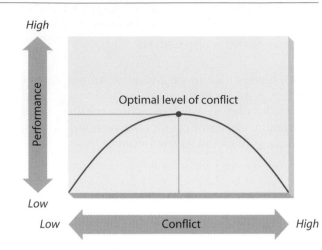

As long as conflict is being handled in a cordial and constructive manner, it is likely to be serving a useful purpose in the organization. On the other hand, when working relationships are being disrupted and the conflict has reached destructive levels, it has probably become dysfunctional and needs to be addressed.[24] We discuss ways of dealing with such conflict later in this chapter.

Figure 13.5 depicts the general relationship between conflict and performance for a group or organization. If there is absolutely no conflict in the group or organization, its members may become complacent and apathetic. As a result, group or organization performance and innovation may begin to suffer. A moderate level of conflict among group or organization members, on the other hand, can spark motivation, creativity, innovation, and initiative; it can even raise performance. Too much conflict, though, can produce such undesirable results as hostility and lack of cooperation, which lower performance. The key for managers is to find and maintain the optimal amount of conflict that fosters performance. Of course, what constitutes optimal conflict varies with both the situation and the people involved.[25]

Causes of Conflict

Conflict may arise in both interpersonal and intergroup relationships. Occasionally, conflict between individuals and groups may be caused by particular organizational strategies and practices. A third arena for conflict is between an organization and its environment.

Interpersonal Conflict

Conflict between two or more individuals is almost certain to occur in any organization, given the great variety in perceptions, goals, attitudes, and so forth among its members. William Gates, founder and CEO of Microsoft, and Kazuhiko Nishi, a former business associate from Japan, ended a long-term business relationship because of interpersonal conflict. Nishi accused Gates of becoming too political, while Gates charged that Nishi became unpredictable and erratic in his behavior.[26]

A frequent source of interpersonal conflict in organizations is what many people call a "personality clash"—when two people distrust each other's motives, dislike each other, or for some other reason simply cannot get along.[27] Conflict may also arise between people who have different beliefs or perceptions about some aspect of their work or their organization. For example, one manager might want the organization to require that all employees use Microsoft Office software, in order to promote standardization. Another manager might believe that a variety of software packages should be allowed, in order to recognize individuality.[28]

Conflict can also result from excess competitiveness among individuals. Two people vying for the same job, for example, may resort to political behavior in an effort to gain an advantage. If either competitor sees the other's behavior as inappropriate, accusations are likely to result. Even after the "winner" of the job is determined, such conflict may continue to undermine interpersonal relationships, especially if the reasons given in selecting one candidate are ambiguous or open to alternative explanations. Robert Allen resigned as CEO of Delta Airlines a few years ago as an indirect result of his disagreeing with other key executives about how best to reduce the carrier's costs. After he began looking for a replacement for one of his rivals without the approval of the firm's board of directors, the resulting conflict and controversy left him no choice but to leave.[29]

Intergroup Conflict

Conflict between two or more organizational groups is also quite common. For example, the members of a firm's marketing group may disagree with the production group over product quality and delivery schedules. Two sales groups may disagree over how to meet sales goals, and two groups of managers may have different ideas about how best to allocate organizational resources.

Many intergroup conflicts arise more from organizational causes than from interpersonal causes. In Chapter 6, we described three forms of group interdependence—pooled, sequential, and reciprocal. Just as increased interdependence makes coordination more difficult, it also increases the potential for conflict. For example, recall that in sequential interdependence, work is passed from one unit to another. Intergroup conflict may arise if the first group turns out too much work (the second group will fall behind), too little work (the second group will not meet its own goals), or poor-quality work.

At one J.C. Penney department store, conflict arose between stockroom employees and sales associates. The sales associates claimed that the stockroom employees were slow in delivering merchandise to the sales floor so that it could be priced and shelved. The stockroom employees, in turn, claimed that the sales associates were not giving them enough lead time to get the merchandise delivered and failed to understand that they had additional duties besides carrying merchandise to the sales floor.

Just like people, different departments often have different goals, and these goals may be incompatible. A marketing goal of maximizing sales, achieved partially by offering many products in a wide variety of sizes, shapes, colors, and models, probably conflicts with a production goal of minimizing costs, achieved partially by long production runs of a few items. Reebok recently confronted this very situation. One group of managers wanted to introduce a new sportswear line as quickly as possible, but other managers wanted to expand more deliberately and cautiously. Because the two groups were not able to reconcile their differences effectively, conflict between the factions led to quality problems and delivery delays that plagued the firm for months.

Competition for scarce resources can also lead to intergroup conflict. Most organizations—especially universities, hospitals, government agencies, and

CONCEPT CHECK 13.6

Describe a case of interpersonal conflict that you have observed in an organization. Describe a case of intergroup conflict that you have observed. In each case, was the conflict beneficial or harmful to the organization, and why?

businesses in depressed industries—have limited resources. In one New England town, for example, the public works department and the library battled over funds from a federal construction grant. The Buick, Pontiac, and Chevrolet divisions of General Motors have frequently fought over the right to manufacture various new products developed by the company.

Conflict Between Organization and Environment

Conflict that arises between one organization and another is called *interorganizational conflict.* A moderate amount of interorganizational conflict resulting from business competition is, of course, expected, but sometimes conflict becomes more extreme. For example, the owners of Jordache Enterprises, Inc., and Guess?, Inc., battled in court for years over ownership of the Guess? label, allegations of design theft, and several other issues.[30] Similarly, General Motors and Volkswagen once went to court to resolve a bitter conflict that spanned more than four years. It all started when a key GM executive, Jose Ignacio Lopez de Arriortua, left GM for a position at Volkswagen. GM claimed that he took with him key secrets that could benefit its German competitor. After the messy departure, dozens of charges and counter-charges were made by the two firms, and only a court settlement was able to put the conflict to an end.[31]

Conflict can also arise between an organization and other elements of its environment. For example, an organization might experience conflict with a consumer group over claims that the group makes about its products. McDonald's faced this problem a few years ago when it published nutritional information about its products that omitted details about fat content. A manufacturer might conflict with a governmental agency such as OSHA. For example, the firm's management may believe it is in compliance with OSHA regulations, whereas officials from the agency itself feel that the firm is not in compliance. Or a firm might conflict with a supplier over the quality of raw materials. The firm may think the supplier is providing inferior materials, whereas the supplier is convinced that the materials are adequate. Finally, individual managers may obviously have disagreements with groups of workers. For example, a manager may think her workers are doing poor-quality work and that they are unmotivated. The workers, on the other hand, may believe they are performing adequately and that the manager is doing a poor job of leading them.

TEST PREPPER 13.3   ANSWERS CAN BE FOUND ON P. 442

True or False?

_____ 1. Certain kinds of conflict are beneficial to an organization.

_____ 2. Conflict between beef producers and the Federal Department of Agriculture is an example of intergroup conflict.

_____ 3. When finance and operations departments disagree on issues, it is called intergroup conflict.

_____ 4. Conflict can arise between an organization and elements of its environment, such as a consumer group. But since this conflict is outside the organization, it can generally be overlooked.

Online Study Center
ACE the Test
ACE Practice Tests 13.3

MANAGING CONFLICT IN ORGANIZATIONS

4▶ *Describe how organizations manage conflict.*

How do managers cope with all this potential conflict? Fortunately, there are ways to stimulate conflict for constructive ends, to control conflict before it gets out of hand, and to resolve it if it does. Here we look at ways of managing conflict.[32]

Stimulating Conflict

In some cases managers may decide that they should try to stimulate some conflict (for reasons noted previously). There are a few common methods for doing this:

1. An organization may stimulate conflict by placing individual employees or groups in competitive situations. For example, managers can establish sales contests, incentive plans, bonuses, or other competitive stimuli to spark competition. As long as the ground rules are equitable and all participants perceive the contest as fair, the conflict created by the competition is likely to be constructive because each participant will work hard to win (thereby enhancing some aspect of organizational performance).

2. Another useful method for stimulating conflict is to bring in one or more outsiders who will shake things up and present a new perspective on organizational practices. Outsiders may be new employees, current employees assigned to an existing work group, or consultants or advisors hired on a temporary basis. Of course, this action can also provoke resentment from insiders who feel they were qualified for the position. The Beecham Group, a British company, once hired an executive from the United States for its CEO position, expressly to change how the company did business. His arrival heralded new ways of doing things and generated new enthusiasm for competitiveness. Unfortunately, however, certain valued employees chose to leave Beecham because they resented some of the changes that were made.

3. Changing established procedures, especially procedures that have outlived their usefulness, can also stimulate conflict. Such actions cause people to reassess how they perform their job and whether they perform it correctly. For example, one university president announced that all vacant staff positions could be filled only after written justification had received his approval. Conflict arose between the president and the department heads, who felt they were having to do more paperwork than was necessary. Most requests were approved, but because department heads now had to think through their staffing needs, a few unnecessary positions were appropriately eliminated.

Controlling Conflict

There are also several common methods managers can use to control conflict.

1. Expand the resource base. Suppose a top manager receives two budget requests for $100,000 each. If she has only $180,000 to distribute, the stage is set for conflict because each group will feel its proposal is worth funding and will be unhappy if it is not fully funded. If both proposals are indeed worthwhile, it may be possible for her to come up with the extra $20,000 from some other source and thereby avoid difficulty.

2. Use techniques that enhance coordination.
   - Making use of the managerial hierarchy
   - Relying on rules and procedures
   - Enlisting liaison people
   - Forming task forces
   - Integrating departments

   At the J.C. Penney store mentioned earlier, the conflict between salesroom associates and stockroom employees was addressed by providing salespeople with clearer forms on which to specify the merchandise they needed and in what sequence they needed different items. If one coordination technique does not have the desired effect, a manager might shift to another one.

3. Focus employee attention on higher-level, or superordinate, goals as a way of eliminating lower-level conflict. When labor unions such as the United Auto Workers make wage concessions to ensure the survival of the U.S. automobile industry, they are responding to a superordinate goal. Their immediate goal may be higher wages for members, but they realize that without the automobile industry, their members would not even have jobs.

4. Try to ensure that employees with incompatible personalities and work habits do not have to work together continuously. For instance, two valuable subordinates, one a chain smoker and the other a vehement antismoker, should probably not be required to work together in an enclosed space. If conflict does arise between incompatible individuals, a manager might seek an equitable transfer for one or both of them to other units.

Resolving and Eliminating Conflict

Online Study Center
Improve Your Grade
Video Segment

Despite everyone's best intentions, conflict will sometimes flare up. If it is disrupting the workplace, creating too much hostility and tension, or otherwise harming the organization, attempts must be made to resolve it.

1. Avoidance, the act of ignoring conflict in the hopes that it will go away, may sometimes be effective in the short run for some kinds of interpersonal disagreements. However, it does little to resolve long-run or chronic conflict. Even more pernicious, though, is "smoothing"—minimizing the conflict and telling everyone that things will "get better." Often the conflict will only worsen as people continue to brood over it.

2. Compromise is striking a middle-range position between two extremes. This approach can work if it is used with care, but in most compromise situations someone wins and someone loses. Budget problems are one of the few areas amenable to compromise, because of their objective nature. Assume, for example, that additional resources are not available to the manager mentioned earlier. She has $180,000 to divide, and each of two groups claims to need $100,000. If the manager believes that both projects warrant funding, she can allocate $90,000 to each. The fact that the two groups have at least been treated equally may minimize the potential conflict.

3. The confrontational approach to conflict resolution—also called *interpersonal problem solving*—consists of bringing the parties together to address the conflict. The parties discuss the nature of their conflict and attempt to reach an agreement or a solution. Such confrontation requires a reasonable degree of maturity on the part of the participants, and the manager must structure the situation carefully. If handled well, this approach can be an effective means of resolving conflict. In recent years, many organizations have experimented with a technique called *alternative dispute resolution*, using a team of employees to arbitrate conflict in this way.[33]

Regardless of the approach, organizations and their managers must realize that conflict must be addressed if it is to serve constructive purposes and be prevented from bringing about destructive consequences. Conflict is inevitable in organizations, but its effects can be constrained with proper attention. For example, Union Carbide sent two hundred of its managers to a three-day workshop on conflict management. The managers engaged in a variety of exercises and discussions to learn with whom they were most likely to come in conflict and how they should try to resolve it. As a result, managers later reported that hostility and resentment had diminished and that employees reported more pleasant working relationships.[34]

TEST PREPPER 13.4

ANSWERS CAN BE FOUND ON P. 442

True or False?

_____ 1. Sales have been flat the past three months. Increasing competition will control interpersonal conflict and lead to better sales.

_____ 2. Three ways to resolve and eliminate conflict are avoiding conflict, convincing conflicting parties to compromise, and bringing the parties in conflict together to address and negotiate conflict.

_____ 3. "Smoothing" over conflict and simply reassuring people that things will get better is an effective way to resolve conflict.

Multiple Choice

_____ 4. All of the following are possible ways to control conflict in organizations EXCEPT _____.
   a. expanding the resource base
   b. setting supraordinate goals
   c. changing established procedures
   d. matching the personalities and work habits of employees
   e. enhancing coordination of interdependence

_____ 5. Roy Disney resigned from the Disney board of directors because he did not agree with Michael Eisner, the CEO and chairman. Eventually the chairmanship was taken away from Eisner. What were the two men experiencing?
   a. Expected role conflict
   b. Person-role conflict
   c. Intrasender conflict
   d. Interpersonal conflict
   e. Interrole conflict

Online Study Center
ACE the Test
ACE Practice Tests 13.4

BUILDING EFFECTIVE CONCEPTUAL SKILLS

Exercise Overview

Groups and teams are becoming ever more important in organizations. This exercise will give you an opportunity to practice your conceptual skills as they apply to work teams in organizations.

Exercise Background

Several highly effective groups exist outside the boundaries of typical business organizations. For example, a basketball team, a military squadron, a government policy group such as the president's Cabinet, a student committee, and the leadership of a church or religious organization are all teams.

Online Study Center
Improve Your Grade
Exercises: Building Effective Skills

Exercise Task

1. Use the Internet to identify an example of a real team. Choose one that (a) is not part of a normal for-profit business and (b) you can argue is highly effective.

2. Determine the reasons for the team's effectiveness. (*Hint:* Use a search engine to look for websites sponsored by that group and for current articles from news sources.) Consider team characteristics and activities, such as role structure, norms, cohesiveness, and conflict management.

3. What can a manager learn from this particular team? How can the factors that account for its success be used in a business setting?

Individual Versus Group Performance

Purpose

This exercise demonstrates the benefits that working as a group can bring to accomplishing a task.

Introduction

You will be asked to do the same task both individually and as part of a group.

Instructions

Part 1: You will need a pen or pencil and an 8½" × 11" sheet of paper. Working alone, do the following:

1. Write the letters of the alphabet in a vertical column down the left side of the paper: A–Z.

2. Your instructor will randomly select a sentence from any written document and read out loud the first 26 letters in that sentence. Write these letters in a vertical column immediately to the right of the alphabet column. Everyone should then have identical sets of 26 two-letter combinations.

3. Working alone, think of a famous person whose initials correspond to each pair of letters and write that person's name next to the letters; for example, "MT Mark Twain." You will have ten minutes. Only one name per set is allowed. One point is awarded for each legitimate name, so the maximum score is 26 points.

4. After time expires, exchange your paper with another member of the class and score each other's work. The instructor will settle disputes about the legitimacy of names. Keep your score for use later in the exercise.

Part 2: Your instructor will divide the class into groups of five to ten. All groups should have approximately the same number of members. Each group now follows the procedure given in part 1. Again, write the letters of the alphabet down the left side of the sheet of paper, this time in reverse order: Z–A. Your instructor will dictate a new set of letters for the second column. The time limit and scoring procedure are the same. The only difference is that the groups will generate the names.

Part 3: Each team identifies the group member who came up with the most names. The instructor places these "best" students into one group. Then all groups repeat part 2, but this time the letters from the reading will be in the first column, and the alphabet letters will be in the second column.

Part 4: Each team calculates the average individual score of its members on part 1 and compares it with the team score from parts 2 and 3. Your instructor will put the average individual score and team scores for each group on the board.

Follow-up Questions

1. Do the average individual scores and the team scores differ? What are the reasons for this difference, if any?

2. Although the team scores in this exercise usually are higher than the average individual scores, under what conditions might individual averages exceed group scores?

Source: Adapted from "Alphabet Names" by William Mulford in *The 1979 Annual Handbook for Group Facilitators* by John E. Jones and H. W. Pfeiffer, eds., pp. 19–20. Reprinted with permission of John Wiley & Sons, Inc.

CLOSING CASE STUDY

Video Game Teams

Microsoft's new Xbox 360, released in November 2005, was very popular, selling 1.5 million units in the first three months. In addition, Sony and Nintendo both announced new game consoles that would be available in 2006. Sales of hardware and accessories accounted for two-thirds of the industry's $31 billion in worldwide sales in 2005. A focus solely on gaming hardware, however, neglects the real growth engine of the industry, the video games themselves.

Video games can be created by the game console makers or third-party developers under contract to a hardware company or even by independents who self-publish. Yet all of the developers rely on teams made up of programmers and designers. The stereotypical image of a computer programmer is one of a brilliant, obsessed, antisocial individual working alone late at night in his or her cubicle. But the reality is quite different. Development of today's extremely complex, multi-faceted games requires the skills and abilities of dozens of workers with various skills. In addition, the game development process is usually stressful, takes one to three years, and costs millions of dollars, making team processes critically important yet challenging for video game developers.

Development teams are led by a producer, who functions in the same way as a director of a movie. The producer is responsible for choosing team members, establishing a team vision and specific goals, and supporting each group of professionals in order to obtain their best artistic and technical efforts. Laura Fryer, a producer at Microsoft, led a team for the development of *Crimson Skies* that consisted of programmers, artists, designers, sound designers, testers, writers, and marketers. Each of these components was itself a team-within-a-team. For example, programmers included experts in systems architecture, graphics, artificial intelligence, networking, and user interfaces. The subteams were assigned specialized tasks. "*Crimson Skies* was set in the 1930s," says Fryer, "so we needed dialogue consistent with that time [from the script writers]." Games must be compatible with multiple formats, including traditional game consoles, portable devices, and personal computers. Adapting the games to these formats requires additional skill sets.

> *"The team dynamic is critical [when developing video games]."*
>
> —Laura Fryer, executive producer, Microsoft Game Studios

Moreover, the specialized teams must also work harmoniously with the other subteams. Fryer claims that, when developing video games, "the team dynamic is critical." Managing group conflict is essential, as is team communication. Fryer says that she often hears, "Your group didn't understand" or "My group isn't valued."

Another important challenge is the competitive nature of the video game development process. Publishers take a chance that a game will be a hit with players. Although the per unit costs are low, upfront costs are extremely high, resulting in many games that do not make much profit beyond their development costs. Furthermore, game developers typically announce ship dates for new games at the industry's annual Electronic Entertainment Expo (E3) convention, held in May. Developers are then held to tough deadlines, resulting in a lot of overtime, or "crunch time," as the industry refers to it.

A video game development team is dependent on other teams, especially marketing and hardware production. This can create friction and conflict. For example, when Xbox 360 was initially released, a shortage of components limited production and sales. "Consumers unable to find Xbox 360 hardware did not purchase as many current-generation software titles as expected," says Colin Sebastian, a game industry analyst.

The future of video games is taking the industry in the direction of super-large teams, ones made up of thousands or even millions of online users. Alternate reality games, called "ARGs," mesh complicated stories, puzzles, and graphics to create an intriguing and addictive fantasy experience. The designer for the ARG "Last Call Poker," Elan Lee, says, "That was the only game I ever made where I followed the community hourly. Any change I made to any Web site was noticed and absorbed immediately. It was like exploring a living body." "We don't tell the story; they discover and tell the story to each other," says Jordan Lee, the game producer. "It goes through the filter of their millions of minds, so it's never the same in the end as what we wrote."

According to Lucas Conley, a *Fast Company* writer, the video game industry shows "the classic struggles of businesses making things up as they go along: landing funding, building and managing teams, and bringing products to markets." This sounds remarkably like the personal computer industry just a few years ago. Chances are the video game industry will follow the same pattern—rapid innovation in hardware until the point of diminishing returns, increasing standardization, and, ultimately, a reliance on software as the main profit generator.

Certainly Microsoft's Xbox experience fits that pattern. Over the next year, Microsoft intends to sell 5 million Xboxes worldwide at prices ranging from $300 to $400. The company also plans to sell about 3 million games per month, at around $60 apiece. With over $3 billion in yearly revenues, you can bet that video games will be an increasingly important part of Microsoft's strategy—and that means continued emphasis on teamwork.

Case Questions

1. What kinds of roles do team members at Microsoft fulfill? In your opinion, are team members likely to experience role ambiguity, conflict, and/or overload? Why or why not?

2. Consider the factors that increase or decrease group cohesiveness. Do you think Microsoft game development teams have high or low cohesiveness? Explain.

3. What types of conflict might team members at Microsoft experience? Give one example from the case for each type.

Case References

John Borland, ""A Novelist Turned Gaming Innovator," *CNet News*, December 15, 2005, www.news.com on February 14, 2006; Lucas Conley, "Reading List: Smartbomb," *Fast Company*, November 2005, www.fastcompany.com on February 14, 2006; Laura Fryer, "Adventures in Game Development," presentation at the U.S. Military Academy at West Point on November 3, 2004 (quote); Kris Graft, "Gaming Industry Growing Pains," *BusinessWeek*, February 14, 2006, www.businessweek.com on February 15, 2006; Jay Greene, "Microsoft's News of Many Parts," *BusinessWeek*, January 27, 2006, www.businessweek.com on February 15, 2006; Chris Morris, "More Than 325,000 Xbox 360s Already Sold," *Money*, December 14, 2005, www.cnnmoney.com on February 15, 2006; Stephen H. Wildstrom, "Xbox: A Winner Only at Games," *BusinessWeek*, December 12, 2005, www.businessweek.com on February 14, 2006.

LEARNING OBJECTIVE REVIEW

Online Study Center
Improve Your Grade
–Learning Objective Review
–Audio Chapter Review
–Study Guide to Go

Online Study Center
ACE the Test
Audio Chapter Quiz

▶ *Define and identify types of groups and teams in organizations, discuss reasons why people join groups and teams, and list the stages of group and team development.*

- A group is two or more people who interact regularly to accomplish a common purpose or goal.

- General kinds of groups in organizations are
    functional groups
    informal or interest groups
    task groups
    teams (groups of workers that function as a unit, often with little or no supervision)

- People join functional groups and teams to pursue a career.

- People join informal or interest groups because of
    interpersonal attraction   group goals
    group activities   need satisfaction
    potential instrumental benefits

- The stages of team development include
    testing and dependence
    an initial lack of unity and uneven interaction patterns
    development of group cohesion
    focusing on the problem at hand

2 *Identify and discuss four essential characteristics of groups and teams.*

- Four important characteristics of teams are
    - role structures   cohesiveness
    - behavioral norms   informal leadership

- Role structures emerge as a result of the development of role episodes and may include a task specialist and a socioemotional specialist. They may be disrupted by
    - role ambiguity   role conflict   role overload

- Norms are standards of behavior for group members.

- Cohesiveness is the extent to which members are loyal and committed to the team and to one another. Several factors can increase or reduce team cohesiveness.

- The relationship between performance norms and cohesiveness is especially important.

- Informal leaders are those leaders whom the group members themselves choose to follow.

3 *Discuss interpersonal and intergroup conflict in organizations.*

- Conflict is a disagreement between two or more people, groups, or organizations.

- Either too little or too much conflict may hurt performance, but an optimal level of conflict may improve performance.

- Interpersonal and intergroup conflict in organizations may be caused by personality differences or by particular organizational strategies and practices.

- Organizations may encounter conflict with one another and with various elements of the environment.

4 *Describe how organizations manage conflict.*

- Three methods of managing conflict, each of which is appropriate under certain circumstances, are to stimulate it, control it, or resolve and eliminate it.

Online Study Center   **RESOURCES**

Prepare for Class, Improve Your Grade, and ACE the Test. These Student Achievement resources include:

ACE Practice Tests	Interactive Skills Assessments	Study Guide to Go
End of Chapter Exercises	Knowledgebank	Video Segments
Glossaries (visual and print)	Reviews (audio and print)	Summaries/Outlines
Flashcards		

To access these learning and study tools, go to: **college.hmco.com/pic/griffinSAS**

JetBlue has become the darling of the airline industry.

4 Identify and distinguish between two opposing forms of structural control.

3 Describe budgets and other tools for financial control.

2 Identify and explain the three forms of operations control.

1 Explain the purpose of control, identify different types of control, and describe the steps in the control process.

> *"We know we're not perfect, but we will always aspire to learn from every situation and improve."*
>
> —David Neeleman, CEO, JetBlue

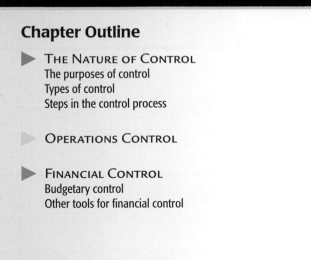

Chapter Outline

▶ **THE NATURE OF CONTROL**
The purposes of control
Types of control
Steps in the control process

▷ **OPERATIONS CONTROL**

▶ **FINANCIAL CONTROL**
Budgetary control
Other tools for financial control

▶ **STRUCTURAL CONTROL**
Bureaucratic control
Decentralized control

▶ **STRATEGIC CONTROL**
Integrating strategy and control
International strategic control

▶ **MANAGING CONTROL IN ORGANIZATIONS**
Characteristics of effective control
Resistance to control
Overcoming resistance to control

Online Study Center
Prepare for Class
Chapter Outline

6 ▶ *Identify characteristics of effective control, why people resist control, and how managers can overcome this resistance.*

5 ▶ *Discuss the relationship between strategy and control, including international strategic control.*

Out of the Blue

The airline industry is one of the most challenging industries for managers. Skills in scheduling, purchasing, customer service, and mechanical maintenance are required. Teams of diverse individuals, from pilots to baggage handlers, must be coordinated. Fixed costs for planes and equipment are high and revenues uncertain. Competition is intense, with fierce price wars. In this hostile environment, few companies thrive—five major airlines were in bankruptcy in 2005. How, then, has JetBlue, founded in 2000, become one of the most profitable airlines in the United States?

First and foremost, credit CEO David Neeleman's planning skills. Neeleman founded Morris Air, a discount carrier based in

PRACTICING MANAGER'S TERMS

control   *p. 369*
controller   *p. 373*
control standard   *p. 373*
operations control   *p. 376*
preliminary control   *p. 376*
screening control   *p. 377*
postaction control   *p. 377*

financial control   *p. 378*
budget   *p. 378*
financial statement   *p. 381*
balance sheet   *p. 381*
income statement   *p. 382*
ratio analysis   *p. 382*
financial audit   *p. 382*
structural control   *p. 383*
bureaucratic control   *p. 384*
decentralized control   *p. 385*
strategic control   *p. 386*

You should be able to define and use terms that are part of the practicing manager's vocabulary, as well as those that are integral in the language of management.

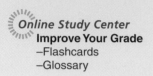

Online Study Center
Improve Your Grade
—Flashcards
—Glossary

Salt Lake City. In 1993 Southwest Airlines bought Morris Air for $128 million. Neeleman worked briefly at Southwest and then was fired. He planned to beat rival Southwest at its own game. He consulted—and in some cases hired—experienced managers from competitors. He copied elements of Southwest's discount strategy, such as point-to-point scheduling and use of nonunion employees. Then he added some extras: reserved seats, upscale snacks, leather seats, XM radio, and seat-back televisions with DirecTV. "JetBlue is not merely a clone of Southwest Airlines; it is the new gold standard among low-cost carriers," claims industry consultant James Craun.

Neeleman, with his extensive industry expertise, focuses his attention on the few significant factors that can make or break his company. He hires younger, less experienced workers and gives them stock options in lieu of high wages. JetBlue also fills up its planes and gets more flying hours out of each aircraft. Maintenance costs are low because the planes are all brand new. Even the luxurious leather seats are cost-effective—they are easier to clean. On-time arrival is critical for customer service, so Neeleman's pager beeps any time a flight is more than one minute late. He even wears his pager to bed. In 2005, JetBlue earned top marks in four of five quality measures, such as on-time performance and accuracy in baggage handling, displacing Southwest Airlines.

Neeleman's dedication to monitoring the airline's performance is matched by his passion for feedback. He jumps on a plane once a week or so, serving drinks and loading baggage. Along the way, he smiles politely at praise but asks passengers to tell him more about their complaints. No concern is too small or too large, from a desire for better biscotti to a request for flights to Chicago. Customers' suggestions are taken seriously. A frequent flyer program, a service desired by travelers, was added in July 2002. Neeleman gives employees the autonomy to make customer service decisions immediately. "Employees at other airlines get so caught up in procedure—rules, rules, rules—that they often forget there is a paying customer there," Neeleman asserts. JetBlue passengers, for example, receive discount coupons and free accommodations if their flight is diverted, compensation that rival airlines do not always provide.

JetBlue's success is clear. But the real question is: Can that success be sustained? Expansion is the trap that ensnared many now-failed airline ventures. As increasing size leads to increasing complexity, Neeleman will have to guard against inefficiencies and too much bureaucracy. Costs will surely rise, as planes age and low-paid workers demand raises. Unionization will probably occur, further increasing labor costs. Growth will mean borrowing to buy more planes and that will increase debt expense. "In a lot of places now, there's no low-fare nonstop service," claims Neeleman. "That creates some opportunities for us." The airline has taken advantage of some of those opportunities, adding numerous cities and its first international destinations. Yet JetBlue will have a harder and harder time finding opportunities as it grows.

The CEO welcomes the challenge. "We're only as good as our last arrival. . . . Customer feedback, the good and the bad, is critical to accomplishing our goal of getting better as we get bigger," he says. "We know we're not perfect, but we will always aspire to learn from every situation and improve." Under Neeleman's guidance, the sky may indeed be the limit for JetBlue.[1]

David Neeleman has almost single-handedly made JetBlue one of the twenty-first century's first success stories. One key to his accomplishments has been a well-constructed business model detailing how he wanted his business to be managed. Another key has been effective control systems that serve their intended purpose. In a nutshell, effective control helps managers like David Neeleman decide where they want their business to go, point it in that direction, and create systems to keep it on track. Ineffective control, on the other hand, can result in a lack of focus, weak direction, and poor overall performance.

Online Study Center
Improve Your Grade
Video Segment

As we noted in Chapter 1, control is one of the four basic managerial functions that provide the organizing framework for this book. This is the first of two chapters devoted to this important area. In the first section of the chapter we examine the nature of control, including its purposes, the different types of control, and the steps in the control process. Next we consider the four levels of control that most organizations must employ in order to remain effective: operations, financial, structural, and strategic control. We conclude by discussing the characteristics of effective control, noting why some people resist control and describing what organizations can do to overcome this resistance. The remaining two chapters in this part focus on managing operations and managing information.

THE NATURE OF CONTROL

1 *Explain the purpose of control, identify different types of control, and describe the steps in the control process.*

Control is the regulation of organizational activities so that some targeted element of performance remains within acceptable limits. Without this regulation, organizations have no indication of how well they are performing in relation to their goals. Control, like a ship's rudder, keeps the organization moving in the proper direction. At any point in time, it compares where the organization is in terms of performance (financial, productive, or otherwise) to where it is supposed

control The regulation of organizational activities in such a way as to facilitate goal attainment.

to be. Like a rudder, control provides an organization with a mechanism for adjusting its course if performance falls outside of acceptable boundaries. For example, FedEx has a performance goal of delivering 99.75 percent of its packages on time. If on-time deliveries fall to 99 percent, control systems will alert managers to the problem so that they can make necessary adjustments in operations to restore the target level of performance. An organization without effective control procedures is not likely to reach its goals—or, if it does reach them, to know that it has!

The Purposes of Control

As Figure 14.1 illustrates, control provides an organization with ways to adapt to environmental change, to limit the accumulation of error, to cope with organizational complexity, and to minimize costs. These four functions of control are worth a closer look.

1. *Adapting to environmental change.*   In today's complex and turbulent business environment, all organizations must contend with change.[2] If managers could establish goals and achieve them instantaneously, control would not be needed. But between the time a goal is established and the time it is reached, many things can happen in the organization and its environment to disrupt movement toward the goal—or even to change the goal itself. A properly designed control system can help managers anticipate, monitor, and respond to changing circumstances.[3] In contrast, an improperly designed system can result in organizational performance that falls far below acceptable levels.

   For example, Michigan-based Metalloy, a forty-six-year-old, family-run metal-casting company, signed a contract to make engine-seal castings for NOK, a big Japanese auto parts maker. Metalloy was satisfied when its first 5,000-unit production run yielded 4,985 acceptable castings and only 15 defective ones. NOK, however, was quite unhappy with this performance and insisted that Metalloy raise its standards. In short, global quality standards are such that customers demand near-perfection from their suppliers. A properly designed control system can help managers such as those at Metalloy stay better attuned to rising standards.

2. *Limiting the accumulation of error.*   Small mistakes and errors do not often seriously damage the financial health of an organization. Over time, however, small errors may accumulate and become very serious. For example, Whistler Corporation, a large radar detector manufacturer, was once faced with such

---

FIGURE 14.1

The Purposes of Control

Control is one of the four basic management functions in organizations. The control function, in turn, has four main purposes. Properly designed control systems can fulfill each of these purposes.

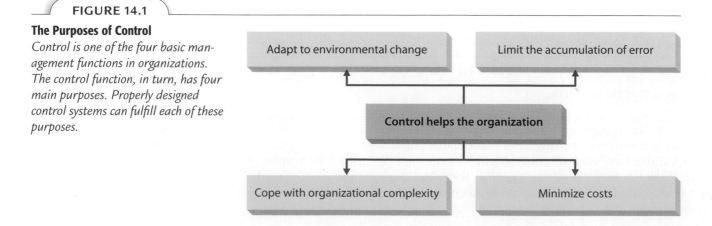

rapidly escalating demand that it essentially stopped worrying about quality. The defect rate rose from 4 percent to 9 percent to 15 percent and eventually reached 25 percent. One day, a manager realized that 100 of the firm's 250 employees were spending all their time fixing defective units and that $2 million worth of inventory was awaiting repair. Had the company adequately controlled quality as it responded to increased demand, the problem would never have reached such shocking proportions. Similarly, Fleetwood Enterprises, a large manufacturer of recreational vehicles, suffered because its managers did not adequately address several small accounting and production problems years earlier. As these small problems grew into large ones, the firm struggled with how to correct them.[4]

3. *Coping with organizational complexity.*   When a firm purchases only one raw material, produces one product, has a simple organization design, and enjoys constant demand for its product, its managers can maintain control with a very basic and simple system. But a business that produces many products from myriad raw materials and has a large market area, a complicated organization design, and many competitors needs a sophisticated system in order to maintain adequate control. When large firms merge, the short-term results are often disappointing. The typical reason for this is that the new enterprise is so large and complex that the existing control systems are simply inadequate. Daimler-Benz and Chrysler faced just this problem when they merged to create DaimlerChrysler.

4. *Minimizing costs.*   When it is practiced effectively, control can also help reduce costs and boost output. For example, Georgia-Pacific Corporation, a large wood products company, learned of a new technology that could be used to make thinner blades for its saws. The firm's control system was used to calculate the amount of wood that could be saved from each cut made by the thinner blades relative to the costs that the firm would incur to replace the existing blades. The results were impressive—the wood that is saved by the new blades each year fills eight hundred rail cars. As Georgia-Pacific discovered, effective control systems can eliminate waste, lower labor costs, and improve output per unit of input. In their bids to reduce costs, businesses are cutting back on everything from health insurance coverage to overnight shipping to business lunches for clients.[5]

Types of Control

The examples of control given thus far have illustrated the regulation of several organizational activities, from producing quality products to coordinating complex organizations. Organizations practice control in a number of different areas and at different levels, and the responsibility for managing control is widespread.

Areas of Control

Most organizations define areas of control in terms of the four basic types of resources they use: physical, human, information, and financial resources.[6]

1. *Physical resources.*   Includes inventory management (stocking neither too few nor too many units in inventory), quality control (maintaining appropriate levels of output quality), and equipment control (supplying the necessary facilities and machinery).

CONCEPT CHECK 14.1

Many organizations today are involving lower-level employees in control. Give at least two examples of specific actions that a lower-level worker could take to help his or her organization better adapt to environmental change. Then do the same for limiting the accumulation of error, coping with organizational complexity, and minimizing costs.

2. *Human resources.* Includes selection and placement, training and development, performance appraisal, and compensation.

3. *Information resources.* Includes sales and marketing forecasting, environmental analysis, public relations, production scheduling, and economic forecasting.

4. *Financial resources.* Involves managing the organization's debt so that it does not become excessive, ensuring that the firm always has enough cash on hand to meet its obligations but does not have excess cash in a checking account, and ensuring that receivables are collected and bills are paid on a timely basis.

Online Study Center
Improve Your Grade
Career Snapshot 14.1

In many ways, the control of financial resources is the most important area, because financial resources are related to the control of all the other resources in an organization. Maintaining too much inventory leads to excessive storage costs; poor selection of personnel leads to termination and rehiring expenses; inaccurate sales forecasts lead to disruptions in cash flows and other financial effects. Financial issues tend to pervade most control-related activities.

Levels of Control

Just as control can be broken down by area, Figure 14.2 shows that it can also be broken down by level within the organizational system.

1. *Operations control* focuses on the processes the organization uses to transform resources into products or services.[7] Quality control is one type of operations control.

2. *Financial control* is concerned with the organization's financial resources. Monitoring receivables to make sure customers are paying their bills on time is an example of financial control.

3. *Structural control* is concerned with how effectively the elements of the organization's structure are serving their intended purpose. Monitoring the administrative ratio to make sure that staff expenses do not become excessive is an example of structural control.

4. *Strategic control* focuses on how effectively the organization's corporate, business, and functional strategies are helping the organization meet its goals. For example, if a corporation has been unsuccessful in implementing its strategy of related diversification, its managers need to identify the reasons for this failure and either change the strategy or renew their efforts to implement it. We discuss these four levels of control more fully later in this chapter.

FIGURE 14.2

Levels of Control

Managers use control at several different levels. The most basic levels of control in organizations are strategic, structural, operations, and financial control. Each level must be managed properly if organization control at large is to be as effective as possible.

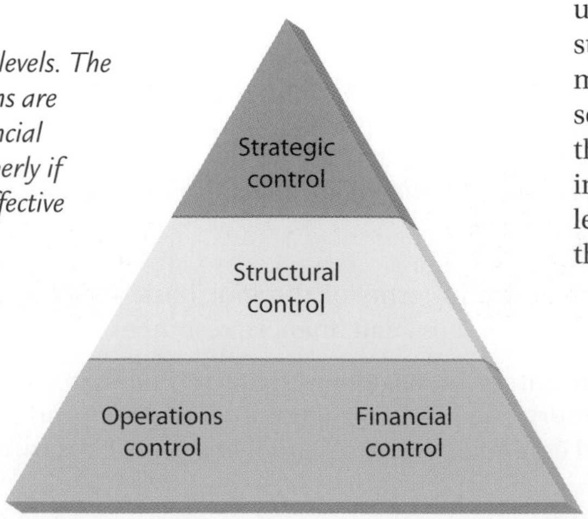

Responsibilities for Control

Traditionally, managers have been responsible for overseeing the wide array of control systems and concerns in organizations. They decide which types of control the organization will use, and they implement control systems and take actions on the basis of the information provided by control systems. Thus ultimate responsibility for control rests with all managers throughout an organization.

Most larger organizations also have one or more specialized managerial positions called *controller*. A **controller** is responsible for helping line managers with their control activities, for coordinating the organization's overall control system, and for gathering and assimilating relevant information. Many businesses that use a divisional organization design have several controllers: one for the corporation and one for each division. The job of controller is especially important in organizations where control systems are complex.[8]

In addition, many organizations are beginning to use operating employees to help maintain effective control. Indeed, employee participation is often used as a vehicle for allowing operating employees an opportunity to help facilitate organizational effectiveness. For example, Whistler Corporation increased employee participation in an effort to turn its quality problems around. To start with, the quality control unit, which had been responsible for checking product quality at the end of the assembly process, was eliminated. Next, all operating employees were encouraged to check their own work and were told that they would be responsible for correcting their own errors. As a result, Whistler has eliminated its quality problems and is now highly profitable once again.

controller An official in an organization who helps line managers with control activities.

CONCEPT CHECK 14.2

How can a manager determine whether his or her firm needs improvement in control? If improvement is needed, how can the manager tell what type of control (operations, financial, structural, or strategic) needs improvement?

Steps in the Control Process

Regardless of what types or levels of control systems an organization needs, there are four fundamental steps in any control process.[9] These are illustrated in Figure 14.3.

Establishing Standards

A **control standard** is a target against which subsequent performance will be compared.[10] Standards established for control purposes should be expressed in

control standard A target against which subsequent performance will be compared.

FIGURE 14.3

Steps in the Control Process

Having an effective control system can help ensure that an organization achieves its goals. Implementing a control system is a systematic process that generally proceeds through four interrelated steps.

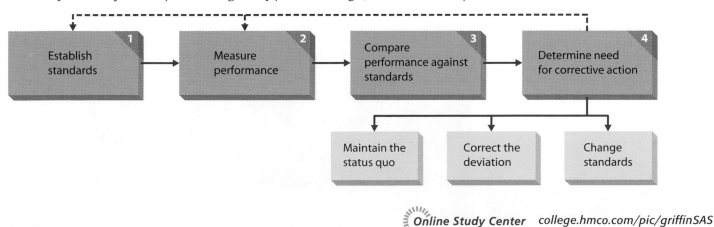

1. Establish standards
2. Measure performance
3. Compare performance against standards
4. Determine need for corrective action

Maintain the status quo

Correct the deviation

Change standards

measurable terms. Employees at a Taco Bell fast-food restaurant, for example, work toward the following service standards:

1. A minimum of 95 percent of all customers will be greeted within three minutes of their arrival.

2. Preheated tortilla chips will not sit in the warmer more than thirty minutes before they are served to customers or discarded.

3. Empty tables will be cleaned within five minutes after being vacated.

Note that standard 1 above has a time limit of three minutes and an objective target of 95 percent of all customers. In standard 3, the objective target of "all" empty tables is implied.

Control standards should also be consistent with the organization's goals. Taco Bell has organizational goals involving customer service, food quality, and restaurant cleanliness. A control standard for a retailer such as a Home Depot should be consistent with its goal of increasing its annual sales volume by 25 percent within five years. A hospital trying to shorten the average hospital stay for a patient will have control standards that reflect an improvement on current averages. A university reaffirming its commitment to academics might adopt a standard of graduating 80 percent of its student athletes within five years of their enrollment. Control standards can be as narrow or as broad as the level of activity to which they apply and must follow logically from organizational goals and objectives.

A final aspect of establishing standards is identifying performance indicators. Performance indicators are measures of performance that provide information that is directly relevant to what is being controlled. For example, suppose an organization is following a tight schedule in building a new plant. Relevant performance indicators might include buying a site, selecting a building contractor, and ordering equipment. Monthly sales increases are not, however, directly relevant. On the other hand, when control is focused on revenue, monthly sales increases are relevant, whereas buying land for a new plant is less relevant.

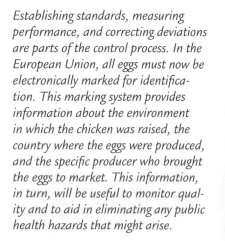

Establishing standards, measuring performance, and correcting deviations are parts of the control process. In the European Union, all eggs must now be electronically marked for identification. This marking system provides information about the environment in which the chicken was raised, the country where the eggs were produced, and the specific producer who brought the eggs to market. This information, in turn, will be useful to monitor quality and to aid in eliminating any public health hazards that might arise.

Measuring Performance

Performance measurement is a constant, ongoing activity for most organizations. For control to be effective, performance measures must be valid. Daily, weekly, and monthly sales figures measure sales performance, and production performance may be expressed in terms of unit cost, product quality, or volume produced. Employees' performance is often measured in terms of quality or quantity of output, but for many jobs, measuring performance is not so straightforward.

A research and development scientist at Merck, for example, may spend years working on a single project before achieving a breakthrough. A manager who takes over a business when it is on the brink of failure may need months or even years to turn things around. Valid performance measurement, however difficult to obtain, is nevertheless vital to effective control, and performance indicators usually can be developed. The scientist's progress, for example, may be partially assessed by peer review, and the manager's success may be evaluated by assessing her ability to convince creditors that she will eventually restore profitability.

Comparing Performance Against Standards

Performance may be higher than, lower than, or identical to the standard. In some cases comparison is easy. The goal of each product manager at General Electric is to make the product either number one or number two (on the basis of total sales) in its market. Because this standard is clear and total sales are easy to calculate, it is relatively simple to determine whether this standard has been met. Sometimes, however, comparisons are less clear-cut. If performance is lower than expected, the question is how much deviation from standards to allow before taking remedial action. For example, is increasing sales by 7.9 percent close enough when the standard was 8 percent?

The timetable for comparing performance to standards depends on a variety of factors, including the importance and complexity of what is being controlled. For longer-run and higher-level standards, annual comparisons may be appropriate. In other circumstances, more frequent comparisons are necessary. For example, a business with a severe cash shortage may need to monitor its on-hand cash reserves daily.

Considering Corrective Action

Decisions regarding corrective action draw heavily on a manager's analytic and diagnostic skills. After performance has been compared with control standards, one of three actions is appropriate:

1. *Maintain the status quo (do nothing).*   This is preferable when performance essentially matches the standards.

2. *Correct the deviation.*   Taking action to correct the deviation and bring it closer to the standard is the most common form of corrective action.

3. *Change the standards.*   Changing an established standard usually is necessary if the standard was set too high or too low at the outset. This is apparent, for example, when large numbers of employees routinely beat a production standard by a wide margin or when no employees ever meet the standard. Also, standards that seemed perfectly appropriate when they were established may need to be adjusted because circumstances have since changed.

TEST PREPPER 14.1

ANSWERS CAN BE FOUND ON P. 442

True or False?

_____ 1. Between the time a goal is established and the time it is reached, many things can happen in the organization and its environment to disrupt movement toward the goal. Sometimes even the goal itself is changed.

_____ 2. Strategic control is focused on how elements of the organization's structure are serving their intended purpose.

_____ 3. The standard bearer is the person in the organization who helps line managers with their control activities.

Multiple Choice

_____ 4. Which of the following is NOT the purpose of a control system?
   a. Limit error accumulation
   b. Cope with complexity
   c. Minimize revenue
   d. Adapt to change
   e. Minimize costs

_____ 5. Middle managers are primarily responsible for which level of control?
   a. Strategic   d. Financial
   b. Structural   e. All of the above
   c. Operations

_____ 6. What is the third step in the control process?
   a. Compare performance against standards
   b. Establish standards
   c. Determine need for corrective action
   d. Measure performance
   e. Change standards

_____ 7. A university reaffirming its commitment to academics sets a graduation goal of 90 percent of students within a five-year time span. This is an example of a(n)_____.
   a. operating control
   b. control standard
   c. financial control
   d. labor control
   e. controller standard

_____ 8. When DaimlerChrysler decided to reduce its advertising for the PT Cruiser because demand was greater than production capability, DaimlerChrysler was at which step in the control process?
   a. Compare performance against standards
   b. Establish standards
   c. Determine need for corrective action
   d. Measure performance
   e. Maintain status quo

Online Study Center
ACE the Test
ACE Practice Tests 14.1

OPERATIONS CONTROL

▷ 2 | *Identify and explain the three forms of operations control.*

operations control Control of the processes the organization uses to transform resources into products or services.

One of the four levels of control practiced by most organizations, **operations control**, is concerned with the processes the organization uses to transform resources into products or services. As Figure 14.4 shows, the three forms of operations control—preliminary, screening, and postaction control—occur at different points in relation to the transformation processes used by the organization.

preliminary control Operations control that attempts to monitor the quality or quantity of financial, physical, human, and information resources before they actually become part of the system.

1. **Preliminary control** concentrates on the resources—financial, material, human, and information—that the organization brings in from the environment. Preliminary control attempts to monitor the quality or quantity of these resources before they enter the organization. Firms such as PepsiCo and General Mills hire only college graduates for their management training program, and even then only after applicants satisfy several interviewers and selection criteria. In this way, they control the quality of the human resources entering the organization. When Sears orders merchandise to be manufactured under its own brand name, it specifies rigid standards of quality, thereby controlling physical inputs. Organizations also control financial and information resources. For example, privately held companies such as UPS and Mars limit

FIGURE 14.4

Forms of Operations Control

Most organizations develop multiple control systems that incorporate all three basic forms of control. For example, the publishing company that produced this book screens inputs by hiring only qualified employees, typesetters, and printers (preliminary control). In addition, quality is checked during the transformation process, such as after the manuscript is typeset (screening control), and the outputs—printed and bound books—are checked before they are shipped from the bindery (postaction control).

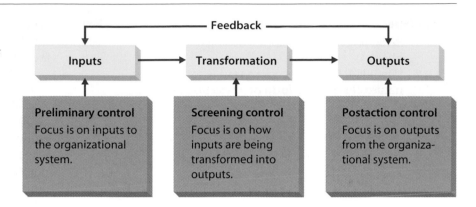

the extent to which outsiders can buy their stock, and television networks verify the accuracy of news stories before they are broadcast.

2. **Screening control** focuses on meeting standards for product or service quality or quantity during the actual transformation process itself. Screening control relies heavily on feedback. For example, in a Dell Computer assembly factory, computer system components are checked periodically as each unit is being assembled. This is done to ensure that all the components that have been assembled up to that point are working properly. The periodic quality checks provide feedback to workers so that they know what, if any, corrective actions to take. Because they are useful in identifying the cause of problems, screening controls tend to be used more often than other forms of control.

3. **Postaction control** focuses on the outputs of the organization after the transformation process is complete. Corning's old system was postaction control—final inspection after the product was completed. Although Corning abandoned its postaction control system, this still may be an effective method of control, primarily when a product can be manufactured in only one or two steps or when the service is fairly simple and routine. Although postaction control alone may not be as effective as preliminary or screening control, it can provide management with information for future planning. For example, if a quality check of finished goods indicates an unacceptably high defect rate, the production manager knows that he or she must identify the causes and take steps to eliminate them. Postaction control also provides a basis for rewarding employees. Recognizing that an employee has exceeded personal sales goals by a wide margin, for example, may alert the manager that a bonus or promotion is in order.

screening control Operations control that relies heavily on feedback processes during the transformation of resources into products or services.

postaction control Operations control that monitors the outputs or results after the transformation of resources into products or services is complete.

Most organizations use more than one form of operations control. For example, Honda's preliminary control includes hiring only qualified employees and specifying strict quality standards when ordering parts from other manufacturers. Honda uses numerous screening controls in checking the quality of components during assembly of cars. And a final inspection and test drive as each car rolls off the assembly line is part of the company's postaction control.[11] Indeed, most successful organizations employ a wide variety of techniques to facilitate operations control.

TEST PREPPER 14.2

ANSWERS CAN BE FOUND ON P. 442

True or False?

_____ 1. Screening controls happen during the input phase.

_____ 2. When H & R Block checks a tax file for client signature, it is using a form of postaction control.

Multiple Choice

_____ 3. The part of the organizational system that focuses on output control is called _____ control.
   a. transformation   d. postaction
   b. preliminary   e. feedback
   c. screening

_____ 4. Research that goes into writing a book is an example of which type of control?
   a. Transformation   d. Postaction
   b. Preliminary   e. Feedback
   c. Screening

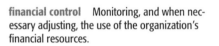

Online Study Center
ACE the Test
ACE Practice Tests 14.2

FINANCIAL CONTROL

3 *Describe budgets and other tools for financial control.*

financial control   Monitoring, and when necessary adjusting, the use of the organization's financial resources.

Financial control is the control of financial resources as they flow into the organization (revenues, shareholder investments), are held by the organization (working capital, retained earnings), and flow out of the organization (pay, expenses). Businesses must manage their finances so that revenues are sufficient to cover costs and still return a profit to the firm's owners. Not-for-profit organizations such as universities have the same concerns: Their revenues (from tax dollars or tuition) must cover operating expenses and overhead. Dickson Poon is a Chinese investor who has profited by relying heavily on financial control. He buys distressed upscale retailers such as Britain's Harvey Nichols and the United States' Barneys, imposes strict financial controls to correct problems, and begins generating hefty profits. A complete discussion of financial management is beyond the scope of this book, but we will examine the control provided by budgets and other financial control tools.

Online Study Center
Improve Your Grade
Career Snapshot 14.2

Budgetary Control

budget   A plan expressed in numerical terms.

A **budget** is a plan expressed in numerical terms.[12] Organizations establish budgets for the following:

▌ Work groups

▌ Departments

▌ Divisions

▌ The whole organization

The usual time period for a budget is one year, although breakdowns of budgets by the quarter or month are also common. Budgets are generally expressed in financial terms, but they may occasionally be expressed in units of output, time, or other quantifiable factors.

   Because of their quantitative nature, budgets provide the following assets for organizations:

▌ They act as yardsticks for measuring performance and facilitate comparisons across departments, between levels in the organization, and from one time period to another.

Current Trends Are Not Sustainable

Percent of GDP

- Discretionary Spending
- Net Interest
- Mandatory
- Total Revenues

Financial control is critically important in all organizations. Director of the U.S. Office of Management and Budget Joshua B. Bolten is shown here briefing reporters on the 2007 budget. Charts and graphs such as the one Bolten is using are commonly used to chart and track income and expenses so that decision makers have a visual sense of trends. For instance, the bar chart Bolten is using illustrates that government spending is increasing across different categories but revenues are not keeping pace. Hence, from a control perspective, the budget deficit continues to grow.

▌ They help managers coordinate resources and projects (because they use a common denominator, usually dollars).

▌ They help define the established standards for control.

▌ They provide guidelines about the organization's resources and expectations.

▌ They enable the organization to evaluate the performance of managers and organizational units.

Types of Budgets

Most organizations develop and make use of three different kinds of budgets—financial, operating, and nonmonetary budgets. Table 14.1 summarizes the characteristics of each of these.

1. A *financial budget* indicates where the organization expects to get its cash for the coming time period and how it plans to use it. Because financial resources are critically important, the organization needs to know where those resources will be coming from and how they are to be used. The financial budget provides answers to both of these questions. Customary sources of cash include sales revenue, short- and long-term loans, the sale of assets, and the issuance of new stock.

2. An *operating budget* is concerned with planned operations within the organization. It outlines what quantities of products or services the organization intends to create and what resources will be used to create them. IBM creates an operating budget that specifies how many of each model of its personal computer will be produced each quarter.

3. A *nonmonetary budget* is simply a budget expressed in nonfinancial terms, such as units of output, hours of direct labor, machine hours, or square-foot allocations. Nonmonetary budgets are most commonly used by managers at the lower levels of an organization. For example, a plant manager can schedule work more effectively knowing that he or she has 8,000 labor hours to allocate in a week, rather than trying to determine how best to spend $86,451 in wages in a week.

Online Study Center
Improve Your Grade
–Visual Glossary 14.1
–Visual Glossary 14.2

TABLE 14.1

Types of Budgets

Type of Budget	What the Budget Shows
Financial Budget	*Sources and Uses of Cash*
Cash-flow or cash budget	All sources of cash income and cash expenditures in monthly, weekly, or daily periods
Capital expenditures budget	Costs of major assets such as a new plant, machinery, or land
Balance sheet budget	Forecast of the organization's assets and liabilities in the event that all other budgets are met
Operating Budget	*Planned Operations in Financial Terms*
Sales or revenue budget	Income the organization expects to receive from normal operations
Expense budget	Anticipated expenses for the organization during the coming time period
Profit budget	Anticipated differences between sales or revenues and expenses
Nonmonetary Budget	*Planned Operations in Nonfinancial Terms*
Labor budget	Hours of direct labor available for use
Space budget	Square feet or square meters of space available for various functions
Production budget	Number of units to be produced during the coming time period

Developing Budgets

Traditionally, budgets were developed by top management and the controller and were then imposed on lower-level managers. Although some organizations still follow this pattern, many contemporary organizations now allow all managers to participate in the budget process. As a starting point, top management generally issues a call for budget requests, accompanied by an indication of overall patterns that the budgets may take. For example, if sales are expected to drop in the next year, managers may be told up front to prepare for cuts in operating budgets.

As Figure 14.5 shows, the heads of all operating units typically submit budget requests to the head of their division. An operating unit head might be a department manager in a manufacturing or wholesaling firm or a program director in a social service agency. The division heads might include plant managers, regional sales managers, or college deans. The division head integrates and consolidates the budget requests from operating unit heads into one overall division budget request. A great deal of interaction among managers usually takes place at this stage, as the division head coordinates the budgetary needs of the various departments.

Division budget requests are then forwarded to a budget committee. The budget committee is usually composed of top managers. The committee reviews budget requests from several divisions, and once again, duplications and inconsistencies are corrected. Finally, the budget committee, the controller, and the CEO review and agree on the overall budget for the organization, as well as specific budgets for each operating unit. These decisions are then communicated back to each manager.

Strengths and Weaknesses of Budgeting

Budgets offer a number of advantages:

▌ Budgets facilitate effective control. Placing dollar values on operations enables managers to monitor operations better and to pinpoint problem areas.

▌ Budgets facilitate coordination and communication between departments because they express diverse activities in a common denominator (dollars).

CONCEPT CHECK 14.3

Describe how a budget is created in most organizations. How does a budget help a manager with financial control?

FIGURE 14.5

Developing Budgets in Organizations

Most organizations use the same basic process to develop budgets. Operating units are requested to submit their budget requests to divisions. These divisions, in turn, compile unit budgets and submit their own budgets to the organization. An organizational budget is then compiled for approval by the budget committee, controller, and CEO.

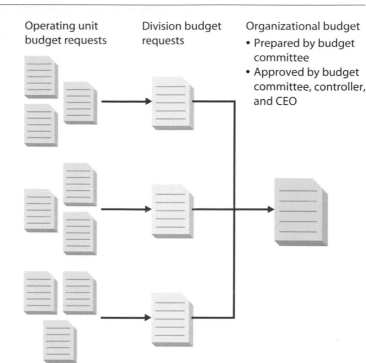

Operating unit budget requests

Division budget requests

Organizational budget
• Prepared by budget committee
• Approved by budget committee, controller, and CEO

▐ Budgets help maintain records of organizational performance and are a logical complement to planning. In other words, as managers develop plans, they should simultaneously consider control measures to accompany them.

▐ Organizations can use budgets to link plans and control by first developing budgets as part of the plan and then using those budgets as part of control.

Budgets have several weaknesses, as well:

▐ Some managers apply budgets too rigidly. Budgets are intended to serve as frameworks, but managers sometimes fail to recognize that changing circumstances may warrant budget adjustments.

▐ The process of developing budgets can also be very time-consuming.

▐ Budgets may limit innovation and change. When all available funds are allocated to specific operating budgets, it may be impossible to procure additional funds to take advantage of an unexpected opportunity.

Online Study Center
Improve Your Grade
Career Snapshot 14.3

Other Tools for Financial Control

Although budgets are the most common means of financial control, three other useful tools are financial statements, ratio analysis, and financial audits.

1. **Financial statements** are a profile of some aspect of an organization's financial circumstances. There are commonly accepted and required ways that financial statements must be prepared and presented.[13] The two most basic financial statements, which are prepared and used by virtually all organizations, are a balance sheet and an income statement.
   • The **balance sheet** lists the assets and liabilities of the organization at a specific point in time, usually the last day of an organization's fiscal year. For example, the balance sheet may summarize the financial condition of

financial statement A profile of some aspect of an organization's financial circumstances.

balance sheet A list of the assets and liabilities of an organization at a specific point in time.

an organization on December 31, 2007. Most balance sheets are divided into current assets (assets that are relatively liquid, or easily convertible into cash), fixed assets (assets that are longer-term in nature and less liquid), current liabilities (debts and other obligations that must be paid in the near future), long-term liabilities (debts and obligations payable over an extended period of time), and stockholders' equity (the owners' claim against the firm's assets).

income statement   A summary of an organization's financial performance over a period of time.

- Whereas the balance sheet reflects a snapshot profile of an organization's financial position at a single point in time, the **income statement** summarizes financial performance over a period of time, usually one year. For example, the income statement might be for the period January 1, 2007, through December 31, 2007. The income statement summarizes the firm's revenues less its expenses to report net income (profit or loss) for the period. Information from the balance sheet and income statement is used in computing important financial ratios.

ratio analysis   The calculation of one or more financial ratios to assess some aspect of the organization's financial health.

2. **Ratio analysis** is the calculation of one or more financial ratios to assess some aspect of the financial health of an organization. Organizations use a variety of different financial ratios as part of financial control.
   - *Liquidity ratios* indicate how liquid (how easily converted into cash) an organization's assets are.
   - *Debt ratios* reflect the organization's ability to meet long-term financial obligations.
   - *Return ratios* show managers and investors how much return the organization is generating relative to its assets.
   - *Coverage ratios* help estimate the organization's ability to cover interest expenses on borrowed capital.
   - *Operating ratios* indicate the effectiveness of specific functional areas rather than of the total organization.

Online Study Center
Improve Your Grade
Visual Glossary 14.4

financial audit   An independent appraisal of an organization's accounting, financial, and operational systems.

3. **Financial audits** are independent appraisals of an organization's accounting, financial, and operational systems. The two major types of financial audits are the external audit and the internal audit.
   - *External audits* are financial appraisals conducted by experts who are not employees of the organization.[14] External audits are typically concerned with determining that the organization's accounting procedures and financial statements are compiled in an objective and verifiable fashion. The organization contracts with certified public accountants (CPAs) for this service. The CPAs' main objective is to verify for stockholders, the IRS, and other interested parties that the methods by which the organization's financial managers and accountants prepare documents and reports are legal and proper. External audits are so important that publicly held corporations are required by law to have external audits regularly, as assurance to investors that the financial reports are reliable.

     Unfortunately, flaws in the auditing process played a major role in the downfall of Enron and several other major firms. The problem can be attributed in part to auditing groups' facing problems with conflicts of interest and eventually losing their objectivity. For instance, Enron was such an important client for its auditing firm, Arthur Andersen, that the auditors started letting the firm take liberties with its accounting systems for fear that, if they were too strict, Enron might take its business to

For example, denim pants were not allowed. Similarly, athletic shoes could be worn as long as they were not white. And all shirts had to have a collar. Nordstrom, the department store chain, is also moving toward bureaucratic control as it works to centralize all of its purchasing in an effort to lower costs.[17] Similarly, Home Depot is moving more toward bureaucratic control in order to cut its costs and more effectively compete with its hard-charging rival, Lowe's.[18]

Decentralized Control

Decentralized control, in contrast, is an approach to organizational control characterized by informal and organic structural arrangements. As Figure 14.6 shows, its goal is employee commitment to the organization. Accordingly, it relies heavily on group norms and a strong corporate culture and gives employees the responsibility for controlling themselves. Employees are encouraged to perform beyond minimally acceptable levels. Organizations using this approach are generally relatively flat. They direct rewards at group performance and favor widespread employee participation.

Levi Strauss practices decentralized control. The firm's managers use groups as the basis for work and have created a culture wherein group norms help facilitate high performance. Rewards are subsequently provided to the higher-performing groups and teams. The company's culture also reinforces contributions to the overall team effort, and employees have a strong sense of loyalty to the organization. Levi's has a flat structure, and power is widely shared. Employee participation is encouraged in all areas of operation. Another company that uses this approach is Southwest Airlines. When Southwest made the decision to "go casual," the firm resisted the temptation to develop dress guidelines. Instead, managers decided that it would allow employees to exercise discretion over their attire and would deal with clearly inappropriate situations on a case-by-case basis.

decentralized control An approach to organizational control based on informal and organic structural arrangements.

CONCEPT CHECK 14.4

Are the differences between bureaucratic control and decentralized control related to differences in organization structure? If so, how? If not, why not?

TEST PREPPER 14.4

ANSWERS CAN BE FOUND ON P. 442

True or False?

_____ 1. The two major forms of structural control—bureaucratic control and decentralized control—represent opposite ends of a continuum.

_____ 2. Structural control is aimed at ensuring that the organization is maintaining an effective alignment with its environment and is moving toward achieving its long-term goals.

_____ 3. Organizations that use decentralized control are less formal than bureaucratic control organizations.

Multiple Choice

_____ 4. Organizations that use a bureaucratic control system typically require all EXCEPT which of the following?
  a. Employee compliance
  b. A reward system directed at individuals
  c. A flat structure with shared influence
  d. Strict rules
  e. Formal control

Online Study Center
ACE the Test
ACE Practice Tests 14.4

STRATEGIC CONTROL

5   *Discuss the relationship between strategy and control, including international strategic control.*

Given the obvious importance of an organization's strategy, it is also important that the organization assess how effective that strategy is in helping the organization meet its goals.[19] To do this requires that the organization integrate its strategy and control systems. This is especially true for the global organization.

Integrating Strategy and Control

strategic control Monitoring, and when necessary adjusting, how effectively the organization's strategies are helping the organization meet its goals and align with its environment.

Strategic control generally focuses on five aspects of organizations—structure, leadership, technology, human resources, and information and operational control systems. For example, an organization should periodically examine its structure to determine whether that structure is facilitating attainment of the strategic goals being sought. Suppose a firm using a functional (U-form) design has an established goal of achieving a sales growth rate of 20 percent per year. However, performance indicators show that it is currently growing at a rate of only 10 percent per year. Detailed analysis might reveal that the current structure is depressing growth in some way (for example, by slowing decision making and inhibiting innovation) and that a divisional (M-form) design would be more likely to bring about the desired growth (by speeding decision making and promoting innovation).

In this way, strategic control focuses on the extent to which the strategy implemented achieves the organization's strategic goals. If, as outlined above, one or more avenues of implementation are inhibiting the attainment of goals, that approach to implementation should be changed. Consequently, the firm might find it necessary to alter its structure, replace key leaders, adopt new technology, modify its human resources, or change its information and operational control systems. For example, IKEA, the Swedish furniture manufacturer, experienced disappointing performance from its internationalization strategy. As a consequence, the company changed how it manages its international operations and has begun enjoying much better results.

A few years ago IKEA, the Swedish furniture manufacturer, developed a strategy calling for aggressive internal expansion. But subsequent performance results based on this strategy were disappointing. As a result, the company developed new methods for managing its international operations and developed new criteria for locating international retail outlets. Now IKEA is performing more effectively.

International Strategic Control

Because of both their relatively large size and the increased complexity associated with international business, global organizations must take an especially pronounced strategic view of their control systems. One very basic question that has to be addressed is whether to manage control from a centralized or a decentralized perspective.[20] Under a centralized system, each organizational unit around the world is responsible for frequently reporting the results of its performance to headquarters. Managers from the home office often visit foreign branches to observe firsthand how the units are functioning.

BP, Unilever, Procter & Gamble, and Sony all use this approach. They believe that centralized control is effective because it allows the home office to keep better informed of the performance of foreign units and to maintain more control over how decisions are made. For example, BP discovered that its Australian subsidiary was not billing its customers for charges as quickly as were its competitors. By shortening the billing cycle, BP now receives customer payments five days earlier than before. Managers believe that they discovered this oversight only because of a centralized financial control system.

In organizations that use a decentralized control system, foreign branches are allowed to report less frequently and in less detail. For example, each unit may submit summary performance statements on a quarterly basis and provide full statements only once a year. Similarly, visits from the home office are less frequent and less focused on monitoring and assessing performance. IBM, Ford, and Shell all use this approach. Because Ford practices decentralized control of its design function, European designers have developed several innovative automobile design features. Managers believe that if control had been more centralized, these designers would not have had the freedom to develop their new ideas.

TEST PREPPER 14.5

ANSWERS CAN BE FOUND ON P. 442

True or False?

_____ 1. A bureaucratic global organization will typically require branch offices to give reports less often and in less detail than a decentralized global firm.

_____ 2. Control should be integrated with planning from the very beginning.

Multiple Choice

_____ 3. Strategic control systems generally focus on which aspect of an organization?
   a. Structure   d. Information
   b. Leadership   e. All of the above
   c. Technology

Online Study Center
ACE the Test
ACE Practice Tests 14.5

MANAGING CONTROL IN ORGANIZATIONS

6 ▷ *Identify characteristics of effective control, why people resist control, and how managers can overcome this resistance.*

Effective control, whether at the operations, financial, structural, or strategic level, successfully regulates and monitors organizational activities. To use the control process, managers must recognize the characteristics of effective control and understand how to identify and overcome occasional resistance to control.[21]

Characteristics of Effective Control

Control systems tend to be most effective when they are integrated with planning and when they are flexible, accurate, timely, and objective.

▌ *Integration with planning.* The more explicit and precise the link between planning and control, the more effective the control system is. The best way to integrate planning and control is to account for control as plans develop. In other words, as goals are set during the planning process, attention should be paid to developing standards that will reflect how well the plan is realized.

▌ *Flexibility.* The control system itself must be flexible enough to accommodate change. Consider, for example, an organization whose diverse product line requires seventy-five different raw materials. The company's inventory control system must be able to manage and monitor current levels of inventory for all seventy-five materials. When a change in product line changes the number of raw materials needed, or when the required quantities of the existing materials change, the control system should be flexible enough to handle the revised requirements. The alternative—designing and implementing a new control system—is an avoidable expense.

▌ *Accuracy.*   Managers make a surprisingly large number of decisions on the basis of inaccurate information. Field representatives may hedge their sales estimates to make themselves look better. Production managers may hide costs to meet their targets. Human resource managers may overestimate their minority-recruiting prospects to meet affirmative action goals. In each case, the information that other managers receive is inaccurate, and the results of inaccurate information may be quite dramatic. If sales projections are inflated, a manager might cut advertising (thinking it is no longer needed) or increase advertising (to build further momentum). Similarly, a production manager who is unaware of hidden costs may quote a sales price much lower than desirable. Or a human resource manager may speak out publicly on the effectiveness of the company's minority recruiting, only to find out later that these prospects have been overestimated. In each case, the result of inaccurate information is inappropriate managerial action.

▌ *Timeliness.*   Timeliness does not necessarily mean quickness. Rather, it describes a control system that provides information as often as is necessary. Retail organizations usually need sales results daily so that they can manage cash flow and adjust advertising and promotion. In contrast, they may require information about complete physical inventory only quarterly or annually. In general, the more uncertain and unstable the circumstances, the more frequently measurement is needed.

▌ *Objectivity.*   The control system should provide information that is as objective as possible. To appreciate this, imagine the task of a manager responsible for control of his organization's human resources. He asks two plant managers to submit reports. One manager notes that morale at his plant is "okay," that grievances are "about where they should be," and that turnover is "under control." The other reports that absenteeism at her plant is running at 4 percent, that sixteen grievances have been filed this year (compared with twenty-four last year), and that turnover is 12 percent. The second report will nearly always be more useful than the first. Of course, managers also need to look beyond the numbers when assessing performance. For example, a plant manager may be boosting productivity and profit margins by putting too much pressure on workers and using poor-quality materials. As a result, impressive short-run gains may be overshadowed by longer-run increases in employee turnover and customer complaints.

Resistance to Control

Managers sometimes make the mistake of assuming that the value of an effective control system is self-evident to employees. This is not always so, however. Many employees resist control, especially if they feel overcontrolled, if they think control is inappropriately focused or rewards inefficiency, or if they are uncomfortable with accountability.

▌ *Overcontrol.*   Overcontrol becomes especially problematic when the control directly affects employee behavior. An organization that instructs its employees when to come to work, where to park, when to have morning coffee, and when to leave for the day exerts considerable control over people's daily activities. Yet many organizations attempt to control not only these but other aspects of work behavior as well. Of particular relevance in recent years is some companies' effort to control their employees' access to private e-mail and the Internet during work hours. Some companies have no policies governing these activities, some attempt to limit them, and some attempt to forbid them altogether.[22]

Troubles arise when employees perceive these attempts to limit their behavior as unreasonable. A company that tells its employees how to dress, how to arrange their desks, and how to wear their hair may meet with still more resistance. Employees at DaimlerChrysler used to complain because if they drove a non-DaimlerChrysler vehicle, they were forced to park in a distant parking lot. People felt that these efforts to control their personal behavior (what kind of car to drive) were excessive. Managers eventually removed these controls and now allow open parking.

▌ ***Inappropriate focus.***   The control system may be too narrow, or it may focus too much on quantifiable variables and leave no room for analysis or interpretation. A sales standard that encourages high-pressure tactics to maximize short-run sales may do so at the expense of goodwill from long-term customers. Such a standard is too narrow. A university reward system that encourages faculty members to publish large numbers of articles but fails to consider the quality of the work is also inappropriately focused. Employees resist the intent of the control system by focusing their efforts only at the performance indicators being used.

▌ ***Rewards for inefficiency.***   Imagine two operating departments that are approaching the end of the fiscal year. Department 1 expects to have $25,000 of its budget left over; department 2 is already $10,000 in the red. As a result, department 1 is likely to have its budget cut for the next year ("They had money left, so they obviously got too much to begin with"), and department 2 is likely to get a budget increase ("They obviously haven't been getting enough money"). Thus department 1 is punished for being efficient, and department 2 is rewarded for being inefficient. (No wonder departments commonly hasten to deplete their budgets as the end of the year approaches!) As with inappropriate focus of control, people resist the intent of this control and behave in ways that run counter to the organization's intent.

▌ ***Too much accountability.***   Effective controls allow managers to determine whether or not employees successfully discharge their responsibilities. If standards are properly set and performance is accurately measured, managers know when problems arise and which departments and individuals are responsible. People who do not want to be answerable for their mistakes or who do not want to work as hard as their boss might like therefore resist control. For example, American Express has a system that provides daily information on how many calls each of its customer service representatives handles. If one representative has typically worked at a slower pace and handled fewer calls than other representatives, that individual's deficient performance can more easily be pinpointed.

"The dip in sales seems to coincide with the decision to eliminate the sales staff."

In recent years, many organizations have sought ways to more effectively manage the size of their workforce, often through workforce reductions. Eliminating unnecessary or redundant jobs is indeed an effective strategy. But businesses sometimes go too far, eliminating jobs that have a detrimental impact on the company. One executive noted that his firm had eliminated the fat but then cut out some muscle too! The managers shown here may have also fallen prey to that same mistake—cutting their sales force so much that their revenues have declined significantly.

Overcoming Resistance to Control

Perhaps the best way to overcome resistance to control is to create effective control to begin with. If control systems are properly integrated with organizational planning and if the controls are flexible, accurate, timely, and objective, the organization will be less likely to overcontrol, to focus on inappropriate standards, or to reward inefficiency. Two other ways to overcome resistance are encouraging employee participation and developing verification procedures.

1. *Encourage employee participation.* We noted in Chapter 7 that participation can help overcome resistance to change. By the same token, when employees are involved with planning and implementing the control system, they are less likely to resist it. For instance, employee participation in planning, decision making, and quality control at the Chevrolet Gear and Axle plant in Detroit has resulted in increased employee concern for quality and a greater commitment to meeting standards.

2. *Develop verification procedures.* Multiple standards and information systems provide checks and balances in control and allow the organization to verify the accuracy of performance indicators. Suppose a production manager argues that she failed to meet a certain cost standard because of increased prices of raw materials. A properly designed inventory control system will either support or contradict her explanation. Suppose that an employee who was fired for excessive absences argues that he was not absent "for a long time." An effective human resource control system should have records that support the termination. Resistance to control declines when such verification procedures are in place, because they protect both employees and management. If the production manager's claim about the rising cost of raw materials is supported by the inventory control records, she will not be held solely accountable for failing to meet the cost standard, and some action will probably be taken to lower the cost of raw materials.

CONCEPT CHECK 14.5

Why do some people resist control? How can managers help overcome this resistance?

TEST PREPPER 14.6

ANSWERS CAN BE FOUND ON P. 442

True or False?

_____ 1. Strict adherence to control is essential for control effectiveness.

_____ 2. An organization that tracks the number of copies made by each employee at the copy machine may create too much accountability and resistance to control.

_____ 3. Multiple standards and information systems provide checks and balances in control and allow the organization to verify the accuracy of performance indicators.

Multiple Choice

_____ 4. Managers may sometimes make the mistake of assuming that the value of an effective control system is self-evident to employees. Which of the following is NOT a cause of resistance to control?
a. Overcontrol
b. Inappropriate focus
c. Rewards for inefficiency
d. Too much accountability
e. Too much employee participation

Online Study Center
ACE the Test
ACE Practice Tests 14.6

BUILDING EFFECTIVE TIME-MANAGEMENT SKILLS

Online Study Center
Improve Your Grade
Exercises: Building Effective Skills

Exercise Overview

Time-management skills—a manager's ability to prioritize work, to work efficiently, and to delegate appropriately—play a major role in the control function. That is, a manager can use time-management skills to control his or her own work more effectively. This exercise will help demonstrate the relationship between time-management skills and control.

Exercise Background

You are a middle manager in a small manufacturing plant. Today is Monday, and you have just returned from a week of vacation. The first thing you discover is that your assistant will not be in today. His aunt died, and he is out of town at the funeral. He did, however, leave you the note shown below.

Exercise Task

With the information above as context, do the following:

1. Prioritize the work that needs to be done by sorting the information in your assistant's list into three categories: very timely, moderately timely, and less timely.

2. Are importance and timeliness the same thing?

3. What additional information must you acquire before you can begin to prioritize this work?

4. How would your approach differ if your assistant were in today?

Dear Boss:

Sorry about not being here today. I will be back tomorrow. In the meantime, here are some things you need to know:

1. Ms. Glinski [your boss] wants to see you today at 4:00.
2. The shop steward wants to see you as soon as possible about a labor problem.
3. Mr. Bateman [one of your big customers] has a complaint about a recent shipment.
4. Ms. Ferris [one of your major suppliers] wants to discuss a change in delivery schedules.
5. Mr. Prescott from the Chamber of Commerce wants you to attend a breakfast meeting on Wednesday to discuss our expansion plans.
6. The legal office wants to discuss our upcoming OSHA inspection.
7. Human resources wants to know when you can interview someone for the new supervisor's position.
8. Jack Williams, the machinist you fired last month, has been hanging around the parking lot, and his presence is making some employees uncomfortable.

Learning About "Real" Control

Online Study Center
Improve Your Grade
–Exercises: Experiential Exercise
–Interactive Skills Self-Assessment

Purpose

The purpose of this exercise is to give you additional insights into how organizations deal with fundamental control issues.

Instructions

Step 1: Working individually, interview a manager, owner, or employee of an organization. The individual can be a local entrepreneur, a manager in a larger company, or an administrator at your college or university, among other choices. If you currently work, interviewing your boss would be excellent.

Using your own words, ask these general questions:

1. In your organization, what are the most important resources to control?

2. Who is primarily responsible for control?

3. Which level of control is most important to your organization? (Briefly describe the three levels of operations control.)

4. Do you use budgets? If so, what kinds and in what ways?

5. Which of these types of control does your organization most typically use? (Briefly describe bureaucratic and decentralized control.)

6. Have you had any instances in which employees resisted control? Can you explain why and what you did about it?

Step 2: Form small groups of four or five. Then do the following:

1. Have each member describe the organization and manager interviewed and the interview findings.

2. Identify as many commonalities across findings as possible.

3. Summarize the differences you found.

4. Select one group member to report your group's experiences to the rest of the class.

Wake Up, "Zombies"!

If the U.S. economy is "sluggish," then the Japanese economy must be described as "comatose." The world's second-largest economy is suffering from a host of problems: Banks are overloaded with bad loans, the Tokyo real estate market bubble has burst, and stock prices have lost much of their value. In addition, the government props up failing businesses through low-cost or no-cost loans, a practice that only increases distrust of the system. "This kind of intervention can work in the short term. But from a long-term point of view it has terrible implications: Investors understand that the market is artificial, and accordingly they pull back," states analyst Jean-Marie Eveillard.

Yet many of the problems plaguing Japanese corporations today are not related to economic or political woes but, rather, to poor management. "Ninety percent of the Japanese economy is made up of domestic companies that are low-tech and low-productivity," claims consultant Masao Hirano. However, a few pioneering firms are starting to demonstrate that "by becoming better focused, [Japanese companies] can survive and even prosper," says analyst Satoru Oyama.

Cosmetics maker Shiseido held too much inventory and had overly high expenses, leading to a $550 million loss over two years. But rather than calling for a government bailout, Shiseido executives focused on

> *"We're showing other Japanese companies that it's possible to reverse a slide."*
>
> —Seiji Nishimori, former chief logistics officer, Shiseido

fundamental improvements. Better technology allowed them to control and forecast inventory more effectively. They cut costs throughout the corporation and curtailed their product line. After Shiseido returned to profitability, former chief logistics officer Seiji Nishimori boasted, "We're showing other Japanese companies that it's possible to reverse a slide."

Canon, the world's leading maker of copiers and laser printers, has also taken a disciplined approach to performance improvement. CEO Fujio Mitarai replaced every manufacturing line at the firm's twenty-nine Japanese factories with small, self-directed teams of half a dozen workers that do the work that was previously done by thirty laborers. The teams discovered more efficient inventory management techniques, and Canon was able to close twenty of its thirty-four parts warehouses. "Manufacturing is where most of the costs lie," Mitarai claims. Canon earnings improved by 53 percent, enabling Mitarai to conclude, "We're much more profitable today because of these changes."

The success of notable high performers such as multinational Toyota has caused Japanese firms to realize the benefits of global cost-competitiveness. High-tech companies are abandoning manufacturing and shifting their attention to R&D to counteract an influx of inexpensive electronics from China, Taiwan, and Korea. For example, NEC has moved out of the unprofitable semiconductor chip–making business and focused on more lucrative cell phones and software. Sharp, too, has given up on low-margin PC monitors and refocused its operations on innovative products such as liquid crystal displays for PDAs. Sony is working on revolutionary new computer chips while reducing its investment in consumer electronics.

All three companies say they have changed their approach and now listen to their consumers more closely. "We were proud of our great technology, and just pumped out products without thinking of our customers' needs," says NEC director Kaoru Tosaka. "Now, we're emphasizing efficiency, profits, and clients."

These companies are an exception in Japan, where so-called zombie firms are bailed out over and over again by a government that fears unemployment and chaos if businesses fail. But the zombies need to heed the lessons these stellar firms have learned. Watch inventory. Cut costs where possible. Use information technology more effectively. Simplify product lines. Experiment with new ways of organizing. Shut down money-losing businesses. Choose areas where the firm can add value. Listen to customer feedback. If the zombies could adopt these suggestions, the Japanese—and the rest of the world—would surely benefit.

Case Questions

1. Use the case to find at least one example of each purpose of control—adapting to environmental change, limiting the accumulation of error, coping with organizational complexity, and minimizing costs. What are the consequences for firms that do not achieve these purposes?

2. List every improvement that is mentioned in the case—for example, closing warehouses and adopting customers' suggestions. For each item, tell whether it represents preliminary, screening, or postaction control. Then tell whether it represents operations, financial, structural, or strategic control.

3. Japanese firms are likely to encounter a great deal of resistance to change as they attempt to improve their control. What advice would you give to managers whose workers are resisting efforts to improve control?

Case References

"2005 Annual Report," Shiseido website, www.shiseido.co.jp on February 15, 2006; Clay Chandler, "Japan's Horror Show," *Fortune*, November 10, 2002, www.fortune.com on February 15, 2003; Irene M. Kunii, "Quick Studies," *BusinessWeek*, November 18, 2002, pp. 48–49 (quote p. 48); Justin Lahart, "Bank of Japan to Buy Stocks," *CNN/Money*, September 18, 2002, www.cnnmoney.com on February 15, 2003.

LEARNING OBJECTIVE REVIEW

☼ *Online Study Center*
Improve Your Grade
–Learning Objective Review
–Audio Chapter Review
–Study Guide to Go

☼ *Online Study Center*
ACE the Test
Audio Chapter Quiz

1 ▶ *Explain the purpose of control, identify different types of control, and describe the steps in the control process.*

- Control is the regulation of organizational activities so that some targeted element of performance remains within acceptable limits.

- Control provides ways to
  - adapt to environmental change
  - limit the accumulation of errors
  - cope with organizational complexity
  - minimize costs

- Control can focus on the following resources:
  - physical   information
  - human   financial

- Control includes the following levels:
  - operations   structural
  - financial   strategic

- Control is the function of
  - managers
  - controllers
  - operating employees

- The steps in the control process are
  - establishing standards of expected performance
  - measuring actual performance
  - comparing performance to the standards
  - evaluating the comparison and taking appropriate action

2 ▶ *Identify and explain the three forms of operations control.*

- Operations control focuses on the processes the organization uses to transform resources into products or services.

- There are three types of operations control:
  - preliminary control: concerned with the resources that serve as inputs to the system
  - screening control: concerned with the transformation processes used by the organization
  - postaction control: focuses on the outputs of the organization

- Most organizations need multiple control systems because no one system alone can provide adequate control.

3 ▶ *Describe budgets and other tools for financial control.*

- Financial control focuses on controlling the organization's financial resources.

- The foundation of financial control is budgets—plans expressed in numerical terms.

- Most organizations rely on the following budgets:
  - financial
  - operating
  - nonmonetary

- Budgets are generally produced first in the smaller operating units and finally at the organization level.

- Financial statements, various kinds of ratios, and external and internal audits are also important tools that organizations use as part of financial control.

4 ▶ *Identify and distinguish between two opposing forms of structural control.*

- Structural control addresses how well an organization's structural elements serve their intended purpose.

- There are two contrasting forms of structural control:
  - bureaucratic control: relatively formal and mechanistic
  - decentralized control: informal and organic

- Most organizations use a form of organizational control that falls somewhere between these two extremes.

5 ▶ *Discuss the relationship between strategy and control, including international strategic control.*

- Strategic control focuses on how effectively the organization's strategies are succeeding in helping the organization meet its goals.

- The integration of strategy and control is generally achieved through
  - organization structure
  - leadership
  - technology
  - human resources
  - information and operational control systems

- International strategic control is also important for multinational organizations.
- Organizations must decide whether to practice centralized or decentralized control.

---

6 ▶ *Identify characteristics of effective control, why people resist control, and how managers can overcome this resistance.*

- One way to increase the effectiveness of control is to fully integrate planning and control.
- The control system should be
    flexible
    accurate
    timely
    objective

- Employees may resist organizational controls because of
    overcontrol
    inappropriate focus
    rewards for inefficiency
    a desire to avoid accountability
- Managers can overcome this resistance by
    improving the effectiveness of controls
    allowing employee participation
    developing verification procedures

Online Study Center **RESOURCES**

Prepare for Class, Improve Your Grade, and ACE the Test. These Student Achievement resources include:

ACE Practice Tests	Interactive Skills Assessments	Study Guide to Go
End of Chapter Exercises	Knowledgebank	Video Segments
Glossaries (visual and print)	Reviews (audio and print)	Summaries/Outlines
Flashcards		

To access these learning and study tools, go to: **college.hmco.com/pic/griffinSAS**

Intel is acutely aware of new technologies. Chief Executive Officer Paul Otellini is shown here at the launch of the firm's new Core Duo chip. Intel claims the Core Duo chip has lower power requirements and higher performance. The processor, which has two computing engines built into a single chip, is expected to enable smaller, living-room-friendly Viiv systems and will power the next-generation mobile platform, the Centrino Duo.

1 ▸ *Describe and explain the nature of operations management.*

2 ▸ *Identify and discuss the components involved in designing effective operations systems.*

3 ▸ *Discuss organizational technologies and their role in operations management.*

4 ▸ *Identify and discuss the components involved in implementing operations systems through supply chain management.*

> *"The point is to move the whole product line . . . to a more competitive performance position . . . rather than lower the price to be competitive."*
> —Gordon Moore, founder of Intel and creator of Moore's Law

Chapter Outline

Online Study Center
Prepare for Class
Chapter Outline

6 ▶ *Explain the meaning and importance of managing productivity, productivity trends, and ways to improve productivity.*

5 ▶ *Explain the meaning and importance of managing quality and total quality management.*

Competing
Through Operations

In 1965, when color televisions were rare and slide rules prevailed, engineer Gordon Moore predicted, "Integrated circuits will lead to such wonders as home computers, automatic controls for automobiles, and personal portable communications equipment." Moore also noted that the number of transistors (roughly equivalent to processing capacity) on a semiconductor chip was doubling each year. This statement was interpreted by others to mean that capacity *must* double yearly, and it became known as "Moore's Law." (Today, the doubling time is actually closer to two

PRACTICING MANAGER'S TERMS

operations management *p. 400*
manufacturing *p. 400*
service organization *p. 401*
product-service mix *p. 402*
capacity *p. 402*
facilities *p. 403*
location *p. 403*
layout *p. 403*
technology *p. 405*
automation *p. 405*
robotics *p. 408*

Online Study Center
Improve Your Grade
  —Flashcards
  —Glossary

robot *p. 408*
supply chain management *p. 409*
purchasing management *p. 410*
inventory control *p. 410*
just-in-time (JIT) method *p. 411*
quality *p. 412*
Malcolm Baldridge Award *p. 413*
total quality management (TQM)
  (quality assurance) *p. 413*
benchmarking *p. 415*
outsourcing *p. 415*
ISO 9000:2000 *p. 416*
statistical quality control (SQC)
  p. 417
productivity *p. 418*

KEY TERMS

product layout *p. 404*
process layout *p. 404*
fixed-position layout *p. 404*
cellular layout *p. 405*
computer-assisted
  manufacturing *p. 407*
value-added analysis *p. 415*
cycle time *p. 416*
ISO 14000 *p. 417*

You should be able to define and use terms that are part of the practicing manager's vocabulary, as well as those that are integral in the language of management.

years.) Moore went on to found Intel, the semiconductor chip maker that successfully applied his law to its design and manufacturing operations.

Even though Moore never intended his observation to become a "law," former Intel CEO Craig Barrett used it to goad his employees to higher performance. "Every time we don't live up to Moore's Law, somebody else does," Barrett told his researchers. "We don't adhere to Moore's Law for the hell of it," Barrett adds. "We dangle Moore's Law in front of the new young minds . . . and say, 'Hey, your predecessors were smart enough to figure this out for the past 20 or 30 years—why aren't you?'" Former vice president of technology Sunlin Chou thinks that the law is "a self-fulfilling prophecy." He states, "In the end, Moore's Law is a philosophy as well as a strategy. It gives us the confidence to believe in the future."

Intel's faith in Moore's Law has led it to take risks in the development of innovative new products. In Ireland, the firm built its largest-ever fabrication plant, a $2.5-billion facility to produce the new Itanium chips. In 2006, that plant will double in size, while other plants in Israel and Arizona are due to come on line next year. Former CEO Andy Grove claims that "capacity is strategy." Worldwide, 80 percent of PCs contain Intel microprocessors, trouncing number-two Advanced Micro Devices (AMD). Intel's advantage lies in its superior design—its Pentium 4 processor has speeds of up to 3 gigahertz, whereas AMD's best efforts still fall short of 2. Barrett believes that Intel can build enough capacity to drive rivals out of the industry. Some, like analyst Jonathon Joseph, worry that Intel may be overbuilding. "Intel has a phobia about capacity," Joseph claims. "They're very concerned that they'll miss the next upturn [in demand for chips]. . . . They aimed forward to hit the duck, and the duck isn't there." Intel plans to shut down older plants as it opens new ones to keep capacity at a sustainable level.

The state-of-the-art factory employs flexible manufacturing to ensure that the plant can produce the next generation of chips. Intel's new facilities will "copy exactly" the design of the first, a cornerstone of the chip maker's innovation strategy. Chou explains, "Once we come up with a manufacturing process, we don't let the chip design team tinker with it." The copy-exactly technique ensures that new facilities become productive immediately and that they do not introduce any new errors into the exacting process of chip fabrication. Moore emphasizes the importance of "copy exactly," saying, "it takes a couple of years out of the life span of a generation of products. That in turn allows us to set a faster pace of innovation for our competitors to keep up with."

Another key piece of Intel's operations strategy is constant innovation, even if that means cannibalizing sales of older products. The new Itanium, for example, will replace the Pentium. During the transition, Pentium chips will be cheaper, but as Itanium production increases, Intel will cease manufacturing Pentiums. Moore says, "The point is to move the whole product line, not just a single part, to a more competitive performance position . . . rather than lower the price to be competitive."

Even as the first factory is nearing completion, Intel's R&D teams have begun work on the next-generation processors. The manufacturer is also bringing the efficiencies of Moore's Law to the manufacture of communications chips. These chips are currently made in small batches to meet each assembler's unique requirements. Intel is working to place standardized wireless and computing technology on the same chip. The semiconductors create a national wireless communications network that provides wireless connectivity to any device, anywhere in the United States.

It is a foregone conclusion that Intel will dominate chip design and manufacture for the foreseeable future. However, much of the demand for high-tech chips is now in telecommunications and flash memory, markets dominated by Samsung and other Asian firms. Intel has mastered the art of high-tech manufacturing. Can it master the challenge of expanding those skills into new markets?[1]

Managers at Intel have made innovation a hallmark of their company's operations. This innovation, in turn, has allowed them to charge premium prices and earn superior profits. But to be successful with this strategy, the firm must also maintain its position as industry leader. And Intel seems to be doing just that by relying heavily on operations management as a centerpiece of its overall strategy.

In this chapter we explore operations management, quality, and productivity. We first introduce operations management and discuss its role in general management and organizational strategy. The next three sections discuss the design of operations systems, organizational technologies, and implementing operations systems. We then introduce and discuss various issues in managing for quality and total quality. Finally, we discuss productivity, which is closely related to quality.

THE NATURE OF OPERATIONS MANAGEMENT

1 ▸ *Describe and explain the nature of operations management.*

Operations management is at the core of what organizations do as they add value and create products and services. But what exactly are operations? And how are they managed? **Operations management** is the set of managerial activities used by an organization to transform resource inputs into products and services. For instance, when Dell Computer buys electronic components, assembles them into PCs, and then ships them to customers, it is engaging in operations management.

operations management The total set of managerial activities used by an organization to transform resource inputs into products, services, or both.

The Importance of Operations

Operations is an important functional concern for organizations, because efficient and effective management of operations goes a long way toward ensuring competitiveness and overall organizational performance, as well as quality and productivity. Inefficient or ineffective operations management, on the other hand, will almost inevitably lead to poorer performance and lower levels of both quality and productivity.

In an economic sense, operations management creates value and utility of one type or another, depending on the nature of the firm's products or services. If the product is a physical good, such as a Harley-Davidson motorcycle, operations creates value and provides "form utility" by combining many dissimilar inputs (sheet metal, rubber, paint, combustion engines, and human skills) to make something (a motorcycle) that is more valuable than the actual cost of the inputs used to create it. The inputs are converted from their incoming form into a new physical form. This conversion is typical of manufacturing operations and essentially reflects the organization's technology.

In contrast, the operations activities of American Airlines create value and provide time and place utility through the airline's services. The airline transports passengers and freight according to agreed-upon departure and arrival places and times. Other service operations, such as a Coors beer distributorship or a Gap retail store, create value and provide place and possession utility by bringing together the customer and products made by others. Although the organizations in these examples produce different kinds of products or services, their operations processes share many important features.[2]

Online Study Center
Improve Your Grade
Career Snapshot 15.1

Manufacturing and Production Operations

Because manufacturing once dominated U.S. industry, the entire area of operations management used to be called production management. **Manufacturing** is a form of business that combines and transforms resources into tangible outcomes that are then sold to others. The Goodyear Tire & Rubber Company is a manufacturer because it combines rubber and chemical compounds and uses blending equipment and molding machines to create tires.

During the 1970s, manufacturing entered a long period of decline in the United States, primarily because of foreign competition. United States firms had grown lax and sluggish, and new foreign competitors arrived on the scene with better equip-

manufacturing A form of business that combines and transforms resource inputs into tangible outcomes.

ment and much higher levels of efficiency. For example, steel companies in the Far East were able to produce high-quality steel for much lower prices than were U.S. companies such as Bethlehem Steel and U.S. Steel (now USX Corporation). Faced with a battle for survival, many companies underwent a long and difficult period of change by eliminating waste and transforming themselves into leaner and more efficient and responsive entities. They reduced their workforce dramatically, closed antiquated or unnecessary plants, and modernized their remaining plants. In the last decade, their efforts have started to pay dividends, as U.S. business has regained its competitive position in many different industries. Although manufacturers from other parts of the world are still formidable competitors, and U.S. firms may never again be competitive in some markets, the overall picture is much better than it was just a few years ago. And prospects continue to look bright.[3]

Service Operations

During the decline of the manufacturing sector, tremendous growth in the service sector kept the U.S. economy from declining at the same rate. A **service organization** is one that transforms resources into an intangible output and creates time or place utility for its customers. For example, Merrill Lynch makes stock transactions for its customers, Avis leases cars to its customers, and your local hairdresser cuts your hair. In 1947 the service sector was responsible for less than half of the U.S. gross national product (GNP). By 1975, however, this figure reached 65 percent, and by 2000 it was over 75 percent. The service sector was responsible for almost 90 percent of all new jobs created in the United States during the 1990s. Managers have come to see that many of the tools, techniques, and methods that are used in a factory are also useful to a service firm. For example, managers of automobile plants and hair salons both have to decide how to design their facility, identify the best location for it, determine optimal capacity, make decisions about inventory storage, establish procedures for purchasing raw materials, and set standards for productivity and quality.

service organization An organization that transforms resources into services.

CONCEPT CHECK 15.1

How can a service organization use techniques from operations management? Give specific examples from your college or university (a provider of educational services).

The Role of Operations in Organizational Strategy

It should be clear by this point that operations management is very important to organizations. Beyond its impact on such factors as competitiveness, quality, and productivity, it also directly influences the organization's overall level of effectiveness. For example, the deceptively simple strategic decision of whether to stress high quality regardless of cost, lowest possible cost regardless of quality, or some combination of the two has numerous important implications. A highest-possible-quality strategy will dictate state-of-the-art technology and rigorous control of product design and materials specifications. A combination strategy might call for lower-grade technology and less concern about product design and materials specifications. Just as strategy affects operations management, so, too, does operations management affect strategy. Suppose that a firm decides to upgrade the quality of its products or services. The organization's ability to implement the decision is dependent in part on current production capabilities and other resources. If existing technology will not permit higher-quality work, and if the organization lacks the resources to replace its technology, increasing quality to meet the new standards will be difficult.

True or False?

_____ 1. Operations management is the total set of managerial activities used by an organization to transform resource inputs into products, services, or both.

_____ 2. Because manufacturing once dominated U.S. industry, the entire area of operations management used to be called production management.

Online Study Center
ACE the Test
ACE Practice Tests 15.1

Multiple Choice

_____ 3. A manufacturing organization creates which type of utility?
a. Time
b. Tangible
c. Intangible
d. Place
e. All of the above

DESIGNING OPERATIONS SYSTEMS

2 | *Identify and discuss the components involved in designing effective operations systems.*

The problems, challenges, and opportunities faced by operations managers revolve around the acquisition and utilization of resources for conversion. Their goals include both efficiency and effectiveness. A number of issues and decisions must be addressed as operations systems are designed. The most basic ones are product-service mix, capacity, and facilities.

Determining Product-Service Mix

product-service mix How many and what kinds of products or services (or both) a firm offers.

A natural starting point in designing operations systems is determining the **product-service mix**. This decision flows from corporate, business, and marketing strategies. Managers have to make a number of decisions about their products and services, starting with how many and what kinds to offer.[4] Procter & Gamble, for example, makes regular, tartar-control, whitening, and various other formulas of Crest toothpaste and packages them in several different sizes of tubes, pumps, and other dispensers. Decisions also have to be made about the level of quality desired, the optimal cost of each product or service, and exactly how each is to be designed. GE, for example, recently reduced the number of parts in its industrial circuit breakers from 28,000 to 1,275. This whole process was achieved by carefully analyzing product design and production methods.

Capacity Decisions

capacity The amount of products, services, or both that can be produced by an organization.

The **capacity** decision involves choosing the amount of products, services, or both that can be produced by the organization. Determining whether to build a factory capable of making 5,000 or 8,000 units per day is a capacity decision. So, too, is deciding whether to build a restaurant with 100 or 150 seats, or a bank with five or ten teller stations. The capacity decision is truly a high-risk one because of the uncertainties of future product demand and the large monetary stakes involved. An organization that builds capacity exceeding its needs may commit resources (capital investment) that will never be recovered. Alternatively, an organization can build a facility with a smaller capacity than expected demand. Doing so may result in lost market opportunities, but it may also free capital resources for use elsewhere in the organization.

a 747 would require an enormous plant, so instead the airplane itself remains stationary, and people and machines move around it as it is assembled.

▌ A **cellular layout** is used when families of products can follow similar flow paths. It is a relatively new approach to facilities design. A clothing manufacturer, for example, might create a cell, or designated area, dedicated to making a family of pockets, such as pockets for shirts, coats, blouses, and slacks. Although each kind of pocket is unique, the same basic equipment and methods are used to make all of them. Hence, all pockets might be made in the same area and then delivered directly to different product layout assembly areas where the shirts, coats, blouses, and slacks are actually being assembled.

> **cellular layout** A physical configuration of facilities used when families of products can follow similar flow paths.

TEST PREPPER 15.2

ANSWERS CAN BE FOUND ON P. 442

True or False?

_____ 1. An example of a capacity decision made by the Girl Scouts would be how many troops an area could support.

_____ 2. When an organization determines how many and what kinds of products or services (or both) to offer, it is determining the layout configuration.

Multiple Choice

_____ 3. When Ford Motor Company designed the Focus automobile, it designed a straight-line flow of work for assembling the automobiles. This was an example of which layout?
  a. Process   d. Cellular
  b. Fixed-position   e. Automation
  c. Product

_____ 4. A hospital represents what type of facilities layout?
  a. Process   d. Cellular
  b. Fixed-position   e. Automation
  c. Product

Online Study Center
ACE the Test
ACE Practice Tests 15.2

ORGANIZATIONAL TECHNOLOGIES

3 ▷ *Discuss organizational technologies and their role in operations management.*

One central element of effective operations management is technology. In Chapter 2 we defined **technology** as the set of processes and systems used by organizations to convert resources into products or services.

> **technology** The methods available for converting resources into products or services.

Manufacturing Technology

Numerous forms of manufacturing technology are used in organizations. In Chapter 6 we discussed the research of Joan Woodward. Recall that Woodward identified three forms of technology—unit or small-batch, large-batch or mass-production, and continuous-process technology.[5] Each form of technology was thought to be associated with a specific type of organization structure. Of course, newer forms of technology not considered by Woodward also warrant attention. Three of these are automation, computer-assisted manufacturing, and robotics.

Automation

Automation, the most recent step in the development of machines and machine-controlling devices, is the process of designing work so that it can be completely or

> **automation** The process of designing work so that it can be completely or almost completely performed by machines.

almost completely performed by machines. Because automated machines operate quickly and make few errors, they increase the amount of work that can be done. Thus automation helps to improve products and services and fosters innovation. Machine-controlling devices have been around since the 1700s. James Watt, a Scottish engineer, invented a mechanical speed control to regulate the speed of steam engines in 1787. The Jacquard loom, developed by a French inventor, was controlled by paper cards with holes punched in them. Early accounting and computing equipment was controlled by similar punched cards.

Automation relies on the following:

▌ Feedback and Information: the flow of information from the machine back to the sensor

▌ Sensors: the parts of the system that gather information and compare it to preset standards

▌ A control mechanism: the device that sends instructions to the automatic machine

Early automatic machines were primitive, and the use of automation was relatively slow to develop. These elements are illustrated by the example in Figure 15.2.

The big move to automate factories began during World War II. The shortage of skilled workers and the development of high-speed computers combined to create tremendous interest in automation. Programmable automation (the use of computers to control machines) was introduced during this era, far outstripping conventional automation (the use of mechanical or electromechanical devices to control machines). The automobile industry began to use automatic machines for a variety of jobs. In fact, the term *automation* came into use in the 1950s in the automobile industry. The chemical and oil-refining industries also began to use computers to regulate production. During the 1990s, automation became a major element in the manufacture of computers and computer components, such as electronic chips and circuits. It is this computerized, or programmable, automation that presents the greatest opportunities and challenges for management today.

The impact of automation on people in the workplace is complex. In the short term, people whose jobs are automated may find themselves without a job. In the long term, more jobs are created than are lost. Nevertheless, not all companies

CONCEPT CHECK 15.3

"Automation is bad for the economy, because machines will eventually replace nearly all human workers, creating high unemployment and poverty." Do you agree or disagree? Explain your answer.

FIGURE 15.2

A Simple Automatic Control Mechanism

All automation includes feedback, information, sensors, and a control mechanism. A simple thermostat is an example of automation. Another example is Benetton's distribution center in Italy. Orders are received, items pulled from stock and packaged for shipment, and invoices prepared and transmitted—all with no human intervention.

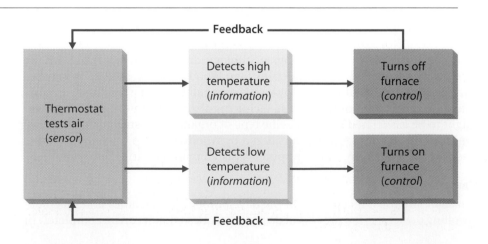

are able to help displaced workers find new jobs, so the human costs are sometimes high. In the coal industry, for instance, automation has been used primarily in mining. The output per miner has risen dramatically ever since the 1950s. The demand for coal, however, has decreased, and productivity gains resulting from automation have lessened the need for miners. Consequently, many workers have lost their jobs, and the industry has not been able to absorb them. In contrast, in the electronics industry, the rising demand for products has led to increasing employment opportunities despite the use of automation.[6]

Computer-Assisted Manufacturing

Computer-assisted manufacturing is technology that relies on computers to design or manufacture products. There are several forms of computer-assisted manufacturing.

computer-assisted manufacturing A technology that relies on computers to design or manufacture products.

▌ *Computer-aided design (CAD)* is the use of computers to design parts and complete products and to simulate performance so that prototypes need not be constructed. Boeing uses CAD technology to study hydraulic tubing in its commercial aircraft. Japan's automotive industry uses it to speed up car design. Oneida Ltd., the table flatware firm, used CAD to design a new spoon in only two days.[7]

▌ *Computer-aided manufacturing (CAM)* is usually combined with *CAD* to ensure that the design moves smoothly to production. The production computer shares the design computer's information and is able to have machines with the proper settings ready when production is needed. A CAM system is especially useful when reorders come in, because the computer can quickly produce the desired product, prepare labels and copies of orders, and send the product out to where it is wanted.

▌ *Computer-integrated manufacturing (CIM)* is closely related to the above approach. In CIM, CAD and CAM are linked together, and computer networks automatically adjust machine placements and settings to enhance both the complexity and the flexibility of scheduling. In settings that use these technologies, all manufacturing activities are controlled by the computer network. Because the network can access the company's other information systems, CIM is both a powerful and a complex management control tool.

▌ *Flexible manufacturing systems (FMS)* usually have robotic work units or workstations, assembly lines, and robotic carts or some other form of computer-controlled transport system to move material as needed from one part of the system to another. FMS like the one in use at Ford Motor Company transformed an English factory producing Ford Escorts into a Jaguar plant making its new Jaguar X-TYPE luxury cars. Using traditional methods, the plant would have been closed, its workers laid off, and the facility virtually rebuilt from the ground up. But, by using FMS, Ford was able to keep the plant open and running continuously while new equipment was being installed and its workers were being retrained in small groups.[8]

These systems are not without disadvantages, however. For example, because they represent fundamental change, they also generate resistance. Additionally, because of their tremendous complexity, CAD systems are not always reliable. CIM systems are so expensive that they raise the breakeven point for firms using them. This means that the firm must operate at high levels of production and sales to be able to afford the systems.

Robotics

robotics The science and technology involved in the construction, maintenance, and use of robots.

robot Any artificial device that is able to perform functions ordinarily thought to be appropriate for human beings.

Computerized **robotics** is another trend in manufacturing technology. A **robot** is any artificial device that is able to perform functions ordinarily thought to be appropriate for human beings. Robotics is the science and technology of the construction, maintenance, and use of robots. The use of industrial robots has steadily increased since 1980 and is expected to continue to increase slowly as more companies recognize the benefits that accrue to users of industrial robots.[9]

Welding was one of the first applications for robots, and it continues to be the area in which most applications occur. In second place and close behind is materials handling. Other applications include machine loading and unloading, painting and finishing, assembly, casting, and such machining applications as cutting, grinding, polishing, drilling, sanding, buffing, and deburring. DaimlerChrysler, for instance, recently replaced about two hundred welders with fifty robots on an assembly line and increased productivity about 20 percent. The use of robots in inspection work is increasing. They can check for cracks and holes, and they can be equipped with vision systems to perform visual inspections.

Robots are also beginning to move from the factory floor to other applications. At the Long Beach Memorial Hospital in California, brain surgeons are assisted by a robot arm that drills into the patient's skull with excellent precision. Some newer applications involve remote work. For example, the use of robot submersibles controlled from the surface can help divers in remote locations. Surveillance robots fitted with microwave sensors can do things that a human guard cannot do, such as "seeing" through nonmetallic walls and in the dark. In other applications, automated farming (called "agrimation") uses robot harvesters to pick fruit from a variety of trees.

Robots are also used by small manufacturers. One robot slices carpeting to fit the inside of custom vans in an upholstery shop. Another stretches balloons flat so that they can be spray-painted with slogans at a novelties company. These robots are lighter, faster, stronger, and more "intelligent" than those used in heavy manufacturing and are the types that more and more organizations will be using in the future.

Service Technology

Hotels use increasingly sophisticated technology to accept and record room reservations. Universities use new technologies to electronically store and provide access to books, scientific journals, government reports, and articles. Hospitals and other health-care organizations use new forms of service technology to manage patient records, dispatch ambulances, and monitor vital signs. Restaurants use technology to record and fill customer orders, order food and supplies, and prepare food. Given the increased role that service organizations are playing in today's economy, even more technological innovations are certain to be developed in the years to come.[10]

Managing service technology and operations has become increasingly important to managers as the service sector continues to grow and become more competitive. Managers in service organizations have come to recognize that many of the same concepts and techniques pioneered in manufacturing can help them as well.

True or False?

_____ 1. Oneida could use a cellular layout to manufacture forks, knives, and spoons in a similar flow path.

_____ 2. Computer-aided manufacturing systems use robots to move materials from one part of the system to another and convert the system as needed.

_____ 3. Reserving a flight using the Internet is an example of service technology.

Multiple Choice

_____ 4. Any artificial device that is able to perform functions ordinarily thought to be appropriate for human beings is called _____.
  a. automation   c. CAM
  b. CAD   d. CIM   e. robotics

_____ 5. _____ can generate resistance to the system because it represents fundamental change.
  a. FMS   c. CAM   e. All of the
  b. CAD   d. CIM   above

_____ 6. Which of the following is an area where robotics has not been applied?
  a. Brain surgery   d. Welding
  b. Financial planning   e. Picking fruit
  c. Law enforcement

Online Study Center
ACE the Test
ACE Practice Tests 15.3

IMPLEMENTING OPERATIONS SYSTEMS THROUGH SUPPLY CHAIN MANAGEMENT

4   *Identify and discuss the components involved in implementing operations systems through supply chain management.*

After operations systems have been properly designed and technologies developed, they must be put into use by the organization. Their basic functional purpose is to control transformation processes to ensure that relevant goals are achieved in such areas as quality and costs. Operations management has a number of special purposes within this control framework, including purchasing and inventory management. Indeed, this area of management has become so important in recent years that a new term—*supply chain management*—has been coined. Specifically, **supply chain management** can be defined as the process of managing operations control, resource acquisition and purchasing, and inventory so as to improve overall efficiency and effectiveness.[11]

supply chain management The process of managing operations control, resource acquisition, and inventory so as to improve overall efficiency and effectiveness.

Operations Management as Control

One way of using operations management as control is to coordinate it with other functions. Monsanto Company, for example, established a consumer products division that produces and distributes fertilizers and lawn chemicals. To facilitate control, the operations function was organized as an autonomous profit center. Monsanto finds this effective because its manufacturing division is given the authority to determine not only the costs of creating the product but also the product price and the marketing program.

In terms of overall organizational control, a division like the one used by Monsanto should be held accountable only for the activities over which it has decision-making authority. It would be inappropriate, of course, to make operations accountable for profitability in an organization that stresses sales and market share over quality and productivity. Misplaced accountability results in ineffective organizational control, to say nothing of hostility and conflict. Depending on the strategic role of operations, then, operations managers are accountable for different kinds of results. For example, in an organization using bureaucratic control, accountability will be spelled out in rules and regulations. In a decentralized system, it is likely to be understood and accepted by everyone.

Within operations, managerial control ensures that resources and activities achieve primary goals such as a high percentage of on-time deliveries, low unit-production cost, or high product reliability. Any control system should focus on the elements that are most crucial to goal attainment. For example, firms in which product quality is a major concern (as it is at Rolex) might adopt a screening control system to monitor the product as it is being created. If quantity is a higher priority (as it is at Timex), a postaction system might be used to identify defects at the end of the system without disrupting the manufacturing process itself.

Purchasing Management

purchasing management Management concerned with buying materials and resources needed to produce products and services.

Purchasing management is concerned with buying the materials and resources needed to create products and services. In many ways, purchasing is at the very heart of effective supply chain management. The purchasing manager for a retailer like Sears is responsible for buying the merchandise the store will sell. The purchasing manager for a manufacturer buys raw materials, parts, and machines needed by the organization. Large companies such as GE, IBM, and Siemens have large purchasing departments.[12] The manager responsible for purchasing must balance a number of constraints. Buying too much ties up capital and increases storage costs. Buying too little might lead to shortages and high reordering costs. The manager must also make sure that the quality of what is purchased meets the organization's needs, that the supplier is reliable, and that the best possible financial terms are negotiated.

Many firms have recently changed their approach to purchasing as a means to lower costs and improve quality and productivity. In particular, rather than relying on hundreds or even thousands of suppliers, many companies are reducing their number of suppliers and negotiating special production-delivery arrangements.[13] For example, the Honda plant in Marysville, Ohio, found a local business owner looking for a new opportunity. They negotiated an agreement whereby he would start a new company to mount car stereo speakers into plastic moldings. He delivers finished goods to the plant three times a day, and Honda buys all he can manufacture. Thus he has a stable sales base, Honda has a local and reliable supplier, and both companies benefit.

Inventory Management

inventory control Managing the organization's raw materials, work in process, finished goods, and products in transit.

Inventory control, also called *materials control,* is essential for effective operations management. The four basic kinds of inventories are as follows:

1. Raw material
2. Work in process
3. Finished goods
4. In transit

As shown in Table 15.1, the sources of control over these inventories are as different as their purposes. Work-in-process inventories, for example, are made up of partially completed products that need further processing; they are controlled by the shop-floor system. In contrast, the quantities and costs of finished-goods

TABLE 15.1

Inventory Types, Purposes, and Sources of Control

JIT is a recent breakthrough in inventory management. With JIT inventory management, materials arrive just as they are needed. JIT therefore helps an organization control its raw materials by reducing the amount of space it must devote to storage.

Type	Purpose	Source of Control
Raw materials	Provide the materials needed to make the product.	Purchasing models and systems
Work in process	Enable overall production to be divided into stages of manageable size.	Shop-floor control systems
Finished goods	Provide ready supply of products on customer demand and make possible long, efficient production runs.	High-level production scheduling systems in conjunction with marketing
In transit (pipeline)	Distribute products to customers.	Transportation and distribution control systems

inventories are under the control of the overall production scheduling system, which is determined by high-level planning decisions. In-transit inventories are controlled by the transportation and distribution systems.

Like most other areas of operations management, inventory management has changed notably in recent years. One particularly important breakthrough is the **just-in-time (JIT) method**. First popularized by the Japanese, the JIT system reduces the organization's investment in storage space for raw materials and in the materials themselves. Historically, manufacturers built large storage areas and filled them with materials, parts, and supplies that would be needed days, weeks, and even months in the future. A manager using the JIT approach orders materials and parts more often and in smaller quantities, thereby reducing investment in both storage space and actual inventory. The ideal arrangement is for materials to arrive just as they are needed—or just in time.[14]

just-in-time (JIT) method   An inventory system that has necessary materials arriving as soon as they are needed (just in time) so that the company's investment in storage space and inventory is minimized and the production process is not interrupted.

TEST PREPPER 15.4

ANSWERS CAN BE FOUND ON P. 442

True or False?

_____ 1. Purchasing management applies to items in transit or in a pipeline.

_____ 2. JIT requires high levels of coordination and cooperation between companies.

Multiple Choice

_____ 3. The process of managing operations control, resource acquisition, and inventory so as to improve overall efficiency and effectiveness is called _____.
- a. supply chain management
- b. purchasing management
- c. inventory management
- d. finished-goods management
- e. pipeline management

_____ 4. Inventory control applies to which of the following?
- a. Raw materials
- b. Work in process
- c. Finished goods
- d. In transit (pipeline)
- e. All of the above

_____ 5. What does JIT stand for?
- a. Job-in-trouble
- b. Just-in-time
- c. Job-in-transit
- d. Just-in-transit
- e. Job-in-time

Online Study Center
ACE the Test
ACE Practice Tests 15.4

Online Study Center   college.hmco.com/pic/griffinSAS

MANAGING TOTAL QUALITY

> 5 *Explain the meaning and importance of managing quality and total quality management.*

Quality and productivity have become major determinants of business success or failure today and are central issues in managing organizations.[15] But, as we will see, achieving higher levels of quality is not easy. Simply ordering that quality be improved is about as effective as waving a magic wand.[16] The catalyst for its emergence as a mainstream management concern was foreign business, especially Japanese. And nowhere was it more visible than in the auto industry. During the energy crisis in the late 1970s, many people bought Toyotas, Hondas, and Nissans because they were more fuel-efficient than U.S. cars. Consumers soon found, however, that not only were the Japanese cars more fuel-efficient, but they were also of higher quality than U.S. cars. Parts fit together better, the trim work was neater, and the cars were more reliable. Thus, after the energy crisis subsided, Japanese cars remained formidable competitors because of their reputation for quality.

Quality plays a major role in today's competitive business environment. The Vermont Agency of Agriculture recently required that all Vermont maple syrup be labeled as Vermont grade, rather than U.S. grade, or simply as amber or fancy. And if a company has Vermont in its name, the label must disclose where the syrup came from. Consumers who buy the syrup will now know for certain that they're getting the real thing.

quality   The totality of features and characteristics of a product or service that bear on its ability to satisfy stated or implied needs.

The Meaning of Quality

The American Society for Quality Control defines **quality** as the totality of features and characteristics of a product or service that bear on its ability to satisfy stated or implied needs.[17] Quality has several basic dimensions. For example, a durable and reliable product is of higher quality than a product with less durability and reliability.

▌ *Performance.*   A product's primary operating characteristic; examples are automobile acceleration and a television's picture clarity

▌ *Features.*   Supplements to a product's basic functioning characteristics, such as power windows on a car

▌ *Reliability.*   A probability of not malfunctioning during a specified period

▌ *Conformance.*   The degree to which a product's design and operating characteristics meet established standards

▌ *Durability.*   A measure of product life

▌ *Serviceability.*   The speed and ease of repair

▌ *Aesthetics.*   How a product looks, feels, tastes, and smells

▌ *Perceived quality.*   As seen by a customer

Quality is also relative. For example, a Lincoln is a higher-grade car than a Ford Taurus, which, in turn, is a higher-grade car than a Ford Focus. The difference in quality stems from differences in design and other features. The Focus, however, is considered a high-quality car relative to its engineering specifications and price. Likewise, the Taurus and Lincoln may also be high-quality cars, given their standards and prices. Thus quality is both an absolute and a relative concept.

Quality is relevant for both products and services. Although its importance for products such as cars and computers was perhaps recognized first, service firms ranging from airlines to restaurants have also come to see that quality is a vitally

CONCEPT CHECK 15.4

Think of a firm that, in your opinion, provides a high-quality service or product. What attributes of the product or service shaped your perception of its high quality? Do you think that everyone would agree with your judgment? Why or why not?

important determinant of their success or failure. Service quality, as we will discuss later in this chapter, has thus also become a major competitive issue in U.S. industry today.[18]

The Importance of Quality

To help underscore the importance of quality, the U.S. government created the **Malcolm Baldridge Award**, named after a former secretary of commerce who championed quality in U.S. industry. The award, administered by an agency of the Commerce Department, is given annually to firms that achieve major improvements in the quality of their products or services. In other words, the award is based on changes in quality, as opposed to absolute quality. In addition, numerous other quality awards have been created. For example, the Rochester Institute of Technology and *USA Today* award their Quality Cup not to entire organizations but to individual teams of workers within organizations. Quality is also an important concern for individual managers and organizations for three very specific reasons: competition, productivity, and costs.[19]

Malcolm Baldridge Award   Award named after a former secretary of commerce and given to firms that achieve major quality improvements.

1. *Competition.*   Quality has become one of the most competitive points in business today. Ford, DaimlerChrysler, General Motors, and Toyota, for example, all argue that their own cars and trucks are higher in quality than the cars and trucks of the others. And American, United, and Continental Airlines each claims that it provides the best and most reliable service. Indeed, it seems that virtually every U.S. business has adopted quality as a major point of competition. Thus a business that fails to keep pace may find itself falling behind not only foreign competition but also other U.S. firms.[20]

2. *Productivity.*   Managers have come to recognize that quality and productivity are related. In the past, many managers thought that they could increase output (productivity) only by decreasing quality. Managers today have learned the hard way that such an assumption is nearly always wrong. If a firm installs a meaningful quality enhancement program, three things are likely to result. First, the number of defects is likely to decrease, occasioning fewer returns from customers. Second, because the number of defects goes down, resources (materials and people) dedicated to reworking flawed output will be decreased. Third, because making employees responsible for quality reduces the need for quality inspectors, the organization is able to produce more units with fewer resources.

Online Study Center
Improve Your Grade
Video Segment

3. **Costs.**   Improved quality also lowers costs. Poor quality results in higher returns from customers, high warranty costs, and lawsuits from customers injured by faulty products. Future sales are lost because of disgruntled customers. An organization with quality problems often has to increase inspection expenses just to catch defective products.

Total Quality Management

Once an organization makes a decision to enhance the quality of its products and services, it must then decide how to implement this decision. The most pervasive approach to managing quality has been called **total quality management**, or **TQM** (sometimes called quality assurance)—a real and meaningful effort by an organization to change its whole approach to business in order to make quality a guiding factor in everything the organization does.[21] Figure 15.3 highlights the major ingredients of TQM.

total quality management (TQM) (quality assurance)   A strategic commitment by top management to change its whole approach to business in order to make quality a guiding factor in everything it does.

FIGURE 15.3

Total Quality Management

Quality is one of the most important issues facing organizations today. Total quality management, or TQM, is a comprehensive effort to enhance the quality of an organization's product or service. TQM involves the five basic dimensions shown here. Each is important and must be addressed effectively if the organization expects to increase quality significantly.

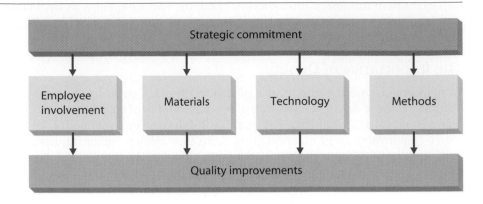

▌ *Strategic commitment,* the starting point for TQM, is important for several reasons.
1. The organization culture must change to reflect the idea that quality is not just an ideal but an objective goal that must be pursued.[22]
2. A decision to pursue the goal of quality carries with it some real costs—such as expenditures for new equipment and facilities. Thus, without a commitment from top management, quality improvement will prove to be just a slogan or a gimmick, and little or no real change will occur.

▌ *Employee involvement,* another critical ingredient in TQM, involves making the person doing the job responsible for making sure it is done right.[23] By definition, then, employee involvement is a critical component in improving quality. Work teams, discussed in Chapter 13, are common vehicles for increasing employee involvement.

▌ *Materials* improvement is another important part of TQM. Suppose that a company that assembles stereos buys chips and circuits from another company. If the chips have a high failure rate, consumers will return defective stereos to the company whose nameplate appears on them, not to the company that made the chips. The stereo firm then loses in two ways: refunds to customers and a damaged reputation. As a result, many firms have increased the quality requirements they impose on their suppliers as a way of improving the quality of their own products.

▌ *Technology,* in various new forms, is also useful in TQM programs. Automation and robots, for example, can often make products with higher precision and better consistency than people can. Investing in higher-grade machines capable of doing jobs more precisely and reliably often improves quality. For example, Nokia has achieved notable improvements in product quality by replacing many of its machines with new equipment. Similarly, most U.S. auto and electronics firms make regular investments in new technology to help boost quality.

▌ *Methods,* or operating systems used by the organization during the actual transformation process, can improve product and service quality. American Express Company, for example, has found ways to cut its approval time for new credit cards from twenty-two days to only a few hours. This results in improved service quality.

CONCEPT CHECK 15.5

Some quality gurus claim that high-quality products or services are those that are error-free. Others claim that high quality exists when customers' needs are satisfied. Still others claim that high-quality products or services must be innovative. Do you subscribe to one of these views? If not, how would you define quality?

TQM Tools and Techniques

Beyond the strategic context of quality, managers can also rely on several specific tools and techniques for improving quality. Among the most popular today are value-added analysis, benchmarking, outsourcing, reducing cycle times, ISO 9000:2000 and ISO 14000, and statistical quality control.

■ **Value-added analysis** is the comprehensive evaluation of all work activities, materials flows, and paperwork to determine the value that they add for customers. Such an analysis often reveals wasteful or unnecessary activities that can be eliminated without jeopardizing customer service. For example, during a value-added analysis, Hewlett-Packard determined that its contracts were unnecessarily long, confusing, and hard to understand. The firm subsequently cut its standard contract form down from twenty pages to two pages and experienced an 18 percent increase in its computer sales.

value-added analysis The comprehensive evaluation of all work activities, materials flows, and paperwork to determine the value that they add for customers.

■ **Benchmarking** is the process of learning how other firms do things in an exceptionally high-quality manner. Some approaches to benchmarking are simple and straightforward. For example, Xerox routinely buys copiers made by other firms and takes them apart to see how they work. This enables the firm to stay abreast of improvements and changes that its competitors are making. When Ford was planning a new automobile model, it pinpointed the four hundred features that customers identified as being most important to them. It then determined what competing cars did the best job on each feature. Ford's goal was to equal or surpass each of its competitors on those four hundred features. Other benchmarking strategies are more indirect. For example, in seeking applications that they can employ in their own businesses, many firms study how L.L. Bean manages its mail-order business, how Disney recruits and trains employees, and how FedEx tracks packages.[24]

benchmarking The process of learning how other firms do things in an exceptionally high-quality manner.

Online Study Center
Improve Your Grade
Knowledgebank 15.1

■ **Outsourcing** is the process of subcontracting services and operations to other firms that can perform them more cheaply or better. If a business performs each and every one of its own administrative and business services and operations, it is almost certain to be doing at least some of them in an inefficient or low-quality manner. If those areas can be identified and outsourced, the firm will save money and achieve a higher-quality service or operation.[25] For example,

outsourcing Subcontracting services and operations to other firms that can perform them more cheaply or better.

Effective total quality management requires major commitments from an organization. Thorough and rigorous quality checks and inspections are often a fundamental part of quality management. But managers who pay only lip service to inspections, such as the managers illustrated here checking water quality, should not be surprised later when they discover major quality problems throughout their organization. Only by using objective and rigorous statistical quality control measures can the firm be assured of bringing high-quality products and services to the marketplace.

cycle time The time that an organization needs to accomplish activities such as developing, making, and distributing products or services.

ISO 9000:2000 A set of quality standards created by the International Organization for Standardization and revised in 2000.

until recently Eastman Kodak handled all of its own computing operations. Now, however, those operations are subcontracted to IBM, which handles all of Kodak's computing. The result is that Kodak has higher-quality computing systems and operations for less money than it was spending before.

▎ If a business can reduce its **cycle time** (the time needed by the organization to develop, make, and distribute products or services[26]), quality will often improve. A good illustration of the power of cycle time reduction comes from General Electric. At one point the firm needed six plants and three weeks to produce and deliver custom-made industrial circuit breaker boxes. By analyzing and reducing cycle time, GE became able to deliver the same product in three days, and only a single plant is involved. Table 15.2 identifies a number of basic suggestions that have helped companies reduce the cycle time of their operations. For example, GE found it better to start from scratch with a remodeled plant. GE also wiped out the need for approvals by eliminating most managerial positions and set up teams as a basis for organizing work.

▎ **ISO 9000:2000** is a set of quality standards created by the International Organization for Standardization; the standards were revised and updated in 2000. These standards cover such areas as product testing, employee training, record keeping, supplier relations, and repair policies and procedures. Firms that want to meet these standards apply for certification and are audited by a company chosen by the organization's domestic affiliate (in the United States, this is the American National Standards Institute). These auditors review every aspect of the firm's business operations in relation to the standards. Many firms report that merely preparing for an ISO 9000 audit has been helpful. Many firms today, including General Electric, DuPont, Eastman Kodak, British Telecom, and Philips Electronics, are urging—or in some cases requiring—that their suppliers obtain ISO 9000 certification.[27] All told, more than 140 countries have adopted ISO 9000 as a national standard, and more than 400,000 certificates of compliance

---

TABLE 15.2

Guidelines for Increasing the Speed of Operations

Many organizations today are using speed for competitive advantage. Listed in this table are six common guidelines that organizations follow when they want to shorten the time it takes to get things done. Not every manager can do all of these things, but most managers can do some of them.

1. Start from scratch. (It is usually easier than trying to do faster what the organization does now.)
2. Minimize the number of approvals needed to do something. The fewer people who have to approve something, the faster approval will get done.
3. Use work teams as a basis for organization. Teamwork and cooperation work better than individual effort and conflict.
4. Develop and adhere to a schedule. A properly designed schedule can greatly increase speed.
5. Do not ignore distribution. Making something faster is only part of the battle.
6. Integrate speed into the organization's culture. If everyone understands the importance of speed, things will naturally get done quicker.

Adapted from Brian Dumaine, "How Managers Can Succeed Through Speed," *Fortune*, February 13, 1989. Copyright © 1989 Time, Inc. All rights reserved.

have been issued. **ISO 14000** is an extension of the same concept to environmental performance. Specifically, ISO 14000 requires that firms document how they are using raw materials more efficiently, managing pollution, and reducing the impact of their operations on the environment.

▌ **Statistical quality control (SQC)** is concerned primarily with managing quality.[28] Moreover, it is a set of specific statistical techniques that can be used to monitor quality. *Acceptance sampling* involves sampling finished goods to ensure that quality standards have been met. Acceptance sampling is effective only when the percentage of products that should be tested (for example, 2, 5, or 25 percent) is correctly determined. This decision is especially important when the test renders the product useless. Flash cubes, wine, and collapsible steering wheels, for example, are consumed or destroyed during testing. Another SQC method is *in-process sampling*. In-process sampling involves evaluating products during production so that needed changes can be made. The painting department of a furniture company might periodically check the tint of the paint it is using. The company can then adjust the color as necessary to conform to customer standards. The advantage of in-process sampling is that it allows problems to be detected before they accumulate.

ISO 14000 A set of standards for environmental performance.

statistical quality control (SQC) A set of specific statistical techniques that can be used to monitor quality; includes acceptance sampling and in-process sampling.

> **TEST PREPPER 15.5**

ANSWERS CAN BE FOUND ON P. 442

True or False?

_____ 1. In the United States it is more expensive to replace the battery on a Volvo than it is on a Ford. This is an example of reliability.

_____ 2. A business that fails to keep pace in quality may find itself falling behind not only foreign competition but also U.S. competition.

_____ 3. Total quality management is a strategic commitment by line employees to change the organization's approach to business by making quality a guiding factor in everything it does.

_____ 4. ISO 9000:2000 requires that firms document how they are using raw materials more efficiently, managing pollution, and reducing their impact on the environment.

_____ 5. Total statistical control (TSC) is a set of specific statistical techniques that can be used to monitor quality, including acceptance sampling and in-process sampling.

Multiple Choice

_____ 6. Which of the following is not a dimension of quality?
   a. Performance   d. Aesthetics
   b. Features   e. Serviceability
   c. Price

_____ 7. The smell of a new car is part of which measure of quality?
   a. Price   d. Aesthetics
   b. Features   e. Perceived quality
   c. Conformance

_____ 8. The Malcolm Baldridge Award is awarded based on _____.
   a. quality control   d. CIM
   b. inventory control e. FMS
   c. advanced technology

_____ 9. When Raytheon contracts all of its relocation operations with local suppliers, it is using _____.
   a. ISO 9000:2000
   b. benchmarking
   c. outsourcing
   d. SQC
   e. inventory management

_____ 10. When you order a pizza from the Pizza Barn, they use your phone number to reference your past order and ask if you would like any of those items. This is an example of _____.
   a. outsourcing   d. service technology
   b. benchmarking   e. SQC
   c. ISO 9000:2000

Online Study Center
ACE the Test
ACE Practice Tests 15.5

MANAGING PRODUCTIVITY

6 ▶ *Explain the meaning and importance of managing productivity, productivity trends, and ways to improve productivity.*

Although the current focus on quality by American companies is a relatively recent phenomenon, managers have been aware of the importance of productivity for several years. The stimulus for this attention was a recognition that the gap between productivity in the United States and productivity in other industrialized countries was narrowing. This section describes the meaning of productivity and underscores its importance. After summarizing recent productivity trends, we suggest ways in which organizations can increase their productivity.

The Meaning of Productivity

productivity An economic measure of efficiency that summarizes the value of what is produced relative to the value of the resources used to produce it.

In a general sense, **productivity** is an economic measure of efficiency that summarizes the value of outputs relative to the value of the inputs used to create them.[29] Productivity can be and often is assessed at different levels of analysis and in different forms.

Levels of Productivity

By level of productivity we mean the units of analysis used to calculate or define productivity.

▌ *Aggregate productivity* is the total level of productivity achieved by a country.

▌ *Industry productivity* is the total productivity achieved by all the firms in a particular industry.

▌ *Company productivity,* just as the term suggests, is the level of productivity achieved by an individual company.

▌ *Unit productivity* and *individual productivity* refer to the productivity achieved by a unit or department within an organization and to the level of productivity attained by a single person.

Forms of Productivity

There are many different forms of productivity. *Total factor productivity* is defined by the following formula:

$$\text{Productivity} = \frac{\text{Outputs}}{\text{Inputs}}$$

Total factor productivity is an overall indicator of how well an organization uses all of its resources, such as labor, capital, materials, and energy, to create all of its products and services. The biggest problem with total factor productivity is that all the ingredients must be expressed in the same terms—dollars (it is difficult to add hours of labor to number of units of a raw material in a meaningful way). Total factor productivity also gives little insight into how things can be changed to improve productivity. Consequently, most organizations find it more useful to calculate a partial productivity ratio. Such a ratio uses only one category of resource. For example, labor productivity could be calculated by this simple formula:

$$\text{Labor Productivity} = \frac{\text{Outputs}}{\text{Direct Labor}}$$

This method has two advantages.

1. It is not necessary to transform the units of input into some other unit.
2. This method provides managers with specific insights into how changing different resource inputs affects productivity.

Suppose that an organization can manufacture 100 units of a particular product with 20 hours of direct labor. The organization's labor productivity index is 100/20, or 5 (5 units per labor hour). Now suppose that worker efficiency is increased (through one of the ways to be discussed later in this chapter) so that the same 20 hours of labor result in the manufacture of 120 units of the product. The labor productivity index increases to 120/20, or 6 (6 units per labor hour), and the firm can see the direct results of a specific managerial action.

The Importance of Productivity

Managers consider it important that their firm maintain high levels of productivity for a variety of reasons. Firm productivity is a primary determinant of an organization's level of profitability and, ultimately, of its ability to survive. If one organization is more productive than another, it will have more products to sell at lower prices and have more profits to reinvest in other areas. Productivity also partially determines people's standard of living within a particular country. At an economic level, businesses consume resources and produce goods and services. The goods and services created within a country can be used by that country's own citizens or exported for sale in other countries. The more goods and services the businesses within a country can produce, the more goods and services the country's citizens will have. Even goods that are exported result in financial resources' flowing back into the home country. Thus the citizens of a highly productive country are likely to have a notably higher standard of living than the citizens of a country with low productivity.

Online Study Center
Improve Your Grade
Knowledgebank 15.2

Productivity Trends

The United States has one of the highest levels of productivity in the world. Sparked by global competitive pressures, however, U.S. business has begun to focus more attention on productivity. For example, General Electric's dishwasher plant in Louisville has cut its inventory requirements by 50 percent, reduced labor costs from 15 percent to only 10 percent of total manufacturing costs, and cut product development time in half. As a result of these kinds of efforts, productivity trends have now leveled out, and U.S. workers are generally maintaining their lead in most industries.[30]

One important factor that has hurt U.S. productivity indices has been the tremendous growth of the service sector in the United States. Although this sector grew, its productivity levels did not. One part of this problem is related to measurement. For example, it is fairly easy to calculate the number of tons of steel produced at a steel mill and divide it by the number of labor hours used; it is more difficult to determine the output of an attorney or a certified public accountant. Still, virtually everyone agrees that improving productivity in the service sector is the next major hurdle facing U.S. business.[31]

Figure 15.4 illustrates manufacturing productivity growth since 1970 in terms of annual average percentage of increase. As you can see, that growth slowed during the 1970s but began to rise again in the late 1980s. Some experts believe that

FIGURE 15.4

Manufacturing and Service Productivity Growth Trends

Both manufacturing productivity and service productivity in the United States continue to grow, although manufacturing productivity is growing at a faster pace. Total productivity, therefore, also continues to grow.

U.S. Bureau of Labor Statistics.

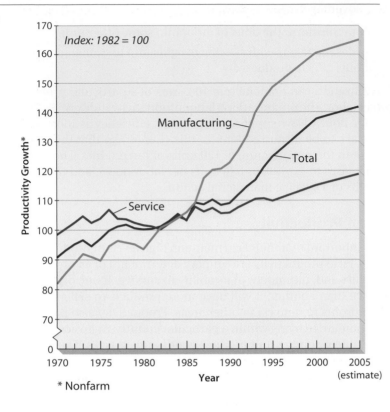

productivity both in the United States and abroad will continue to improve at even more impressive rates. Their confidence rests on technology's potential ability to improve operations.

Improving Productivity

How does a business or industry improve its productivity? Numerous specific suggestions made by experts generally fall into two broad categories: improving operations and increasing employee involvement.

Improving Operations

There are many ways in which firms can improve operations:

▮ *Spending more on research and development.*   R&D helps identify new products, new uses for existing products, and new methods for making products. And each of these contributes to productivity. For example, Bausch & Lomb almost missed the boat on extended-wear contact lenses because the company had neglected R&D. When it became apparent that its major competitors were almost a year ahead of Bausch & Lomb in developing the new lenses, management made R&D a top priority. As a result, the company made several scientific breakthroughs, shortened the time needed to introduce new products, and greatly enhanced both total sales and profits—and all with a smaller workforce than the company used to employ. Even though other countries are greatly increasing their R&D spending, the United States continues to be the world leader in this area.

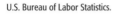
Online Study Center
Improve Your Grade
Career Snapshot 15.2

■ *Reassessing and revamping their transformation facilities.*   We noted earlier how one of GE's modernized plants does a better job than six antiquated ones. Just building a new factory is no guarantee of success, of course, but IBM, Ford, Caterpillar, and many other businesses have achieved dramatic productivity gains by revamping their production facilities. Facilities refinements are not limited to manufacturers. Most McDonald's restaurants now have drive-through windows, and many have moved soft-drink dispensers out to the restaurant floor so that customers can get their own drinks. Each of these moves is an attempt to increase the speed with which customers can be served, and thus to increase productivity.

Increasing Employee Involvement

There are numerous ways in which firms can increase employee involvement:

■ *Participation.*   As we noted earlier, participation can enhance quality and boost productivity. For example, an individual worker can be given a bigger voice in how she does her job, a formal agreement of cooperation can be drawn up between management and labor, or the entire organization may become committed to total involvement. GE eliminated most of the supervisors at its one new circuit breaker plant and put control in the hands of workers.

■ *Training employees to perform a number of different jobs.*   Such cross-training allows the firm to function with fewer workers because workers can be transferred easily to areas where they are most needed. At one Motorola plant, 397 of 400 employees have learned at least two skills under a similar program.

■ *Rewards.*   Firms must reward people for learning new skills and using them proficiently. At Motorola, for example, workers who master a new skill are assigned for five days to a job requiring them to use that skill. If they perform with no defects, they are moved to a higher pay grade, and then they move back and forth between jobs as they are needed. If there is a performance problem, they receive more training and practice. This approach is fairly new, but preliminary indicators suggest that it can increase productivity significantly. Many unions resist such programs because they threaten job security and reduce a person's identification with one skill or craft.

TEST PREPPER 15.6

ANSWERS CAN BE FOUND ON P. 442

True or False?

_____ 1. Virtually everyone agrees that improving service sector productivity is the next major hurdle facing U.S. business.

Multiple Choice

_____ 2. The productivity achieved by a department within an organization is classified at what level of productivity?
- a. Aggregate
- b. Industry
- c. Company
- d. Unit
- e. Individual

_____ 3. Output equals $1,000, input equals $200, and direct labor equals 100 hours. Calculate the labor productivity.
- a. 5
- b. $10/hour
- c. $3.33/hour
- d. $2/hour
- e. $1,000

Online Study Center
ACE the Test
ACE Practice Tests 15.6

BUILDING EFFECTIVE COMMUNICATION SKILLS

Online Study Center
Improve Your Grade
Exercises: Building Effective Skills

Exercise Overview

Communication skills reflect a manager's ability to convey ideas and information to others and to receive ideas and information from others. This exercise develops your communication skills in addressing issues of quality.

Exercise Background

Assume that you are a customer service manager of a large auto parts distributor. The general manager of a large auto dealer, one of your best customers, wrote the letter shown below. It will be your task to write a letter in response.

Dear Customer Service Manager:

On the first of last month, ABC Autos submitted a purchase order to your firm. Attached to this letter is a copy of the order. Unfortunately, the parts shipment that we received from you did not contain every item on the order. Further, that fact was not noted on the packing slip that accompanied your shipment, and ABC was charged for the full amount of the order.

To resolve the problem, please send the missing items immediately. If you are unable to do so by the end of the week, please cancel the remaining items and refund the overpayment. In the future, if you ship a partial order, please notify us at that time and do not bill for items not shipped.

I look forward to your reply and a resolution to my problem.

Sincerely,

A. N. Owner

A. N. Owner, ABC Autos
Attachment: Purchase Order 00001

Exercise Task

1. Write an answer to this letter, assuming that you now have the parts available.

2. How would your answer differ if ABC Autos were not a valued customer?

3. How would your answer differ if you found out that the parts were in the original shipment but had been stolen by one of your delivery personnel?

4. How would your answer differ if you found out that the owner of ABC Autos made a mistake and that, in fact, the order was filled correctly by your workers?

5. Referring to your answers to the questions above, list the important components of responding effectively to a customer's quality complaint—the tone of the letter, expressing an apology, suggesting a solution, and so on. Explain how you incorporated these components into your response.

Preparing the Fishbone Chart

Online Study Center
Improve Your Grade
  –Exercises: Experiential Exercise
  –Interactive Skills Self-Assessment

Purpose

The fishbone chart is an excellent procedure for identifying possible causes of a problem. It provides you with knowledge that you can use to improve the operations of any organization. This skill exercise focuses on the *administrative management model* and helps you develop the *monitor role*. One of the skills of the monitor is the ability to analyze problems.

Introduction

Japanese quality circles often use the fishbone "cause-and-effect" graphical technique to initiate the resolution of a group work problem. Quite often the causes are clustered in categories such as materials, methods, people, and machines. The fishbone technique is usually accomplished in the following six steps:

1. Write the problem in the "head" of the fish (the large block).
2. Brainstorm the major causes of the problem and list them on the fish "bones."
3. Analyze each main cause and write in minor sub-causes on bone sub-branches.
4. Reach consensus on one or two of the major causes of the problem.
5. Explore ways to correct or remove the major causes.
6. Prepare a report or presentation explaining the proposed change.

Instructions

Your instructor will provide you with further instructions.

The fishbone will look something like this:

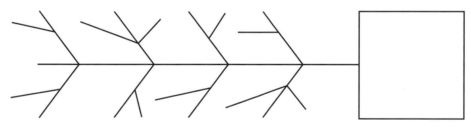

Source: Adapted from *Exercises in Management* by Linda Morable, pp. 141–145.
Copyright © 2005 by Houghton Mifflin Company. Used with permission.

Small Is Beautiful

The new Mini is a hit, with 40,000 cars sold in the U.S. in 2005. Three years after its initial introduction into the American market, the car is still oversold, with every new vehicle committed to a specific buyer. The Mini was trendy during the 1960s, but it lost its appeal and went out of production in 2000. However, BMW acquired and reintroduced the brand in 2001.

The look remains the same, yet every aspect of the auto has been reengineered. One of BMW's priorities was to use modern, efficient manufacturing techniques. BMW also wanted to ensure that the entire process would be friendly to the environment and to workers. Another goal was to offer customers the ability to customize their cars and also to meet the differing requirements of many countries. "Every car is built to order," says Rachel Stevens, a logistics coordinator. "We don't build cars to park them in the field."

A just-in-time logistics system at the Oxford, U.K., Mini plant is important in meeting those goals. BMW relies on a variety of subassemblies of 2,415 different parts that can be used in various combinations. A Mini can be made with any of twelve body shells, twenty-seven wheels, four engines, three transmissions, left- or right-hand drive, and so on. Logistics are further complicated by the use of over two hundred suppliers, only half based in England. Therefore, the company keeps from three hours to five days' worth of parts in the warehouse. Deliveries to the factory floor are made continuously. Stevens says, "We only get what we want and we get it when we need it."

Just-in-time systems can be difficult to use for products with seasonal demand. BMW, however, allows workers to "bank" hours during peak production times, then to "cash in" during slack times. Each work team organizes its schedule to meet work demands, making BMW one of the only companies to offer flextime for assembly-line workers.

Robotics and other automation are key elements too, with 228 robots performing 80 percent of the assembly. When manual assembly is required, the tools are electric instead of air-driven. This is more expensive but allows better precision and is quieter and safer. The entire factory is organized around a single line. "There's no way to take a car out of the chain," says

"Every car is built to order. We don't build cars to park them in the field."

—Rachel Stevens,
logistics manager, BMW

Rainer Bickman, an assembly director. The car and all of its parts are bar-coded to ensure perfect matching. The entire body is submerged in a tank of paint, a high-tech process that wastes only 10 percent of the paint, as compared to 75 percent wastage with an ordinary spray process.

Most quality inspections are done right on the assembly line throughout the process, as welds are created, parts are joined, and options added. Lasers perform precise measurements and compare the car's geometry to the desired standard. A sample of finished autos is inspected, but since rework is expensive, efforts are made to detect problems early.

Workers at each step in the assembly focus on the satisfaction of not only the ultimate purchaser, but also of workers in the assembly process. Andy Lambert, a technology manager, says, "We look after our internal customers." Lambert mentions, for example, that a rough edge on a weld could hurt a worker in a later step of the process and so must be sanded smooth. Workers serve on quality teams that set standards and share information about best practices. A sophisticated system tracks each vehicle to the workers who assembled it, increasing accountability: BMW can discover who worked on any car that is later found to be defective.

Fewer errors lead to lower costs by resulting in less rework and, ultimately, in fewer warranty claims. Worker-friendly policies reduce costs too, through reduced injuries, absenteeism, and turnover. In addition, because the facility creates little pollution, the costs of regulatory compliance are driven down. Finally, the flexibility and speed of the processes allow purchasers to customize their cars and allow BMW to charge higher prices.

BMW's new car wins praise as well as sales. "The Mini is one of the most significant cars . . . of the last

20 years," says *Automobile Magazine* editor Mark Giles. Other automakers are jumping on the bandwagon. The next few years should show a sharp increase in the number and variety of small cars sold in the United States. Yet BMW, with its flexible and efficient manufacturing system, has a distinctive competency that will be hard to beat.

Case Questions

1. How do BMW's facilities, logistics, and operations decisions help the company to realize its goals?
2. What benefits does BMW get from its use of automation and robotics? What benefits do workers get? What are the potential problems or limitations?
3. Describe BMW's quality efforts at its Oxford plant. What ingredients of TQM is BMW using?

Case References

Martin Ashcroft, "A Mini Adventure," *The Manufacturer* (U.K.), November 2003, www.themanufacturer.com on February 10, 2006 (quote); "Manufacturing Facilities," BMW website, www.bmwgroup.com on February 8, 2006; David Kiley, "The Mini Bulks Up," January 19, 2006, *Business-Week*, www.businessweek.com on February 8, 2006; Mark Malaczynski, "History of the Mini Cooper," *Out Motoring*, www.outmotoring.com on February 10, 2006; Micheling Maynard, "Carmakers' Big Idea: Think Small," *New York Times*, February 5, 2006, pp. 1–7; Jean McGregor, "High-Tech Achiever: Mini USA," *Fast Company*, October 2004, www.fastcompany.com on February 8, 2006.

Online Study Center
Improve Your Grade
 –Learning Objective Review
 –Audio Chapter Review
 –Study Guide to Go

Online Study Center
ACE the Test
 Audio Chapter Quiz

LEARNING OBJECTIVE REVIEW

1 *Describe and explain the nature of operations management.*

- Operations management is the set of managerial activities that organizations use in creating their products and services.
- Operations management plays an important role in an organization's strategy and is important to both manufacturing and service organizations.

2 *Identify and discuss the components involved in designing effective operations systems.*

- The starting point in using operations management is designing appropriate operations systems.
- Key decisions that must be made in the design of operations systems involve product-service mix, capacity, and facilities.

3 *Discuss organizational technologies and their role in operations management.*

- Technology plays a key role in manufacturing quality and includes the following techniques:
   automation
   computer-aided manufacturing
   robotics
- Technology is as relevant to service organizations as it is to manufacturing organizations.

4 *Identify and discuss the components involved in implementing operations systems through supply chain management.*

- After an operations system has been designed and put in place, it must be implemented.
- Major areas of interest during the use of operations systems are
   control
   purchasing
   inventory management

- Supply chain management is a comprehensive view of managing all of these activities in a more efficient manner.

5 ▶ *Explain the meaning and importance of managing quality and total quality management.*

- Quality, a major consideration for all managers today, is important because it affects
    competition
    productivity
    costs
- Total quality management (TQM) is a comprehensive, organization-wide effort to enhance quality in a variety of ways.
- Tools for TQM include value-added analysis, benchmarking, outsourcing, reducing cycle time, ISO 9000:2000 and ISO 14000, and statistical quality control.

6 ▶ *Explain the meaning and importance of managing productivity, productivity trends, and ways to improve productivity.*

- Productivity, a major concern to managers, is a measure of how efficiently an organization is using its resources to create products or services.
- Most firms prefer to use a partial productivity ratio to calculate productivity.
- The United States is a world leader in individual productivity, but firms still work to achieve productivity gains.
- Productivity can be improved by improving operations and increasing employee involvement.

⚙ *Online Study Center* RESOURCES

Prepare for Class, Improve Your Grade, and ACE the Test. These Student Achievement resources include:

ACE Practice Tests	Interactive Skills Assessments	Study Guide to Go
End of Chapter Exercises	Knowledgebank	Video Segments
Glossaries (visual and print)	Reviews (audio and print)	Summaries/Outlines
Flashcards		

To access these learning and study tools, go to: **college.hmco.com/pic/griffinSAS**

ENDNOTES

Chapter 1

1. Michael V. Copeland, "The League of Extraordinary Young Executives," *Business 2.0,* money.cnn.com on January 12, 2006; Ben Elgin, "Google's Search for Simplicity," *BusinessWeek,* October 3, 2005, www.businessweek.com on January 6, 2006; Ben Elgin, "Managing Google's Idea Factory," *BusinessWeek,* October 3, 2005, www.businessweek.com on January 6, 2006; "Corporate Information," "Marissa Mayer," Google website, www.google.com on January 12, 2006; Roben Farzad and Ben Elgin, "Googling for Gold," *BusinessWeek,* December 5, 2005, www.businessweek.com on January 6, 2006; "Google's Internet Doctor," *Red Herring,* June 6, 2005, www.redherring.com on January 12, 2006; Linda Tischler, "The Beauty of Simplicity," *Fast Company,* November 2005, www.fastcompany.com on January 6, 2006 (quote).

2. Fred Luthans, "Successful vs. Effective Real Managers," *Academy of Management Executive,* May 1988, pp. 127–132. See also "The Best Performers," *The Business Week 50,* April 5, 2004, pp. 73–92.

3. Rosemary Stewart, "Middle Managers: Their Jobs and Behaviors," in Jay W. Lorsch, ed., *Handbook of Organizational Behavior* (Englewood Cliffs, NJ: Prentice-Hall, 1987), pp. 385–391.

4. John P. Kotter, "What Effective General Managers Really Do," *Harvard Business Review,* March–April 1999, pp. 145–155.

5. See Robert L. Katz, "The Skills of an Effective Administrator," *Harvard Business Review,* September–October 1974, pp. 90–102, for a classic discussion of several of these skills.

6. See "I'm Late, I'm Late, I'm Late," *USA Today,* November 26, 2002, pp. 1B, 2B.

7. For a recent discussion of the importance of time-management skills, see David Barry, Catherine Durnell Cramton, and Stephen J. Carroll, "Navigating the Garbage Can: How Agendas Help Managers Cope with Job Realities," *Academy of Management Executive,* May 1997, pp. 26–42.

8. Gary Hamel and C. K. Prahalad, "Competing for the Future," *Harvard Business Review,* July–August 1994, pp. 122–128.

9. James Waldroop and Timothy Butler, "The Executive as Coach," *Harvard Business Review,* November–December 1996, pp. 111–117.

10. Terence Mitchell and Lawrence James, "Building Better Theory: Time and the Specification of When Things Happen," *Academy of Management Review,* vol. 26, no. 4, 2001, pp. 530–547; see also Clayton Christensen and Michael Raynor, "Why Hard-Nosed Executives Should Care About Management Theory," *Harvard Business Review,* September 2003, pp. 67–75.

11. Peter F. Drucker, "The Theory of the Business," *Harvard Business Review,* September–October 1994, pp. 95–104; see also Christensen and Raynor, "Why Hard-Nosed Executives."

12. "Why Business History?" *Audacity,* Fall 1992, pp. 7–15. See also Alan L. Wilkins and Nigel J. Bristow, "For Successful Organization Culture, Honor Your Past," *Academy of Management Executive,* August 1987, pp. 221–227.

13. Daniel Wren, *The Evolution of Management Theory,* 4th ed. (New York: Wiley, 1994); Page Smith, *The Rise of Industrial America* (New York: McGraw-Hill, 1984).

14. Martha I. Finney, "Books That Changed Careers," *HRMagazine,* June 1997, pp. 141–145.

15. See Harriet Rubin, *The Princessa: Machiavelli for Women* (New York: Doubleday/Currency, 1997). See also Nanette Fondas, "Feminization Unveiled: Management Qualities in Contemporary Writings," *Academy of Management Review,* January 1997, pp. 257–282.

16. Alan M. Kantrow, ed., "Why History Matters to Managers," *Harvard Business Review,* January–February 1986, pp. 81–88.

17. Wren, *Evolution of Management Theory.*

18. Henri Fayol, *General and Industrial Management,* trans. J. A. Coubrough (Geneva, Switzerland: International Management Institute, 1930).

19. Max Weber, *Theory of Social and Economic Organizations,* trans. T. Parsons (New York: Free Press, 1947); Richard M. Weis, "Weber on Bureaucracy: Management Consultant or Political Theorist?" *Academy of Management Review,* April 1983, pp. 242–248.

20. Wren, *Evolution of Management Theory,* pp. 255–264.

21. Elton Mayo, *The Human Problems of an Industrial Civilization* (New York: Macmillan, 1933); Fritz J. Roethlisberger and William J. Dickson, *Management and the Worker* (Cambridge, MA: Harvard University Press, 1939).

22. Abraham Maslow, "A Theory of Human Motivation," *Psychological Review,* July 1943, pp. 370–396.

23. Douglas McGregor, *The Human Side of Enterprise* (New York: McGraw-Hill, 1960).

24. Sara L. Rynes and Christine Quinn Trank, "Behavioral Science in the Business School Curriculum: Teaching in a Changing Institutional Environment," *Academy of Management Review,* vol. 24, no. 4, 1999, pp. 808–824.

25. See Gregory Moorhead and Ricky W. Griffin, *Organizational Behavior,* 8th ed. (Boston: Houghton Mifflin, 2007), for a recent review of current developments in the field of organizational behavior.

26. Wren, *Evolution of Management Thought,* Chapter 21.

27. For more information on systems theory in general, see Ludwig von Bertalanffy, C. G. Hempel, R. E. Bass, and H. Jonas, "General Systems Theory: A New Approach to Unity of Science," I–VI, *Human Biology,* vol. 23, 1951, pp. 302–361. For systems theory as applied to organizations, see Fremont E. Kast and James E. Rosenzweig, "General Systems Theory: Applications for Organizations and Management," *Academy of Management Journal,* December 1972, pp. 447–465. For a recent update, see Donde P. Ashmos and George P. Huber, "The Systems Paradigm in Organization Theory: Correcting the Record and Suggesting the Future," *Academy of Management Review,* October 1987, pp. 607–621.

28. Kathleen M. Eisenhardt and D. Charles Galunic, "Coevolving—At Last, a Way to Make Synergies Work," *Harvard Business Review,* January–February 2000, pp. 91–103.

29. Fremont E. Kast and James E. Rosenzweig, *Contingency Views of Organization and Management* (Chicago: Science Research Associates, 1973).

30. "The Business Week Best-Seller List," *BusinessWeek,* November 4, 2002, p. 26.

Chapter 2

1. "Coffeehouses U.S. 2004," *Prepared Foods*, February 2004; Cora Daniels, "Mr. Coffee," *Fortune*, April 14, 2003, pp. 139–143; Chester Dawson, "Online Extra: Q&A with Starbucks' Howard Schultz," *BusinessWeek*, September 9, 2002, www.businessweek.com on November 18, 2002; Christina W. Passariello, "The Java Joint That's Swallowing France," *BusinessWeek*, September 11, 2002, www.businessweek.com on November 18, 2002; Kevin Helliker and Shirley Leung, "Despite the Jitters, Most Coffeehouses Survive Starbucks," *Wall Street Journal*, September 24, 2002, pp. A1, A11 (quote p. A1); Stanley Holmes, "Planet Starbucks," *BusinessWeek*, September 9, 2002, pp. 100–110; "Not a Johnny-Come-Latte," *USA Today*, September 9, 2003, p. 3B; Andy Serwer, "Hot Starbucks to Go," *Fortune*, January 26, 2004, pp. 60–74, "Timeline" Starbucks website, www.starbucks.com on December 19, 2005.
2. See Jay B. Barney and William G. Ouchi (eds.), *Organizational Economics* (San Francisco: Jossey-Bass, 1986), for a detailed analysis of linkages between economics and organizations.
3. "How Prosperity Is Reshaping the American Economy," *BusinessWeek*, February 14, 2000, pp. 100–110.
4. See "Firms Brace for a Worker Shortage," *Time*, May 6, 2002, p. 44.
5. Richard N. Osborn and John Hagedoorn, "The Institutionalization and Evolutionary Dynamics of Interorganizational Alliances and Networks," *Academy of Management Journal*, April 1997, pp. 261–278. See also "More Companies Cut Risk by Collaborating with Their 'Enemies,'" *Wall Street Journal*, January 31, 2000, pp. A1, A10.
6. "The Best & Worst Boards," *BusinessWeek*, October 7, 2002, pp. 104–114. See also Amy Hillman and Thomas Dalziel, "Boards of Directors and Firm Performance: Integrating Agency and Resource Dependence Perspectives," *Academy of Management Review*, vol. 23, no. 3, 2003, pp. 383–396.
7. "Curves Ahead," *Wall Street Journal*, March 10, 1999, pp. B1, B10.
8. See Norman Barry, *Business Ethics* (West Lafayette, IN: Purdue University Press, 1999).
9. Thomas Donaldson and Thomas W. Dunfee, "Toward a Unified Conception of Business Ethics: An Integrative Social Contracts Theory," *Academy of Management Review*, vol. 19, no. 2, 1994, pp. 252–284.
10. William Dill, "Beyond Codes and Courses," *Selections*, Fall 2002, pp. 21–23.
11. See "Restoring Trust in Corporate America," *BusinessWeek*, June 24, 2002, pp. 30–35.
12. "Is It Rainforest Crunch Time?" *BusinessWeek*, July 15, 1996, pp. 70–71; "Yo, Ben! Yo, Jerry! It's Just Ice Cream," *Fortune*, April 28, 1997, p. 374.
13. "Legal But Lousy," *Fortune*, September 2, 2002, p. 192.
14. Lynn Sharp Paine, "Managing for Organizational Integrity," *Harvard Business Review*, March–April 1994, pp. 106–115.
15. "Battling 'Donor Dropsy,'" *Wall Street Journal*, July 19, 2002, pp. B1, B4.
16. David M. Messick and Max H. Bazerman, "Ethical Leadership and the Psychology of Decision Making," *Sloan Management Review*, Winter 1996, pp. 9–22.
17. "Ethics in Action: Getting It Right," *Selections*, Fall 2002, pp. 24–27.
18. See Janet P. Near and Marcia P. Miceli, "Whistle-Blowing: Myth and Reality," *Journal of Management*, vol. 22, no. 3, 1996,

pp. 507–526, for a recent review of the literature on whistle-blowing. See also Michael Gundlach, Scott Douglas, and Mark Martinko, "The Decision to Blow the Whistle: A Social Information Processing Framework," *Academy of Management Review*, vol. 28, no. 1, 2003, pp. 107–123.
19. For instance, see "The Complex Goals and Unseen Costs of Whistle-Blowing," *Wall Street Journal*, November 25, 2002, pp. A1, A10.
20. "A Whistle-Blower Rocks an Industry," *BusinessWeek*, June 24, 2002, pp. 126–130.
21. "The *Fortune* Global 5 Hundred—World's Largest Corporations," *Fortune*, July 21, 2003, pp. 106–119.
22. "The *Fortune* Global 5 Hundred Ranked Within Industries," *Fortune*, July 21, 2003, pp. 106–119.
23. *Hoover's Handbook of American Business 2006* (Austin, TX: Hoover's Business Press, 2006), pp. 200–201, 578–579.
24. Kenichi Ohmae, "The Global Logic of Strategic Alliances," *Harvard Business Review*, March–April 1989, pp. 143–154.
25. For an excellent discussion of the effects of NAFTA, see "In the Wake of Nafta, a Family Firm Sees Business Go South," *Wall Street Journal*, February 23, 1999, pp. A1, A10.
26. Terrence E. Deal and Allan A. Kennedy, *Corporate Cultures: The Rights and Rituals of Corporate Life* (Reading, MA: Addison-Wesley, 1982).
27. Jay B. Barney, "Organizational Culture: Can It Be a Source of Sustained Competitive Advantage?" *Academy of Management Review*, July 1986, pp. 656–665.
28. For example, see Carol J. Loomis, "Sam Would Be Proud," *Fortune*, April 17, 2000, pp. 131–144.
29. See Carol Loomis, "The Tragedy of General Motors," *Fortune*, February 20, 2006, pp. 58–75.
30. Why Wells Fargo Is Circling the Wagons," *Wall Street Journal*, June 9, 1997, pp. 92–93.

Chapter 3

1. "2005 Annual Report," Nike, www.nike.com on November 10, 2005 (quote); Bethany McLean, "Nike Goes Toe to Toe with Adidas/Reebok Combo," *Fortune*, August 4, 2005, www.fortune.com on November 10, 2005; "CS First Boston Lowers Foot Locker to 'Neutral,'" *BusinessWeek*, December 20, 2002, www.businessweek.com on January 4, 2003; Matthew Boyle, "How Nike Got Its Swoosh Back," *Fortune*, June 11, 2002, www.fortune.com on January 4, 2003; "Sweatshops: Finally, Airing the Dirty Linens," *BusinessWeek*, June 23, 2003, pp. 100–102; Patricia O'Connell, "A Jog with Nike's New Team," *BusinessWeek*, October 28, 2002, www.businessweek.com on January 4, 2002; Stanley Holmes, "How Nike Got Its Game Back," *BusinessWeek*, November 4, 2002, pp. 129–131.
2. See Peter J. Brews and Michelle R. Hunt, "Learning to Plan and Planning to Learn: Resolving the Planning School/Learning School Debate," *Strategic Management Journal*, vol. 20, 1999, pp. 889–913.
3. Max D. Richards, *Setting Strategic Goals and Objectives*, 2nd ed. (St. Paul, MN: West, 1986).
4. Jim Collins, "Turning Goals into Results: The Power of Catalytic Mechanisms," *Harvard Business Review*, July–August 1999, pp. 71–81.
5. Kenneth R. Thompson, Wayne A. Hochwarter, and Nicholas J. Mathys, "Stretch Targets: What Makes Them Effective?" *Academy of Management Executive*, August 1997, pp. 48–58.
6. "A Methodical Man," *Forbes*, August 11, 1997, pp. 70–72.

7. John A. Pearce II and Fred David, "Corporate Mission Statements: The Bottom Line," *Academy of Management Executive*, May 1987, p. 109.

8. See Charles Hill and Gareth Jones, *Strategic Management*, 6th ed. (Boston: Houghton Mifflin, 2004).

9. For early discussions of strategic management, see Kenneth Andrews, *The Concept of Corporate Strategy*, rev. ed. (Homewood, IL: Dow Jones–Irwin, 1980); and Igor Ansoff, *Corporate Strategy* (New York: McGraw-Hill, 1965). For more recent perspectives, see Michael E. Porter, "What Is Strategy?" *Harvard Business Review*, November–December 1996, pp. 61–78; Kathleen M. Eisenhardt, "Strategy as Strategic Decision Making," *Sloan Management Review*, Spring 1999, pp. 65–74; and Sarah Kaplan and Eric Beinhocker, "The Real Value of Strategic Planning," *Sloan Management Review*, Winter 2003, pp. 71–80.

10. *Hoover's Handbook of American Business 2006* (Austin, TX: Hoover's Business Press, 2006), pp. 894–895.

11. Jim Rohwer, "GE Digs into Asia," *Fortune*, October 2, 2000, pp. 164–178.

12. For a discussion of the distinction between business- and corporate-level strategies, see Charles Hill and Gareth Jones, *Strategic Management: An Integrated Approach*, 6th ed. (Boston: Houghton Mifflin, 2004).

13. Jay Barney, "Firm Resources and Sustained Competitive Advantage," *Journal of Management*, June 1991, pp. 99–120.

14. "If It's on the Fritz, Take It to Jane," *BusinessWeek*, January 27, 1997, pp. 74–75.

15. Michael Beer and Russell Eisenstat, "How to Have an Honest Conversation About Your Business Strategy," *Harvard Business Review*, February 2004, pp. 82–89.

16. Porter, *Competitive Strategy*. See also Colin Campbell-Hunt, "What Have We Learned About Generic Competitive Strategy? A Meta-Analysis," *Strategic Management Journal*, vol. 21, 2000, pp. 127–154.

17. Ian C. MacMillan and Rita Gunther McGrath, "Discovering New Points of Differentiation," *Harvard Business Review*, July–August 1997, pp. 133–136.

18. Alfred Chandler, *Strategy and Structure: Chapters in the History of the American Industrial Enterprise* (Cambridge, MA: MIT Press, 1962); Richard Rumelt, *Strategy, Structure, and Economic Performance* (Cambridge, MA: Division of Research, Graduate School of Business Administration, Harvard University, 1974); Oliver Williamson, *Markets and Hierarchies* (New York: Free Press, 1975).

19. K. L. Stimpert and Irene M. Duhaime, "Seeing the Big Picture: The Influence of Industry, Diversification, and Business Strategy on Performance," *Academy of Management Journal*, vol. 40, no. 3, 1997, pp. 560–583.

20. See Chandler, *Strategy and Structure*; Yakov Amihud and Baruch Lev, "Risk Reduction as a Managerial Motive for Conglomerate Mergers," *Bell Journal of Economics*, 1981, pp. 605–617.

21. "Did Somebody Say McBurrito?" *BusinessWeek*, April 10, 2000, pp. 166–170.

22. See Constantinoes C. Markides and Peter J. Williamson, "Corporate Diversification and Organizational Structure: A Resource-Based View," *Academy of Management Journal*, April 1996, pp. 340–367.

23. See Barry Hedley, "A Fundamental Approach to Strategy Development," *Long Range Planning*, December 1976, pp. 2–11; Bruce Henderson, "The Experience Curve-Reviewed. IV: The Growth Share Matrix of the Product Portfolio," *Perspectives*, no. 135 (Boston: Boston Consulting Group, 1973).

24. Michael G. Allen, "Diagramming G.E.'s Planning for What's WATT," in Robert J. Allio and Malcolm W. Pennington, eds., *Corporate Planning: Techniques and Applications* (New York: AMACOM, 1979). The limitations of this approach are discussed in R. A. Bettis and W. K. Hall, "The Business Portfolio Approach: Where It Falls Down in Practice," *Long Range Planning*, March 1983, pp. 95–105.

25. Unilever to Sell Specialty-Chemical Unit to ICI of the U.K. for About $8 Billion," *Wall Street Journal*, May 7, 1997, pp. A3, A12; "For Unilever, It's Sweetness and Light," *Wall Street Journal*, April 13, 2000, pp. B1, B4.

26. James Brian Quinn, Henry Mintzberg, and Robert M. James, *The Strategy Process* (Englewood Cliffs, NJ: Prentice-Hall, 1988).

27. Vasudevan Ramanujam and N. Venkatraman, "Planning System Characteristics and Planning Effectiveness," *Strategic Management Journal*, vol. 8, no. 2, 1987, pp. 453–468.

28. K. A. Froot, D. S. Scharfstein, and J. C. Stein, "A Framework for Risk Management," *Harvard Business Review*, November–December 1994, pp. 91–102.

29. Michael Watkins and Max Bazerman, "Predictable Surprises: The Disasters You Should Have Seen Coming," *Harvard Business Review*, March 2003, pp. 72–81.

Chapter 4

1. "2004 Annual Report," "2002 Annual Report," Cephalon website, www.cephalon.com on December 19, 2005 (quote from 2002 annual report); Andrew Pollack, "A Biotech Outcast Awakens," *New York Times*, October 20, 2002, pp. BU1, BU13; "Cephalon, Inc. Reports Third Quarter 2002 Financial Results," *PRNewswire*, November 6, 2002, hoovnews.hoovers.com on January 8, 2003; "Cephalon Submits Supplemental New Drug Application for Provigil," *PRNewswire*, December 23, 2002, hoovnews.hoovers.com on January 8, 2003; "Testing in Humans," U.S. Food and Drug Administration website, www.fda.gov on January 8, 2003.

2. Richard Priem, "Executive Judgment, Organizational Congruence, and Firm Performance," *Organization Science*, August 1994, pp. 421–432.

3. "Ford Grabs Big Prize as Steep Losses Force BMW to Sell Rover," *Wall Street Journal*, March 17, 2000, pp. A1, A8.

4. Paul Nutt, "The Formulation Processes and Tactics Used in Organizational Decision Making," *Organization Science*, May 1993, pp. 226–240.

5. See Michael Mankins and Richard Steele, "Stop Making Plans; Start Making Decisions," *Harvard Business Review*, January 2006, pp. 89–102.

6. For a review of decision making, see E. Frank Harrison, *The Managerial Decision Making Process*, 5th ed. (Boston: Houghton Mifflin, 1999).

7. Jerry Useem, "Decisions, Decisions," *Fortune*, June 27, 2005, pp. 55–154.

8. See "How Goodyear Blew Its Chance to Capitalize on a Rival's Woes," *Wall Street Journal*, February 19, 2003, pp. A1, A10.

9. George P. Huber, *Managerial Decision Making* (Glenview, IL: Scott, Foresman, 1980).

10. See Paul D. Collins, Lori V. Ryan, and Sharon F. Matusik, "Programmable Automation and the Locus of Decision-Making Power," *Journal of Management*, vol. 25, 1999, pp. 29–53, for an example.

11. Huber, *Managerial Decision Making*. See also David W. Miller and Martin K. Starr, *The Structure of Human Decisions* (Englewood Cliffs, NJ: Prentice-Hall, 1976); Alvar Elbing, *Behavioral Decisions in Organizations*, 2nd ed. (Glenview, IL: Scott, Foresman, 1978).
12. "Taking the Angst Out of Taking a Gamble," *BusinessWeek*, July 14, 1997, pp. 52–53.
13. Gerard P. Hodgkinson, Nicola J. Bown, A. John Maule, Keith W. Glaister, and Alan D. Pearman, "Breaking the Frame: An Analysis of Strategic Cognition and Decision Making Under Uncertainty," *Strategic Management Journal*, vol. 20, 1999, pp. 977–985.
14. "Andersen's Fall from Grace Is a Tale of Greed and Miscues," *Wall Street Journal*, June 7, 2002, pp. A1, A6.
15. Glen Whyte, "Decision Failures: Why They Occur and How to Prevent Them," *Academy of Management Executive*, August 1991, pp. 23–31.
16. Kenneth Brousseau, Michael Driver, Gary Hourihan, and Rikard Larsson, "The Seasoned Executive's Decision-Making Style," *Harvard Business Review*, February 2006, pp. 111–120.
17. "The Wisdom of Solomon," *Newsweek*, August 17, 1987, pp. 62–63.
18. "Making Decisions in Real Time," *Fortune*, June 26, 2000, pp. 332–334.
19. Herbert A. Simon, *Administrative Behavior* (New York: Free Press, 1945). Simon's ideas have been refined and updated in Herbert A. Simon, *Administrative Behavior*, 3rd ed. (New York: Free Press, 1976) and Herbert A. Simon, "Making Management Decisions: The Role of Intuition and Emotion," *Academy of Management Executive*, February 1987, pp. 57–63.
20. Patricia Corner, Angelo Kinicki, and Barbara Keats, "Integrating Organizational and Individual Information Processing Perspectives on Choice," *Organization Science*, August 1994, pp. 294–302.
21. Kimberly D. Elsbach and Greg Elofson, "How the Packaging of Decision Explanations Affects Perceptions of Trustworthiness," *Academy of Management Journal*, vol. 43, 2000, pp. 80–89.
22. Eugene Sadler-Smith and Erella Shefy, "The Intuitive Executive: Understanding and Applying 'Gut-Feel' in Decision-Making," *Academy of Management Executive*, vol. 18, 2004, pp. 76–91.
23. Charles P. Wallace, "Adidas—Back in the Game," *Fortune*, August 18, 1997, pp. 176–182.
24. Barry M. Staw and Jerry Ross, "Good Money After Bad," *Psychology Today*, February 1988, pp. 30–33; D. Ramona Bobocel and John Meyer, "Escalating Commitment to a Failing Course of Action: Separating the Roles of Choice and Justification," *Journal of Applied Psychology*, vol. 79, 1994, pp. 360–363.
25. Mark Keil and Ramiro Montealegre, "Cutting Your Losses: Extricating Your Organization When a Big Project Goes Awry," *Sloan Management Review*, Spring 2000, pp. 55–64.
26. Gerry McNamara and Philip Bromiley, "Risk and Return in Organizational Decision Making," *Academy of Management Journal*, vol. 42, 1999, pp. 330–339.
27. See Brian O'Reilly, "What It Takes to Start a Startup," *Fortune*, June 7, 1999, pp. 135–140, for an example.
28. Martha I. Finney, "The Catbert Dilemma—The Human Side of Tough Decisions," *HRMagazine*, February 1997, pp. 70–78.
29. Edwin A. Locke, David M. Schweiger, and Gary P. Latham, "Participation in Decision Making: When Should It Be Used?" *Organ-izational Dynamics*, Winter 1986, pp. 65–79; Nicholas

Baloff and Elizabeth M. Doherty, "Potential Pitfalls in Employee Participation," *Organizational Dynamics*, Winter 1989, pp. 51–62.
30. "The Art of Brainstorming," *BusinessWeek*, August 26, 2002, pp. 168–169.
31. Andre L. Delbecq, Andrew H. Van de Ven, and David H. Gustafson, *Group Techniques for Program Planning* (Glenview, IL: Scott, Foresman, 1975); Michael J. Prietula and Herbert A. Simon, "The Experts in Your Midst," *Harvard Business Review*, January–February 1989, pp. 120–124.
32. Norman P. R. Maier, "Assets and Liabilities in Group Problem Solving: The Need for an Integrative Function," in J. Richard Hackman, Edward E. Lawler, III, and Lyman W. Porter, eds., *Perspectives on Business in Organizations*, 2nd ed. (New York: McGraw-Hill, 1983), pp. 385–392.
33. Anthony L. Iaquinto and James W. Fredrickson, "Top Management Team Agreement About the Strategic Decision Process: A Test of Some of Its Determinants and Consequences," *Strategic Management Journal*, vol. 18, 1997, pp. 63–75.
34. Tony Simons, Lisa Hope Pelled, and Ken A. Smith, "Making Use of Difference: Diversity, Debate, and Decision Comprehensiveness in Top Management Teams," *Academy of Management Journal*, vol. 42, 1999, pp. 662–673.
35. Richard A. Cosier and Charles R. Schwenk, "Agreement and Thinking Alike: Ingredients for Poor Decisions," *Academy of Management Executive*, February 1990, pp. 69–78.
36. Irving L. Janis, *Groupthink*, 2nd ed. (Boston: Houghton Mifflin, 1982).
37. Ibid.

Chapter 5

1. "About Our Company," Pret A Manger website, www.pret .com on December 11, 2005; Ian Parker, "An English Sandwich in New York," *The Guardian* (London), August 9, 2002, www .guardian.co.uk on January 13, 2003 (quote); Julie Forster, "Thinking Outside the Burger Box," *BusinessWeek*, September 16, 2002, pp. 66–67; Milton Moskowitz and Robert Levering, "100 Great Companies to Work for in Europe: Pret A Manger," *Fortune*, January 22, 2002, www.fortune.com on January 13, 2003; Scott Kirshner, "Recipe for Reinvention," *Fast Company*, April 2002, pp. 38–42.
2. "The 400 Richest People in America," *Forbes*, September 9, 2005, p. 214.
3. Murray B. Low and Ian MacMillan, "Entrepreneurship: Past Research and Future Challenges," *Journal of Management*, June 1988, pp. 139–159.
4. U.S. Department of Commerce, *Statistical Abstract of the United States: 1999* (Washington, DC: U.S. Census Bureau, 1999).
5. "Small Business 'Vital Statistics,'" www.sba.gov/aboutsba/on May 24, 2000.
6. Ibid.
7. Ibid.
8. Amar Bhide, "How Entrepreneurs Craft Strategies That Work," *Harvard Business Review*, March–April 1994, pp. 150–163.
9. *Hoover's Handbook of American Business 2006* (Austin, TX: Hoover's Business Press, 2006), pp. 889–890; Wendy Zellner, "Peace, Love, and the Bottom Line," *BusinessWeek*, December 7, 1998, pp. 79–82.
10. Nancy J. Lyons, "Moonlight Over Indiana," *Inc.*, January 2000, pp. 71–74.

11. "Three Biker-Entrepreneurs Take on Mighty Harley," *New York Times*, August 20, 1999, p. F1; see also "Easy Riders," *Forbes*, April 19, 2004, pp. 94–96.

12. The importance of discovering niches is emphasized in Charles Hill and Gareth Jones, *Strategic Management: An Integrative Approach*, 6th ed. (Boston: Houghton Mifflin, 2004).

13. Gregory Patterson, "An American in . . . Siberia?" *Fortune*, August 4, 1997, p. 63; "Crazy for Crunchies," *Newsweek*, April 28, 1997, p. 49.

14. "'Ship Those Boxes; Check the Euro!'" *Wall Street Journal*, February 7, 2003, pp. C1, C7.

15. "Cheap Tricks," *Forbes*, February 21, 2000, p. 116.

16. U.S. Department of Commerce, *Statistical Abstract of the United States: 1999* (Washington, DC: Bureau of the Census, 1999). See also "Too Much Ventured, Nothing Gained," *Fortune*, November 25, 2002, pp. 135–144.

17. "Internet Industry Surges 'Startling' 62%," *USA Today*, June 6, 2000, p. 1B.

18. *The Economist World in Figures 2006* (London: Profile Books, 2006), pp. 234–236.

19. See *The Wall Street Journal Almanac 1999*, pp. 179, 182 and *The Economist World in Figures 2006*, pp. 234–236.

20. "Women Increase Standing as Business Owners," *USA Today*, June 29, 1999, p. 1B.

21. Norman M. Scarborough and Thomas W. Zimmerer, *Effective Small Business Management: An Entrepreneurial Approach*, 6th ed. (Upper Saddle River, NJ: Prentice-Hall, 2000), pp. 412–413.

22. "Expert Entrepreneur Got Her Show on the Road at an Early Age," *USA Today*, May 24, 2000, p. 5B.

Chapter 6

1. "About Us," "Comedy Central Launches on iTunes," "Viacom Completes Separation," Viacom website, January 1, 2006, www.viacom.com on January 17, 2006; Josh Bernoff and Jim Nail, "Dismantling the TV Schedule," *CNET*, November 8, 2005, www.news.com on January 17, 2006; Ronald Grover, "In Media, Size Does Matter," *BusinessWeek*, April 13, 2005, www.businessweek.com on January 17, 2006 (quote); Leo Hindery Jr., "Time Warner: No Disassembly Required," *BusinessWeek*, January 1, 2006, www.businessweek.com on January 17, 2006; Paul R. La Monica, "Media's Musical Chairs," *CNN Money*, January 6, 2006, www.cnnmoney.com on January 17, 2006; Tom Lowry, "The World of the Superniche," *BusinessWeek*, November 7, 2005, www.businessweek.com on January 17, 2006; Tom Lowry, "TV's New Parallel Universe," *BusinessWeek*, November 14, 2005, www.businessweek.com on January 17, 2006; Emily Thornton, "Breaking Up Isn't Always the Answer," *BusinessWeek*, January 10, 2006, www.businessweek.com on January 17, 2006; "UPN, WB to Combine for New Network," *CBS News*, January 24, 2006, www.cbsnews.com on January 25, 2006.

2. See Kathleen M. Eisenhardt and Shona L. Brown, "Patching—Restitching Business Portfolios in Dynamic Markets," *Harvard Business Review*, May–June 1999, pp. 106–115, for a related discussion.

3. Ricky W. Griffin, *Task Design* (Glenview, IL: Scott, Foresman, 1982).

4. M. D. Kilbridge, "Reduced Costs Through Job Enlargement: A Case," *Journal of Business*, vol. 33, 1960, pp. 357–362.

5. R. W. Griffin and G. McMahon, "Motivation Through Job Design," in *Organizational Behavior: The State of the Science* (New York: Lawrence Erlbaum Associates, 1994), pp. 23–44.

6. Kilbridge, "Reduced Costs Through Job Enrichment: A Case."

7. Frederick Herzberg, *Work and the Nature of Man* (Cleveland, OH: World Press, 1966).

8. J. Richard Hackman and Greg R. Oldham, *Work Redesign* (Reading, MA: Addison-Wesley, 1980).

9. "Some Plants Tear Out Long Assembly Lines, Switch to Craft Work," *Wall Street Journal*, October 24, 1994, pp. A1, A4.

10. Richard L. Daft, *Organization Theory and Design*, 8th ed. (Cincinnati, OH: South-Western, 2004).

11. David D. Van Fleet and Arthur G. Bedeian, "A History of the Span of Management," *Academy of Management Review*, 1977, pp. 356–372.

12. James C. Worthy, "Factors Influencing Employee Morale," *Harvard Business Review*, January 1950, pp. 61–73.

13. Dan R. Dalton, William D. Todor, Michael J. Spendolini, Gordon J. Fielding, and Lyman W. Porter, "Organization Structure and Performance: A Critical Review," *Academy of Management Review*, January 1980, pp. 49–64.

14. See Jerry Useem, "Welcome to the New Company Town," *Fortune*, January 10, 2000, pp. 62–70, for a related discussion.

15. See Daft, *Organization Theory and Design*.

16. William Kahn and Kathy Kram, "Authority at Work: Internal Models and Their Organizational Consequences," *Academy of Management Review*, vol. 19, no. 1, 1994, pp. 17–50.

17. Carrie R. Leana, "Predictors and Consequences of Delegation," *Academy of Management Journal*, December 1986, pp. 754–774.

18. Kevin Crowston, "A Coordination Theory Approach to Organizational Process Design," *Organization Science*, March–April 1997, pp. 157–166.

19. James Thompson, *Organizations in Action* (New York: McGraw-Hill, 1967). For a recent discussion, see Bart Victor and Richard S. Blackburn, "Interdependence: An Alternative Conceptualization," *Academy of Management Review*, July 1987, pp. 486–498.

20. Jay R. Galbraith, *Designing Complex Organizations* (Reading, MA: Addison-Wesley, 1973) and *Organizational Design* (Reading, MA: Addison-Wesley, 1977).

21. Paul R. Lawrence and Jay W. Lorsch, "Differentiation and Integration in Complex Organizations," *Administrative Science Quarterly*, March 1967, pp. 1–47.

22. Max Weber, *Theory of Social and Economic Organizations*, trans. T. Parsons (New York: Free Press, 1947).

23. Paul Jarley, Jack Fiorito, and John Thomas Delany, "A Structural Contingency Approach to Bureaucracy and Democracy in U.S. National Unions," *Academy of Management Journal*, vol. 40, no. 4, 1997, pp. 831–861.

24. Joan Woodward, *Industrial Organization: Theory and Practice* (London: Oxford University Press, 1965).

25. Joan Woodward, *Management and Technology, Problems of Progress Industry*, no. 3 (London: Her Majesty's Stationery Office, 1958).

26. Tom Burns and G. M. Stalker, *The Management of Innovation* (London: Tavistock, 1961).

27. Paul R. Lawrence and Jay W. Lorsch, *Organization and Environment* (Homewood, IL: Irwin, 1967).

28. Edward E. Lawler III, "Rethinking Organization Size," *Organizational Dynamics*, Autumn 1997, pp. 24–33. See also Tom Brown, "How Big Is Too Big?" *Across the Board*, July–August 1999, pp. 14–20.

29. Derek S. Pugh and David J. Hickson, *Organization Structure in Its Context: The Aston Program I* (Lexington, MA: D.C. Heath, 1976).

30. "Can Wal-Mart Get Any Bigger?" *Time*, January 13, 2003, pp. 38–43.

31. Robert H. Miles and Associates, *The Organizational Life Cycle* (San Francisco: Jossey-Bass, 1980). See also "Is Your Company Too Big?" *BusinessWeek*, March 27, 1989, pp. 84–94.

32. Douglas Baker and John Cullen, "Administrative Reorganization and Configurational Context: The Contingent Effects of Age, Size, and Change in Size," *Academy of Management Journal*, vol. 36, no. 6, 1993, pp. 1251–1277. See also Kevin Crowston, "A Coordination Theory Approach to Organizational Process Design," *Organization Science*, March–April 1997, pp. 157–168.

33. Oliver E. Williamson, *Markets and Hierarchies* (New York: Free Press, 1975).

34. Ibid.

35. Michael E. Porter, "From Competitive Advantage to Corporate Strategy," *Harvard Business Review*, May–June 1987, pp. 43–59.

36. Williamson, *Markets and Hierarchies*.

37. Jay B. Barney and William G. Ouchi, eds., *Organizational Economics* (San Francisco: Jossey-Bass, 1986); Robert E. Hoskisson, "Multidivisional Structure and Performance: The Contingency of Diversification Strategy," *Academy of Management Journal*, December 1987, pp. 625–644. See also Bruce Lamont, Robert Williams, and James Hoffman, "Performance During 'M-Form' Reorganization and Recovery Time: The Effects of Prior Strategy and Implementation Speed," *Academy of Management Journal*, vol. 37, no. 1, 1994, pp. 153–166.

38. Stanley M. Davis and Paul R. Lawrence, *Matrix* (Reading, MA: Addison-Wesley, 1977).

39. Ibid.

40. See Lawton Burns and Douglas Wholey, "Adoption and Abandonment of Matrix Management Programs: Effects of Organizational Characteristics and Interorganizational Networks," *Academy of Management Journal*, vol. 36, no. 1, pp. 106–138.

41. See Michael Hammer and Steven Stanton, "How Process Enterprises Really Work," *Harvard Business Review*, November–December 1999, pp. 108–118.

42. Raymond E. Miles, Charles C. Snow, John A. Mathews, Grant Miles, and Henry J. Coleman, Jr., "Organizing in the Knowledge Age: Anticipating the Cellular Form," *Academy of Management Executive*, November 1997, pp. 7–24.

43. "The Horizontal Corporation," *BusinessWeek*, December 20, 1993, pp. 76–81; Shawn Tully, "The Modular Corporation," *Fortune*, February 8, 1993, pp. 106–114.

44. "Management by Web," *BusinessWeek*, August 28, 2000, pp. 84–96.

45. Peter Senge, *The Fifth Discipline* (New York: Free Press, 1993). See also David Lei, John W. Slocum, and Robert A. Pitts, "Designing Organizations for Competitive Advantage: The Power of Unlearning and Learning," *Organizational Dynamics*, Winter 1999, pp. 24–35.

Chapter 7

1. "Best Companies to Work For," *Fortune*, January 20, 2003, www.fortune.com on January 27, 2003; Dave Carpenter, "Sears' Earnings Rise, Helped by Lands' End," *AP Business*, January 16, 2003, hoovnews.hoovers.com on January 27, 2003; Heesun Wee, "The Solid Ground Under Lands' End," *BusinessWeek*, December 7, 2001, www.businessweek.com on January 27, 2003; Joel Grover, "Sears Boosts Brand Image with Lands' End Purchase," *Shopping Center World*, June 1, 2002, shoppingcenterworld.com on January 27, 2003 (quote); Keith Regan, "Can Lands' End Bring Sears Up to Speed Online?" *E-Commerce Times*, May 20, 2002, www.ecommercetimes.com on January 27, 2003; "Message from the Chairman," Sears Holdings website, December 6, 2005, www.searsholdings.com on January 18, 2006; Robert Berner, "Sears–Lands' End: The Seams May Show," *BusinessWeek*, May 16, 2002, www.businessweek.com on January 27, 2003.

2. For an excellent review of this area, see Achilles A. Armenakis and Arthur G. Bedeian, "Organizational Change: A Review of Theory and Research in the 1990s," *Journal of Management*, vol. 25, no. 3, 1999, pp. 293–315.

3. For additional insights into how technological change affects other parts of the organization, see P. Robert Duimering, Frank Safayeni, and Lyn Purdy, "Integrated Manufacturing: Redesign the Organization Before Implementing Flexible Technology," *Sloan Management Review*, Summer 1993, pp. 47–56.

4. Joel Cutcher-Gershenfeld, Ellen Ernst Kossek, and Heidi Sandling, "Managing Concurrent Change Initiatives," *Organizational Dynamics*, Winter 1997, pp. 21–38.

5. Michael A. Hitt, "The New Frontier: Transformation of Management for the New Millennium," *Organizational Dynamics*, Winter 2000, pp. 7–15. See also Michael Beer and Nitin Nohria, "Cracking the Code of Change," *Harvard Business Review*, May–June 2000, pp. 133–144; Clark Gilbert, "The Disruption Opportunity," *MIT Sloan Management Review*, Summer 2003, pp. 27–32.

6. See Warren Boeker, "Strategic Change: The Influence of Managerial Characteristics and Organizational Growth," *Academy of Management Journal*, vol. 40, no. 1, 1997, pp. 152–170.

7. Alan L. Frohman, "Igniting Organizational Change from Below: The Power of Personal Initiative," *Organizational Dynamics*, Winter 1997, pp. 39–53.

8. Nandini Rajagopalan and Gretchen M. Spreitzer, "Toward a Theory of Strategic Change: A Multi-Lens Perspective and Integrative Framework," *Academy of Management Review*, vol. 22, no. 1, 1997, pp. 48–79.

9. Anne Fisher, "Danger Zone," *Fortune*, September 8, 1997, pp. 165–167.

10. John P. Kotter and Leonard A. Schlesinger, "Choosing Strategies for Change," *Harvard Business Review*, March–April 1997, p. 106.

11. Clayton M. Christensen and Michael Overdorf, "Meeting the Challenge of Disruptive Change," *Harvard Business Review*, March–April 2000, pp. 67–77.

12. "To Maintain Success, Managers Must Learn How to Direct Change," *Wall Street Journal*, August 13, 2002, p. B1.

13. See Eric Abrahamson, "Change Without Pain," *Harvard Business Review*, July–August 2000, pp. 75–85. See also Gib Akin and Ian Palmer, "Putting Metaphors to Work for Change in Organizations," *Organizational Dynamics*, Winter 2000, pp. 67–76.

14. Erik Brynjolfsson, Amy Austin Renshaw, and Marshall Van Alstyne, "The Matrix of Change," *Sloan Management Review*, Winter 1997, pp. 37–54.

15. "Time for a Turnaround," *Fast Company*, January 2003, pp. 55–61.

16. See Connie J. G. Gersick, "Revolutionary Change Theories: A Multilevel Exploration of the Punctuated Equilibrium Paradigm," *Academy of Management Review*, January 1991, pp. 10–36.

17. See Gerald Andrews, "Mistrust, the Hidden Obstacle to Empowerment," *HRMagazine*, November 1994, pp. 66–74, for a good illustration of how resistance emerges.

18. Arnon E. Reichers, John P. Wanous, and James T. Austin, "Understanding and Managing Cynicism About Organizational Change," *Academy of Management Executive*, February 1997, pp. 48–59.

19. See Paul R. Lawrence, "How to Deal with Resistance to Change," *Harvard Business Review*, January–February 1969, pp. 4–12, 166–176, for a classic discussion.

20. Benjamin Schneider, Arthur P. Brief, and Richard A. Guzzo, "Creating a Climate and Culture for Sustainable Organizational Change," *Organizational Dynamics*, Spring 1996, pp. 7–19.

21. Paul Bate, Raza Khan, and Annie Pye, "Towards a Culturally Sensitive Approach to Organization Structuring: Where Organization Design Meets Organization Development," *Organization Science*, March–April 2000, pp. 197–211.

22. "Founding Clan Vies with Outside 'Radical' for the Soul of Toyota," *Wall Street Journal*, May 5, 2000, pp. A1, A12.

23. David Kirkpatrick, "The New Player," *Fortune*, April 17, 2000, pp. 162–168.

24. "Mr. Ryder Rewrites the Musty Old Book at Reader's Digest," *Wall Street Journal*, April 18, 2000, pp. A1, A10.

25. Thomas A. Stewart, "Reengineering—The Hot New Managing Tool," *Fortune*, August 23, 1993, pp. 41–48.

26. Richard Beckhard, *Organization Development: Strategies and Models* (Reading, MA: Addison-Wesley, 1969), p. 9.

27. W. Warner Burke, "The New Agenda for Organization Development," *Organizational Dynamics*, Summer 1997, pp. 7–20.

28. Wendell L. French and Cecil H. Bell, Jr., *Organization Development: Behavioral Science Interventions for Organization Improvement*, 2nd ed. (Englewood Cliffs, NJ: Prentice-Hall, 1978).

29. "Memo to the Team: This Needs Salt!" *Wall Street Journal*, April 4, 2000, pp. B1, B14.

30. Constantinos Markides, "Strategic Innovation," *Sloan Management Review*, Spring 1997, pp. 9–24. See also James Brian Quinn, "Outsourcing Innovation: The New Engine of Growth," *Sloan Management Review*, Summer 2000, pp. 13–21.

31. L. B. Mohr, "Determinants of Innovation in Organizations," *American Political Science Review*, 1969, pp. 111–126; G. A. Steiner, *The Creative Organization* (Chicago: University of Chicago Press, 1965); R. Duncan and A. Weiss, "Organizational Learning: Implications for Organizational Design," in B. M. Staw, ed., *Research in Organizational Behavior*, vol. 1 (Greenwich, CT: JAI Press, 1979), pp. 75–123; J. E. Ettlie, "Adequacy of Stage Models for Decisions on Adoption of Innovation," *Psychological Reports*, 1980, pp. 991–995.

32. See Alan Patz, "Managing Innovation in High Technology Industries," *New Management*, September 1986, pp. 54–59.

33. See Willow A. Sheremata, "Centrifugal and Centripetal Forces in Radical New Product Development Under Time Pressure," *Academy of Management Review*, vol. 25, no. 2, 2000, pp. 389–408. See also Richard Leifer, Gina Colarelli O'Connor, and Mark Rice, "Implementing Radical Innovation in Mature Firms: The Role of Hubs," *Academy of Management Executive*, vol. 15, no. 3, 2001, pp. 102–113.

34. Dorothy Leonard and Jeffrey F. Rayport, "Spark Innovation Through Empathic Design," *Harvard Business Review*, November–December 1997, pp. 102–115.

35. See Steven P. Feldman, "How Organizational Culture Can Affect Innovation," *Organizational Dynamics*, Summer 1988, pp. 57–68.

36. See Gifford Pinchot III, *Intrapreneuring* (New York: Harper & Row, 1985).

Chapter 8

1. "100 Best Companies to Work For," "Hall of Fame," *Fortune*, January 20, 2006, www.fortune.com on January 21, 2006; "Benefits," "Culture and Philosophy," "Grants Program," "Join Our Winning Team," "REI Earns Top 10 Ranking," "REI Facts," "Testimonials," REI website, www.rei.com on January 21, 2006 (quote); Dale Buss, "REI: Working Out," *BusinessWeek*, November 15, 2005, www.businessweek.com on January 21, 2006; Monica Soto Ouchi, "Sally Jewell: Team Player at Her Peak," *The Seattle Times*, March 23, 2005, www.seattletimes.com on January 21, 2006; Alison Overholt, "Smart Strategies: Putting Ideas to Work," *Fast Company*, April 2004, www.fastcompany.com on January 21, 2006.

2. For a complete review of human resource management, see Angelo S. DeNisi and Ricky W. Griffin, *Human Resource Management*, 3rd ed. (Boston: Houghton Mifflin, 2007).

3. Patrick Wright and Gary McMahan, "Strategic Human Resources Management: A Review of the Literature," *Journal of Management*, June 1992, pp. 280–319.

4. Augustine Lado and Mary Wilson, "Human Resource Systems and Sustained Competitive Advantage: A Competency-based Perspective," *Academy of Management Review*, vol. 19, no. 4, 1994, pp. 699–727.

5. David Lepak and Scott Snell, "Examining the Human Resource Architecture: The Relationships Among Human Capital, Employment, and Human Resource Configurations," *Journal of Management*, vol. 28, no. 4, 2002, pp. 517–543.

6. "While Hiring at Most Firms Chills, Wal-Mart's Heats Up," *USA Today*, August 26, 2002, p. 1B.

7. James A. Breaugh and Mary Starke, "Research on Employee Recruiting: So Many Studies, So Many Remaining Questions," *Journal of Management*, vol. 26, no. 3, 2000, pp. 405–434.

8. "Pumping Up Your Past," *Time*, June 10, 2002, p. 96.

9. Frank L. Schmidt and John E. Hunter, "Employment Testing: Old Theories and New Research Findings," *American Psychologist*, October 1981, pp. 1128–1137.

10. Robert Liden, Christopher Martin, and Charles Parsons, "Interviewer and Applicant Behaviors in Employment Interviews," *Academy of Management Journal*, vol. 36, no. 2, 1993, pp. 372–386.

11. Paul R. Sackett, "Assessment Centers and Content Validity: Some Neglected Issues," *Personnel Psychology*, vol. 40, 1987, pp. 13–25.

12. See Angelo S. DeNisi and Avraham N. Kluger, "Feedback Effectiveness: Can 360-Degree Appraisals Be Improved?" *Academy of Management Executive*, vol. 14, no. 1, 2000, pp. 129–139.

13. Barry R. Nathan, Allan Mohrman, and John Milliman, "Interpersonal Relations as a Context for the Effects of Appraisal Interviews on Performance and Satisfaction: A Longitudinal Study," *Academy of Management Journal*, June 1991, pp. 352–369.

14. "Goodyear to Stop Labeling 10% of Its Workers as Worst," *USA Today*, September 12, 2002, p. 1B.

15. "To Each According to His Needs: Flexible Benefits Plans Gain Favor," *Wall Street Journal*, September 16, 1986, p. 29.

16. For an example, see "A Female Executive Tells Furniture Maker What Women Want," *Wall Street Journal*, June 25, 1999, pp. A1, A11.

17. Patricia L. Nemetz and Sandra L. Christensen, "The Challenge of Cultural Diversity: Harnessing a Diversity of Views to Understand Multiculturalism," *Academy of Management Review*, vol. 21, no. 2, 1996, pp. 434–462. See also "Generational Warfare," *Forbes*, March 22, 1999, pp. 62–66.

18. Christine M. Riordan and Lynn McFarlane Shores, "Demographic Diversity and Employee Attitudes: An Empirical Examination of Relational Demography Within Work Units," *Journal of Applied Psychology*, vol. 82, no. 3, 1997, pp. 342–358.

19. Barbara Presley Nobel, "Reinventing Labor," *Harvard Business Review*, July–August 1993, pp. 115–125.

20. John A. Fossum, "Labor Relations: Research and Practice in Transition," *Journal of Management*, Summer 1987, pp. 281–300.

21. "How Wal-Mart Keeps Unions at Bay," *BusinessWeek*, October 28, 2002, pp. 94–96.

22. Max Boisot, *Knowledge Assets* (Oxford, U.K.: Oxford University Press, 1998).

23. Thomas Stewart, "In Search of Elusive Tech Workers," *Fortune*, February 16, 1998, pp. 171–172.

24. "Need for Computer Experts Is Making Recruiters Frantic," *New York Times*, December 18, 1999, p. C1.

25. "FBI Taps Retiree Experience for Temporary Jobs," *USA Today*, October 3, 2002, p. 1A.

26. "When Is a Temp Not a Temp?" *BusinessWeek*, December 7, 1998, pp. 90–92.

Chapter 9

1. "The New Science of Happiness," *Time*, January 17, 2006, pp. A2–A15; Pamela Kruger, "Betrayed by Work," *Fast Company*, November 1999, www.fastcompany.com on February 1, 2003; Jody Miller and Matt Miller, "Get a Life!" *Fortune*, November 16, 2005, www.fortune.com on January 19, 2006; Andrea Sachs, "Wedded to Work," *Time*, September 2002, p. A21; Ilene Philipson, "Work Is Life," PsychotherapistResources.com website, November 2001, www.psychotherapistresources.com on February 1, 2003 (quote); Jerry Useem, "Welcome to the New Company Town," *Fortune*, January 10, 2000, www.fortune.com on February 1, 2003.

2. Lynn McGarlane Shore and Lois Tetrick, "The Psychological Contract as an Explanatory Framework in the Employment Relationship," in C. L. Cooper and D. M. Rousseau, eds., *Trends in Organizational Behavior* (London: John Wiley, 1994).

3. Elizabeth Wolfe Morrison and Sandra L. Robinson, "When Employees Feel Betrayed: A Model of How Psychological Contract Violation Develops," *Academy of Management Review*, January 1997, pp. 226–256.

4. Lawrence Pervin, "Personality," in Mark Rosenzweig and Lyman Porter, eds., *Annual Review of Psychology*, vol. 36 (Palo Alto, CA: Annual Reviews, 1985), pp. 83–114; S. R. Maddi, *Personality Theories: A Comparative Analysis*, 4th ed. (Homewood, IL: Dorsey, 1980).

5. L. R. Goldberg, "An Alternative 'Description of Personality': The Big Five Factor Structure," *Journal of Personality and Social Psychology*, vol. 59, 1990, pp. 1216–1229.

6. Michael K. Mount, Murray R. Barrick, and J. Perkins Strauss, "Validity of Observer Ratings of the Big Five Personality Factors," *Journal of Applied Psychology*, vol. 79, no. 2, 1994,

pp. 272–280; Timothy A. Judge, Joseph J. Martocchio, and Carl J. Thoreson, "Five-Factor Model of Personality and Employee Absence," *Journal of Applied Psychology*, vol. 82, no. 5, 1997, pp. 745–755.

7. J. B. Rotter, "Generalized Expectancies for Internal vs. External Control of Reinforcement," *Psychological Monographs*, vol. 80, 1966, pp. 1–28. See also Simon S. K. Lam and John Schaubroeck, "The Role of Locus of Control in Reactions to Being Promoted and to Being Passed Over: A Quasi Experiment," *Academy of Management Journal*, vol. 43, no. 1, 2000, pp. 66–78.

8. Marilyn E. Gist and Terence R. Mitchell, "Self-Efficacy: A Theoretical Analysis of Its Determinants and Malleability," *Academy of Management Review*, April 1992, pp. 183–211.

9. T. W. Adorno, E. Frenkel-Brunswick, D. J. Levinson, and R. N. Sanford, *The Authoritarian Personality* (New York: Harper & Row, 1950).

10. Jon L. Pierce, Donald G. Gardner, and Larry L. Cummings, "Organization-based Self-Esteem: Construct Definition, Measurement, and Validation," *Academy of Management Journal*, vol. 32, 1989, pp. 622–648.

11. See Daniel Goleman, *Emotional Intelligence: Why It Can Matter More Than IQ* (New York: Bantam Books, 1995).

12. Daniel Goleman, "Leadership That Gets Results," *Harvard Business Review*, March–April 2000, pp. 78–90.

13. Leon Festinger, *A Theory of Cognitive Dissonance* (Palo Alto, CA: Stanford University Press, 1957).

14. See John J. Clancy, "Is Loyalty Really Dead?" *Across the Board*, June 1999, pp. 15–19.

15. Patricia C. Smith, L. M. Kendall, and Charles Hulin, *The Measurement of Satisfaction in Work and Behavior* (Chicago: Rand-McNally, 1969).

16. "Companies Are Finding Real Payoffs in Aiding Employee Satisfaction," *Wall Street Journal*, October 11, 2000, p. B1.

17. For research work in this area, see Jennifer M. George and Gareth R. Jones, "The Experience of Mood and Turnover Intentions: Interactive Effects of Value Attainment, Job Satisfaction, and Positive Mood," *Journal of Applied Psychology*, vol. 81, no. 3, 1996, pp. 318–325; Larry J. Williams, Mark B. Gavin, and Margaret Williams, "Measurement and Nonmeasurement Processes with Negative Affectivity and Employee Attitudes," *Journal of Applied Psychology*, vol. 81, no. 1, 1996, pp. 88–101.

18. Kathleen Sutcliffe, "What Executives Notice: Accurate Perceptions in Top Management Teams," *Academy of Management Journal*, vol. 37, no. 5, 1994, pp. 1360–1378.

19. See H. H. Kelley, *Attribution in Social Interaction* (Morristown, NJ: General Learning Press, 1971), for a classic treatment of attribution.

20. For a recent overview of the literature on stress, see Frank Landy, James Campbell Quick, and Stanislav Kasl, "Work, Stress, and Well-Being," *International Journal of Stress Management*, vol. 1, no. 1, 1994, pp. 33–73.

21. Hans Selye, *The Stress of Life* (New York: McGraw-Hill, 1976).

22. M. Friedman and R. H. Rosenman, *Type A Behavior and Your Heart* (New York: Knopf, 1974).

23. "Work & Family," *BusinessWeek*, June 28, 1993, pp. 80–88.

24. Richard S. DeFrank, Robert Konopaske, and John M. Ivancevich, "Executive Travel Stress: Perils of the Road Warrior," *Academy of Management Executive*, vol. 14, no. 2, 2000, pp. 58–67.

25. "Breaking Point," *Newsweek*, March 6, 1995, pp. 56–62. See also "Rising Job Stress Could Affect Bottom Line," *USA Today*, July 28, 2003, p. 18.

26. See Richard W. Woodman, John E. Sawyer, and Ricky W. Griffin, "Toward a Theory of Organizational Creativity," *Academy of Management Review*, April 1993, pp. 293–321.

27. John Simons, "The $10 Billion Pill," *Fortune*, January 20, 2003, pp. 58–68.

28. Christina E. Shalley, Lucy L. Gilson, and Terry C. Blum, "Matching Creativity Requirements and the Work Environment: Effects on Satisfaction and Intentions to Leave," *Academy of Management Journal*, vol. 43, no. 2, 2000, pp. 215–223. See also Filiz Tabak, "Employee Creative Performance: What Makes It Happen?" *Academy of Management Executive*, vol. 11, no. 1, 1997, pp. 119–122.

29. "That's It, I'm Outa Here," *BusinessWeek*, October 3, 2000, pp. 96–98.

30. See Philip M. Podsakoff, Scott B. MacKenzie, Julie Beth Paine, and Daniel G. G. Bacharah, "Organizational Citizenship Behaviors: A Critical Review of the Theoretical and Empirical Literature and Suggestions for Future Research," *Journal of Management*, vol. 26, no. 3, 2000, pp. 513–563, for recent findings on this behavior.

31. Dennis W. Organ, "Personality and Organizational Citizenship Behavior," *Journal of Management*, vol. 20, no. 2, 1994, pp. 465–478; Mary Konovsky and S. Douglas Pugh, "Citizenship Behavior and Social Exchange," *Academy of Management Journal*, vol. 37, no. 3, 1994, pp. 656–669; and Jacqueline A.M. Coyle-Shapiro, "A Psychological Contract Perspective on Organizational Citizenship," *Journal of Organizational Behavior*, vol. 23, 2002, pp. 927–946.

32. See Anne O'Leary-Kelly, Ricky W. Griffin, and David J. Glew, "Organization-Motivated Aggression: A Research Framework," *Academy of Management Review*, January 1996, pp. 225–253; See also Ricky W. Griffin and Yvette Lopez, "'Bad Behavior' in Organizations: A Review and Typology for Future Research," *Journal of Management*, December 2005, pp. 988–1005.

Chapter 10

1. "2004 Financial Report," "Beyond the Headlines," "What Is Doctors Without Borders?" Doctors Without Borders website, www.doctorswithoutborders.org on January 23, 2006; "About DNDI," Drugs for Neglected Diseases Initiative website, www.dndi.org on January 20, 2006; Nicolas de Torrenté, "The Professionalization and Bureaucratization of Humanitarian Action," Social Sciences Research Institute website, March 23, 2005, www.ssrc.org on January 20, 2006; Carlotta Gall, "Afghan Aid Killings: Suspect, No Arrests," *The New York Times*, April 10, 2005, www.nytimes.com on January 20, 2006; Karin Moorhouse and Wei Cheng, *No One Can Stop the Rain*, Insomniac Press, April 2005; Cynthia M. Piccolo, "Across Careers and Continents," MedHunters website, www.medhunters.com on January 20, 2006; Kristin Rothwell, Nurse Zone website, www.nursezone.com on January 20, 2006; Nayana Somaiah, "Keep Up the Fight, Nigerians!" MedHunters website, www.medhunters.com on January 20, 2006; Stephanie Strom, "As Disaster Follows Disaster, Relief Groups Feel the Strain," *The New York Times*, October 13, 2005, www.nytimes.com on January 20, 2006.

2. Richard M. Steers, Gregory A. Bigley, and Lyman W. Porter, *Motivation and Leadership at Work*, 6th ed. (New York: McGraw-Hill, 1996). See also Maureen L. Ambrose and Carol T. Kulik, "Old Friends, New Faces: Motivation Research in the 1990s," *Journal of Management*, vol. 25, no. 3, 1999, pp. 231–292.

3. See Nigel Nicholson, "How to Motivate Your Problem People," *Harvard Business Review*, January 2003, pp. 57–67.

4. See Jeffrey Pfeffer, *The Human Equation* (Cambridge, MA: Harvard Business School Press, 1998).

5. See Eryn Brown, "So Rich So Young—But Are They Really Happy?" *Fortune*, September 18, 2000, pp. 99–110, for a recent discussion of these questions.

6. Abraham H. Maslow, "A Theory of Human Motivation," *Psychological Review*, vol. 50, 1943, pp. 370–396; Abraham H. Maslow, *Motivation and Personality* (New York: Harper & Row, 1954). Maslow's most recent work is Abraham H. Maslow and Richard Lowry, *Toward a Psychology of Being* (New York: Wiley, 1999).

7. For a review, see Craig Pinder, *Work Motivation in Organizational Behavior* (Upper Saddle River, NJ: Prentice-Hall, 1998).

8. Frederick Herzberg, Bernard Mausner, and Barbara Snyderman, *The Motivation to Work* (New York: Wiley, 1959); Frederick Herzberg, "One More Time: How Do You Motivate Employees?" *Harvard Business Review*, January–February 1987, pp. 109–120 (reprinted in *Harvard Business Review*, January 2003, pp. 87–98).

9. Robert J. House and Lawrence A. Wigdor, "Herzberg's Dual-Factor Theory of Job Satisfaction and Motivation: A Review of the Evidence and a Criticism," *Personnel Psychology*, Winter 1967, pp. 369–389; Victor H. Vroom, *Work and Motivation* (New York: Wiley, 1964). See also Pinder, *Work Motivation*.

10. David C. McClelland, *The Achieving Society* (Princeton, NJ: Van Nostrand, 1961); David C. McClelland, *Power: The Inner Experience* (New York: Irvington, 1975).

11. Victor H. Vroom, *Work and Motivation* (New York: Wiley, 1964).

12. "Starbucks' Secret Weapon," *Fortune*, September 29, 1997, p. 268.

13. J. Stacy Adams, "Towards an Understanding of Inequity," *Journal of Abnormal and Social Psychology*, November 1963, pp. 422–436.

14. See Edwin A. Locke, "Toward a Theory of Task Performance and Incentives," *Organizational Behavior and Human Performance*, vol. 3, 1968, pp. 157–189.

15. Gary P. Latham and J. J. Baldes, "The Practical Significance of Locke's Theory of Goal Setting," *Journal of Applied Psychology*, vol. 60, 1975, pp. 187–191.

16. B. F. Skinner, *Beyond Freedom and Dignity* (New York: Knopf, 1971).

17. Fred Luthans and Robert Kreitner, *Organizational Behavior Modification and Beyond: An Operant and Social Learning Approach* (Glenview, IL: Scott, Foresman, 1985).

18. David J. Glew, Anne M. O'Leary-Kelly, Ricky W. Griffin, and David D. Van Fleet, "Participation in Organizations: A Preview of the Issues and Proposed Framework for Future Analysis," *Journal of Management*, vol. 21, no. 3, 1995, pp. 395–421.

19. Baxter W. Graham, "The Business Argument for Flexibility," *HRMagazine*, May 1996, pp. 104–110.

20. A. R. Cohen and H. Gadon, *Alternative Work Schedules: Integrating Individual and Organizational Needs* (Reading, MA: Addison-Wesley, 1978).

21. Daniel Wren, *The Evolution of Management Theory*, 4th ed. (New York: Wiley, 1994).

22. "When Money Isn't Enough," *Forbes*, November 18, 1996, pp. 164–169.

23. Jacquelyn DeMatteo, Lillian Eby, and Eric Sundstrom, "Team-Based Rewards: Current Empirical Evidence and Directions for Future Research," in L. L. Cummings and Barry Staw, eds., *Research in Organizational Behavior*, vol. 20 (Greenwich, CT: JAI Press, 1998), pp. 141–183.

24. Theresa M. Welbourne and Luis R. Gomez-Mejia, "Gainsharing: A Critical Review and a Future Research Agenda," *Journal of Management*, vol. 21, no. 3, 1995, pp. 559–609.

25. Harry Barkema and Luis Gomez-Mejia, "Managerial Compensation and Firm Performance: A General Research Framework," *Academy of Management Journal*, vol. 41, no. 2, 1998, pp. 135–145.

26. Rajiv D. Banker, Seok-Young Lee, Gordon Potter, and Dhinu Srinivasan, "Contextual Analysis of Performance Impacts of Outcome-Based Incentive Compensation," *Academy of Management Journal*, vol. 39, no. 4, 1996, pp. 920–948.

27. M. Blair, "CEO Pay: Why Such a Contentious Issue?" *The Brookings Review*, Winter 1994, pp. 23–27.

28. Steve Kerr, "The Best-Laid Incentive Plans," *Harvard Business Review*, January 2003, pp. 27–40.

29. "Now It's Getting Personal," *BusinessWeek*, December 16, 2002, pp. 90–92.

Chapter 11

1. Anthony Bianco, "Ken Lay's Audacious Ignorance," *Business-Week*, February 6, 2006, www.businessweek.com on February 1, 2006 (quote); Geoffrey Colvin, "The Other Victims of Bernie Ebbers's Fraud," *CNN Money*, August 8, 2005, www.cnnmoney .com on January 28, 2006; Krysten Crawford, "Ex-WorldCom CEO Ebbers Guilty," *CNN Money*, March 15, 2005, www .cnnmoney.com on January 28, 2006; Marcy Gordon, "Four Indicted in Sham General Re–AIG Deal," *Associated Press*, February 2, 2006, www.businessweek.com on January 28, 2006; Marc Gunther, "Spotting the Next Tyco," *CNN Money*, November 3, 2005, www.cnnmoney.com on January 28, 2006; David Henry, Mike France, and Louis Lavelle, "The Boss on the Sidelines," *BusinessWeek*, April 25, 2005, www.businessweek .com on January 28, 2006; Christopher Palmieri, "The Case Against Qwest's Nacchio," *BusinessWeek*, December 21, 2005, www.businessweek.com on January 28, 2006.

2. See Ronald A. Heifetz and Donald L. Laurie, "The Work of Leadership," *Harvard Business Review*, January–February 1997, pp. 124–134. See also Arthur G. Jago, "Leadership: Perspectives in Theory and Research," *Management Science*, March 1982, pp. 315–336; and "The New Leadership," *BusinessWeek*, August 28, 2000, pp. 100–187.

3. Gary A. Yukl, *Leadership in Organizations*, 3rd ed. (Englewood Cliffs, NJ: Prentice-Hall, 1994), p. 5. See also Gregory G. Dess and Joseph C. Pickens, "Changing Roles: Leadership in the 21st Century," *Organizational Dynamics*, Winter 2000, pp. 18–28.

4. John P. Kotter, "What Leaders Really Do," *Harvard Business Review*, May–June 1990, pp. 103–111 (reprinted in *Harvard Business Review*, December 2001, pp. 85–93). See also Daniel Goleman, "Leadership That Gets Results," *Harvard Business Review*, March–April 2000, pp. 78–88; and Keith Grints, *The Arts of Leadership* (Oxford, U.K.: Oxford University Press, 2000).

5. John R. P. French and Bertram Raven, "The Bases of Social Power," in Dorwin Cartwright, ed., *Studies in Social Power* (Ann Arbor: University of Michigan Press, 1959), pp. 150–167.

6. Bennett J. Tepper, "Consequences of Abusive Supervision," *Academy of Management Journal*, vol. 43, no. 2, 2000, pp. 178–190.

7. Bernard M. Bass, *Bass & Stogdill's Handbook of Leadership*, 3rd ed. (Riverside, NJ: Free Press, 1990).

8. Shelley A. Kirkpatrick and Edwin A. Locke, "Leadership: Do Traits Matter?" *Academy of Management Executive*, May 1991, pp. 48–60. See also Robert J. Sternberg, "Managerial Intelligence: Why IQ Isn't Enough," *Journal of Management*, vol. 23, no. 3, 1997, pp. 475–493.

9. Rensis Likert, *New Patterns of Management* (New York: McGraw-Hill, 1961); Rensis Likert, *The Human Organization* (New York: McGraw-Hill, 1967).

10. The Ohio State studies stimulated many articles, monographs, and books. A good overall reference is Ralph M. Stogdill and A. E. Coons, eds., *Leader Behavior: Its Description and Measurement* (Columbus, OH: Bureau of Business Research, Ohio State University, 1957).

11. Edwin A. Fleishman, E. F. Harris, and H. E. Burt, *Leadership and Supervision in Industry* (Columbus, OH: Bureau of Business Research, Ohio State University, 1955).

12. Robert R. Blake and Jane S. Mouton, *The Managerial Grid* (Houston: Gulf Publishing, 1964); Robert R. Blake and Jane S. Mouton, *The Versatile Manager: A Grid Profile* (Homewood, IL: Dow Jones-Irwin, 1981).

13. Fred E. Fiedler, *A Theory of Leadership Effectiveness* (New York: McGraw-Hill, 1967).

14. Chester A. Schriesheim, Bennett J. Tepper, and Linda A. Tetrault, "Least Preferred Co-Worker Score, Situational Control, and Leadership Effectiveness: A Meta-Analysis of Contingency Model Performance Predictions," *Journal of Applied Psychology*, vol. 79, no. 4, 1994, pp. 561–573.

15. Fiedler, *A Theory of Leadership Effectiveness*; Fred E. Fiedler and M. M. Chemers, *Leadership and Effective Management* (Glenview, IL: Scott, Foresman, 1974).

16. For recent reviews and updates, see Lawrence H. Peters, Darrell D. Hartke, and John T. Pohlmann, "Fiedler's Contingency Theory of Leadership: An Application of the Meta-Analysis Procedures of Schmidt and Hunter," *Psychological Bulletin*, vol. 97, pp. 274–285; and Fred E. Fiedler, "When to Lead, When to Stand Back," *Psychology Today*, September 1987, pp. 26–27.

17. Martin G. Evans, "The Effects of Supervisory Behavior on the Path-Goal Relationship," *Organizational Behavior and Human Performance*, May 1970, pp. 277–298; Robert J. House and Terence R. Mitchell, "Path-Goal Theory of Leadership," *Journal of Contemporary Business*, Autumn 1974, pp. 81–98. See also Yukl, *Leadership in Organizations*.

18. For a recent review, see J. C. Wofford and Laurie Z. Liska, "Path-Goal Theories of Leadership: A Meta-Analysis," *Journal of Management*, vol. 19, no. 4, 1993, pp. 857–876.

19. Victor H. Vroom and Arthur G. Jago, *The New Leadership* (Englewood Cliffs, NJ: Prentice-Hall, 1988).

20. Ibid.

21. George Graen and J. F. Cashman, "A Role-Making Model of Leadership in Formal Organizations: A Developmental Approach," in J. G. Hunt and L. L. Larson, eds., *Leadership Frontiers* (Kent, OH: Kent State University Press, 1975), pp. 143–165; Fred Dansereau, George Graen, and W. J. Haga, "A Vertical Dyad Linkage Approach to Leadership Within Formal Organizations: A Longitudinal Investigation of the Role-Making

Process," *Organizational Behavior and Human Performance*, vol. 15, 1975, pp. 46–78.

22. See Kathryn Sherony and Stephen Green, "Coworker Exchange: Relationships Between Coworkers, Leader-Member Exchange, and Work Attitudes," *Journal of Applied Psychology*, vol. 87, no. 3, 2002, pp. 542–548.

23. Steven Kerr and John M. Jermier, "Substitutes for Leadership: Their Meaning and Measurement," *Organizational Behavior and Human Performance*, December 1978, pp. 375–403.

24. See Charles C. Manz and Henry P. Sims, Jr., "Leading Workers to Lead Themselves: The External Leadership of Self-Managing Work Teams," *Administrative Science Quarterly*, March 1987, pp. 106–129. See also "Living Without a Leader," *Fortune*, March 20, 2000, pp. 218–219.

25. See Robert J. House, "A 1976 Theory of Charismatic Leadership," in J. G. Hunt and L. L. Larson, eds., *Leadership: The Cutting Edge* (Carbondale: Southern Illinois University Press, 1977), pp. 189–207. See also Jay A. Conger and Rabindra N. Kanungo, "Toward a Behavioral Theory of Charismatic Leadership in Organizational Settings," *Academy of Management Review*, October 1987, pp. 637–647.

26. Stratford P. Sherman, "Donald Trump Just Won't Die," *Fortune*, August 13, 1990, pp. 75–79.

27. David A. Nadler and Michael L. Tushman, "Beyond the Charismatic Leader: Leadership and Organizational Change," *California Management Review*, Winter 1990, pp. 77–97.

28. James MacGregor Burns, *Leadership* (New York: Harper & Row, 1978). See also Rajnandini Pillai, Chester A. Schriesheim, and Eric J. Williams, "Fairness Perceptions and Trust as Mediators for Transformational and Transactional Leadership: A Two-Sample Study," *Journal of Management*, vol. 25, no. 6, 1999, pp. 897–933.

29. Kenneth Labich, "The Seven Keys to Business Leadership," *Fortune*, October 24, 1988, pp. 100–112.

30. Jerry Useem, "Tape + Light Bulbs = ?" *Fortune*, August 12, 2002, pp. 127–132.

31. "The Best (& Worst) Managers of the Year," *BusinessWeek*, January 13, 2003, pp. 58–92.

32. See Kurt Dirks and Donald Ferrin, "Trust in Leadership," *Journal of Applied Psychology*, vol. 87, no. 4, 2002, pp. 611–628.

33. Jeffrey Pfeffer, *Power in Organizations* (Marshfield, MA: Pitman Publishing, 1981), p. 7.

34. Timothy Judge and Robert Bretz, "Political Influence Behavior and Career Success," *Journal of Management*, vol. 20, no. 1, 1994, pp. 43–65.

35. Victor Murray and Jeffrey Gandz, "Games Executives Play: Politics at Work," *Business Horizons*, December 1980, pp. 11–23; Jeffrey Gandz and Victor Murray, "The Experience of Workplace Politics," *Academy of Management Journal*, June 1980, pp. 237–251.

36. Don R. Beeman and Thomas W. Sharkey, "The Use and Abuse of Corporate Power," *Business Horizons*, March–April 1987, pp. 26–30.

37. "How Ebbers Kept the Board in His Pocket," *BusinessWeek*, October 14, 2002, pp. 138–139.

38. See William L. Gardner, "Lessons in Organizational Dramaturgy: The Art of Impression Management," *Organizational Dynamics*, Summer 1992, pp. 51–63; Elizabeth Wolf Morrison and Robert J. Bies, "Impression Management in the Feedback-Seeking Process: A Literature Review and Research

Agenda," *Academy of Management Review*, July 1991, pp. 522–541.

39. See Chad Higgins, Timothy Judge, and Gerald Ferris, "Influence Tactics and Work Outcomes: A Meta-Analysis," *Journal of Organizational Behavior*, vol. 24, 2003, pp. 89–106.

40. Murray and Gandz, "Games Executives Play."

41. Stefanie Ann Lenway and Kathleen Rehbein, "Leaders, Followers, and Free Riders: An Empirical Test of Variation in Corporate Political Involvement," *Academy of Management Journal*, December 1991, pp. 893–905.

Chapter 12

1. Michelle Conlin, "E-Mail Is So Five Minutes Ago," *BusinessWeek*, November 28, 2005, www.businessweek.com on February 1, 2006; Michelle Delio, "The Internet: It's Full of Holes," *Wired News*, February 6, 2001, www.wired.com on February 11, 2003 (quote); Heidi L. McNeil and Robert M. Kort, "Discovery of E-Mail and Other Computerized Information," Scottsdale Law website, www.scottsdalelaw.com on October 29, 2002; Gretchen Morgenson, "Analyze This: What Those Analysts Said in Private," *New York Times*, September 15, 2002, p. BU2; Joseph Nchor, "Self-Policing of Email Marketing Industry May Work," *Email Today*, www.emailtoday.com on February 10, 2003; Kevin Poulsen, "New York Times Internal Network Hacked," *BusinessWeek*, February 27, 2002, www.businessweek.com on February 10, 2003.

2. Henry Mintzberg, *The Nature of Managerial Work* (New York: Harper & Row, 1973).

3. See Michael H. Zack, "Managing Codified Knowledge," *Sloan Management Review*, Summer 1999, pp. 45–58.

4. Edward W. Desmond, "How Your Data May Soon Seek You Out," *Fortune*, September 1997, pp. 149–154.

5. Mintzberg, *The Nature of Managerial Work*.

6. Reid Buckley, "When You Have to Put It to Them," *Across the Board*, October 1999, pp. 44–48.

7. "'Did I Just Say That?!' How to Recover from Foot-in-Mouth," *Wall Street Journal*, June 19, 2002, p. B1.

8. "Executives Who Dread Public Speaking Learn to Keep Their Cool in the Spotlight," *Wall Street Journal*, May 4, 1990, pp. B1, B6.

9. Mintzberg, *The Nature of Managerial Work*.

10. Buckley, "When You Have to Put It to Them."

11. See "Watch What You Put in That Office Email," *BusinessWeek*, September 30, 2002, pp. 114–115.

12. Nicholas Varchaver, "The Perils of E-mail," *Fortune*, February 17, 2003, pp. 96–102; "How a String of E-Mail Came to Haunt CSFB and Star Banker," *Wall Street Journal*, February 28, 2003, pp. A1, A6.

13. A. Vavelas, "Communication Patterns in Task-Oriented Groups," *Journal of the Acoustical Society of America*, vol. 22, 1950, pp. 725–730; Jerry Wofford, Edwin Gerloff, and Robert Cummins, *Organizational Communication* (New York: McGraw-Hill, 1977).

14. Nelson Phillips and John Brown, "Analyzing Communications in and Around Organizations: A Critical Hermeneutic Approach," *Academy of Management Journal*, vol. 36, no. 6, 1993, pp. 1547–1576.

15. Walter Kiechel, III, "Breaking Bad News to the Boss," *Fortune*, April 9, 1990, pp. 111–112.

16. Mary Young and James Post, "How Leading Companies Communicate with Employees," *Organizational Dynamics*, Summer 1993, pp. 31–43.

17. For one example, see Kimberly D. Elsbach and Greg Elofson, "How the Packaging of Decision Explanations Affects Perceptions of Trustworthiness," *Academy of Management Journal,* vol. 43, no. 1, 2000, pp. 80–89.

18. Donald A. Marchand, William J. Kettinger, and John D. Rollins, "Information Orientation: People, Technology, and the Bottom Line," *Sloan Management Review,* Summer 2000, pp. 69–79.

19. Mary Cronin, "Ford's Intranet Success," *Fortune,* March 30, 1998, p. 158.

20. Walter Kiechel, III, "Hold for the Communicaholic Manager," *Fortune,* January 2, 1989, pp. 107–108.

21. Those Bawdy E-mails Were Good for a Laugh—Until the Ax Fell," *Wall Street Journal,* February 4, 2000, pp. A1, A8.

22. Keith Davis, "Management Communication and the Grapevine," *Harvard Business Review,* September–October 1953, pp. 43–49.

23. "Spread the Word: Gossip Is Good," *Wall Street Journal,* October 4, 1988, p. B1.

24. See David M. Schweiger and Angelo S. DeNisi, "Communication with Employees Following a Merger: A Longitudinal Field Experiment," *Academy of Management Journal,* March 1991, pp. 110–135.

25. Nancy B. Kurland and Lisa Hope Pelled, "Passing the Word: Toward a Model of Gossip and Power in the Workplace," *Academy of Management Review,* vol. 25, no. 2, 2000, pp. 428–438.

26. See Tom Peters and Nancy Austin, *A Passion for Excellence* (New York: Random House, 1985).

27. Albert Mehrabian, *Non-verbal Communication* (Chicago: Aldine, 1972).

28. Michael B. McCaskey, "The Hidden Messages Managers Send," *Harvard Business Review,* November–December 1979, pp. 135–148.

29. David Givens, "What Body Language Can Tell You That Words Cannot," *U.S. News & World Report,* November 19, 1984, p. 100.

30. Edward J. Hall, *The Hidden Dimension* (New York: Doubleday, 1966).

31. For a detailed discussion of improving communication effectiveness, see Courtland L. Bovee, John V. Thill, and Barbara E. Schatzman, *Business Communication Today,* 7th ed. (Upper Saddle River, NJ: Prentice-Hall, 2003).

32. See "You Have (Too Much) E-mail," *USA Today,* March 12, 1999, p. 3B.

33. Justin Fox, "The Triumph of English," *Fortune,* September 18, 2000, pp. 209–212.

34. Joseph Allen and Bennett P. Lientz, *Effective Business Communication* (Santa Monica, CA: Goodyear, 1979).

35. See "Making Silence Your Ally," *Across the Board,* October 1999, p. 11.

36. Boyd A. Vander Houwen, "Less Talking, More Listening," *HRMagazine,* April 1997, pp. 53–58.

37. For a discussion of these and related issues, see Eric M. Eisenberg and Marsha G. Witten, "Reconsidering Openness in Organizational Communication," *Academy of Management Review,* July 1987, pp. 418–426.

Chapter 13

1. Eric Adelson, "Shani-Chad Duel a Catch-22 for Speedskating," *ESPN Magazine,* February 21, 2006, www.espn.com on February 21, 2006; "Banned Austrian Coach at Center of Doping Drama," *Time,* February 21, 2006, www.time.com on February 21, 2006; Aditi Kinkhabwala, "Olympic Insanity," *Sports Illustrated,* February 21, 2006, www.si.com on February 21, 2006;

Tim Layden, "Downhill Spiral," *Sports Illustrated,* February 13, 2006, www.si.com on February 21, 2006; Larry McShane, "Emily Hughes Makes Olympic Debut Tonight," Associated Press, www.ap.org on February 21, 2006; Pritha Sarkar, "Athletes Give Village Thumbs Down," Reuters, February 7, 2006, www.reuters.com on February 21, 2006; Bob Simon, "Golden Boy Bode Miller," *CBS News,* January 8, 2006, www.cbsnews.com on February 21, 2006.

2. See Gregory Moorhead and Ricky W. Griffin, *Organizational Behavior,* 7th ed. (Boston: Houghton Mifflin, 2004), for a review of definitions of groups.

3. Dorwin Cartwright and Alvin Zander, eds., *Group Dynamics: Research and Theory,* 3rd ed. (New York: Harper & Row, 1968).

4. Rob Cross, Nitin Nohria, and Andrew Parker, "Six Myths About Informal Networks—And How to Overcome Them," *Sloan Management Review,* Spring 2002, pp. 67–77.

5. Robert Schrank, *Ten Thousand Working Days* (Cambridge, MA: MIT Press, 1978); Bill Watson, "Counter Planning on the Shop Floor," in Peter Frost, Vance Mitchell, and Walter Nord, eds., *Organizational Reality,* 2nd ed. (Glenview, IL: Scott, Foresman, 1982), pp. 286–294.

6. "After Layoffs, More Workers Band Together," *Wall Street Journal,* February 26, 2002, p. B1.

7. Bradley L. Kirkman and Benson Rosen, "Powering Up Teams," *Organizational Dynamics,* Winter 2000, pp. 48–58.

8. Brian Dumaine, "Payoff from the New Management," *Fortune,* December 13, 1993, pp. 103–110.

9. "Why Teams Fail," *USA Today,* February 25, 1997, pp. 1B, 2B.

10. Brian Dumaine, "The Trouble with Teams," *Fortune,* September 5, 1994, pp. 86–92. See also Susan G. Cohen and Diane E. Bailey, "What Makes Teams Work: Group Effectiveness Research from the Shop Floor to the Executive Suite," *Journal of Management,* vol. 23, no. 3, 1997, pp. 239–290.

11. Marvin E. Shaw, *Group Dynamics—The Psychology of Small Group Behavior,* 4th ed. (New York: McGraw-Hill, 1985).

12. "How to Avoid Hiring the Prima Donnas Who Hate Teamwork," *Wall Street Journal,* February 15, 2000, p. B1.

13. See Connie Gersick, "Marking Time: Predictable Transitions in Task Groups," *Academy of Management Journal,* June 1989, pp. 274–309. See also Avan R. Jassawalla and Hemant C. Sashittal, "Building Collaborative Cross-Functional New Product Teams," *Academy of Management Review,* vol. 13, no. 3, 1999, pp. 50–60.

14. See Michael Campion, Gina Medsker, and A. Catherine Higgs, "Relations Between Work Group Characteristics and Effectiveness: Implications for Designing Effective Work Groups," *Personnel Psychology,* Winter 1993, pp. 823–850, for a review of other team characteristics.

15. David Katz and Robert L. Kahn, *The Social Psychology of Organizations,* 2nd ed. (New York: Wiley, 1978), pp. 187–221. See also Greg L. Stewart and Murray R. Barrick, "Team Structure and Performance: Assessing the Mediating Role of Intrateam Process and the Moderating Role of Task Type," *Academy of Management Journal,* vol. 43, no. 2, 2000, pp. 135–148, and Michael G. Pratt and Peter O. Foreman, "Classifying Managerial Responses to Multiple Organizational Identities," *Academy of Management Review,* vol. 25, no. 1, 2000, pp. 18–42.

16. See Travis C. Tubre and Judith M. Collins, "Jackson and Schuler (1985) Revisited: A Meta-Analysis of the Relationships Between Role Ambiguity, Role Conflict, and Job Performance," *Journal of Management,* vol. 26, no. 1, 2000, pp. 155–169.

17. Robert L. Kahn, D. M. Wolfe, R. P. Quinn, J. D. Snoek, and R. A. Rosenthal, *Organizational Stress: Studies in Role Conflict and Role Ambiguity* (New York: Wiley, 1964).

18. Daniel C. Feldman, "The Development and Enforcement of Group Norms," *Academy of Management Review*, January 1984, pp. 47–53.

19. "Companies Turn to Peer Pressure to Cut Injuries as Psychologists Join the Battle," *Wall Street Journal*, March 29, 1991, pp. B1, B3.

20. James Wallace Bishop and K. Dow Scott, "How Commitment Affects Team Performance," *HRMagazine*, February 1997, pp. 107–115.

21. Anne O'Leary-Kelly, Joseph Martocchio, and Dwight Frink, "A Review of the Influence of Group Goals on Group Performance," *Academy of Management Journal*, vol. 37, no. 5, 1994, pp. 1285–1301.

22. Suzy Wetlaufer, "Common Sense and Conflict," *Harvard Business Review*, January–February 2000, pp. 115–125.

23. Kathleen M. Eisenhardt, Jean L. Kahwajy, and L. J. Bourgeois III, "How Management Teams Can Have a Good Fight," *Harvard Business Review*, July–August 1997, pp. 77–89.

24. Thomas Bergmann and Roger Volkema, "Issues, Behavioral Responses and Consequences in Interpersonal Conflicts," *Journal of Organizational Behavior*, vol. 15, 1994, pp. 467–471.

25. Robin Pinkley and Gregory Northcraft, "Conflict Frames of Reference: Implications for Dispute Processes and Outcomes," *Academy of Management Journal*, vol. 37, no. 1, 1994, pp. 193–205.

26. "How 2 Computer Nuts Transformed Industry Before Messy Breakup," *Wall Street Journal*, August 27, 1996, pp. A1, A10.

27. Bruce Barry and Greg L. Stewart, "Composition, Process, and Performance in Self-Managed Groups: The Role of Personality," *Journal of Applied Psychology*, vol. 82, no. 1, 1997, pp. 62–78.

28. "Rumsfeld's Abrasive Style Sparks Conflict with Military Command," *USA Today*, December 10, 2002, pp. 1A, 2A.

29. "Delta CEO Resigns After Clashes with Board," *USA Today*, May 13, 1997, p. B1.

30. "A 'Blood War' in the Jeans Trade," *BusinessWeek*, November 13, 1999, pp. 74–81.

31. Peter Elkind, "Blood Feud," *Fortune*, April 14, 1997, pp. 90–102.

32. See Patrick Nugent, "Managing Conflict: Third-Party Interventions for Managers," *Academy of Management Executive*, vol. 16, no. 1, 2002, pp. 139–148.

33. "Solving Conflicts in the Workplace Without Making Losers," *Wall Street Journal*, May 27, 1997, p. B1.

34. "Teaching Business How to Cope with Workplace Conflicts," *BusinessWeek*, February 18, 1990, pp. 136, 139.

Chapter 14

1. "2004 Annual Report," "Welcome From Our CEO," JetBlue website, www.jetblue.com on February 19, 2006 (quote); Robert Barker, "Is JetBlue Flying Too High?" *BusinessWeek*, April 29, 2002, www.businessweek.com on February 14, 2003; Julia Boorstin, "JetBlue's IPO Takes Off," *Fortune*, April 29, 2002, www.fortune.com on February 14, 2003; Paul C. Judge, "How Will Your Company Adapt?" *Fast Company*, November 2001, www.fastcompany.com on February 14, 2003; Melanie Wells, "Lord of the Skies," *Forbes*, October 14, 2002, pp. 130–138.

2. Thomas A. Stewart, "Welcome to the Revolution," *Fortune*, December 13, 1993, pp. 66–77.

3. William Taylor, "Control in an Age of Chaos," *Harvard Business Review*, November–December 1994, pp. 64–70.

4. "Fleetwood: Not a Happy Camper Company," *BusinessWeek*, October 9, 2000, pp. 88–90.

5. "An Apple a Day," *BusinessWeek*, October 14, 2002, pp. 122–125; "More Business People Say: Let's Not Do Lunch," *USA Today*, December 24, 2002, p. 1B; David Stires, "The Breaking Point," *Fortune*, March 3, 2003, pp. 107–114.

6. Mark Kroll, Peter Wright, Leslie Toombs, and Hadley Leavell, "Form of Control: A Critical Determinant of Acquisition Performance and CEO Rewards," *Strategic Management Journal*, vol. 18, no. 2, 1997, pp. 85–96.

7. Sim Sitkin, Kathleen Sutcliffe, and Roger Schroeder, "Distinguishing Control from Learning in Total Quality Management: A Contingency Perspective," *Academy of Management Review*, vol. 19, no. 3, 1994, pp. 537–564.

8. Robert Lusch and Michael Harvey, "The Case for an Off-Balance-Sheet Controller," *Sloan Management Review*, Winter 1994, pp. 101–110.

9. Edward E. Lawler III and John G. Rhode, *Information and Control in Organizations* (Pacific Palisades, CA: Goodyear, 1976).

10. Charles W. L. Hill, "Establishing a Standard: Competitive Strategy and Technological Standards in Winner-Take-All Industries," *Academy of Management Executive*, vol. 11, no. 2, 1997, pp. 7–16.

11. "An Efficiency Guru Refits Honda to Fight Auto Giants," *Wall Street Journal*, September 15, 1999, p. B1.

12. See Belverd E. Needles, Jr., Henry R. Anderson, and James C. Caldwell, *Principles of Accounting*, 9th ed. (Boston: Houghton Mifflin, 2004).

13. Ibid.

14. Ibid.

15. Jeremy Kahn, "Do Accountants Have a Future?" *Fortune*, March 3, 2003, pp. 115–117.

16. William G. Ouchi, "The Transmission of Control Through Organizational Hierarchy," *Academy of Management Journal*, June 1978, pp. 173–192; Richard E. Walton, "From Control to Commitment in the Workplace," *Harvard Business Review*, March–April 1985, pp. 76–84.

17. "Nordstrom Cleans Out Its Closets," *BusinessWeek*, May 22, 2000, pp. 105–108.

18. Patricia Sellers, "Something to Prove," *Fortune*, June 24, 2002, pp. 88–98.

19. Peter Lorange, Michael F. Scott Morton, and Sumantra Ghoshal, *Strategic Control* (St. Paul, MN: West, 1986). See also Joseph C. Picken and Gregory G. Dess, "Out of (Strategic) Control," *Organizational Dynamics*, Summer 1997, pp. 35–45.

20. See Hans Mjoen and Stephen Tallman, "Control and Performance in International Joint Ventures," *Organization Science*, May–June 1997, pp. 257–265.

21. See Diana Robertson and Erin Anderson, "Control System and Task Environment Effects on Ethical Judgment: An Exploratory Study of Industrial Salespeople," *Organization Science*, November 1993, pp. 617–629, for a recent study of effective control.

22. "Workers, Surf at Your Own Risk," *BusinessWeek*, June 12, 2000, pp. 105–106.

Chapter 15

1. Cliff Edwards, "A Weaker David to Intel's Goliath," *BusinessWeek*, October 21, 2002, p. 48; Michael Kanellos, "Intel to Expand Irish Manufacturing Facilities," *CNet News*, May 19, 2004, www.news.com on February 12, 2006; Tom Krazit, "Intel

Plans New 300mm Manufacturing Plant for Arizona," *Info-World*, July 25, 2005, www.infoworld.com on February 12, 2006; John Markoff and Steve Lohr, "Intel's Huge Bet Turns Iffy," *New York Times*, September 29, 2002, pp. BU1, BU12, BU13; Brent Schlender, "How Intel Took Moore's Law from Idea to Ideology," *Fortune*, October 27, 2002, www.fortune.com on February 17, 2003 (quote); Brent Schlender, "Intel's $10 Billion Gamble," *Fortune*, November 11, 2002, pp. 90–102.

2. Paul M. Swamidass, "Empirical Science: New Frontier in Operations Management Research," *Academy of Management Review*, October 1991, pp. 793–814.

3. See Anil Khurana, "Managing Complex Production Processes," *Sloan Management Review*, Winter 1999, pp. 85–98.

4. For an example, see Robin Cooper and Regine Slagmulder, "Develop Profitable New Products with Target Costing," *Sloan Management Review*, Summer 1999, pp. 23–34.

5. Joan Woodward, *Industrial Organization: Theory and Practice* (London: Oxford University Press, 1965).

6. See "Tight Labor? Tech to the Rescue," *BusinessWeek*, March 20, 2000, pp. 36–37.

7. "Computers Speed the Design of More Workaday Products," *Wall Street Journal*, January 18, 1985, p. 25.

8. "New Plant Gets Jaguar in Gear," *USA Today*, November 27, 2000, p. 4B.

9. "Thinking Machines," *BusinessWeek*, August 7, 2000, pp. 78–86.

10. James Brian Quinn and Martin Neil Baily, "Information Technology: Increasing Productivity in Services," *Academy of Management Executive*, vol. 8, no. 3, 1994, pp. 28–37.

11. See Charles J. Corbett, Joseph D. Blackburn, and Luk N. Van Wassenhove, "Partnerships to Improve Supply Chains," *Sloan Management Review*, Summer 1999, pp. 71–82, and Jeffrey K. Liker and Yen-Chun Wu, "Japanese Automakers, U.S. Suppliers, and Supply-Chain Superiority," *Sloan Management Review*, Fall 2000, pp. 81–93.

12. See "Siemens Climbs Back," *BusinessWeek*, June 5, 2000, pp. 79–82.

13. See M. Bensaou, "Portfolios of Buyer-Supplier Relationships," *Sloan Management Review*, Summer 1999, pp. 35–44.

14. "Just-in-Time Manufacturing Is Working Overtime," *BusinessWeek*, November 8, 1999, pp. 36–37.

15. "Quality—How to Make It Pay," *BusinessWeek*, August 8, 1994, pp. 54–59.

16. Rhonda Reger, Loren Gustafson, Samuel DeMarie, and John Mullane, "Reframing the Organization: Why Implementing Total Quality Is Easier Said Than Done," *Academy of Management Review*, vol. 19, no. 3, 1994, pp. 565–584.

17. Ross Johnson and William O. Winchell, *Management and Quality* (Milwaukee: American Society for Quality Control, 1989).

See also Carol Reeves and David Bednar, "Defining Quality: Alternatives and Implications," *Academy of Management Review*, vol. 19, no. 3, 1994, pp. 419–445, and C. K. Prahalad and M. S. Krishnan, "The New Meaning of Quality in the Information Age," *Harvard Business Review*, September–October 1999, pp. 109–120.

18. "Quality Isn't Just for Widgets," *BusinessWeek*, July 22, 2002, pp. 72–73.

19. W. Edwards Deming, *Out of the Crisis* (Cambridge, MA: MIT Press, 1986).

20. David Waldman, "The Contributions of Total Quality Management to a Theory of Work Performance," *Academy of Management Review*, vol. 19, no. 3, 1994, pp. 510–536.

21. Thomas Y. Choi and Orlando C. Behling, "Top Managers and TQM Success: One More Look After All These Years," *Academy of Management Executive*, vol. 11, no. 1, 1997, pp. 37–48.

22. James Dean and David Bowen, "Management Theory and Total Quality: Improving Research and Practice Through Theory Development," *Academy of Management Review*, vol. 19, no. 3, 1994, pp. 392–418.

23. Edward E. Lawler, "Total Quality Management and Employee Involvement: Are They Compatible?" *Academy of Management Executive*, vol. 8, no. 1, 1994, pp. 68–79.

24. Jeremy Main, "How to Steal the Best Ideas Around," *Fortune*, October 19, 1992, pp. 102–106.

25. See James Brian Quinn, "Strategic Outsourcing: Leveraging Knowledge Capabilities," *Sloan Management Review*, Summer 1999, pp. 8–22.

26. Thomas Robertson, "How to Reduce Market Penetration Cycle Times," *Sloan Management Review*, Fall 1993, pp. 87–96.

27. Ronald Henkoff, "The Hot New Seal of Quality," *Fortune*, June 28, 1993, pp. 116–120. See also Mustafa V. Uzumeri, "ISO 9000 and Other Metastandards: Principles for Management Practice?" *Academy of Management Executive*, vol. 11, no. 1, 1997, pp. 21–28.

28. Paula C. Morrow, "The Measurement of TQM Principles and Work-Related Outcomes," *Journal of Organizational Behavior*, July 1997, pp. 363–376.

29. John W. Kendrick, *Understanding Productivity: An Introduction to the Dynamics of Productivity Change* (Baltimore: Johns Hopkins, 1977).

30. "Why the Productivity Revolution Will Spread," *BusinessWeek*, February 14, 2000, pp. 112–118. See also "Productivity Grows in Spite of Recession," *USA Today*, July 29, 2002, pp. 1B, 2B; "Productivity's Second Wind," *BusinessWeek*, February 17, 2003, pp. 36–37.

31. Michael van Biema and Bruce Greenwald, "Managing Our Way to Higher Service-Sector Productivity," *Harvard Business Review*, July–August 1997, pp. 87–98.

ANSWERS TO TEST PREPPERS

Chapter 1

Test Prepper 1.1
1. F   2. F   3. T   4. D   5. B   6. B   7. B

Test Prepper 1.2
1. T   2. F   3. T   4. F   5. A   6. C
7. E   8. D

Test Prepper 1.3
1. T   2. T   3. T   4. T   5. A   6. A

Chapter 2

Test Prepper 2.1
1. T   2. F   3. T   4. C   5. A   6. B   7. D

Test Prepper 2.2
1. T   2. F   3. F   4. A   5. E   6. C   7. A

Test Prepper 2.3
1. T   2. T   3. T   4. T   5. D   6. E

Test Prepper 2.4
1. F   2. T   3. T   4. C

Chapter 3

Test Prepper 3.1
1. F   2. F   3. T   4. E   5. D   6. B

Test Prepper 3.2
1. F   2. T   3. F   4. C   5. D

Test Prepper 3.3
1. T   2. T   3. A   4. C

Test Prepper 3.4
1. F   2. T   3. T   4. A   5. B   6. D

Test Prepper 3.5
1. F   2. C

Test Prepper 3.6
1. T   2. A   3. C

Chapter 4

Test Prepper 4.1
1. F   2. T   3. B   4. B   5. E

Test Prepper 4.2
1. F   2. F   3. T   4. A   5. E

Test Prepper 4.3
1. F   2. E   3. A   4. D   5. E

Test Prepper 4.4
1. F   2. T   3. F   4. F   5. A   6. C   7. B

Chapter 5

Test Prepper 5.1
1. F   2. C   3. C

Test Prepper 5.2
1. T   2. T   3. B   4. D

Test Prepper 5.3
1. T   2. T   3. T   4. B   5. A   6. E   7. B

Test Prepper 5.4
1. F   2. F   3. F   4. D   5. A

Test Prepper 5.5
1. T   2. F   3. F   4. D   5. E

Chapter 6

Test Prepper 6.1
1. F   2. T   3. F   4. C   5. E   6. B   7. C

Test Prepper 6.2
1. F   2. A

Test Prepper 6.3
1. T   2. F   3. F   4. A   5. D   6. B

Test Prepper 6.4
1. T   2. T   3. A   4. C

Test Prepper 6.5
1. F   2. B   3. C

Chapter 7

Test Prepper 7.1
1. T   2. F   3. F   4. E   5. A

Test Prepper 7.2
1. T   2. F   3. A   4. D

Test Prepper 7.3
1. F   2. T   3. F   4. E   5. E   6. D

Test Prepper 7.4
1. F   2. T   3. T   4. C   5. E   6. E

Chapter 8

Test Prepper 8.1
1. F   2. F   3. F   4. A   5. E   6. E

Test Prepper 8.2
1. F   2. A   3. A   4. A

Test Prepper 8.3
1. T   2. T   3. F   4. F   5. C   6. D   7. E

Test Prepper 8.4
1. T   2. T   3. D   4. D

Test Prepper 8.5
1. F   2. A   3. E

Test Prepper 8.6
1. F   2. F   3. T   4. C

Test Prepper 8.7
1. F   2. E

Chapter 9

Test Prepper 9.1
1. F   2. D   3. C

Test Prepper 9.2
1. F   2. T   3. T   4. B   5. E   6. A

Test Prepper 9.3
1. F   2. C   3. E   4. E

Test Prepper 9.4
1. T   2. D

Test Prepper 9.5
1. F   2. T   3. T   4. D   5. C

Test Prepper 9.6
1. T   2. T   3. F   4. C   5. E

Test Prepper 9.7
1. F   2. F   3. C

Chapter 10

Test Prepper 10.1
1. T   2. E   3. B

Test Prepper 10.2
1. F   2. F   3. F   4. C   5. B   6. C

Test Prepper 10.3
1. T   2. T   3. F   4. C   5. D   6. B

Test Prepper 10.4
1. F   2. C   3. B   4. C

Test Prepper 10.5
1. F   2. T   3. C

Test Prepper 10.6
1. F   2. T   3. T   4. A

Chapter 11

Test Prepper 11.1
1. F   2. T   3. T   4. T   5. E   6. A   7. B

Test Prepper 11.2
1. F   2. F   3. A   4. C

Test Prepper 11.3
1. T   2. F   3. E   4. C   5. D   6. B

Test Prepper 11.4
1. F   2. F   3. E

Test Prepper 11.5
1. T   2. T   3. B

Test Prepper 11.6
1. F   2. T   3. T   4. E   5. C   6. E

Chapter 12

Test Prepper 12.1
1. T   2. F   3. T   4. E   5. C

Test Prepper 12.2
1. F   2. F   3. T   4. E   5. B   6. C   7. D
8. C   9. A

Test Prepper 12.3
1. T   2. T   3. F   4. F   5. T   6. F   7. A
8. A   9. B

Test Prepper 12.4
1. T   2. E   3. E   4. E

Test Prepper 12.5
1. F   2. T   3. B   4. B

Chapter 13

Test Prepper 13.1
1. F   2. T   3. C   4. A   5. D   6. D

Test Prepper 13.2
1. F   2. T   3. T   4. F   5. B   6. E
7. B   8. E

Test Prepper 13.3
1. T   2. F   3. T   4. F   5. D

Test Prepper 13.4
1. F   2. T   3. F   4. C

Chapter 14

Test Prepper 14.1
1. T   2. F   3. F   4. C   5. B   6. A
7. B   8. C

Test Prepper 14.2
1. F   2. T   3. D   4. B

Test Prepper 14.3
1. F   2. T   3. A   4. A   5. A   6. B

Test Prepper 14.4
1. T   2. F   3. T   4. C

Test Prepper 14.5
1. F   2. T   3. E

Test Prepper 14.6
1. F   2. T   3. T   4. E

Chapter 15

Test Prepper 15.1
1. T   2. T   3. B

Test Prepper 15.2
1. T   2. F   3. C   4. A

Test Prepper 15.3
1. T   2. F   3. T   4. E   5. E   6. B

Test Prepper 15.4
1. F   2. T   3. A   4. E   5. B

Test Prepper 15.5
1. F   2. T   3. F   4. F   5. F   6. C   7. D
8. A   9. C   10. D

Test Prepper 15.6
1. T   2. D   3. B

Name Index

ORGANIZATION AND PRODUCT INDEX

Subject Index